ROUTE SHOWN THUS
ROAD
RAIL
SEA
FRONTIERS ·········

Subotitsa

R. Tisa

Novi Sad
Karlovtsi
RUSHKA GORA
Ravanitsa
Krushedol
Zemun
BELGRADE
Avala
Topola

R. Drina

VIA

THE SHUMADIYA

Kragujevats
Parachin

Ushitse
evo
Vishegrad

Studenitsa

Kolashin
Andriyevitsa
Petch
Vikshitch
nye
LAKE PLAV
Dechani
ishan
Perast
Iselinye
Riyeka
Podgoritsa
dya
L. SCUTARI
Scutari

R. Drin
Tetovo

Prizren

Durazzo

Tirana

Debar

Struga
Ochrid
Resan
L. OCHRID
Sv. Naum
L. PRESPA

ALBANIA

Kossovska Mitrovitsa
PLAIN OF KOSSOVO
Prishtina
Grachanitsa

ROUMANIA

Danube

Nish

R. Isker

R. Morava

SOFIA

BULGARIA

TSERNA GORA
Kumanovo
OVCHE POLYE SHEEPS FIELD
Skoplje
Veles

BABUNA MT.
Gostivar
Prilep

Bitolj
Kaymakchalan

R. Vardar

RUPEL PASS
L. DOIRAN

R. Struma

SALONIKA

GREECE

Black Lamb and Grey Falcon

To John

from Drew

— So many places to see.

OTHER BOOKS BY REBECCA WEST

NOVELS

The Return of the Soldier

Harriet Hume

The Judge

The Thinking Reed

SHORT STORIES

The Harsh Voice

BIOGRAPHY

St. Augustine

CRITICISM

Henry James

The Strange Necessity

IN COLLABORATION WITH LOW

Lions and Lambs

The Rake's Progress

BLACK LAMB
AND
GREY FALCON

A Journey through Yugoslavia

BY

REBECCA WEST

MCMXLI : THE VIKING PRESS : NEW YORK

TO MY FRIENDS IN YUGOSLAVIA,
WHO ARE NOW ALL DEAD OR ENSLAVED

Καὶ τὴν ποθεινὴν πατρίδα παράσχου αὐτοῖς,
Παραδείσου πάλιν ποιῶν πολίτας αὐτούς.

Grant to them the Fatherland of their desire,
and make them again citizens of Paradise.

Note on Pronunciation

The spelling of Yugoslavian names presents a serious problem. The Serbo-Croat language is spoken in all parts of Yugoslavia described in this book; but to write it the Serbs use the Cyrillic alphabet (which is much the same as the Russian, but simpler) and the Croats use the Latin alphabet. Most foreign writers on Yugoslavia follow the Croatian spelling, but this is not satisfactory. The Cyrillic alphabet is designed to give a perfect phonetic rendering of the Slav group of languages, and provides characters for several consonants which other groups lack. The Latin alphabet can only represent these consonants by clapping accents on other consonants which bear some resemblance to them; and the Croation usage still further confuses the English eye by using "c" to represent not "s" and "k" but "ts," and "j" for "y." I have found that in practice the casual English reader is baffled by this unfamiliar use of what looks familiar and is apt to pass over names without grasping them clearly. I have therefore done my best to transliterate all Yugoslavian names into forms most likely to convey the sound of them to English ears. Cetinje is written here as Tsetinye, Jajce as Yaitse, Peč as Petch, Šestinje as Shestinye. Kosovo I have written Kossovo, though the Serbo-Croat language uses no double consonants, because we take them as a sign that the preceding vowel is short.

This is a rough and ready method, and at certain points it has broken down. The Cyrillic alphabet provides special characters for representing liquid consonants; the Latin alphabet can only indicate these by adding "j" to the consonant, and this is extremely confusing at the end of a word. In pronouncing "Senj" the speaker says "Sen," then starts to say a "y" sound, and stops half-way. The English reader, seeing "Senj," pronounces it "Senge" to rhyme with "Penge." But the spelling "Seny" makes him pronounce it as a disyllable; and if the suggestion of the Royal Geographical Society is adopted and the word is spelled "Sen' " he is apt for some strange reason to interpret this sign as a Scotch "ch." I have therefore regarded the problem as insoluble, and have left such words spelt in the Croatian fashion, with the hope that readers will take the presence of the letter "j" as warning that there are dark phonetic doings afoot. In "Bitolj," I may add, the "l" has almost entirely disappeared, having only a short "y" sound.

I have also given up any attempt to transliterate "Sarajevo" or "Skoplje." For one thing "Sarajevo" is a tragically familiar form; and for another, it is not a pure Slav word, and has the Turkish word "*saraï*," a fortress, embedded in it, with a result hardly to be conveyed by any but a most uncouth spelling. It is pronounced something like "Sa-raï-ye-vo," with a faint accent on the second syllable, and a short "e." As for "Skoplje," the one way one must not pronounce it is the way the English reader will certainly pronounce it if it is spelt "Skoplye." The "o" is short, and all the letters after it are combined into a single sound. I have committed another irregularity by putting an "e" into the word "Tsrna," so often found in place-names. This makes is easier for the English reader to grasp that the vowel sound in the rolled "r" comes before it and not after.

R. W.

Contents

VOLUME I

VOLUME II

Illustrations in Volume I

Illustrations in Volume II

J'exige un vrai bonheur, un vrai amour, une vraie contrée où le soleil alterne avec la lune, où les saisons se déroulent en ordre, où de vrais arbres portent de vrais fruits, où de vrais poissons habitent les rivières, et de vrais oiseaux le ciel, où la vraie neige découvre de vraies fleurs, où tout sort est vrai, vrai, véritable. J'en ai assez de cette lumière morne, de ces campagnes stériles, sans jour, sans nuit, où ne survivent que les bêtes féroces et rapaces, où les lois de la nature ne fonctionnent plus.

JEAN COCTEAU: *Les Chevaliers de la Table Ronde*

Fluellen: I think it is in Macedon where Alexander is porn. I tell you, captain, if you look in the maps of the 'orld, I warrant you sall find, in the comparisons between Macedon and Monmouth, that the situations, look you, is both alike. There is a river in Macedon; and there is also moreover a river at Monmouth: it is called Wye at Monmouth; but it is out of my prains what is the name of the other river; but 'tis all one, 'tis alike as my fingers is to my fingers, and there is salmons in both.

SHAKESPEARE: *King Henry the Fifth*

PROLOGUE

I RAISED myself on my elbow and called through the open door into the other wagon-lit:

"My dear, I know I have inconvenienced you terribly by making you take your holiday now, and I know you did not really want to come to Yugoslavia at all. But when you get there you will see why it was so important that we should make this journey, and that we should make it now, at Easter. It will all be quite clear, once we are in Yugoslavia."

There was, however, no reply. My husband had gone to sleep. It was perhaps as well. I could not have gone on to justify my certainty that this train was taking us to a land where everything was comprehensible, where the mode of life was so honest that it put an end to perplexity. I lay back in the darkness and marvelled that I should be feeling about Yugoslavia as if it were my mother country, for this was 1937, and I had never seen the place till 1936. Indeed, I could remember the first time I ever spoke the name "Yugoslavia" and that was only two and a half years before, on October the ninth, 1934.

It was in a London nursing-home. I had had an operation, in the new miraculous way. One morning a nurse had come in and given me an injection, as gently as might be, and had made a little joke which was not very good but served its purpose of taking the chill off the difficult moment. Then I picked up my book and read that sonnet by Joachim du Bellay which begins "*Heureux qui, comme Ulysse, a fait un beau voyage.*" I said to myself, "That is one of the most beautiful poems in the world," and I rolled over in my bed, still thinking that it was one of the most beautiful poems in the world, and found that the electric light was burning and there was a new nurse standing at the end of my bed. Twelve hours had passed in that moment. They had taken me upstairs to a room far above the roofs of London, and had cut me about for three hours and a half, and had brought me down again, and now I was merely sleepy, and not at all sick, and still half-rooted in my pleasure in the poem, still listening to a voice speaking through the ages, with barest economy that somehow is the most lavish melody: "*Et en quelle saison*

1

Revoiray-je le clos de ma pauvre maison, Qui m'est une province, et beaucoup d'avantage?"

I had been told beforehand that it would all be quite easy; but before an operation the unconscious, which is really a shocking old fool, envisages surgery as it was in the Stone Age, and I had been very much afraid. I rebuked myself for not having observed that the universe was becoming beneficent at a great rate. But it was not yet wholly so. My operation wound left me an illusion that I had a load of ice strapped to my body. So, to distract me, I had a radio brought into my room, and for the first time I realized how uninteresting life could be and how perverse human appetite. After I had listened to some talks and variety programmes, I would not have been surprised to hear that there are householders who make arrangements with the local authorities not to empty their dustbins but to fill them. Nevertheless there was always good music provided by some station or other at any time in the day, and I learned to swing like a trapeze artist from programme to programme in search of it.

But one evening I turned the wrong knob and found music of a kind other than I sought, the music that is above earth, that lives in the thunderclouds and rolls in human ears and sometimes deafens them without betraying the path of its melodic line. I heard the announcer relate how the King of Yugoslavia had been assassinated in the streets of Marseille that morning. We had passed into another phase of the mystery we are enacting here on earth, and I knew that it might be agonizing. The rags and tags of knowledge that we all have about us told me what foreign power had done this thing. It appeared to me inevitable that war must follow, and indeed it must have done, had not the Yugoslavian Government exercised an iron control on its population, then and thereafter, and abstained from the smallest provocative action against its enemies. That forbearance, which is one of the most extraordinary feats of statesmanship performed in post-war Europe, I could not be expected to foresee. So I imagined myself widowed and childless, which was another instance of the archaic outlook of the unconscious, for I knew that in the next war we women would have scarcely any need to fear bereavement, since air raids unpreceded by declaration of war would send us and our loved ones to the next world in the breachless unity of scrambled eggs. That thought did not then occur to me, so I rang for my nurse, and when she came I cried to her, "Switch on the telephone! I must speak to my husband at once. A most terrible thing has happened. The King of Yugoslavia has been assassinated." "Oh, dear!" she replied. "Did you know him?" "No," I said. "Then why," she asked, "do you think it's so terrible?"

Her question made me remember that the word "idiot" comes from a Greek root meaning private person. Idiocy is the female defect: intent on their private lives, women follow their fate through a darkness deep as that cast by malformed cells in the brain. It is no worse than the male defect, which is lunacy: they are so obsessed by public affairs that they see the world as by moonlight, which shows the outlines of every object but not the details indicative of their nature. I said, "Well, you know, assassinations lead to other things!" "Do they?" she asked. "Do they not!" I sighed, for when I came to look back on it my life had been punctuated by the slaughter of royalties, by the shouting of newsboys who have run down the streets to tell me that someone has used a lethal weapon to turn over a new leaf in the book of history. I remember when I was five years old looking upward at my mother and her cousin, who were standing side by side and looking down at a newspaper laid on a table in a circle of gaslight, the folds in their white pouched blouses and long black skirts kept as still by their consternation as if they were carved in stone. "There was the Empress Elizabeth of Austria," I said to the nurse, thirty-six years later. "She was very beautiful, wasn't she?" she asked. "One of the most beautiful women who ever lived," I said. "But wasn't she mad?" she asked. "Perhaps," I said, "perhaps, but only a little, and at the end. She was certainly brilliantly clever. Before she was thirty she had given proof of greatness." "How?" she asked. To her increasing distress I told her, for I know quite a lot of Habsburg history, until I saw how bored she was and let her go and leave me in darkness that was now patterned by the lovely triangle of Elizabeth's face.

How great she was! In her early pictures she wears the same look of fiery sullenness we see in the young Napoleon: she knows that within her there is a spring of life and she is afraid that the world will not let it flow forth and do its fructifying work. In her later pictures she wears a look that was never on the face of Napoleon. The world had not let the spring flow forth and it had turned to bitterness. But she was not without achievements of the finest sort, of a sort, indeed, that Napoleon never equalled. When she was sixteen she came, a Wittelsbach from the country bumpkin court of Munich, to marry the young Emperor of Austria and be the governing prisoner of the court of Vienna, which was the court of courts since the French Revolution had annulled the Tuileries and Versailles. The change would have made many women into nothing. But five years later she made a tour of Lombardy and Venetia at Franz Josef's side which was in many ways a miracle. It was, in the first place, a miracle of courage, because he and his officials had made these provinces loathe them for their brutality and inefficiency. The young girl sat with unbowed head in theatres that became silent as the grave at her coming, that were black with mourning worn to insult her, and she walked unperturbed through streets that emptied before her as if she were the plague. But when she came face to face with any Italians there occurred to her always the right word and gesture by which she uncovered her nature and pled: "Look, I am the Empress, but I am not evil. Forgive me and my husband and Austria for the evil we have done you, and let us love one another and work for peace between us."

It was useless, of course. Her successes were immediately annulled by the arrests and floggings carried out by the Habsburg officials. It was inevitable that the two provinces should be absorbed in the new kingdom of Italy. But Elizabeth's sweetness had not been merely automatic, she had been thinking like a liberal and like an Empress. She knew there was a real link between Austria and Hungary, and that it was being strained by misgovernment. So the next year she made a journey through Hungary, which was also a matter of courage, for it was almost as gravely disaffected as Lombardy and Venetia, and afterwards she learned Hungarian, though it is one of the most difficult of languages, cultivated the friendship of many important Hungarians, and acquainted herself with the nature of the concessions desired by Hungary. Her plans fell into abeyance when she parted from Franz Josef and travelled for five years. But in 1866 Austria was defeated by the Prussians, and she came back to console her husband, and then she induced him to create the Dual Monarchy and give autonomy to Hungary. It was by this device alone that the Austro-Hungarian Empire was able to survive into the twentieth century, and both the idea and the driving force behind the execution belonged to Elizabeth. That was statesmanship. Nothing of Napoleon's making lasted so long, nor was made so nobly.

Elizabeth should have gone on and medicined some of the other sores that were poisoning the Empire. She should have solved the problem of the Slav populations under Habsburg rule. The Slavs were a people, quarrelsome, courageous, artistic, intellectual, and profoundly perplexing to all other peoples, who came from Asia into the Balkan Peninsula early in the Christian era and were Christianized by Byzantine influence. Thereafter they founded violent and magnificent kingdoms of infinite promise in Bulgaria, Serbia, and Bosnia, but these were overthrown when the Turks invaded Europe in the fourteenth century, and

all were enslaved except the Slavs on the western borders of the Peninsula. These lived under the wing of the great powers, of Venice and Austria and Hungary, which was a doubtful privilege, since they were used
as helots and as man-power to be spent without thrift against the Turks.
Now all of these were under the Austro-Hungarian Empire, the Czechs
and the Croats, and the Slovenes and the Slovaks and the Dalmatians;
and they were alike treated oppressively, largely because the German-
Austrians felt a violent, instinctive loathing of all Slavs and particularly
of the Czechs, whose great intelligence and ability made them dangerous competitors in the labour market. Moreover, Serbia and Bulgaria had
thrown off the Turkish yoke during the nineteenth century and had
established themselves as free states, and the reactionary parties in Austria and Hungary feared that if their Slav populations were given liberty
they would seek union with Serbia under Russian protection. Therefore
they harried the Slavs as much as they could, by all possible economic
and social penalties, tried with especial venom to destroy their languages,
and created for themselves an increasing amount of internal disorder
which all sane men saw to carry a threat of disruption. It might have
saved the Empire altogether, it might have averted the war of 1914, if
Elizabeth had dealt with the Slavs as she dealt with the Hungarians. But
after thirty she did no more work for the Empire.

Her work stopped because her marriage, which was the medium for
her work, ceased to be tolerable. It appears probable, from the evidence
we have, that Elizabeth could not reconcile herself to a certain paradox
which often appears in the lives of very feminine women. She knew that
certain virtues are understood to be desirable in women: beauty, tenderness, grace, house-pride, the power to bear and rear children. She believed that she possessed some of these virtues and that her husband loved
her for it. Indeed, he seemed to have given definite proof that he loved
her by marrying her against the will of his mother, the Archduchess
Sophie. And she thought that because he loved her he must be her friend.
In that she was artless. Her husband, like many other human beings, was
divided between the love of life and the love of death. His love of life
made him love Elizabeth. His love of death made him love his abominable mother, and give her an authority over Elizabeth which she horribly misused.

The Archduchess Sophie is a figure of universal significance. She was
the kind of woman whom men respect for no other reason than that
she is lethal, whom a male committee will appoint to the post of hospital
matron. She had none of the womanly virtues. Especially did she lack

tenderness. There is no record of her ever having said a gentle word to the girl of sixteen whom her son brought home to endure this trouble-some greatness, and she arranged for the Archbishop who performed their marriage ceremony to address an insulting homily to the bride, bidding her remember that she was a nobody who had been called to a great position, and try to do her best. In politics she was practised in every kind of folly that most affronted the girl's instinctive wisdom. She was always thrusting the blunt muzzle of her stupidity into conclaves of state, treading down intelligent debate as a beast treads down the grass at a gate into mud, undermining the foundations of the Empire by insist-ing that everybody possible should be opposed and hurt. She was per-sonally responsible for some very ugly persecutions: one of her victims was the peasant philosopher Konrad Deubler. She was also a great slut. She had done nothing to reform the medievalism of the Austrian Palaces. It was the middle of the nineteenth century when Elizabeth came to Vienna, but both at the Winter Palace and the Summer Palace, at the Hofburg and Schönbrunn, was she expected to perform her excretory functions at a commode behind a screen in a passage which was patrolled by a sentry. The Archduchess Sophie saw to it that the evil she did should live after her by snatching Elizabeth's children away from her and allowing her no part in their upbringing. One little girl died in her care, attended by a doctor whom Elizabeth thought old-fashioned and incompetent; and the unhappy character of the Crown Prince Rudolf, restless, undisciplined, tactless, and insatiable, bears witness to her in-ability to look after their minds.

After Franz Josef had lost Elizabeth by putting this inferior over her and proving that love is not necessarily kind, he showed her endless kindness and indulgence, financing her wanderings and her castle-buildings with great good temper and receiving her gladly when she came home; and it seems she had no ill-feeling against him. She intro-duced the actress, Katherina Schratt, into his life very much as a woman might put flowers into a room she felt to be dreary. But she must have hated him as the Habsburg of Habsburgs, the centre of the imbecile sys-tem, when on January the thirtieth, 1889, Rudolf was found dead in his shooting-box at Mayerling beside the body of a girl of seventeen named Mary Vetsera. This event still remains a mystery. Mary Vetsera had been his mistress for a year and it is usually supposed that he and she had agreed to die together because Franz Josef had demanded they should part. But this is very hard to believe. Mary Vetsera was a very fat and plain little girl, bouncing with a vulgar ardour stimulated by improper

French novels, which had already led her into an affair with an English officer in Egypt; and it seems unlikely that Rudolf, who was a man of many love-affairs, should have thought her of supreme value after a year's possession, particularly considering that he had spent the night before he went to Mayerling with an actress to whom he had long been attached. It would seem much more probable that he had taken his life or (which is possible if his farewell notes were forged) been murdered as a result of troubles arising from his political opinions.

Of these we know a great deal, because he wrote a great number of articles for anonymous publication in the *Neues Wiener Tageblatt* and an even greater number of letters to its editor, a gifted Jew named Moritz Szeps. These show that he was a fervent liberal and loathed the Habsburg system. He loathed the expanding militarism of Germany, and prophesied that a German alliance would mean the destruction of Austria, body and soul; and he revered France with its deeply rooted culture and democratic tradition. He was enraged by anti-Semitism and wrote one of his most forcible articles against a gang of aristocrats who after a drunken orgy had gone round the Ghetto of Prague smashing windows, and had been let off scot free by the police. He was scandalized by the corruption of the banks and law-courts, and by the lack of integrity among high officials and politicians, and most of all by the Austro-Hungarian Empire. "As a simple onlooker," he wrote, "I am curious to know how such an old and tough organism as the Austrian Empire can last so long without cracking at the joints and breaking into pieces." Particularly was he eager to deal with the Slav problem, which had now grown even more complicated. Bosnia and Herzegovina had driven out the Turks and had been cheated of the freedom they had thus won by the Treaty of Berlin, which had given the Austro-Hungarian Empire the right to occupy and administer them. This had enraged the Slavs and given Serbia a grievance, so it was held by reactionaries to be all the more necessary to defend Austrian and Hungarian privileges. Rudolf had shown what he felt early in his career: when Franz Josef had appointed him colonel he had chosen to be attached to a Czech regiment with middle-class officers which was then stationed in Prague.

Whatever the explanation of Mayerling it must have raised Elizabeth's impatience with Vienna to loathing. The situation was unmitigated waste and ruin. She had never achieved a happy relationship with her son, although there was a strong intellectual sympathy between them, because of the early alienating influence of the Archduchess Sophie, and the Habsburgs had spoiled what they had not let her save. Rudolf had been forced for dynastic reasons into a marriage with a tedious Belgian princess, an acidulated child with golden hair, small eyes, and the conservative opinions one would expect from a very old member of the Carlton Club. She was literally a child; at the time of her wedding she had not yet shown the signs of womanhood. Owing to a slip in the enormously complicated domestic machinery of the Habsburgs she and her young bridegroom, who was only twenty-two, had been sent for their honeymoon to a remote castle which had been left servantless and unprepared. This ill-begun marriage had gone from bad to worse, and both husband and wife tortured and were tortured in turn. But it was the Habsburg situation, not merely the specific wrongs the Habsburgs brought on Rudolf, that was his ruin. Chamberlains fussed, spies scribbled, the police bullied and nagged, everybody knew where everybody else was at every moment of the day; Franz Josef rose at four each morning and worked on official papers for twelve or fourteen hours; and not a minute's thought was given to correcting the evils that were undermining the foundations of the Empire. Rudolf, as any intelligent member of the family must have done, tried to remedy this. Either he made some too ambitious plan and was detected and killed himself or was killed, or from discouragement he soused himself with brandy till it seemed proper to die for a plump little hoyden of seventeen. Now he lay dead, and the Austro-Hungarian Empire was without a direct or satisfactory heir.

Elizabeth lived nine years after her son's death, as drearily as any other of the unemployed. Then, perhaps as a punishment for having turned her back on the Slav problem, the key to Eastern Europe, a Western problem slew her. For the newspaper my mother and her cousin spread in the gaslight was wrong when it said that the man who killed her, Luccheni, was a madman. It is true that he said that he had killed Elizabeth because he had vowed to kill the first royal person he could find, and that he had gone to Évian to stab the Duke of Orléans but had missed him and had come back to Geneva to get Elizabeth instead; and this is an insane avowal, for no benefit whatsoever could be derived by anybody from the death of either of these people. But for all that Luccheni was not mad. Many people are unable to say what they mean only because they have not been given an adequate vocabulary by their environment; and their apparently meaningless remarks may be inspired by a sane enough consciousness of real facts.

There is a phase of ancient history which ought never to be forgotten by those who wish to understand their fellow-men. In Africa during the fourth century a great many Christians joined a body of schismatics known as the Donatists who were wrecking the Church by maintaining that only sacraments administered by a righteous priest were valid, and that a number of contemporary priests had proved themselves un-righteous by showing cowardice during the persecutions of Diocletian. They raved: for according to the Church Christ is the real dispenser of the sacraments, and it is inconceivable that a relationship prescribed by Him could break down through the personality of the mediator, and in many cases the tales were scandalmongering. But though these people raved they were not mad. They were making the only noises they knew to express the misery inflicted on them by the economic collapse of the Western Roman Empire. Since there was no economic literature there was no vocabulary suitable to their misery, so they had to use the vo-cabulary given them by the Church; and they screamed nonsense about the sacraments because they very sensibly recognized that the Western Roman Empire was going to die, and so were they.

It was so with Luccheni. He performed his meaningless act out of his consciousness of what is perhaps the most real distress of our age. He was an Italian born in Paris of parents forced to emigrate by their pov-erty and trodden down into an alien criminal class: that is to say, he belonged to an urban population for which the existing forms of gov-ernment made no provision, which wandered often workless and al-ways traditionless, without power to control its destiny. It was indeed most appropriate that he should register his discontent by killing Eliza-beth, for Vienna is the archetype of the great city which breeds such a population. Its luxury was financed by an exploited peasant class bled so white that it was ready to send its boys into the factories and the girls into service on any terms. The beggars in the streets of Vienna, who, the innocent suppose, were put there by the Treaty of St. Germain, are descendants of an army as old as the nineteenth century. Luccheni said with his stiletto to the symbol of power, "Hey, what are you going to do with me?" He made no suggestions, but cannot be blamed for it. It was the essence of his case against society that it had left him unfit to offer suggestions, unable to form thoughts or design actions other than the crudest and most violent. He lived many years in prison, almost until his like had found a vocabulary and a name for themselves and had as-tonished the world with the farce of Fascism.

So Elizabeth died, with a terrible ease. All her life her corsets had deformed and impeded her beautiful body, but they did not protect her from the assassin's stiletto. That cut clean through to her heart. Even so her imperial rank had insulated her from emotional and intellectual achievement, but freely admitted sorrow. And it would not leave her alone after her death. She had expressed in her will a solemn desire to be buried in the Isle of Corfu, but for all that Franz Josef had her laid in the Habsburg vault at the Capucin church of Vienna, fifteenth in the row of Empresses. The Habsburgs did not restrict themselves to the fields of the living in the exercise of their passion for preventing people from doing what they liked. Rudolf also asked that he might not be buried among his ancestors, but he had to yield up his skeleton; and the Prime Minister himself, Count Taaffe, called on Mary Vetsera's mother and asked her not to pray beside her daughter's grave, and received many police reports on her refusal to abandon this practice, which seems innocent enough even from the point of view of the court, since the whole of Vienna already knew how the girl had died. This was the kind of matter the Austrian Secret Police could handle. In the more important matter of keeping royal personages alive they were not nearly so successful.

After that Austria became a quiet place in Western eyes. Proust has pointed out that if one goes on performing any action, however banal, long enough, it automatically becomes "wonderful": a simple walk down a hundred yards of village street is "wonderful" if it is made every Sunday by an old lady of eighty. Franz Josef had for so long risen from his camp bed at four o'clock in the morning and worked twelve or fourteen hours on his official papers that he was recognized as one of the most "wonderful" of sovereigns, almost as "wonderful" as Queen Victoria, though he had shown no signs of losing in age the obstinacy and lack of imagination that made him see it as his duty to preserve his court as a morgue of etiquette and his Empire as a top-heavy anachronism. He was certain of universal acclamation not only during his life but after his death, for it is the habit of the people, whenever an old man mismanages his business so that it falls to pieces as soon as he dies, to say, "Ah, So-and-so was a marvel! He kept things together so long as he was alive, and look what happens now he has gone!" It was true that there was already shaping in his court a disaster that was to consume us all; but this did not appear to English eyes, largely because Austria was visited before the war only by our upper classes, who in no country noticed anything but horses, and Austrian horses were good.

The next time the red light of violence shone out it seemed of no importance, an irrelevant horror. When I was ten years old, on June the eleventh, 1903, Alexander Obrenovitch, King of Serbia, and his wife Draga were murdered in the Palace at Belgrade, and their naked bodies thrown out of their bedroom into the garden. The Queen's two brothers and two Ministers were also killed. The murder was the work of a number of Army officers, none of whom was then known outside Serbia, and the main characters were not interesting. Alexander was a flabby young man with pince-nez who had a taste for clumsy experiments in absolutism, and his wife, who strangely enough belonged to the same type as Mary Vetsera, though she had in her youth been far more beautiful, was understood to have the disadvantages of being disreputable, having an ambitious family, and lying under the suspicion of having tried to palm off a borrowed baby as an heir to the throne. There can be no question that these people were regarded with terrified apprehension by the Serbians, who had freed themselves from the Turk not a hundred years before and knew that their independence was perpetually threatened by the great powers. The crime lingered in my mind only because of its nightmare touches. The conspirators blew open the door of the Palace with a dynamite cartridge which fused the electric lights, and they stumbled about blaspheming in the darkness, passing into a frenzy of cruelty that was half terror. The King and Queen hid in a secret cupboard in their bedroom for two hours, listening to the searchers grow cold, then warm, then cold again, then warm, and at last hot, and burning hot. The weakly King was hard to kill: when they threw him from the balcony they thought him doubly dead from bullet wounds and sword slashes, but the fingers of his right hand clasped the railing and had to be cut off before he fell to the ground, where the fingers of his left hand clutched the grass. Though it was June, rain fell on the naked bodies in the early morning as they lay among the flowers. The whole of Europe was revolted. Edward VII withdrew his Minister and most of the great powers followed his example.

That murder was just a half-tone square, dimly figured with horror, at the back of my mind: a Police News poster or the front page of a tabloid, seen years ago. But now I realize that when Alexander and Draga fell from that balcony the whole of the modern world fell with them. It took some time to reach the ground and break its neck, but its fall started then. For this is not a strictly moral universe, and it is not true that it is useless to kill a tyrant because a worse man takes his place. It has never been more effectively disproved than by the successor of Alexander Obrenovitch. Peter Karageorgevitch came to the throne under every possible disadvantage. He was close on sixty and had never seen Serbia since he left it with his exiled father at the age of fourteen; he had been brought up at Geneva under the influence of Swiss liberalism and had later become an officer in the French Army; he had no experience of statecraft, and he was a man of modest and retiring personality and simple manners, who had settled down happily at Geneva, to supervise the education of his three motherless children and pursue mildly bookish interests. It appears to be true that though he had told the conspirators of his readiness to accept the Serbian throne if Alexander Obrenovitch vacated it, he had had no idea that they proposed to do anything more violent than force an abdication; after all, his favourite author was John Stuart Mill. The Karageorgevitch belief in the sacredness of the dynasty brought him back to Belgrade, but it might have been safely wagered that he would need all the support he could get to stay there. He was entirely surrounded by the conspirators whose crime he abhorred, and he could not dismiss them, because in sober fact they numbered amongst them some of the ablest and most public-spirited men in Serbia; and with these fierce critics all about him perfectly capable of doing what they had done before, he had to keep order in a new and expanding country, vexed with innumerable internal and external difficulties.

But Peter Karageorgevitch was a great king. Slowly and soberly he proved himself one of the finest liberal statesmen in Europe, and later, in the Balkan wars which drove the Turk out of Macedonia and Old Serbia, he proved himself a magnificent soldier. Never was there worse luck for Europe. Austria, with far more territory than she could properly administer, wanted more and had formed her Drang nach Osten, her Hasten to the East policy. Now the formidable new military state of Serbia was in her way, and might even join with Russia to attack her. Now, too, all the Slav peoples of the Empire were seething with discontent because the free Serbians were doing so well, and the German-Austrians hated them more than ever. The situation had been further complicated since Rudolf's day because the Empire had affronted Slav feeling by giving up the pretence that Bosnia and Herzegovina were provinces which she merely occupied and administered, and formally annexing them. This made many Slavs address appeals to Serbia, which, as was natural in a young country, sometimes answered boastfully.

The situation was further complicated by the character of the man who had succeeded Rudolf as the heir to the Imperial Crown, the Archduke Franz Ferdinand of Este. This unlovable melancholic had upset all sections of the people by his proposals, drafted and expressed without the slightest trace of statesmanship, to make a tripartite monarchy of the Empire, by forming the Slavs into a separate kingdom. The reactionaries felt this was merely an expression of his bitter hostility towards the Emperor and his conservatism; the Slavs were unimpressed and declared they would rather be free, like Serbia. The reaction of Austria to this new situation was extravagant fear. The Austrian Chief of General Staff, Conrad von Hötzendorf, was speaking for many of his countrymen and most of his class when he ceaselessly urged that a preventive war should be waged against Serbia before she became more capable of self-defence. He and his kind would not have felt this if Alexander Obrenovitch had not been murdered and given place to a better man, who made a strong and orderly Serbia.

Then on June the twenty-eighth, 1914, the Austro-Hungarian Government allowed Franz Ferdinand to go to Bosnia in his capacity of Inspector-General of the Army to conduct manœuvres on the Serbian frontier. It was strange that he should wish to do this, and that they should allow him, for that is St. Vitus's Day, the anniversary of the battle of Kossovo in 1389, the defeat of the Serbs by the Turks which meant five hundred years of enslavement. That defeat had been wiped out in the Balkan War by the recapture of Kossovo, and it was not tactful to remind the Serbs that some of their people were still enslaved by a foreign power. But Franz Ferdinand had his wish and then paid a visit to Sarajevo, the Bosnian capital, where the police gave him quite insufficient protection, though they had been warned that attempts were to be made on his life. A Bosnian Serb named Princip, who deeply resented Austro-Hungarian misrule, was able without any difficulty to shoot him as he drove along the street, and accidentally killed his wife as well. It must be noted that he was a Serb and not a Serbian. A Croat is a Catholic member and a Serb an Orthodox member of a Slav people that lies widely distributed south of the Danube, between the Adriatic and Bulgaria, and north of the Greek mountains. A Serbian is a subject of the kingdom of Serbia, and might be a Croat, just as a Croatian-born inhabitant of the old Austrian province of Croatia might be a Serb. But Princip had brought his revolver from Belgrade, and though he had been given it by a private individual and not by the Government, the Austro-Hungarian Empire used this as a pretext to declare war on Serbia. Other powers took sides and the Great War started.

Of that assassination I remember nothing at all. Every detail of Elizabeth's death is clear in my mind, of the Belgrade massacre I keep a blurred image, but I cannot recall reading anything about the Sarajevo *attentat* or hearing anyone speak of it. I was then very busy being an idiot, being a private person, and I had enough on my hands. But my idiocy was like my anæsthetic. During the blankness it dispensed I was cut about and felt nothing, but it could not annul the consequences. The pain came afterwards.

So, that evening in 1934, I lay in bed and looked at my radio fearfully, though it had nothing more to say that was relevant, and later on the telephone talked to my husband, as one does in times of crisis if one is happily married, asking him questions which one knows quite well neither he nor anyone else can answer and deriving great comfort from what he says. I was really frightened, for all these earlier killings had either hastened doom towards me or prefigured it. If Rudolf had not died he might have solved the Slav problem of the Austro-Hungarian Empire and restrained its imperialist ambition, and there might have been no war. If Alexander Obrenovitch had not been killed Serbia might never have been strong enough to excite the Empire's jealousy and fear, and there might have been no war. The killing of Franz Ferdinand was war itself. And the death of Elizabeth had shown me the scourge of the world after the war, Luccheni, Fascism, the rule of the dispossessed class that claims its rights and cannot conceive them save in terms of empty violence, of killing, taking, suppressing.

And now there was another killing. Again it was in the South-East of Europe, where was the source of all the other deaths. That seemed to me strange, in 1934, because the Slav problem then seemed to have been satisfactorily settled by the war. The Czechs and the Slovaks had their pleasant democratic state, which was working well enough except for the complaints of the Sudeten Germans who under the Habsburgs had been pampered with privileges paid for by their Slav neighbours. The Slovenes and the Croats and the Dalmatians and the Montenegrins were now united in the kingdom of the South Slavs, which is what Yugoslavia means; and though the Slovenes and Croats and the Dalmatians were separated in spirit from the Serbs by their Catholicism and the Montenegrins hankered after their lost independence, the state had seemed to be finding its balance. But here was another murder, another threat that man was going to deliver himself up to pain, was going to serve death instead of life.

A few days later my husband told me that he had seen a news film which had shown with extraordinary detail the actual death of the King of Yugoslavia, and as soon as I could leave the nursing-home I went and saw it. I had to go to a private projection room, for by that

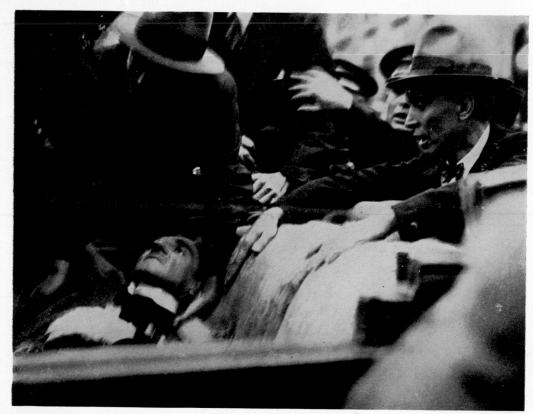

DEATH OF ALEXANDER KARAGEORGEVITCH, KING OF YUGOSLAVIA,
Marseille, October 9, 1934

THE ARCHDUKE FRANZ FERDINAND AND SOPHIE CHOTEK
leaving the Town Hall of Sarajevo, after the civic reception, June 28, 1914. In front of the Archduke
sits General Potiorek, Governor of Bosnia; beside him is his Adjutant, Lieutenant-Colonel Merizzi

time it had been withdrawn from the ordinary cinemas, and I took the opportunity to have it run over several times, while I peered at it like an old woman reading the tea-leaves in her cup. First there was the Yugoslavian warship sliding into the harbour of Marseille, which I know very well. Behind it was that vast suspension bridge which always troubles me because it reminds me that in this mechanized age I am as little able to understand my environment as any primitive woman who thinks that a waterfall is inhabited by a spirit, and indeed less so, for her opinion might from a poetical point of view be correct. I know enough to be aware that this bridge cannot have been spun by a vast steel spider out of its entrails, but no other explanation seems to me as plausible, and I have not the faintest notion of its use. But the man who comes down the gangway of the ship and travels on the tender to the quay, him I can understand, for he is something that is not new. Always the people have had the idea of the leader, and sometimes a man is born who embodies this idea.

His face is sucked too close to the bone by sickness to be tranquil or even handsome, and it would at any time have suggested a dry pedantry, unnatural in a man not far advanced in the forties. But he looks like a great man, which is not to say that he is a good man or a wise man, but is to say that he has that historic quality which comes from intense concentration on an important subject. What he is thinking of is noble, to judge from the homage he pays it with his eyes, and it governs him entirely. He does not relapse into it when the other world fails to interest him; rather does he relapse into noticing what is about him when for a moment his interior communion fails him. But he is not abstracted, he is paying due respect to the meeting between France and Yugoslavia. Indeed he is bringing to the official occasion a naïve earnestness. When Monsieur Barthou, the French Foreign Minister, comes and greets him, it is as if a jolly priest, fully at ease in his orders, stands before the altar beside a tortured mystical layman. Sometimes, too, he shows by a turn of the head, by a dilation of the pinched nostrils, that some aspect of the scene has pleased him.

About all his reactions there is that jerky quickness which comes of long vigilance. It was natural. He had been a soldier from boyhood, and since the Great War he had perpetually been threatened with death from within, by tuberculosis, and with death from without, by assassination at the hand of Croats or Macedonians who wanted independence instead of union with Serbia. But it is not fear that is his preoccupation. That, certainly, is Yugoslavia. He has the look of one of those men who claim that they rule by divine right whether they be kings or presidents, because their minds curve protectively over their countries with the inclusiveness of the sky. When one sees President Roosevelt one is sure that he is thinking about America; sometimes his thought may be soft and loose, but it is always dedicated to the same service. Those who saw Lenin say that he was always thinking of Russia; even when his thought was hard and tight it knew the same dedication. In our own King George V we recognized that piety.

Now King Alexander is driving down the familiar streets, curiously unguarded, in a curiously antique car. It can be seen from his attempt to make his stiff hand supple, from a careless flash of his careful black eyes, it can be seen that he is taking the cheers of the crowd with a childish seriousness. It is touching, like a girl putting full faith in the compliments that are paid to her at a ball. Then his preoccupation veils his brows and desiccates his lips. He is thinking of Yugoslavia again, with the nostalgia of an author who has been interrupted in writing his new book. He might be thinking, "*Heureux qui, comme Ulysse, a fait un beau voyage. . . .*" But then the camera leaves him. It recedes. The sound-track records a change, a swelling astonishment, in the voice of the crowd. We see a man jumping on the footboard of the car, a soldier swinging a sword, a revolver in the hand of another, a straw hat lying on the ground, a crowd that jumps up and down, up and down, smashing something flat with its arms, kicking something flat with its feet, till there is seen on the pavement a pulp covered with garments. A lad in a sweater dodges before his captors, his defiant face unmarked by fear, although his body expresses the very last extreme of fear by a creeping, writhing motion. A view of the whole street shows people dashed about as by a tangible wind of death.

The camera returns to the car and we see the King. He is lying almost flat on his back on the seat, and he is as I was after the anæsthetic. He does not know that anything has happened, he is still half rooted in the pleasure of his own nostalgia. He might be asking, "*Et en quelle saison Revoiray-je le clos de ma pauvre maison, Qui m'est une province, et beaucoup d'avantage?*" It is certain that he is dying, because he is the centre of a manifestation which would not happen unless the living had been shocked out of their reserve by the presence of death. Innumerable hands are caressing him. Hands are coming from everywhere, over the back of the car, over the sides, through the windows, to caress the dying King, and they are supremely kind. They are far kinder than faces can be, for faces are Marthas, burdened with many cares because of their close connexion with the mind, but these hands express the mindless sympathy of living flesh for flesh that is about to die, the pure physical basis for pity. They are men's hands, but they move tenderly as the hands of women fondling their babies, they stroke his cheek as if they were washing it with kindness. Suddenly his nostalgia goes from him. His pedantry relaxes. He is at peace, he need not guard against death any more.

Then the camera shows an official running wildly down a street in top hat and frock-coat, demonstrating the special ridiculousness of middle-aged men, who have the sagging, anxious faces and protruding bellies appropriate to pregnancies, but bring forth nothing. It would be a superb ending for a comic film. Then we see again the warship and the harbour, where the President of the Republic stands with many men around him, who are all as naïvely earnest as only one man was when that ship first came into the harbour. Now there is no jolly priest confident that he has the sacred mysteries well in hand: Barthou by now was also dead. All these men look as the King looked at his coming, as if there lay behind the surface of things a reality which at any moment might manifest itself as a eucharist to be partaken of not by individuals, but by nations. The coffin containing the man through which this terrible sacrament has been dispensed to France is carried on board, and the warship takes it away from these people, who stand in a vast circle, rigid with horror and reverence. They are intensely surprised that the eucharist was of this nature, but the King of Yugoslavia had always thought it might be so.

I could not understand this event, no matter how often I saw this picture. I knew, of course, how and why the murder had happened. Luccheni has got on well in the world. When he killed Elizabeth, over forty years ago, he had to do his own work in the world, he had to travel humbly about Switzerland in search of his victims, he had but one little two-edged dagger as tool for his crime, and he had to pay the penalty. But now Luccheni is Mussolini, and the improvement in his circumstances can be measured by the increase in the magnitude of his crime. In Elizabeth the insecure and traditionless town-dweller struck down the symbol of power, but his modern representative has struck down power itself by assuming itself and degrading its essence. His offence is not that he has virtually deposed his king, for kings and presidents who cannot hold their office lose thereby the title to their kingdoms and republics. His offence is that he made himself dictator without binding himself by any of the contractual obligations which civilized man has imposed on his rulers in all creditable phases of history and which give power a soul to be saved. This cancellation of process in government leaves it an empty violence that must perpetually and at any cost outdo itself, for it has no alternative idea and hence no alternative activity. The long servitude in the slums has left this kind of barbarian without any knowledge of what man does when he ceases to be violent, except for a few uncomprehending glimpses of material prosperity. He therefore can conceive of no outlet for his energies other than the creation of social services which artificially and unnaturally spread this material prosperity among the population, in small doses that keep them happy and dependent; and, for his second string, there is the performance of fantasias on the single theme of brute force. All forms of compulsion are practised on any element within the state that is resistant or is even suspected of retaining consciousness of its difference from the dominating party; and all living beings outside the state are conceived as enemies, to be hated and abused, and in ideal conditions to be robbed and murdered. This aggressiveness leads obviously to the establishment of immense armed forces, and furtively to incessant experimentation with methods of injuring the outer world other than the traditional procedure of warfare.

These methods, as time went on and Mussolini developed his foreign policy, included camps where Croats and Macedonians who objected to incorporation with Yugoslavia, or who were simply rogues, were trained as terrorists in the use of bombs and small arms and financed to use the results of that training in raids on Yugoslavia in the alleged service of their separatist campaigns. There could be no more convincing proof of the evil wrought on our civilization by the great cities and their spawn, for in not one state in pre-war Europe could there have been found any such example of an institution designed to teach the citizens of another state to murder their rulers. The existence of these camps and the necessity felt by human beings to practise any art they have learned explain the assassination of King Alexander without properly conveying its indecency. For Italy instructed her satellite, Hungary, to follow her example, and a notorious camp was established near the Yugoslav-Hungarian border at Yanka Puszta. Honour often seems a highly artificial convention, but life in any level of society where it has been abandoned astonishes by its tortuousness. When the Italians sent assassins from their training camps to murder the King, they went to great pains to make it appear that his murderers came from Yanka Puszta, even inducing a Macedonian assassin who had been associated with the Hungarian camp to come to Marseille and be killed, so that his dead body could be exhibited as proof of the conspirators' origin. It is a measure of the inevitable frivolity of a state governed by Fascist philosophy that the crime was entirely wasted and was committed only because of a monstrous miscalculation. Mussolini had believed that with the King's death the country would fall to pieces and be an easy prey to a foreign invader. But if Croat discontent had been a thousand times more bitter than it was, it would still have remained true that people prefer to kill their tyrants for themselves; and actually the murder shocked Yugoslavia into a unity it had not known before. So there was not war; there was nothing except the accomplishment of a further stage in the infiltration of peace with the depravity of war, which threatens now to make the two hardly distinguishable.

But the other participator in the event remained profoundly mysterious. At each showing of the film it could be seen more plainly that he had not been surprised by his own murder. He had not merely known of it as a factual possibility, he had realized it imaginatively in its full force as an event. But in this matter he seemed more intelligent than his own intelligence. Men of action often take an obstinate pride in their own limitations, and so, too, do invalids; and his face hinted that he, being both sick and soldierly, had combined the two forms of fault. All that I could read of his reign confirmed this indication and showed him as inflexible and slow. Yet there was in him this great wisdom, which brought him to the hour of his death sustained by a just estimate of what it is to die, and by certain magnificent conceptions such as kingliness and patriotism. It would be an enigma were it not that an individual had other ways of acquiring wisdom than through his own intellectual equipment. He can derive it, as it were, through the pores from the culture of his race. Perhaps this peculiar wisdom, which appeared on the screen as definitely as the peculiar sanity of Françoise Rosay or the peculiar narcissism of Garbo, was drawn by the King of Yugoslavia from the kingdom of Yugoslavia, from the South Slavs.

As to that I could form no opinion, for I knew nothing about the South Slavs, nor had I come across anybody who was acquainted with them. I was only aware that they formed part of the Balkan people, who had played a curious role in the history of British benevolence before the war and for some time after it. They had been, till they severally won their independences at various times in the nineteenth and twentieth centuries, the Christian subjects of the Turkish or Ottoman Empire,

which had kept them in the greatest misery by incompetent administration and very cunningly set each section of them at odds with all the
others, so that they could never rise in united rebellion. Hence each
people was perpetually making charges of inhumanity against all its
neighbours. The Serb, for example, raised his bitterest complaint against
the Turk, but was also ready to accuse the Greeks, the Bulgarians, the
Vlachs, and the Albanians of every crime under the sun. English persons,
therefore, of humanitarian and reformist disposition constantly went out
to the Balkan Peninsula to see who was in fact ill-treating whom, and,
being by the very nature of their perfectionist faith unable to accept
the horrid hypothesis that everybody was ill-treating everybody else,
all came back with a pet Balkan people established in their hearts as
suffering and innocent, eternally the massacree and never the massacrer.
The same sort of person, devoted to good works and austerities, who is
traditionally supposed to keep a cat and a parrot, often set up on the
hearth the image of the Albanian or the Bulgarian or the Serbian or the
Macedonian Greek people, which had all the force and blandness of
pious fantasy. The Bulgarians as preferred by the Buxton brothers, and
the Albanians as championed by Miss Durham, strongly resembled Sir
Joshua Reynolds's picture of the Infant Samuel.

But often it appeared that the Balkans had forced piety to work on
some very queer material. To hear Balkan-fanciers talk about each
other's Infant Samuel was to think of some painter not at all like Sir
Joshua Reynolds, say Hieronymus Bosch. The cats and parrots must
often have been startled. In 1912 there was a dispute, extravagantly inappropriate to those who took part in it, as to whether Mr. Prochaska,
the Austrian Consul in a town named Prizren, had or had not been castrated by the Serbs. Mr. Prochaska, an unusually conscientious public
servant, furthered his country's anti-Serbian policy by allowing it to be
supposed that he had. Miss Durham, born in 1863, the daughter of a
Fellow of the Royal College of Surgeons, a pupil at Bedford College,
and an exhibitor at the Royal Institute of Painters in Water-colours, who
had been led by her humanitarian passion to spend nearly all her life
in the Balkans and was strongly anti-Serbian, made the astonishing
statement that a party of Serbian officers whom she had met at a railway
station had informed her that they themselves had operated on Mr.
Prochaska. It is interesting to speculate on what the Fellow of the Royal
College of Surgeons or the staff of Bedford College would have thought
of this announcement. The controversy raged until Professor Seton-
Watson, who had no favourite among the Balkan peoples, but was

strongly anti-Austrian, stated that he had himself had access to a confidential account from Mr. Prochaska, which made it clear that the operation had not been performed at all. In no other circumstances could one imagine that gentle and elevated character receiving communications which afforded that kind of information. No other cause espoused by liberals so completely swept them off their feet by its own violence. The problems of India and Africa never produced anything like the jungle of savage pamphlets that sprang up in the footsteps of the Liberals who visited Turkey in Europe under the inspiration of Gladstone.

Violence was, indeed, all I knew of the Balkans: all I knew of the South Slavs. I derived the knowledge from memories of my earliest interest in Liberalism, of leaves fallen from this jungle of pamphlets, tied up with string in the dustiest corners of junk-shops, and later from the prejudices of the French, who use the word *"Balkan"* as a term of abuse, meaning a *rastaquouère* type of barbarian. In Paris, awakened in a hotel bedroom by the insufficiently private life of my neighbours, I have heard the sound of three slashing slaps and a woman's voice crying through sobs, *"Balkan! Balkan!"* Once in Nice, as I sat eating langouste outside a little restaurant down by the harbour, there were some shots, a sailor lurched out of the next-door bar, and the proprietress ran after him, shouting, *"Balkan! Balkan!"* He had emptied his revolver into the mirror behind the bar. And now I was faced with the immense nobility of the King in the film, who was certainly *Balkan, Balkan*, but who met violence with an imaginative realization which is its very opposite, which absorbs it into the experience it aims at destroying. But I must have been wholly mistaken in my acceptance of the popular legend regarding the Balkans, for if the South Slavs had been truly violent they would not have been hated first by the Austrians, who worshipped violence in an imperialist form, and later by the Fascists, who worship violence in a totalitarian form. Yet it was impossible to think of the Balkans for one moment as gentle and lamb-like, for assuredly Alexander and Draga Obrenovitch and Franz Ferdinand and his wife had none of them died in their beds. I had to admit that I quite simply and flatly knew nothing at all about the south-eastern corner of Europe; and since there proceeds steadily from that place a stream of events which are a source of danger to me, which indeed for four years threatened my safety and during that time deprived me for ever of many benefits, that is to say I know nothing of my own destiny.

That is a calamity. Pascal wrote: "Man is but a reed, the most feeble thing in nature; but he is a thinking reed. The entire universe need not arm itself to crush him. A vapour, a drop of water, suffices to kill him. But if the universe were to crush him, man would still be more noble than that which killed him, because he knows that he dies and the advantage which the universe has over him; the universe knows nothing of this." In these words he writes the sole prescription for a distinguished humanity. We must learn to know the nature of the advantage which the universe has over us, which in my case seems to lie in the Balkan Peninsula. It was only two or three days distant, yet I had never troubled to go that short journey which might explain to me how I shall die, and why. While I was marvelling at my inertia, I was asked to go to Yugoslavia to give some lectures in different towns before universities and English clubs, and this I did in the spring of 1936.

It was unfortunate that at the end of my journey I went to Greece and was stung by a sand-fly and got dengue fever, which is also known, and justly so, as breakbone fever. On the way back I had to rest in a *Kurhaus* outside Vienna, and there they thought me so ill that my husband came out to fetch me home. He found me weeping in my bedroom, though this is a town governed by its flowers, and as it was May the purple and white lilacs were as thick along the streets as people watching for a procession, and the chestnut trees were holding their candles to the windows of the upper rooms. I was well enough to be out, but I was sitting in a chair with a heap of coarse linen dresses flung over my knees and feet. I showed them to my husband one by one, saying in remorse, "Look what I have let them do!" They were dresses which I had bought from the peasants in Macedonia, and the Austrian doctor who was treating me had made me have them disinfected, though they were quite clean. But the nurse who took them away had forgotten what was to be done with them, and instead of putting them under the lamp she had given them to the washerwoman, who had put them in strong soak. They were ruined. Dyes that had been fixed for twenty years had run and now defiled the good grain of the stuff; stitches that had made a clean-cut austere design were now sordid smears. Even if I could have gone back immediately and bought new ones, which in my weakness I wanted to do, I would have it on my conscience that I had not properly protected the work of these women which should have been kept as a testimony, which was a part of what the King had known as he lay dying.

"You must not think me stupid," I said to my husband; "you cannot understand why I think these dresses important; you have not been there." "Is it so wonderful there?" he asked. "It is more wonderful than

I can tell you," I answered. "But how?" he said. I co[...]
all clearly. I said, "Well, there is everything there. [...]
have. But that seems very little." "Do you mean that [...]
very little," he asked, "or the whole of the West?" "[...]
West," I said, "here too." He looked at the butter[...]
houses between the chestnut trees and laughed. "Beeth[...]
and Schubert wrote quite a lot of music in this town," [...]
were none of them happy," I objected. "In Yugoslavi[...]
husband, smiling, "everybody is happy." "No, no," I [...]
but . . ." The thing I wanted to tell him could not b[...]
because it was manifold and nothing like what one is acc[...]
municate by words. I stumbled on, "Really, we are n[...]
West as we think we are. Or, rather, there is much v[...]
which the people in the Balkans have got in quantity. [...]
you would think they had nothing. The people who ma[...]
looked as if they had nothing at all. But if these imbeci[...]
spoiled this embroidery you would see that whoever [...]
than we have." I saw the blue lake of Ochrid, the mosq[...]
the walled town of Korchula, and it appeared possible th[...]
to find words for what I wanted to say because it was [...]
never sure of the reality of what I see, if I have seen [...]
know that until it has firmly established its objective ex[...]
pressing my senses and my memory, I am capable of [...]
into the service of a private dream. In a panic I said, "I [...]
Yugoslavia, this time next year, in the spring, for Easter."

JOURNEY

JOURNEY

strongly anti-Austrian, stated that he had himself had access to a confidential account from Mr. Prochaska, which made it clear that the operation had not been performed at all. In no other circumstances could one imagine that gentle and elevated character receiving communications which afforded that kind of information. No other cause espoused by liberals so completely swept them off their feet by its own violence. The problems of India and Africa never produced anything like the jungle of savage pamphlets that sprang up in the footsteps of the Liberals who visited Turkey in Europe under the inspiration of Gladstone.

Violence was, indeed, all I knew of the Balkans: all I knew of the South Slavs. I derived the knowledge from memories of my earliest interest in Liberalism, of leaves fallen from this jungle of pamphlets, tied up with string in the dustiest corners of junk-shops, and later from the prejudices of the French, who use the word *"Balkan"* as a term of abuse, meaning a *rastaquouère* type of barbarian. In Paris, awakened in a hotel bedroom by the insufficiently private life of my neighbours, I have heard the sound of three slashing slaps and a woman's voice crying through sobs, *"Balkan! Balkan!"* Once in Nice, as I sat eating langouste outside a little restaurant down by the harbour, there were some shots, a sailor lurched out of the next-door bar, and the proprietress ran after him, shouting, *"Balkan! Balkan!"* He had emptied his revolver into the mirror behind the bar. And now I was faced with the immense nobility of the King in the film, who was certainly *Balkan, Balkan,* but who met violence with an imaginative realization which is its very opposite, which absorbs it into the experience it aims at destroying. But I must have been wholly mistaken in my acceptance of the popular legend regarding the Balkans, for if the South Slavs had been truly violent they would not have been hated first by the Austrians, who worshipped violence in an imperialist form, and later by the Fascists, who worship violence in a totalitarian form. Yet it was impossible to think of the Balkans for one moment as gentle and lamb-like, for assuredly Alexander and Draga Obrenovitch and Franz Ferdinand and his wife had none of them died in their beds. I had to admit that I quite simply and flatly knew nothing at all about the south-eastern corner of Europe; and since there proceeds steadily from that place a stream of events which are a source of danger to me, which indeed for four years threatened my safety and during that time deprived me for ever of many benefits, that is to say I know nothing of my own destiny.

That is a calamity. Pascal wrote: "Man is but a reed, the most feeble thing in nature; but he is a thinking reed. The entire universe need not arm itself to crush him. A vapour, a drop of water, suffices to kill him. But if the universe were to crush him, man would still be more noble than that which killed him, because he knows that he dies and the advantage which the universe has over him; the universe knows nothing of this." In these words he writes the sole prescription for a distinguished humanity. We must learn to know the nature of the advantage which the universe has over us, which in my case seems to lie in the Balkan Peninsula. It was only two or three days distant, yet I had never troubled to go that short journey which might explain to me how I shall die, and why. While I was marvelling at my inertia, I was asked to go to Yugoslavia to give some lectures in different towns before universities and English clubs, and this I did in the spring of 1936.

It was unfortunate that at the end of my journey I went to Greece and was stung by a sand-fly and got dengue fever, which is also known, and justly so, as breakbone fever. On the way back I had to rest in a *Kurhaus* outside Vienna, and there they thought me so ill that my husband came out to fetch me home. He found me weeping in my bedroom, though this is a town governed by its flowers, and as it was May the purple and white lilacs were as thick along the streets as people watching for a procession, and the chestnut trees were holding their candles to the windows of the upper rooms. I was well enough to be out, but I was sitting in a chair with a heap of coarse linen dresses flung over my knees and feet. I showed them to my husband one by one, saying in remorse, "Look what I have let them do!" They were dresses which I had bought from the peasants in Macedonia, and the Austrian doctor who was treating me had made me have them disinfected, though they were quite clean. But the nurse who took them away had forgotten what was to be done with them, and instead of putting them under the lamp she had given them to the washerwoman, who had put them in strong soak. They were ruined. Dyes that had been fixed for twenty years had run and now defiled the good grain of the stuff; stitches that had made a clean-cut austere design were now sordid smears. Even if I could have gone back immediately and bought new ones, which in my weakness I wanted to do, I would have it on my conscience that I had not properly protected the work of these women which should have been kept as a testimony, which was a part of what the King had known as he lay dying.

"You must not think me stupid," I said to my husband; "you cannot understand why I think these dresses important; you have not been there." "Is it so wonderful there?" he asked. "It is more wonderful than

I can tell you," I answered. "But how?" he said. I could not tell him at all clearly. I said, "Well, there is everything there. Except what we have. But that seems very little." "Do you mean that the English have very little," he asked, "or the whole of the West?" "The whole of the West," I said, "here too." He looked at the butter-yellow baroque houses between the chestnut trees and laughed. "Beethoven and Mozart and Schubert wrote quite a lot of music in this town," he said. "But they were none of them happy," I objected. "In Yugoslavia," suggested my husband, smiling, "everybody is happy." "No, no," I said, "not at all, but . . ." The thing I wanted to tell him could not be told, however, because it was manifold and nothing like what one is accustomed to communicate by words. I stumbled on, "Really, we are not as rich in the West as we think we are. Or, rather, there is much we have not got which the people in the Balkans have got in quantity. To look at them you would think they had nothing. The people who made these dresses looked as if they had nothing at all. But if these imbeciles here had not spoiled this embroidery you would see that whoever did it had more than we have." I saw the blue lake of Ochrid, the mosques of Sarajevo, the walled town of Korchula, and it appeared possible that I was unable to find words for what I wanted to say because it was not true. I am never sure of the reality of what I see, if I have seen it only once; I know that until it has firmly established its objective existence by impressing my senses and my memory, I am capable of conscripting it into the service of a private dream. In a panic I said, "I must go back to Yugoslavia, this time next year, in the spring, for Easter."

JOURNEY

WE spent the night at Salzburg, and in the morning we had time to visit the house where Mozart was born, and look at his little spinet, which has keys that are brown and white instead of white and black. There the boy sat, pleased by its prettiness and pleased by the sounds he drew from it, while there encircled him the rage of his father at this tiresome, weak, philandering son he had begotten, who would make no proper use of his gifts; and further back still the indifference of his contemporaries, which was to kill him; and further back still, so far away as to be of no use to him, our impotent love for him. That was something we human beings did not do very well. Then we went down to the railway station and waited some hours for the train to Zagreb, the capital of Croatia. When it at last arrived, I found myself in the midst of what is to me the mystery of mysteries. For it had left Berlin the night before and was crammed with unhappy-looking German tourists, all taking advantage of the pact by which they could take a substantial sum out of the country provided they were going to Yugoslavia; and I cannot understand the proceedings of Germans. All Central Europe seems to me to be enacting a fantasy which I cannot interpret.

The carriages were so crowded that we could find only one free seat in a first-class compartment, which I took, while my husband sat down in a seat which a young man had just left to go to the restaurant car for lunch. The other people in the compartment were an elderly business man and his wife, both well on in the fifties, and a manufacturer and his wife, socially superior to the others and fifteen to twenty years younger. The elderly business man and his wife, like nearly everybody else on the train, were hideous; the woman had a body like a sow, and the man was flabby and pasty. The manufacturer was very much better-looking, with a direct laughing eye, but he was certainly two stone overweight, and his wife had been sharpened to a dark keen prettiness by some Hungarian strain. The business man's wife kept leaving her

27

seat and running up and down the corridor in a state of great distress, lamenting that she and her husband had no Austrian schillings and therefore could not get a meal in the restaurant car. Her distress was so marked that we assumed that they had eaten nothing for many hours, and we gave her a packet of chocolate and some biscuits, which she ate very quickly with an abstracted air. Between mouthfuls she explained that they were travelling to a Dalmatian island because her husband had been very ill with a nervous disorder affecting the stomach which made him unable to make decisions. She pointed a bitten bar of chocolate at him and said, "Yes, he can't make up his mind about anything! If you say, 'Do you want to go or do you want to stay?' he doesn't know." Grieving and faithful love shone in her eyes. My husband was very sympathetic, and said that he himself had nervous trouble of some sort. He even alleged, to my surprise, that he had passed through a similar period of not knowing his own mind. Sunshine, he said, he had found the only cure.

But as she spoke her eyes shifted over my husband's shoulders and she cried, "Ah, now we are among beautiful mountains! *Wunderbar! Fabelhaft! Ach*, these must be the Dolomites!" "No, these are not the Dolomites," said my husband, "this is the valley that runs up to Bad Gastein," and he told her that in the sixteenth century this had been a district of great wealth and culture, because it had been a gold-mining centre. He pointed out the town of Hof Gastein and described the beautiful Gothic tombs of mineowners in the church there, which are covered with carvings representing stages of the mining process. Everybody in the carriage listened to this with sudden, proud, exclamatory delight; it was as if they were children, and my husband were reading them a legend out of a book about their glorious past. They seemed to derive a special pious pleasure from the contemplation of the Gothic; and they were also enraptured by the perfection of my husband's German.

"But it is real German German!" they said, as if they were complimenting him on being good as well as clever. Suddenly the manufacturer said to him, "But have you really got first-class tickets?" My husband said in surprise, "Yes, of course we have; here they are." Then the manufacturer said, "Then you can keep the seat where you are sitting, for the young man who had it has only a second-class ticket!" The others all eagerly agreed. "Yes, yes," they said, "certainly you must stay where you are, for he has only a second-class ticket!" The business man's wife jumped up and stopped a passing ticket-collector and told him about it with great passion and many defensive gestures towards us, and he too became excited and sympathetic. He promised that, as lunch was now finished and people were coming back from the restaurant car, he would wait for the young man and eject him. It was just then that the business man's wife noticed that we were rising into the snowfields at the head of the pass and cried out in rapture. This too was *wunderbar* and *fabelhaft*, and the whole carriage was caught up into a warm lyrical ecstasy. Snow, apparently, was certified in the philosophy as a legitimate object for delight, like the Gothic. For this I liked them enormously. Not only was it an embryonic emotion which, fully developed and shorn of its sentimentality, would produce great music of the Beethoven and Brahms and Mahler type, but it afforded an agreeable contrast to the element I most dislike. If anyone in a railway carriage full of English people should express great enjoyment of the scenery through which the train was passing, his companions would feel an irresistible impulse not only to refrain from joining him in his pleasure, but to persuade themselves that there was something despicable and repellent in that scenery. No conceivable virtue can proceed from the development of this characteristic.

At the height of this collective rhapsody the young man with the second-class ticket came back. He had been there for a minute or two before anybody, even the ticket-collector, noticed his presence. He was standing in the middle of the compartment, not even understanding that his seat had been taken, as my husband was at the window, when the business man's wife became aware of him. "Oho-o-o-o!" she cried with frightful significance; and everybody turned on him with such vehemence that he stood stock-still with amazement, and the ticket-collector had to pull him by the sleeve and tell him to take his luggage and be gone. The vehemence of all four Germans was so intense that we took it for granted that it must be due to some other reason than concern for our comfort, and supposed the explanation lay in the young man's race and personality, for he was Latin and epicene. His oval olive face was meek with his acceptance of the obligation to please, and he wore with a demure coquetry a suit, a shirt, a tie, socks, gloves, and a hat all in the colours of coffee-and-cream of various strengths. The labels on his suitcase suggested he was either an actor or a dancer, and indeed his slender body was as unnaturally compressed by exercise as by a corset. Under this joint attack he stood quite still with his head down and his body relaxed, not in indifference, but rather because his physical training had taught him to loosen his muscles when he was struck so that he should fall light. There was an air of practice about him, as if he were thoroughly used to being the object of official hostility, and a kind of passive, not very noble fortitude; he was quite sure he would survive this, and would be able to walk away unhurt. We were distressed, but could not believe we were responsible, since the feeling of the Germans was so passionate; and indeed this young man was so different from them that it was conceivable they felt as hippopotami at the Zoo might feel if a cheetah were introduced into their cage.

By the time he had left us the train was drawing in to Bad Gastein. The business man's wife was upset because she could get nothing to eat there. The trolleys carrying chocolate and coffee and oranges and sandwiches were busy with another train when we arrived, and they started on our train too late to arrive at our carriage. She said that she did not mind so much for herself as for her husband. He had had nothing since breakfast at Munich except some sausages and coffee at Passau and some ham sandwiches at Salzburg. As he had also eaten some of the chocolate and biscuits we had given her, it seemed to us he had not done so badly for a man with a gastric ailment. Then silence fell on her, and she sat down and dangled her short legs while we went through the very long tunnel under the Hohe Tauern mountains. This tunnel represents no real frontier. They were still in Austria, and they had left Germany early that morning. Yet when we came out on the other side all the four Germans began to talk quickly and freely, as if they no longer feared something. The manufacturer and his wife told us that they were going to Hertseg Novi, a village on the South Dalmatian coast, to bathe. They said he was tired out by various difficulties which had arisen in the management of his business during the last few months. At that the business man put his forehead down on his hand and groaned. Then they all laughed at their own distress; and they all began to tell each other how badly they had needed this holiday they were taking, and what *pension* terms they were going to pay, and by what date they had to be back in Germany, and to discuss where they were allowed to go as tourists and how much money they would have been allowed if they had gone to other countries and in what form they would have had to take it. The regulations which bound them were obviously of an inconvenient intricacy, for they frequently disputed as to the details; and indeed they frequently uttered expressions of despair at the way they were hemmed in and harried.

They talked like that for a long time. Then somebody came and told the business man's wife that she could, after all, have a meal in the restaurant car. She ran out in a great hurry, and the rest of us all fell silent. I read for a time and then slept, and woke up just as the train was running into Villach, which is a lovely little Austrian town set on a river. At Villach the business man's wife was overjoyed to find she could buy some sausages for herself and her husband. All through the journey she was eating voraciously, running after food down the corridor, coming back munching something, her mouth and bust powdered with crumbs. But there was nothing so voluptuous as greed about all this eating. She was simply stoking herself with food to keep her nerves going, as ill and tired people drink. Actually she was an extremely pleasant and appealing person: she was all goodness and kindness, and she loved her husband very much. She took great pleasure in bringing him all this food, and she liked pointing out to him anything beautiful that we were passing. When she had got him to give his attention to it, she looked no more at the beautiful thing but only at his face. When we were going by the very beautiful Wörther See, which lay under the hills, veiled by their shadows and the dusk so that one could attribute to it just the kind of beauty one prefers, she made him look at it, looked at him looking at it, and then turned to us and said, "You cannot think what troubles he has had!" We made sympathetic noises, and the business man began to grumble away at his ease. It appeared that he owned an apartment house in Berlin, and had for six months been struggling with a wholly unforeseen and inexplicable demand for extra taxes on it. He did not allege that the tax was unjust. He seemed to think that the demand was legal enough, but that the relevant law was so complicated, and was so capriciously interpreted by the Nazi courts, that he had been unable to foresee how much he would be asked for, and was still quite at a loss to calculate what might be exacted in the future. He had also had a great deal of trouble dealing with some undesirable tenants, whose conduct had caused frequent complaints from other tenants, but who were members of the Nazi Party. He left it ambiguous whether he had tried to evict the undesirable tenants and had been foiled by the Nazis, or if he had been too frightened even to try to get redress.

At that the manufacturer and his wife sighed, and said that they could understand. The man spoke with a great deal of reticence and obviously did not want to give away exactly what his business was, lest he get into difficulties; but he said with great resentment that the Nazis had put a director into his company who knew nothing and was simply a Party man in line for a job. He added, however, that what he really minded was the unforeseeable taxes. He laughed at the absurdity of it all, for he was a brave and jolly man; but the mere fact that he stopped giving us details of his worries, when he was obviously extremely expansive by temperament, showed that his spirit was deeply troubled. Soon he fell silent and put his arm round his wife. The two had an air of being united by a great passion, an unusual physical sympathy, and also by a common endurance of stress and strain, to a degree which would have seemed more natural in far older people. To cheer him up the wife told us funny stories about some consequences of *Hitlerismus*. She described how the hairdresser's assistant who had always waved her hair for her had one morning greeted her with tears, and told her that she was afraid she would never be able to attend to her again, because she was afraid she had failed in the examination which she had to pass for the right to practise her craft. She had said to the girl, "But I am sure you will pass your examination, for you are so very good at your work." But the girl had answered, "Yes, I am good at my work! Shampooing can I do, and water-waving can I do, and marcelling can I do, and oil massage can I do, and hair-dyeing can I do, but keep from mixing up Göring's and Goebbels's birthday, that can I not do." They all laughed at this, and then again fell silent.

The business man said, "But all the young people, they are solid for Hitler. For them all is done."

The others said, "*Ja, das ist so!*" and the business woman began, "Yes, our sons," and then stopped.

They were all of them falling to pieces under the emotional and intellectual strain laid on them by their Government, poor Laocoöns strangled by red tape. It was obvious that by getting the population into this state the Nazis had guaranteed the continuance of their system; for none of these people could have given any effective support to any rival party that wanted to seize power, and indeed their affairs, which were thoroughly typical, were in such an inextricable state of confusion that no sane party would now wish to take over the government, since it would certainly see nothing but failure ahead. Their misery seemed to have abolished every possible future for them. I reflected that if a train were filled with the citizens of the Western Roman Empire in the fourth century they would have made much the same complaints. The reforms of Diocletian and Constantine created a condition of exorbitant and unforeseeable taxes, of privileged officials, of a complicated civil administration that made endless demands on its subjects and gave them very little security in return. The Western

Romans were put out of their pain by the invasion of the Goths. But these people could not hope for any such release. It was like the story of the man who went to Dr. Abernethy, complaining of hopeless melancholy, and was advised to go and see the famous clown, Grimaldi. "I am Grimaldi," he said. These men and women, incapable of making decisions or enforcing a condition where they could make them, were the Goths.

It was dark when we crossed the Yugoslavian frontier. Handsome young soldiers in olive uniforms with faces sealed by the flatness of cheekbones asked us questions softly, insistently, without interest. As we steamed out of the station, the manufacturer said with a rolling laugh, "Well, we'll have no more good food till we're back here again. The food in Yugoslavia is terrible." "*Ach*, so we have heard," wailed the business man's wife, "and what shall I do with my poor man! There is nothing good at all, is there?" This seemed to me extremely funny, for food in Yugoslavia has a Slav superbness. They cook lamb and sucking-pig as well as anywhere in the world, have a lot of freshwater fish and broil it straight out of the streams, use their vegetables young enough, have many dark and rich romantic soups, and understand that seasoning should be pungent rather than hot. I said, "You needn't worry at all. Yugoslavian food is very good." The manufacturer laughed and shook his head. "No, I was there in the war and it was terrible." "Perhaps it was at that time," I said, "but I was there last year, and I found it admirable." They all shook their heads at me, smiling, and seemed a little embarrassed. I perceived they felt that English food was so far inferior to German that my opinion on the subject could not be worth having, and that I was rather simple and ingenuous not to realize this. "I understand," ventured my husband, "that there are very good trout." "*Ach*, no!" laughed the manufacturer, waving his great hand. "They call them trout, but they are something quite different; they are not like our good German trout." They all sat, nodding and rocking, entranced by a vision of the warm goodness of German life, the warm goodness of German food, and of German superiority to all non-German barbarity.

A little while later my husband and I went and had dinner in the wagon-restaurant, which was Yugoslavian and extremely good. When we came back the business man was telling how, sitting at his desk in his office just after the war, he had seen the bodies of three men fall past his windows, Spartacist snipers who had been on his roof and had been picked off by Government troops; how he had been ruined in the inflation, and had even sold his dog for food; how he had made a fortune again, by the refinancing of a prosperous industry, but had never enjoyed it because he had always been afraid of Bolshevism, and had worried himself ill finding the best ways of tying it up safely; and now he was afraid. He had spent the last twenty-three years in a state of continuous terror. He had been afraid of the Allies; he had been afraid of the Spartacists; he had been afraid of financial catastrophe; he had been afraid of the Communists; and now he was afraid of the Nazis.

Sighing deeply, he said, evidently referring to something about which he had not spoken, "The worst of life under the Nazis is that the private citizen hasn't any liberty, but the officials haven't any authority either." It was curious that such a sharply critical phrase should have been coined by one whose attitude was so purely passive; for he had spoken of all the forces that had tormented him as if they could not have been opposed, any more than thunder or lightning. He seemed, indeed, quite unpolitically minded. When he complained of the inflation, my husband tried to console him by saying that the sufferings he and others had undergone at that time may have been severe, but they had at least been of immense service to Germany; that Helfferich had been justified in his heroic plan, since it had wiped out the internal debt and cleared the ground for enterprising people to make a new and triumphant industrialism. But the business man, though he had himself actually been one of those enterprising men, did not show any interest in the idea. He seemed quite unused to regarding anything that the state did as having a cause or any but the most immediate effect.

Just then I happened to see the name of a station at which we were stopping, and I asked my husband to look it up in a time-table he had in his pocket, so that we might know how late we were. And it turned out that we were very late indeed, nearly two hours. When my husband spoke of this all the Germans showed the greatest consternation. They realized that this meant they would almost certainly get into Zagreb too late to catch the connexion which would take them the twelve hours' journey to Split, on the Dalmatian coast, and in that case they would have to spend the night at Zagreb. It was not easy to see why they were so greatly distressed. Both couples were staying in Yugoslavia for some weeks and the loss of a day could not mean much to them; and they could draw as they liked on their dinars in the morning. The business man's wife was adding another agony to the strain of the situation. For it was still just possible that we might get to Zagreb in time to bundle into the Split train, and she was not sure if she ought to do that, as her husband was so tired. The necessity for making a decision on this plan caused her real anguish; she sat wringing her poor red hands. To us it seemed the obvious thing that they should simply make up their minds to stay the night, but it was not at all obvious to them. She looked so miserable that we gave her some biscuits, which she crammed into her mouth exactly like an exhausted person taking a pull of brandy. The other two had decided to stay at Zagreb, but they were hardly in a better state. Consciousness of their own fatigue had rushed upon them; they were amazed at it, they groaned and complained.

I realized again that I would never understand the German people. The misery of these travellers was purely amazing. It was perplexing that they should have been surprised by the lateness of the train. The journey from Berlin to Zagreb is something like thirty hours, and no sensible person would expect a minor train to be on time on such a route in winter, particularly as a great part of it runs through the mountains. It also seemed to me odd that the business man's wife should take it as an unforeseen horror that her husband, who had been seriously ill and was not yet recovered, should be tired after sitting up in a railway carriage for a day and a night. Also, if she had such an appetite why had she not brought a tin of biscuits and some ham? And how was it that these two men, who had successfully conducted commercial and industrial enterprises of some importance, were so utterly incompetent in the conduct of a simple journey? As I watched them in complete mystification, yet another consideration came to horrify them. "And what the hotels in Zagreb will be like!" said the manufacturer. "Pig-sties! Pig-sties!" "Oh, my poor husband!" moaned the business man's wife. "To think he is to be uncomfortable when he is so ill!" I objected that the hotels in Zagreb were excellent; that I myself had stayed in an old-fashioned hotel which was extremely comfortable and that there was a new and huge hotel that was positively American in its luxury. But they would not listen to me. "But why are you going to Yugoslavia if you think it is all so terrible?" I asked. "Ah," said the manufacturer, "we are going to the Adriatic coast where there are many German tourists and for that reason the hotels are good."

Then came a climactic mystification. There came along the first Yugoslavian ticket-collector, a red-faced, ugly, amiable Croat. The Germans all held out their tickets, and lo and behold! They were all second-class. My husband and I gaped in bewilderment. It made the campaign they had conducted against the young man in coffee-and-cream clothes completely incomprehensible and not at all pleasing. If they had been nasty people it would have been natural enough; but they were not at all nasty, they loved each other, tranquillity, snow, and their national history. Nevertheless they were unabashed by the disclosure of what my husband and I considered the most monstrous perfidy. I realized that if I had said to them, "You had that young man turned out of the carriage because he had a second-class ticket," they would have nodded and said, "Yes," and if I had gone on and said, "But you yourselves have only second-class tickets," they would not have seen that the second statement had any bearing on the first; and I cannot picture to myself the mental life of people who cannot perceive that connexion.

But as we gaped we were plunged into yet another mystification. The Croat ticket-collector told the Germans that they must pay the difference between the first-class and the second-class fares from the frontier. It amounted to very little, to only a few marks a head. The Germans protested, on the ground that not enough second-class carriages had been provided in Berlin, but the Croat explained that that was not his business, nor the Yugoslavian Railway Company's. The German authorities made up the train, and it was their fault if it were not properly constituted. The Yugoslavian Railway Company simply accepted the train, and on its line passengers must pay for the seats they occupied. At that the manufacturer winked at him and held out a hand to him with a bribe in it. The Croat was so poor, his hand curved for it in spite of himself. But he explained that he could not settle it that way, because an inspector might come along, and he would lose his job, for on this matter the company was really strict. The manufacturer persisted, smiling. I nearly bounced out of my seat, for the ticket-collector was so poor that he was grinning with desire for the money, while his eyebrows were going up in fear. It was not fair to tempt him to take this risk. I also wondered how these people, who were sure that Yugoslavia was a land of barbarians, dared put themselves on the wrong side of the law within a few hours of crossing the frontier.

As I wondered, the ticket-collector suddenly lost his temper. His red face became violet, he began to shout. The Germans showed no resentment and simply began to get the money together; yet if anybody had shouted at me like that, I should have shouted back, no matter how much in the wrong I was. In this they showed a marked superiority over me. But in their efforts to make payment they became again flatly incomprehensible. They could pay it in marks, and the amount was much less than the marks they had been allowed to take out of the country, and had in fact taken. Nevertheless they had great difficulty in paying, for the incredible reason that not one of them knew exactly where his money was. They had to turn out pockets and bags and purses, they had to give each other change, they had to do reckonings and correct each other, and they groaned all the time at this inconvenience which was entirely their own fault.

I got up and went out into the corridor. It was disconcerting to be rushing through the night with this carriageful of unhappy muddlers, who were so nice and so incomprehensible, and so apparently doomed to disaster of a kind so special that it was impossible for anybody not of their blood to imagine how it could be averted. It added to their eerie quality that on paper these people would seem the most practical and sensible people. Their businesses were, I am sure, most efficiently conducted. But this only meant that since the Industrial Revolution capitalism has grooved society with a number of deep slots along which most human beings can roll smoothly to a fixed destination. When a man takes charge of a factory the factory takes charge of him, if he opens an office it falls into a place in a network that extends over the whole world and so long as he obeys the general trend he will not meet any obvious disaster; but he may be unable to meet the calls that daily life outside this specialist area makes on judgment and initiative. These people fell into that category. Their helplessness was the greater because they had plainly a special talent for obedience. In the routine level of commerce and industry they must have known a success which must have made their failure in all other phases of their being embittering and strange. Now that capitalism was passing into a decadent phase and many of the grooves along which they had rolled so happily were worn down to nothing, they were broken and beaten, and their ability to choose the broad outlines of their daily lives, to make political decisions, was now less than it had been originally. It was inevitable that the children of such muddlers, who would themselves be muddlers, would support any system which offered them new opportunities for profitable obedience, which would pattern society with new grooves in place of the old, and would never be warned by any instinct for competence and self-preservation if that system was leading to universal disaster. I tried to tell myself that these people in the carriage were not of importance, and were not typical, but I knew that I lied. These were exactly like all Aryan Germans I had ever known; and there were sixty millions of them in the middle of Europe.

"This is Zagreb!" cried the Germans, and took all their luggage down from the racks. Then they broke into excessive cries of exasperation and distress because it was not Zagreb, it was Zagreb-Sava, a suburb three or four miles out of the main town. I leaned out of the window. Rain was falling heavily, and the mud shone between the railway tracks. An elderly man, his thin body clad in a tight-fitting, flimsy overcoat, trotted along beside the train, crying softly, "Anna! Anna! Anna!" He held an open umbrella not over himself but at arm's length. He had not brought it for himself, but for the beloved woman he was calling. He did not lose hope when he found her nowhere in all the long train, but turned and trotted all the way back, calling still with anxious sweetness, "Anna! Anna! Anna!" When the train steamed out he was trotting along it for a third time, holding his umbrella still further away from him. A ray of light from an electric standard shone on his white hair, on the dome of his umbrella, which was streaked with several rents, and on the strong spears of the driving rain. I was among people I could understand.

CROATIA

CROATIA

Zagreb I

THEY were waiting in the rain on the platform of the real Zagreb, our three friends. There was Constantine, the poet, a Serb, that is to say a Slav member of the Orthodox Church, from Serbia. There was Valetta, a lecturer in mathematics at Zagreb University, a Croat, that is to say a Slav member of the Roman Catholic Church, from Dalmatia. There was Marko Gregorievitch, the critic and journalist, a Croat from Croatia. They were all different sizes and shapes, in body and mind.

Constantine is short and fat, with a head like the best-known satyr in the Louvre, and an air of vine-leaves about the brow, though he drinks little. He is perpetually drunk on what comes out of his mouth, not what goes into it. He talks incessantly. In the morning he comes out of his bedroom in the middle of a sentence; and at night he backs into it, so that he can just finish one more sentence. Automatically he makes silencing gestures while he speaks, just in case somebody should take it into his head to interrupt. Nearly all his talk is good, and sometimes it runs along in a coloured shadow show, like Heine's *Florentine Nights*, and sometimes it crystallizes into a little story the essence of hope or love or regret, like a Heine lyric. Of all human beings I have ever met he is the most like Heine: and since Heine was the most Jewish of writers it follows that Constantine is Jew as well as Serb. His father was a Jewish doctor of revolutionary sympathies, who fled from Russian Poland about fifty years ago and settled in a rich provincial town in Serbia and became one of the leaders of the medical profession, which has always been more advanced there than one might have supposed. His mother was also Polish Jewish, and was a famous musician. He is by adoption only, yet quite completely, a Serb. He fought in the Great War very gallantly, for he is a man of great physical courage, and to him Serbian history is his history, his life is a part of the life of the Serbian people. He is now a Government official; but that is not the reason why he believes in Yugoslavia. To him a state of Serbs, Slovenes, and

Croats, controlled by a central government in Belgrade, is a necessity if these peoples are to maintain themselves against Italian and Central European pressure on the west, and Bulgarian pressure, which might become in effect Central European pressure, on the east.

Valetta comes from a Dalmatian town which was settled by the Greeks some hundreds of years before Christ, and he has the strong delicacy and the morning freshness of an archaic statue. They like him everywhere he goes, Paris and London and Berlin and Vienna, but he is hall-marked as a Slav, because his charm is not associated with any of those defects that commonly go with it in other races. He might suddenly stop smiling and clench his long hands, and offer himself up to martyrdom for an idea. He is anti-Yugoslavian; he is a federalist and believes in an autonomous Croatia.

Gregorievitch looks like Pluto in the Mickey Mouse films. His face is grooved with grief at the trouble and lack of gratitude he has encountered while defending certain fixed and noble standards in a chaotic world. His long body is like Pluto's in its extensibility. As he sits in his armchair, resentment at what he conceives to be a remediable injustice will draw him inches nearer to the ceiling, despair at an inevitable wrong will crumple him up like a concertina. Yugoslavia is the Mickey Mouse this Pluto serves. He is ten years older than Constantine, who is forty-six, and thirty years older than Valetta. This means that for sixteen years before the war he was an active revolutionary, fighting against the Hungarians for the right of Croats to govern themselves and to use their own language. In order that the Croats might be united with their free brother Slavs the Serbs, he endured poverty and imprisonment and exile. Therefore Yugoslavia is to him the Kingdom of Heaven on earth. Who speaks more lightly of it spits on those sixteen years of sorrow, who raises his hand against it violates the Slav sacrament. So to him Constantine, who was still a student in Paris when the Great War broke out, and who had been born a free Serb, seems impious in the way he takes Yugoslavia for granted. There is the difference between them that there was between the Christians of the first three centuries, who fought for their faith when it seemed a lost cause, and the Christians of the fourth century, who fought for it when it was victorious.

And to Gregorievitch, Valetta is quite simply a traitor. He is more than an individual who has gone astray, he is the very essence of treachery incarnate. Youth should uphold the banner of the right against unjust authority, and should practise that form of obedience to God which is rebellion against tyranny; and it seems to Gregorievitch that Valetta is betraying that ideal, for to him Yugoslavia represents a supreme gesture of defiance against the tyranny of the Austro-Hungarian Empire. Only a sorcerer could make him realize that the Austro-Hungarian Empire ceased to be when Valetta was six years old, and that he has never known any other symbol of unjust authority except Yugoslavia.

They are standing in the rain, and they are all different and they are all the same. They greet us warmly, and in their hearts they cannot greet each other, and they dislike us a little because it is to meet us that they are standing beside their enemies in the rain. We are their friends, but we are made from another substance. The rich passions of Constantine, the intense, graceful, selected joys and sorrows of Valetta, and Gregorievitch's gloomy Great Danish nobility are all cut from the same primary stuff, though in very dissimilar shapes. Sitting in our hotel room, drinking wine, they showed their unity of origin. A door opens, they twitch and swivel their heads, and the movement is the same. When these enemies advance on each other, they must move at the same tempo.

My husband has not met any of them before. I see him transfixed by their strangeness. He listens amazed to Constantine's beautiful French, which has preserved in it all the butterfly brilliances of his youth, when he was one of Bergson's favourite students, and was making his musical studies with Wanda Landowska. He falls under the spell of Constantine. He strains forward to hear the perfect phrase that is bound to come when Constantine's eyes catch the light, and each of his tight black curls spins on his head, and his lips shoot out horizontally, and his hands grope in the air before him as if he were unloosing the neckcloth of the strangling truth. Now Constantine was talking of Bergson and saying that it was to miss the very essence in him to regard him only as a philosopher. He was a magician who had taken philosophy as his subject matter. He did not analyse phenomena, he uttered incantations that invoked understanding. "We students," said Constantine, "we were not the pupils of a great professor, we were the sorcerer's apprentices. We did strange things that are not in most academic courses. On Sundays we would talk together in the forest of Fontainebleau, all day long sometimes, reconstituting his lectures by pooling our memories. For, you see, in his class-room it was not possible to take notes. If we bent our heads for one moment to take down a point, we missed an organic phrase, and the rest of the lecture appeared incomprehensible. That shows he was a magician. For what is the essential of a spell? That if one word is left out it is no longer a spell. I was able to recognize that at once, for in my town, which is Shabats, there were three houses in a row, and in one house lived my father who was the greatest doctor in our country, and in the next there lived a priest who was the greatest saint in my country, and in the next there lived an old woman who was the greatest witch in my country, and when I was a little boy I lived in the first of these houses and I went as I would into the other two, for the holy man and the witch liked me very much, and I tell you in each of these houses there was magic, so I know all about it as most men do not."

A line of light ran along the dark map of Europe we all of us hold in our minds; at one end a Serbian town, unknown to me as Ur, peopled with the personnel of fairy-tales, and at the other end the familiar idea of Bergson. My husband, I could see, was enraptured. He loves to learn what he did not know before. But in a minute I could see that he was not so happy. Valetta had said that he was making plans for our pleasure in Yugoslavia, and that he hoped that we would be able to go up into the snow mountains, particularly if we liked winter sports. My husband said he was very fond of Switzerland, and how he enjoyed going over there when he was tired and handing himself over to the care of the guides. "Yes, the guides are so good for us, who are over-civilized," said Constantine. "They refresh us immensely, when we are with them. For they succeed at every point where we fail. We can be responsible for what we love, our families and our countries, and the causes we think just, but where we do not love we cannot muster the necessary attention. That is just what the guides do, with such a wealth of attention that it amounts to nothing comparable to our attention at all, to a mystical apprehension of the whole universe.

"I will give you," he said, "an example. I made once a most beautiful journey in Italy with my wife. She is a German, you know, and she worships Goethe, so this was a pilgrimage. We went to see where he had lived in Venice and Rome, and she was so delighted, you cannot believe, delighted deep in herself, so that her intuition told her many things. 'That is the house where he lived!' she cried in Venice, jumping up and down in the gondola, and it was so. At length we came to Naples, and we took a guide and went up Vesuvius, because Goethe went up Vesuvius. Do you remember the passage where he says he was on the edge of a little crater, and he slipped? That was much in my wife's mind, and suddenly it was given to her to know by intuition that a certain little crater we saw was that same one where Goethe had slipped, so before we could stop it she ran down to it. I saw, of course, that she might be killed at any moment, so I ran after her. But so did the guide, though she was nothing to him. And then came the evidence of this mystic apprehension which is given by the constant vigilance of a guide's life. Just then this crater began to erupt, and the lava burst out here and there and here. But always the guide knew where it was coming, and took us to the left or the right, wherever it was not. Sometimes there was barely time for us to be there for more than a second; that was proved afterwards because the soles of our shoes were scorched. For three-quarters of an hour we ran thus up and down, from right to left and from left to right, before we could get to safety; and I was immensely happy the whole time because the guide was doing something I could not have done, which it is good to do!"

During the telling of this story my husband's eyes rested on me with an expression of alarm. It was apparent from Constantine's tone that nothing in the story had struck him as odd except the devotion of the guide to his charges. "Are not her friends very dotty?" he was plainly asking himself. "Is this how she wants to live?" But the conversation took a businesslike turn, and we were called on to consider our plans. We must meet So-and-so and Such-and-such, of course. It became obvious from certain reticences that the strained relations between Croats and Serbs were making themselves felt over our plans. For So-and-so, it appeared, would not meet Such-and-such, and that, it could be deduced, was the reason. Suddenly such reticences were blown away by a very explicit wrangle about Y., the editor of a certain newspaper. "Oh, you should meet him, he would interest you," said Valetta. "Yes, he has a very remarkable mind," admitted Constantine. "No," exploded Gregorievitch. They squabbled for a time in Serbian. Then Gregorievitch shrugged his shoulders and said to us, with heavy lightness, "Y. is not an honest man, that is all!" "He is perfectly honest," said Valetta coldly. "Gregorievitch, you are an impossibilist," said Constantine mildly. "Let our English guests judge," said Pluto grimly.

It appeared that one day some years before, Pluto had rung up Y. and reminded him that next week was the centenary of a certain Croat poet, and asked him if he would like an article on him. Y. said that he would, and Pluto sent an article four columns long, including two quotations concerning liberty. But the article had to be submitted to the censor, who at that particular time and in that particular place happened to be Pluto. He sent it back to Y. cut by a column and a half, including both quotations. Then, if we would believe it, Y. had rung up Pluto on the telephone and been most abusive, and never since then had he accepted one single article from Pluto. "Surely," said Pluto, immensely tall and grey and wrinkled, "he must have seen that I had to do what I did.

To be true to myself as a critic I had to write the article as I did. But to be true to myself as a censor, I had to cut it as I did. In which capacity did he hope that I would betray my ideals?" As he related this anecdote his spectacles shone with the steady glare of a strong man justly enraged.

But that story I could understand. It proceeds not, as might be thought, from incoherence but from a very high and too rigid sense of order. There lingers here a survival of an old attitude towards status that the whole world held, in days which were perhaps happier. Now, we think that if a man takes an office, he will modify it according to what he is as a man, according to his temperament and official standards. But then it was taken for granted that a man would modify his temperament and his ethical standards according to his office, provided it were of any real importance. In the third and fourth centuries Christian congregations were constantly insisting on electing people as bishops who were unwilling to accept the office, perhaps for some such valid reason as that they were not even Christians, but who seemed to have the ability necessary for the semi-magisterial duties of the episcopacy. Sometimes these men were so reluctant that the congregations were obliged to kidnap them and ordain them forcibly. But once they were installed as bishops, they often performed their duties admirably. They had a sense of social structure, they were aware that bishops, who had by then taken over most of the civil administration that the crumbling Roman Empire could no longer handle, must work well if society was not to fall to pieces. Even so Gregorievitch must have been conscious, all his life, of the social value of patriotic poets and, for the last unhappy twenty years, of censors. Therefore it seemed to him that he must do his best in both capacities, not that he should modify his performances to uphold the consistence of his personality. That I could perfectly understand; but it was so late I did not feel able to explain it to my husband, whom I saw, when I forced open my eyelids, undressing slowly, with his eyes set pensively on the window-curtains, wondering what strange city they were going to disclose next day.

Zagreb II

BUT the morning showed us that Zagreb was not a strange city at all. It has the warm and comfortable appearance of a town that has been well aired. People have been living there in physical, though not political, comfort for a thousand years. Moreover it is full of those vast toast-coloured buildings, barracks and law courts and municipal offices, which are an invariable sign of past occupancy by the Austro-Hungarian Empire; and that always means enthusiastic ingestion combined with lack of exercise in pleasant surroundings, the happy consumption of coffee and whipped cream and sweet cakes at little tables under chestnut trees. But it has its own quality. It has no grand river, it is built up to no climax; the hill the old town stands on is what the eighteenth century used to call "a moderate elevation." It has few very fine buildings except the Gothic Cathedral, and that has been forced to wear an ugly nineteenth-century overcoat. But Zagreb makes from its featureless handsomeness something that pleases like a Schubert song, a delight that begins quietly and never definitely ends. We believed we were being annoyed by the rain that first morning we walked out into it, but eventually we recognized we were as happy as if we had been walking in sunshine through a really beautiful city. It has, moreover, the endearing characteristic, noticeable in many French towns, of remaining a small town when it is in fact quite large. A hundred and fifty thousand people live in Zagreb, but from the way gossips stand in the street it is plain that everybody knows who is going to have a baby and when. This is a lovely spiritual victory over urbanization.

There was a wide market-place, where under red and white umbrellas peasants stood sturdy and square on their feet, and amazed us by their faces, which are as mobile and sensitive as if they were the most culti-vated townspeople. The women wore, and were the first to do so I have ever seen anywhere in the world, neither skirt nor trousers, but two broad aprons, one covering the front part of the body and one the back, and overlapping at the sides, and underneath showed very brave red woollen stockings. They gave the sense of the very opposite of what we mean by the word "peasant" when we use it in a derogatory sense, think-ing of women made doltish by repeated pregnancies and a lifetime spent in the service of oafs in villages that swim in mud to the thresholds every winter. This costume was evolved by women who could stride along if they were eight months gone with child, and who would dance in the mud if they felt like it, no matter what any oaf said.

They lived under no favour, however. They all spoke some German, so we were able to ask the prices of what they sold; and we could have bought a sackful of fruit and vegetables, all of the finest, for the equivalent of two shillings: a fifth of what it would have fetched in a Western city. This meant desperate, pinching poverty, for the manufactured goods in the shops are marked at nearly Western prices. But they looked gallant, and nobody spoke of poverty, nobody begged. It was a sign that we were out of Central Europe, for in a German and Austrian town where the people were twice as well off as these they would have perpetually complained. But there were signs that we were near Central Europe. There were stalls covered with fine embroidered handkerchiefs and table linen, which was all of it superbly executed, for Slav women have a captive devil in their flying fingers to work wonders for them. But the design was horrible. It was not like the designs I had seen in other parts of Yugoslavia, in Serbia and Macedonia; it was not even as good as the designs on the dresses of the peasant women who were standing by the stalls, inferior though they were. It was severely naturalistic, and attempted to represent fruit and flowers, and it followed the tradition of Victorian Berlin woolwork. In other words, it showed German influence.

I felt impatient. I was getting no exhilaration out of being here, such as I had hoped for in coming to Yugoslavia. For a rest I went and stood on the steps of the statue in the middle of the square. Looking at the inscription I saw that it was a statue of the Croat patriot, Yellatchitch, and I reflected that if the Croats had not succeeded in cheering me up they had other achievements to their credit. For this is one of the strangest statues in the world. It represents Yellatchitch as leading his troops on horseback and brandishing a sword in the direction of Budapest, in which direction he had indeed led them to victory against the Hungarians in 1848; and this is not a new statue erected since Croatia was liberated from Hungary. It stood in the market-place, commemorating a Hungarian defeat, in the days when Hungary was master of Croatia, and the explanation does not lie in Hungarian magnanimity. It takes the whole of Croatian history to solve the mystery.

The Croats were originally a Slav tribe who were invited by the Emperor Heraclius to free the Dalmatian coast and the Croatian hinterland from the Avars, one of the most noxious pillaging hordes who operated

MARKET-PLACE AT ZAGREB

The Walls of Rab

from a centre on the Danube far and wide: they created an early currency crisis by collecting immense tributes in gold, year after year, from all surrounding peoples. That was well on into the decadence of the Western Roman Empire, in the seventh century. They then stayed on as vassals of the Empire, and when its power dissolved they declared themselves independent; and they had their own kings who acknowledged the suzerainty of the Pope. Very little is known about them in those days, except that they were not a barbarous people, but had inherited much of the elaborate Byzantine ritual. The last of their kings was crowned about the time of the Norman Conquest. He left no kin, and civil war followed among the Croat nobles. For the sake of peace they recognized as their sovereign Coloman, King of Hungary, who asserted the triple claim of conquest, election, and inheritance; the last was doubtful, but the other two were fair enough. It is a thing to be noted, the age of legalism in these parts. It is our weakness to think that distant people became civilized when we looked at them, that in their yesterdays they were brutish.

Coloman was crowned *Rex Hungariæ Croatiæ atque Dalmatiæ*. For two centuries the two kingdoms led an independent and co-equal existence under the same crown. Their peoples were not likely to assimilate. They were racially unrelated: the Hungarians or Magyars are a people of far Asiatic origin, akin to the Finns, the Bulgars, and the Turks, and the Croats are Slav, akin to the Serbs, the Russians, the Poles, and the Czechs. Neither is meek; each is passionately attached to his own language; and the Hungarians are fierce and warlike romantics whereas the Croats are fierce and warlike intellectuals. Nothing could make them sympathetic, but their position in Central Europe made the close alliance of a dual monarchy desirable. But it was not cast-iron. In the fourteenth century Coloman's line died out, and the Croats would not accept the king elected by the Hungarians but crowned their own choice in Zagreb Cathedral, and the union was restored only after six years, when the Hungarians accepted the Croat King. But the son of that King was Louis the Great, and he was predominantly Hungarian in blood, and more in feeling. The Croats had to take a second place.

Many of us think that monarchy is more stable than a republican form of government, and that there is a special whimsicality about modern democracies. We forget that stable monarchies are the signs of genius of an order at least as rare in government as in literature or music, or of stable history. Monarchy without these conditions is whimsical to the point of mania. The stock was not fruitful as among commoners, perhaps because princesses were snatched as brides before puberty lest others make the useful alliance first; and in no rank does stock breed true and merit follow merit. If on a king's death he should leave an idiot heir or none, the nobles would send, perhaps far away, to a man whose fame lay in violence, in order to avoid war among themselves. He would rule them with the coldness of an alien, and it might be that in his loins there was working this genetic treachery, to leave them masterless at his death. He was in any case sure to be afflicted with the special malady of kings, which was poverty; the reluctance we feel about paying income tax is only the modern expression of a human incapacity to see the justice of providing for corporate expenses which is as old as the species itself. Here his alien blood made itself felt. Terrified of his insecure position in a strange land, he asked little of the nobles and came down like a scourge on the peasants, and was tempted to plunder them beyond need and without mercy. That is to say, he demanded certain sums from the nobles and made no provisions for social justice which prevented the nobles from wringing them out of the peasants and keeping their private treasures intact. There was the still graver danger that the king's alien blood would let him make contracts to their disadvantage with foreign powers. This danger was very grave indeed. For though there is a popular belief that negotiations to take the place of warfare are a modern invention, nothing could be further from the truth. The Middle Ages were always ready to lay down the sword and sign an agreement, preferably for a cash payment. An alien king was always particularly likely to sell a slice of his lands and people for a sum that would shore up his authority.

It is not comfortable to be an inhabitant of this globe. It never has been, except for brief periods. The Croats have been peculiarly uncomfortable. Louis the Great was a Frenchman, one of the house of Anjou; he married Elizabeth, a Slav, the daughter of a Bosnian king. When Louis died he left two daughters, and nearly all Hungary and Dalmatia recognized as their queen the elder, Mary, who was to govern under the regency of her mother. But certain Croatian and Hungarian barons were against her, and called to the throne her father's cousin, King Charles of Naples. It is to be noted that these Croatian barons were a strange and ungodly lot, with so little care for their people and, indeed, so little resemblance to them that they might be guessed to be alien. This whole territory had been devastated again and again by Asiatic invaders, and it is supposed that many of these nobles were the descendants of various roving brigands, men of power, who had seized land from the exhausted population as the invaders receded; some of them were certainly by origin Italian, German, and Goth, and in some cases themselves Asiatic. King Charles was crowned King of Hungary and Croatia, and four years afterwards was assassinated by the widow Elizabeth. He was succeeded by his son, Ladislas, a fantastical adventurer. He was faced by Elizabeth and her daughter, Mary, and her betrothed, another alien, Sigismond of Luxembourg, a son of the Emperor Charles of Germany, for whom they desired the crown. Thereafter for fifty years the country agonized under these aliens, who were, however, inevitable at this phase of history. The people screamed with pain. They were tortured, imprisoned, famined; and their national soul was violated. Ladislas, though he had never been crowned, sold Dalmatia to the Republic of Venice for a hundred thousand ducats; and though Sigismond was eventually crowned, he was never in a position to assert his legal rights and recover his possessions. This meant that an enormous number of warlike, thriftless, bucolic intellectuals fell under the control of a community of merchants; and that the Croats of Croatia were thereafter the more helpless against Hungary by this division from their Dalmatian brothers.

Sigismond bore the Croats a grudge, because certain of their nobles had aided Ladislas against him. There was then and thereafter no separate coronation for Croatia. She had to be satisfied with a separate *diploma inaugurale*, a document setting forth the king's oath to his subjects and the privileges he intended to give them. But it is to be observed that she had to be satisfied. Dismembered as she was, she still had enough military power to make her able to bargain. Only as time went on these things mattered less. From the south-east the Turks pressed on and on. In 1453 they took Constantinople. In 1468 they were threatening the Dalmatian coast. Thereafter the Croats and the Hungarians were engaged in a perpetual guerrilla warfare to defend their lands. In 1526 the Hungarians fought the Turks in the battle of Mohacs, without calling on the Croats for aid, out of pride and political cantankerousness among the nobles. They were beaten and the King killed. Now Croatia was quite alone. It had to fall back on Austria, which was then governed by Ferdinand of Habsburg, and it offered him the throne on a hereditary basis.

The Germans have always hated the Slavs. More than that, they have always acted hatefully towards them. Now the Croats began to learn this lesson. Croatia was ruined economically, because the Turks were to their north-east, their east, and their south-east, so they were at Austria's mercy. Austria used her power to turn them into the famous Military Confines, where the whole male population between the ages of sixteen and sixty were treated as a standing army to defend the Austrian Empire. They were given certain privileges which were chiefly legal fictions; but for the very reason that they were isolated from the rest of Europe they lingered in the legalistic Middle Ages and enjoyed these fictions. They were sunk in wretched poverty. At the end of the sixteenth century there was a peasants' rising, which was suppressed with the greatest cruelty conceivable. The leader was killed at a mock coronation. The crown set on his head was of white-hot iron. Thereafter, between Austrian tyranny and Turkish raids, the Croats lived submissively, until 1670, when a number of the Croat nobles formed a conspiracy against the Habsburgs. It is curious to observe that these aliens, noted before for their indifference to the interests of their people, had in the years of misfortune grown truly nationalist. They were discovered and beheaded; and their lands were given to Austrian and Italian families, to whom the peasants were simply brute beasts for exploitation.

Meanwhile there developed among the Croats one of the most peculiar passions known in history: a burning, indestructible devotion to the Habsburgs. Because of the historic union with Hungary they sent their Ban, which is to say their Governor, to sit in the Hungarian Diet, while it sat in exile and when it sat again in Budapest, after the Turks had been driven out. But they had their independence; they ratified separate treaties, and nobody said them nay. They used this power to put the Habsburgs firmly on the throne. When Charles VI had no son he put forward the Pragmatic Sanction, which declared that the house of Habsburg could inherit through the female line, and gave the succession to his daughter Maria Theresa. If this had been resisted by the highly militarized state of Croatia other parts of the Empire might have followed suit; but the Croats eagerly accepted. They received a characteristic return. The aristocracy of Hungary was lawless and disobedient, after a hundred and fifty years of demoralization under Turkish rule. Maria Theresa tore up the constitution to please them, and put Croatia under them as a slave state: not as *regnum socium,* not as a companion state, but as *partes adnexæ,* annexed territory. Since the Croatian nobles had been destroyed there was now nobody to lead a revolt. The imported aristocracy felt a far greater kinship with the Hungarians of their own class than with the peasants on their lands.

So the eighteenth century went by with the Croats enslaved by Hungary, and their passion for Austria idiotically stable. The increasing incapacity of the Habsburgs led to the crisis of 1848. Among other follies Francis I and Metternich had the unhappy idea of closing the Hungarian

Diet for fourteen years, an oppressive act which had raised Hungarian national feeling to fever point. It oddly happened that inherent in Hungarian nationalism was a contempt and loathing for all nationalist sentiments felt by any other people in all conceivable circumstances. This is proved by their extraordinary attitude to the language issue. It infuriated them that they should be forced to speak German and should not be allowed to speak their own language, Magyar; but they were revolted by the idea that any of their neighbours, the Croats, Serbs, or Slovaks, should speak their own language, or indeed anything but Magyar. The famous Hungarian patriot, Lajos Kossuth, showed vehemence on this point that was simply not sane, considering he had not one drop of Hungarian blood in his veins and was purely Slovak. When he took charge of the Nationalist Party he announced it as part of his programme to destroy the identity of Croatia. He declared he would suppress the Croatian language by the sword, and introduced an electoral bill which omitted the name of Croatia and described her departments as Hungarian counties.

The Croats showed their love and trust in Austria once more. They sent a deputation to Vienna to ask the Emperor Ferdinand for divorce from Hungary and direct subordination to the Habsburgs, and to suggest that a young officer named Yellatchitch should be appointed Ban of Croatia. The Emperor behaved with the fluttering inefficiency of the German tourists on the train. He was on the eve of a cataclysm in European history. He was surrounded by revolutionary Viennese, by discontented Czechs, by disloyal Hungarians; the only faithful subjects within sight were the Croats. But he hesitated to grant the deputation its requests, and indeed would have refused them had it not been that certain persons in court circles had taken a liking to Yellatchitch. After Yellatchitch was appointed he spent six months in organizing anti-Hungarian feeling throughout Croatia, and then in September 1848 he marched across the frontier at the head of fifty thousand Croat soldiers and defeated a Hungarian army that was hurrying to Austria to aid the Viennese revolutionaries against the Habsburgs. Nobody has ever said that the Hungarians were not magnificent fighters, but this time the Croats were at least as good, and they had the advantage of meeting an adversary under an insane leader. They did not even have to go on holding the Hungarians at bay, for Kossuth was inspired to the supreme idiocy of formally announcing that the Habsburgs were deposed and that he was ruler of Hungary. Up till then the programme of the revolutionaries had simply been autonomy within the Austrian Empire. This

extension meant that Russia felt bound to intervene. Those who fear
Bolshevist Russia because of its interventions in the affairs of other
countries, which are so insignificant that they have never been rewarded
with success, forget that Tsarist Russia carried foreign intervention to a
pitch that has never been equalled by any other power, except the modern Fascist states, and that she held it as her right to defend the dynastic
principle wherever it was threatened. Kossuth's proclamation meant that
the Tsar immediately poured a hundred and eighty thousand Russians
into Hungary. By summer-time in 1849 Kossuth was a fugitive in
Turkey.

Yellatchitch and the Croats had saved the Austrian Empire. They got
exactly nothing for this service, except this statue which stands in Zagreb
market-square. The Habsburgs were still suicidal. They were bent on
procuring the dissolution of their Empire, on raping time and begetting
on her the Sarajevo assassination. Instead of giving the Croats the autonomy they demanded they now made them wholly subject to the central
government, and they freed them from Magyarization to inflict on them
the equal brutality of Germanization. And then, ultimately, they practised on them the supreme treachery. When the Dual Monarchy was
framed to placate Hungary, the Croats were handed over to the Hungarians as their chattels. I do not know of any nastier act than this in
history.[1] It has a kind of lowness that is sometimes exhibited in the sexual
affairs of very vulgar and shameless people: a man leaves his wife and
induces a girl to become his mistress, then is reconciled to his wife and to
please her exposes the girl to some public humiliation. But, all the same,
Austria did not forget 1848 and Lajos Kossuth. It left the statue there,
just as a reminder. So the Croat helots stood and touched their caps to
their Hungarian masters in the shadow of the memorial of the Croat
General who led them to victory against a Hungarian army. That is the
strangest episode of sovereignty I have ever chanced upon in any land.

Well, what did all this story mean to the people in Croatia, the people
I was looking at, the people who had been selling me things? I had come
to Yugoslavia because I knew that the past has made the present, and I
wanted to see how the process works. Let me start now. It is plain that it
means an amount of human pain, arranged in an unbroken continuity appalling to any person cradled in the security of the English or American
past. Were I to go down into the market-place, armed with the powers
of witchcraft, and take a peasant by the shoulders and whisper to him,
"In your lifetime, have you known peace?" wait for his answer, shake his

---

[1] It must be remembered that this journal was written in 1937.

shoulders and transform him into his father, and ask him the same question, and transform him in his turn to his father, I would never hear the word "Yes," if I carried my questioning of the dead back for a thousand years. I would always hear, "No, there was fear, there were our enemies without, our rulers within, there was prison, there was torture, there was violent death."

And they had no compensation in their history, for that never once formed a historic legend of any splendid magnitude. It was a record of individual heroism that no nation could surpass, but it had never shaped itself into an indestructible image of triumph that could be turned to as an escape from present failure. The Croats have always been superb soldiers; but their greatest achievements have been merged in the general triumphs of the armies of the Habsburgs, who were at pains that they should never be extricated and distinguished, and their courage and endurance were shown most prodigious in engagements with the Turks which were too numerous and too indecisive to be named in history or even preserved with any vividness in local tradition. The only outstanding military victory to their credit was the rout of the Hungarians commemorated by Yellatchitch's statue, and this might as well have been a defeat. Again we must go for an analogy to the sexual affairs of individuals. As we grow older and see the ends of stories as well as their beginnings, we realize that to the people who take part in them it is almost of greater importance that they should be stories, that they should form a recognizable pattern, than that they should be happy or tragic. The men and women who are withered by their fates, who go down to death reluctantly but without noticeable regrets for life, are not those who have lost their mates prematurely or by perfidy, or who have lost battles or fallen from early promise in circumstances of public shame, but those who have been jilted or were the victims of impotent lovers, who have never been summoned to command or been given any opportunity for success or failure. Art is not a plaything, but a necessity, and its essence, form, is not a decorative adjustment, but a cup into which life can be poured and lifted to the lips and be tasted. If one's own existence has no form, if its events do not come handily to mind and disclose their significance, we feel about ourselves as if we were reading a bad book. We can all of us judge the truth of this, for hardly any of us manage to avoid some periods when the main theme of our lives is obscured by details, when we involve ourselves with persons who are insufficiently characterized; and it is possibly true not only of individuals, but of nations. What would England be like if it had not its immense Valhalla of kings and heroes, if it had not its Elizabethan and its Victorian ages, its thousands of incidents which come up in the mind, simple as icons and as miraculous in their suggestion that what England has been it can be again, now and for ever? What would the United States be like if it had not those reservoirs of triumphant will-power, the historical facts of the War of Independence, of the giant American statesmen, and of the pioneering progress into the West, which every American citizen has at his mental command and into which he can plunge for revivification at any minute? To have a difficult history makes, perhaps, a people who are bound to be difficult in any conditions, lacking these means of refreshment. "But perhaps," said my husband, "it does not matter very much."

Zagreb III

BUT it matters. He saw, before we went to bed that night, that what happened to these people matters a great deal. As we stood on the steps of the statue there came towards us Constantine, treading delicately among the pigeons that cover all the pavement in the market-square where there are not stalls. He brought his brows together in censure of two of these pigeons which, in spite of the whirling traffic all around them, had felt the necessity to love. "*Ah, les Croates!*" he murmured, shaking his head; and as we laughed he went on, "And I can see that you two also are thinking of committing a misdemeanour of taste. Not so gross, but still a misdemeanour. You are thinking of going up to look at the Old Town, and that is quite wrong. Up there are villas and palaces, which must not be seen in the morning. In the evening, when the dusk is sentimental, we shall go and peer through the gateways and you shall see colonnades and pediments more remote than those of Rome, because they are built in the neo-classical style that was the mode in Vienna a hundred to a hundred and fifty years ago, and you shall see our little Slav contribution, for in the walled garden before the house we will see iron chairs and tables with nobody sitting at them, and you will recognize at a glance that the person who is not sitting there is straight out of Turgeniev. You cannot look at Austria as it was the day before yesterday, at us Slavs as we were yesterday, by broad daylight. It is like the pigeons. But come to the Cathedral, which is so beautiful that you may see it now or any other time."

So we went up the steep street into the Cathedral Square, and looked for a time at the Archbishop's palace, with its squat round towers under their candle-extinguisher tops, and then went through the Cathedral's nineteenth-century false front into the dark and stony plant forms of the Gothic interior. It has been cut about as by a country dressmaker, but it has kept the meditative integrity of darkness considering light, the mathematical aspiration for something above mathematics, which had been the core of its original design, and at that moment it housed the same intense faith that had built it. This was Easter Eve; the great cross had been taken down from the altar and lay propped up before the step, the livid and wounded Christ wincing in the light of the candles set at His feet. It was guarded by two soldiers in the olive uniform of the Yugoslavian Army, who leaned on their rifles as if this was a dead king

of earth lying in state. As I looked at them, admiring the unity enjoyed
by a state which fights and believes it has a moral right to fight, and
would give up either fighting or religion if it felt the two inconsistent, I
saw that they were moved by a deep emotion. Their lips were drawn
outward from their clenched teeth, they were green as if they were sea-
sick. "Are they tired? Do they have to guard the cross for a long time?"
I asked cautiously. "No," said Constantine, "not for more than an hour
or two. Then others come." "Then they are really looking like that," I
pressed, "because it is a great thing for them to guard the dead Christ?"
"Certainly," he replied. "The Croats are such Catholics as you never did
see, not in France, not in Italy; and I think you ask that question because
you do not understand the Slavs. If we did not feel intensely about
guarding the dead Christ we should not put our soldiers to do it, and indeed they would not do it if we put them there, they would go away and
do something else. The custom would have died if it had not meant a
great deal to us." For a long time we watched the wincing Christ and the
two boys with bowed heads, who swayed very slightly backwards and
forwards, backwards and forwards, like candle-flame in a room where
the air is nearly still. I had not been wrong. In Yugoslavia there was an
intensity of feeling that was not only of immense and exhilarating force,
but had an honourable origin, proceeding from realist passion, from
whole belief.

We were to learn after that something about the intellectual level of
Croatia. In a restaurant beside the Cathedral people awaited us for lunch:
a poet and playwright, author of dramas much larger than life, larger
even than art, which make *Othello* seem plotless and light-minded, who
looks like Mr. Pickwick, and his wife, who had the beauty of a Burne-
Jones, the same air of having rubbed holes in her lovely cheeks with her
clenched knuckles. They looked up at us absently, said that they had
found the poems of Vaughan the Silurist in an anthology of English
poems and thought him one of the greatest poets, and, while ordering us
an immense meal of which goose-liver and apple sauce were the centre-
piece, threw over us the net of an extremely complicated conversation
about literature. "We think," said the playwright, "that the greatest
writers of recent times are Joseph Conrad, Maxim Gorki, and Jack London." We blenched. We thought that in fact these people could have
no taste, if they could think both Vaughan and Jack London great. We
were wrong. The playwright was actually a real poet, and he did not expect anything but poetic forms to satisfy the highest canons of art. Writers like Shaw and Wells and Péguy and Gide did not seem to him artists

at all: they wrote down what one talks in cafés, which is quite a good thing to do if the talk is good enough, but is not serious, because it deals with something as common and renewable as sweat. But pure narration was a form of great importance, because it gathered together experiences that could be assimilated by others of poetic talent and transmuted into higher forms; and he liked Conrad and Jack London and Maxim Gorki because they were collecting experiences which were rare, which they had investigated thoroughly by undergoing them themselves, and which they had tested with an abnormal sensitiveness. But the playwright and his wife had been wondering whether Conrad was not in a class alone, because of the feeling of true tragedy that ran through his works. It never blossomed into poetry, but was it not so definitely the proper subject matter of poetry that he might claim to be, so to speak, on the commissariat of the poetic army?

"No," said my husband suddenly, "Conrad has no sense of tragedy at all, but only of the inevitable, and for him the inevitable was never the fulfilment of a principle such as the Greek *ananke*, but a *déroulement* of the consequences of an event." An example of this, he said, is the story "Duel" in *A Set of Six*, in which the original event is commonplace, bringing no principle whatsoever into play, and the inevitable consequences are so far-reaching that they are almost ludicrous. But there is no factor involved that might come into operation, that indeed must come into operation so generally in human affairs that as we identify it we feel as if a new phase of our destiny has been revealed to us. The playwright's wife said that this was true but irrelevant. To her there was a sense of tragedy implied in Conrad's work not by factual statement but by the rhythm of his language. "Tchk! Tchk!" said Constantine. "A great symphony must have its themes as well as the emotional colour given by its orchestration. And listen . . ." He said the sense of inevitability in a work of art should be quite different from the scientific conception of causality, for if art were creative then each stage must be new, must have something over and above what was contained in the previous stages, and the connexion between the first and the last must be creative in the Bergsonian sense. He added that it is to give this creativeness its chance to create what is at once unpredictable and inevitable that an artist must never interfere with his characters to make them prove a moral point, because this is to force them down the path of the predictable. "Yes, that is what Tolstoy is always doing," said the playwright, "and all the same he convinces us he is a great artist." "I feel he is not a great artist," I said, "I feel he might have been the greatest of all artists, but instead chose to be the second greatest of renegades after Judas." "I, too!" said the poet, who had just sat down at the table. "I, too!"

The bottles thick about us, we stayed in the restaurant till it was five o'clock. We were then discussing Nietzsche's attitude to music. At eight we were back in the same restaurant, dining with an editor leader of the Croat party which is fighting for autonomy under a federal system, and his wife. Valetta was there, but Constantine was not. The editor, though he himself was a Serb by birth, would not have sat down at the same table with an official of the Yugoslavian Government. And Gregorievitch was not there, not only for that reason, but because he would not have sat down at the same table as the editor, whom he regarded as evil incarnate. He had come in for a glass of brandy that evening, and on hearing where we were to spend the evening he had become Pluto dyspeptic, Pluto sunk in greenish gloom, caterpillar-coloured because of the sins of the world. Yet this editor also would have died for the Slav cause, and had indeed undergone imprisonment for its sake before the war. He is still facing grave danger, for he was running his movement from the point of view of an English pre-war liberal, who abhorred all violence, and he not only attacked the Yugoslavian Government for the repressive methods it used against Croatia, but also those Croats who used violence against the Government and who accepted Hungarian and Italian support for terrorism. He does not mind thus risking the loss of his only friends. He is a great gentleman, an intellectual and a moralist, and has carved himself, working against the grain of the wood, into a man of action.

As we talked of the political situation there ran to our table a beautiful young Russian woman, who could be with us only half an hour because she was supervising a play of hers about Pushkin which had been put on at the National Theatre a few nights before and was a failure. She brought the news that this amazing Easter had now produced a blizzard. On her golden hair and perfect skin and lithe body in its black dress snowflakes were melting, her blood running the better for it; and failure was melting on her like a snowflake also, leaving her glowing. "They are hard on my play!" she cried, choked with the ecstatic laughter of Russian women. "*Ce n'est pas bien, ce n'est pas mal, c'est médiocre!*" The editor, smiling at her beauty and her comet quality, tried to upbraid her for her play. The drama, he said, was a great mystery, one of the most difficult forms of art. All men of genius have tried their hand at a play at some time, and he had read most of them. These people, I realized, could make such universal statements. Both the editor and his wife knew, and knew well, in addition to their native Serbo-Croat, English, French, German, Italian, Russian, Latin, and Greek.

Nearly all these dramas, the editor continued, were bad. The drama demanded concentration on themes which by their very nature tempted to expansion, and only people with a special gift for craftsmanship could handle this problem. And one enormously increased this difficulty if, as she had done, one chose as one's theme a great man, for what could be more obstinately diffused than the soul of a great man? Often, indeed, the soul of a great man refused to be reduced to the terms necessary even for bare comprehension. And especially was this true of Pushkin. Which of us can understand Pushkin? At that the editor and the editor's wife and Valetta and the Russian all began to talk at once, their faces coming close together in a bright square about the middle of the table. The talk had been in French, it swung to Serbo-Croat, it ended in Russian. My husband and I sat tantalized to fury. We knew Pushkin only by translation; we found *Evgenye Onegin* like something between *Don Juan* and Winthrop Mackworth Praed, and we liked his short stories rather less than Nathaniel Hawthorne's; and obviously we are wrong, for because of limitations of language we are debarred from seeing something that is obvious to unsealed eyes as the difference between a mule and a Derby winner.

But the Russian stood up. She had to go back to the theatre to supervise the crowd that in the last scene of the play wept outside Pushkin's house while he was dying. It was plainly the real reason that she was leaving us, and not an excuse. There was nothing more indicative of the high level of culture among these people than their capacity to discuss the work of one amongst them with complete detachment. But before she went she made a last defence. For a short time she had found herself united in experience with Pushkin, and even if that union covered only a small part of Pushkin, it was worth setting down, it might give a clue to the whole of him. Looking past her at her beauty, in the odd way that men do, the editor said, though only to tease her, "Experience indeed! Are you sure you have enough experience? Do you think you have lived enough to write?" She answered with an air of evasion suggesting that she suspected she might some day have a secret but was too innocent to know what it was, though she was actually a married woman at the end of her twenties, if not in her early thirties: "I will not argue that, because the connexion between art and life is not as simple as that!" But then her face crinkled into laughter again, "Sometimes the connexion between art and life is very close! Think of it, there is a woman in the crowd in this last scene whose cries always give a lead to the others and have indeed given the end of the play much of its effect, they are always so sad. The audience cannot hear the words the actors in the crowd are using, they only catch the accent of the whole sentence. And as this woman has caught the very accent of anxious grief, I listened to what she had to say. And she was crying, 'Oh, God! Oh, God! Let Pushkin die before the last bus leaves for my suburb!' " She turned from us laughing, but turned back again: "That's something I don't like! There is a mockery inherent in the art of acting, the players must make everybody weep but themselves; if they don't weep they must jeer inside themselves at the people who do weep!" She shuddered, wishing she had never written the play, never had tried her luck in the theatre, a child who had chosen the wrong birthday treat. She brushed the sadness from her mouth and went away, laughing. This, so far as talk was concerned, was a representative day in Zagreb.

Shestine

"THIS is a very delightful place," said my husband the next morning. It was Easter Sunday, and the waiter had brought in on the breakfast-tray dyed Easter eggs as a present from the management, and we were realizing that the day before had been wholly pleasant. "Of course, Austria did a lot for the place," said an Englishman, a City friend of my husband's, who was staying in the hotel and had come to have breakfast. "I suppose so," said my husband, and then caught himself up. "No, what am I saying? It cannot be so, for this is not in the remotest degree like Austria. Austrians do sit in cafés for hours, and they talk incessantly, but they have not this raging polyglot intellectual curiosity, they have not this way of turning out universal literature on the floor as if it were a rag-bag, which indeed it is, and seeking for a fragment that is probably not there, but is probably part of an arcanum of literature that exists only in their own heads. In cultured Vienna homes they often give parties to hear the works of great writers read aloud: only a few months ago I spent an evening at the house of a Viennese banker, listening to the poems of Wildgans. But it would be impossible to read aloud to a party of Yugo-slavs, unless one bound and gagged the guests beforehand."

There came into the room Constantine and Gregorievitch, who was still a little cold to us because of the company we had kept on the previous night. "What has Austria done for you?" asked my husband. "Nothing," said Constantine; "it has not the means. What can a country without history do for a people with a glorious history like the Serbs?" "I was talking of Croatia," said my husband. Gregorievitch said anxiously, as if he had been detecting himself looking in the mirror, "The answer stands." "But the Austrians have their history," objected my husband. "No," said Gregorievitch, "we are its history. We Slavs in general, we Croats in particular. The Habsburgs won their victories with Czechs, with Poles, and, above all, with Croats. Without us the Austrians would have no history, and if we had not stood between them and the Turks, Vienna would now be a Moslem city." The Englishman laughed, as if a tall story that knew its own height had been told. Gregorievitch looked at him as if he had blasphemed. "Is it a little thing that only yesterday it was decided that Europe should not be Islamized?" he asked. "What does he mean?" asked the Englishman. "That the Turks besieged Vienna in

63

1683 and were turned back," said my husband, "and that if they had not
been turned back it is possible that they would have swept across all Europe." "Is that true?" asked the Englishman. "Yes," said my husband.
"But it's not yesterday," said the Englishman. "To these people it is,"
said my husband, "and I think they are right. It's uncomfortably recent,
the blow would have smashed the whole of our Western culture, and we
shouldn't forget that such things happen." "But ask them," said the Englishman, "if Austria did not do a lot for them in the way of sanitary services." Gregorievitch looked greenly into the depths of the mirror as if
wondering how he showed not signs of gaiety but signs of life under
the contamination of these unfastidious English. "Your friend, who
showed no emotion at the thought of the spires of Vienna being replaced
by minarets, doubtless would expect us to forgive the Austrians for
building oubliettes for our heroes so long as they built us chalets for our
necessities. Are you sure," he said, speaking through his teeth, "that you
really wish to go to hear mass at the village of Shestine? It is perhaps not
the kind of expedition that the English find entertaining?"

We drove through a landscape I have often seen in Chinese pictures:
wooded hills under snow looked like hedgehogs drenched in icing sugar.
On a hill stood a little church, full to the doors, bright inside as a garden,
glowing with scarlet and gold and blue and the unique, rough, warm
white of homespun, and shaking with song. On the women's heads were
red handkerchiefs printed with yellow leaves and peacocks' feathers,
their jackets were solidly embroidered with flowers, and under their
white skirts were thick red or white woollen stockings. Their men were
just as splendid in sheepskin leather jackets with appliqué designs in
dyed leathers, linen shirts with fronts embroidered in cross-stitch and
fastened with buttons of Maria Theresa dollars or lumps of turquoise
matrix, and homespun trousers gathered into elaborate boots. The splendour of these dresses was more impressive because it was not summer.
The brocade of a rajah's costume or the silks of an Ascot crowd are
within the confines of prudence, because the rajah is going to have a
golden umbrella held over him and the Ascot crowd is not far from
shelter, but these costumes were made for the winter in a land of unmetalled roads, where snow lay till it melted and mud might be knee-deep,
and showed a gorgeous lavishness, for hours and days, and even years had
been spent in the stuffs and skins and embroideries which were thus put
at the mercy of the bad weather. There was lavishness also in the singing
that poured out of these magnificently clad bodies, which indeed transformed the very service. Western church music is almost commonly

petitioning and infantile, a sentiment cozening for remedy against sickness or misfortune, combined with a masochist enjoyment in the malady, but this singing spoke of health and fullness.

The men stood on the right of the church and the women on the left. This is the custom also in the Orthodox Church, and it is reasonable enough. At a ceremony which sets out to be the most intense of all contacts with reality, men and women, who see totally different aspects of reality, might as well stand apart. It is inappropriate for them to be mixed as in the unit of the family, where men and women attempt with such notorious difficulty to share their views of reality for social purposes. From this divided congregation came a flood of song which asked for absolutely nothing, which did not ape childhood, which did not pretend that sour is sweet and pain wholesome, but which simply adored. If there be a God who is fount of all goodness, this is the tribute that should logically be paid to Him; if there be only goodness, it is still a logical tribute. And again, the worship, like their costume, was made astonishing by their circumstances. These people, who had neither wealth nor security, nor ever had had them, stood before the Creator, and thought not what they might ask for but what they might give. To be among them was like seeing an orchard laden with apples or a field of ripe wheat, endowed with a human will and using it in accordance with its own richness.

This was not simply due to these people's faith. There are people who hold precisely the same faith whose worship produces an effect of poverty. When Heine said that Amiens Cathedral could have been built only in the past, because the men of that day had convictions, whereas we moderns have only opinions, and something more than opinions are needed for building a cathedral, he put into circulation a half-truth which has done a great deal of harm. It matters supremely what kind of men hold these convictions. This service was impressive because the congregation was composed of people with a unique sort of healthy intensity. At the end we went out and stood at the churchyard gate, and watched the men and women clumping down a lane to the village through the deep snow, with a zest that was the generalized form of the special passion they had exhibited in the church. I had not been wrong about what I had found among the Yugoslavs.

"Are they not beautiful, the costumes of Croatia?" asked Gregorievitch, his very spectacles beaming, his whole appearance made unfamiliar by joy. "Are they not lovely, the girls who wear them, and are not the young men handsome? And they are very pious." "Yes," I said, "I have never heard a mass sung more fervently." "I do not mean that," he said irritably, "I meant pious in their Croat patriotism." It appeared that the inhabitants of Shestine wore these wonderful clothes not from custom but from a positive and virile choice. They would naturally wear ordinary Western European clothes, as most other peasants round Zagreb do, but they are conscious that the great patriot Anton Starchevitch is buried in the graveyard of their church, and they know that to him everything Croatian was precious. We went and stood by his tomb in the snow, while Gregorievitch, taller than ever before though not erect, hung over its railings like a weeping willow and told us how Starchevitch had founded the Party of the Right, which defied both Austria and Hungary and attempted to negotiate his country back to the position of independence it had enjoyed eight hundred years before. "It was Starchevitch's motto, 'Croatia only needs God and the Croats,' " said Gregorievitch. "For thirty years when the glamour and wealth and triumphant cruelty of nineteenth-century Hungary might have tempted us young Croats to forget our country, he made us understand that if we forgot the tradition of our race we lost our souls as if by sin." We were conscious of the second coat that lies about a snow-covered world, the layer of silence; we smelt the wood-smoke from the village below. "As a child I was taken to see him," said Gregorievitch, his voice tense as if he were a Welsh evangelist; "we all drew strength from him." Constantine, looking very plump and cosy, announced, "His mother was a Serb." "But she had been received at the time of her marriage into the True Church," said Gregorievitch, frowning.

We moved away, and as Constantine and I stepped into the snow-drifts of the lane we passed three men, dark as any Hindu, carrying drums and trumpets. "*Ohé!* Here are the gipsies," said Constantine, and we smiled at them, seeing pictures of some farm kitchen crammed with people in dresses brighter than springtime, all preparing with huge laughter to eat mountains of lamb and pig and drink wells of wine. But the men looked at us sullenly, and one said with hatred, "Yes, we are gipsies." Both Constantine and I were so startled that we stopped in the snow and gaped at each other, and then walked on in silence. In the eastern parts of Yugoslavia, in Serbia and in Macedonia, the gipsies are proud of being gipsies, and other people, which is to say the peasants, for there are practically none other, honour them for their qualities, for their power of making beautiful music and dancing, which the peasant lacks, and envy them for being exempt from the necessities of toil and order which lie so heavily on the peasant; and this has always been my natural attitude to those who can please as I cannot. It was inconceivable to both Constantine and myself that the gipsies should have thought we held them in contempt or that we should have expressed contempt aloud if we had felt it.

The whole world was less delightful. The snow seemed simply weather, the smell of the wood-smoke gave no pleasure. "I tell you, Central Europe is too near the Croats," said Constantine. "They are good people, very good people, but they are possessed by the West. In Germany and Austria they despise the gipsies. They have several very good reasons. The art of the gipsies commands no respect, for the capitalist system has discredited popular art, and only exploits virtuosos. If I go and play Liszt's scaramoucheries very fast, thump-thump-thump and tweedle-tweedle-tweedle, they will think more of it than the music those three men play, though it is perfectly adapted to certain occasions. Also the gipsies are poor, and the capitalist system despises people who do not acquire goods. Also the West is mad about cleanliness, and the gipsies give dirt its rights, perhaps too liberally. We Serbs are not bourgeois, so none of these reasons make us hate the gipsies, and, believe me, our world is more comfortable."

I looked back at the gipsies, who were now breasting the hill, huddled under the harsh wind that combed its crest. Life had become infinitely poorer since we left church. The richness of the service had been consonant with an order of society in which peasants and gipsies were on an equal footing and there was therefore no sense of deprivation and need; but here was the threat of a world where everybody was needy, since the moneyed people had no art and the people with art had no money. Something alien and murderous had intruded here into the Slav pattern, and its virtue had gone out of it.

Two Castles

YES, the German influence was like a shadow on the Croat World. We were to learn that again the next day. Gregorievitch had arranged to take us on Easter Monday into the country, with Constantine and Valetta and some young Croat doctors. It is a sign of the bitterness felt by the Croats against the Serbs that because we were in the company of Constantine and Gregorievitch, who were representatives of the Yugoslavian ideas, very few Croats would meet us: and Valetta, who came to see us because of an existing friendship with me, was slightly embarrassed by the situation, though he concealed it. These Croat doctors were ready to come with us, because it was our intention to visit first a castle belonging to a great Hungarian family who still used it as a residence for a part of the year, and then to go on to another castle, once owned by the same family, but now used as a sanatorium for tuberculosis by a Health Insurance Society. This gave them a professional excuse. But it snowed all through the night of Easter Sunday, and we woke to an Arctic morning, so we telephoned to ask Valetta and these doctors to come all the same and have breakfast, though the expedition would obviously have to be cancelled. They came and proved to be delightful young men, graduates of Zagreb University, with hopes of post-graduate work in Vienna and Berlin and Paris, and we were having a pleasant conversation over our coffee and boiled eggs when the door opened and Gregorievitch came in, and we saw that we had done wrong.

It is of the highest importance that the reader should understand Gregorievitch. If it were not for a small number of Gregorievitches the eastern half of Europe (and perhaps the other half as well) would have been Islamized, the tradition of liberty would have died for ever under the Habsburgs, the Romanoffs, and the Ottoman Empire, and Bolshevism would have become anarchy and not a system which may yet be turned to many uses. His kind has profoundly affected history, and always for the better. Reproachfully his present manifestation said to us, "Are you not ready yet?" We stared up at him, and my husband asked, "But is not the weather far too bad?" He answered, "The sun is not shining, but the countryside will be there all the same, will it not? And the snow is not too deep." "Are you sure?" my husband asked doubtfully. "I am quite sure," answered Gregorievitch. "I have rung up a friend of mine, a

68

general who has specialized in mechanical transport, and I have told him the make of our automobiles, and he is of the opinion that we will be able to visit both castles."

There, as often before and after, Gregorievitch proved that the essential quality of Slavs is not, as might be thought, imagination. He is characteristically, and in an endearing way, a Slav, but he has no imagination at all. He cannot see that the factual elements in an experience combine into more than themselves. He would not, for example, let us go to the theatre at Zagreb. "No, I will not get you tickets," he said with a repressed indignation, like a brawl in a crypt, "I will not let you waste your money in that way. Since you cannot follow Serbo-Croat easily even when it is spoken slowly, and your husband does not understand it at all, what profit can it be for you to go to our theatre?" He envisaged attendance at a play as an attempt to obtain the information which the author has arranged for the characters to impart to the audience by their words and actions; and that the actions could be used as a basis for guesswork to the words, that the appearance of the actors, the inflections of their voices, and the reactions they elicited from the audience, could throw light not only on the play but the culture of which it was a part was beyond his comprehension. So now he conceived of an expedition to the country as being undertaken for the purpose of observing the physical and political geography of the district, and this could obviously be pursued in any climatic conditions save those involving actual physical discomfort. Nevertheless the Slav quality of passion was there, to disconcert the English or American witness, for it existed in a degree which is found among Westerners only in highly imaginative people. As he stood over us, grey and grooved and Plutoish, he palpitated with the violence of his thought, "These people will go away without seeing the Croatian countryside, and some day they may fail Croatia for the lack of that knowledge." His love of Croatia was of volcanic ardour; and its fire was not affected by his knowledge that most of the other people who loved Croatia were quite prepared, because he favoured union with the Serbs, to kill him without mercy in any time of crisis.

We rose, abashed, and filed out to the automobiles; and indeed at first the weather was not too bad. We went out of the town in a light drizzle, passing a number of women who were hurrying to market. They wore red kerchiefs on their heads, red shawls and white skirts, and carried red umbrellas in one hand, while with the other they pulled their skirts high over their red woollen stockings, so high that some showed their very clean white drawers of coarse linen edged with elaborate *broderie an-*

glaise. There was a Breughel-like humour about their movements, as if they were stylizing their own struggles with nature; their faces showed that there was nothing brutish about them. This was very marked among the old women. Slavs grow old more beautifully than the people of other races, for with the years their flesh clings closer to the bone instead of sagging away from it. This ribbon of laughing peasants ran beside us in an unbroken comic strip, right out into the country, where they exercised their humour with extreme good temper, for the automobiles raised fans of liquid mud on each side of them, and everyone we met had to jump some distance into deep snow to keep their clothes dry and clean. But they all made a joke of it. In one village, where the plaster houses were all painted a deep violet which was given great depth and vibrancy by the snow and the grey sky, a lovely young girl laughingly put her umbrella in front of her and mocked us and herself with clownish gestures that were exquisitely graceful and yet very funny.

Then we saw nobody on the roads. The snow began to fall thickly and to lie. People at the door of a cottage smiled, waved, shivered theatrically, and banged the door. We passed through a broad valley paved with the dark glass of floods. In the driving snow a birch wood looked like a company of dancing naked nymphs. Then there was another Chinese landscape of wooded hills furred with snow, that went on for a long time; they were unwinding the whole scroll for us to see. Here and there the scroll was damaged. The painting of the woods stopped abruptly, and we could see nothing but the silk on which the artist worked; the hills were hidden, and there was nothing but the mist. Sometimes it parted and we saw a gross-towered, butter-coloured *Schloss*. They told us what Austrian or Hungarian family had lived there, and what it was now: a textile factory, a canning plant, a convalescent home.

It grew colder. We stopped in a little town and went into the hotel, and warmed ourselves with plum brandy, which is the standard oddtime drink in Yugoslavia. The landlord spoke to us proudly of the place, telling us they had a beautiful memorial to some Croat patriots in the market-place, and that not far away they had found the skeleton of a prehistoric man. We said that we knew how that had happened. The poor man had been taken for a nice drive in the country by Gregorievitch. This delighted Gregorievitch; it was pathetic to see how pleased he was because the young Croats could lay aside their hatred of Yugoslavia and joke with him for a little. He was very happy indeed when, because he had pretended to be aggrieved, we drank another round of plum brandies to his honour. Then we started out again, into hillier country where the snow was still deeper. At the top of a hill our automobile stuck in a snowdrift. Peasants ran out of a cottage near by, shouting with laughter because machinery had made a fool of itself, and dug out the automobile with incredible rapidity. They were doubtless anxious to get back and tell a horse about it.

Thereafter the snow was so thick on the wooded hills that the tree-trunks were mere lines and the branches were finer than any lines drawn by a human hand. No detail was visible in the houses of the villages at the base of the hills. They were blocks of soft black shadow edged with the pure white fur of the snow on the roofs. Above the hills there was a layer of mist that drew a dull white smudge between this pure black-and-white world and the dark-grey sky. There was no colour anywhere except certain notes of pale bright gold made by three things. So late was this snowfall that the willows were well on in bud; their branches were too frail to carry any weight of snow, and the buds were too small to be discernible, so each tree was a golden-green phantom against the white earth. There were also certain birds that were flying over the fields, bouncing in the air as if they were thrown by invisible giants at play; their breasts were pale gold. And where the snow had been thickest on the banks of the road it had fallen away in a thick crust, showing primroses. They were the same colour as the birds' breasts. Sometimes the road ran over a stream, and we looked down on the willows at its edge. From this aspect the snow their green-gold branches supported looked like a white body prostrate in woe, an angel that had leaped down in suicide from the ramparts of the sky.

We saw no one. Once a horse, harsh grey against a white field, gave way to that erotic panic peculiar to its species, which rolls the eye not only in fear but enjoyment, that seeks to be soothed with an appetite revealing that it plainly knows soothing to be possible, and pursues what it declares it dreads. It leaped the low hedge and fled along the road before us; and out of a farm on the further side of the field there ran a man, splendid in a sapphire sheepskin jacket, who remembered to close the door behind him as carefully as if it were not merely an extreme of temperature he were shutting out, but an actual destroying element of fire. When he caught the horse and dragged it off the road, our chauffeur shouted our thanks and regrets to him; but he made no answer. He stood still with the horse pressing back its head against his shoulder, in voluptuous exaggeration of its distress, and from the contraction of the man's brows and his lips it could be seen that he was barely conscious of the situation which he was remedying, and could think of nothing but the intense cold. To the eye the world seemed unified by the spreading whiteness of the snow, yet actually each horse, even each person, was shut off from all others in an abnormal privacy by this pricking, burning icy air.

We passed through a village, still as midnight at midday, and stone-blind, every door and window closed. "Think of it," said Valetta; "in all those cottages there are sitting nothing but dukes and duchesses, barons and baronesses." The peasants here had received an emperor handsomely when by the stupidity of his nobles he had found himself tired and wounded and humpy and alone after a day's hunting, and he ennobled the whole village by patents of perfect validity. And a little further on was our journey's end. We got out of the automobile and found ourselves at a lodge gateway with extravagant stables behind it, and what were recognizably "grounds" beyond, the kind of grounds that were made in England during the nineteenth century after the Georgian and Regency schools of landscape gardening, shrubby and expensive and futile; these sloped to the base of an extremely steep sugar-loaf hill which had something like Balliol on the top of it. As we gaped a mist swooped on us and all was suddenly veiled by the whirling confetti of a gentle snowstorm. Not unnaturally, nobody was about.

"What can have happened to them all?" asked Gregorievitch. He went and pounded on the door of the porter's lodge, and when an astonished face appeared at the upper windows he demanded, "And where is Nikolai? Why is Nikolai not here to meet us?" "He is up at the castle," said the porter; "he did not think you would be coming." "Thought we were not coming!" exclaimed Gregorievitch. "What made him think we were not coming?" It had distressed him very much to find that Valetta and the Croats and my husband and I seemed unable to grasp the common-sense point of view that if one wanted to see a castle one went and saw it, no matter what the weather, since the castle would certainly be there, no matter what the weather; but he had excused it because we were by way of being intellectuals and therefore might be expected to be a little fanciful. Here, however, were quite simple people who were talking the same sort of nonsense. He said testily, "Well, we will go up and find him for ourselves." We climbed the sugar-loaf hill by whimsically contrived paths and stone steps, among fir trees that were striped black and white like zebras, because of the branches and the layer of white snow that lay on each of them, while the porter, who was now invisible to us through the snow, cried up to the castle, "Nico-lai! Nikolai! They have come!" I was warm because I was wearing a squirrel coat, but all the men were shaking with cold, and we were all up to our knees in snow. At last we came to a walk running round some ramparts, and Nikolai, who was a very handsome young peasant with golden hair and blue eyes framed by long lashes, dropped the broom with which he had been trying to clear a path for us and ran towards Gregorievitch, crying, "How brave you are to make such a journey in this weather!" "Lord above us," said Gregorievitch, "what does everybody mean? Open the door, open the door!"

When the door was opened the point of this fierce Arctic journey proved to be its pointlessness. For indeed there was nothing in the castle to match the wildness of the season, of the distraught horses and the wavering birds, of Gregorievitch and his people. A fortress six hundred years old had been encased in a vast building executed in that baronial style which owed so much more to literary than to architectural inspiration, having been begotten by Sir Walter Scott; and though the family which owned it had been unusually intelligent, and free-minded to the point of being Croatian patriots, their riches had brought them under the cultural influence of the Austro-Hungarian Empire. So there were acres of walls covered from floor to ceiling with hunting trophies. These never, in any context, give an impression of fullness. I remembered the story of the old Hungarian count who was heard to mutter as he lay dying, "And then the Lord will say, 'Count, what have you done with your life?' and I shall have to say, 'Lord, I have shot a great many animals.' Oh, dear! Oh, dear! It doesn't seem enough." Nobody but the fool despises hunting, which is not only a pleasure of a high degree, but a most valuable form of education in any but a completely mechanized state. Marmont, who was one of Napoleon's most intelligent marshals, explains in his memoirs that he was forced to hunt every day from two o'clock to nightfall from the time he was twelve, and this put him into such perfect training that no ordeal to which he was subjected in all his military career ever disconcerted him. But as a sole offering to the Lord it was not enough, and it might be doubted if this was the right kind of hunting. These trophies spoke of nineteenth-century sport, which was artificial, a matter of reared beasts procured for the guns by peasants, and so essentially sedentary that the characteristic sportsman of the age, commemorated in photographs, had a remarkable paunch.

There was also a clutterment of the most hideous furniture of the sort that was popular in the Austro-Hungarian Empire in the second half of the nineteenth century, walloping stuff bigger than any calculations of use could have suggested, big in accordance with a vulgar idea that bigness is splendid, and afflicted with carving that made even the noble and austere substance of wood ignoble as fluff. It would have been interesting to know where they had put the old furniture that must have been displaced by these horrors. One of the most beautiful exhibitions in Vienna, the Mobiliendepot, in the Mariahilfestrasse, was composed chiefly of the Maria Theresa and Empire furniture which the Emperor Franz Josef and the Empress Elizabeth banished to their attics when they had refurnished their palaces from the best firms in the Tottenham Court Road.

There were also a great many bad pictures of the same era: enormous flushed nudes which would have set a cannibal's mouth watering; immense and static pictures showing what historical events would have looked like if all the personages had been stuffed first; and one of the family had over-indulged in the pleasures of amateur art. She herself had been a woman of enormous energy; a fashionable portrait painter had represented her, full of the uproarious shire-horse vitality common to the women admired by Edward VII, standing in a pink-satin ball dress and lustily smelling a large bouquet of fat roses in a massive crystal vase, apparently about to draw the flowers actually out of the water by her powerful inhalations. This enormous energy had covered yards of the castle walls with pictures of Italian peasant girls holding tambourines, lemon branches, or amphoræ, which exactly represented what is meant by the French word "*niaiserie*."

There were also some portraits of male members of the family, physically superb, in the white-and-gold uniform of Hungarian generals, solemnized and uplifted by the belief that they had mastered a ritual that served the double purpose of establishing their personal superiority and preserving civilization as they knew it; it was as pathetic to see them here as it would be to go into the garret of a starving family to see the picture of some of its members who had been renowned on the stage as players of kings and emperors. It might be said that though all these things were poor in themselves, they represented a state superior to the barbaric origins of Croatian society. But it was not so, for the family portraits which depicted the generations of the late sixteenth and seventeenth centuries showed people with their heads held high by pride and their features organized by intelligence, set on canvas by artists at least as accomplished and coherent in vision as the painters of our Tudor portraits. They gave documentary proof that German influence had meant nothing but corruption.

The corruption was profound. I left my companions at one point and turned back to a bedroom, to look again from its windows on an enchanting view of a little lake, now a pure sheet of snow, which lay among some groves below the sugar-loaf hill. I found Gregorievitch sitting on the window-sill, with his back to the view, looking about him at the hideous pictures and furniture with a dreamy and absorbed expression. "It would be very pleasant to live this way," he said, without envy, but with considerable appetite. This was the first time I had heard him say anything indicating that he had ever conceived living any life other than his own, which had been dedicated to pain and danger and austerity; and I could be sure that it was not the money of the people who lived in the castle, not the great fires that warmed them or the ample meals they ate, it was their refinement that he envied, their access to culture. I had never thought before what mischief a people can suffer from domination by their enemies. This man had lived his whole life to free Croatia from Hungarian rule; he had been seduced into exalting Hungarian values above Croatian values by what was an essential part of his rebellion. He had had to tell himself and other people over and over again that the Hungarians were taking the best of everything and leaving the worst to the Croats, which was indeed true so far as material matters were concerned. But the human mind, if it is framing a life of action, cannot draw fine distinctions. He had ended by believing that the Hungarians had had the best of everything in all respects, and that this world of musty antlers and second-rate pictures and third-rate furniture was superior to the world where peasants sang in church with the extreme discriminating fervour which our poets envy, knowing themselves lost without it, and wore costumes splendid in their obedience to those principles of design which our painters envy, knowing themselves lost without instinctive knowledge of them.

On the way to the sanatorium the party was now more silent. The young men were hungry, we had all of us wet feet, the sky threatened more snow, and the houses were now few and widely scattered. We could understand enough to realize that it was worrying them a little that if the automobiles broke down we should have a long distance to walk before we found shelter. Nobody, however, seemed to blame Gregorievitch. It was felt that he was following his star.

It was not till after an hour and a half that we arrived at the sanatorium, which was a fine baroque castle set on a hill, once owned by the same family which had owned the other castle, but now abandoned because the lands all around it had been taken away and given to peasant tenants under the very vigorous Agrarian Reform Scheme which the Yugoslavian Government put into effect after the war. This visit was less of an anticlimax than the other, for here was the real Slav quality. As we came to the gates a horde of people rushed out to meet us, and as my husband, who finds one of his greatest pleasures in inattention, had never grasped that this castle had been converted into a sanatorium, he believed them to be the family retainers, and wondered that such state could be kept up nowadays. But they were only the patients. They rushed out, men and women and children, all mixed together, some wearing ordinary Western costume, and some in peasant costume; some of the men wore the Moslem fez, for the Health Insurance Society which manages the sanatorium draws its members from all over Yugoslavia. They looked strangely unlike hospital patients. There was not the assumption of innocence which is noticeable in all but the wilder inmates of an English institution, the tramps and the eccentrics; not the pretence that they like starched sheets as a boundary to life, that the authority of doctors and nurses is easy to accept and reasonable in action, that a little larking is the only departure from hospital routine they could possibly desire, that they were as Sunday-school children mindful of their teachers. These people stood there, dark, inquisitive, critical, our equals, fully adult.

This was, of course, partly due to their racial convictions. Many of them came from parts of Yugoslavia where there is still no trace of a class system, where there are only peasants. They had therefore not the same sense that in going into hospital a worker placed himself in the hands of his superior, and that he must please him by seeming undangerous. But also, as it appeared when he went into the doctor's room, the theory of illness was not the same as in a Western European hospital. We found there the superintendent, who was a Serb though long resident in Croatia and pro-Croat in politics, and his three Croat assistants who all had an oddly unmedical air to English eyes. I do not mean that they looked unbusinesslike; on the contrary, each of them had a sturdy air of competence and even power. But there was in their minds no vista of shiny hospital corridors, leading to Harley Street and the peerage, with blameless tailoring and courtesy to patients and the handling of committees as subsidiary obligations, such as appears before most English doctors. There was no sense that medical genius must frustrate its own essential quality, which is a fierce concentration on the truth about physical problems, by cultivating self-restraint and a conventional blankness which are incompatible with any ardent pursuit. These people had an air of pure positiveness which amounted to contentiousness. They might have been bull-fighters.

They were bull-fighters, of course. The bull was tuberculosis. The formalities of our reception were got over in a minute. Had I been visiting a sanatorium in England cold and with wet feet I would have had to go to the matron's room, and time would have been wasted. Here we shook hands, hurried to the radiators, sat down on them, took off our shoes, and pressed our stocking soles against the warm iron, while the doctors talked their tauromachy around us. Did we know that tuberculosis was the scourge of Southern Slavs? It had to be so, because the country was being rapidly industrialized. Peasants came to the town blankly ignorant of hygiene, drawn by wages that looked high on paper and were in fact far too low to buy proper housing or clothing; and there was still so little hospital treatment that a tuberculosis case was as likely as not to remain untreated and spread infection. And this was not because they were Balkans. They said that with a sudden leap of fire to their eyes, which could be understood by anyone who has heard Germans or Austrians use the adjective "*Balkan*," with a hawking excess of gross contempt. We English, they said, had had just as much tuberculosis at the beginning of the nineteenth century.

I have acquired, painfully enough, some knowledge of sanatoria; and looking round me as they talked, I could see that in a way this sanatorium was frightful and, in another, most excellent. The first door we opened showed us the anachronistic character of the building in which it had been installed. We stepped suddenly into the opaque darkness, the inconquerable midday chill, of the family chapel, with a gilt and bosomy baroque Virgin and half a dozen cherubs ballooning above the altar, and two of the family gaunt in marble on their tombs. A congregation of nuns, each a neat little core to a great sprawling fruit of black-and-white robes, swivelled round on their knees to see who the intruders might be, and the Mother Superior, with a gesture of hospitality completely in consonance with the air of the presiding Virgin behind the altar, ceased the chanting of the service until we had ended our visit. Such a gesture had probably not been made in Western Europe for three hundred years. I do not believe it is easy to convert to hospital use a seventeenth-century castle built on three stories round an immense courtyard, with immensely high rooms and floors of stone and marble, and to staff it with people so much in accord with that same century that to them everything on the margin of hygiene, the whole context of life in which the phrase of science appears, must have been wholly incomprehensible.

But the place was clean, fantastically clean, clean like a battleship. There at least was something that an English hospital authority would have had to approve; perhaps, however, the only thing he could. The patients within doors were shocking to Western theories as they had been when they had met us out of doors on our arrival. They were evidently preoccupied with the imaginative realization of their sickness, and no one was attempting to interfere with them in their pleasure. This was a visiting day; and in what had been the grand drawing-room of the ladies of the castle, a large apartment adorned with sugary, Italianate, late nineteenth-century murals representing the islands of the blest, women sat holding their handkerchiefs to their lips with the plangent pathos of *la dame aux camélias*, and men assumed the sunrise mixed with sunset glamour of the young Keats, while their families made no attempt to distract them from these theatrical impersonations but watched with sympathy, as audiences should. The patients who had no visitors were resting; and when we went into the wards they were lying on their beds, the quilts drawn over their mouths, the open windows showing a firmament unsteadily yet regularly cleft by the changing stripes of snowfall. Shivering, they stared at us, their eyes enormous over the edges of their quilts, enjoying at its most dramatic the sense of the difference between our health and their disease; and indeed in the dark beam of their hypnotic and hypnotized gaze the strangeness of their plight became newly apparent, the paradox of the necessity which obliged them to accept as a saviour the cold which their bodies believed to be an enemy, and to reject as death the warmth which was the known temperature of life. The doctors beside us appeared to take for granted this atmosphere of poetic intensity, and made none of the bouncing gestures, none of the hollow invocations to optimism which in England are perpetually inflicted on any of the sick who show consciousness of their state. The tolerance of these doctors, indeed, was wide. As we passed along a corridor overlooking the courtyard, there trembled, in one of the deep recesses each window made in the thickness of the wall, a shadow that was almost certainly two shadows, fused by a strong preference. "Yes," said the superintendent, "they sometimes fall in love, and it is a very good thing. It sometimes makes all the difference, they get a new appetite for living, and then they do so well." That was the answer to all our Western scruples. The patients were doing so well. Allowed to cast themselves for great tragic roles, they were experiencing the exhilaration felt by great tragic actors. It was not lack of control, lack of taste, lack of knowledge that accounted for permission of what was not permitted in the West. Rather was it the reverse. Our people could not have handled patients full of the dangerous thoughts of death and love; these people had such resources that they did not need to empty their patients of such freight.

The doctors themselves were living richly. They were enjoying the sense of power which comes to the scientist when he applies his knowledge to a primitive people. They talked of the peasants as of beautiful and vigorous animals that have to be coaxed and trapped and bludgeoned into submitting to the treatment which will keep alive the flame in their bodies without which they will have neither beauty nor vigour. So, of course, do any colonial administrators; but these doctors cared for loveliness with the uncorrupted eye of an unmechanized race, and though they were divided from the patients by the gulf that divides a university graduate from a peasant, that gulf was bridged by the consciousness that they all were Slavs and that their forbears had all been peasants together. Each of these doctors was a magician who was working his spells to save his father and his mother. It is this same situation, I imagine, which is responsible for the peculiar enthusiasm shown by officials engaged in the social services in Soviet Russia. This is often regarded as a specific effect of a Communist regime, but it could certainly be matched all over the Balkans, in all the Baltic provinces that were formerly under the Tsardom, and in Turkey. The old and the new sometimes make an intoxicating fusion. These doctors were enchanted with their X-ray department and their operating theatre where they had a pretty record of successful collapses of the lung, and they were enchanted, too, when they hurried us down the corridors, down a staircase of stone so old that it was black as iron, and through a door of wood so old that it shone as glass, to a vast kitchen, obscure in its great vaulted roof, glowing near the fires which were roaring like the night wind in a forest. At long tables half as thick as tree-trunks, pretty nuns in white robes put the last touches to that state of order which women make twice a day after meals and live only to unmake. The prettiest one of all we found in a store-room half the size of my flat in London, standing by a table covered with the little sweet biscuits made of nuts and meringue and fine pastry which are loved in every Slav country. We caught her eating one. She swallowed it in a gulp, and faced out the men's roar of laughter in the most serene confusion imaginable, smiling, with some tiny crumbs caught in the fair down on her upper lip. It was then that somebody remembered that our dinner was ready for us.

We were taken up to the doctors' mess and set before a further exhibition of antique plenty. There was a river of plum brandy somewhere near, it seemed. Then, to begin with, there was a platter of cold meat such as I never expected to eat in my life again. There was sucking-pig so delicate that it could be spread on bread like butter, and veal and ham and sausage and tongue, all as superb in their austerer way, and slabs of butter and fat cheese. Then there were pancakes, stuffed with chopped steak and mushrooms and chickens' livers, and then spring chicken served with a border of moist and flavoursome rice on a bed of young vegetables, and it appeared that there was also a river of white wine near by. And then there was a compote of quinces, cherries, and peaches, served with a stack of little biscuits, like the one we had found the pretty nun eating. We ate and drank enormously. Valetta said in my ear, "You really must eat, you know. They will think you dislike their food if you do not. It is our Slav custom to give our guests too much to eat, as a kind of boastfulness, and of course out of good-will, and the guests show how strong they are by eating it. We are really a very primitive people, I am afraid." I did not complain, and we ate without interruption, save when a nun put her head round the door, and with round eyes cried out an announcement. The superintendent spoke to one of the younger doctors, who took off his coat, rolled up his sleeves, and ran from the room at the double. "Two of the patients have been talking politics," explained the superintendent; "it is not allowed, but sometimes they do it. However it is not really serious, they have no weapons. But go on eating, go on eating. All our food is raised on the land belonging to the sanatorium or round it, and prepared by our good nuns. And mind you, the patients have the same food as you are having. This is a feast for distinguished visitors, of course, but at all times we give them plenty, for it is cheap and we have no need to skimp it." "Yes," said another of the doctors, waving his glass at me, "we send the patients home five and ten and fifteen kilos heavier."

Here was the authentic voice of the Slav. These people hold that the way to make life better is to add good things to it, whereas in the West we hold that the way to make life better is to take bad things away from it. With us, a satisfactory hospital patient is one who, for the time being at least, has been castrated of all adult attributes. With us, an acceptable doctor is one with all asperities characteristic of gifted men rubbed down by conformity with social standards to a shining, cornerless blandness. With us, a suitable hospital diet is food from which everything toxic and irritant has been removed, the eunuchized pulp of steamed fish and stewed prunes. Here a patient could be adult, primitive, dusky, defensive; if he chose to foster a poetic fantasy or personal passion to tide him over his crisis, so much the better. It was the tuberculosis germ that the doctor wanted to alter, not the patient; and that doctor himself might be just like another man, provided he possessed also a fierce intention to cure. To him the best hospital diet would be that which brought the most juices to the mouth; and there was not the obvious flaw in the argument that one might think, for the chicken and the compote were the standard dishes of any nursing-home, but these were good to eat. One of the doctors raised his glass to me; I raised my glass to him, enjoying the communion with this rich world that added instead of subtracting. I thought of the service at Shestine, and its unfamiliar climate. The worshippers in Western countries come before the altar with the desire to subtract from the godhead and themselves; to subtract benefits from the godhead by prayer, to subtract their dangerous adult qualities by affecting childishness. The worshippers at Shestine had come before the altar with a habit of addition, which made them pour out the gift of their adoration on the godhead, which made them add to themselves by imaginative realization the divine qualities which they were contemplating in order to adore. The effect had been of enormous, reassuring natural wealth; and that was what I had found in Yugoslavia on my first visit. I had come on stores of wealth as impressive as the rubies of Golconda or the gold of Klondike, which took every form except actual material wealth. Now the superintendent was proposing the health of my husband and myself, and when he said, "We are doing our best here, but we are a poor country," it seemed to me he was being as funny as rich people who talk to their poor relations about the large amount they have to pay in income tax.

"But since they have this Slav abundance here and at Shestine," I wondered, "why have I had so little enjoyment of it since I arrived?"

But my attention was caught by a crack that had suddenly begun to fissure the occasion. The superintendent had been telling my husband and me what pleasure he had in welcoming us to Croatia, when Gregorievitch had leaned across the table and corrected him. "To Yugoslavia," he said in the accents of a tutor anxious to recall his pupil to truth and accuracy. There fell a silence. "To Yugoslavia," he repeated. Severity still lived in his brows, which he brought together by habit. But his eyes were stricken; so does an old dog look when it hopes against hope that the young master will take him out on a walk. After another silence, the superintendent said, "Yes, I will say that I welcome them to Yugoslavia. Who am I, being a Serb, to refuse this favour to a Croat?" They all laughed kindly at Gregorievitch after that; but there had sounded for an instant the authentic wail of poverty, in its dire extreme, that is caused by a certain kind of politics. Such politics we know very well in Ireland. They grow on a basis of past injustice. A proud people acquire a habit of resistance to foreign oppression, and by the time they have driven out their oppressors they have forgotten that agreement is a pleasure and that a society which has attained tranquillity will be able to pursue many delightful ends. There they continue to wrangle, finding abundant material in the odds and ends of injustices that are left over from the period of tyranny and need to be tidied up in one way or another. Such politics are a leak in the community. Generous passion, pure art, abstract thought, run through it and are lost. There remain only the obstinate solids which cannot be dissolved by argument or love, the rubble of hate and prejudice and malice, which are of no price. The process is never absolute, since in all lands some people are born with the inherent sweetness which closes that leak, but it can exist to a degree that alarms by the threat of privation affecting all the most essential goods of life; and in Croatia I had from time to time felt very poor.

Zagreb IV

THERE is no end to political disputation in Croatia. None.

Because we were walking near the vegetable market we trod on a mosaic of red and green cabbage leaves, orange peel, and grey stone. I directed the attention of Valetta and Constantine to its beauty, and I even became ecstatic over it; but I could not distract them from their heavy sense of disagreement. I had to admit that the experience I was offering them was perhaps insufficiently interesting, so when I found myself in front of a cage where a grey-and-pink parrot sat before a card index of destinies, I was glad to cry, "Let us have our fortunes told!" But Constantine and Valetta each looked at the bird with eyes smouldering with hope that the other would have no future whatsoever. So I put in my dinar and the bird picked out a card; and when I gave it to Valetta, he burst out laughing and threw it back to me. "Oh, wise bird! It says, 'You are surrounded by the wrong friends, you must get rid of them at once!'" He waved his cap and went laughing through the crowd. "Till you have obeyed, it is good-bye!" he cried over his shoulder; and then suddenly grave, lest we should think he had really turned against us, he said, "And I shall come to see you tonight, about seven."

They had quarrelled all through lunch. We had spent the morning going round the sights of the town with a Croat lady and Constantine, and over the soup we told Valetta how much we had liked her; and Constantine exploded: "I did not like her. She is not a true Slav. Did you hear what she told you when you were at the Health Co-operative Society Clinic? She said that all such things were very well looked after in the Austrian times. Yes, and she said it regretfully." "Well, it was so," said Valetta. "Yes, it was so," said Constantine, "but we must not regret it. No true Slav would regret it. That is to say no true human being would say it, for if a true human being is a Slav, he knows that to be a Slav is what is important, for that is the shape which God has given him, and he should keep it. The Austrians sometimes pampered you, and sometimes the Hungarians, so that each should play you off against the others. Benefits you get so are filth, and they spoil your shape as a Slav. It is better to have nearly nothing at all, and be a freeman with your brother Slavs." He paused, but Valetta was silent and went on eating. "Do you not think it is better?" Constantine asked him. He nodded slightly. "Well, if you do not feel that strongly you can feel nothing at all!" said Constantine a little louder. "Oh, yes, I feel it strongly," said Valetta, quite softly, and then, more softly still, "It would be much better for us to be freemen with our brother Slavs."

For a moment Constantine was satisfied and went on eating. Then he threw down his knife and fork. "What is that you are saying? It *would* be better . . . You mean it is not so?" "I mean it is not quite so," said Valetta. "How is it not so?" asked Constantine, lowering his head like a bull. Valetta shrugged his shoulders. Constantine collapsed quite suddenly, and asked pathetically, "But are we not brothers, we Croats and Serbs?" "Yes," said Valetta. He was speaking softly, not, as a stranger might have thought, out of guile, but out of intense feeling. He was quite white. "But in Yugoslavia," he said painfully, "it is not so. Or, rather, it is as if the Serbs were the elder brother and we Croats the younger brother, under some law as the English, which gives the elder everything and the younger nothing." "Oh, I know what you think!" groaned Constantine. "You think that all your money goes to Belgrade, and you get hardly anything of it back, and we flood your country with Serb officials, and keep Croats out of all positions of real power. I know it all!"

"You may know it all," said Valetta, "but so do we: and it is not a thing we can be expected to overlook." "I do not ask you to overlook it," said Constantine, beginning to roar like a bull, "I ask you to look at it. You did not have the spending of your money before, when you were under Hungary. All your money was sent to Budapest to landlords or to tax-collectors, and you got some railways, yes, and some hospitals, yes, and some roads, yes, but not costing one-half of your money, and you got also Germanization and Magyarization, you got the violation of your soul. But now you are a part of Yugoslavia, you are a part of the kingdom of the South Slavs, which exists to let you keep your soul, and to guard that kingdom we must have an army and a navy to keep Hungary and Italy in their places, and we must give Serbia many things she did not have because Serbia was fighting the Turk when you were standing safe behind us, and we must do much for Bosnia, because the Hungarians did nothing there, and we must do everything for Macedonia, because the Turks were there till 1912, and we must drain marshes and build schools and make military roads, and it is all for you as well as for us, but you will not see it!"

"Yes, I see it," said Valetta, "but if you want to found a strong and civilized Yugoslavia you should have brought the Serb schools up to

the Croat level instead of bringing the Croat schools down to Serb level."
"But now you show you see nothing at all," wailed Constantine; "it is a
question of money! It is more important that one should have good
schools everywhere than that part of the country should have very good
schools. A chain is as strong as its weakest link. What good is it to you in
Croatia that your boys and girls can read the Hindustani and paint like
Raphael if the young men in Macedonia go bang-bang all night at whoever because they do not know anything else to do?" "We might feel
more confidence that our money went to build schools in Macedonia if
it did not go through Belgrade," said Valetta. "You must forgive us for
fearing that a great deal of it sticks in Belgrade." "Of course it sticks in
Belgrade!" said Constantine, his voice going high, though it is low by
nature. "We must make a capital. We must make a capital for your sake,
because you are a South Slav! All Western Europeans despise us because
we have a little capital that is not chic. They are wrong, for there is no
reason why we should have a big capital, for we are a peasant state. But
you must give these people what they want, and they are like children,
it is the big shining thing that impresses them. Do you not remember
how before the war the Austrian Ministers treated us like dirt, because
Vienna is a place of baroque palaces and we had nothing but our poor
town that had a Turkish garrison till fifty years ago, though it meant
nothing, for at the appointed time we came down on them like a hammer
on nutshells?"

"If it were only ministries and hotels that were being built in Belgrade,
we Croats might approve," said Valetta, "but we understand that there
are many private houses which are being built for people who have been
connected with politics." "It is not true, I swear it is not true," cried
Constantine. "Are you telling me," asked Valetta, "that all Serb officials
are honest?" Constantine rocked in his seat. "I am all for chonesty," he
said, giving the *h* its guttural sound, "I am a very chonest man." And that
is true: during his life he has had the unquestioned administration of
much money, and never has one penny stuck to his fingers. "And I admit," he continued heavily, "that in our Serbia there are sometimes people who are not chonest. But how could we do? There are not enough
people in our country to take on the administration, so many of us were
killed in the war. Ninety per cent," he wailed, "ninety per cent of our
university students were killed in the war." And that, too, I learned
afterwards, is true. "Then why do you not draw on us Croats for officials?" asked Valetta. "There are many Croats whom nobody in the
world would dare to call untrustworthy." "But how can we let you

Croats be officials?" spluttered Constantine. "You are not loyal!" "And how," asked Valetta, white to the lips, "can we be expected to be loyal if you always treat us like this?" "But I am telling you," grieved Constantine, "how can we treat you differently till you are loyal?"

It is an absolute deadlock; and the statement of it filled the heart with desolation. Constantine pushed away his plate and said, "Valetta, I will tell you what is the matter with you." "But we can see nothing the matter with either of you," I intervened. "After we left you at the Health Co-operative Clinic the Croat lady took us to the Ethnographical Museum. What genius you Slav peoples have! I have never seen such a wealth of design, provoked by all sorts of objects always to perfection. A dress, an Easter egg, a butter-churn." I knew that my intervention was feeble, but it was the best I could do. I find that this always happens when I try to interrupt Slavs who are quarrelling. They draw all the energy out of the air by the passion of their debate, so that anything outside its orbit can only flutter trivially. "I will tell you what is the matter with you," repeated Constantine, silencing me with his hand. "Here in Croatia you are lawyers as well as soldiers. You have been good lawyers, and you have been lawyers all the time. For eight hundred years you have had your *procès* against Hungary. You have quibbled over phrases in the *diploma inaugurale* of your kings, you have wrangled about the power of your Ban, you have sawed arguments about *regna socia* and *partes adnexæ*, you have chattered like jackdaws over your rights under the Dual Monarchy, you have covered acres of paper discussing the Hungaro-Croatian compromise. And so it is that you are now more lawyers than soldiers, for it is not since the eighteenth century that you have fought the Turks, and you fought against the Magyars only a little time. But now we are making Yugoslavia we must feel not like lawyers but like soldiers, we must feel in a large way about the simple matter of saving our lives. You must cast away all your little rights and say that we have a big right, the right of the Slavs to be together, and we must sacrifice all our rights to protect that great right."

Valetta shrugged his shoulders once more. "What have you against that?" roared Constantine. "I will tell you what is the matter with you. You are an intellectual, you are all intellectuals here in the bad sense. You boast because Zagreb is an old town, but that it is a great pity for you. Everywhere else in Serbia is a new town, and though we have novelists and poets and all, they have now been in no town not more than not one generation." (This is good Serbian grammar, which piles up its negatives.) "So what the peasant knows they also know. They know that one must not work against, one must work with. One ploughs the earth that would not be ploughed, certainly, but one falls in with the earth's ideas so much as to sow it with seed in the spring and not in the winter or in the summer. But in the town you do not know that, you can go through life and you can work against all, except the motor car and the railway train and the tram, them you must not charge with your head down, but all other things you can. So you are intellectuals. The false sort that are always in opposition. My God, my God, how easy it is to be an intellectual in opposition to the man of action! He can always be so much cleverer, he can always pick out the little faults. But to make, that is more difficult. So it is easier to be a critic than to be a poet." He flung down a fork suddenly. "But I should say it is easier to be a bad critic. To be a good critic you must make sometimes and know how it is in your own self to make well or badly. That is why I am a great critic. I am also a great poet. But you are not poets, you Croats, you do not make. You are always little and clever, you are always in opposition winning points as if it were a game." He flung himself on his jam pancakes like a hungry lion, then, with his mouth full, roared again, "All of you in Zagreb are the same. I have been in the cafés every night and the Croats all say to me, 'It is disgusting, the trade pact you in Belgrade have made with Italy!' And who are the Croats, who took Italian help to kill our King, who are howling always that your peasants are so poor, to attack us if we swallow our pride and for the sake of getting the peasants a little money make a trade pact with the Italians? *Ach,* in all your little ways you are very terrible."

For a time Valetta did not answer. It is a considerable part of the Croat argument that Croats do not shout in restaurants and do not speak at all with their mouths full. "You would say we were well governed here?" he asked presently. "You would say that nobody is arrested without cause and thrown into prison and treated barbarously? You would say that nobody has been tortured in Croatia since it became Yugoslavia?" He was trembling, and such sick horror passed across his face that I am sure he was recollecting atrocities which he had seen with his own eyes, at which his own bowels had revolted. Constantine nearly cried. "Ah, God! it is their fault," he pled, indicating my husband and myself with his thumb. "These English are hypocrites, they pretend you govern people without using force, because there are many parts of the Empire where they govern only people who want to be governed. It is not necessary to use force in Canada and Australia, so they pretend that there is the general rule, though in India where the people do not want to be governed many people are beaten and imprisoned. And for that I do not blame the English. It must be done if one race has to have power over another; that is why it is wrong for one race to have power over another, and that is why we must have a Yugoslavia, a self-governing kingdom of the South Slavs, and why we should make all possible sacrifices for Yugoslavia." "I see the argument," said Valetta; "we are to let Serbs torture us Croats, because under Yugoslavia we are not to be tortured by the Italians and Hungarians." "Oh, God! Oh, God!" cried Constantine, "I am glad that I am not a Croat, but a Serb, for though I myself am a very clever man, the Serbs are not a very clever people; that has not been their business, their business has been to drive out the Turks and keep their independence from the Austrians and the Germans, so their strong point is that they can open doors by butting them with their heads. Believe me, in such a position as ours—that is more important. But, my God, my God, do you know what I feel like doing when I talk to you Croats? I feel like rolling up my coat and lying down in the middle of the street, and putting my head on my coat, and saying to the horses and motor cars, 'Drive on, I am disgusted.' What is so horrible in this conversation is that you are never wrong, but I am always right, and we could go on talking like this for ever, till the clever way you are never wrong brought death upon us." "Some have died already," said Valetta.

Zagreb V

THE rest of the afternoon was to prove to us that Constantine was to some extent right, and that the Croat is weakened by Austrian influence as by a profound malady.

When Valetta had left us in front of the parrot's cage, Constantine said, "Now we must hurry, for we have two things to do this afternoon. We must see the treasury of the Cathedral and then we must go to the dancer who has promised to dance for us in her apartment." He walked beside us very glumly, looking at the pavement, and then burst out: "I do not know why you trouble yourself with that young man, he is not of importance, he is quite simply a Croat, a typical Croat." After a silence we came to the square in front of the Cathedral. He burst out again: "They do appalling things and they make us do appalling things, these Croats. When God works through the Croats He works terribly. I will tell you what once happened in the war. There was a hill in Serbia that we were fighting for all night with the Austrian troops. Sometimes we had it, and sometimes they had it, and at the end we wholly had it, and when they charged us we cried to them to surrender, and through the night they answered, 'The soldiers of the Empire do not surrender,' and it was in our own tongue they spoke. So we knew they were our brothers the Croats, and because they were our brothers we knew that they meant it, and so they came against us, and we had to kill them, and in the morning they all lay dead, and they were all our brothers."

Just then, the face of the Cathedral rose pearly-brown above us. Constantine tiptoed to the sacristan and said that we wanted to see the treasury, and there began a scurrying quest for the key. A sacristan in ordinary breeches and shirt-sleeves was carrying away the tubs of oleanders that had decorated the altar during Easter. His face was pursed with physical effort and an objection to it, and the oleander branches waved about him like the arms of a vegetable Sabine. "They are a long time seeking the key," said Constantine wearily, leaning against a pillar and looking up to its high flowering. "I would not have you think that the Croats are not good people. All Slavs are good people. They were the best soldiers in the Austro-Hungarian Empire. All, all said so, on all the fronts. Hey, what is this?" A priest had come to say that the key had had to be sent for, that it would come soon. He then ran towards a little door through which five or six other people ran constantly during the next quarter of an hour, on errands connected with the finding of the key. "Now I as a Serb do not think it is as important that the key should be found quickly as you English would do," said Constantine, "but I would point out to you that in Zagreb also the key is not found in the quick English tempo. Yet I am sure that here they say to you all day, 'We are not as the Serbs in Belgrade, here we are businesslike, we do things as they are done in Vienna.' " And it was true. So they had said to us constantly in the banks and hotels and museums.

At last a priest came with the key in his hand, and took us up a stone staircase to the treasury which had an enormous safe-door, affixed after the theft of a tenth-century ivory diptych, which was discovered some years later in the museum at Cleveland, Ohio. The safe-door took quite a long time to open, it was so very elaborate. Then the priest went in and immediately ran out with a chalice of which he was evidently very proud, though it was not very distinguished late sixteenth-century work. For some reason all Croat priests both in Croatia and Dalmatia have a special liking for dull Renaissance work. Byzantine work they value for its antiquity only, and its lavish use of precious metals, and medieval work they usually despise for its uncouthness. The priest was quite ecstatic about this chalice, which he put down on a little rickety table on the landing outside the treasury, and made us stand and admire it for some time. Then he said that we must see the jewelled mitre of a sixteenth-century bishop, and he showed us into the treasury. After we had looked at the silver we were shown the diptych, which is pleasing but not satisfying, because it lacks spaciousness. The figures are the right hieroglyphics; they could spell out a magic message, but they do not, because they are so crowded it is like a poem printed with the words run together. We were shown also the sham diptych which was substituted by the thief for the real one so that the theft went undetected for some days. This was a surprising story, for though the copy reproduced all the details of the original, it was with such infidelity, such falsity of proportion and value, that the two were quite unlike in effect. It is possible that the copy was carved in some centre of craftsmanship, perhaps in Italy, by somebody who had never seen the original but worked from a photograph.

While we were discussing this the priest uttered a sharp cry and ran out of the room, while Constantine burst into laughter. He explained, "He has remembered that he has left the chalice on the table outside." I said, "But why do you laugh? It is a thing that any of us might have done." "But it is not," said Constantine. "Your husband would not have done it at all, because he is English. You might or might not have done it, because you are a woman, and so of course you have no very definite personality. But I would have been sure to do it, and the priest was sure to do it. But because I am a Serb I know I am sure to do it, while because he is a Croat he thinks he is like a German or an Englishman and will not do it. Of course I must laugh. It is the same funny thing as about the key."

When the priest came back he showed us the illuminated Psalters and Bibles; and in one of them we fell on the record of what is always pleasing, a liberal and humanist soul which found perfect satisfaction and a refuge from troubled times in the Church. On the margins of his holy book he painted towns set on bays where it would be good to swim, meadows where spring had smiled four hundred years and was not tired, and rosy nudes with their flesh made sound by much passive exercise. We would have thought that the man who painted so was at ease with the world had we not turned a page and found proof that he was nothing of the kind. With unbroken sweetness but in perplexed misery, he painted a hunter lying asleep in the woods and peopled the glades with his dream. The hunter is spitted before a lively fire by hinds who sniff in the good roasting smell, while hares chase hounds lather-mouthed with fright and cram their limp bodies into baskets, and by every stroke of the brush it is asked, "What are blue seas and the spring and lovely bodies so long as there are pain and cruelty?" He spoke to us for one second out of the past and instantly returned there, for the priest preferred that we look at his vestments rather than at his books. "And indeed they are very beautiful," said Constantine. They were of embroidered damask and stamped velvet, for the most part of Italian provenance, some as old as the sixteenth century. "But how poor they look!" I said. "You are hard to please," he said. "No, I am not," I said, "but compared to the design we saw in the Ethnographical Museum these seem so limited and commonplace."

I was not flattering Constantine. These designs on the vestments were of that Renaissance kind which, if one sees them in a museum and tries to draw them, distress one by their arbitrariness. They partake neither of naturalism nor of geometrical pattern; they often depict flowers set side by side to make harmonies of colour and united by lines whose unpleasant lack of composition is disguised by those harmonies. The designs in the Slav embroideries are based on sound line, on line that is potent and begets as it moves, so that in copying it the pencil knows no

opposition; it is, as Constantine would say, "working with." Also the
Slav designs have great individuality while keeping loyal to a defined
tradition, whereas the Italian designs follow a certain number of defined
models. "You are right," said Constantine benignly. "We are a wonderful people. That is why we want to be Slavs and nothing else. All else is
too poor for us. But now we must go to the dancer; she is having the
accompanist specially for us, so we must not be late."

The dancer lived on the top floor of a modern apartment house. The
blond floor of her practice room shone like a pool under the strong light
from the great windows, and though her accompanist had not yet come,
she was swaying and circling over it like a bird flying low over the
water, as swallows do before rain. She turned at the end of the room
and danced back to greet us. She had that vigorous young beauty that
seems to carry its keen cold about with it. Her eyes were bright and her
cheeks glowed as if she were not really here, as if she were running on
her points up the cornices of a snow peak to a fairy ice-palace. She had
the most relevant of beauties for her trade, the bird foot that born dancers have, that Nijinsky had to perfection. Before she got to us she stopped
and pointed to a gilded laurel wreath that hung on the wall. As she
pointed with her right hand her left heel moved a thought backwards,
and the result was perfection. I went up and looked at the wreath and
found that she had been awarded it at some Berlin dance festival. "That
is why we have come," said Constantine; "she won the second prize at
the great Folk-Dance Festival. It is a great honour."

My husband said, "Please tell her we think her dress most beautiful.
Is it a Croatian peasant dress?" "*Ach*, no!" said Constantine. "But no, my
God, I am wrong, it is." He went down on his knees and looked at the
skirt. It was of white linen embroidered with red and white flowers of
a very pure design. "Yes," he said, "it is a Croatian peasant girl, but she
has adapted it to Western ideas. She has made it much lighter. Well, we
shall see. Here comes the accompanist." We watched the girl's feet move
like nothing substantial, like the marks on eddying water. Her skirts
flowed round her in rhythms counter to the rhythms of her feet, and,
smiling, she held out her hands to invisible partners to share in this dear
honourable drunkenness. Out of the air she conjured them till they were
nearly visible, frank and hearty fellows that could match her joke with
joke, till shyness came and made all more delicate, and for a second all
laughter vanished and she inscribed on the air her potentiality for romance. Her head and bosom hung backwards from the stem of her waist

like a flower blown backwards, but for fear that this wind blow too strongly she called back the defence of laughter, and romped again.

When she stopped we all applauded; but as soon as she went away to change her dress Constantine said to me, "It is terrible, is it not?" "Yes, it is very shocking," I said, "but I thought it must be so from her dress." My husband said, "I do not know what you mean. It seems to me we have been watching a very accomplished dance of little or no imaginative distinction, but I cannot understand why anybody should consider it as shocking." "No, of course you cannot understand, but your wife can, because she has been in Serbia and Macedonia, and she knows how it is natural for a Slav woman to dance. She knows that with us a woman must not dance like this. It does not go with any of our ideas. A woman must not spring about like a man to show how strong she is and she must not laugh like a man to show how happy she is. She has something else to do. She must go round wearing heavy clothes, not light at all, but heavy, heavy clothes, so that she is stiff, like an icon, and her face must mean one thing, like the face of an icon, and when she dances she must move without seeming to move, as if she were an icon held up before the people. It is something you cannot understand, but for us it is right. Many things in our culture accord with it." "Is this something that is taken for granted and spoken about, or have you just thought of it?" asked my husband. "I have just thought of putting it like this," said Constantine, laughing, "but that is nothing against it, for I am a demoniac man like Goethe, and my thoughts represent the self-consciousness of nature. But indeed your wife will tell you it is so." "Yes," I said, "he is right. They shuffle round as if they were dead, but somehow it looks right."

When the dancer came back she was committing a worse offence against Slav convention. It happens that Lika, which is a district of Dalmatia, in the Karst, that is to say on the bare limestone mountains, breeds a kind of debonair Highlander, rather hard to believe in, so like is he to the kind of figure that a Byron-struck young lady of the early nineteenth century drew in her album. The girl's dress was a principal-boy version of this, a tight bodice and kilt of oatmeal linen, with a multicoloured sporran, and she wore the typical male Lika head-dress, a cap with an orange crown, a black rim, and a black lock of fringe falling over the ear and nape of the neck on the right side. It suited her miraculously, and her legs were the shape of perfection. But the rhythm of her dance was very quick and springing; it was in fact a boy's dance, and she danced it as a girl wanting to emphasize that she was a girl by performing a characteristically male process. She ended standing on the tips of her toes, with her left hand on her hip and her right forefinger touching her chin, her eyebrows raised in coyness; there was never anything less androgynous.

But the attempt to juggle with the two aspects of human sexuality was not the reason why this dance was distressing in its confusion. It was a distress not new to me—I have felt it often in America. I have at times felt suddenly sickened when a coloured dancer I have been watching has used a step or gesture that belongs to "white" dancing; even if the instant before they had been wriggling in an imitation sexual ecstasy and passed into a dull undulation of the Loie Fuller sort or the chaste muscular bound of a ballet movement, the second seemed more indecent than the first, and I have often experienced the same shock when I have seen white dancers borrow the idiom of coloured dancers. There is nothing unpleasant in the gesture known as "cherry-picking," provided it is a Negro or Negress who performs it; the dancer stands with feet apart and knees bent, and stretches the arms upwards while the fingers pull an invisible abundance out of the high air. But it is gross and revolting, a reversion to animalism, when it is performed by a white person. That same feeling of inappropriateness amounting to cultural perversion afflicted me slightly when I saw this girl's first dance, more severely when I saw her second, and to a painful degree in the third, which she did to show us that she could do more than mere folk-dances. It was that cabaret chestnut, the dance of the clockwork doll, which is an imaginative cliché of the stalest sort, never again to be more amusing than the riddle "When is a door not a door?" And this was the most excruciating rendering of it that I have ever seen. This Croat girl was so noble a creature that when she did a silly thing she looked far sillier than the silly do. At the end of her dance she ran across the shining floor and stood with her bare arm resting on the golden wreath, her reflection broken loveliness at her feet. "Some day I will make them give me the first prize," she laughed. "The poor little one," said Constantine, "she should be like an icon, your wife will tell you."

Zagreb VI

WE went up the hill and looked at the archaic statues on the porch of St. Mark's Church, which is a battered old spiritual keep that has been built and rebuilt again and again since the thirteenth century. "This old square is the heart of the town," said Constantine. "Zagreb is the heart of Croatia, and St. Mark's Square is the heart of Zagreb, and I think that only once did it fall, and then to the Tartars, to whom all fell. But now they have renamed it the Square of Stefan Raditch, after the great leader of the Croat Peasant Party, who was shot in the Belgrade Parliament in 1928. Here in Croatia they say we Serbs did it, they say our King Alexander plotted it," said Constantine, his voice rising to a wail, "but it is not so. He was shot by a mad Montenegrin deputy whom he had accused of corruption. The Montenegrins are a Homeric people, they do not understand modern life; they think that if a man attacks your honour you kill him, and it is well. But the Croats do not know that, for they will never travel; they have no idea of going any further than Dalmatia. And why would King Alexander want to kill Raditch? He knew very well that if Raditch were killed the Croats would go mad and would make with the Italians and the Hungarians to kill him also. And so they did. And that is a thing to remember when the King is blamed for suspending the constitution. Always King Alexander knew that he would be killed. It is proof of the lack of imagination of all you English liberals that you forget that a man's policy is a little different when he knows he is going to be killed."

Down in the town we sat and drank chocolate in a café, till Constantine said, "Come you must go. You must not keep Valetta waiting." Since he was staying in the same hotel as we were, and he looked tired, I said, "Come back with us." But he would not. "I will come later," he said, and I am sure he was afraid of meeting Valetta in the lounge and having to admit that Valetta wanted to see us but not him. The Serb, though he seems tough and insensitive, is sometimes childishly hurt by Croat coldness. Some French friends of mine who once attended an international congress of some sort at Zagreb were in the company of a Serb, a middle-aged diplomat, when somebody came into the room with the news that the Croat hospitality committee was not going to ask the Serb delegates to the banquet which was going to terminate the proceedings. The Serb diplomat burst into tears. This story is the sadder because every Croat, who thinks of the Serb as the gendarme who tortures him, would disbelieve it.

When we got to our hotel we found Valetta waiting for us, and we took him up to our room and drank plum brandy, pleased to see him again though we had seen him so recently. He stood by the window, pulled the curtains apart, and grimaced at the snow that fell aslant between us and the electric standards. "What a terrible Easter we have given you!" he laughed, and raised his glass to his lips, smiling on us with the radiance that is usually the gift of traitors, but means nothing in him but kindness and good faith. He went on to apologize for the violence with which he had spoken at lunch-time. "I could not help it," he said. "I know that Constantine is a wonderful man, but he is all for Belgrade, and you will understand how we are bound to feel about that. I am so afraid that as you are just passing through the country, you will not see what we Croats have to suffer. Of course everything is better since 1931, when the King gave us back some sort of constitution; and since the King died it has improved still further. But it is still terrible.

"You cannot think," he said, as we all gathered round the fire with our glasses on our knees, "what the censorship here is like. Do you know that that little pamphlet about the Dictatorship of the Proletariat, which was a kind of three-cornered debate between Stalin and Shaw and Wells, has been suppressed? Think of the absurdity of it! Of course that hardly matters, for it is imported and it could not be called an epoch-making work, but what does matter is that our own great people are persecuted. You have heard of X. Y.? He is a dramatist, and he is really by far the greatest living writer we have. But he is a Communist. Well, never can we see his plays at our theatre. They simply will not let them be performed. And it matters not only for us, but for him, because he is miserably poor. And he is not allowed to make money any way, for when some people arranged for him to give a lecture here in one of our big halls and had sold all the tickets, the police prevented it twenty-four hours before, on the ground that if there were a riot in the hall they could not undertake to keep order. Now, that is sheer nonsense. We Croats might riot about all sorts of things, but we would not riot because X. Y. was giving a lecture. And really, I am not exaggerating, all this means that the great X. Y. is starving."

"But wait a minute," said my husband. "Is it only the Yugoslavian Government that did not want X. Y. to speak? Is there not a chance

that the Croat Clerical Party was also rather anxious that he shouldn't?"
Valetta looked uncomfortable. "Yes, it is so," he said. "They would be
against any Communist, wouldn't they?" pressed my husband. "And
they would be in favour of a strict censorship, wouldn't they?" "Yes,"
said Valetta. "Then when you fight for free speech and a free press, you
Croats are not only fighting the Serbs, you are also fighting your own
Clerical Party?" "That is so," agreed Valetta; and he added sadly, "Our
Clerical Party is very violent." There he was guilty of an understatement. The Croatian Clerical Party is not a force that can easily be regarded as proceeding from God. It is a party with a long pedigree of
mischief-makers, for it descends from the nineteenth-century Party
of the Right, which was led by Anton Starchevitch, and its successor,
the Party of Pure Right, which was led by Dr. Josef Frank. Both these
parties were violently bigoted in their pietism, and professed the most
vehement antagonism to the Jews (which implied antagonism to liberalism) and to the Orthodox Church (which, as all Serbs are Orthodox,
implied antagonism to the Serbs).

There is to be noted, as evidence against the Austro-Hungarian Empire, the neurotic quality of its rebels. It is as if the population were so
drugged and depleted that they never raised their voice unless they were
stung by some inner exasperation. It has been mentioned that Kossuth,
the Magyar patriot and scourge of the Slavs, was himself pure Slovak
and had no Magyar blood in his veins. Even so, Starchevitch, who loathed
the Serbs, was himself, as Constantine had told us beside his grave, born
of a Serb mother, and Dr. Frank, whose anti-Semitism was frenzied, was
a Jew. Such Slav patriots as these were meat and drink to the Austro-
Hungarian Empire, who hated her Slav subjects. They made it easy for
her to rule according to that counsel of Hell, *Divide et impera*. The
famous Ban Khuen-Héderváry, whose rule of Croatia was infamously
cruel, made a point of granting the Serb minority in Croatia special
privileges, so that the Croats would be jealous of them, and there was
thus no danger of Serbs and Croats joining together in revolt against
Hungarian rule.

The state of mind this produced in the populace can be read in one
of the numerous trials that disgraced the Austro-Hungarian Empire so
far as Croatia was concerned from the beginning of the twentieth century till the war. This was the famous "Agram trial" (Agram was the
Austrian name for Zagreb) which arraigned fifty-three Serbs of Croatia for conspiracy with the free Serbs of Serbia against the Austro-
Hungarian Empire. The charge was flagrant nonsense, cooked up by the

Ban, Baron Rauch, a stupid brute, and Count Aehrenthal, the Austrian Foreign Minister, who belonged to the company of Judas and Fouché; but for evidence they never had to turn to Austrians or Magyars. Nearly all the two hundred and seventy witnesses brought by the prosecution, who were nearly all flagrantly perjured, were Croats. They were all willing to swear away the lives of their fellow-Slavs to the authorities they hated; yet there is no difference between Croats and Serbs except their religion.

The Croat Clerical Party, therefore, has always worked with a motive power of anti-Serb hatred, which naturally created its material. The Serbs retorted with as bad as they got, and the Orthodox Church showed no example of tolerance to the Roman Catholics. The greatest of nineteenth-century Slav patriots of the pacific sort, Bishop Strossmayer, once announced his intention of visiting Serbia, and the Serbian Government had to make the shameful confession that it could not guarantee his personal safety. But the greatest stimulus to anti-Serb feeling has lain outside Croatia, in the Roman Catholic Church itself. During the last sixty years or so the Vatican has become more and more Ultramontane, more and more predominantly Italian in personnel; and since the war of 1914 it has become more and more terrified of Communism. Can the Roman Catholic Church really be expected to like Yugoslavia?—to like a state in which Croats, who used to be safely amalgamated with Catholic Austrians and Hungarians, are outnumbered by Orthodox Serbs, who are suspected of having no real feeling of enmity towards Bolshevist Russia?

There are two indications, one small and one massive, of the Roman Catholic attitude to Yugoslavia. In all Slav countries there have been for many years gymnastic societies for young Slavs, called "Sokols," or "The Hawks," after an original made in Czechoslovakia, where boys and girls are given physical training and instructed in their nationalist tradition and the duties of a patriot. These are, indeed, the models from which the Italian Fascisti copied the Balilla and Avanguardisti. After the war, the Roman Catholic Church started rival societies called "The Eagles" in both Croatia and Slovenia. It is extremely difficult to see what motive there can have been behind this move except to weaken the state loyalty of the Roman Catholic Yugoslavs; the Church could not possibly fear that the Sokols would interfere with the religious views of their members, for the Czech and Croatian Sokols had always been predominantly Catholic. The more important indication of the pro-Italian and anti-Slav attitude of the Roman Catholic Church is her callousness towards the unhappy Slovenes who were incorporated in Italy under the Peace Treaty. These six hundred thousand people are the worst-treated minority in Europe except the German Tirolese. "Have bugs a nationality when they infest a dwelling? That is the historical and moral position of the Slovenes living within our borders," once said the *Popolo d'Italia*. The 1929 Concordat which Pope Pius XI signed with Mussolini did not adequately protect the religious rights of the Slav minority, and the Slovenes no longer enjoy the right, which they prized highly, of using the Slovene liturgy in the churches. The Slav so loves his language that this was a gesture of hostility to the Slav soul.

It is, therefore, not sensible to trust the Roman Catholic Croat to like and understand the Orthodox Serb, or even to discourage the artificial hatred that has been worked up between them in the past. "Do you not think, Valetta," said my husband, "that the Belgrade Government knows this, and therefore bargains with the Church, giving it assistance in its anti-Communist campaign on condition that it keeps the anti-Serb and Croatian Separatist Movement within bounds?" Valetta hesitated. "It may be so," he said, his long fingers fiddling with the fringe of a cushion. "And there is another thing," said my husband; "there is the present Concordat." [1] He paused. In 1937 all the Serbian parts of Yugoslavia were up in arms because the Government had signed a Concordat with Pope Pius which gave the Roman Catholic Church immense advantages over the Orthodox Church: in any town where the Roman Catholics were in an absolute majority over the Serbs all the schools without exception were to be Roman Catholic; the child of a Roman Catholic mother and an Orthodox father was to be brought up as a Roman Catholic even if the mother were received into the husband's Church; it was to be far easier for Roman Catholic soldiers to practise their religion than for the Orthodox soldiers, and so on. The terms were so grossly favourable to the Roman Catholics that the Government made it very difficult for the Serb public or for foreigners to obtain the text of the Concordat. "Yes," sighed Valetta, "this wretched Concordat. We none of us want it here, in Croatia, you know."

"Yes, I do not think you Croats want it," said my husband, "but your Church does. And don't you feel that the Church would never have been able to extort such terms from the Belgrade Government if it had not been able to trade some favours in return? I suspect very strongly

---

[1] This Concordat was abandoned in 1938 because of the fierce opposition of the Serbs and the lukewarm attitude of the Croats. It was entirely the project of the Vatican.

that it has said to the Belgrade Government, 'If you give us these concessions we will see to it that the Croatian Peasant Party never seriously menaces the stability of the Yugoslavian state.' " Valetta rocked himself uneasily, "Oh, surely not, surely not," he murmured. "But for what other reason can the Belgrade Government have granted this preposterous Concordat?" pressed my husband. "I cannot imagine," said Valetta. "Oh, I suppose you are right!" He rose and went to the window and drew back the curtains, and looked again on the bright snow that drove out of the darkness through the rays of the street lamps.

"Is it not the tragedy of your situation here," suggested my husband, "that you Croats are for the first time discovering that your religion and your race run counter to one another, and that you are able to evade that discovery by putting the blame on the constitution of Yugoslavia? The Croats, like all Slavs, are a democratic and speculative people. You lived for long under the Habsburgs, whom you could blame for every interference with individual liberty. Since the great pro-Croat Strossmayer was a Bishop you could even think of the Roman Catholic Church as the arch-opponent of the Habsburgs, and therefore the protector of liberty. Now the Habsburgs are swept away you should see the Roman Catholic Church as it is: not at all democratic, not at all in favour of speculative thought; far more alarmed by the vaguest threat of social revolution than by any actual oppression, provided it is of monarchical or totalitarian origin, and wholly unsympathetic with any need for free expression but its own. You should proceed to the difficult task of deciding whether you can reconcile yourself to this bias of the Church for the sake of the spiritual benefits it confers upon you. But you are postponing this task by letting the Church throw the blame for all its suppressions of free speech and free press on Belgrade."

"It is possible that you are right," said Valetta, coming back and taking his seat by the fire. "Nothing is ever clear-cut here." "Do you never get down to a discussion of first principles?" asked my husband. "This business of social revolution, how is it regarded by the Croat politicians such as Matchek of the Croat Peasant Party?" "We never speak of such things, it is too soon," said Valetta. "But if they want to become a separate autonomous canton, surely they must have some idea of the kind of society they want to found?" "No," answered Valetta, "it is felt that it would be premature to discuss such things. Oh, I know it is wrong and naïve and foolish, but that is how our people feel."

That is how they had always felt, the Croat leaders. There lay on the table a wad of papers which was the result of my efforts, practised over some weeks, to discover what opinions had been held by the greatest of Croat leaders, the murdered Stefan Raditch. Those efforts had been fruitless, except so far as they provided a proof of the essential unity of the Slavs. For Raditch was the spit and image of Tolstoy. He talked nonsense as often as not, but nobody minded; they all listened and felt exalted. It was his habit to speak in parables that were apt to be childish and obscure, and his speeches sometimes lasted for half a day and usually contained matter that was entirely contrary to human experiences; but his audiences adored him as a sage and a saint, and would have died for him. What was peculiarly Croat in him was his appeal to the peasants as a representative of the country as against the town. This was his own invention. Before the war it was possible to meet all the other Croat politicians by frequenting the Zagreb cafés and restaurants, but both Raditch and his brother Anton, who was almost as famous, made it a strict rule never to enter a café or a restaurant. This was to mark themselves off from the bourgeoisie as specifically peasant. This would not have been impressive in any other part of Yugoslavia than Croatia, where alone is there a bourgeoisie which has existed long enough to cut itself off from the peasantry. It would have evoked dislike and impatience in Serbia or Bosnia or Macedonia, where the poorest peasant is accustomed to sit in cafés.

In the minds of his followers Raditch must have sown confusion and little else. He spoke always as if he had a plan by which the Croat peasant was instantly to become prosperous, whereas there is no man in the world, not even Stalin, who would claim to be able to correct in our own time the insane dispensation which pays the food-producer worst of all workers. The only practical step Raditch ever proposed was the abolition of a centralized Yugoslavian Government and the establishment of a federalism which would have left the economic position of the Croat peasant exactly where it was. The rest was a mass of violent inconsistencies. Probably nobody but St. Augustine has contradicted himself so often or so violently.

He was pro-Habsburg; at the outbreak of the war he made a superb speech calling on the Croats to defend their Emperor, and his sentiments did not really change after the peace. But he constantly preached that the Croats should form a republic within the kingdom of Yugoslavia, on the grounds that the proletariat was better off in a republic than in a monarchy. Not only was he simultaneously pro-Habsburg and republican, he had friendly correspondence with Lenin and made a triumphal progress through Russia. Though he expressed sympathy with Bolshe-

vist ideas, he had stern race theories, which made him despise many of
the inhabitants of the southern parts of Yugoslavia and reproach the
Serbs bitterly for admitting to Government posts such people as Vlachs,
an ancient and quite respectable shepherd tribe of the Balkans. It is said,
however, that he made the visit to Russia not from any ideological motive but because like all Slavs he loved to travel, and though he had lived
in Vienna and Berlin and Paris (where he had taken university degrees,
for no more than Tolstoy was he a piece of peasantry straight out of the
oven) and had visited London and Rome, he had never been in Moscow.

Whatever the reason may have been, the visit did not help him to give a
definition to the Croat mind, particularly as shortly afterwards he became
a close friend of King Alexander of Yugoslavia, whom he alternately
reproached for his interference with Parliamentarianism and urged to
establish a military dictatorship. Meanwhile he robbed the Croats of
any right to complain that the Serbs refused to let them take any part
in the government by ordering the Croat deputies to abstain from taking
their seats in the Belgrade Parliament, when the wiser course would
have been to leave them as an obstructionist and bargaining body. Some
idea of Raditch can be formed by an effort to imagine an Irish politician
with Parnell's personal magnetism, who was at one and the same time an
agrarian reformer, a Stuart legitimist, a republican, a Communist sym-
pathizer, an advocate of the Aryan race theory, and a close friend of the
King of England, to whom he recommended Liberalism and Fascism
as he felt like it, and who withdrew the Irish members from St. Stephen's
while himself constantly visiting London. It is no wonder that his party,
even under his successor Matchek, has formed only the vaguest programmes.

"Nothing," said Valetta, "has any form here. Movements that seem
obvious to me when I am in Paris or London become completely inconceivable when I am here in Zagreb. Here nothing matters except the
Croat-Serb situation. And that, I own, never seems to get any further."
"But this is something very serious," said my husband, "for a movement
might rush down on you here, say from Germany, and sweep away the
Croat-Serb situation and every other opportunity for debate." "You are
perfectly right," said Valetta. "I know it, I know it very well. But I do
not think anything can be done." And of course nothing can be done.
A great empire cannot bring freedom by its own decay to those corners
in it where a subject people are prevented from discussing the funda-
mentals of life. The people feel like children turned adrift to fend for
themselves when the imperial routine breaks down; and they wander to

and fro, given up to instinctive fears and antagonisms and exaltation until reason dares to take control. I had come to Yugoslavia to see what history meant in flesh and blood. I learned now that it might follow, because an empire passed, that a world full of strong men and women and rich food and heady wine might nevertheless seem like a shadow-show: that a man of every excellence might sit by a fire warming his hands in the vain hope of casting out a chill that lived not in the flesh. Valetta is a clean-cut person; he is for gentleness and kindness and fastidiousness against clod-hopping and cruelty and stupidity, and he would make that choice in war as well as in peace, for his nature is not timid. But he must have something defined that it is possible to be gentle and kind and fastidious about. Here, however, there is none, and therefore Valetta seems a little ghostly as he sits by our hearth; and I wonder if Zagreb is not a city without substance, no more solid than the snow-flakes I shall see next time Valetta strolls to the window and pulls the curtain, driving down from the darkness into the light of the street lamps. This is what the consequences of Austrian rule mean to individual Croats.

Zagreb VII

POLITICS, always politics. In the middle of the night, when there is a rap on our bedroom door, it is politics. "It may be a telegram," said my husband, springing up and fumbling for the light. But it was Constantine. "I am afraid I am late, I am very late. I have been talking in the cafés with these Croats about the political situation of Yugoslavia; someone must tell them, for they are quite impossible. But I must tell you that I will be leaving tomorrow for Belgrade, very early, earlier than you will go to Sushak, for they have telephoned to me and say that I must go back, they need me, for there is no one who works so well as me. I would have left you a note to tell you that, but there was something I must explain to you. I have spoken not such good things of Raditch who was killed and of Matchek who is alive—you had better put on your dressing-gown, for I will be some time explaining this to you—but I want to make you understand that though they are not at all clever men and cannot understand that there must be a Yugoslavia, they are chonest. They would neither of them take money from the Italians and Hungarians. They and their followers would spit on such men as go to be trained in terrorism at the camps in Italy and Hungary. These were quite other men, let me tell you. . . ."

Nevertheless we had woken as early as it was light, and my husband said to me, "We have never seen Mestrovitch's statue of the great Croat patriot, Bishop Strossmayer; it is in the public garden just outside this hotel. Let us go and look at it now." So we dressed in the dawn, said "Excuse me" to the charwomen that were scrubbing the hall, and found the Bishop among the dark bushes and drab laurels of the unilluminated morning. But his beauty, even under the handling of one whose preference for rude strength must have been disconcerted by its delicacy, was a light by itself. Mestrovitch had given up his own individuality and simply reproduced the Bishop's beauty, veiling it with a sense of power, and setting horns in the thick wavy hair, after the manner of Michael Angelo's Moses. I would like to know if Mestrovitch ever saw his model: he probably did, for Strossmayer lived until he was ninety in the year 1905.

This dazzling creature had then completed fifty-six years of continuous heroic agitation for the liberation of the Croats and as the fearless

denunciator of Austro-Hungarian tyranny. Because of his brilliant performances as a preacher and a scholar he was at thirty-four made the
Bishop of Djakovo, a see which included a vast stretch of the Slav-
inhabited territory of the Empire; and he immediately declared himself
as a passionate pro-Croat. It is an indication of the wrongs suffered by
the Croats that the revenues of this bishopric were enormous, though the
poverty and ignorance of the peasants were so extreme that they shocked
and actually frightened travellers. He amazed everyone by spending
these enormous revenues on the Croats. While Hungary was trying to
Magyarize the Croats by forbidding them to use their own language,
and as far as possible deprived them of all but the most elementary education, he financed a number of secondary schools and seminaries for
clerics, where the instructions were given in Serbo-Croat; he endowed
many South Slav literary men and philologists, both Croats and Serbs,
and, what was most important, he insisted on the rights of the Croats
and the Slovenes to use the Slav liturgy instead of the Latin. This last was
their ancient privilege, for which they had bargained with Rome at the
time of their conversion by Cyril and Methodius in the ninth century,
when they were a free people. He founded the University of Zagreb,
which was necessary not only for educational reasons but to give the
Croats a proper social status; for in the Austro-Hungarian Empire, as in
Germany and in the United States, graduation at a university has a class
value; it is the mental equivalent of a white collar. Since the Croats had
a university they could not be despised as peasants. He was able to raise
pro-Slav feeling in the rest of Europe, for he was the friend of many
distinguished Frenchmen, and he was the admired correspondent of
Lord Acton and Mr. Gladstone.

In all this lifelong struggle he had the support of no authority. He
stood alone. Though Pope Leo XIII liked and admired him, the Ultramontane Party, which wanted to dye the Church in the Italian colours,
loathed him because he was one of the three dissentients who voted
against the Doctrine of Papal Infallibility. On this matter he was of the
same mind as Lord Acton, but was at odds with his nearer Catholic
neighbours. These hated him because he defended the right of the Slavs
to have their liturgy said in their own tongue. They also found him
lamentably deficient in bigotry. When he sent a telegram of brotherly
greetings to the head of the Orthodox Church in Russia on the occasion
of the millenary of the Slav apostle Methodius, his fellow-Catholics, particularly the Hungarians, raged against this as an insult to the Holy See.
The sense of being part of a universal brotherhood, of being sure of

finding a family welcome in the furthest land, is one of the sweetest benefits offered by the Roman Catholic Church to its members. He had none of this enjoyment. He had only to leave his diocese to meet coldness and insolence from those who should have been his brothers.

The Austro-Hungarian Empire could not persecute Strossmayer to his danger. The Croats loved him too well, and it was not safe to have a belt of disaffected Slavs on the border of Serbia, the free Slav state. But it nagged at him incessantly. When he went to open the Slav Academy in Zagreb the streets were thronged with cheering crowds, but the Government forbade all decorations and illuminations. It took him fifteen years to force on Vienna the University of Zagreb; the statutes were not sanctioned till five years after the necessary funds had been collected. During the negotiations which settled the terms on which Croatia was to submit to Hungary, after Hungary had been given a new status by Elizabeth's invention of the Dual Monarchy, Strossmayer was exiled to France. At the height of the trouble over his telegram to the Orthodox Church about Methodius, he was summoned to Sclavonia, a district of Hungary, where the Emperor Franz Josef was attending manœuvres; and Franz Josef took the opportunity to insult him publicly, though he was then seventy years of age. This was a bitter blow to him, for he loved Austria, and indeed was himself of Austrian stock, and he wished to preserve the Austro-Hungarian Empire by making the Croats loyal and contented instead of rebels who had the right on their side. Again and again he warned the Emperor of the exact point at which his power was going to disintegrate: of Sarajevo. He told him that if the Austrians and Hungarians misgoverned Bosnia they would increase the mass of Slav discontent within the Empire to a weight that no administration could support and the Habsburg power must fall.

But what is marvellous about this career is not only its heroism but its gaiety. Strossmayer was a child of light, exempt from darkness and terror. In person he resembled the slim, long-limbed, and curled Romeo in Delacroix's *Romeo and Juliet,* and the Juliet he embraced was all grace. The accounts given by European celebrities of the visits they had to him read richly. The foreigner arrived after a night journey at a small station, far on the thither side of civilization, and was received by a young priest followed by a servant described as "a pandour with long moustachios dressed in the uniform of a hussar," who put him into a victoria drawn by four dappled greys of the Lipizaner strain which is still to be seen in the Spanish Riding School at Vienna. Twenty-two miles they did in two hours and a half, and at the end, near a small market town, reached a true palace. It was nineteenth-century made, and that was unfortunate, particularly in these parts. There is a theory that the decay of taste is somehow linked with the growth of democracy, but it is completely disproved by the Austro-Hungarian Empire, which in its last eighty years grew in fervour for absolutism and for Messrs. Maple of Tottenham Court Road. But there was much here worthy of any palace. There was a magnificent avenue of Italian poplars, planted by the Bishop in his young days; there was a superb park, landscaped by the Bishop himself; there were greenhouses and winter gardens, the like of which the eastward traveller would not see again until he had passed through Serbia and Bulgaria and Roumania and had found his way to the large estates in Russia.

The guest breakfasted by an open window admitting the perfume of an adjacent acacia grove, on prodigious butter and cream from the home farm, on Viennese coffee and rolls made of flour sent from Budapest. Later he was taken to worship in the Cathedral which the Bishop had built, where peasants proudly wearing Slav costumes were hearing the Slav liturgy. Then there was the return to the palace, and a view of the picture gallery, hung with works of art which Strossmayer had collected in preparation for the museum at Zagreb. It is an endearing touch that he confessed he was extremely glad of the imperial opposition which had delayed the foundation of this museum, so that he had an excuse for keeping these pictures in his own home. After an excellent midday dinner the Bishop exhibited his collection of gold and silver crucifixes and chalices of Slav workmanship, dating from the tenth to the fourteenth century, pointing out the high level of civilization which they betokened. Then the Bishop would take the visitor round his home farm, to see the Lipizaner horses he bred very profitably for the market, the Swiss cattle he had imported to improve the local stock, and the model dairy which was used for instructional purposes, and he would walk with him in his deer park, at one corner of which he had saved from the axes of the woodcutters a tract of primeval Balkan forest, within a palisade erected to keep out the wolves which still ravaged that part of the world. Before supper the visitor took a little rest. The Bishop sent up to him a few reviews and newspapers: *The Times, La Revue des Deux Mondes*, the *Journal des Economistes, La Nuova Antologia*, and so on.

After supper, at which the food and drink were again delicious, there were hours of conversation, exquisite in manner, stirring in matter. Strossmayer spoke perfect German, Italian, Czech, Russian, and Serbian, and a peculiarly musical French which bewitched the ears of Frenchmen;

but it was in Latin that he was most articulate. It was his favourite medium of expression, and all those who heard him use it, even when they were such scholars as the Vatican Council, were amazed by the loveliness he extracted from that not so very sensuous language. About his conversation there seems to have been the clear welling beauty of the first Latin hymns. The early Christians and he alike were possessed by an ardour which was the very quality needed to transcend the peculiar limitations of that tongue. It was an ardour which, in the case of Strossmayer, led to a glorious unfailing charity towards events. He spoke of his beloved Croats, of the victories of their cause, of his friendships with great men, as a lark might sing in mid-air; but of his struggles with Rome and the Habsburgs he spoke with equal joy, as a triumphant athlete might recall his most famous contests. His visitors, who had travelled far to reassure him in his precarious position, went home in a state of reassurance such as they had never known before.

This is not a character in life as we know it: it belongs to the world that hangs before us just so long as the notes of a Mozart aria linger in the ear. According to our dingy habit, which is necessary enough, considering our human condition, we regard him with suspicion, we look for the snake beneath the flower. All of us know what it is to be moonstruck by charmers and to misinterpret their charm as a promise that now, at last, in this enchanting company, life can be lived without precaution, in the laughing exchange of generosities; and all of us have found later that that charm made no promise and meant nothing, absolutely nothing, except perhaps that their mothers' glands worked very well before they were born. Actually such men often cannot understand generosity at all, since the eupeptic quality which is the cause of their charm enables them to live happily without feeling the need for sweetening life by amiable conduct. They often refrain from contemptuous comment on such folly because they have some use for the gifts of the generous, but even then they usually cannot contain their scorn at what seems a crazy looseness, an idiot interference with the efficient mechanism of self-interest. Hence the biographies of charmers are often punctuated by treachery and brutality of a most painful kind. So we wait for the dark passages in Strossmayer's story. But they do not come.

It appears that he turned on the spiritual world the same joyous sensuality with which he chose chalices, Italian pictures, horses, cattle, coffee, and flowers. He rejected brutality as if it were a spavined horse, treachery as if it had been chicory in the coffee. His epicureanism did not fail under its last and supreme obligation, so much more difficult than the harshest vow of abstinence taken by ascetics: he preferred love to hate, and made sacrifices for that preference. The sole companions left to him were the Croats; for them he had forsaken all others. But he never hesitated to oppose the Croat leaders over certain errors tending to malice and persecution, which sprung up here as they are bound to do in every movement of liberation. Though he risked everything to free the Croats from the dominance of the Austro-Hungarian Empire, he would not suffer any attempt to raise hatred among the Slavs against the Austrians or the Hungarian peoples; nor did he ever let ill be spoken of the Emperor Franz Josef. Nor, though he was a most fervent propagandist for the Roman Catholic faith, would he have any hand in the movement to persecute the Orthodox Church which set the Croat against the Serb. He set himself another problem of enormous delicacy in his opposition to anti-Semitism, which was here an inevitable growth, since the feudal system kept the peasants bound to the land and thereby gave the Jews a virtual monopoly of trade and the professions. For thirty-six years, smiling, he dared deny his friends all titbits to feed the beast in their bosoms, and lived in peril of making them his enemies, though he loved friendship above all things. Out of the political confusion of Croatia which makes for the endless embitterment and impoverishment I have described, this creature had derived sweetness and well-being.

"That is one of the most beautiful lives recorded in modern history," said my husband. We left the lovely statue smiling under the heavy rain.

On the railway station we found the good Gregorievitch and Valetta waiting to say good-bye to us. They stood side by side on the platform, these two enemies, the early morning rain dripping on their turned-up coat collars. Valetta laughed and wriggled as the drops of water trickled down his neck, but Gregorievitch merely bowed beneath the torrents. "Nothing is as it used to be," he said stoically; "even the seasons are changed." We did not wonder that he correlated his political disappointments with the weather. The previous day we had seen him link them with phenomena fated, it might have been imagined, to be connected with absolutely nothing, to be themselves alone.

We had gone, Constantine and my husband and myself, to take tea with Gregorievitch at his little flat on the hill beyond the Cathedral. His apartment and his family were the work of that God whose creations Tchekov described. Gregorievitch's wife was nearly as tall and quite as thin as he was, and every minute or so she put her hand to her head in a gesture of apprehension so uncontrolled that it disturbed her front hair, which rose in that tangled palisade called a transformation, familiar to us on the brows of nineteenth-century minor royalties, and finally fixed it at an angle of about sixty degrees to her fine and melancholy features. This would have been comic had she not been a creature moulded in nobility, and had it not been probable that that gesture had become a habit in the early days of her marriage, when Gregorievitch was as young as Valetta, and there was a Hungarian Ban in Zagreb, and every knock at the door might mean, and more than once had meant, that police officers had come to arrest him.

There was also a daughter, very short, very plump, very gay, an amazing production for the Gregorievitches. It was as if two very serious authors had set out to collaborate and then had published a limerick. We had heard about her: she wanted to marry a young officer, but could not because Army regulations forbade him to take a bride with a dowry below a certain sum, and the bank in which Gregorievitch had put his savings declared a moratorium. But she laughed a great deal, and wore a dress printed with little yellow flowers. That was not all in the little flat. There was also a small white poodle, which was pretty and neatly clipped, but old and careworn. It barked furiously when we entered; on Sunday afternoon it was evidently accustomed to repose itself and considered visitors a disorderly innovation. Quivering with rage, it watched while we were shown the sitting-room and the little library which opened off it through an arch. These rooms were full of heavy Austrian furniture with stamped leather cushions and embroidered mats, and they were suffused with a curious nostalgia, as if far older people were living in them than was the case. In the library several tables were entirely covered with thousands of typewritten pages: there must have been at least three-quarters of a million words. Gregorievitch told us that this was the typescript of his book on his war experiences, but it was only half finished, and now he had begun to doubt if it was morally justifiable to write it. To make conversation, since everybody was very silent, my husband looked at the bookshelves and seeing that many of the volumes were well worn, said, "I suppose you love your books very much?" Gregorievitch thought for some time and then said, "No." The conversation dropped again.

"Ah! Ah! Ah!" cried Constantine, pointing his forefinger. We all wheeled about and saw that the poodle was relieving itself on the carpet. The poor creature was making the only protest it could concerning its shattered repose; but it must be admitted that the spectacle was extremely obscene, for its froth of white curls over its clipped limbs recalled a ballerina. Gregorievitch and his wife started forward with tragic faces. The dog got up on its hind legs and clung onto Gregorievitch's hand, barking in weak defiance, putting his case about the sacredness of Sunday afternoon. But Gregorievitch inclined from his great height a face of solemn censure, as if it were a child or even a man who were at fault, while his wife beat the poodle with a small stick which had been brought from the hall by the daughter, who was now no longer laughing. Gregorievitch's expression reminded me of the words St. Augustine once addressed to a Donatist bishop whom he was persecuting: "If you could see the sorrow of my heart and my concern for your salvation, you would perhaps take pity on your own soul."

The dog was put out into the passage: but the incident could not be considered as ended. There remained in the middle of the carpet the results of its protest. We endeavoured to take the matter lightly, but we found that the Gregorievitches were evidently hurt by our frivolity; it was as if we had chanced to be with them when a son of theirs had returned home drunk or wearing the badge of the Croat Separatist Party, and we had tried to tamper with the horror of the moment by laughter. The atmosphere was tense beyond bearing; so Constantine, who had assumed an air of gravity, walked to the piano in the manner of an official taking charge in an emergency, and played a majestic motet by Bach, which recognizes the fact of tragedy and examines it in the light of an intuitive certainty that the universe will ultimately be found to be reasonable. The Gregorievitches, who had sunk into two armchairs facing each other, sat with their arms and legs immensely extended before them, nodding their heads to the music and showing signs of deriving sober comfort from its message. There entered presently with a brush and dust-pan an elderly servant, in peasant costume, who was grinning from ear to ear at the joke the dog's nature had played on the gentry.

As she proceeded with her task Constantine passed into the calmer and less transcendental music of a Mozart sonata, suitable to the re-establishment of an earthly decorum; and when she left the room he played a brief triumphal passage from Handel and then rose from the piano. Madame Gregorievitch bowed to him, as if to thank him for having handled a social catastrophe with the tact of a true gentleman, and he acknowledged the bow very much as Heine might have done. She then began to converse with me on general topics, on the exceptionally severe weather and its effect on the social festivities of Zagreb. Meanwhile her husband took mine aside, ostensibly to show him a fine print representing the death of an early Croatian king, but really to murmur in a voice hoarse with resentment that he had owned both the poodle's father and grandmother, and that neither of them would ever have dreamed of behaving in such a way. "Nothing, man or beast, is as it was. Our ideals, think what has happened to our ideals . . . what has happened to our patriots. . . ."

But for dear Valetta it is not all politics. He is a man of letters, he is a poet. What he could give the world, if there could only be peace in Croatia! But how is there to be peace in Croatia? It is said by some that it could be imposed overnight, if the Serbs of Yugoslavia could nerve themselves to grant federalism on the Swiss model. That would change the twilit character of Croatian history, it would give the Croats a sense of having at last won a success, it would give their national life a proper form. That, however, could never be a true solution. But supposing Croatia got her independence, and the peasants found they were still poor, surely there would be a movement towards some form of social revolution; and surely then the bourgeoisie and the conservatives among the peasants would try to hand their country over to some foreign power, preferably Nazi or Fascist, for the sake of stability. Surely, too, the Roman Catholic Church would be pleased enough if Croatia left its union with Orthodox Yugoslavia. And if that happened there would be no more peace in Croatia, for either Gregorievitch or Valetta. They were both true Slavs, and they would neither of them be able to tolerate foreign domination, firstly because it was foreign, and secondly because it was Fascist. Suddenly they looked to me strange and innocent, like King Alexander of Yugoslavia in the first part of the film, as he was in the boat and on the quay at Marseille. I pulled down the window so that I could see them better, my two dear friends who were each other's enemies, who might yet be united to each other, far more closely than they could ever be to me, by a common heroic fate. Such a terrible complexity has been left by the Austro-Hungarian Empire, which some desire to restore; such a complexity, in which nobody can be right and nobody can be wrong, and the future cannot be fortunate.

DALMATIA

DALMATIA

Sushak

THE train went through a countryside dark with floods; and then there was no countryside, but something like an abstract state of ill-being, a mist that made the land invisible but was not visible itself. Then we pulled up to mountains that were deep under new snow. Here trees became curious geometrical erections; white triangles joined each branch-tip to the trunk. I saw one branch break under its burden and fall in a scattery powder of what had wrecked it. Valleys that I had seen in summer-time and knew to be rocky deserts strewn with boulders the size of automobiles were level as lakes and swansdown white. I grumbled at it, for I had wanted my husband to see the crocuses that I had seen the year before lying under the trees like dapples of mauve sunshine, and all the red anemones springing among the lion-coloured stones. I kept on saying, "It will be all right when we get to Dalmatia, when we come to the coast." But in the early afternoon we caught sight of the Adriatic across barren, snow-streaked hills, and it looked like one of the bleaker Scottish lochs. Sky and islands and sea alike were bruise-coloured.

Well, I will own it. The grimness of the day was not all to blame. No weather can make the Northern Dalmatian coast look anything but drear. The dreariness is so extreme that it astounds like luxuriance, it gluts the mind with excess of deprivation. The hills are naked. That exclusion of everything but rock that we English see only in a quarry face is here general. It is the landscape. Tracks lead over this naked rock, but it is hard to believe that they lead anywhere; it seems probable that they are traced by desperate men fleeing from barrenness, and doomed to die in barrenness. And indeed these bald hills mean a great deal of desperation. The rainfall sweeps down their slopes in torrents and carries away the soil instead of seeping into it and fertilizing it. The peasants collect what soil they can from the base of the hills and carry it up again and pack it in terraces; but there is not enough soil and the terraces are often swept away by the torrents.

The human animal is not competent. That is the meaning of the naked Dalmatian hills. For once they were clothed with woods. These the earliest inhabitants of Dalmatia, the Illyrians and Romans, axed with an innocent carelessness; and the first Slav settlers were reckless too, for they came from the inexhaustible primeval forest of the Balkan Peninsula. Then for three hundred years, from about the time of the Norman Conquest to 1420, the Hungarians struggled with the Venetians for the mastery of this coast, and the nations got no further with their husbandry. Finally the Venetian Republic established its claim, and thereafter showed the carelessness that egotistic people show in dealing with other people's property.

They cut down what was left of the Dalmatian forests to get timbers for their fleet and piles for their palaces; and they wasted far more than they used. Venetian administration was extremely inefficient, and we know not only from Slav complaints but from the furious accusation of the Republic against its own people that vast quantities of timber were purloined by minor officials and put on the market, and that again and again supplies were delivered at the dockyard so far beyond all naval needs that they had to be let rot where they lay. After this wholesale denudation it was not easy to grow the trees again. The north wind, which blows great guns here in winter, is hard on young plantations; and the peasant as he got poorer relied more and more on his goat, a vivacious animal insensible to the importance of afforestation. The poor peasant is also sometimes a thief, and it is easier to steal a young tree than a fully grown one. So, for all the Yugoslavian Government can do, the mainland and the islands gleam like monstrous worked flints.

Bare hills, and young men that shout, both the product of human incompetence, of misgovernment. That is the immediate impression given by North Dalmatia. We met our first young man very soon after we got to Sushak. We strolled for a time round the port, which has a brown matter-of-fact handsomeness, and then we drove off to Trsat, a village two or three miles up on the heights behind Sushak, which is visited by countless thousands every year, for the sake of the church.

This is not interesting in itself, or even pleasing, except for a charming triangular piazza in front of it, which is edged by horse-chestnuts. But it has the supreme claim on the attention of marking the site where the Holy House, in which the Virgin Mary and Jesus and St. Joseph lived at Nazareth, rested for three years and seven months, from the year 1291 to 1294, on its way to Loretto, where it now is.

This is a story that enchants me. It gives a new meaning to the phrase "God moves in a mysterious way"; and the picture of the little house floating through space is a lovely example of the nonsensical function of religion, of its power to cheer the soul by propounding that the universe is sometimes freed from the burden of necessity, which inspires all the best miracles. It has often grieved the matter-of-fact. One English priest named Eustace who visited Loretto at the beginning of the nineteenth century wrote that many of the more sensible of his faith were extremely distressed by the story, and "suppose the holy house to have been a cottage or log building long buried in a pathless forest, and unnoticed in a country turned almost into a desert by a succession of civil wars, invasions and revolutions, during the space of ten or twelve centuries." It won't do. The place where the Holy House rested at Trsat is a very short distance indeed from the castle where the Frankopan family were living at the time. We must admit that sometimes human beings quite simply lie, and indeed it is necessary that they should, for only so can poets who do not know what poetry is compose their works.

We pushed on to the Frankopan castle, which is the historical equivalent of a stall in the Caledonian Market. It is a huddle of round and square towers, temples and dungeons and dwelling-houses packed within battlements under an excess of plants and creepers due to neglect rather than luxuriousness. The earliest masonry that has been found is Illyrian, and much is Roman, of the time of Julius Cæsar. We climbed a Roman tower to see Sushak lying brown by the blue sea, and the dark ravine that runs up from the town to split a mountain range on the high sky-line.

We numbered seven, the little party that was exploring the castle: ourselves, a middle-aged Frenchman and his blonde sopranoish wife, a German honeymoon couple, aggrieved and agonized, as Germans often are nowadays, at contact with foreigners, and a darkly handsome young man, a Dalmatian on holiday from some town further down the coast, who had early detached himself, and was seen only occasionally in the distance, a silhouette on the edge of the round tower after we had left it, or a shadow treading down the brambles at the entrance to the dungeons. We forgot him totally in a great wonder that came upon us when we were looking at the dwelling-house made in the castle by an early nineteenth-century Austrian general of Irish birth, Marshal Nugent. The Nugents had the custom, like the English who live in the West Indies and the early settlers in the southern states, of burying their dead on their premises. But whereas those other exiles buried their dead in their gardens, the Nugents set theirs in niches of the house, above ground, their coffins set upright behind slabs of marble.

That I found puzzling. The only people I have ever heard of as being buried upright are the ancient Irish, whose monotony of mind made them wish to be discovered at the Day of Judgment ready to face their enemies; but the Nugents are English by origin, and never saw Ireland till the days of Queen Elizabeth. But we soon forgot that bewilderment in another. The gardener was telling us that there was buried among the Nugents a stranger, a something that he described in a rapid phrase which we could not at first grasp. Incredulously we repeated his phrase: "*La zia del Signore Bernard Shaw?*" "*Si, signore.*" We still felt a need for verification, and repeated it in other languages: "*La tante de Monsieur Bernard Shaw?*" "*Die Tante von Herrn Bernard Shaw?*" "*Tetka od Gospodina Bernarda Shawa?*" This was the hour for which Olendorff has waited a hundred years. Always the gardener nodded; and there, on the tomb, which indeed had a blue-veined elegance not inappropriate to Bernard Shaw himself, there was carved "Jane Shaw." But before we could find out how she came to be there, the dark young man was suddenly amongst us again, shouting at the top of his voice.

He had found, it seemed, a notice behind some creepers, on a wall, stating that the price of admission to the castle was five dinars, and we had all been charged ten. A dinar is about a penny; and I fancy that there was some reasonable explanation of the incident, the tariff had changed. But the young man was terribly enraged. All the resentment that most people feel in their whole lives is not greater than what he felt on this one point. "*Zehn dinar!*" he cried, speaking in German so that we might understand and collaborate with him in fury. "*Zehn dinar ist viel, zehn dinar ist zu teuer, ist viel zu teuer!*" He switched back to Serbo-Croat, so that he could make his accusations against the gardener with the unhampered vigour of a man using his native tongue. "You are an Austrian!" he screamed at him. "You are an Italian!" Rage ran through his whole body and out of his tongue. It was plainly an exercised gift, a precious function proudly developed. His gift mastered him, he could not endure the iniquity of this place; he had to leave us. Shouting protests to an invisible person, leaping higher and higher as if to keep in contact with his own soaring cries, he rushed away from us, away from the castle of the Frankopans, towards the place where the house of innocence had rested for what appears to have been the insufficient period of three years and seven months.

"Maniac," said the Frenchman. "Frightful!" said his wife. "Savages!"

said the German couple. They were wrong. He was simply the product
of Dalmatian history: the conquest of Illyria by Rome, of Rome by the
barbarians; then three hundred years of conflict between Hungary and
Venice; then four hundred years of oppression by Venice, with the war
against Turkey running concurrently for most of that time; a few years
of hope under France, frustrated by the decay of Napoleon; a hundred
years of muddling misgovernment by Austria. In such a shambles a
man had to shout and rage to survive.

Let me try to understand the plight of this people. Because this is a
story that no Westerner can know of himself, no Englishman, no American. Let us consider what the Frankopans were. They are said to have
been of Italian origin, to be affiliated with the Frangipani family of
Rome; but that is almost certainly a late invention. They were typical
Dalmatian nobles: of unknown origin, probably aliens who had come
down on the Slavs when these were exhausted by barbarian invasions,
and were themselves of barbarian blood. Certainly they owed their
ascendancy not to virtue nor to superior culture, but to unusual stead-
fastness in seeing that it was always the other man who was beheaded
or tossed from the window or smothered. They lived therefore in an
agony of fear. They were liable to armed attack by Vienna or Hungary
if ever they seemed to be favouring one rather than the other. Their
properties were temptations to pirates. Their followers, and even their
own families, were themselves living in continual fear, and were therefore apt to buy their safety by betraying their overlord to his strongest
enemy; so overlords could trust nobody. We know a great deal about
one Count Ivan Frankopan, in the fifteenth century. He was the eldest
of nine sons: the other eight all conspired against him. To protect himself he used a device common in that age of legalist division: he made
the Venetian Republic his heir. Thus it was not to the advantage of his
brothers, or any other private person, to assassinate him. But when he
seized the fortresses of two of his brothers he found that they were
protected by a similar testamentary precaution; they had made the
Count of Hungary their heir. He fled across the sea to an island named
Krk, which was his. Then he went mad. He conceived the idea that
he must have an infinite amount of money to save him from disaster.
He robbed his peasants of their last coins. He murdered refugees who
landed on his island in flight from the Turk, for the sake of their little
stores. The Venetian Commissioner was ceded the island by its horrified
inhabitants on condition that he take the poor lunatic away.

The bare hills around the castle told us what followed that: four centuries of selfish exploitation. Then, with the French occupation, there was hope. The gardener showed us with pride a neat nineteenth-century neo-classical temple, built with the fidelity to antique classicism that does not deceive the eye for an instant, so obvious is it that the builders belonged to a later civilization that had learned to listen to orchestral music and to drink tea from fine cups. There is a cross at the apex of the pediment and two well-bosomed matrons sit on its slopes, one decapitated by an idiot bomb dropped by one of d'Annunzio's planes when he was holding Sushak's neighbour, Fiume. Across the frieze of this temple is written "*Mir Yunaka*," which I translated to my husband perhaps more often than was absolutely necessary, for I am delighted with my minute knowledge of the Serbian language. Peace to the Heroes, it means. This temple was erected during the French occupation which gave Dalmatia a peace for eight years. Eight years out of all time. No longer.

For in 1806 Napoleon had still much of his youthful genius. It made him take over this territory after he had defeated Austria, and found the two provinces of High and Low Illyria that comprised Croatia, and Dalmatia, and Slovenia, as well as the Slav districts behind Trieste that are now Italian. He had the idea of forming a civilized Slav state, to include in time the Christian provinces of Turkey, which should make South-Eastern Europe stable, pacific, and pro-French. He made Marshal Marmont the Governor of these Illyrian provinces, and it was an excellent appointment. Though Marmont was a self-satisfied prig, he was an extremely competent and honourable man, and he loved Dalmatia. His passion for it was so great that in his memoirs, his style, which was by nature dropsically pompous, romps along like a boy when he writes of his Illyria. He fell in love with the Slavs; he defended them against their Western critics. They were not lazy, he said indignantly, they were hungry. He fed them, and set them to build magnificent roads along the Adriatic, and crowed like a cock over the accomplishment. They were not savages, either, he claimed: they had had no schools, and he built them plenty. When he saw they were fervent in piety, he fostered their religious institutions, though he himself conceived faith as buckram to stiffen the Army Regulations.

Marmont would have spent all his life in paternal service of Dalmatia had his been the will that determined this phase of history. But he could achieve less and less as time went on, and when he resigned in 1811 the commerce of the country was in ruins, the law courts were paralysed by corruption, the people were stripped to the skin by tax-collectors, and there was no sort of civil liberty. For he was only Marmont, a good and just and sensible man whom no one would call great. But none denied the greatness of Napoleon, who was neither good, nor just, nor sensible.

There is a school of historians today who claim with semi-erotic ardour that Napoleon's benevolence and wisdom never failed. It is hard to know how this view can survive a reading of his correspondence with Marmont on the subject of the Illyrian provinces. The style of his letters is curiously frivolous and disagreeable. He addresses Marmont with the provocative mock insolence of a homosexual queen; and there is nothing in the content to redeem this impression. By this time he had forgotten everything about his empire except the crown. He showed complete indifference to the welfare of the French troops he had left in Dalmatia, and refused to sanction the expenditure Marmont insisted was necessary to keep them healthy in this barren coast of extreme weather, and he was completely unresponsive to Marmont's desire to build up a virile and loyal population and bring it into the fold of civilization. As time went on, he ignored Marmont's letters altogether, and his exchequer grudged every halfpenny sent to Dalmatia. Finally, for no other purpose than pure offensiveness, he re-drafted the constitution of the provinces and reduced the post of Governor to a mere prefectship. Marmont could do nothing but resign and go back to the Army. Yet he was a born colonial administrator, and this is one of the rarest forms of genius.

The men Napoleon sent to Dalmatia to replace Marmont prove his odd sluttishness. First was General Bertrand, who was later to share his Emperor's captivity on St. Helena. He deserved it for his treatment of the Dalmatians. To a race of mystics, who had been granted a special revelation of Christianity, because they had had to defend it against Islam, he applied the petty and shallow proscriptions of French eighteenth-century anti-clericalism. On these same mystics, who were also, though the West lacked the scholarship to know it, accomplished jurists, dowered with laws and customs springing from ancient tradition and beautifully adapted to local necessities, he forced the new legislative cure-all, the Code Napoléon. But Bertrand was far better than his successor. Junot, the Duke of Abrantès, brought his career to its only possible climax at the Governor's palace in the delicious Slovenian town of Lyublyana. He gave a state ball, and came down the great marble staircase, under the blazing chandeliers, stark naked and raving mad. But there was yet to come Fouché, the Duke of Otranto: a renegade priest, one of the most pitiless butchers of the Revolution, and in his capacity as the Minister of Police the worst of all traitors, Judas only excepted. He loathed Napoleon yet loved him, was never loyal to him, yet could never bring himself to betray him finally. There was here some nasty coquetry of spirit, some purulent corruption of love. Because his master was by then a beaten man, Fouché came out to Dalmatia in a yeast of loyalty, and indeed was inspired to glorious courage. In this far country, while Napoleon's future crumbled in the West, Fouché acted all day the secure administrator and dawdled through the routine of governorship, and by night worked with frenzy on the plans for evacuation. "Step by step, therefore, without losses," writes one of his biographers, "he withdraws to Venice, bringing away intact or almost intact from the short-lived Illyria, its officials, its funds, and much valuable material." All very marvellous; but not by any accountancy could it be judged honest to withdraw "funds and much valuable material" from that hungry country, which had beggared itself saving the West from the Turkish invasion.

I did not wonder that the young man shouted as he ran down the road, shouted as if he must go mad, did not the world at last abandon its bad habit and resolve into mercy, justice, and truth.

Senj

THE next morning we woke early, prodigiously early, so that before we embarked on our little steamer we could cross the bridge over the river that leads from Sushak to Fiume. There we found a town that has the quality of a dream, a bad headachy dream. Its original character is rotund and sunburnt and solid, like any pompous southern port, but it has been hacked by treaties into a surrealist form. On a ground plan laid out plainly by sensible architects for sensible people, there is imposed another, quite imbecile, which drives high walls across streets and thereby sets contiguous houses half an hour apart by detour and formality. And at places where no frontiers could possibly be, in the middle of a square, or on a bridge linking the parts of a quay, men in uniform step forward and demand passports, minatory as figures projected into sleep by an uneasy conscience.

"This has meant," said my husband as we wandered through the impeded city, "infinite suffering to a lot of people," and it is true. Because of it many old men have said to their sons, "We are ruined," many lawyers have said to widows, "I am afraid there will be nothing, nothing at all." All this suffering is due, to a large part, to English inefficiency. The Treaty of London, signed by the Allies and Italy in 1915, was intended as a bribe to induce the Italians to come into the war on the Allied side, and it promised them practically the whole Adriatic seaboard of the Austro-Hungarian Empire and all but one of the Adriatic islands. It was made by Lord Oxford and Lord Grey, and it reflected the greatest discredit on them and on the officials of the Foreign Office. For it handed over to a new foreign yoke the Slav inhabitants of this territory, who were longing to rise in revolt against the Central Powers in support of the Allies; and an Italian occupation of the Adriatic coast was a threat to the safety of Serbia, who of all the Allies had made the most sacrifices. These were good reasons why the Italians should not have Dalmatia, and there were no reasons why they should, for the Italian population was negligible.

Mercifully the Treaty of London was annulled at Versailles, largely through the efforts of Lloyd George and President Wilson. But it had done its work. It had given Italian greed a cue for inordinacy; it started her wheedling and demanding and snatching. So she claimed Fiume on the ground that the inhabitants were Italian, and proved it by taking a census of the town, excluding one part which housed twenty-five per cent of the population. The Italian Government was discouraged by European opinion from acting on that peculiar proof, but thereafter d'Annunzio marched his volunteers into Fiume, in an adventure which, in mindlessness, violence, and futility exactly matched his deplorable literary works, and plunged it into anarchy and bloodshed. He was made to leave it, but the blackmail had been started. Yugoslavia had to buy peace, and in 1920 she conceded Italy the capital of Dalmatia, Zara, three Dalmatian islands, and the hinterland behind Trieste, and she entered into arrangements concerning Fiume which, in the end, left the port as it is.

All this is embittering history for a woman to contemplate. I will believe that the battle of feminism is over, and that the female has reached a position of equality with the male, when I hear that a country has allowed itself to be turned upside-down and led to the brink of war by its passion for a totally bald woman writer. Years ago, in Florence, I had marvelled over the singular example of male privilege afforded by d'Annunzio. Leaning from a balcony in the Lung' arno I had looked down on a triumphal procession. Bells rang, flags were waved; flowers were thrown, voices swelled in ecstasy; and far below an egg reflected the rays of the May sunshine. Here in Fiume the bald author had been allowed to ruin a city: a bald-headed authoress would never be allowed to build one. Scowling, I went on the little steamer that was taking us and twenty other passengers and as many cattle and sheep southwards to the island of Rab, and we set off in a cold dither of spray.

The bare hills shone like picked bones. I fell asleep, for we had risen at six. Then my husband shook me by the shoulder and said, "You must come up on deck. This is Senj." I followed him and stared at the port, which was like many others in Spain and Italy: from the quayside high buttoned-up houses washed in warm colours and two or three campaniles struggled up a hill towards a ruined fortress, the climbing mass girt in by city walls. I groaned, remembering that the climbing mass certified man to be not only incompetent but beastly, that here the great powers had mocked out of their own fullness at another's misery and had shown neither gratitude nor mercy.

Senj was the home of the Uskoks. These are not animals invented by Edward Lear. They were refugees. They were refugees like the Jews and Roman Catholics and liberals driven out by Hitler. They found, as these have done, that when one door closed on them others that should have been open suddenly were not. These were driven out of their homes, out of the fellowship of Christendom, out of the world of virtue, into an accursed microcosm where there was only sin. They were originally Slavs of blameless character who fled before the Turks as they swept over Bulgaria and Serbia and Bosnia, and formed a strange domestic army, consisting of men, women, and children, that fought many effective rearguard actions over a period of many years. Finally they halted at the pass over the Dalmatian mountains, behind the great port of Split, and for five years from 1532 they held back the Turks single-handed. Then suddenly they were told by their Christian neighbours to abandon the position. Venice, which had just signed a pact with Turkey, and was a better friend to her than Christian historians like to remember, convinced Austria that it would be wise to let Turkey have the pass as a measure of appeasement.

Then the Uskoks came down to the coast and settled in this little town of Senj, and performed a remarkable feat. Up till then they had displayed courage and resolution of an unusual order. But they now showed signs of genius. Some of them were from the southern coast of Dalmatia, down by Albania, but most of them were inland men. In any case they can have had few marine officers. But in a short time they had raised themselves to the position of a naval power.

This was not a simple matter of savage daring. The Uskoks had unusual talent for boat-building. They devised special craft to suit the special needs of the Dalmatian coast, which resembled those with which the ancient Illyrians used to vex the Roman fleet: light boats that could navigate the creeks and be drawn up on the beach where there was no harbour. They also developed extraordinary powers of seamanship which enabled them to take advantage of the situation of Senj. Just here the channel between the mainland and the island of Krk widens to ten miles or so, which makes a fairway for the north wind, and it meets another channel that runs past the tail of the island to the open sea, so the seas roar rougher here than elsewhere on the coast. It was so when we came into Senj; a wave larger than any we had met before slapped against the quay. The Uskoks developed a technique of using this hard weather as a shield against their enemies, while they ran through it unperturbed. Therefore they chased the Turkish ships up and down the Adriatic, stripped them, and sunk them; and year by year they grew cleverer at the game. This success was amazing, considering they numbered at most two thousand souls. If the Venetian fleet had been directed by men of the quality of the Uskoks the Turks might have been driven out of

European waters, which would have meant out of Europe, in the middle of the sixteenth century.

Venice, however, was in her decline, which was really more spiritual than economic. Her tragedies were due to maladministration and indecisive politics rather than to actual lack of means.

She tried to placate Turkey in another way. She stopped attacking her at sea. To the Uskoks this capitulation of the great Christian powers must have seemed the last word in treachery. They had, within the memory of all those among them who were middle-aged or over, been driven from their homes by the Turks in atrocious circumstances; and they had believed that in harrying the Turks they were not only avenging their wrongs but were serving God and His Son. They had often been blessed by the Church for their labours, and Gregory XIII had even given them a large subsidy. But now they were treated as enemies of Christendom, for no other crime than attacking its enemies. And not only were they betrayed in the spirit, they were betrayed in the body. How were they to live? Till then they had provided for themselves, quite legitimately, since the Turks had dispossessed them of all their homes, by booty from Turkish ships. But now all that was over. The Christian powers had no suggestions to make. The plight of a refugee, then as now, provoked the feeling that surely he could get along somehow. There was nothing for the Uskoks to do except defy Venice and Austria, and attack their ships and the Turks' alike.

It seems certain that to see the story of the Uskoks thus is not to flatter them. For nearly thirty years they lived in such a state of legitimate and disciplined warfare that they attacked only Turkish ships. It is not until 1566 that there is the first record of an Uskok attack on a Christian ship. Thereafter, of course, the story is very different. They became gangsters of the sea. They developed all the characteristics of gunmen: a loyalty that went unbroken to the death, unsurpassable courage, brutality, greed, and, oddly enough, thriftlessness. Just as a Chicago racketeer who has made an income of five figures for many years will leave his widow penniless, so the Uskoks, who helped themselves to the richest loot the sea ever carried, always fell into penury if they survived to old age. Also they were looted, as thieves often are, by the honest. It is said that they bribed the very highest Austrian officials, even in the seat of government itself at Graz; and that a Jewish merchant might recognize there on a great lady's breast a jewel which he had seen snatched by a robber's hand on the Adriatic. Because of this traffic, it is alleged, the Austrians did little to restrain the Uskoks after they had become pirates. In any case it is certain that Venetian officials often bought the Uskoks' prizes from them and marketed them at a profit in Venice.

In a very short time the moral confusion of these people was complete. At Christmas and Easter every year there were expeditions financed by the whole of Senj. Everybody, the officials, the soldiers, the private families, the priests and monks, paid their share of the expenses and drew a proportionate share of the booty. The Church received its tithe. This would be funny if murder had not been a necessary part of such expeditions, and if barbarity did not spread from heart to heart as fire runs from tree to tree in a forest in summer. Some of the later exploits of the Uskoks turn the stomach; they would knife a living enemy, tear out his heart, and eat it. Not only did the perpetrators of these acts lose their own souls, but the whole level of Slav morality was debased, for the Dalmatian peasant knew the Uskok's origin and could not blame him. And the infection spread more widely. All the villains of Europe heard that there was good sport to be had in the Adriatic, and the hardier hurried to Senj. It testifies to the unwholesomeness of Renaissance Europe that some of these belonged to the moneyed classes. When a party of Uskoks were hanged in Venice in 1618 nine of them were Englishmen, of whom five were gentlemen in the heraldic sense of the word, and another was a member of one of the noblest families in Great Britain.

It is sometimes very hard to tell the difference between history and the smell of skunk. Both Venice and Austria used the degradation of these men as extra aces in their cheating game. The Austrians pretended to want to suppress them, but rather liked to have them harrying Venice. Venice sacrificed them to her friendship with Turkey, but that friendship was a sham; she never really wept over those Turkish ships. Also she liked to have a legitimate source of grievance against Austria. The insincerity of both parties was proven by their refusal to grant the Uskoks' demand, which was constantly presented during a period of fifty years, that they should be transported to some inland place and given a chance to maintain themselves either by tilling the soil or by performing military duties. Again and again the poor wretches explained that they had no means of living except by piracy, and that they would abandon it at once if they were shown any other way of getting food. But Venice and Austria, though one was still wealthy and the other was becoming wealthier every day, haggled over the terms of each settlement and let it go. Once there was put forward a scheme of selling the forests of pine and beech that in those days still grew round

Senj, and using the proceeds to build fortresses on the Austrian frontiers which would be manned by Uskoks. It fell through because neither power would agree to make an initial payment amounting to something like fifty pounds. At the same time the Uskoks were not allowed to go to any country which was prepared to make room for them. They were strictly forbidden to enlist in foreign service. They were shut up in piracy as in jail by powers that affected to feel horror at their crimes.

In the end their problem was settled in the course of an odd war between Austria and Venice, in which the Uskoks were used as a pretext by several people who wanted a fight. This war, which was almost nothing and led to nothing, lasted three years and must have brought an infinity of suffering to the wretched Dalmatian peasant. But, mercifully, as it was supposed to be about the Uskoks, the Peace Treaty had to deal with them. A good many were hanged and beheaded and the rest were transported, as they themselves had requested for fifty years, to the interior. But the method of their transport was apparently unkind. There were no stout fortresses built for them, or hopeful villages, for no certain trace of them can be found. Some say their descendants are to be found on the Alps at the very southern end of Austria; others have thought to recognize them on the slopes of a mountain in North Italy. It is to be feared that their seed was scattered on stony ground. That is sad, for the seed was precious.

We went down to the little dining-saloon and had a good, simple, coarse, well-flavoured luncheon. Opposite us sat a young man, handsome and angry, the very spit and image of the one at Trsat who had cried out to his God about the ten dinars; and indeed they were of the same breed. For this one thrust away his plate as soon as it was brought to him with a gesture of fury. "This soup is cold!" he shouted, his brows a thick straight line. "This soup is as cold as the sea!" But he was not shouting at the soup. He was shouting at the Turks, at the Venetians, at the Austrians, at the French, and at the Serbs (if he was a Croat) or at the Croats (if he was a Serb). It was good that he shouted. I respected him for it. In a world where during all time giants had clustered to cheat his race out of all their goods, his forefathers had survived because they had the power to shout, to reject cold soup, death, sentence to piracy, exile on far mountain slopes.

Rab

THE sea was green and hard as glass; the crests of the waves were *chevaux de frise* between us and a horizon of pure, very pale-green light, and dark-bronze islands. Our destination, the isle of Rab, lay before us, its mountains bare as Krk, its shores green as spring itself. As we came closer to it my husband said, "It is only scrub, of course, low woods and scrub." But a little later he exclaimed, "Only scrub, indeed! Just smell it! Well, I have heard of this but I never quite believed it." It was still distant by half a mile or so, but the scent of myrtle and rosemary and thyme was as strong and soothing a delight as sunshine. Through this lovely invisible cloud we rode slowly into the harbour of Rab, and found ourselves in one of the most beautiful cities of the world. It is very little. One can see it all at once, as if it were a single building; and that sight gives a unique pleasure. Imagine finding a place where one heard perpetually a musical phrase which was different every time one moved a few steps, and was always exquisite. At Rab something comparable happens to the sight. The city covers a ridge overlooking the harbour. It is built of stone which is sometimes silver, sometimes at high noon and sunset, rose and golden, and in the shadow sometimes blue and lilac, but is always fixed in restraint by its underlying whiteness. It is dominated by four campaniles, set at irregular intervals along the crest of the ridge. From whatever point one sees it these campaniles fall into a perfect relationship with each other and the city. We sat under a pine tree on the shore and ate oranges, and the city lay before us, making a statement that was not meaningless because it was not made in words. There we undressed and swam out fifty yards, and we stopped and trod water, because the town was making another lovely statement. From every yard of the channel that divides it from its neighbour islands, from every yard of the roads that wind among the inland farms and olive terraces to the bald mountains in the centre of the island, the city can be seen making one of an infinite series of statements. Yet it achieves this expressiveness with the simplest of means: a grey horizontal oblong with four smaller vertical oblongs rising from it. Euclid never spoke more simply.

This island is within sight of the barbarized home of the Frankopans, is set in a sea polluted by the abominations of the Turks and the Uskoks.

It is therefore astonishing that there is nothing accidental about the beauty of Rab; that in the fissure of this bare land there should be art and elegance of the most refined and conscious sort. Though Rab is no larger than many villages, it is a city, a focus of culture, a fantasy made by man when he could do more with his head and hands than is absolutely necessary for survival. There is a noble white square by the harbour, where balconies are supported by tiers of three lions set one upon another, pride upon pride, and façades are aristocratic in their very proportions, being broad enough to be impressive yet not too broad for respect towards neighbouring properties. From this square streets run up to the ridge of the town or along its base; and the richness of the doorways and windows and columns makes each seem a passage in some private magnificence. In one doorway stone grows as fern fronds above the pilasters, enwreaths with flowers a coat of arms, and edges the shield above with forms delicate as wheat-ears. Above another doorway, opening into a cloistered garden, cupids hold ropes of laurel flowing from a shield and helmet on which an eagle broods. One cupid holds forth his rope of laurel with a gesture that expresses the ambition of the Renaissance. "To humanity be the kingdom, the power, and the glory." Each of these doorways has begun to feel the weight of five centuries; in the first the columns are straddling apart, in the second a stone has fallen and left a gap through which a flower pokes a scarlet head. But this shabbiness, which is not at all tainted by dirt, is very much what a great emperor might permit in the homelier parts of his palace.

There is the same sense of private magnificence about the Cathedral of Rab. On the ridge there is a little square, with bastions and cliffs falling deeply to the shore on the further side; between the tall soldierly flowers of the aloes and the swords of their leaves the eyes fall on the sea and its scattered islands. Here stands the cathedral built of rose and white marble in alternate courses, ornamented with blind arches of a lovely span. It is no bigger than many a private chapel; and it has an air of not knowing what strangers are. That was the theory. Without, the horror, the pirate, the Turk; within, an enclosed community within an enclosed community, a small city upon an island. One arranges one's house with a certain lavishness and confidence when one believes that it is going to be visited only by familiars, and this Cathedral is therefore at once domestic and elegant. It is Venetian in spirit, which is not to say that it is actually the work of Venetian hands: our English Norman and Gothic churches derive from France but were not built by Frenchmen. It recalls the bone-white architectural backgrounds of Carpaccio and Bellini, that delicate frame of a world which is at once pious and playful, luxurious and simple-minded. Its interior might have been designed by a maker of masks, who with infinite reverence conceived the high mass as the supreme mask. The stage is set high above the onlookers: six high steps lead up to the choir, where stalls of heraldic pomp indicate that those who sit there are the servants of a great lord, and another flight mounts to the altar, which is sheltered and magnified by a tall baldacchino.

This is a part of an older church, a thousand years old, built in the time of Slav independence. It is one of the utmost elegance imaginable. Its six supporting columns are of fine cipollino marble, and its canopy is carved from one great block of stone, but it is weightless as a candle-flame because of the exquisiteness of its design and execution. Round its six arches are garlands carved more finely than the emblems on the patricians' doorways in the town below, which is as it should be, since this is the palace of the patrician above all patricians. The pyramided roof of the baldacchino is painted a tender red, the vault above it is painted a tender blue, just such colours as grace the festivities of a much later Venice in the paintings of Paolo Veronese. The community that built this Cathedral was so civilized that it could conceive a God who would be pleased not by the howlings of His worshippers and the beating of their breasts, but by their gaiety, by their accomplishment, by their restraint and dignity. At one time the island of Rab paid an annual tribute to the Doge of ten pounds of silk. In this building it paid a tribute of silken elegance to the Doge of Doges.

Because it was noon they came to close the Cathedral. We went out blinking into the sunlight, which for a moment was falling strong between thunderclouds; and a group of women smiled at us and gave us some greetings in Italian, though they were visibly not Italian. For they were completely lacking in Latin facility. They had that flat, unfeigned, obstinate look about the cheekbones, which is the mark of the Slav, and their bodies were unpliable. But they were not of a harsh race that had usurped the home of gentler beings perished through gentleness. These people, and none other, had made Rab. Over the Cathedral doorway the builders had set a Pietà, a Madonna holding her dead son in her arms, and she was as these women. With a stiff spine, with her chin high, she sits and holds a Christ that is dead, truly dead—for if he were not, where would be the occasion for all the excitement?—dead as mutton, dead as the skinned lamb which one of the women was holding like a baby. This Madonna is as sorrowful as sorrow; her son is dead as death. There is here the fullest acceptance of tragedy, there is no refusal to recognize the essence of life, there is no attempt to pretend that the bitter is the sweet. One must not pull wool over the eyes if one is in danger; for it goes badly with one when the sword falls unless one has a philosophy which has contemplated the fact of death.

Above our heads a bell gave out the hour, and I jumped with surprise. The women laughed indulgently, sleepily; there was a semblance of noon heat settling down on the city. It was the Campanile of St. Christopher, the most beautiful of the four towers of Rab. It is said of the big bell, as it is said of many old ones, that when it was being cast the citizens came to the foundry and dropped their gold and silver ornaments into the melting-pot; and certainly its tone is much mollified for metal; it might be the voice of a dove that had grown old and great and wise. Leaning back against the wall of a palace and looking up at the campanile my husband said: "Look at the thing. It is made on a Euclidean recipe. There are four stories. On the lowest is a doorway. On the next are on each wall two windows, each divided by a shaft. On the next there are two windows, each divided by two columns; on the highest there is one window divided by three columns; above that is a balustrade of seventeen columns, every fifth one somewhat stouter. Above is the spire. How did that man who built this tower seven hundred years ago know that these severe shapes would affect my eyes as a chime of joy-bells would affect my ear? He must have been a man of incredible cunning to make this stony promise of a fluid world, this geometric revelation of a universe in which there is not an angle."

Out in the country round the city of Rab there are no revelations. There is a mystery. It is formulated also in stone, but not in worked stone, in the terrible naked stone of Dalmatia, in the terrible earth that here lies shallow and infirm of purpose as dust, and in the terrible faces of the people, who are all like crucified Christs. Everywhere there are terraces. High up on the bare mountains there are olive terraces; in the valleys there are olive terraces; in the trough of the valleys there are walled fields where an ordinary crop of springing corn or grass strikes one as an abnormal profusion like a flood. On these enclosures black figures work frenetically. From a grey sky reflected light pours down and makes of every terrace and field a stage on which these black figures play each their special drama of toil, of frustration, of anguish. As we passed by on the stony causeway, women looked up at us, from the fields, their faces furrowed with all known distresses. By their sides lambs skipped in gaiety and innocence, and goats skipped in gaiety but without innocence, and at their feet the cyclamens shone mauve; the beasts and flowers seemed fortunate because they are not human, as those who have passed within the breath of a plague and have escaped it. From the olive terraces the men looked down with faces contracted by the greatest effort conceivable; and the trees they stood upon, though the droughts of summer and the salt hurricanes of winter had twisted them to monstrous corkscrews, also seemed fortunate by comparison. Sometimes we met people on these causeways who begged from us without abjectness, without anything but hunger. Their lean hands came straight out before them. Their clothes asked alms louder than they did, making it plain that here were the poorest of creatures, peasants who had not the means to make a peasant costume, to proclaim that in their village they had skill and taste and their own way of looking at things. They wore undifferentiated black rags.

Here, out in the country, the islanders spoke Serbo-Croat; half an hour from the city gates we found peasants who knew only a few words of Italian. These are true, gaunt Slavs, wholly without facility, with that Slav look of being intuitionally aware of the opposite of the state in which they found themselves at the moment, and therefore being more painfully affected by it if it were disagreeable. The poor have at the back of their sunken eyes a shining picture of wealth, the sick know what it is to be sound, and as the unhappy weep the scent of happiness dilates their nostrils. This unfamiliar way of bearing misery gave them a certain unity in our eyes; but there were also marked differences between them, which were terrible because they depended to such a startling degree on the geographical variations, necessarily not very great, which can be observed here within a few hundred yards of each other. That we noticed on our first walk in the island. We followed a stony causeway along the barren lower slopes of a ridge that ran towards an estuary, and there the people who were working on the fields and who begged from us were thin and slow-moving, glaring in misery. Then we came to a village set on firm ground above the estuary, which could draw on the wealth of both the sea and the rich earth among the river's mouth; and here the people were stouter and brisker.

And so it was throughout our walk, rich, poor, rich, poor. Once we found ourselves on the shore of a land-locked bay, broken with a magnificent cliff, round which there was plainly no road at all. We came on an old man in patched clothes sitting under a pine tree watching some goats, on a little headland made into a harbour by a few blocks of stone. He concerned himself in our plight as if he were our host.

It was inconceivable that he could have begged from us. There came presently a young fisherman in a rowing-boat, who rowed us across waters that were swimming with the first sunset colours to the village on the other side of the bay, and took his just fare, and would not have taken money for any other cause.

But when we had walked half a mile or so from where we landed we were on barren and wind-swept lands again, and we met an old man, who was like the old man on the headland as one pea and another, and he was begging shamelessly and very pitifully. He had gathered some flowers from the hedgerows and stood there in the dusk on the chance of some tourist coming along, which might justly be called an off-chance, as all the tourists on the island were middle-aged Germans who never moved a mile from the city. All this part was very poor. We met ragged and listless men and women hurrying through the twilight without zest, leaden-footed with hunger. Nevertheless there bloomed suddenly before us the lovely gallant human quality of fantasy, which when necessity binds it down with cords leaps up and exercises its choice where it would have seemed there was nothing to choose, which in destitution dares to prefer this to that and likes its colours bright. We came on a group that was standing lapped in pleasure all across the causeway in front of a young man who was showing off his new suit. They were peering at it and fingering it and exclaiming over it, as well they might, for though it was conventionally tailored in Western fashion it was cut from emerald velveteen. It was the time of dusk when colours liquefy and clot, when in a garden the flowers become at once more solid and more glowing; the suit was a pyre of green flame, about which the black figures pressed insubstantially, yet with ecstatic joy.

The poverty of the island was made plainer still to us the next day. Our first expedition had been over the northern part of the island, which is more or less protected from the north wind by high ground; but this time we walked to the south, where there is no shelter from the blast that rakes the channel between Rab and its neighbour island. Here is a land and a people that are not only grim but desperate. Most of the houses are very large; some of them are almost fortress size, for the customs of land tenure make it convenient for a whole family to live under the same roof, even to several degrees of cousinship. There is something specially terrifying about a house that is very big and very poor, a Knole or Blenheim of misery. At the dark open door of one such home, that seemed to let out blackness rather than let in light, there waited a boy of seven or eight with flowers in his hand for the tourist. My husband thrust down into his pocket, brought up three dinars and one half-dinar, and peered to see what they were. The child shuddered with suspense, broke down, put out his little hand and snatched, and ran into the house. But he had not snatched the four coins. He had snatched just one dinar; his fear had been lest my husband should give him the half-dinar. Later we passed a blind beggar, crouched on a bank with a little girl beside him. To him we gave ten dinars, that is tenpence. The little girl shook him and shouted into his ear and gave him the coin to feel, and then shook him again, furious that he could not realize the miraculous good fortune that had befallen him; but he went on muttering in complaint.

The most heartrending figure we saw was not mendicant. It was a woman, middle-aged and of dignified physique, who was sitting on a stone wall, some distance from the road, in an attitude of despair. When we passed the place on our return, half an hour later, she was still sitting there. And there was here too an outbreak of fantasy, of the human capacity for laughter and wonder and invention. At a fork in the path near by we found a knot of men pausing for gossip, and turning aside from their talk to laugh at the antics of the lambs they were leading to market. They dropped an amused eye on the pale butter-coloured waves in the white lambs' fleeces, the nigger-brown waves in the black lambs' fleeces, on the nearly closed curves the lambs described when they leaped clear off the ground and silly fore-paws dangling from a young and flexible backbone almost met silly hind-paws. These people have not been anæsthetized by loutishness.

The day we left the island we climbed its highest peak. We were led by a well-mannered and intelligent man, whose rags were wretched, though he lived in a huge house and was evidently co-heir to a property of some extent. At the top there was a glory of clean salt air, and intense but unwounding light; for here we are not so far from Greece, where the light is a benediction, and one can go out at noon till near high summer without wearing glasses. Below us lion-coloured islands lay in a dark-blue sea. To the east the mainland raised violet-grey mountains to a dense superior continent of white clouds; to the west the long outer islands lay like the scrolls angels hold up in holy pictures. We leaned on a gate. It was necessary; for the first time I was on a hill where it was impossible to find a place to sit down without inflicting on oneself innumerable sharp wounds. As we rested we tried to account for the state of the island. There is no apparent reason why it should be so poor. There is plenty of fish in this part of the Adriatic, including very good mackerel; there are many parts of the island where oil and wine and corn can be produced, and sheep and swine can be raised. It is said that the population is too lazy to work. There was in the city of Rab a Viennese Jew who managed a photographic store, and he told us that. "They would rather beg than put their hands to a plough," he had said, but his spectacles gleamed with smug pleasure as he spoke, and he was expressing nothing but adherence to the disposition of the German subjects of the Austrian Empire to hate and despise all subjects of other races. A Serb doctor who was working in Rab told us that the islanders could not be expected to work on the food they got; and I remembered that Marmont wrote in his memoirs that the laziness of the Dalmatians was notorious, but entirely disappeared when he set them down to build roads on regular and adequate rations.

The reason for the island's melancholy lies not in its present but in its past. It is only now, since the war, since Dalmatia became a part of a Slav state, that it has had a chance to enjoy the proper benefits of its economic endowment; and since then there have been such overwhelming catastrophes in the world market that no community could live without tragic discomfort unless it could fall back on accumulations which it had stored in earlier days. That Rab has never been able to do. Some of the factors which have hindered her have been real acts of God, not to be circumvented by man. She has been ravaged by plague. But for the most part what took the bread out of Rab's mouth was empire. The carelessness and cruelty that infects any power when it governs a people not its own without safeguarding itself by giving the subjects the largest possible amount of autonomy, afflicted this island with hunger and thirst. Venice made it difficult for Dalmatian fishermen to make their profit in the only way it could be made before the day of refrigeration; the poor wretches could not salt their fish, because salt was a state monopoly and was not only extremely expensive but badly distributed. Moreover Venice restricted the building of ships in Dalmatia. It was her definite policy to keep the country poor and dependent. She admitted this very frankly, on one occasion, by ordering the destruction of all the mulberry trees which were grown for feeding silk-worms and all the olive trees. This law she annulled, because the Dalmatians threatened an insurrection, but not until a great many of the mulberry trees had been cut down; and indeed she found herself able to attend to the matter by indirect methods. Almost all Dalmatian goods, except corn, which paid an export duty of ten per cent, had to be sold in Venice at prices fixed by the Venetians; but any power that Venice wanted to propitiate, Austria, Ancona, Naples, Sicily, or Malta, could come and sell its goods on the Dalmatian coast, an unbalanced arrangement which ultimately led to grave currency difficulties. All these malevolent fiscal interferences created an unproductive army of *douaniers*, which in turn created an unproductive army of smugglers.

This was cause enough that Rab should be poor; but there was a further cause which made her poorer still. It is not at all inappropriate that the men and women on these Dalmatian islands should have faces which recall the crucified Christ. The Venetian Republic did not always fight the Turks with arms. For a very long time they contented themselves with taking the edge off the invaders' attack by the payment of immense bribes to the officials and military staff of the occupied territories. The money for these was not supplied by Venice. It was drawn from the people of Dalmatia. After the fish had rotted, some remained sound; after the corn had paid its ten per cent, and the wool and the wine and the oil had been haggled down in the Venetian market, some of its price returned to the vender. Of this residue the last ducat was extracted to pay the tribute to the Turks. These people of Dalmatia gave the bread out of their mouths to save us of Western Europe from Islam; and it is ironical that so successfully did they protect us that those among us who would be broad-minded, who will in pursuit of that end stretch their minds till they fall apart in idiocy, would blithely tell us that perhaps the Dalmatians need not have gone to that trouble, that an Islamized West could not have been worse than what we are today. Their folly is certified for what it is by the mere sound of the word "Balkan" with its suggestion of a disorder that defies human virtue and intelligence to accomplish its complete correction. I could confirm that certificate by my own memories: I had only to shut my eyes to smell the dust, the lethargy, the rage and hopelessness of a Macedonian town, once a glory to Europe, that had too long been Turkish. The West has done much that is ill, it is vulgar and superficial and economically sadist; but it has not known that death in life which was suffered by the Christian provinces under the Ottoman Empire. From this the people of Rab had saved me: I should say, are saving me. The woman who sat on the stone wall was in want because the gold which should have been handed down to her had bought my safety from the Turks. Impotent and embarrassed, I stood on the high mountain and looked down on the terraced island where my saviours, small and black as ants, ran here and there, attempting to repair their destiny.

Split I

SPLIT, alone of all cities in Dalmatia, has a Neapolitan air. Except
for a few courtyards in its private houses, it does not exhibit the spirit
of Venice, which is at once so stately and so materialist, like a proud
ghost that has come back to remind men that he failed for a million. It
recalls Naples, because it also is a tragic and architecturally magnificent
sausage-machine, where a harried people of mixed race have been forced
by history to run for centuries through the walls and cellars and sewers
of ruined palaces, and have now been evicted by a turn of events into
the open day, neat and slick and uniform, taking to modern clothes and
manners with the adaptability of oil, though at the same time they are
set apart for ever from the rest of the world by the arcana of language
and thoughts they learned to share while they scurried for generations
close-pressed through the darkness.

Split presents its peculiar circumstances to the traveller the minute he
steps ashore. We left the great white liner, the *King Alexander*, that
had brought us through the night from Rab, and the history of the
place was on our right and our left. On the left was the marine market,
where fishing-boats are used for stalls; men who must be a mixture of
sailor and retailer bring goods over from the islands, take their boats
head-on to the quay, and lay out their wares in little heaps on the prows.
Pitiful little heaps they often are, of blemished apples, rags of vegetables,
yellowish boards of dried fish, but the men who sell them are not pitiful. They look tough as their own dried fish, and stand by with an air
of power and pride. This coast feeds people with other things than
food; it grudges them the means of life, but lets them live. On our right
was a row of shops, the cafés and rubbisheries which face any port:
the houses that rise above them were squeezed between the great
Corinthian columns in the outer gallery of Diocletian's palace.

For Split is Diocletian's palace: the palace he built himself in 305,
when, after twenty years of imperial office, he abdicated. The town has
spread beyond the palace walls, but the core of it still lies within the
four gates. Diocletian built it to be within suburban reach of the Roman
town of Salonæ, which lies near by on the gentle slopes between the
mountains and the coastal plain. The site had already been occupied by
a Greek settlement, which was called Aspalaton, from a fragrant shrub

still specially abundant here. In the seventh century the Avars, that tribe of barbarian marauders who were to provoke a currency crisis in the Middle Ages because they looted so much gold from Eastern and Central Europe and hoarded it, came down on Dalmatia. They swept down on Salonæ and destroyed it by fire and sword. The greater part of the population was killed, but some had time to flee out to the islands, which gave them the barest refuge. What they suffered in those days from cold and hunger and thirst is still remembered in common legend. In time they crept back to the mainland, and found nothing left more habitable than the ruins of Diocletian's palace. There they made shelters for themselves against the day when there should be peace. They are still there. Peace never came. They were assailed by the Huns, the Hungarians, the Venetians, the Austrians, and some of them would say that with the overcoming of those last enemies they still did not win peace; and during these centuries of strife the palace and the fugitives have established a perfect case of symbiosis. It has housed them, they are now its props. After the war there was a movement to evacuate Split and restore the palace to its ancient magnificence by pulling down the houses that had been wedged in between its walls and columns; but surveyors very soon found out that if they went all Diocletian's work would fall to the ground. The people that go quickly and darkly about the streets have given the stone the help it gave them.

"I would like to go into the palace at once," said my husband, "and I greatly wish we could have brought Robert Adam's book of engravings with us." That thought must occur to many people who go to Split. Adam's book on Diocletian's palace is one of the most entertaining revelations of the origins of our day, pretty in itself and an honour to its author. He came here from Venice in 1757, and made a series of drawings which aimed at showing what the palace had been like at the time of its building, in order to obtain some idea of "the private edifices of the ancients." The enterprise took a great deal of perseverance and courage, for all idea of the original plan had been lost centuries before. He had to trace the old walls through the modern buildings, and was often hindered by the suspicions of both the inhabitants and the authorities. The Venetian Governor of the town was quite sure he was a spy and wanted to deport him, but the Commander-in-chief of the Venetian garrison, who happened to be a Scotsman, and one of his Croat officers were sufficiently cultured to recognize Adam for what he was, and they got him permission to carry on his work under the supervision of a soldier.

The indirect results were the best of Georgian architecture, with its emphasis on space and variety and graceful pomp; often when we look at a façade in Portman Square or a doorway in Portland Place, we are looking at Roman Dalmatia. The direct result was this book of enchanting drawings—some of them engraved by Bartolozzi—which, though serviceably accurate, are beautiful examples of the romantic convention's opinion that an artist should be allowed as much latitude in describing a landscape as an angler is allowed in describing a fish. The peaks of Dalmatia are shown as monstrous fencers lunging at the black enemy of the sky; the Roman cupolas and columns have the supernatural roundness of a god's attack of mumps; vegetation advances on ruins like infantry; and peasants in fluent costumes ornament the foreground with fluent gestures, one poor woman, whom I specially remember bringing every part of her person into play, including her bust, in order to sell a fowl to two turbaned Jews, who like herself are plainly Veronese characters in reduced circumstances. In the corner of certain drawings are to be seen Adam himself and his French assistant, Clérisseau, sketching away in their dashing tricornes and redingotes, very much as one might imagine the two young men in *Così fan tutte*. It is delightful to find a book that is a pretty book in the lightest sense, that pleases like a flower or a sweetmeat, and that is also the foundation for a grave and noble art which has sheltered and nourished us all our days.

"Yes," I said to my husband, "it is disgusting that one cannot remember pictures and drawings exactly. It would have been wonderful to have the book by us, and see exactly how the palace struck a man of two centuries ago, and how it strikes us, who owe our eye for architecture largely to that man." "Then why did we not bring the book?" asked my husband. "Well, it weighs just over a stone," I said. "I weighed it once on the bathroom scales." "Why did you do that?" asked my husband. "Because it occurred to me one day that I knew the weight of nothing except myself and joints of meat," I said, "and I just picked that up to give me an idea of something else." "Well, well!" said my husband. "It makes me distrust Fabre and all other writers on insect life when I realize how mysterious your proceedings would often seem to a superior being watching them through a microscope. But tell me, why didn't we bring it, even if it does weigh a little over a stone? We have a little money to spare for its transport. It would have given us pleasure. Why didn't we do it?" "Well, it would have been no use," I said; "we couldn't have carried anything so heavy as that about the streets." "Yes, we could," said my husband; "we could have hired a wheelbarrow and pushed it about from point to point." "But people would have thought we were mad!" I exclaimed. "Well, would they?" countered my husband. "That's just what I'm wondering. In fact, it's what made me pursue the subject. These Slavs think all sorts of things natural that we think odd; nothing seems to worry them so long as it satisfies a real desire. I was wondering if they could take a thing like this in their stride; because after all we feel a real desire to look at Adam's book here." "I don't know," I said, "but there is Philip Thomson standing in the doorway of our hotel, and we can ask him."

Philip Thomson teaches English to such inhabitants of Split as wish to learn it. He is a fine-boned, fastidious, observant being, very detached except in his preference for Dalmatia over all other parts of the world, and for Split over all other parts of Dalmatia. We had morning coffee with him, good unnecessary elevenses, in the square outside our hotel, a red stucco copy of a Venetian piazza, with palm trees in it, which is quite a happy effort, and we put the question to him. "Oh, but they'd think it very odd here, if you went about the streets trundling a book in a wheelbarrow and stopping to look at the pictures in it, very odd indeed," said Philip. "You evidently don't understand that here in Split we are very much on parade. We're not a bit like the Serbs, who don't care what they do, who laugh and cry when they feel like it, and turn cartwheels in the street if they want exercise. That's one of the reasons we don't like the Serbs. To us it seems self-evident that a proud man must guard himself from criticism every moment of the day. That's what accounts for the most salient characteristic of the Splitchani, which is a self-flaying satirical humour; better laugh at yourself before anybody else has time to do it. But formality is another result. I suppose it comes of being watched all the time by people who thought they were better than you, the Dalmatians, the Hungarians and the Venetians and the Austrians."

"But all this," Philip continued, "brings to light one very strange thing about Split. Did you notice how I answered you off-hand, as if Split had a perfectly definite character, and I could speak for the whole of its inhabitants? Well, so I could. Yet that's funny, for the old town of Split was a tiny place, really not much more than the palace and a small overflow round its walls, and all this town you see stretching over the surrounding hills and along the coast is new. A very large percentage of the population came here after the war, some to work, some as refugees from the Slav territories which have been given to Italy. Do you see that pretty dark woman who is just crossing the square? She is one of my star pupils and she belongs to a family that left Zara as soon as it was handed over to the Italians, like all the best families of the town. Now Zara has quite a different history, and, from all I hear, quite a different atmosphere. But this woman and her family, and all the others who migrated with her, have been completely absorbed by Split. They are indistinguishable from all the natives, and I have seen them in the process of conversion. It's happened gradually but surely. It's a curious victory for a system of manners that, so far as I can see, has nothing to do with economics. For people here are not rich, yet there is considerable elegance."

This is, indeed, not a rich city. Later we lunched with Philip in a restaurant which though small was not a mere bistro, which was patronized by handsome and dignified people who were either professional or commercial men. For the sweet course we were given two apiece of palatschinken, those pancakes stuffed with jam which one eats all over Central Europe. The Balkans inherited the recipe from the Byzantines, who ate them under the name of palacountas. We could eat no more than one, for the meal, as almost always in these parts, had been good and abundant. "Shall I put the palatschinken in paper for the Herrschaft to take home with them?" asked the waiter. We thought not. But the waiter doubted our sincerity. "Is it because they are strangers," he asked Philip, "and do not know that we are always delighted to do this sort of thing for our clients? Down in the new hotels, I fully understand, they would be disagreeable about it, such institutions being, as we know, founded on extravagance and ostentation. But here we are not like that, we know that what God gave us for food was not meant to be wasted, so the Herrschaft need not be shy." "I do not think that they are refusing your kind offer because they are shy," said Philip resourcefully, "you see they are staying at one of the big hotels, and they will have to dine there anyway, so really the palatschinken would be of very little use to them."

The waiter accepted this, and went away, but soon came back. "But if the Herrschaft took them away with them," he insisted, "then they would not order a whole dinner. They could just take the soup and a meat dish, and afterwards they could go upstairs and have these instead of dessert." "Thank you very much for your kind thought," said Philip, still not at a loss. "I think, however, that my friends are *en pension*." "But it would be nice," said the waiter, "if the lady felt hungry in the night, for her to be able to put out her hand and find a piece of cold palatschinken by her bed." I shall never think he was right; but his kindly courtesy was something to be remembered, and his sense, not hysterical but quietly passionate, of economy as a prime necessity. In Diocletian's palace, throughout the ages, a great many very well-mannered people must have learned to draw in their belts very tight upon occasion; and certainly they would be encouraged to be mannerly by their surroundings, which, even today, speak of magnificent decorum.

It is not, of course, remarkable as an example of Roman architecture. It cannot hold a candle to the Baths of Caracalla, or the Forum, or the Palatine. But it makes an extraordinary revelation of the continuity of history. One passes through the gate that is squeezed between the rubbisheries on the quayside straight into antiquity. One stands in the colonnaded courtyard of a fourth-century Roman palace; in front is the entrance to the imperial apartments, to the left is the temple which was Diocletian's mausoleum, now the Cathedral, and to the right is the Temple of Æsculapius, just as a schoolboy learning Latin and as old ladies who used to go to the Royal Academy in the days of Alma Tadema would imagine it. Only the vistas have been filled in with people. Rather less than one-fifth of the population of Split, which numbers forty-four thousand, lives in the nine acres of the palace precincts; but the remaining four-fifths stream through it all day long, because the passages which pierce it from north to south and from east to west are the most convenient ways to the new parts of the town from the harbour. The fifth that lives within the palace packs the sides of these crowded thoroughfares with houses set as closely as cells in a honeycomb, filling every vacant space that was left by Diocletian's architects. One cannot, for example, see the Temple of Æsculapius as one stands in the fine open courtyard as it was intended one should do; the interstices on that side of the peristyle have been blocked by Venetian Gothic buildings, which project balconies on a line with the entablatures of neighbouring columns and open doorways just beside their bases.

Yet there is no sense of disorder or vandalism. It would be as frivolous to object to the adaptations the children of the palace have made to live as it would be to regret that a woman who had reared a large and glorious family had lost her girlish appearance. That is because these adaptations have always been made respectfully. So far as the walls stood they have been allowed to stand; there has been no destruction for the sake of pilfering material for new buildings. It is, therefore, as real an architectural entity, as evident to the eye of the beholder, as the Temple or Gray's Inn. There is only one blot on it, and that is not the work of necessity. In the middle of the peristyle of the imperial apartments, this superb but small open space, there has been placed a statue by Mestrovitch of a fourth-century bishop who won the Slavs the right to use the liturgy in their own tongue. Nobody can say whether it is a good statue or not. The only fact that is observable about it in this position is that it is twenty-four feet high. A more ungodly misfit was never seen. It reduces the architectural proportions of the palace to chaos, for its head is on a level with the colonnades, and the passage in which it stands is only forty feet wide. This is hard on it, for on a low wall near by there lies a black granite sphinx from Egypt, part of the original decorations of the palace, but far older, seventeen hundred years older, of the great age of Egyptian sculpture; and though this is not five feet long its compact perfection makes the statue of the bishop gangling and flimsy, lacking in true mass, like one of those marionettes one may sometimes see through the open door of a warehouse in Nice, kept against next year's carnival.

It cannot be conceived by the traveller why Mestrovitch wanted this statue to be put here, or why the authorities humoured him. If the step was inspired by nationalist sentiment, if it is supposed to represent the triumph of the Slav over Roman domination, nobody present can have known much history. For Diocletian's palace commemorates a time when the Illyrians, the native stock of Dalmatia, whose blood assuredly runs in the veins of most modern Dalmatians, had effective control of the Roman Empire; it commemorates one of the prettiest of time's revenges. Rome destroyed, for perhaps no better reason than that she was an empire and could do it, the ancient civilization of Illyria. But when she later needed sound governors to defend her from barbarian invaders, Illyria gave her thirteen rulers and defenders, of whom only one was a failure. All the others deserved the title they were given, *restitutores orbis*; even though it turned out that the earth as they knew it was not restorable. Of these the two greatest were Diocletian and Constantine; and some would say that Diocletian was the greater of the two.

His mausoleum is exquisitely appropriate to him. It is a domed building, octagonal outside and circular within. It is naughtily designed. Its interior is surrounded by a double row of columns, one on top of the other, which have no functional purpose at all; they do nothing except support their own overelaborate entablatures and capitals, and eat up much valuable space in doing so. Diocletian came to Rome when the rose of the world was overblown, and style forgotten. It must originally have been pitchy dark, for all the windows were made when it was centuries old. Because of this blackness and something flat-footed and

Oriental in the design, some have thought that Diocletian did not build it as a temple or as a mausoleum. They have suspected that he, who was first and foremost a soldier and turned by preference to the East, was a follower of the bloody and unspiritual but dramatic religion of Mithraism, the Persian cult which had been adopted by the legionaries, and that here he tried to make a mock cavern, an imitation of the grottoes in which his fellow-soldiers worshipped the god that came out of the Sun. But not only is the building otiose and dank, it is oddly executed. It is full of incongruities such as a lack of accord between capitals and entablatures, which were committed because the architects were using the remains of older buildings as their material, and had to join the pieces as best they could. Diocletian had done much the same for the Roman Empire. He took the remains of a social and political structure and built them into a new and impressive-looking edifice.

In this palace of old oddments put together to look like new, this imperial expert in makeshifts must have had some better moments. His edicts show that he was far too intelligent not to realize that he had not made a very good job of his cobbling. He was a great man wholly worsted by his age. He probably wanted real power, the power to direct one's environment towards a harmonious end, and not fictitious power, the power to order and be obeyed; and he must have known that he had not been able to exercise real power over Rome. It would have been easier for him if what we were told when we were young was true, and that the decay of Rome was due to immorality. Life, however, is never as simple as that, and human beings rarely so potent. There is so little difference between the extent to which any large number of people indulge in sexual intercourse, when they indulge in it without inhibitions and when they indulge in it with inhibitions, that it cannot often be a determining factor in history. The exceptional person may be an ascetic or a debauchee, but the average man finds celibacy and sexual excess equally difficult. All we know of Roman immorality teaches us that absolute power is a poison, and that the Romans, being fundamentally an inartistic people, had a taste for pornography which they often gratified in the description of individuals and families on which that poison had worked.

Had general immorality been the cause of the decay of the Empire, Diocletian could have settled it; he was a good bullying soldier. But the trouble was pervasive and deep-rooted as couch-grass. Rome had been a peasant state, it had passed on to feudal capitalism, the landowners and the great industrialists became tyrants; against this tyranny the bour-

geoisie and the proletariat revolted. Then the bourgeoisie became the
tyrants. They could bribe the town proletariat with their leavings, but
the peasants became their enemies. The army was peasant, for country
stock is healthier. Therefore, in the third century, there was bitter strife
between the Army and the bourgeoisie. Then came the Illyrian emperors, *restitutores orbis*. Order, it was said, was restored.

But this, the greatest of the Illyrian emperors, must have known that
this was not true: that, on the contrary, disorder had been stabilized. His
edicts had commanded in the peremptory tone of the parade-ground that
every man in the Empire should stay by his post and do his duty, fulfilling this and that public obligation and drawing this and that private
reward. There was genius in his plan. But it was a juggler's feat of bal-
ancing, no more. It corrected none of the fundamental evils of Roman
society. This could hardly be expected, for Diocletian had been born
too late to profit by the discussion of first principles which Roman culture had practised in its securer days; he had spent his whole life in
struggles against violence which led him to a preoccupation with compulsion. He maintained the Empire in a state of apparent equilibrium for
twenty-one years. But the rot went on. The roads fell into ruin. The
land was vexed with brigands and the sea with pirates. Agriculture was
harried out of existence by demands for taxation in kind and forced
labour, and good soil became desert. Prices rose and currency fell; and
to keep up the still enormously costly machinery of the central administration the remnants of the moneyed class were skinned by the tax-
collector. The invasion of the barbarians was an immediate danger, but
only because the Empire was so internally weakened by its economic
problems. Of these nobody knew the solution at the beginning of the
fourth century, and indeed they have not been solved now, in the middle of the twentieth century.

For some strange reason many have written of Diocletian's resignation
of imperial power and retirement to his native Illyria as if it were an
unnatural step which required a special explanation. Some of the pious
have thought that he was consumed by remorse for his persecution of
the Christians, but nothing could be less likely. Immediately after his
election as Emperor he had chosen to share his power with an equal
and two slightly inferior colleagues, in a system which was known as
the Tetrarchy; and it was one of his colleagues, Galerius, who was responsible for what are falsely known as the persecutions of Diocletian.
But nothing could be more comprehensible than that he should, just
then, have wanted rest and his own country. He was fifty-nine, and had

been exceedingly ill for a year; and he had twenty-one years of office
behind him. He had had a hard life. He had come from a peasant home
to enlist in one of the two Dalmatian legions, and since then he had
borne an increasing burden of military and legislative responsibility.
Violence must have disgusted such an intelligent man, but he had had to
avail himself of it very often. In order to be chosen Cæsar by the military council he had had to whip out his sword and drive it into the
breast of a fellow-officer who might have been a rival. So often, indeed,
had he had to avail himself of violence that he must have feared he would
himself become its victim at the end. A society which is ruled by the
sword can never be stable, if only because the sword is always passing
from hand to hand, from the ageing to the young.

In the halls of his palace, which must have been extremely cold and
sunless, as they were lit only by holes in the roof, he cannot have found
the peace he sought. The disorder of the world increased. The members
of the Tetrarchy wrangled; some died and were replaced by others not
less contentious. They split the Empire between their greeds, and suddenly, improbably, they dipped their fingers into Diocletian's blood.
He had a wife called Prisca and a daughter called Valeria, who were
very dear to him. Both had become Christians. We know of no protest
against this on the part of Diocletian. Valeria's hand he had disposed of
in circumstances that bring home the psychological differences between
antiquity and the modern world. When he had been chosen as Emperor he had elected to share his power first with Maximian alone, then
with two other generals, Galerius and Constantius Chlorus. When these
two last were admitted to the sovereign authority, Diocletian adopted
Galerius and Maximian adopted Constantius Chlorus, and each adopted
father gave his daughter to his adopted son, though this meant that each
had to repudiate his existing wife.

The marriage of Valeria must have been sufficiently horrible; for
Galerius was a brute whose violence precipitated him from disaster to
disaster, and he was bitterly anti-Christian. But she found solace in
caring for his illegitimate son, Candidianus, and at last Galerius died,
issuing on his deathbed an edict which put an end to the persecution of
the Christians. She might have then enjoyed some happiness had she not
been left a very rich woman. This made Galerius's successor, Maximin
Daia, want to marry her, although he had a wife. When she refused he
brought fraudulent legal proceedings against her. All her goods were
confiscated, her household was broken up, some of her women friends
were killed, and she and the boy Candidianus were sent into exile in the

deserts of Syria. It is only in some special and esoteric sense that women are the protected sex.

From these dark halls Diocletian appealed for mercy to the man whom his own invention of the Tetrarchy had raised to power. He entreated Maximin Daia to allow Valeria to come back to Aspalaton. He was refused. But later it seemed that Valeria was safe, for Maximin Daia died, and she and Candidianus were able to take refuge with another of the four Cæsars, Licinius, who first received them with a kindliness that was natural enough, since he owed his advancement to the dead Galerius. It looked as if they would find permanent safety with him. But suddenly he turned against them and murdered the boy for no other reason than that he was a cruel and stupid man and bloodshed was fashionable just then. Valeria managed to escape in the dress of a plebeian, and disappeared. To Diocletian, fond father though he was, this may have brought no special shattering shock. It may have seemed but one shadow in the progress of a night that was engulfing all. For Diocletian was receiving letters that were pressing him to visit Licinius and his ally, the Cæsar Constantine. He excused himself, pleading illness and old age. The invitations became ominously insistent. He was in danger of being involved in a dispute among the Tetrarchs. Sooner or later one side or other would have his blood. He died, it is thought by self-administered poison, some time between 313 and 316. The earlier date is to be hoped for; in that case he would not have heard that in 314 his daughter was found in hiding at Salonika and there beheaded and thrown into the sea.

What did Diocletian feel when all this was happening to him? Agony, of course. It is an emotion that human beings feel far more often than is admitted; and it is not their fault. History imposes it on us. There is no use denying the horrible nature of our human destiny. Diocletian must have felt one kind of agony because he was a healthy peasant, and his bowels must have slid backwards and forwards like a snake when he doubted the safety of his daughter; another because though he had been born a peasant he had been born a peasant into a civilized world, and faculties developed in civilization are revolted when they have to apprehend experiences provided by barbarism; and another because it is always terrible to advance from particular success to particular success and be faced at last with general defeat, and he had passed from achievement to achievement only to see the negation of all his achievements decreed by impersonal forces which, if he had been truly imperial and the right object of worship by the common man, he should have anticipated and forestalled. How did he endure all these agonies? If he went for comfort into the building which was afterwards his mausoleum, and if it was, as some think, the Temple of Jupiter, he can have found little enough. Paganism, when it was not rural and naïvely animist, or urban and a brake applied to the high spirits of success, must have been an empty form, claiming at its most ambitious to provide just that stoicism which an exceptional man might find for himself and recognize as inadequate. If the building was a Mithraic grotto, then he must have looked at the governing sculpture of the god slitting the throat of the bull and he must have said to himself, "Yes, the world is exactly like that. I know it. Blood flows, and life goes on. But what of it? Is the process not disgusting?" And Mithras would give no answer.

It is possible that Diocletian found his comfort in the secular side of his palace, in its splendour. Some have thought that he built it for the same reason that he had built his baths in Rome, to give work to the vast number of proletarians that were hungry and idle. But these grandiose public works would not have come into Diocletian's mind had he not been in love with magnificence, and indeed he had demonstrated such an infatuation while he was Emperor by his elaboration of court ceremonial. It had grown more and more spectacular during the last century or so, and he gave its gorgeousness a fixed and extreme character. There was more and more difficulty in gaining access to the sacred person of the Emperor, and those who were given this privilege had to bow before him in an act of adoration as due to the holy of holies. The Emperor, who was by then a focus of unresolvable perplexities, stood providing a strongly contrary appearance in vestments stiff with richness and insignia glittering with the known world's finest precious stones and goldsmith's work; and his visitor, even if the same blood ran in his veins, had to kneel down and touch a corner of the robe with his lips.

Diocletian, who had prescribed this ritual, must certainly have derived some consolation from the grandeur of Aspalaton, the great arcaded wall it turned to the Adriatic, its four separate wards, each town size, and its seventeen watch-towers, its plenitude of marble, its colonnades that wait for proud processions, its passages that drive portentously through darkness to the withdrawn abode of greatness. Robes stiff with embroidery help the encased body to ignore its flimsiness; a diadem makes the head forget that it has not yet evolved the needed plan of action. In a palace that lifts the hard core out of the mountains to make a countryside impregnable by wind and rain, it would seem untrue that we can build ourselves no refuge against certain large movements of destiny. But there was a consideration which may have disturbed Diocletian as he tried to sustain himself on Aspalaton. It was not Rome, which he had visited only once, that had given him his conception of magnificence as an aid to the invincibility of government. He had drawn it from Persia, where he had been immensely impressed by the vast palaces and their subtle and evocative ceremonial. But he had visited Persia as an invader, to destroy the Sassanian kings. The symbol that he depended upon he had himself proved invalid.

After his death he remained corporeally in possession of the palace, his tomb resting in the centre of the mausoleum. Thirty years or so later, a woman was put to death for stealing the purple pall from his sarcophagus, a strange, crazy crime, desperate and imaginative, a criticism in which he would by now have concurred, for the walls of the Empire which he had failed to repair had fallen and let a sea of catastrophe wash over his people. The Adriatic was ravaged by Vandal pirates, and Rome had been sacked by the barbarians three times in sixty years; the Huns had devastated the Danube, and Salonæ was crowded with refugees. But this was for the meantime a little ledge of safety, and ordinary life went on and seemed to prove that there was some sense in the idea of building a palace for shelter. Illyria had always been noted for its textiles. There is a statue of the Emperor Augustus in the Capitoline Museum at Rome, which has on its shield the figure of an Illyrian; he is wearing a knee-length tunic, beltless but with sleeves, and ornamented by bands running from the shoulders to the lower hem. This is our first knowledge of the dalmatic. In the third century the Pope ordered that all martyrs should be buried in it, and it is still worn by all deacons and officiating bishops in the Western church, and by English kings at their coronation. No matter what bestial tricks history might be playing, there were always looms at work in Illyria. A considerable corner of Aspalaton was taken up by a large factory, operated by female labour, which turned out uniforms for the Roman Army as well as civilian material.

But other events proved that a palace is no shelter at all. In the middle of the fifth century there arose a Dalmatian of genius, Marcellinus, who served the army loyally on condition that he was allowed to rule Dalmatia as an independent kingdom owing allegiance to the Emperor. It is possible that the Empire might have survived as a federation of such states, modest in extent and governed by men of local ambitions on the old Roman principles of efficiency and public spirit. Marcellinus took up his residence in Diocletian's palace, and with his courage and wisdom and energy in the defence of his people filled it again with recognizable majesty. But after thirteen years of benign brilliance he went in the service of the Emperor to Sicily, for the purpose of leading an expedition against the Vandals in Africa; and there he was murdered by order of Ricimer, a German general who was one of the barbarians who were destroying Rome from within. They had no use for local potentates who would build up the Empire by raising their territories to military and economic strength; they wanted it as a defenceless field of exploitation for an international army. The last of the *restitutores orbis* had not found safety where he might accomplish his work.

A few years later his nephew, who was called by that name, Julius Nepos, Julius the Nephew, and had ruled Dalmatia in his uncle's place, was called to be Emperor of the West. It was not an encouraging invitation. "Cocky, cocky, come and be killed." But since it was issued by the Emperor of the East he did not dare to refuse. He had at once to oust a competitor, whom he consoled for his defeat by making him Bishop of Salonæ; chroniclers with a sense of the picturesque describe him tearing off his rival's imperial insignia and delivering him over to a barber who cut his tonsure and a priest who gave him the episcopal consecration. It was a practical step, since it prevented his rival avenging himself. Julius the Nephew had no chance to show his quality, for he was faced by an infinity of hostile barbarians, within and without the Empire, and he made a fatal error by summoning his Dalmatian Commander-in-chief, Orestes, to govern Gaul. This Orestes was an Illyrian adventurer who had at one time been secretary to Attila the Hun. It can never have been a satisfactory reference. But he had established himself in the Roman order by marrying a patrician's daughter, and he was able to turn on his master and declare his own son Romulus Emperor.

Julius the Nephew went back to Aspalaton and there lived for five years. Meanwhile Orestes was murdered by a barbarian general, Odoacer, who formed a curious plan of supporting the cause of Romulus, whose youth and beauty he much admired, and acting as the power behind the throne. In 480 two Dalmatian counts, Victor and Ovida, one a Romanized Illyrian and the other a barbarian, made their way into Diocletian's palace and treacherously killed Julius. He was the last legitimately elected Emperor of the West. His assassins had been moved by the hope of pleasing Odoacer; the barbarian Ovida wished to make himself King of Dalmatia, and he needed imperial support. But Odoacer was as hostile to regional rulers as the other murderer, Ricimer, and at the end of a punitive war on Dalmatia he killed Ovida with his own hand.

Later he himself was killed by Theodoric, King of the Ostrogoths, who after signing a treaty with him invited him to a banquet and then ran him through with a sword, and massacred all his men. Murder. Murder. Murder. Murder.

It was about this time that the sarcophagus of Diocletian disappeared. For about a hundred and seventy years it was visible, firmly planted in the middle of the mausoleum, described by intelligent visitors. Then it suddenly is not there any more. It is suggested that a party of revengeful Christians threw it into the sea; but that is an action comprehensible only in a smouldering minority, and Christianity had been the official religion of the Roman Empire since the time of the Emperor's death. Nor can it be supposed that the sarcophagus was destroyed by the Avar invaders, for they did not reach the coast until a couple of centuries later. Probably the occasion of its disappearance was far less dramatic. The everyday routine of life persisted in Aspalaton, however many barbarians committed murder; in the textile factory the shuttles crossed and recrossed the loom. Without doubt it continued to be necessary that Diocletian's mausoleum should be cleaned and repaired, and it may well have happened that one day the owner of a yard near by said, "Yes, you can put it down there," watching it reverently, and wondering that he should be the guardian of such a holy thing. It may be also that the workmen who laid it down did not come back, that there was a threat to the city from land or sea which called them and the authorities who employed them and the owner of the yard himself to the defence. Soon it might be that people would say of the sarcophagus, "I wonder when they will come and take it back"; but continued unrest may have made it advisable that the treasures of the temples should be kept dispersed. Later it might be that a break in a chain of family confidences, due to violent death or flight or even sudden natural death, would leave the sarcophagus unidentified and only vaguely important. Some day a woman would say of it, "I really do not know what that is. It is just something that has always been here; and it is full of old things." She spoke the truth. It was full of old things: the bones of Diocletian the man, the robes of Diocletian the Emperor, the idea of a world order imposed on the peoples by superior people, who were assumed to know because they could act. Aspalaton, the palace of the great Restorer of the Earth, had passed away. It had become Split, a city lived in by common people, who could establish order within the limits of a kitchen or a workshop or a textile factory, but had been monstrously hindered in the exercise of that capacity by the efforts of the superior people who establish world order.

I have no doubt that one day Diocletian's sarcophagus will turn up in the cellars of some old and absent-minded family of Split; and in the cellars of the Dalmatian mind, the foundation on which its present philosophy is built, the old Emperor is to be found also. We in England have an unhistoric attitude to our lives, because every generation has felt excitement over a clear-cut historical novelty, which has given it enough to tell its children and grandchildren without drawing on its father's and grandfather's tales. In all these impressive events the central government has played a part which was, at any rate, not tragically disgraceful, at least so far as our own country is concerned, and was often very creditable. We think of the national organization that controls the public services throughout the country as ambitious on the whole to give the common man every opportunity to exercise his ability for keeping order in his own sphere.

It would not be so, however, if the last clear-cut event in English history had been the departure of the Roman legionaries in 420; and if there had followed a period of internal disorder which the battle of Hastings had perpetuated to our own day, by inaugurating a series of attempts at invasion and settlement by imperialistic Continental powers. Then the idea of the state would seem to us like wine, a delight that must be enjoyed only in moderation lest it lead to drunkenness and violence, uproar and want. We would know that some degree of national organization is necessary, and that dominance is the most exquisite of luxuries, but we would think of kings and statesmen as mischief-makers whose failure drove us from time to time out of our houses into ditches, to feed on roots and berries. The difference in our attitude can be computed if we try to imagine what our reaction to the word "queen" would be if we had had no Victoria or Elizabeth, or even Anne, and that Boadicea had had a determining effect on English history.

So it is with the Splitchani, and indeed with all Dalmatians. They are aware of Diocletian's failure to restore the earth, and what it cost them. Therefore their instinct is to brace themselves against any central authority as if it were their enemy. The angry young men run about shouting. But they have Illyrian blood as well as Slav; they are of the same race that produced Diocletian and the other *restitutores orbis*. They are profoundly sensitive to the temptation of power. Therefore they cannot break their preoccupation with the central authority. The young men cannot sit down and get angry about something else. The stranger will be vastly mistaken if he regards this attitude as petulant barbarism. It is an extremely sensible reaction to his experience, and it has helped him to protect his rights under the rule of empires which were indifferent or hostile to him. It might yet be of enormous service to humanity if the world were threatened by an evil domination.

Split II

DIOCLETIAN'S mausoleum was transformed into a cathedral during the eighth century. It is still obviously a pagan edifice, though the Christians fitted it in the thirteenth century with a good bell-tower, and with fine carved doors that show twenty-eight scenes from the life of Christ, and have gone on filling it with pious objects till it has something of a box-room air. There is a superb pulpit of the same date as the tower and the doors, splendid with winged beasts, and two good fifteenth-century tombs, one showing a Flagellation of Christ, the work of George the Dalmatian, who is alluded to as Georgio Orsini by those who want to show this coast as a Slav wilderness redeemed by Venetian culture, with no other justification than that a son or nephew of his called himself by that name. One can look at nothing in Dalmatia, not even a Flagellation of Christ, without being driven back to the struggle of Slav nationalism. The history of the Cathedral is dominated by it; here was the centre of the movement, which has been for the most part successful, for the use of the Slav liturgy.

There were, however, two ecclesiastics of Split who were of importance to the rest of the world. There was the Archdeacon Thomas of Spalato, in the thirteenth century, who wrote an excellent history of his own times and was the only contemporary foreigner known to have seen St. Francis of Assisi, and heard him preach; and there was the seventeenth-century Archbishop Mark Antony de Dominis, who was typically Slav in being at once an intellectual and incredibly naïve. He came from the city of Rab, from one of its exquisite Gothic palaces. Though he was an archbishop, and added to the mausoleum its present choir, his main interest lay in scientific studies; and he hit on the discovery of the solar spectrum one day while he was saying mass, more than half a century before Newton. Much of Descartes's work is founded on his, and Goethe writes of him in his book on the theory of colour. Unfortunately he became interested in matters of religion, which was a fatal mistake for a Renaissance prelate of his kind. Soon he became convinced of the truth of Protestantism, and through the influence of his friend, Sir Henry Wotton, the author of "You meaner beauties of the night," who was then the English Ambassador to Venice, he was appointed Dean of Windsor and Master of the Savoy and

Vicar of West Ilsley, up on the Berkshire downs. He then published a tremendous attack on the Roman Catholic Church under the title of *De republica ecclesiastica*. But doubts vexed him, and he came to the conclusion that he was wrong. In touching abandonment to the Slav belief that people are not really unreasonable, he went to Rome to talk about it to the Pope. That Pope died and was succeeded by one less tolerant. Dominis was thrown into the Castle of St. Angelo and died in its dungeons. Later the Inquisition tried him for heresy and found him guilty, so dug up his corpse and burned it together with his writings.

But though the religious life of Split is obscured by its nationalism in the historical annals, we must remember that much of human activity goes unrecorded. There is great piety among the Splitchani. We noted it that night when the Professor came to dine with us. The Professor is a great Latinist and was the pupil, assistant, and close friend of Bulitch, the famous scholar who spent his life working on the antiquities of Split and Salonæ. He is in his late sixties, but has the charm of extreme youth, for he comes to a pleasure and hails it happily for what it is without any bitterness accumulated from past disappointments, and he believes that any moment the whole process of life may make a slight switch-over and that everything will be agreeable for ever. His manners would satisfy the standards of any capital in the world, but at the same time he is exquisitely, pungently local. "Thank you, I will have no lobster," he said to us. "I am sure it is excellent, but, like many of my kind, who have had to renounce robust health along with the life of action, I have a weak digestion." He then emptied his pepper-pot into his soup till its surface became completely black. "See," he said, "how carefully I eat. I never neglect to take plenty of pepper, since it is excellent for the health. What, did you not know that? But I assure you, one can hardly live long unless one eats a great deal of pepper." I was enchanted; the Abbé Fortis, who made a tour of the coast in the eighteenth century, expressed amazement at the enormous quantities of pepper eaten by the Dalmatians, and their faith in it as a medicament.

Being so much a child of his country, he had of course to speak of nationalism, and indeed what he said brought home to me more than anything else the extreme unsuitability, the irksomeness of the last subjection which the Dalmatians had had to yield to an external authority. Here was a man who was the exact Adriatic equivalent of an Oxford don; he would by nature have found all his satisfaction in the pursuit of learning. But from his youth and through all his adult years he had been an active member of a party that existed to organize revolt against the Austrian Government; and there was none of his large and respectable family who had not been as deeply engaged in rebellion as himself. "One of my brothers," he told us, "was very well known as a Dalmatian patriot, for he had trouble that was reported in the newspapers all over Europe. For he was a priest, and the Austrians expelled him from Dalmatia though he had a parish. Still he did not suffer very much from that, for the great Bishop Strossmayer took him under his protection and gave him a parish near Zagreb.

"How fortunate for me all that trouble was!" he exclaimed, beaming. "For when I was going to the University at Vienna to make my studies Bishop Strossmayer invited me to see him. And that is the most wonderful thing that happened to me in my whole life. It was a very long time ago, for I was then only nineteen years old, but I have forgotten nothing of it. The room seemed bright as an altar at Easter when I went in, but that was not so much because of the chandeliers, which were indeed superb, but because of the company. There was Bishop Strossmayer himself, who was amazing in his handsomeness and elegance, and also there were at least twenty other people, who were all notable, great aristocrats of our race, or scholars, or artists, or foreigners of eminence, or women of superb beauty and great distinction. It is well known that Bishop Strossmayer was deeply respectful to the beauty of women, as to all the beauties of creation.

"But do not think that this was a mere worldly dinner-party. The great man imposed on it his own superiority. First we stood at the table, and he himself said grace in his exquisite Latin, which was Latin as no one else has spoken it, as the angels may speak it. Then we sat down, and as we ate a young priest read us a passage from the Gospel of St. John, and then a fable from Æsop. Then the Bishop started the conversation, which, though the party was so large, was nevertheless general and brilliant beyond imagination. It was his own doing, of course, yet it did not seem so. It all appeared to happen quite naturally. It was as if the birds in a wood should start singing and their notes should combine to form utterances of a wisdom unsurpassed by the philosophers. Alas! It is terrible that such a perfect thing should have been, and should be no longer. I suppose all the people who were there are dead, except some of the women; for I was much the youngest man there. But that feeling over what is gone the ancients knew well, and expressed better than we can." He murmured scraps of Latin verse. It was very characteristically Slav that he said nothing of having been troubled by social embarrassment at this dinner-party. In any other country, a boy of nineteen, not rich, from a provincial town, would have felt timid at a dinner-party given in a capital by one of the most famous men of the time. But Serbs and Croats alike are an intensely democratic people. There are few class distinctions, and Split, being a free and ancient city, would not feel inferior to Zagreb, for all its size and comparative wealth. Nevertheless, perhaps Bishop Strossmayer had his part in the boy's ease.

"I speak foolishly," said the Professor, when he started to talk again, "if I imply that the Bishop Strossmayer was an inspiration to me, for, to tell the truth, I have never been inspired. I have committed no great action, nor have I needed to. For the Austrian Government never persecuted us in the grand manner, it never called on us to be heroes, it merely pricked us with pins, and all we had to do was to be gentlemen and philosophers. My worst time was during the war, and that was not so bad." It appeared that as soon as Austria declared war on Serbia all the men in Split who had shown signs of hostility to the Austrian Government, which is to say all prominent or even respectable citizens, were arrested and sent on tour through Austria and Hungary to be shown off publicly as Serbian prisoners of war. "I who know German as my own tongue," said the Professor, "had to stand there while they described me as an Orthodox priest—that was because of my beard. Certain circumstances concerning that imprisonment were indeed very disagreeable. But let us not remember that, but the good things the war brought us. It brought us our freedom and it brought us many friends. Yes, many English friends. For many English sailors and soldiers came here after the war, and we liked them very much. I suppose you do not know Admiral William Fisher?" "No," said my husband, "but I know his brother, H. A. L. Fisher, the Warden of New College, who is a great historian and one of the most charming people in the world." "So is this man! So is this man!" cried the Professor. "He came here with the fleet several times, and I grew to love him like a brother. I tell you, he is like a hero of old!"

His eyes were glowing. Here, as in Serbia, there is very little effeminacy, and no man puts himself under suspicion by praising another; so one is sometimes aware of a strong current of love running from man to man, from comrade to comrade, from hero to hero. The Professor spoke long of Admiral Fisher, of his solid qualities, his wisdom and patience, and of his lovely lightnesses, his capacity for a gay Homeric cunning, and his tremendous laughter. "Ah!" he sighed at last, "I have spoken so much of my friend that without noticing it I have drunk a great deal of red wine. This will not be healthy, unless I drink a lot of black coffee. Is this coffee strong?" "I am afraid it is," I said, "terribly strong." "Why are you afraid?" asked the Professor. "The stronger it is the healthier it is. Did you not know that?"

After the Professor and my husband had talked for a while of their favourite editions of the classics they fell silent; and I said, "I have asked Philip Thomson to come in afterwards. He could not come to dinner as he had a lesson, but he is coming in at ten. I hope you will like him." "I have not met him," said the Professor, "but I know him by sight, and I am sure I will like him." "Yes, he has a charming, sensitive appearance," I said. "It is not that I mean," said the Professor. "I am sure I will like him because he is a very pious Catholic. I have noticed that he is most pious in his observances, and during Lent I have gone into my church several times and found him praying like a little child." And when Philip Thomson came in he greeted him with a special confidential and yet reticent friendliness, as if he knew they had in common certain experiences which, however, cannot be shared.

To start the conversation we talked of what we meant to do in Split before we set off southwards down the coast. "You really must go up to the park on Mount Marian, that hill below the town," said Philip; "it is most beautiful up there among the pines, looking over the sea and the islands." "Yes, indeed," I said. "I was there last year, and I want to go again. It interested me to see that in Robert Adam's drawings there isn't a tree on the hill, it is just bare rock. I suppose the Austrians planted it." "They did not!" cried the Professor, leaping from his chair. "And shall I tell you who did? I myself, I did it. I found in the archives uncontestable proof that there were once trees on that hill, which were cut down to make Venetian galleys. So I formed the idea that there could be trees there again, and I started a society to do it. Many people thought it was madness and my poor wife received anonymous letters saying that I should be put into a lunatic asylum. But I collected the money, and, believe me, it was Dalmatians who gave it. No, the Austrians did nothing for us, nor the Venetians either. We took the Venetian style of architecture, that is all; and I should not even say that if I were striving to be accurate. It would be more truthful to say that the Venetians and the Dalmatians both drew from the same sources inspiration towards a new movement. . . ."

We were back again at Slav nationalism; but we left it for that permanent and mystical preoccupation which lies deeper in the Dalmatian mind. "I do not think that the Venetians have left any permanent mark on the life of the people," said the Professor, "except perhaps the Venetian habit of blasphemy. Do you not find it dreadful, Mr. Thomson, the oaths that one must hear as one walks in the streets of Split?" "I find it most terrible," said Philip; "they use the holy names in a way that makes one clap one's hands over one's ears." They shook their heads gravely; and I saw the unusual spectacle of a foreigner born to the Catholic faith matching in fervour an English convert. In the Professor I recognized the same Slavic religious passion that had made dark and glowing the voices of the men and women singing mass at Shestine; but it seemed to me that in him it was not only sweetened by the great sweetness of his personality, but also that it was given a special intensity by the long dolorous life of his town, and its reflections upon its tragedy, its refusal to take the sorrow and waste of it at their face value.

It is not to be doubted, as one goes about Split, that this walled city has such a life, far more concentrated than the life of our diffuse Western towns; and that it has been engaged in a continuous effort to find a noble interpretation of its experience through piety. The Professor took us the next morning to the Golden Gate of the palace, which is most recognizably what it was in the days of Diocletian, a very handsome, creeper-hung matter of niches and pillarets and a narrow door, which modern times have pierced with an unending thread of neat and supple Splitchani hurrying down to the harbour. Near this Gate we climbed a stairway, and a door was opened by a nun, who led us up more stairs into a little church built in the thickness of the palace walls. It is about eleven hundred years old, and though it is defaced by hideous *bondieuseries* of the modern Roman Catholic Church, it remains infinitely touching because of its slender stone screen, because of the carvings on that screen which write in shapes as fresh as dew the faith of a people that they have found a beneficent magic to banish the horrors of life. Beside us the nun spoke on and on to the Professor, her voice stilled with amazement, in words that also were as fresh as dew. She was telling him that the Mother Superior of that tiny order which guards this Church of St. Martin was growing very old and very sick, but was showing great fortitude. Though she spoke calmly she took nothing for granted; this might have been the first time that pain and fortitude had shown themselves on earth. She was among those who will not suffer any event merely to happen, who must examine it with all the force of the soul and trace its consequences, and seek, against all probability, an explanation of the universe that is as kind as human kindness.

We went, later in the morning, to another church, built in honour of the Virgin Mary actually within one of the gates, over an archway. It is not specially interesting; one has seen its like all over Southern Europe, grey and pliant in its line, a gentle boast that if one has but faith it needs no more than the strength of a lily to withstand life. This, like many of the smaller churches in the Dalmatian towns, belongs to a confraternity; about twenty townsmen sustained it, used it as the centre of their devotions and the means of their charity, and there married their wives and christened their children and were buried. It was shown to us by one of this confraternity, a plasterer, who had left his work to do the Professor this courtesy. Wearing his working clothes, which were streaked with white plaster, he stood still and stiff like a page in a more than royal household, showing subjects the throne-room, the plain transmitter of a tradition which we had recognized earlier that day.

We had recognized it in the Temple of Æsculapius, which lies on the other side of the courtyard from Diocletian's mausoleum and is now the baptistery. This change would not have surprised Diocletian, for the last glimpse that we have of his personal life is his irritation at the refusal of his Christian stone-masons to make him a statue of Æsculapius. There we saw a tenth-century stone slab, roughly carved, which is said by some to represent the adoration of Christ and by others the homage paid to a Croatian king by his subjects. It does not matter which it is. What is important is that the sculptor, wishing to depict magnificence, whether earthly or supernatural, saw it in Byzantine terms. After the Western Roman Empire had collapsed Dalmatia had thirty years of dangerous independence and then fell under the Eastern Empire, under Byzantium. That Empire was a real fusion of Church and State; the Emperor was given absolute power over his subjects only because he professed absolute subjection to God, and the ceremonial of his court was a religious ritual. That slab exists to show that this conception of government by holy ballet deeply impressed the imagination of the governed people, even on its furthermost frontiers.

The devout grace of the workman, which, though it had an instinctive basis, had been borne as far from that by art and discipline as the Guards have been removed in their drill from the primitive emotion of ferocity, proved that the Byzantine tradition had made other signs of vitality than mere diffusion. This man was a Slav. The fair hair, the high cheekbones, the sea-blue eyes showed it. Byzantium had struck new roots in the race that had come into the Balkans from the mid-Russian plains as pure barbarians, untouched by anything that had happened during the first centuries of the Christian era, and apparently as inaccessible to Christian influence as any race on earth. Without pity, they killed and tortured; without purpose, they burned and laid waste. They came down to the Dalmatian coast on a mission of ruin, in the company of the Huns and Avars. But it happened that the Huns and the Avars turned on and reduced them to slaves, and they rose in revolt. Angry young men ran about shouting. They were heard by the Byzantine Emperor Heraclius, who promised that if they drove the Huns and Avars out of Illyria they might settle the land as vassals of the Empire. He imposed a further condition: that they must adopt Christianity. Who could have foretold that out of this marriage of convenience between the Slav people and the Church would flower a great passion? Who could have foretold that a horde of murderers and marauders would be also addicts to spiritual pursuits and the use of the intellect, believers in magic and the existence of a reality behind appearances, who would perform any ritual and carry on any argument that promised a revelation of the truth? History sometimes acts as madly as heredity, and her most unpredictable performances are often her most glorious.

Salonæ

THIS was the grimmest Easter; and when the Professor took us up to the remains of the great Roman city, Salonæ, which should be one of the prettiest sights in the whole world, it was nothing of the sort. Its pillars and steps and sarcophagi lie among rich grass and many flowers under the high olive terraces overlooking the sea and its many islands, the very spot which Horace would have liked to visit with a footman carrying a lunch basket behind him. It is one of the disharmonies of history that there is nothing that a Roman poet would have enjoyed more than a Roman ruin, with its obvious picturesqueness and the cue it gives for moralizing. But we could not enjoy it at all, for sharp rain scratched our faces all the four miles we drove from Split, and at Salonæ it grew brutal and we were forced into a little house, all maps and inscriptions, built by the great Bulitch to live in while he was superintending the diggings, and since his death converted into a museum.

We were not alone. The house was packed with little girls, aged from twelve to sixteen, in the care of two or three nuns. They were, like any gathering of their kind in any part of the world, more comfortable to look at than an English girls' school. They were apparently waiting quite calmly to grow up. They expected it, and so did the people looking after them. There was no panic on anybody's part. There were none of the unhappy results which follow the English attempt to make all children look insipid and docile, and show no signs whatsoever that they will ever develop into adults. There were no little girls with poked chins and straight hair, aggressively proud of being plain, nor were there pretty girls making a desperate precocious proclamation of their femininity. But, of course, in a country where there is very little homosexuality it is easy for girls to grow up into womanhood.

But I wondered what the little dears were learning up at Salonæ. I suspected that they were receiving an education with a masculine bias. Indeed, I knew it, for they were being educated by nuns, who are women who have accepted the masculine view of themselves and the universe, who show it by being the only members of their sex who go into fancy dress and wear uniforms as men love to do. I feared that in this particular background they might be instilling into their charges some monstrous male rubbish. It was even possible that they were teach-

ing them the same sort of stuff about the Romans which I learned when
I was at school: panegyrics of dubious moral value, unsupported by evidence. There is, Heaven knows, enough to be said in their favour without
any sacrifice of honesty. I can bear witness to it. I was at school in Scotland, and therefore, owing to the strange dispensations of that country
in regard to the female, learned Latin and no Greek, a silly, lopsided way
of being educated. But even for this one-eyed stance on the classics I
am grateful, though I was slow-witted at learning that and all other languages, and have forgotten most of what I knew. It gave me the power
to find my way about the Romance languages; it gave me a sense of the
past, a realization that social institutions such as the law do not happen
but are made; it gave, and gives, me considerable literary rapture. I like
a crib, indeed some might say that I need a crib; but once I have it I
enjoy my Latin verse enormously. To this day I am excited as I read
that neatest possible expression of the wildest possible grief:

*Floribus Austrum
Perditus et liquidis immisi fontibus apros.*

It also seems to me that the modern mind cannot be fully understood
until one has gone back to Latin literature and seen what European culture was like before it was injected with the ideas of St. Augustine.

But I regret that to give me this pleasure and information my teachers
should have found it necessary to instruct me, with far more emphasis
than was justified by the facts in their or anybody else's possession, that
the Roman Empire was a vast civilizing force which spread material
and moral well-being all over the ancient world by its rule. I was taught
that this was no mere accident: that the power to extend their rule by
military means sprang from an intellectual and moral genius that made
them able to lay down the best way of living for the races they subdued.
I find these assumptions firmly embedded in the mass of literature written by people who received a classical education, especially if it had the
same Latin bias as mine, and expressed even more passionately in literature written by people who have not had any education at all. Every
year I grow more critical of them. We have no real evidence that the
peoples on which the Roman Empire imposed its civilization had not
pretty good civilizations of their own, better adapted to local conditions. The Romans said they had not; but posterity might doubt the
existence of our contemporary French and English culture if the Nazis
destroyed all records of them. We may at least suspect from the geniuses
of African stock who appear within the Roman Empire that when Rome

destroyed Carthage, dragging the plough three times through the land, she destroyed her equal or even her superior. The great work by Monsieur Camille Julian on the history of Gaul suggests that when Rome came to France she frustrated the development of a civilization of the first order; and Strzygowski doubts whether she did not bring disorganization to the Germanic tribes. It appears probable from the researches of the last few years, which have discovered codes of law, far from rudimentary, among all the contemporaries of the Romans, even to the nomads, that they might have got on with their social institutions very satisfactorily if they had not been obliged to fight against the external efforts at their betterment. And it seems very probable that Rome was able to conquer foreign territories because she had developed her military genius at the expense of precisely those qualities which would have made her able to rule them. Certainly she lacked them to such an extent that she was unable to work out a satisfactory political and economic policy for Rome itself and perished of that failure.

I am sure of it, those little girls were being taught that they should be proud because Split was the heir to a Roman city. Yet neither I nor anybody else knows whether or not the conquest of Illyria by the Romans was not a major disaster, the very contrary to an extension of civilization. Illyria had its past. It was linked with Greek history, and had a double tie with Macedonia of alternate enmity and alliance. Alexander the Great had Illyrian princesses for his mother and grandmother, and he and his father both fought great campaigns against their country. In the Roman period we know little about Illyria save from Roman sources, but even they suggest a considerable culture. They had an extremely able and heroic queen, Teüta, who was not the sort of monarch that can be raised from a tribe in skins; and while she and her subjects are accused of piracy, examination proves this a reference to efforts, which history would regard as creditable if they had been undertaken by the Romans, to conquer the Adriatic archipelago. It is also brought up against Teüta that she murdered two of three Roman ambassadors who were sent to accuse her people of unmannerly ways at sea. But it is said that these were murdered by brigands outside the Illyrian frontiers; and some heed had better be given to Polybius, a Roman of the Romans, when he explains why the Senate once made war on the Illyrians:

Since the Romans had expelled Demetrios of Pharos from Illyria they had completely neglected the Adriatic seaboard; and on another hand the Senate wished to avoid at all costs that the Italians became effeminate during a longstanding peace because it was more than eleven years since the Persian war and the Macedonian Expedition had ended. In undertaking a campaign against the Dalmatians they would reawaken the fighting spirit of the people at the same time that they would give the Illyrians a lesson and would force them to submit to the domination of Rome. Such were the reasons why Rome declared war on the Dalmatians; but the excuse which was given to the other nations was the insolence with which they had treated the ambassadors.

Little girls of Salonæ, try to work out this sum on your fingers. It took Rome two hundred and fifty years of war to bring peace to the Illyrians. Then they had fifty years or so of disturbance, and a hundred years of peace, which I cannot but think they could have procured for themselves, since they had then to take over the government of Rome and provide the long line of Illyrian emperors. They were then precipitated into an abyss of unrest and catastrophe, of which the worst feature, the barbarian invasions, owed its horror largely to Roman expansion. If Italy had been content with herself as a unit and had developed on a solid economic basis, and if Illyria had been allowed to look after her own affairs, they might have put up a far more effective resistance to the invaders. No, the sum does not work out. Remember, when the nuns tell you to beware of the deceptions of men who make love to you, that the mind of man is on the whole less tortuous when he is love-making than at any other time. It is when he speaks of governments and armies that he utters strange and dangerous nonsense to please the bats at the back of his soul. This is all to your disadvantage, for in love-making you might meet him with lies of equal force, but there are few repartees that the female governed can make to the male governors.

Nevertheless, it was sweet for all of us, nuns and the little dears, the Professor and my husband and me, to go out when the rain had stopped and walk among the Roman ruins of Salonæ. Grey and silver were the olive leaves shining in the timid sunlight, dark grey the wet ruins, silvergrey the tall spiked aloes, and blacker than green the cypresses, black the mountains behind us, silver the sea that lay before us, and grey the islands that streaked it; and at our feet storm-battered flowers looked like scraps of magenta paper. The Professor was gay, as birds are after rain. He read us inscriptions, lending them a sweetness that was not in their meaning from the enjoyment of Latinism which had been mellowing in his soul since his youth, and guiding us to the stony stubs and plinths and stairways of temples, baths, churches, the city walls, the city gate, that had been battered less by time than by wars. Again and again

THE CATHEDRAL AT RAB

A Dalmatian Doorway:
it can be seen from this photograph what influence the architecture which Robert
Adam saw on his visit to the Dalmatian coast had on Georgian architecture

this place had been taken and retaken by the Goths and the Huns before the Avars finally smashed it in 639. It is for this reason that the churches in this city have the majesty of a famous battle-field. Here Christianity's austere message that it is better not to be a barbarian, even if victory lies with barbarism, was tested in the actual moment of impact with barbarians, in face of a complete certainty that victory was to be with barbarism. In the baptistery of the Cathedral the chamber round the font still stands. There can still be seen the steps down which the naked men, glistening with the holy oil and reeling with the three days' fast, descended to the holy waters, to be immersed in them three times and lifted out, glorious in the belief that the death that was closing in on them was magically changed to joy and salvation. From the most coldly rationalist point of view it must be pronounced that they were not mistaken. Complete victory was given here to the barbarians; on this spot they followed their nature in all its purity of destructiveness, its zeal of cruelty. But the gentle virtue of the Professor, the dedicated fineness of the plasterer in the confraternity chapel, showed that the stock of the christened men lived still and had not been brutalized.

It was right that the nuns should be trailing the little dears round the site of this miracle of which they formed a part. But I passed one of the nuns and remarked, as I had done before, that the rank and file of the female religious order present an unpleasing appearance because they have assumed the expression of credulity natural and inevitable to men, who find it difficult to live without the help of philosophical systems which far outrun ascertained facts, but wholly unsuitable to women, who are born with a faith in the unrevealed mystery of life and can therefore afford to be sceptics. I feared very much that the nuns' charges would be fed a deal of nonsense along with the bread of truth. They would be taught, for example, to honour those claims of the Church which reflect no reality and spring from certain masculine obsessions of its ecclesiastics: such as its pretension to be unchanging, to have attained in its first years a wisdom about all matters, eternal and temporal, of which it has made a progressive disclosure, never contradicting itself. We are, of course, at liberty to imagine that the Church would be a nobler institution if it knew no alteration; even so it does no harm if we dream that we could all be much happier if our bodies remained for ever young and fair. But these are day-dreams and nothing else, for the Church changes, and we grow old. There was evidence of it, written here on the wet grey stone.

"Look," said the Professor, "this is one of our most interesting tombs,

which is also very touching." Here a husband had laid to rest his beloved wife; and in the inscription he boasted that he had brought her to
his home when she was eighteen and had lived beside her in chastity for
thirty-three years. His very grief itself must have been made serene by
his consciousness that by their abstinence they had followed the approved Christian course. These were the days when Theodore the Con-
script was enraged against paganism because Juno had twelve children.
To some this multiplication of divinities might seem as beautiful as the
birth of a new constellation, but this Christian it made cry shame on "a
goddess who littered like a sow"; and he died for his opinion, frustrat-
ing the intended moderation of the authorities by firing her temple.
About this time St. Jerome declared that he valued marriage only because it produced virgins, and advised a widow against remarriage in
terms which remind us that he was Dalmatian, and that the inhabitants
of this coast have never been noted for understatement. "The trials of
marriage," he told the Lady Furia, "you have learned in the married
state; you have been surfeited to nausea as though with the flesh of
quails. Your mouth has tasted the bitterest of gall, you have voided the
sour unwholesome food, you have relieved a heaving stomach. Why
would you put into it again something which has already proved harm-
ful to you? The dog is turned to his own vomit again and the washed
sow to her wallowing in the mire." This married pair of Salonæ, eager
for salvation, must have believed that they could not be denied some
measure of it, since they had allowed themselves to be groomed in
barrenness by the Church.

They would have felt amazement had they known that, some few
centuries later, the Church would have persecuted them, even to death,
for such wedded chastity. For over this coast there was to spread from
the hinterland of the Balkan Peninsula the Puritan heresy known as
Paulicianism or Patarenism or Bogomilism or Catharism, knowing certain local and temporal variations under these names, but all impassioned
over the necessity of disentangling the human spirit from the evilness of
matter and convinced that this was immensely facilitated by the practice
of virginity. It had the advantage of appealing to that love of the disagreeable which is one of the most unpleasant characteristics of humanity, and it became a serious rival to the orthodox churches, which attacked it not only by reason but by fire and sword. Since it laid such
emphasis on virginity, the ecclesiastical authorities came down like
wolves on any married pairs whom gossip reported as not availing themselves of their marital privileges. So far was this recognized as a test

that a man accused of heresy is said to have brought forward as proof
of his orthodoxy that he drank wine and ate meat and swore and lay
with his wife. Therefore this couple of Salonæ, had they practised this
wedded chastity on the same spot five or six hundred years later, would
not have been granted thirty-three years to do it in. They would have
had a fate indistinguishable from that of the Christian martyrs whom
they revered, but they would have ranked as pagans or lower. Yet even
that change in the Church's attitude they might have felt as less con-
founding than the later change, which would have regarded it as a matter of indifference whether they lived in abstinence or not, provided
that they did not prevent the begetting of children in any intercourse
they might have. That yawn in the face of their thirty-three years
might have seemed worse than martyrdom.

It might have been sad to watch the little dears in their blue coats and
straw hats being inducted into male superstition among the sarcophagi
on a dampish day; but the Professor took us to a tomb that gave reason
for hope that they would suffer no harm, being protected by their own
female nature. The Latin of the inscription was so bad that it must have
been erected at a time when the ancient world was suffering its last
agony. In that hour, when the earth trembled and the columns were
falling, a good creature set up this stone in honour of her departed husband. He was so strong, she said, that she had twins some months after
he had died, and she had loved him very much. Finally, with a tremendous gesture she put out her arm and drew together two conceptions of the universe to shield him from all dangers, and commended him
to the mercy of both Jesus Christ and the Parcæ. She did what she could
before the darkness came, acting out of sound sense and good feeling,
though with a tendency to idealize virility; and we may suppose that the
little dears would do as much, whatever they were taught.

Trogir

THE steamer which makes the hour's journey from Split to Trogir was full of Germans, and I wondered more and more at the impossibility of learning the truth. I have been given to understand, partly by what I have read and heard, and partly by parades I have seen in Germany, that Germans are a race of beautiful athletes tense with will, glossy with efficiency, sinister with aggressiveness. The German tourists who had surrounded us in every hotel and on every steamer since we got to Dalmatia were either pear-shaped fat or gangling thin, and in any case wore too much flesh packed on the nape of the neck, and were diffident, confused, highly incompetent as travellers, and not at all unkindly. There was, I suppose, no contradiction here, only proof that Germany has been divided into two nations, a pampered young prætorian guard and the badgered, undernourished, unregarded others. These were the others. But they also were of Hitler's Germany; for the steamer dawdled along the coast from portlet to portlet, and on each landing-stage there were standing a crowd of Dalmatians, tall, lean, upright in pride of body. The tourists stared at them and spoke of them as if they were odd and dangerous animals. The German hatred of the Slav had been revived and reinforced.

Across a milk-white sea, with two silver hydroplanes soaring and dipping to our right and left, we came to the town of Trogir, which covers a minute island, lying close to the coast, in the lee of a larger island. It is one of those golden-brown cities: the colour of rich crumbling shortbread, of butterscotch, of the best pastry, sometimes of good undarkened gravy. It stands naked and leggy, for it is a walled city deprived of its walls. The Saracens levelled them, and the Venetians and the Hungarians would never let them be rebuilt. Now it looks like a plant grown in a flower-pot when the pot is broken but the earth and roots still hang together. On the quay stand Slavized Venetian palaces with haremish lattice-work fixed to screen the stone balconies, to show that here West meets East, brought thus far by Byzantine influence and perpetuated by the proximity of the Turks. Behind them lies a proof that life is often at once mad and consistent, in the manner of dreams. Petronius Arbiter's *Satyricon* lives in the mind long after reading as a fevered progression of flights through a cityful of twisting alleys. Trogir's alleys turn and writhe like entrails. It was in Trogir that the codex of the *Satyricon* was found in 1650. It was not written there, of course. If it had been there would be nothing startling in the resemblance between the work and the town. But it came to light here, after centuries of loss. The appropriateness is as exquisite as the colour of the town, as its spires.

The appropriateness went further still: for Petronius Arbiter was by nature a Puritan, who had he been born in due time would have found himself at home as a Paulician or Patarene or Bogomil or Catharist, or in any other of those heresies which were based on the Persian faith of Manichæanism, which held that matter was evil, and sex a particularly evil manifestation of it.

> *Fœda in coitu et brevis voluptas est*
> *Et tædet Veneris statim peractæ.*

Gross and brief is the pleasure of love-making, he says, and consummated passion a shocking bore. He goes on to beg his beloved therefore that they should not mate like mere cattle, but should lie lip to lip and do nothing more, to avoid toil and shame. The meaning of this exhortation lies in *Trimalchio's Supper*, which shows Petronius to have been homosexual and fearful of impotence with women; and perhaps the same explanation lay behind most followers of these heresies. But he rationalized his motives, and so did Trogir. This was an inveterately heretic city.

In its beginning it was a Greek settlement and later a Roman town, and then it was taken over in the Dark Ages by wandering Paulicians. In the twelfth century the town was sacked by the Saracens, and the inhabitants were dispersed among the villages on the mainland. That, however, did not break the tradition of heresy, for when the King of Hungary collected them and resettled them on their island they soon fell under the influence of Catharism, which was sweeping across the Balkan Peninsula from Bulgaria to Bosnia and Herzegovina and the coast. This recurrence is natural enough. Manichæanism—for these heresies might as well be grouped together under the name of their parent— represents the natural reaction of the earnest mind to a religion that has aged and hardened and committed the sin against the Holy Ghost, which is to pretend that all is now known, and there can now be laid down a system of rules to guarantee salvation. In its origin it was a reaction against the extreme fatalism of Zoroastrianism, which held that man's destiny was decided by the stars, and that his only duty was to accom-

plish it in decorum. Passionately Mani created a myth that would show
the universe as a field for moral effort: inspired by Christianity as it had
passed through the filter of many Oriental minds and by a cosmology
invented by an Aramaic astronomer, he imagined that there had been
in the beginning of time a kingdom of light and a kingdom of darkness,
existing side by side without any commixture, and that these had later
been confused, as the result of aggression on the part of the darkness.
This was the origin of the present world, which Mani very aptly called
The Smudge. It became the duty of all men who were on the side of the
light, which was identified with virtue and reason, to recover the particles of light that have become imprisoned in the substance of darkness,
which was identified with vice and brutishness.

This is actually an extremely useful conception of life. But Manichæanism was handicapped by the strictly literal mind of the founder and
his followers, who believed that they were not speaking in allegory but
were describing the hard material facts of the universe. When they
spoke of the signs of the zodiac as dredges bringing up rescued particles
of light to store them in the sun and moon, they meant quite squarely
that that is what they thought the constellations were. This literalness
turned the daily routine of the faithful into a treasure-hunt, sometimes of
an indecorous nature. Excrement was obviously part of the kingdom of
darkness, if ever anything was. Hence it became the duty of the Manichæan priests, the "elect," to take large doses of purgatives, not furtively. This routine became not only ridiculous but dangerous, as the
centuries passed and the ingenious medieval European began to use it
to serve that love of the disagreeable which is our most hateful quality.
Natural man, uncorrected by education, does not love beauty or pleasure or peace; he does not want to eat and drink and be merry; he is on
the whole averse from wine, women, and song. He prefers to fast, to
groan in melancholy, and to be sterile. This is easy enough to understand. To feast one must form friendships and spend money, to be merry
one must cultivate fortitude and forbearance and wit, to have a wife
and children one must assume the heavy obligation of keeping them and
the still heavier obligation of loving them. All these are kinds of generosity, and natural man is mean. His meanness seized on the Manichæan
routine and exploited it till the whole of an infatuated Europe seemed
likely to adopt it, and would doubtless have done so if the Orthodox
and Roman Catholic Churches had not hardened their hearts against it
and counted no instrument too merciless for use, not even mass murder.

It is our tendency to sympathize with the hunted hare, but much that

we read of Western European heretics makes us suspect that here the
quarry was less of a hare than a priggish skunk. In Languedoc there seems
to have been some sort of pleasant transmutation of the faith, but for
the most part heretical Europe presents us with the horrifying spectacle
of countless human beings gladly facing martyrdom for the right to perform cantrips that might have been invented by a mad undertaker. There
was a particularly horrible travesty of extreme unction called the "endura." Every dying person was asked by the priest whether he wanted
to be a confessor or a martyr; if he wanted to be a confessor he remained without food or drink, except for a little water, for three days,
and if he wanted to be a martyr a pillow was held over his mouth while
certain prayers were recited. If he survived in either case he ranked as
a priest. This horrid piece of idiocy was often used as a means of suicide,
a practice to which these heretics were much addicted; but as they believed that to suffer torture in dying would relieve them from it in the
next world, the real enthusiasts preferred for this purpose to swallow
broken glass. The faith also gave encouragement to certain passive methods of murder. The guardians of the sick were urged to extinguish
life when death was near; and how this worked out may be deduced
from a case in France where a woman subjected her infant grandchild
to the endura and then prevented its mother from suckling it till it died.
By this necrophily, and a pervasive nastiness about sex, which went so
far as to forbid a father to be touched by his own daughter, even if he
were very old and she were his nurse, millions were raised to a state of
rapture. The whole of modern history could be deduced from the
popularity of this heresy in Western Europe: its inner sourness, its
preference for hate over love and for war over peace, its courage about
dying, its cowardice about living.

   This cannot have been the whole truth about these heresies. So inherently noble a vision must have produced some nobility, its own particles of light cannot all have been dissolved. But its achievements were
trodden into the dirt by its enemies along with its failures; the Huns
and the Avars never made a cleaner job of devastation than the orthodox armies who were sent against the Albigenses and the Catharists,
and the heretics in the Balkans were spared such demolition only because of the Turkish occupation, which laid waste their institutions just
as thoroughly for quite other reasons. It happens that here in Trogir
there is preserved a specimen of Manichæan culture. In the centre of the
town a cathedral stands in a flagged square. They began building it in
the thirteenth century to replace a cathedral, six hundred years old,

which had been burned by the Saracens, and went on for a couple more centuries. It was for long one of the homes of the Patarene heresy. Its congregation were solidly adepts of the hidden faith, and so too, at least once in its history, was the bishop who officiated at its altar. In the porch to the bell-tower of this cathedral there is a carved portal which is the most massive and pure work of art produced by Manichæanism that I have ever seen. There are, of course, specimens of heretic architecture in France, but those were modified by an existing and flourishing French culture. Here a fresh and vigorous Manichæanism has been grafted on a dying and remote offshoot of Roman and Byzantine culture.

It is the work of a thirteenth-century sculptor called Radovan, or the Joyous One, and it instantly recalls the novels of Dostoevsky. There is the same sense of rich, contending disorder changing oozily from form to form, each one of which the mind strives to grasp, because if it can but realize its significance there will be not order, but a hint of coming order. Above the door are many scenes from the life of Christ, arranged not according to the order of time; in the beginning He is baptized, in the middle He is crucified, in the end He is adored by the Wise Men. These scenes are depicted with a primitive curiosity, but also make a highly cultured admission that that curiosity cannot be wholly gratified. It is as if the child in the artist asked, "What are those funny men doing?" and the subtle man in him answered, "I do not know, but I think . . ." On the outer edge of the door, one to the right and one to the left, stand Adam and Eve, opinions about our deprived and distorting destiny; and they stand on a lion and a lioness, which are opinions about the animal world, and the nature we share with it. In the next column, in a twined confusion, the sculptor put on record the essence of the sheep and the stag, the hippopotamus and the centaur, the mermaid and the apostles; and in the next he shows us the common man of his time, cutting wood, working leather, making sausages, killing a pig, bearing arms. But of these earthly types and scenes the child in the artist asked as eagerly as before, "What are those funny men doing?" and the man answered as hesitantly, "I do not know, but I think . . ."

There we have an attitude which differentiates Manichæanism sharply from orthodox Christianity. If the common man was actually interpenetrated with particles of light, or divinity, as the heretics believed, and if this could be made more or less difficult to recover by his activities, then each individual and his calling had to be subjected to the severest analysis possible. But if the common man has a soul, a recognizable part of himself, as orthodox Christians believe, which is infected with sin through the fall of man and can be cleansed again by faith and participation in the sacraments and adherence to certain ethical standards, then it is necessary not to analyze the individual but to make him follow a programme. This difference corresponds with the difference between Western Europeans and the Slavs, of which many of us receive our first intimations from Dostoevsky. In the West conversation is regarded as a means of either passing the time agreeably or exchanging useful information; among Slavs it is thought to be disgraceful, when a number of people are together, that they should not pool their experience and thus travel further towards the redemption of the world. In the West conduct follows an approved pattern which is departed from by people of weak or headstrong will; but among Slavs a man will try out all kinds of conduct simply to see whether they are of the darkness or of the light. The Slavs, in fact, are given to debate and experiment which to the West seem unnecessary and therefore, since they must involve much that is painful, morbid. This spirit can be recognized also in the curious pressing, exploratory nature of Radovan's imagination.

But there are other resemblances also between Manichæanism and Slavism, between Radovan and Dostoevsky. For one, the lack of climax. The orthodox Christian thinks that the story of the universe has revealed itself in a design that would be recognized as pleasing in a work of finite proportions; a number of people, not too great to be remembered, and all easily distinguishable, enact a drama which begins with the Creation, rises to its peak in the Incarnation, is proceeding to its consummation in the Day of Judgment and the coming of the Kingdom of Heaven. The Manichæan believed that an immense crowd of people, often very difficult to distinguish from one another, are engaged in recovering the strayed particles of light, a process which can come to a climax only when it is finished. This is reflected in Radovan's work by a curious levelness of inspiration, a lack of light and shade in his response to his subject; in the Slav's readiness to carry on a conversation for ever, to stay up all night; in Dostoevsky's continuous, unremitting spiritual excitement.

For another resemblance, there is the seeming paradox of a fierce campaign against evil combined with a tolerance of its nature. We cannot understand this in the West, where we assume that sincere hostility to sin must be accompanied by a reluctance to contemplate it and a desire to annihilate it. But according to the Manichæan faith there was no need to take action against darkness except when it enmeshed the light.

When the kingdom of darkness was existing side by side with the kingdom of light without any commixture, then it was committing no offence. That attitude can be traced in Radovan's faithful reproduction of life's imperfect forms, in Dostoevsky's choice of abnormality as a subject. And there is yet another resemblance which is particularly apparent in the work of Radovan. The columns he carved with the representations of The Smudge are borne on the shoulders of those who are wholly of the darkness, Jews and Turks and pagans. It is put forward solidly and without sense of any embarrassment that there are those who are predestined to pain, contrary to the principles of human justice. Calvin admitted this with agony, but there is none here; and Dostoevsky never complains against the God who created the disordered universe he describes. This is perhaps because the Manichæans, like the Greeks, did not regard God as the Creator, but as the Arranger, or even as the Divine Substance which had to be arranged.

That the West should be wholly orthodox and not at all Manichæan in its outlook on these matters is the consequence of the zeal of the Roman Catholic Church. Quite simply it physically exterminated all communities who would not abandon the heretic philosophy. But the South-East of Europe was so continuously disturbed, first by civil war and Asiatic invasion and then by the Turkish occupation, that the Eastern Church could not set up an effective machine for the persecution of heretics, even if it had had the temperament to do so. There the outward forms of Manichæanism eventually perished, as they were bound to do in time, partly because of the complicated and fantastic nature of its legend and the indecorous and cruel perversions of its ritual; but its philosophy remained, rooted in the popular mind before the Turkish gate closed down between the Balkans and the rest of the world, to travel northwards and influence the new land of Russia, where after several centuries it inspired a generation of giants, to the astonishment of Europe. The Russian novelists of the nineteenth century represented the latest recrudescence of a philosophy that had too much nobility in it ever to perish utterly.

But one wishes one knew how this heresy compared with orthodoxy as a consolation in time of danger: whether the Manichæans of Trogir were as firmly upheld by their faith as the Christians of Salonæ. The Manichæans might claim that it served them better, so far as barbarian invasion was concerned, for they had one of the narrowest escapes from annihilation that is written in all history. The Professor took us on from the Cathedral to see the scene of it. We walked out of the city onto the quay through a gate which still keeps the handsome stone lion of St. Mark that was the sign of Venetian possession, surmounted by the patron saint of Trogir, St. Giovanni Orsini, who was its bishop about the time of the Norman Conquest; he was a remarkable engineer, who was made a saint because he aided the Papacy in its efforts to suppress the Slav liturgy. A bridge crossed a channel hemmed with marble and glazed with the reflection of many cypresses, and joined Trogir to a mainland that showed us a little level paradise under the harsh, bare, limestone hills, where the pepper trees dropped their long green hair over the red walls of villa gardens, and Judas trees showed their stained, uneasy purple flowers through wrought-iron gates. "You see, it came very near, so near that it could not have come any nearer," said the Professor.

He spoke of the time in 1241, just after Radovan had started his portal, when the Mongols, seeking to expand the empire made for them by Genghis Khan, conquered Russia and swept across Europe to Hungary, putting King Bela and his nobles to flight. While he vainly petitioned the other Christian powers to help, the invaders swept on towards Vienna and then swung down to Croatia, burning, looting, killing. King Bela tried to stand firm at Zagreb, and sent his Greek wife and their three children to seek safety on the coast. These were ranging in panic between Split and the fortress of Klish, just behind it in the mountains, when the King joined them, frantic with fear. It is doubtful if even our own times can provide anything as hideous as the Mongol invasion, as this dispensing of horrible death by yellow people made terrible as demons by their own unfamiliarity. It is true that the establishment of the Mongol Empire was ultimately an excellent thing for the human spirit, since it made Asiatic culture available to Europe; but as Peer Gynt said, "Though God is thoughtful for His people, economical, no, that He isn't!"

The King and a tattered, gibbering multitude of nobles and soldiers and priests, bearing with them the body of the saint King Stephen of Hungary, and many holy objects from their churches, trailed up and down the coast. Split received them magnificently, but the King struck away the townsmen's greetings with the fury of a terrified child. The shelter they offered him was useless. They might not know it, but he did. He had seen the Mongols. He demanded a ship to take him out to the islands. Yellow horsemen could not ride the sea. But there was none ready. He shouted his anger and went with his Queen and his train to Trogir, which is within a short distance of many islands. He fled to a neighbouring island, which is still called "The King's Shelter." Some of his followers went with him, but enough stayed in Trogir to carpet the place with sleeping men and women when night fell. Worn out by fatigue, by hunger, by fear, they threw themselves down wherever they could: on the floors of all rooms, in every palace and hovel, all over every church, under Radovan's portal, on the flags of the piazza and the alleys, on the quays. Their treasures cast down beside them, they slept. Every boat too was covered with sleeping bodies and upturned faces, and the rocks of every island.

The Mongols came down on the coast. Nothing could stop them. But at the sea they met a check. They had thought the King must be at Klish or Split, and they were repulsed at both. The shelter offered by the Splitchani was not as negligible as the King had thought. The Mongols were used to unlimited space for their operations, and to attack fortifications from a terrain bounded by the sea or sharply broken ground presented them with a new problem. But they found their way to Trogir; and on to this bridge across the channel they sent a herald who cried out in a loud voice the minatory moral nonsense talked by the aggressor in any age: "Here is the commandment of the Kaïdan, the unconquerable chief of the army: do not uphold the crimes of others, but hand over to us our enemies, lest you be involved in those crimes and perish when you need not." For the herald himself the delivery of this message must have been the supreme moment of his life, either for perverse joy or for pain. For those who heard him tell us that he spoke in Slav as a Slav. He must have been either a traitor or a prisoner. Either he was dooming his own people, whom he loathed, to their ruin, and his words were sweet as honey in his mouth, or he loved his people, and he found his words bitter as gall.

The guards of Trogir made no answer, for they had been ordered by the King to keep silent. Then we find, which is not common, history following a line to which we are accustomed in our private lives. We have all heard spoken tremendous words which must unchain tragedy, we have all recognized the phrase after which there can be nothing but love and happiness; and afterwards nothing has happened, life goes on precisely the same, there is the vacuum of the anticlimax. But in history the pushed boulder usually falls. In Trogir, however, it was not so. After this tremendous moment, nothing happened. The herald cried out his tremendous message, the guards kept silent; and presently the Mongols went home. It is thought that they were considering whether they should ford or bridge the channel, when they received news that their supreme chief, Ogodai, the son of Genghis Khan, had died in Asia, and that the succession was in dispute. They went back at a trot, just taking time to sack and kill on their way, through Southern Dalmatia, where they burned the lovely city of Kotor, and through Bosnia, Serbia, and Bulgaria. Trogir breathed again. The King returned from his islet, and took his nobles and his armies and his priests and the dead St. Stephen and the holy jewels back to Hungary. But the Queen had to stay in Dalmatia for some time, till her two little daughters, Catarina and Margareta, died of a sickness they had contracted during their flight. Their tombs can be seen in Diocletian's mausoleum at Split.

It is the kind of secret that time takes with it: whether the heretics of Trogir leaned on their faith and found it bore them, in those hours when the Mongol sword hung over their heads. But it can be deduced that in a general way it did them no harm, for they came out of the Middle Ages into the Renaissance strong in art and gallant. The interior of the Cathedral, which is two hundred years later than Radovan's work, has a fine form under its immensely rich vault, cut out of stone that has a warm grey bloom; and there is a baptistery, naughtily overdecorated, but with an exquisite series of panels, in each of which a cherub bearing a torch thrusts his way through ponderous closing doors, ostensibly to illustrate some notion concerning immortality, but more probably because the Renaissance had a liking for fine little boys. And everywhere are small but delicious palaces in the Venetian Gothic style, sweetly compact, covered by elegance as by a creeper, with balconies and trellised windows. There is one such, most lovely, facing the Cathedral, the residence of the Chippitch family. It is the very house where there was found the codex of *The Satyricon*. Here in Trogir it is as if events were caught in the rich architecture like wasps in syrup.

When you go into the courtyard of the Chippitch Palace you will find the figureheads of two old ships, one a delicate victory woman, the other a huge cock. Each was made on a long iron stalk, held in a long iron hand. They are violent in character, as if they were made by desperate men. One was the figurehead of the ship manned and financed by Trogir and commanded by Louis Chippitch at the battle of Lepanto in 1571 and the other belonged to the Turkish ship he captured. He put them there when he came home and they have remained there ever since. Again we were made to realize the debt the West owes the people of this coast. The naval power of the Turks was broken at Lepanto and never was reconstituted. What broke it was a fleet composed of one hundred and fourteen Venetian galleys, a hundred and three Spanish galleys, twelve supplied by the Pope, four supplied by the Duke of

Savoy, three from Malta, and seven from the seven Dalmatian towns, although by that time the coast was ravaged and poverty-stricken. Even devastated Rab and Krk sent one apiece. And Trogir's contribution also was a magnificent offering from poverty; for the town was perpetually forced by the Venetians to give money and supplies as bribes to the Turkish military and civil officials on the mainland, and it often knew real need. Not only Rab but Trogir, and indeed every community on this coast, paid in their gold and then blood for the security of the West.

Since Trogir created such beauty and achieved such courage under Venice, the visitor is tempted to believe that foreign dominance was good for Dalmatia. But to think that is to be as superficial as visitors to an orphanage, who at sight of children with washed faces doing neat handwork forget the inevitable wrongs of institutional life. The inhabitants of this coast were looted of their money and their morals by their alien masters. "Come into the Dominican church," said the Professor, "and you will see how savage we were here, how horribly and beautifully savage." In that fine church there is a tomb erected by a noble widow to her murdered husband. Carved as carefully and reverently as any Madonna in a Pietà, an enraged lioness lifts to Heaven a muzzle soft and humid with the hope of vengeance. "It is the vendetta put into stone," said the Professor. "Here the vendetta was a curse as it was in Corsica, because God has made us a very quarrelsome people, and the Hungarians and the Venetians encouraged all our dissensions, so that we should not be a united people and would therefore be more easy for them to subdue."

This policy became more formidable in the fifteenth century, after Trogir had finally become Venetian. Refugees have always presented a grave problem to the countries that have received them. The culture they bring with them must clash with the culture they find established in their new homes. When the Turks overran the Balkan Peninsula some Bosnian and Herzegovinian landowners became Moslems and were left in possession of their lands, but those who clung to their faith fled to Dalmatia. They were pure feudal lords, of a type that had long disappeared from Western Europe, and they could not understand the constitution of the Dalmatian cities, which gave different rights to nobles and citizens, but on that basis defended them with equal justice. The refugees could not understand that they must treat with courtesy lawless men of admittedly inferior social status, and that the nobles also would be against them if they failed to obey this convention; and indeed some of the nobles, who were undemocratic and hated the citizens, were willing to side with the refugees in this. Thus there arose a great deal of civil strife which time would have corrected if the Venetians had not seen in it an opportunity to obey that evil precept, *Divide et impera*. They secretly backed each party against the others, and refrained from any legislative reform that would have sweetened the situation.

But they went in for simpler misconduct. In the seventeenth century Trogir produced a superb example of the learned gentleman of the Renaissance, Giovanni Lucius, or Yovan Lutchitch, a descendant of one of the same Bosnian refugees. He had studied in Rome and devoted his life to research into Croatian and Dalmatian history. His great work *De Regno Dalmatiæ et Croatiæ* is still a classic: he collected a great many original documents, for though he wrote with patriotic passion he was governed by the love of truth. But one of the feuds that Venice encouraged struck him down. A member of a noble family that had long been political enemies of the Lutchitches, Paolo de Andreis, was himself a historian and was himself engaged on a rival work. Dons will be dons, so he informed the authorities that Lutchitch was searching the archives to prove that the Venetians had violated the ancient constitutions of the Dalmatian cities. Later, when the Venetian Governor-general came to visit Trogir and proposed to quarter himself in the Lutchitch Palace, Yovan Lutchitch excused himself on the ground that his sister was gravely ill; and again Andreis went to the authorities, this time to denounce his rival as a liar. Immediately Lutchitch was thrown into prison among common criminals, while a squad of galley slaves cleared his family out of their palace and the Governor-general took possession of it. Lutchitch himself was about to be bastinadoed, but the Bishop of Trogir saved him by appealing to the power of the Church, and got him permission to take refuge in Rome, where he died after thirty-four years of exile, an extravagant punishment for a patriot.

"We have so greatly needed peace, a little peace," said the Professor, "but we have had hardly any. And I will take you now to see a relic of the regime that gave us the fairest promise of it. But I warn you, you will laugh at it, it is not as impressive as it should be." He took us round the wide hem of the city, the space on its quays where the walls used to stand, to the north end of the island. It did not take us long to get there, for this town is incredibly small: one could walk round it in less than ten minutes. "Look at it well!" said the Professor, and we gaped, for what we saw was surprising in this land which is precious about its architecture, which will have nothing that is not superb or ethereal or noble. On a patch of waste ground, beside a medieval tower, there stands a little roofless temple raised on a platform of rough-hewn stones, not at all antique, not at all suggestive of sacrifices to the gods, strongly evocative of an afternoon in the park. Almost it is a bandstand. "Is it not French?" said the Professor. "So neat, so irreverent to the tragic solemnity of the place and its past, so fundamentally admirable. You see the sea used to wash all round it. It is only since we had a Yugoslavia that there have been drained the marshes along the coast which gave the city malaria, and that has involved deepening the main channel and drawing the sea away from this shore. But when Marshal Marmont built this belvedere it was right out among the waves, and he used to sit there with his officers and play cards when it was very hot. That we find very amusing: it is such a light-minded, pleasure-loving thing to do. And yet Marmont was a hero, a great hero, and the only foreign ruler that was truly good for us. Though we find it hard to forgive our conquerors, we could even find it in our hearts to admit that it would have been a good thing if the French had stayed here longer."

It is really a very pretty belvedere; and it has the sacred French air of dealing respectfully and moderately with the little things of life that are not sacred. It is better, yes, it is definitely better, than the muzzle of the lioness wetly throbbing towards the scent of blood. That it knows and has put behind it. The sword was declared superseded in the delicious contentment which was housed here, between the columns, above the rippling Adriatic. For indeed Marmont must have been extraordinarily happy here, for a time. For one thing, he very greatly disliked his wife, and here he was able to treat her extremely well from a very great distance. For another, he adored the place itself, and he was one of those who like the Slav flavour, who find all other peoples insipid by contrast. And he liked the exercise of independent power, as a colonial governor far from home. "He was, of course, a very vain man," said the Professor in a deprecating tone. I wondered why: I have never been able to see why people object to vanity, unless it is associated with blindness to the qualities of others, and it often is not.

But if Marmont was not vain, he was a prig. He must have been very well pleased with himself as he played cards in the belvedere. He was living in accordance with reason and virtue. He might have been very hot, but thanks to this intelligent device he was less hot. He was building up a career, and while many men have had to resort to violence and rapacity to serve their ambition he was at once earning success and disseminating peaceful manners, learning, and hygiene in a land previously barbarian. He did not even compromise his integrity, for he faced quite honestly the moral problem inherent in empire. In his memoirs, which he wrote well for a man of action, he admits that a nation cannot hold alien territories without disingenuous handling of subject populations; he sets down without disguise the plain facts of certain occasions when he found it necessary to play politics and foment misunderstandings among friends in order to establish French authority. It may have happened that, while he waited for a partner to put down a card, he set his eyes on the dancing glass of the Adriatic, or the lion-coloured mountains, trembling like the sea in the heat, and hypnosis made him aware of the question the inner self perpetually asks itself: "What am I doing, and is it good?" The answer he would have overheard would certainly not have been boastful: it might have been proud of the process in which it was engaged, but it would have been modest regarding the extent of its engagement. The universe was in disorder; its sole offensiveness lay in its disorder. Man having been given, whether by a personal or an impersonal force it hardly mattered, a vision of order, he could correct the universe and regiment it into shining harmony. Marmont had pointed his sword at a bulging plinth and bidden it be straight; he had raised his schoolmaster's rod and a fallen column was again erect. He would have claimed no less, but no more, and would have been happy in an exact accountancy of his limited effort.

But the place held a vaster, darker wisdom. On the edge of the city stands this belvedere with its six frail pillars. In the centre of Trogir stands the Cathedral with its portico sombre with the prophecies of Radovan, with his announcement that there is no hope within man, since he is a fusion of light and darkness, like the universe itself; and that he must work for the liberation of the light and not for the reform of the universe, because the universe is evil, by reason of this fusion, and must pass. This is a hard word, hard with the intolerable hardness of mysticism. It is far harder, far more mystical, than the message of orthodox Christianity. It places on man a tremendous obligation to regard his life as a redemptory act, but at the same time it informs him that he is tainted through and through with the substance of damnation, and that the medium through which alone he can perform this act is equally tainted; and it assumes that this obligation is worth accepting and will in fact be crowned with success, simply because of the nature of the abstractions involved, simply because light is light and therefore to be loved.

That it might be as Radovan thought was confirmed by the experience of Marmont; his later card games in the belvedere cannot have been happy at all. Napoleon was called by many The Man, and in his manhood he agreed with the Manichæan conception. He was at first a soldier of the light. Marmont must have felt that in working with him he was driving the darkness engendered by the collapsed Revolution out of France, and out of disturbed Europe. He had, indeed, almost no other grounds for liking the association. It is one of the oddest examples of human irrationality that while most of the people who really knew Napoleon well found him unlovable and something of a bore, innumerable people who were not born until long after his death, and have nothing to go upon except the accounts of these familiars, obstinately adore him; and these have blamed Marmont for coldness and ingratitude to him. But as Marmont explains in his memoirs, he had known Napoleon since his early youth and had never really liked him, and he had no reason to feel gratitude to him, for he had earned every step of his military promotion by concrete achievements that would have been similarly rewarded in any army. He worked with him because they both stood for the same ideal of national order.

The darkness suddenly streamed out of Napoleon's soul; the ray had been white, it was black. There was manifest in his relations with his subordinates the same enjoyment of the exciting discord irrelevant to the theme which is familiar enough as a symptom of sexual degeneration, of incapacity for love. Marmont has recorded in his memoirs, with the exquisite accuracy of a perceptive but unimaginative man, the moment when Napoleon sought to slake his appetite on him, to his perturbation and disgust. During the 1809 campaign Marmont returned to headquarters to report after fighting a brilliant and fatiguing engagement and was received by a scowling and soured Napoleon, who grumbled at him for nearly two and a half hours. When he went back to the hovel where he was billeted he flung himself down in an agony of weariness and humiliation, and was reduced to the extreme of bewildered misery because the room began to fill up with more and more people. Suddenly he found that they had come to congratulate him. The two and a half hours of nagging had been Napoleon's way of adding spice to the promotion of Marmont to the rank of marshal: so might a lover, of the sillier sort, pick a quarrel with the beloved before making her or him a present. But Marmont was interested in the art of war, in France, and in the establishment of the international order he thought most favourable to France; and he could not imagine why his promotion from one rank of the army to another, about which there was nothing unnatural, which was according to routine, should be attended by discourtesy and gross disregard for his feelings. He records it with restraint. Napoleon had long been fallen when he wrote. But behind the well-mannered writing sounds a perplexity. If Napoleon thought I was good enough to be marshal, which was pleasant, why couldn't he have been pleasant about it? Marmont would have liked pleasantness everywhere. The light was in him, seeking to establish its kingdom.

When he first went to Dalmatia it must have seemed that the light in him and in Napoleon was working to free itself from the long captivity it had endured in these darkened lands. A strong and peaceful Illyria emerging from the state of war and anarchy that had lasted since nearly the beginning of recorded time would have shone like the moon coming out of a black cloud. There was a time in Napoleon's life when the whole of Europe appeared to be suffering defeat before France only in order to rise again and put on an immortal brightness. But in a few months the prospect changed. It was as if there had been an eclipse; the Manichæans would have recognized its nature. In Napoleon there seemed now to be nothing but darkness. In Marmont's letters he held up to Napoleon his own conception of a radiant Illyria, part of a transfigured Europe, and asked for support in realizing it, in men, in money, in words. But Napoleon turned away, shutting his eyes as if he could no longer bear the light. He ignored all Marmont's requests and replied in letters hot and sticky with roguishness, or did not reply at all.

In the belvedere Marmont must have found it difficult to keep his mind on his cards. In the end, we know, he threw them in and pushed back his chair and strolled away, to leave Dalmatia for ever. There was fault in him too. He was man also, he was a fusion of good and evil, of light and darkness. Therefore he did not want with his wholeness that there should be a victory of light; he preferred that darkness should continue to exist, and this universe, The Smudge, should not pass away. He showed it, and so did all his reasonable kind, by leaving power in the hands of Napoleon, who had long ceased to be reasonable, who was now seeking disgrace as he had earlier sought glory. He went to Spain, he went to Russia, against the advice of his counsellors, for no other purpose than to make a long journey and be benighted at its end. But the change in him excited no horror in the people; rather their passion for him rose to an orgasm, as if this were the climax to which his glory had been but the preparation. The great men for whom humanity feels ecstatic love need not be good, nor even gifted; but they must display this fusion of light and darkness which is the essential human character; they must even promise, by a predominance of darkness, that the universe shall for ever persist in its imperfection.

After Napoleon had safely led back Europe to the limits of frustration it preferred to paradise, nothing happened in Dalmatia for a hundred years. Austrian rule was sheer negativism. The Slavs were raised up in enmity against the Italian-speaking sections, who were either such descendants of the Roman settlers as had never amalgamated with the Slavs, or Venetian immigrants. There was no coherence; very little trade, since the Austrian railway system was designed to encourage the prosperity of Austria and Hungary and leave the Slav territories isolated from the rest of Europe. In Trogir grass grew in the streets and piazzas. But the tradition of its rich civic life was not broken. After the war this town, like many another on the Dalmatian coast, was coveted by the Italians, who one September night in 1919 sent a small party of soldiers to seize it. It should have been defended by eight Yugoslav soldiers, but these had too ingenuously accepted hospitality of some pro-Italians on the previous evening and were all unconscious. So when the inhabitants woke up in the morning they found their town in possession of Italian soldiers. There were, however, only five families that were pro-Italian; and the rest of the population rushed at the invaders and disarmed them with their bare hands. One woman ran at four men in charge of a machine-gun and took it away from them, and many others chased out runaway Italians who had taken refuge in the courtyards of the houses, beating them with their fists and tearing away their helmets and belts. "I do not tell you their names," said the Professor, "because it is a very disagreeable thing for a lady to have to commit such violent acts, and these were not viragoes, they were ladies. But I can assure you that they bore names which have been distinguished in the annals of Trogir for many centuries, and that they were none of them ignorant of their ancestors' achievements."

It is a very quiet city now: an empty city, for it suffered like Rab from a terrible visitation of the plague, and the population has never replenished itself, because the malaria that raged here till recently caused sterility. But it exists. That is to be noted, for there is a legend all over Europe which leaves not one of its stones standing upon another. Close by the Cathedral there is a loggia which was the ancient hall of justice, undatable because it was built of bits and pieces from the old town which was destroyed by the Saracens and from near-by Roman settlements. It was in ruins during the Austrian occupation, and it was roofed and made decent by the Yugoslav Government. Nevertheless in all anti-Slav circles it has become a symbol of the barbarity of the Yugo-slavs, because of a very small defacement. It happened that on the wall behind the stone table at which the judges used to sit there was placed during the late fifteenth century a winged lion of St. Mark, surrounded by saints and emblems of justice. Every Dalmatian town bears such a symbol at one place or more, on a wall or a gate, or a public building, and always it is beautiful. The lion is always waved and opulent, and reminds one that it was Bronzino and Paris Bordone who first celebrated the type which we know now, in brass instead of gold, as Mae West. To judge from photographs the lion in the loggia was a specially glorious example of its kind, a *lilium auratum* in stone. While the Austrians were in Dalmatia the wind and the rain beat on this lion, but it was properly sheltered after the Yugoslavs had done their repairs.

It unfortunately happened, however, that about Christmastime in 1932 some young men of Trogir got drunk, and their larger, simpler emotions were liberated. They then remembered that the Italians had tried to steal their city, and had not given up the hope of doing so some day; and they inflicted severe damage on this lion and another at the port gate of the town. They were not utterly destroyed. They still exist, in a quite recognizable form, on the walls of a museum. This was one of those incidents which prove it to be a matter of sheer luck that man does not go on all fours, but it obviously had no other significance. Italy, however, took the opportunity to give an extraordinary exhibition of her intentions towards Dalmatia. There took place all over the country dem-onstrations against the Yugoslavian Government, organized by two so-cieties which exist for the purpose of such mischief-making, Dalmatia Irredenta and Pro-Dalmatia. Mussolini himself declared that in the mild hooliganism of the intoxicated young men he saw "the clear expression of a mentality of hate that made no secret of its opposition to Italy. . . . It is a carefully premeditated plan. . . . The responsible parties are to be found among elements of the ruling classes. . . . The lions of Trogir are destroyed, but in their destruction they stand stronger than ever as a living symbol and a certain promise." To keep the peace the Yugo-slavian Government had to eat dirt and, what is worse, harden its tradition of mercilessness towards its own people by suppressing the counter-demonstrations against Italy which naturally took place all over Yugoslavia.

The wickedness and absurdity of Mussolini's proceedings can be estimated if one imagines Great Britain making hostile demonstrations against Ireland because some drunken boys in Cork had destroyed a couple of Union Jacks that had been left there during the English occupation. But that does not quite express the perversity of the Italian attitude, for it must further be remembered that Trogir had not belonged to Venice for a hundred and forty years, at which time it would have been impossible for a Roman or the inhabitant of any other Italian city except Venice to feel any emotion whatsoever regarding an insult to the lion of St. Mark, except perhaps a lively sympathy. This immense forgery of feeling led on to a forgery of fact. There spread all over Italy and into Central Europe, and thence all over the world, a belief that the inhabitants of Trogir had destroyed all the historic beauties of their town, and even their entire town. "What, you went to Trogir?" a refugee German professor said to me in London, after my first visit to Dalmatia. "But it cannot have been worth your while, now that these barbarous Yugoslavs have levelled everything worth looking at to the ground. Ah, if you had only visited it, when I did, two years before the war! You can have no idea how beautiful it was then!" Medieval Europe was ignorant, it believed in unicorns and mermaids, it debated how many angels could dance on the point of a needle. The folly of modern Europe provides us with no agreeable decorative symbols, it does not lead us to debate on the real fact of the different planes of existence. It pretends for mean motives that a city which stands steadily among the moving waters, its old buildings and its old families as they have been for seven hundred years, is not.

Split III

My husband was reading to me from Count Voinovitch's *Histoire de Dalmatie* a fairy story that they tell about the Emperor Diocletian all over this coast and Bosnia and Herzegovina and Montenegro. It is a variant of the story we all know about Midas. It seems that he had a ridiculous physical secret which he could keep from all the world except his barber, a little matter of ears like an ass and horns like a ram. So his barbers shaved him but once, and were never heard of again. At last a barber who was the only son of a widow was told that the next day he must shave the Emperor's beard. He was overcome with horror, but his mother told him not to despair, and made him a little cake moistened with her own milk, and said to him, "While you are shaving the Emperor take a bit of this cake." When he did so, Diocletian smelt the curious odour of the paste, and asked for a piece of it. He liked it, but found the taste peculiar, and felt he knew it yet could not name it. "What did your mother use to moisten this cake?" he asked. "Her own milk," answered the barber. "Then we are brothers and I cannot kill you," said the Emperor. Thereafter the story follows familiar lines: the barber's life is spared, but he is sworn to silence, and he is so inconvenienced by the secret that he murmurs it to a reed, which is made into a flute by the village children and repeats it whenever it is played.

"How characteristic it is of the Slavs to keep on telling this story," said my husband; "it is so packed with criticism of the idea of power. The folk imagination that invented it is responsible to the majesty of the Emperor and his usefulness to the community, and it recognizes that he can exercise power and that his subjects can obey him only if there is a convention that he is superhuman, that he has none of the subhuman characteristics which compose humanity. The Emperor must therefore be permitted to commit acts in defence of this convention which would be repulsive if an individual committed them for his private ends. But here nature speaks, through the mother, who is a superb example of the hatefulness of women as Strindberg sees it. She pulls down what men have built up by an appeal to the primitive facts of life which men have agreed to disregard in order that they may transcend them. She proves to the Emperor that after all he is an individual, that the murder he commits for the sake of maintaining a useful convention may be a social act

but is also fratricide on a basis of reality. But the story does not give her
the victory either, for it gives a warning that, once a breach is made in
that convention, it must fall; what the barber knows the village children
must know before long, and then there must be anarchy. The story is
perfectly balanced; but it shows bias to have preserved it, and that bias
would make it very difficult for Slavs ever to settle down under a government, and lead a *rangé* political life."

"I wonder what the woman really put in the cake," I said, "for it requires a great deal of explanation if the widowed mother of a grown-up
son should have any milk. But what on earth are our friends doing? It is
half-past eight." For we were in our bedroom, waiting for a lady and her
husband, Mr. and Mrs. X., who were to take us to a charity festival in
the town, where there was to be a dance and a cabaret supper, and there
we were to meet other friends of ours, Mr. and Mrs. A., and spend the
evening with the four of them. "Yes, something must have gone wrong,"
said my husband, "for they said they would come at seven." "Then let us
go downstairs and have dinner," I demanded. "No," said my husband,
"if we do that we will eat a lot at dinner because it is so good, and then
we will have to eat more food at the dance, and we are effete Westerners.
If you are hungry, it is your own fault for rejecting the waiter's advice,
and not keeping that nice cold palatschinken by you." And indeed it
was only a few minutes later that Mr. and Mrs. X. sent up a message to
say that they were in the hall of the hotel, but would be glad if we did
not come down but received them in our room, as they wished to speak
to us on a private matter.

As soon as they entered, Mrs. X., who was an exquisite creature made
of moonlight and soot-black shadows, cast from her slimness her heavy
coat, which fell from her like a declaration in recitative. Both she and
her husband, who was himself exceedingly handsome, were in a state
of excitement that recalled Italian opera. It was tragic yet not painful,
it was accomplished and controlled, and yet perfectly sincere. What it
was putting forward as important, it in fact felt to be important. They
both began by apologizing to us deeply, for having kept us waiting, for
not being able to offer us the most intense and comprehensive hospitality
possible. But they had found themselves unable to carry out Mr. A.'s
plan for the evening. Absolutely unable; and it was astonishing that
Mr. A. could have conceived that it should be otherwise. He would
never have put forward such a proposal had he not been exposed to alien
influences, had he not just returned from several years in the United

States and had his wife not been a Czech. This had, naturally enough, no doubt, made him insensitive to the state of public opinion in Split.

When the X.'s had first received Mr. A.'s letter two hours before, they said, warming up nicely, they had looked at each other in horror. For it had presented them with a dilemma. Mr. A. would not have put forward his proposal had it not suited our convenience. Was it therefore their duty to overlook the affront it offered to the public opinion of Split in order to fulfil the Dalmatian ideal of hospitality? To decide this they had visited a friend, a judge ninety years old, of a very ancient Splitchani family, who was a connexion of Mr. X.'s mother. He had told them that he considered the question immensely delicate, but that he understood we had shown signs of sensibility and it was therefore unlikely we would wish them to violate the feeling of their birthplace. The judge had added that as we were travelling abroad instead of being in England at the time of the Coronation, we were probably members of some party which was in opposition to the Government, and would be the more ready to understand their point of view. So Mr. and Mrs. X. had gone to see Mr. and Mrs. A., who had seen their point of view when it was explained to them, and had instantly apologized, but had had to go to the festival all the same, as they had promised to act as judges in some competition; and they had, indeed, framed an alternative plan for the evening which we might perhaps consider, if we were not incensed against hosts who altered their programme of hospitality for the sake of their own honour.

We felt unworthy subject-matter for this excitement, and we realized that there had been some monstrous over-estimation of the delicacy of our sentiments. So might two comfortable toads feel if the later Henry James and Edith Wharton at her subtlest insisted on treating them as equals. "Let me give you some of the brandy I have brought from London," said my husband, and I could see that the poor creature was trying to make a claim to some sort of fineness, even though it were other than that which they were ascribing to us. We all sipped brandy with an air of sustaining ourselves during a crisis. Then they went on to explain that Mr. A. had forgotten that whereas the charitable festival was being held for the benefit of some fund for supplying the poor with medical attention, it was organized by Dr. and Mrs. Y., emigrated Jews from Zara, the Dalmatian town which has been handed over to the Italians, who were almost the only prominent pro-Yugoslavians in the town, and who might use this fund in co-operation with institutions which ought to be ignored, because they had been founded by the Government. The charity festival was therefore being boycotted by all the considerable families in Split, of the social level of Mr. and Mrs. X., or Mr. and Mrs. A. Other people could take us, if we cared to go. But it was impossible, the X.'s assured us in something like a duet by the early Verdi, impossible that they should do so.

We refrained from warning them that some day they might have something really worth worrying about; and we intimated that, as we had promised a very civil shopkeeper friend of ours to go to this festival, we should prefer to keep our promise. This we did, and enjoyed a spectacle of nice-looking young people performing with graceful awkwardness under the eyes of adoring parents, of which we had seen the like in Exeter, in Edinburgh, and in Cleveland, Ohio. There are a few institutions which are universal, and it is pleasant when one proves to be pretty and innocent. But the organizers, the doctor and his wife, were interesting and pathetic. They seemed outside the Splitchani tradition, not because they were Jews, but because they belonged to that warm and idealistic and intelligent breed of Jew that puts its trust in synthesis and centralization. Always they would assume that hatred and stupidity were peculiar local conditions, which any general government would make its business to correct; and this optimism would be reinformed by their knowledge that there does in fact exist a unifying force, which on the whole is benevolent, in science. They were both learning English, and they beamed as they spoke of it. It appeared to them, much more clearly than it did to me, that they were associating themselves with liberalism. But that was only part of their buoyant Utopianism, which believed that if a large enough number of charity festivals of this kind were held, if enough people studied a language other than their own, if enough vows of tolerance were taken by the state, there would be an end to poverty, war, and misery. I could only hope that, holding such inoffensive views in our offensive age, they might be permitted to die in their beds.

Our four friends, the X.'s and the A.'s, met us in the principal café of the town after the entertainment, and we took an early opportunity to ask them why they and their world were against the Yugoslav state. Their first reply was simply to look very handsome. Their eyes widened, their nostrils dilated. The natural exception was Mrs. A., the Czech, who seemed, like ourselves, a little gross by contrast. We were in effect watching racehorses racing, beautiful specialized animals demonstrating their speciality, which was opposition. I had to remind myself that this con-

centration on opposition had substantially contributed to the saving of
Western Europe from Islam. Few of us have as much reason to be thank-
ful to the plainer and blunter virtues as to this cloak-and-sword romanticism that I saw before me; and they themselves owed their very existence to it. Only that had saved them from Rome, from the barbarian
invaders, from the Hungarians and Venetians, from the Turks, from the
Austrians. But all the same a government which was not seeking to
destroy them but to co-operate with them must find this attitude so
maddening that it would be not unnatural did it sometimes behave as if
it were seeking their destruction.

"Tell me," said my husband, "some specific things that you find ob-
jectionable about Yugoslavia." "Belgrade!" exclaimed Mr. and Mrs. X.
in one voice. "This country," Mr. X. explained, "is fantastically and
extraordinarily poor. You would not believe how poor the poor people
in our city are, how poor nearly all the people in the country outside
are. The Government does nothing for us, but they take our taxes and
they spend them in Belgrade. They are putting up whole new streets of
offices, there is not a Ministry that hasn't a palace for its home. Is that
fair, when down here we lack bread?" "It was a wretched little village
before the war," said Mrs. X., "a pig-town. It made one laugh to see it,
particularly if one had been to Zagreb. But now they are turning it into
a place like Geneva, with public buildings six and seven stories high, all
at our expense." "But do you not think that is necessary?" asked my husband. "For it was because Serbia had such a capital as Belgrade was
before the war that the Austrian Foreign Office used to treat the Serb
diplomats as if they were farm labourers come up to the great house
with an impertinent demand." "But the Serbs are not like us," said Mrs.
X. vaguely. "They are not like us, they have not the tradition that we
have here in Split. And how can Belgrade ever be such a beautiful town
as our Split?"

"I see the problem from a different aspect," said Mr. A., "because I
have been in America for a very long time. It does not shock me so
much that Dalmatia should be governed from Belgrade, for I have lived
in Milwaukee for many years, and things went very well there, though
we were governed from Washington, which was far further away from
us than Belgrade is from Split. And I have been to Washington, which is
a fine city, and I know it is right that the government of a great country
should have impressive buildings. But my case against Belgrade is that
it governs badly. Oh, I know there is corruption and graft in American
politics, but you have no idea what it is like here. The trouble is not

only that, as X. says, the money goes to Belgrade, it's what happens to it
when it gets there. It sticks to people's palms in the most disgusting way.
There are ever so many people in Belgrade who have made fortunes,
huge fortunes, by peculation. And that's the only activity in which they
ever show any efficiency. For the idiotic muddle of the administration
is beyond belief."

"It is worse, then, than it was under the Austrians?" asked my husband. They looked at him in astonishment. "Not at all," said Mr. A.;
"the Austrians were not inefficient at all. They were assassins. Look
what they did here with the railways!" They all broke out into cries
of anger and disgust. "Why, think of it," said Mr. X., "the railway
stopped outside Split, so as to make sure we should be nothing of a
port." "And we could not go to Austria except through Budapest," said
Mrs. X. "That was the Hungarian influence, of course," said Mr. A.
"But Austria permitted it," said Mr. X. "Permitted it!" cried Mrs. A.,
the Czech. "Tell me when those who speak German have not rejoiced
in humiliating the Slavs. And there are people in your country," she
said to us, "who are sorry for the German-speaking minorities in Czechoslovakia. There are beings so charitable that they would get up funds
to provide feeding-bottles for baby alligators."

But my husband persisted. "Then you found the Austrians efficient
in what? Assassination only?" "In that certainly," said Mr. A., "but
they were also far more efficient than our present Government in the
everyday routine of administration. Take the case of my family. Several
of them have been university professors. Now, the old ones, who retired under the Austrians, never had any difficulty in getting their pensions. They drew their pay, they retired, they filled in papers, they drew
the appointed sum. Nothing could have been simpler. But now there
is terrible disorder. I have an uncle, a professor of mathematics, who retired months ago. He fulfilled all the requisite formalities, but he has
not yet touched a penny of his pension. The papers have not come
through from Belgrade, for no other reason than sheer muddle." "And it
is so, too, in my profession," said Mr. X. "I am a lawyer, it is the calling
of my family, and some of my older relatives are judges. It is the same
with pensions, and appointments, and even dates for trials, everything
that comes from Belgrade. There is endless bother and muddle. And we
are not accustomed to such things in Split, for here we manage our
affairs simply, it may be, but with a certain distinction." "Ah, yes," said
Mrs. A., "if they would leave us Splitchani to manage our own affairs,
that would be all we ask."

"But there are affairs which are certainly your own, but which equally you cannot manage," said my husband. "You could not yourselves have got rid of Austria, and you cannot yourselves protect yourselves if she comes back, or if Italy wants to establish the same domination over you." They looked at him with preoccupied bright eyes, and said, "Of course, of course." "And though some money must vanish in Belgrade in peculation, since that inevitably happens in every new country," said my husband, "a great deal must be spent in legitimate enterprises. There is, after all, Macedonia and Old Serbia. I have not yet been there, but my wife tells me it has been revolutionized since the days when it was Turkish, that she has seen with her own eyes hundreds of miles of good military roads, whole districts of marshes that have been drained and now are no longer malarial, and many schools and hospitals. All that costs money." "Yes, there was nothing down there in those parts," said Mr. A. without enthusiasm. "They are nearly barbarians," said Mrs. X., wrinkling her nose with distaste. "Have you ever been there?" asked my husband. They shook their heads. Split is two days' easy journey from Old Serbia, three days from the heart of Macedonia. "It is not easy for us to go to such places," said Mrs. X.; "here in Split we have a certain tradition, we would not be at home there."

When we got back to our room in the hotel, my husband said, "All this is very sad. Men and women have died and lived for the ideal of Yugoslavia, the South Slav state; and here are these very charming people chafing with discontent at the realization of it. And so far as I can see, however bad Belgrade may be, they give it no chance to prove its merits. These people are born and trained rebels. They cry out when they see a government as if it were a poisonous snake, and seize a stick to kill it with, and in that they are not being fanciful. All the governments they have known till now have been, so far as they are concerned, poisonous snakes. But all the same that attitude would be a pity, if they happened to meet a government for once who was not a poisonous snake.

"Moreover, I cannot see how these people can ever fit into a modern state. They are essentially the children of free cities. Because all these towns, even while they were exploited and oppressed so far as their external relations were concerned, possessed charters that gave them great freedom to manage their internal affairs. Under the Hungarian crown the towns enjoyed the same sort of freedom, as of a state within a state, that the City of London enjoyed under Henry the First. Their rights were ceaselessly attacked by Venice, but they managed to defend most of them. They were forced to provide men for the Venetian

Army and Navies, and their trade was ruined by the restrictions laid upon it; but they were always to some extent masters at their own firesides. They really cannot conceive of a centralized government at all as otherwise than an evil: and when they got rid of Austria there must have been a childish idea at the back of their minds that they had also got rid of a centralized government, and would return to medieval conditions. Alas! Alas!"

"Look," I said, "I am watching three people talking in the square. They are so very picturesque; come and see them." My husband turned out the light and came and sat beside me on the window-seat. The square was whitewashed with moonlight; the dark shadows took the nineteenth-century Venetian Gothic architecture and by obscuring the detail and emphasizing the general design made it early, authentic, exquisite. On the quay ships slept, as alone among inanimate objects ships can sleep; their lights were dim and dreaming. Between the flaked trunk of a palm tree and the wild-haired shadow of the leaves stood three men of the quick and whippy and secret kind we had seen when we first entered Split, descendants of those who had lived through the angry centuries the lives of rats and mice in the walls of Diocletian's palace. Sometimes we could hear their voices raised in lyrical mockery, and sometimes they made gestures that united them on a platform of heroism and loaded some absent person with ridicule and chains. "Yes, they are wonderful," said my husband. "Though they probably have no noble ideas, they are noble in the intensity of their being, and in the persistency with which they try to identify their standards and the ultimate values of right and wrong. See how they are pretending that behind them, had one but the proper eyesight, could be seen the wings of the hierarchy of angels and the throne itself, and that behind the man they are despising is primeval ooze and chaos. These people are profoundly different from us. They are not at all sentimental, but they are extremely poetic. How they examine everything, and analyse it, and form a judgment on it that engenders a supply of the passion which is their motive power! How I should hate to govern these people who would not accept the idea of government and would insist on examining it, but only as a poet does, from the point of view of his own experience, which is to say that they would reject all sorts of information about it which they ought to consider if they are going to form a just opinion about it."

We watched the three men till a languor showed in their vehemence. They had laughed so much at the fourth man who was not there that any further mockery would seem an anticlimax. The night was left to

SPLIT FROM MOUNT MARIAN

THE GOLDEN DOOR OF DIOCLETIAN'S PALACE

the sleeping ships, to the temporary romantic perfection of the Venetian arcades. "Get into bed," my husband said, "and I will read you the other story which Voinovitch says the Dalmatian peasantry tell about the Emperor Diocletian." It was the prettier of the two. It represents Diocletian's daughter, Valeria, as the victim of her father; not, as in fact she was, as the subject of a good worldly marriage that went maniacally wrong, but with a destiny cut fairy-tale fashion. She had, according to this story, a crowd of suitors, and of these her father chose a prince whom she could not tolerate. So she refused obedience, and upon this her father cast her into one of the dungeons in his palace. But God was on her side. Once a year invisible hands opened the door of her prison, and she travelled through the city clad in cloth of gold, in a shining chariot drawn by winged horses. Her presence was a benediction, and anybody who could stop the chariot and embrace her would be happy all the rest of his life. When Diocletian heard of these visits he sent soldiers to clear the streets, but it could not be done. The people worshipped Valeria and would not be driven away. Then Diocletian decided to kill her. But the walls of her prison melted, and not all his power could discover her. According to this legend, she still lives, and once every hundred years she comes back to her worshippers. It is not known what year of the century she chooses for her visit, but be that as it may, her visit always falls at Christmastide. When they are saying the midnight mass in the Cathedral, a procession of ghosts starts from Salonæ and winds up the road to Split; and at the end the lovely young Valeria rides in her golden coach, still able to give lifelong happiness to all that embrace her. She still, it must be observed, carries on her quarrel with authority. She was at odds with her pagan father, but she does not attend the Christian mass.

"See, this story cuts at the root of the idea of power," said my husband; "it denies all necessary sanctions to authority. For power claims to know what life is going to be about and what prescription to offer, and authority claims to be able to enforce that prescription. But the Slav knows, as this story proves, that life, which is to say Valeria, is in essence unpredictable, that she often produces events for which there is no apt prescription, and that she can be as slippery as an eel when wise men attempt to control her; and they know that it is life, not power or authority, that gives us joy, and this often when she is least predictable. Knowing Valeria, they cannot respect Diocletian; yet they produce Diocletian, they are Diocletian, they know perfectly well that power and authority are necessary."

BOAT

On another great white steamer we glided down the coast to Korchula, and received at one port, and put ashore at another, the older of the two German couples with whom we had travelled from Salzburg to Zagreb. They hastened towards us uttering cries of welcome, excessively glad to see us because their holiday had made them excessively glad about everything. The man no longer looked ill; he seemed bound to his wife by a common novel satisfaction, as if they had been on their honeymoon. "It is so good here," they laughed, "one forgets all one's worries." There seemed fresh evidence for the malignity of the universe in the sight of these Aryans, blossoming in their temporary exile from Germany, when all over England and France and America so many Jews were mourning for the fatherland in a grief visible as jaundice. Another of Dalmatia's angry young men watched them coldly as they disembarked. "I am a hotel manager at Hvar," he said. Hvar is a beautiful town, which lies on an island of the same name. It is noted for the extraordinary sweetness of its air, which is indeed such as might be inhaled over a bed of blossoming roses, and by a perversity rare in the Serbo-Croat tongue it is pronounced "Whar." "Your friends will presently come to me and demand impossible terms. They are a curious people, the Germans. They seem content to travel when we would prefer to stay at home. Where is the pleasure of travelling if you cannot spend freely? Yet these Germans come here and have to count every penny and do not seem at all embarrassed. Now, that is all right if one is a poor student at Zagreb or Vienna, or is ill and has to go to a spa. But for a tourist it seems very undignified." It had struck me before that there are many resemblances between the Slavs and the Spanish, and this spoke with the very voice of Spain, in its expression of the purse-pride which comes not from wealth but from poverty, in its conception of handsome spending as an inherently good thing, to be indulged in, like truthfulness, even against one's economic interest.

The angry young man scowled down at the marbled blue and white water that rushed by our ship. "I have read in Jackson's great book on Dalmatia," said my husband, to soothe him, "that the inhabitants of the island of Hvar added to their income by making a sweet wine called *prosecco*, by distilling rosemary water, and by making an insecticide from the wild chrysanthemum. Do they still do all those pleasant things?" "Not to any extent," answered the young man, his brows enraged. "Now they cultivate the tourist traffic all summer, and talk politics all winter. Politics and politics and politics, I am sick of politics. Why can we never have any peace? Why must there always be all this conflict?" He was as angry as the young man who had been angry with the gardener at Trsat, or the other who had been angry with the cold soup on the boat to Rab, and it was with them that he felt angry. My husband attempted to comfort him by telling him that in England we were suffering from marked deterioration of political life, and even of national character, because we have no effectual opposition. "But here there is nothing but disputes and disputes and disputes!" cried the young man.

There had been standing beside us a middle-aged man in expensive clothes, who was holding up his hand to hide the left side of his face. He now pressed forward and made what was evidently a sharp remark to the angry young hotel manager, who turned to us and said gloomily, "This man, who is a native of Hvar, says that I do wrong to speak to you like this, for it might discourage you from visiting Hvar, and it is certainly the most beautiful place in the world. I hope I have not done that?" The middle-aged man interrupted in German, "Yes, you must not take what he says too seriously, for though we in Hvar are quarrelsome, as all Slavs are (it is the curse that has been laid upon us), that does not alter its extraordinary beauty. You must not miss visiting us, indeed you must not." "We cannot do so now," said my husband, "for we have made definite plans to go to Korchula today. But we will try to stop at Hvar on our way back." "Yes, that you must do! For, though I do not want to be discourteous to a sister island, and indeed all Dalmatia is glorious country, Korchula has little to show compared to Hvar." He began to speak of their main street, which is broad and paved with marble and lined with fifteenth-century palaces weathered to warm gold; of the old Venetian arsenal, that had a dry dock for the galleys below and above a theatre, the first theatre to be built in the Balkans, which is still just as it was in the seventeenth century, though the curtains in the boxes are thin as paper; of the Franciscan monastery that stands on a piny headland, with its picture of the Last Supper which is so marvellous that a Rothschild who had been made an English duke had tried to buy it from the monks for as many sovereigns as would cover the canvas; and of the lovely garden that had been made on the hill above the town, by a pupil of our dear Professor at Split, who had wished to emulate his teacher's achievement in planting the woods on Mount Marian, which is as pretty a testimony to the value of humanist education as I know. During his story there sometimes came to him living phrases which made actual the beauty of his home, and then his hand dropped, no longer feeling it urgent to hide the port-wine stain that ravaged the left side of his face from temple to chin; and when the steamer entered Hvar harbour, and it was as he had said, he let his hand drop by his side.

When these new friends had left us and we were out in midchannel, I picked up a guide-book, but soon laid it down again, saying to my husband peevishly, "This guide-book is written by a member of my sex who is not only imbecile but bedridden. She is wrong about every place we have been to, so wildly wrong that it seems probable that not only can she never have visited any of these particular cities, but that she can have seen no scenery at all, urban or rural." "I think," said my husband, "that that is perhaps something of an over-statement. In any case there is no need for you to keep your eyes down on any guide-book, you might just as well be looking at the islands, which are really becoming very beautiful now that they support some trees. But I rather suspect that you are nervous about coming to Korchula and do not want to face it until the last moment." "Well, neither I do," I admitted. "I must own that I am seriously nervous about it, because I can't believe that it had quite the revelatory quality I thought it had last year. You see, I passed it on my way from Split to Dubrovnik last year. I had been asleep on one of the benches on deck, and I woke suddenly to find that we were lying beside the quay of a little walled town which was the same creamy-fawn colour as some mushrooms and some puppies. It covered a low, rounded peninsula and was surmounted by a church tower, rising from it like a pistil from a flower; and its walls girt it so massively that they might have been thought natural cliffs if a specially beautiful lion of St. Mark had not certified them as works of art.

"Standing on the quayside was a crowd which was more male in quantity and in quality than we are accustomed to in Western Europe. There were very few women, and the men were very handsome with broad shoulders and long legs and straight hair, and an air of unashamed satisfaction with their own good looks which one finds only where there is very little homosexuality. The faces of the crowd were turned away from the steamer. They were all staring up a street that ran down the steepness of the town to the quay. Presently there was a hush, all the window-sashes of the quayside houses were thrown up, and the crowd shuffled apart to make a clear avenue to the gangway. Then there came out of the street and along this alley four men carrying a stretcher on which there lay a girl of about sixteen. The air was so still that there could be heard the quick padding of the stretcher-bearers' feet on the dust, and as they left the street its mouth filled up with people who stood gaping after them. This must have been a notorious tragedy in the town, for the girl was extravagantly beautiful, as beautiful as Korchula itself, and she was very ill. The shadows on her face were blue. She was being taken, a sailor said, to a hospital at Dubrovnik, but I am sure not by her own consent. It was evident that she had wholly lost the will to live. Her hands lay lax and open on the magenta coverlet; and as they turned her stretcher round to manœuvre it onto the gangway, she opened her eyes and looked up at the tall ship in hostility, loathing it because it was something and she wanted nothingness. Behind her the alley closed, the crowd formed into a solid block and stared at us as if we were taking with us a sign and a wonder.

"But the crowd divided again. Another four men hurried along, bearing this time a chair to which there was strapped an old woman, so immensely old that she had nothing to do with the substance of flesh; she seemed to be compounded of glittering intelligence and a substance more than bony, resembling the hard parts of a very aged and gnarled lobster. She looked towards the steamer with an air of unconquerable appetite. It was something, and therefore better than nothingness, which was what she feared. When the stretcher-bearers halted in manœuvring her up the gangway she rose up in her chair, a twisted hieroglyphic expressing the love of life, and uttered an angry sound she might have used to a mule that was stopping in midstream.

"Now that was something worth while seeing for itself. But it also seemed typical of life in Yugoslavia, in the Balkans, because I had been able to see it. In Western Europe or in America it would have been highly unlikely that I would see an old woman or a young girl who were desperately ill, unless they were my relatives or close friends, and then my interest in them as individuals would distract my attention from their general characteristics. I might have guessed, and indeed had done so, from a great many subtle indications, that the appetite for life comes in eating, though not by any simple process of taste. Experience often causes people to pass an adverse judgment on life, and if they fall ill when they still hold this opinion with the violence of youth they may die of it, should their personalities be vehement enough. But if they live long enough they seem to be governed by a kind of second strength, a secret core of vitality. There is a Finnish word, 'sisu,' which expresses this ultimate hidden resource in man which will not be worsted, which takes charge when courage goes and consciousness is blackened, which insists on continuing to live no matter what life is worth. This may mean only that the skeleton wishes to keep its accustomed garment of flesh, that the eyeball fears to feel naked without the many-coloured protection of sight; but it might mean that the whole of us knows some argument in favour of life which the mind has not yet apprehended. But the point is that here in Yugoslavia I did not have to poke about among the detritus of commonplace life to find allusions to this process: an old woman and a young girl came out into the street and gave a dramatic rendering of it in the presence of the people. It is that quality of visibility that makes the Balkans so specially enchanting, and it was at Korchula that I had the first intimations of it. So naturally I am alarmed lest I find the town not so beautiful as I had supposed, and life in the Balkans precisely the same as everywhere else."

Korchula I

WE found, however, that I was perfectly right about Korchula. "And let that be enough for you," said my husband. "As for your other demands that from now on every day will be an apocalyptic revelation, I should drop that, if I were you. You might not like it even if you got it." We were talking as we unpacked in the room we had taken in the hotel on the quay, which is either a converted Venetian palace or built by one accustomed to palaces from birth. A good hotel, it showed that expiatory cleanliness which is found sometimes in southern countries; from early in the morning till late at night, women were on their knees in the corridors as if in prayer, scrubbing and scrubbing, and murmuring to themselves through compressed lips. It was scented with the classic kitchen smell of the Mare Internum, repellent only to the effete, since it asserts that precious plants can live in waterless and soilless country, that even after centuries of strife and misery woman still keeps the spirit to put a pinch of strong flavour in the cook-pot, and that it takes the supreme assault of urban conditions to bring on humanity the curse of a craving for insipidity. Our fellow-guests were a couple of men as floridly grave as wreathed Cæsars, and their two ladies, both in cloaks, who might have been travelling for the same romantic and detective reasons as Donna Anna and Donna Elvira: ornaments of the Sushak wine trade and their wives.

"I will lie down and sleep for half an hour," I said, looking at the clean coarse sheets, bluish and radiant with prodigious laundering. "I will sit here and look at the maps," said my husband, who is much given to that masculine form of auto-hypnosis. But we did neither of these things, for there was a knock at the door and an announcement that two gentlemen of the town, who had received a letter about us from a friend at Split, were waiting for us downstairs. We had no idea who these people might be. My husband imagined mild antiquaries living among the ruins of Korchula like ageing doves; I thought of mildewed Irish squires. We went downstairs and found two handsome men in early middle age telling the hotel-keeper's wife to be sure to cook us a good fish for dinner that night, and give us a certain red wine grown on the island, and it was as if we looked on a Venetian picture come to life, for the heads of all were bowed intently towards the argument, the men's ges-

203

tures were wide and made from expanded chests, the woman promised them obedience with the droop of her whole body. Of the men one had the great head and full body of a Renaissance cardinal, the other had the rejecting crystal gaze of a Sitwell. They dismissed the hotel-keeper's wife with a National Gallery gesture and turned to welcome us. They told us that they would be pleased to act as our guides in the town, and would start now, if we wished, with any destination we pleased. We expressed our gratitude, and said that we would leave it to them where we should go. The gentleman with the Sitwell gaze then said: "Perhaps you would like to see our new steam bakery."

Neither myself nor my husband replied. We both sank into a despondent reverie, wondering why he should think we wanted to see a new steam bakery. We could only suppose that to him we were representatives of a Western civilization that was obsessed with machinery, and perhaps he suspected us of thinking for that reason that in Dalmatia they ate no bread, or only bread prepared in a filthy way. Fortunately the one who looked like a cardinal blanketed the topic by saying, not accurately, "Ah, but you will have seen many, many steam bakeries; you would like better to see our old churches and palaces."

We walked along the quay that runs round the point of the little peninsula, following the walls, and then went up a steep little street, close-packed with palaces, which thrust out balconies to one another or were joined by bridges, into the town. We found it like a honeycomb; it was dripping with architectural richness, and it was laid out in an order such as mathematicians admire. But its spirit was riotous, the honey had fermented and turned to mead. The men who accompanied us had fine manners, and only by a phrase or two did they let us gather that they appreciated how beautiful Korchula must seem to us because they had known the great towns of the West, Berlin and Paris, and found them filthy; but they were not exquisites, they were robust. They climbed the steep streets at a great rate, telling us the historic jokes of the town with gusts of laughter, and apologizing for the silence that they shattered by owning that the city had never repopulated itself after the attack of plague in the sixteenth century, that had taken five thousand citizens out of seven thousand. The one that looked like a Renaissance cardinal had a peculiarly rich and rolling laugh, in which there seemed to join amusement at a particular fact with extreme satisfaction with life in general. Bringing us to a small square in front of the Cathedral, which was smoothly paved and therefore had that air of being within the confines of some noble household, he said, "Here we have always walked

and talked, and often we have talked too loud. That is one thing that
never changes, our archives are full of the priests' complaints that we
talked so loud out here that they could not hear themselves saying mass
in the Cathedral." His laughter rolled. "Also we played ball," said the
Sitwell; "they complained of that also." "That leads to the story of
Jacopo Faganeo," said the Cardinal. "He was a seventeenth-century
Tuscan priest who was a very great preacher, but a very good companion too. The Admiral in command of the Venetian fleet in the Adriatic
got him to take a cruise with him, and when they got here the sailors
came ashore, even to the Admiral and his friends, and we townsmen
challenged them to a game of ball. Nobody was such a good ballplayer as
this priest, so he tucked up his gown and gave a wonderful display, and
we all cheered him. But this scandalized our local priests, and when Lent
came along they refused to let Father Jacopo preach in the Cathedral,
though he was still here with the fleet. However, soon after our Bishop
died, and the Admiral, who had the Pope's ear, paid out our priests by
getting Father Jacopo appointed to fill his place. And a very good Bishop
he was, too."

Then the square must have rung with laughter, with the laughter of
strong men; but it always knew that there was darkness as well as light.
Above the ballplayers rose the Cathedral, which is giraffish because of
the architect's consciousness that he must work on a minute site, but
which owes its strangeness of appearance to the troubled intricacy of
the ornamentation, loaded with tragic speculations of the Slav mind.
For Korchula, like Trogir, is an intensely Slav town. The degree of the
oddity of this ornament can be measured by the sculpture which projects
from the gable above the central door and rose window. It is a power-
fully realistic bust of a richly decked old woman, not a grotesque, but
far too passionate to be, as some suppose, merely the representation of a
fourteenth-century Queen of Hungary who gave money to the Church.
It has the same Dostoevsky quality as Radovan's work at Trogir. Perhaps
it was to exercise this note of metaphysical fantasy that a nineteenth-
century bishop made a jigsaw puzzle of the inside of the Cathedral, inter-
changing the parts and putting in a horrid but matter-of-fact pulpit.
But the outside remains enigmatic in its beauty, partly because it looks
across the square to the roofless ruin of the palace, wild-eyed with windows whose marble traceries are outlined against the sky, wild-haired
with the foliage of trees that had taken root in the angles of the upper
story and grew slantwise out of balconies.

"What is that?" said the Cardinal. "Regrettably enough, it is the home of my family. We burned it to disinfect it, in the sixteenth century, after many of our household had died in the plague, and we have never had the money to rebuild it. But now I will show you another church which you ought to see." It was at the foot of one of the steep streets, a church where the Gothic was melting into the Renaissance, where the architectural spring was over and the summer was warm and drowsy. These people could look on this summer-time with much more satisfaction than we could, for they knew nothing of the winter-time that had followed it with us, they were unaware of Regent Street. But they were specially pleased with this church for another reason which had nothing to do with architecture. They told us that this church was in the care of a confraternity and began to explain to us what these confraternities were; but when they found out that we already knew, they stopped and said no more. They did not tell us that they themselves belonged to this confraternity; but that was evident. With the ease of men who were showing strangers round their own house they took us up a staircase and over a bridge across an alley into the room where the confraternity kept its records and its treasures. There we all sat down, and they smiled about them, gentle and secret smiles. Here they came for the benefit of magic, and enjoyed a mystical, uplifting version of the pleasures of brotherhood. The room was itself an astonishment. It was hung with a score or so of Byzantine icons, in the true colours of icons, that is to say of flame and smoke; with the true message of icons, that is to say of spirit rising from matter with the precise yet immaterial form of a flame. Of these they said, smiling at their own history, "You see, we are a very pious people— all of us—even our sailors." These had, in fact, been looted by good Catholic Korchulans on expeditions that may sometimes have been certified as naval, but were sometimes plainly piratical, from Orthodox shrines. "People come here and try to buy them," said the Cardinal lazily, and laughed into his hand, while his awed eye raked them and found them valid magic.

"But some day there will be no question of our being poor people who can be tempted by foreigners to part with their goods," said the Sitwell. "Nor will we need the tourist traffic though the money will come in welcome," said the Cardinal; "we shall be able to live exactly like other people, on our production, when we have repaired the wrongs that the Venetians and Austrians have done to us. We are not only sailors, we are shipbuilders. But of course we need more wood. We have a lot for Dalmatia, more than you will find on the other islands you have seen, but we still have not enough. Come and see what we are doing about that." We went from a gate on the landward side of the town, down a superb stone staircase, and we found ourselves in a motor bus full of people who knew our guides and were known by them, who by some miraculous adjustment deferred to them and yet behaved as their equals. It was going to a village on the top of the mountain lying south of Korchula, and we left it as it got to the foothills, to take a path into a pinewood. Soon the Cardinal stopped and laid his hand on the thick trunk of a tall pine and said, "These trees were planted by my grandfather when he was mayor." And later, in a further valley he stopped by a slenderer trunk in a lower, thinner wood, and said, "These trees were planted by my father when he was mayor." And later still, in the crease of a spur that stretched towards an unmedicined barrenness, dull ochre rock save for the slightly different monotone of the scrub, we came to a plantation of pine saplings, hardly hip-high. "These are the trees I have planted, now I am mayor," he said. He stood among them spreading his arms wide above them, laughing lazily. "Have I not poor spindly children? But they will grow."

On our way back through the denser pinewoods we came to a terrace, where there were tables and benches for people to sit and eat on their Sunday walks, and because we were tired, having started on our journey in the early morning, we asked if we might rest there for a little. So we sat down on one side of the table, and they on the other, and they told us what they hoped to do for the reafforestation of the island and how the Government had helped them. Then they spoke of how the Venetians had cut down the woods, and how little the Austrians had done to replace them; and as they talked these men, who were essentially aristocrats, assumed the sullenness and shabbiness of conspirators. They muttered bitterly into their fingers, their underlips came forward. Then the Cardinal, suddenly noble once more, looked up at the sky through the trees and cried, "It is better now, it is still difficult, but the chief offence has been removed; we are free, and the work goes well. Are you rested? Shall we return?"

We went all the way back on foot, first by an inlet edged with prosperous modern villas, belonging to rich Croats, and then by a road that would have seemed dusty if it had not passed a monument that flattered my pride. By a very pretty semicircle of stone seats, conceived in the neo-classical tradition, was a tablet giving thanks to the English troops who occupied the island when the French were driven out, and governed it for two years till the Peace of 1815 handed it over with the rest of Dalmatia to Austria. We English were then a different breed. We could

build. We could administer. We gave these islands a democratic institution which they thoroughly enjoyed and followed the French tradition
of efficient public works by making good roads and harbours. Now we
would build tin huts all over the place, would have been compelled from
Downing Street to kick the natives in the face for fear of encouraging
revolutionary movements which did not in fact exist, and would have
ended up with the evil reputation of oppressors without any of the fruits
of oppression.

Something has changed us. The life we lead does not suit us. I knew
it a few minutes later when we were back in Korchula, and our guides
took us into one of the shipyards on the shore. We went through a yard
stacked with wood, that clean, moral substance, and carpeted with shavings, into a shed where three men stood contemplating the unfinished
hull of a motor boat. The overlapping timbers were as neat as the feathers
on a bird's wing, the shape was neat as a bird in flight. It was a pity that
so much beauty should be hidden under the water. Of the three men in
front of it, one held up a blueprint very steadily; another held a rule to
the boat and made measurements; the other watched and spoke with
authority. They were all three beautiful, with thick, straight, fair hair
and bronze skins and high cheekbones pulling the flesh up from their
large mouths, with broad chests and long legs springing from arched
feet. These were men, they could beget children on women, they could
shape certain kinds of materials for purposes that made them masters of
their worlds. I thought of two kinds of men that the West produces:
the cityish kind who wears spectacles without shame, as if they were the
sign of quality and not a defect, who is overweight and puffy, who can
drive a car but knows no other mastery over material, who presses buttons and turns switches without comprehending the result, who makes
money when the market goes up and loses it when the market goes
down; the high-nosed young man, who is somebody's secretary or is in
the Foreign Office, who has a peevishly amusing voice and is very delicate, who knows a great deal but far from all there is to be known about
French pictures. I understand why we cannot build, why we cannot
govern, why we bear ourselves without pride in our international relations. It is not that all Englishmen are like that, but that too many of
them are like that in our most favoured classes.

It is strange, it is heartrending, to stray into a world where men are
still men and women still women. I felt apprehensive many times in Korchula, since I can see no indications that the culture of Dalmatia is going
to sweep over the Western world, and I can see many reasons to fear

that Western culture will in the long run overwhelm Dalmatia. We crossed the road from the shipyard to call on an elderly woman who lived in a house which, a bourgeois kind of palace, had belonged to her husband's family for four hundred years. We were taken through a finely vaulted passage to the garden, where we stood under a pergola of wistaria and looked up at the tracery of the windows, which were greatly enriched by the salty weathering of the stone to an infinity of fine amber and umber tones; for we had been asked to wait till she had finished some pious business she was performing in the private chapel, which stood, an arched and pointed outhouse, among the crowded flowers, close to a niched wall that sheltered a Triton and a nymph. On the steps of the chapel there lay some candles and a match-box and a packet of washing soda on a sheet of newspaper. For a second I took this as an indication that the family fortunes were in decline, but on reflection I wondered what evidence I had that palaces had ever been neat. All historical memoirs portray a union between the superb and the sluttish; and probably tidiness is a creation of the middle classes, who have had their tendency to bare and purging Protestantism reinforced by their panic-stricken acceptance of the germ theory. Boucher's famous portrait of Madame Pompadour reveals that even she, who was the ideal civil servant, kept her personal possessions lying about on the floor. The homely disorder on the chapel steps was therefore simply a proof that this establishment was not yet a museum.

At length the lady of the house came out of the private chapel, followed by the kitchen smells of piety, not less powerful and classic than the kitchen smells of our hotel. She was elderly, though not old; and it could be seen that she had been very lovely; and immediately she began to flirt with my husband. She knew with absolute realism, and had known it, I am sure, from the first moment when the knowledge became necessary to her, that she was too old for love. But she knew that a repetition of the methods by which she had charmed the hearts and intelligences of the men of her time would give him the same pleasure an enthusiastic theatre-goer would feel if a famous old actress rehearsed for him her celebrated performance of Juliet. Therefore we enjoyed again the gaieties in which her voice and face and body had combined to promise her admirers that not only she but all her life was infinitely and unpredictably agreeable. After there had been a long rally of teasing compliment and mockery, a bell tolled somewhere in the town, and we all stopped to listen.

When it ceased there was a silence. My husband breathed deeply, warmed and satisfied by her aged and now sexless charm as one might be by a wine so old that all the alcohol had disappeared, and said, "It is wonderfully quiet." She abandoned her performance and said to him not sentimentally but with an almost peevish recollection of past enjoyment, as one might say that in one's youth one had cared greatly for racing but could no longer get about to the meetings, "It's too quiet. I liked it when there were children about, laughing, and then crying, and then laughing again. That's how it ought to be in a house." She spoke with complete confidence, as one who expresses an opinion held by all the world. A house with children is better than a house without children. That she assumed to be an axiom, on that she had founded all her life and pride. It was as if she were a child herself, a fragile child who had escaped death by a miracle and was boasting of its invulnerability to all ills. Her life had for the most part been secure because in her world men had been proud to be fathers, and had marvelled gratefully at women for being fine-wrought enough to make the begetting of children an excitement and sturdy enough to bear them and rear them, and had thought of the mother of many children as the female equivalent of a rich man. Because these masculine attitudes had favoured her feminine activities, her unbroken pride was lovely as the trumpet of a lily. It might have been different for her if she had been born into a society where men have either lost their desire for children, or are prevented from gratifying it by poverty or the fear of war. There she would have been half hated, and perhaps more than half, for her sex. Her womb, which here was her talisman, would have been a source of danger, which might even strike at the very root of her primal value, and one day make her husband feel that the delight he had known with her was not worth the price he must pay for it. It was terrible that this fate, even if it had failed to engulf her, was certain to annihilate many of her blood, of her kind, and that the threat was implicit in many statements that she made without a shadow of apprehension, as when she told us that her husband and all his forebears had been sea captains, and that her sons were still of the tradition and not of it, for they were agents for great steamship lines.

The Cardinal said to me, "You are looking very tired. Before I take you to our house to meet my parents, we will go to a café on the quay, and you can rest." This seemed to me a peculiar programme, but it was agreeable enough. As we drank very good strong coffee the two men talked again of trees: of the possibility of making many motor boats for the new tourist traffic, of the fishing fleets, of the wrong Italians had done by seizing the southward island, Lagosta, where the fish are spe-

cially plentiful. "The Slavs all left it when the treaty was known," said
the Sitwell. "And they have not been able to repopulate it with Italians,"
said the Cardinal, "for they are idiots, worse than the Austrians. Think
of it, they wanted to colonize the island with Italian fishermen and they
renamed it after an Italian airman who had been killed. Think of doing
a silly thing like that, when you're dealing with peasants. It's such a silly
townsman's trick." His great laughter rolled up out of him. "You're accustomed to deal politically with people in person," said my husband.
"That is a funny idea, for us. Not by the million, through newspapers
and the radio, or by the thousand or hundred in halls, but just in person."
The Cardinal answered modestly, "One does what one can, in order
not to be destroyed. But come and see my father, who is cleverer at it
than I am."

We went back into the town, and had but one more digression. The
Cardinal whisked us into a courtyard gorgeous with two balustraded
galleries. Because it was an orphanage there projected between the pillarets the grave puppy-snouts of interested infant Slavs, while above them
were the draperies and blandness of young nuns. The presence of the
Cardinal produced a squealing babble of homage from the orphans, and
the wheeling and bowing courtesies of the nuns recalled the evolutions
of angels. The institution wailed its disappointment as we left, and the
Cardinal hurried us round a corner up another street, into the medievalism of his home.

The courtyard was dark with its own shadows as well as the dusk, and
ghostly with the pale light filtering down from the still sunlit upper air,
through the gutted palace, burned because of the plague, which formed
its fourth side. It looked even more fantastic than we had thought it in
the Cathedral square. At a window on its ground floor a tree stood like a
woman looking into the courtyard, and on the floors above trees, some
of them clothed with blossom which in this uncertain light was the colour of a grey Persian cat, shot forth from the empty sockets of vanished
rafters in the attitudes of acrobats seeking the trapeze. The courtyard
itself spoke of something even older than this palace, for it was full of
carved stone; slabs bearing inscriptions or low reliefs had been let into
its walls, and there were set about many statues and fragments of statues,
some of which were Roman. It held as well an infinity of growing things,
of flowers bursting from a lead cistern and a sarcophagus, full-fleshed
leafy plants and bronze-backed ferns, a great many of them in little pots
hung on lines of string secured to details of sculpture. We were reminded
of what he had sometimes forgotten during this water-logged spring,

that this was the far South, accustomed to seasons when grass is a recollected miracle and everything that can be coaxed to grow in a flowerpot is a token and a comfort. On the other side of the courtyard, facing the ruin, was another palace, also Venetian Gothic and of the fifteenth century, but intact. Its great door was open, and showed a dark room and another beyond it that was lit by the soft white light of a chandelier. Towards this reserved and even defensive interior the Cardinal now led us. But I delayed to admire the richness of a design impressed on the lead cistern, and he told me, "Those are the arms of my family. But now we do not use such cisterns. We have modern methods. See, there is a great cistern under this courtyard." He brought down his heel on the pavement, making a sharp ringing noise that sent a little bird whirring out of one of the plants back to its home in the ruined palace. "Trees and water," said the Sitwell, "they are more precious to us on the island than gold." "We will have all we want of them under Yugoslavia," said the Cardinal.

We paused again at the door to handle the great knocker, which was perhaps by Giovanni Bologna: it was a Neptune between two rear-uplifted dolphins, magnificent whatever hand had made it. Inside we found the same vein of magnificence, though the proportions here, as everywhere else in the city, were constrained by a want of space; and the furniture showed the influence of nineteenth-century Italy and Austria, which was not without a chignoned and crinolined elegance, but was coarsened by the thick materials it employed, the chenille and rep, the plush and horsehair. In the second room, at a table under the chandelier, sat a white-haired lady, in her sixties, dressed in a black velvet gown. From the stateliness of her greeting we understood why her son had taken us to rest at a café before he brought us into her house. The social life in this palace was extremely formal, that is to say we were expected to play our part in a display of the social art in its highest sense, the art of meeting people with whom one may have little or nothing in common and distilling the greatest possible pleasantness out of the contact without forcing an unreal intimacy. But it was light as air, weightless swordsmanship. The old lady first addressed herself to me with a maternal air that was flattering yet not indecently so, as if the gulf of years between us were greater than it actually was, but not impossibly great. Then, like the lady in the sea captain's palace, she began to address herself to my husband for the excellent reason that she was a woman and he was a man. The performance she gave, however, was probably not modified by time: for the difference in their social status meant that though all her life she must have taken for granted that her beauty was a beacon before the eyes of men, it must have also been her faith that all its sexual implications, to the remotest, must be private to her immediate family. The sea captain's widow was certainly chaste as snow, but it was probable that many men had looked on her and thought it a pity that she was not their wife; but this lady was to such an extreme degree the wife of her husband, the queen of this palace, that she was withdrawn from even such innocent and respectful forms of desire. She made, therefore, since her career was to be a wife and a mother, an exclusively feminine appeal, but it was remote, ethereal, almost abstract.

When her husband came he proved to be as noble-looking as she was; a slender bearded man, with a wolfish alertness odd in a man of his type. It was like seeing Lord Cecil with the springy gait of a matador. He apologized at once, in Italian, for having spoken to his son in Serbo-Croat as he entered the room. "I am afraid," he said, "we had better converse in Italian, but I hope you will not take it as a proof of the truth of the Italian lie that we are Italian on this coast by race and in language. That is propaganda, and mendacious for that. They have the impudence to deny us our blood and our speech, and they have never minded what lies they told. One of them has even inconvenienced us to the point of having to change our name. It happened that though we are pure Slavs our name originally ended in -i, which is not a Slav but an Italian termination, for a surname, for the reason that in the sixteenth century we chose to be known by the Christian name of a member of our family who was a great hero and was killed by the Turks while he was defending Candia. This circumstance, which was to our glory, the Italians attempted to turn to our shame, by pretending that our name proved that we, one of the leading patrician families of Korchula, were of Italian origin. There is no infamy to which they will not stoop."

At that point a decanter of wine and some little cakes were brought in, and we drank to one another's health. My husband explained what a pleasure it was for us to meet them and to see their historic home. It was strange that when they answered they seemed not more proud of the stone glories of their palace than of the little ferns in the pots on the string lines. "Once," said the old gentleman, a gleam coming into his eye, "I had birds as well as plants in my courtyard." His son began to laugh, the old lady held her handkerchief to her lips and pouted and shook her head from side to side. "Very beautiful they looked in their cages, and they sang like angels," went on the old gentleman severely. "But my wife did not like having them there. She did not like it at all.

And that is why they are not there now. Shall I tell the story, Yelitsa? Shall I tell the story? Yes, I had better tell the story. It is something the like of which they will never have heard; never will they have heard of a woman behaving so wickedly."

We were evidently being admitted to a favourite family joke. "Think of it," he told us with much mock horror, "we were entertaining a large company of friends in the courtyard on Easter morning, as is our custom. Suddenly my wife rose and began to walk from cage to cage, opening all the doors and saying, 'Christ is risen, the whole world is rejoicing, rejoice thou also, bird, and fly away home!' And as it was an assembly, I could not jump up and chastise her, and our friends sat and smiled, thinking this was some graceful pious comedy, suitable for Easter. Did ever a woman play such a trick on her husband? I ask you, sir, did your wife ever play such a trick on you?" Her husband, and indeed all of us, gazed at her in adoration through our laughter, and she shrugged her shoulders and said comfortably, "Well, birds in cages, that is something I do not like."

But in no time we were back in the conflict of Dalmatia with history. The old gentleman said to us, "I think you will enjoy your travels amongst us. But you must make allowances. We are in some respects still barbarous simply because we spent so much of our time defending the West. We fought the Turk, and then we fought the Turk, and then we fought the Turk. For that reason we could not throw off the tyranny of Venice, so that it was able to use us as a deathbed, to use our life as a mattress for its decay. The French were better, but they brought with them their taint of revolution. There were some sad scenes, here and in Trogir especially, where the doctrines of Jacobinism caused revolt. But of your countrymen we have only the happiest recollections. Alas, that the peace treaty of 1815 should have made the mistake of handing us over to the Austrian Empire, that unnecessary organization, which should have ceased to exist after the destruction of the Turks, and which survived only to cultivate grossness and frivolity at the expense of her superior subject races." "The Austrians were the worst oppressors of all that we have known," said his son, "for Venice was a dying power during much of her reign over us, and had not the energy to conquer our spirit. But Austria felt in excellent health till the beginning of the Great War, and when she kicked us there was plenty of force in the boot." "Four generations of us were under Austria," said his father, "and always we rebelled against them for that very reason. Not out of their

poverty but out of their wealth the Austrians would not plant our ruined
forests, would not give us water, and taxed salt, so that our fisheries could
not preserve their fish; and they hated those of us who were fortunate
but defended the cause of our less fortunate fellow-Slavs." "But it is
excessively hard on women," said his wife, addressing me, "when the
men are for ever busying themselves with politics."

The old gentleman regarded her tenderly. "My wife pretends to be
frivolous," he said, "but she is really true to the courageous tradition of
Dalmatian womanhood, which indeed has been carried on with peculiar
glory in Korchula. In 1571, when we had been abandoned by our cur of
a Venetian governor, who ran away to Zara, and all our men were fighting at sea, a garrison of women and children successfully defended the
town against the infamous Turkish corsair, Uliz Ali, who by the way
was no Turk, but a renegade, simply another of those Italians. I can say
that my wife has been a worthy successor to those women, for I have
never known her to flinch before danger." "Perhaps I do not," she said,
"but all the same it has sometimes been very boring." Nevertheless, I
could see his view of her was the truth. Her standard expression was one
I had seen before, on the faces of women whose husbands had been pre-
war Russian revolutionaries, or Spanish liberals under Alfonso. The
eyebrows were slightly raised, so that the space between them was fairly
smooth, and the eyelids were lowered: so people look when they expect
at any moment to receive a heavy blow in the face. But her chin was
tilted forward, her lips were resolutely curved in a smile: she mocked
the giver of the blow before he gave it, and removed her soul to a place
where he could not touch it. "Were you ever frightened?" I asked.
"Again and again I had reason to be, on account of the way my husband
behaved," she replied. "But I thank God that by the time my sons were
men we were safe under Yugoslavia."

"You hear in her words what Yugoslavia means to us Dalmatians,"
said the old gentleman. Then he paused. I felt he was searching for words
to say something that had been in his mind since he set eyes on us, and
that he found intensely disagreeable. "I am glad," he continued, "that
you have come to see our Yugoslavia. But I think you have come to see
it too soon. It is what I have fought for all my life, and it is what must be,
and, as my wife tells you, it already means a security such as we have
never known before, not since the beginning of time. But you must remember what Cavour said: 'Now there is an Italy, but we have not yet
got Italians.' It is so with us. We have the machinery of the state in

Yugoslavia, but we have not yet learned how to work it. We have many amongst us who do not understand its possibilities, who are unaware of . . ."—his hands moved in distress—"of what it should be to us Slavs." He began to speak in a slow, braked tone, of the Croatian discontent, and of the Matchek movement; and it was clear from his son's uneasiness and the muting of his wife's gaiety that this household felt itself still girt by enemies, and that this last encirclement was harder to bear than any of the others, since these enemies were of their own blood. These people had remembered they were Slavs for a thousand years, in spite of the threats of empire, and had believed they could not hate their fellow-Slavs. But now they saw their fellow-Slavs conspiring against Yugoslavia and giving Italy its opportunity to impose itself again as their oppressor, it seemed to them that they must hate them, must exterminate them without pity, as in the past they had exterminated renegades of their race who went over to the Turks.

The old gentleman was saying, "You will find it hard to believe, but there are those amongst us who are so misguided as to wish to alienate the Croats from our fellow-Slavs, the Serbs; and indeed there are very great differences between us and the Serbs, differences of manners due to the unfortunate circumstance that they suffered what we did not, centuries of enslavement by the Turks. But they are not only brothers, they have given us enormous gifts. I remember that many years ago your admirable Professor Seton-Watson came to stay with me here, and he said to me, 'You are insane to think of complete Slav independence, all you can hope for is full rights for the Slavs as citizens within the Austro-Hungarian Empire; it is far too strong for any of the Slav powers.' But then he came back early in 1914, just after Serbia had beaten Turkey in the Balkan War, and he said, 'Now it is different. When I see what the Serbs have done against Turkey, I am not at all sure that the Serbs and the Czechs and you Croats will not beat the Austro-Hungarian Army.' He spoke truly. It was the triumph of the Serbs that gave us hope. I find it therefore disgusting that over a slight affair of manners people should disdain their liberators." He spoke as a clear-cut man of action, used to making clear-cut decisions, used to arriving at clear-cut computations which are necessary before a compromise can be arranged. Not in a thousand years would he understand the Croatian world, which had been diluted by the German poison, which was a platform of clouds for drifting personalities, Slav in essence but vague in substance, unclimactic in process.

"And this Matchek movement," cried the old gentleman, "is Bolshevist! It is Communist! What is all this nonsense about the necessity for a social revolution? If there is work the people earn wages and benefit. What other economic problem is there beyond this? If we can build up our fisheries and our shipbuilding on Korchula, then our islanders will have plenty of money and have all they want. What more is there to say about it?" He looked at us with the eyes of an old eagle that is keeping up its authority, yet fears that he may be wrong. He knew that what he was saying was not quite right, but he did not know in what it was wrong. We thought that his predicament was due to his age, but when we looked at his son we found precisely the same expression on his face. He said, without his usual authority, "This is all the work of agitators, such as Mussolini used to be." He probably alluded to the fact that when Mussolini was a Socialist he once organized a dock strike at Split. The experience of these people was very rich.

But in one respect it was very poor. They laboured, I saw, under many advantages—innate gifts, a traditional discipline which had been so ferociously applied through the centuries to cowards and traitors that courage and loyalty now seemed theirs of birthright, a devotion to public interest which made them almost as sacred as priests. But they laboured under one disadvantage. The ideas of the French Revolution had never been talked out in this part of the world. A touch of the Jacobin fever had reached Dalmatia when it was still under Venice, and had been drastically cured, first by the Venetians and later by the French. The year 1848 had brought a revival of revolutionary ideas to all Europe, but not to Dalmatia and Croatia, because the Hungarian uprising had taken an anti-Slav turn under Kossuth, and the Croats were obliged to offend their racial interests by fighting for the Habsburgs and reaction. Nobody in these parts, therefore, had ever discussed the possibility that the doctrine of Liberty, Equality, and Fraternity might be an admirable prescription to maintain the peace in an expanding industrial civilization. They had no means of understanding those believers in their doctrine who have discovered that it is impossible to guarantee liberty, equality, or fraternity to every member of a community while some members hold economic power over others, and who now demand a redistribution of wealth. This family took all the pother for a modern version of something which as Korchulan patricians they understood quite well: a plebeian revolt. Without a qualm they would resist it, for they knew what the people really wanted, and were doing their best to get it for them as fast as possible. Water, that was what they needed, and trees.

Innocent in their misapprehension, bright with charity and public spirit, but puzzled by the noise of some distant riot for which their intimate knowledge of the civic affairs had not prepared them, the father and mother and son sat in the white circle under the chandelier, the darkness in the courtyard beyond now entirely night.

Korchula II

I WOKE early next morning, and heard Ellen Terry speaking as she had spoken at the Theatre Royal, Edinburgh, when I was a little girl. Her voice had lifted imperiously to cry, "Kill Claudio!"—a behest not at all offensive since it was essentially just, yet raising certain problems. It was good that somebody should speak up for simple dealing with evil, although no one who knew all, who had comprehended the whole mystery of good and evil, would say it like that. There was perhaps something about the family I had visited last night which had recalled the speaking of those words. I fell asleep again, and was reawakened by the sound of singing, a little rough and wolfish for mere gaiety. When I went to the window there was a crowd of young men standing on the quay, each carrying a bundle. "They must be conscripts," said my husband, "waiting for a steamer to take them to the mainland." "Yes," I said, "this is the time of year when they start their training. And look, they all look oddly shabby for such clean young men. They are all brisked up to look their best, but at the same time they've all come in their old clothes and left their new ones at home." "Let us wash and dress very quickly, and go down and have a look at them as they go on board."

As we came out of the front door of the hotel, our cups of coffee in our hands, a white steamer came round the peninsula, lovely as a lady and drunk as a lord. She listed deeply landwards, because she already carried a freight of young men, and they had all run to the side to have a look at Korchula. "It is the steamer come to take the conscripts away," said a man standing beside us, in English which had been learned in America. "Yes," we said. "They go to do their military service now on the mainland," he continued. "Yes," we said. "They go now to do their military service for Yugoslavia," he said, "but they are good Dalmatians, they are good Croats. Those songs you have heard them singing are all against the Government." He wore a fixed, almost absent-minded smile that represented derision grown second-nature, having long forgotten its first or any other reason. I remembered something Constantine once told me. "We Slavs love the terrible," he said, "and it happens that when we feel deeply terrible expressions come on our faces. As we love the terrible we keep them there, and they become grins, grimaces, masks that mean nothing. That is one of the things that has happened among the Bolsheviks. Revolution has become a rictus." It has perhaps gone wrong here also.

As the ship drew nearer we heard that the young men leaning over the rail were singing just these same angrily hopeful songs as the young men on the quay, and by the time she came alongside the quay they were joined in one song. Some of those on the ship could not wait to land until the gang-plank was lowered, and, after shouting for the crowd below to fall back, they jumped from the rails to the quay, their bodies full of a goatish vigour, their faces calm and stubborn and withdrawn. They ran past us and came back in an instant carrying yard-long loaves under their arms, and stood quietly, rapt in the exaltation of having started on a new adventure, behind the young men of Korchula, who were standing more restlessly, the new adventure not having begun for them, and the distress of their families being a disagreeable distraction. Unifying these two groups was this dark overhanging cloud of discontented song. We went inside the hotel and buttered ourselves second rolls, and when we returned the boat had taken aboard its load and started out to sea. She was some hundreds of yards from the shore, more drunken than ever, listing still deeper with her increased freight, which was singing now very loudly and crowding to the rails to wave to the residue of their grieving kin, who were now moving along the quay to the round towers at the end of the peninsula so that they would be able to see her again as she left the bay and went out into the main channel; they walked crabwise, with their heads turned sideways, so that they should not miss one second's sight of their beloveds. They were obviously much moved by that obscure agony of the viscera rather than of the mind, or even of the heart, which afflicts the human being when its young goes from it over water, which St. Augustine described for ever in his *Confessions*, in his description of how his mother Monica grieved when he took sail from Africa to Italy. Presently the ship was gone, and the crowd came back, all walking very quickly and looking downwards and wiping their noses.

We found standing beside us the Cardinal, the Sitwell, and a handsome lady who was the Sitwell's wife. It was a pity so far as we were concerned, but it threw an interesting light on the claims of Italy to Dalmatia, and the real orientation of Dalmatia, that this lady spoke no languages but Serbo-Croatian and Russian, which she had acquired from a teacher who had been at the Tsarina's boarding school in Montenegro. They took us down to a motor boat by the quay, and we went out through a blue and white and windy morning for a trip about the island.

Now the city of Korchula was a goldsmith's toy, a tortoise made of precious metals, sitting on its peninsula as on a show-stand, and we were chugging past a suburb of villas, pink and white like sugar almonds. We passed a headland or two and came to a bay wide enough to be noble, and narrow enough to be owned. On its lip were moor and rock, and behind them olive terraces and almond orchards rose to scrub and bleakness. A track ran up to a high village in a crevice of this bleakness, and the Cardinal, laughing, told us that its inhabitants plagued the central and the local authorities for a better road down to this bay. "And we say, 'But why? You have a perfectly good road down to Korchula!' And they say, 'But Korchula is not *our* port. This bay should be *our* port.' So you see the little world is the same as the big world, and both are silly."

In that, and a further bay, we made the boat linger. The green water glittered clean as ice, but gentle. "Could we buy some land?" we asked. "Could we build a villa?" It would be a folly. To get there from London would take two nights and two days by rail and steamer, and I do not suppose that either of us would ever be on easy terms with a language we had learned so late. But the sweet wildness of these bays, and the air rich with sun-baked salt and the scent of the scrub, and the view of the small perfect city, made this one of the places where the setting for the drama is drama enough. "Yes, you could buy it, yes, you could build," they said. "But one thing," said the Cardinal, rather than deceive a stranger, "one thing you will not have in abundance. That is water. But then you could afford to build yourself a big cistern, and it always rains here in winter. That is the trouble, things work in a circle. People here need water if they are to make money. But because they have no money they cannot build cisterns to store water. So they cannot make any more money. All that, however, we shall settle in time."

As we set off to the opposite coast, which looked like an island but was the peninsula of Pelyesatch, the Korchulans still talked of water. "We had a great disappointment," said the Sitwell. "Over at Pelyesatch there is a spring of which the inhabitants have no very great need, and it was thought that we could raise enough money to build a pipe-line across this channel to our island. But alas! we discovered at the last moment that from time to time, and especially during droughts, when we would need it most, the spring ran salt." "You from England," said the Cardinal, "can have no notion of how disappointed we were. Still, we must not complain. When the worst comes to the worst, they send us a ship with a cargo of water down from Split."

As we drew nearer the shore the water under the keel was pale emerald, where the diving sunlight had found sand. We landed on a little stone quay, where fishermen in a boat with a rust-coloured sail called greetings to our friends, as in the Middle Ages plebeians who were yet free men would have greeted nobles, when the dispensation was working well. We stepped out and walked along the coast by a line of small houses and gardens, and the Cardinal said, "This is the village where all retired sea captains come to live if they can possibly manage it." Sea captains are sensible. There was nothing that was not right in this village. There was nothing there which was not quietly guided to perfection by a powerful tradition. Every house was beautiful, and every garden. And they were small, they were not the results of lavish expenditure; and most of them were new, they were not legacies from a deceased perfection.

Even the quite businesslike post-office had an air of lovely decorum. Its path led through a garden which practised a modest and miniature kind of formality, to a small house built of this Dalmatian stone which is homely as cheese and splendid as marble. Within, a cool and clean passage, finely vaulted, was blocked by a high stand of painted iron, proper in every twist of its design, in which were posed flowers that needed special gentleness. A woman, well-mannered and remote, came from the back of the house and talked gravely of some local matter with the Cardinal, while she plucked me a nosegay with precise taste. The people who went by on the road looked like her, the houses we had passed had all been like this. Here man was at ease, he had mastered one part of the business of living so well that it was second nature to him. If we bought that bay over on Korchula we would not know what kind of house to build, we would have to take an infinite amount of thought, and our success would be a matter of hit and miss; and we would have to think of what we wanted our garden to look like. But these people's culture instructed them exactly how best they might live where they must live.

We went next into the garden of a larger and a grander house, which was empty, and from an orange tree the Cardinal broke me a branch laden with both fruit and blossom. "It belongs," he said, looking up at its desolation, "to some Croats, who, poor people, bought it to turn into a hotel without reflecting that they had no money to rebuild it or run it." Though he was so practical, he spoke of this not unimportant negligence as if it were not blameworthy, as if they had just been afflicted with this lapse of memory as they might with measles or loss of sight. I carried my sceptre of oranges along till we came to a church, a little church, the least of churches, that was dwarfed by a cypress which was a third of its breadth and a quarter taller, and itself was no king of trees. Small as it was, this church was recognizably of a superb tradition, and had big brothers that were cathedrals. We stood on the lawn admiring its tiny grandeur, while the Cardinal, who knew that all things were permitted to him everywhere, went to the bell-tower, which stood separate, and pulled the rope. While its deep note still was a pulse in the air, the Cardinal pointed to the road behind us and said, "Look! There is something you will not often see nowadays."

An old gentleman was having his walk, neat and clean, with white mutton-chop whiskers joining the moustaches that ran right across his shining pink face, wearing a short coat and sailorly trousers. He had the air of being a forthright and sensible person, but time was disguising him, for he had checked himself on seeing us from carrying on a conversation with certain phantoms, and age forced him to walk drunkenly. "*Zdravo!*" said the Cardinal, as is the way of Slavs when they meet. "Flourish!" it means. "*Zdravo*," the old man answered, as from the other side of an abyss. "I told you that all retired sea captains wanted to live here. There is one of them; and you may see from his Franz Josef whiskers that he was in the Austrian Navy. I think those side-whiskers on such an old man are the only things coming from Vienna that I really like." We watched the old man totter on his way, and as he forgot us, he resummoned his phantom friends and continued their argument. "God pity us," said the Cardinal. "Yugoslavia must be, but it is almost certain that because of it there is here and there a good soul who feels like a lost dog."

The boat took us for a time round the pale emerald waters close to the beach within a stone's throw of these houses and gardens that would have been theatrical in their perfection if they had not been austere. Then we drew further out and saw how above this hem of fertility round the shore olive groves and almond orchards rose in terraces to bluffs naked except for a little scrub, on which rested a plateau with more olives and almonds and a scattered blackness of cypresses and some villages and churches; and above this were the naked peaks, reflecting the noonlight like a mirror. Then fertility died out. Under the bluffs there was now a slope of scrub that sent out a perfume which I could smell in spite of the flowering orange branch upon my knee; and then a thick forest of cypresses, which for all their darkness and chastity of form presented that extravagant appearance that belongs to a profusion of anything that is usually scarce. Then the mountains dropped to a bay, a shoulder of sheer rock, and on the flat shore lay a pleasant town. "This is Orebitch," said the Cardinal. "Look, there is painted all along the pier, 'Hail and welcome to the Adriatic.' It is the greeting the town made to our poor King Alexander when he sailed up this coast on his way to his death at Marseille. He had no time to stop there, so they paid their respects in this way." We murmured our interest and kept our eyes on that inscription, and not on the other which some daring young man had scratched giant-high on the shoulder of rock above. "*Zhive* Matchek," it read. Long live Matchek, the enemy of Yugoslavia, the emblem of the economic struggle which awakened no sympathy among our friends, though they could feel kindly for Croats who bought hotels without the money to run them, and for old Austrian naval officers, simply because nothing in their experience had prepared them for it.

Across the channel Korchula's lovely form was minute and mellow gold. We started towards it over a sea that was now brighter emerald, among islets which were scattered pieces of Scotland, rugged points of rock and moor with the large air of the Grampians though hardly paddock-wide. Our boat could slip within a foot or two of them, so deep and calm were the waters. Here was one much visited for the seagulls' eggs. As we chugged past the gulls rose and crossed and recrossed the sky above us, wailing against us who were their Turks, their pirates. At another islet a boat was hauled up on a yard of shingle and three fishermen lay sleeping among the scrub, bottles and empty baskets beside them. One heard our boat and lifted his head. His preoccupied eyes, blinking before the noon, found and recognized us; he raised his hand and said "*Zdravo!*" in an absent voice, and sank back with an air of returning to a more real world. The other two did not wake, but stirred defensively, as if guarding their own sleep.

"They will have been fishing since dawn, the good lads," said the Sitwell. We passed another and more barren islet which rose to a flat top, not broad. Perhaps five fishermen might have taken their midday rest there. "Here a famous treaty in our history was signed," said the Cardinal. Men had scrambled out of boats on to this stony turret, barbarian and jewelled, for this coast was as much addicted to precious stones as to violence. Merchants went from island to island, hawking pearls and emeralds among the nobles, and the number of jewellers in the towns was extraordinary. In Korchula there were at one time thirty-two. After a few more such islets we came on a larger island, Badia, which illustrated the enigmatic quality of Dalmatian life. A monastery stands among its pinewoods, where there had been one for nearly a thousand years, though not the same one. Again and again men have gone there to live the contemplative life, and because it lies by the shore on a flatness hard to defend, and is distant from both Korchula and the mainland, pirates have murdered and looted their altars; and always other monks have come in their stead, to be murdered and looted in their turn. This series of pious tragedies continued until the middle of the nineteenth century. This might be comprehensible, were the place the site of some holy event, or were it some desert supremely appropriate to renunciation of the world and union with the supernatural. But Badia has no story other than this curious mutual persistence of monks and pirates, and the monastery lies as comfortably and unspiritually among its gardens as a Sussex manor-house. The history presents an exactly matched sadism and masochism, equally insane in the pursuit of what it finds its perverse pleasure, and nothing more.

Nuns, finding themselves as unwholesomely situated, would have gone home. That I thought before we landed, and I knew it afterwards. For we walked through the well-husbanded gardens, and round the cloisters, which are a mixture of Venetian Gothic and early Renaissance and conventional classic, yet are handled with such genius that they please as if they were of the purest style, and into the church, where the golden stone of the country makes splendour out of a plainish design. There, though this was a Franciscan monastery and a boys' school, a very pretty nun was scrubbing the floor in front of the altar. She sat back on her pleasing little haunches and smiled with proprietary pride while we were shown a wooden cross, brought to Korchula by refugees who had fled here after the Turks had beaten Balkan Christendom at the battle of Kossovo, which showed on each side a realistic Christ in agony, the one manifestly dead, the other manifestly still living. So might a farmer's daughter smile when strangers came to her father's byres to marvel at a two-headed calf. Had she been in charge of the religious establishment when pirates threatened, this and all other holy objects would have been gathered up and stuffed with simple cunning into loads of hay or cabbages and rowed back to safety.

She was sensible. There is nothing precious about this Dalmatian civ-ilization. It rests on a basis of good peasant sense. We left Badia and chugged back to the island of Korchula, to a bay of hills terraced with vineyards and set with fortress-like farms, stocky among their fig and mulberry trees. The roads that joined them ran between thick walls, up great ramps and steps that not all the armies of the world and marching a year could tread down; wine always converts those who deal in it to the belief that all should be made for time to gather up into an ultimate perfection. "On that headland yonder," said the Cardinal, pointing to a moory headland, "was found the tablet which told us who we Korchulans are. An archæologist working there last century found an inscription which gave the names of five hundred Greek colonists who settled there in the third century before Christ." "Was it not a hundred?" asked the Sitwell. "That is not important," said the Cardinal, "what matters is that they were Greek. It means that here is a part of ancient Greece which never was conquered by the Turk, which was never conquered at all in any way that could conquer ancient Greece. For in spite of Hungary and Venice and Austria we have, as you may have noticed, kept ourselves to ourselves." I listened, smiling as at a boast, and then forgot to smile. What was ancient Greece that all the swains adore her? A morning freshness of the body and soul, that will have none of the dust; so it might be said. That was not incongruous with much we had seen since we first took to the water that morning. The claim was perhaps relevant to the extreme propriety of the sea captain's village, the gracefulness of the olive orchards and the almond orchards that had been forced on the mountains, the town of Orebitch and its clear, virile inscription and counter-inscription, the fisherman on the islet, the peasant nun scrubbing the golden stone in front of the altar at Badia, the vineyards and their sturdy forts and redoubts. It was certainly completely in harmony, that claim, with this last island that we visited.

"This you must see," the Sitwell had said; "there is a great quarry there, which has given the stone for some of the most beautiful buildings on our coast. They say the Rector's palace at Dubrovnik came from here." We slid by so near that we could see the weed floating from its rocks, and looked at something that surely could not be a quarry town. There are certain ugly paradoxes that hold good in almost every society; for example, the people who satisfy humanity's most urgent need and grow its food are ill-paid and enjoy little honour. Another is the scurvy treatment of those who hew from the earth its stone, which not only gives shelter but compels those who use it towards decorum; for even the worst architect finds difficulty in committing certain meannesses of design when he is working with stone, and it will help him to fulfil whatever magnificent intentions he may conceive. But in most quarry villages privation can be seen gaining on man like a hungry shark; and in France I have visited one where the workers lived in lightless and waterless holes their hands had broken in the walls of a medieval castle. But here it was not so. The island was like a temple, the village we saw before us was like an altar in a temple.

The village lay on the shore under a long low hill, riven with quarries and planted with some cypresses. The houses were built in proper shapes that would resist the winter gales but were not grim, that did not deny the existence of spring and summer, in stone that was the colour of edible things, of pale honey, of pie-crust, of certain kinds of melon. Flowers did not merely grow here, they were grown. Nasturtiums printed a gold and scarlet pattern on a wall under a window, vine leaves made an awning over a table outside a house where an open door showed a symmetry of stacked barrels. Some men walked down the street, two and then another group of three. Because they knew our friends and thought them worthy, they raised their hands in salutation, then thought no more of us, receding into their own lives as the fisherman had receded into his sleep. Four children, playing with a goat and its kid, looked backwards over their shoulders for a second, and went back to their play. A woman scrubbing a table in her garden straightened her arm and rested on it, wondering who we might be, and when she had rested enough put aside her curiosity and went on with her work. The houses and the people made a picture of a way of life different from what we know in the West, and not inferior.

My power to convey it is limited; a man cannot describe the life of a fish, a fish cannot describe the life of a man. It would be some guide to ask myself what I would have found on the island if we had not been water-strolling past it on our way back to familiarity but had been cast on it for ever. I would not find literacy, God knows. Nearly one-half the population in Yugoslavia cannot read or write, and I think I know in which half these men and women would find themselves. From the extreme æsthetic sensibility shown in the simple architecture of their houses and the planting of their flowers it could be seen that they had not blunted their eyes on print. Nor would I find clemency. This was no sugar-sweet island of the blest; the eyes of these men and women could be cold as stone if they found one not to be valuable, if they felt the need to be cruel they would give way to it, as they would give way to the need to eat or drink or evacuate. Against what I should lack on this island I should count great pleasure at seeing human beings move about with the propriety of animals, with their muscular ease and their lack of compunction. There was to be included in the propriety the gift, found in the lovelier animals, of keeping clean the pelt and the lair. At a close

gaze it could be seen that not in this quarry village either had the dam-
nably incongruous poverty been abolished, but all was clean, all was neat.
But not animal was the tranquillity of these people. They had found
some way to moderate the flow of life so that it did not run to waste,
and there was neither excess nor famine, but a prolongation of delight.
At the end of the village a fisherman sat on a rock with his nets and a
lobster-pot at his feet, his head bent as he worked with a knife on one of
his tools. From the deftness of his movements it could be seen that he
must have performed this action hundreds of times, yet his body was
happy and elastic with interest, as if this were the first time. It was so
with all things on this island. The place had been a quarry for over a
thousand years: it was as if new-built. The hour was past noon; it was as
undimmed as dawn. Some of the men, and a woman who was sitting between her flowers on the doorstep, were far gone in years, but there was
no staleness in them.

On the last rock of the island, a yard or so from the shore, stood a boy,
the reflected ripple of the water a bright trembling line across his naked
chest. He raised his eyes to us, smiled, waved his hand, and receded, receded as they all did, to their inner riches. There passed through my
mind a sentence from Humfry Payne's book on *Archaic Marble Sculpture in the Acropolis*, which, when I verified it, I found to run: "Most
archaic Attic heads, however their personality, have the same vivid look
—a look expressive of nothing so much as the plain fact of their own
animate existence. Of an animate existence lifted up, freed from grossness and decay, by some action taken by the mind, which the rest of the
world cannot practice." I said to the Cardinal, "You have a way of living
here that is special, that is particular to you, that must be defended at all
costs." He answered in a deprecating tone, "I think so." I persisted. "I
do not mean just your architecture and your tradition of letters, I mean
the way the people live." He answered, "It is just that. It is our people,
the way we live." We were running quicker now, past the monastery
among its pinewoods, past the headland where the Greek tablet was
found, and could see the town of Korchula before us. "I should like,"
said the Cardinal, "you to come back and learn to know our peasants.
This business of politics spoils us in the towns, but somebody has to
do it."

It was at this point, when the town had become a matter of identifiable
streets, that the motor boat stopped and began to spin round. The Sitwell said, "We in Korchula are the descendants of a hundred or perhaps
of five hundred Greeks, and we have defended the West against the

Turks, and maybe Marco Polo was one of our fellow-countrymen, but all the same our motor boats sometimes break down." The boatman made tinkering sounds in the bowels of the boat, while the green waters showed their strength and drew us out to the wind-crisped channel. "They will miss the steamer to Dubrovnik," said the Sitwell. "Is it of importance," asked the Cardinal, "that you should be at Dubrovnik today?" "Yes," said my husband. The Cardinal stood up and made a funnel of his hands and hallooed to a rowing-boat that was dawdling in the bright light on the water to our south. Nothing happened, and the Cardinal clicked his tongue against his teeth, and said, "That family has always been slow in the uptake. Always." It would have been amusing to ascertain what he meant by always: probably several centuries. But he continued to halloo, and presently the boat moved towards us. It proved to contain two young persons evidently but lately preoccupied with their own emotions: a girl whose hair was some shades lighter than her bronze skin but of the same tint, and a boy who seemed to have been brought back a thousand miles by the Cardinal's cry, though once he knew what was wanted and we had stepped from our boat to his, he bent to his oars with steady vigour, his brows joined in resolution. The girl, who was sucking the stem of a flower, derived a still contentment from the sight of his prowess, which indeed did not seem to surprise her. Behind us, across a widening space of shining milk-white water, the motor boat we had just left had now become a stately national monument, because the Cardinal remained standing upright, looking down on the boatman. He was quite at ease, since he had got us off to our boat, but he was watching this man, not to reprove him for any fault but to judge his quality. From a distance he resembled one of those stout marble columns in the squares of medieval cities from which the city standard used to be flown.

Dubrovnik (Ragusa) I

"Let us wire to Constantine and ask him to meet us earlier in Sarajevo," I said, lying on the bed in our hotel room. "I can't bear Dubrovnik." "Perhaps you would have liked it better if we had been able to get into one of the hotels nearer the town," said my husband. "Indeed I would not," I said. "I stayed in one of those hotels for a night last year. They are filled with people who either are on their honeymoon or never had one. And at dinner I looked about me at the tables and saw everywhere half-empty bottles of wine with room-numbers scrawled on the labels, which I think one of the dreariest sights in the world." "Yes, indeed," said my husband, "it seems to me always when I see them that there has been disobedience of Gottfried Keller's injunction, '*Lass die Augen fassen, was die Wimper hält von dem goldnen Ueberfluss der Welt*,' 'Let the eyes hold what the eyelids can contain from the golden overflow of the world.' But you might have liked it better if we were nearer the town." "No," I said, "nothing could be lovelier than this."

We were staying in a hotel down by the harbour of Gruzh, which is two or three miles out of Dubrovnik, or Ragusa as it used to be called until it became part of Yugoslavia. The name was changed, although it is pure Illyrian, because it sounded Italian: not, perhaps, a very good reason. Under the windows were the rigging and funnels of the harbour, and beyond the crowded waters was a hillside covered with villas, which lie among their gardens with an effect of richness not quite explicable by their architecture. The landscape is in fact a palimpsest. This was a suburb of Dubrovnik where the nobles had their summer palaces, buildings in the Venetian Gothic style furnished with treasures from the West and the East, surrounded by terraced flower-gardens and groves and orchards, as lovely as Fiesole or Vallombrosa, for here the Dalmatian coast utterly loses the barrenness which the traveller from the North might have thought its essential quality. These palaces were destroyed in the Napoleonic wars, looted and then burned; and on their foundations, in the nineteenth and twentieth centuries, have been built agreeable but undistinguished villas. But that is not the only confusion left by history on the view. The rounded slope immediately above the harbour is covered by an immense honey-coloured villa, with arcades and terraces and balconies hung with wistaria, and tier upon tier of orange trees and cypresses and chestnuts and olives and palms rising to the crest. It makes the claim of solidity that all Austrian architecture made, but it should have been put up in stucco, like our follies at Bath and Twickenham; for it was built for the Empress Elizabeth, who, of course, in her restlessness and Habsburg terror of the Slavs, went there only once or twice for a few days.

"I like this," I said, "as well as anything in Dubrovnik." "That can't be true," said my husband, "for Dubrovnik is exquisite, perhaps the most exquisite town I have ever seen." "Yes," I said, "but all the same I don't like it, I find it a unique experiment on the part of the Slav, unique in its nature and unique in its success, and I do not like it. It reminds me of the worst of England." "Yes," said my husband, "I see that, when one thinks of its history. But let us give it credit for what it looks like, and that too is unique." He was right indeed, for it is as precious as Venice, and deserves comparison with the Venice of Carpaccio and Bellini, though not of Titian and Tintoretto. It should be visited for the first time when the twilight is about to fall, when it is already dusk under the tall trees that make an avenue to the city walls, though the day is only blanched in the open spaces, on the bridge that runs across the moat to the gate. There, on the threshold, one is arrested by another example of the complexity of history. Over the gate is a bas-relief by Mestrovitch, a figure of a king on a horse, which is a memorial to and a stylized representation of King Peter of Serbia, the father of the assassinated King Alexander, he who succeeded to the throne after the assassination of Draga and her husband. It is an admirable piece of work. It would surprise those who knew Mestrovitch's work only from international exhibitions to see how good it can be when it is produced under nationalist inspiration for a local setting. This relief expresses to perfection the ideal ruler of a peasant state. Its stylization makes, indeed, some reference to the legendary King Marko, who is the hero of all Serbian peasants. This king could groom the horse he rides on, and had bought it for himself at a fair, making no bad bargain; yet he is a true king, for no man would daunt him from doing his duty to his people, either by strength or by riches. It is enormously ironic that this should be set on the walls of a city that was the antithesis of the peasant state, that maintained for centuries the most rigid system of aristocracy and the most narrowly bourgeois ethos imaginable. The incongruity will account for a certain coldness shown towards the Yugoslavian ideal in Dubrovnik; which itself appears ironical when it is considered that after Dubrovnik was destroyed by the great powers no force on earth could have come to its rescue except the peasant state of Serbia.

For an ideal first visit the traveller should go into the city and find the light just faintly blue with dusk in the open space that lies inside the gate, and has for its centre the famous fountain by the fifteenth-century Neapolitan architect Onofrio de la Cava. This is a masterpiece, the size of a small chapel, a domed piece of masonry with fourteen jets of water, each leaping from a sculptured plaque set in the middle of a panel divided by two slender pilasters, into a continuous trough that runs all round the fountain: as useful as any horse-trough, and as lovely and elevating as an altar. On the two steps that raise it from the pavement there always lie some carpets with their sellers gossiping beside them. At this hour all cats are grey and all carpets are beautiful; the colours, fused by the evening, acquire richness. On one side of this square is another of the bland little churches which Dalmatians built so often and so well, a town sister of that we had seen in the village where the retired sea captains lived. At this hour its golden stone gives it an air of enjoying its own private sunset, prolonged after the common one. It has a pretty and secular rose-window which might be the brooch for a bride's bosom. Beside it is a Franciscan convent, with a most definite and sensible Pietà over a late Gothic portal. The Madonna looks as if, had it been in her hands, she would have stopped the whole affair; she is in no degree gloating over the spectacular fate of her son. She is not peasant, she is noble; it is hardly possible to consider her as seducible by the most exalted destiny. Facing these across the square is the old arsenal, its façade pierced by an arch; people walk through it to a garden beyond, where lamps shine among trees, and there is a sound of music. For background there are the huge city walls, good as strength, good as honesty.

Ahead runs the main street of the town, a paved fairway, forbidden to wheeled traffic, lined with comely seventeenth-century houses that have shops on their ground floor. At this time it is the scene of the Corso, an institution which is the heart of social life in every Yugoslavian town, and indeed of nearly all towns and villages in the Balkans. All of the population who have clothing up to the general standard—I have never seen a person in rags and patches join a Corso in a town where good homespun or manufactured textiles are the usual wear, though in poverty-stricken districts I have seen an entire Corso bearing itself with dignity in tatters—join in a procession which walks up and down the main street for an hour or so about sunset. At one moment there is nobody there, just a few people going about the shops or sitting outside cafés; at the

next the street is full of all the human beings in the town that feel able
to take part in the life of their kind, each one holding up the head and
bearing the body so that it may be seen, each one chattering and being
a little gayer than in private, each one attempting to establish its individuality. Yet the attempt defeats itself, for this mass of people, moving up and down the length of the street and slowly becoming more and
more like each other because of the settling darkness, makes a human
being seem no more than a drop of water in a stream. In a stream, moreover, that does not run for ever. The Corso ends as suddenly as it begins.
At one instant the vital essence of the town chokes the street with its
coursing; the next, the empty pavement is left to the night.

But while it lasts the Corso is life, for what that is worth in this particular corner of the earth; and here, in Dubrovnik, life still has something of the value it must have had in Venice when she was young. A city
that had made good bread had learned to make good cake also. A city
that had built itself up by good sense and industry had formed a powerful secondary intention of elegance. It is a hundred and thirty years
ago that Dubrovnik ceased to exist as a republic, but its buildings are the
unaltered cast of its magnificence, its people have still the vivacity of
those who possess and can enjoy. Here the urbanity of the Dalmatian
cities becomes metropolitan. Follow this Corso and you will find yourself in the same dream that is dreamed by London and Paris and New
York; the dream that there is no limit to the distance which man can
travel from his base, the cabbage-patch, that there is no pleasure too
delicate to be bought by all of us, if the world will but go on getting
richer. This is not a dream to be despised; it comes from man's more
amiable parts, it is untainted by cruelty, it springs simply from a desire
to escape from the horror that is indeed implicit in all man's simpler relationships with the earth. It cannot be realized in a city so great as London or Paris or New York, or even the later Venice; it was perhaps possible to realize it in a city no larger than Dubrovnik, which indeed
neither was nor is very far from the cabbage-patches. For on any fine
night there are some peasants from the countryside outside the walls
who have come to walk in the Corso.

To taste the flavour of this Corso and this city, it is good to turn for
a minute from the main street into one of the side streets. They mount
steep and narrow to the walls which outline the squarish peninsula on
which the city stands; close-pressed lines of houses—left at this hour to
sleeping children, the old, and servant-maids—which are rich in carved
portals and balconies, and perfumed with the spring. For it took the In-

dustrial Revolution to make man conceive the obscene idea of a town as
nothing but houses. These carved portals and balconies are twined with
flowers that are black because of the evening but would be scarlet by
day, and behind high walls countless little gardens send out their sweetness. Back in the main street the people from these houses and gardens
sweep down towards their piazza, past a certain statue which you may
have seen in other towns, perhaps in front of the Rathaus at Bremen.
Such statues are said to represent the hero Orlando or Roland who defeated the Saracens: they are the sign that a city is part of liberal and
lawful Christendom. To the left of the crowd is the Custom House and
Mint, in which the history of their forebears for three centuries is written in three stories. In the fourteenth century the citizens of the Republic built themselves a Custom House, just somewhere to take in the
parcels; in that age the hand of man worked right, and the courtyard is
perfection. A hundred years later so many parcels had come in that the
citizens were refined folk and could build a second story for literary
gatherings and social assemblies, as lovely as Venetian Gothic could make
it. Prosperity became complicated and lush, the next hundred years
brought the necessity of establishing a handsome Mint on the top floor,
in the Renaissance style; and for sheer lavishness they faced the Custom
House with a loggia. Because the people who did this were of the same
blood, working in a civilization that their blood and none other had
made, these different styles are made one by an inner coherence. The
building has a light, fresh, simple charm.

They mill there darkly, the people of Dubrovnik, the buildings running up above them into that whiteness which hangs above the earth
the instant before the fall of the night, which is disturbed and dispersed
by the coarser whiteness of the electric standards. The Custom House is
faced by the Church of St. Blaise, a great baroque mass standing on a
balustraded platform, like a captive balloon filled with infinity. In front
is an old tower with a huge toy clock: at the hour, two giant bronze
figures of men come out and beat a bell. The crowd will lift their heads
to see them, as their fathers have done for some hundreds of years. Next
to that is the town café, a noble building, where one eats well, looking
on to the harbour; for we have reached the other side of the peninsula
now, the wind that blows in through the archways is salt. Then to the
right is the Rector's palace, that incomparable building, the special glory
of Dubrovnik, and even of Dalmatia, the work of Michelozzo Michel-
ozzi the Florentine and George the Dalmatian, known as Orsini. Simply
it consists of a two-storied building, the ground floor shielded by a

loggia of six arches, the upper floor showing eight Gothic windows. It is imperfect: it once had a tower at each end, and these have gone. Nevertheless, its effect is complete and delightful, and, like all masterpieces of architecture, it expresses an opinion about the activities which are going to be carried on under its roof. Chartres is a speculation concerning the nature of God and of holiness. The Belvedere in Vienna is a speculation concerning political power. With its balanced treatment of its masses and the suggestion of fecundity in its springing arches and proliferating capitals, the Rector's palace puts forward an ideal of an ordered and creative society. It is the most explicit building in an amazingly explicit town, that has also an explicit history, with a beginning and an end. It is another example of the visibility of life which is the special character of Yugoslavia, at least so far as those territories which have not been affected by the Teutonic confusion are concerned.

The Corso says, "This is the city our fathers made." The city says, "These are the men and women we have made." If you should turn aside and go into the café to eat an evening meal, which here should be preferably the *Englische Platte*, an anthology of cold meats chosen by a real scholar of the subject, the implications of this display will keep you busy for the night. There is, of course, the obvious meaning of Dubrovnik. It was quite truly a republic: not a protectorate, but an independent power, the only patch of territory on the whole Dalmatian coast, save for a few unimportant acres near Split, that never fell under the rule of either Hungary or Venice. It was a republic that was a miracle: on this tiny peninsula, which is perhaps half a mile across, was based a great economic empire. From Dubrovnik the caravans started for the overland journey to Constantinople. This was the gateway to the East; and it exploited its position with such commercial and financial and naval genius that its ships were familiar all over the known world, while it owned factories and warehouses in every considerable port of Southern Europe and in some ports of the North, and held huge investments such as mines and quarries in the Balkans. Its history is illuminated by our word "argosy," which means nothing more than a vessel from Ragusa. It is as extraordinary as if the city of London were to have carried out the major part of the commercial achievements of the British Empire up to, say, the reign of Henry VII, with no more territory than itself and about three or four hundred square miles in the home counties which it had gradually acquired by conquest and purchase. That is the primary miracle of Dubrovnik; that and its resistance to Turkey, which for century after century coveted the port as the key to the Adriatic and the invasion of Italy, yet could never dare to seize it because of the diplomatic genius of its defenders.

But as one contemplates the town other issues crowd on the mind. First, the appalling lack of accumulation observable in history, the perpetual cancellation of human achievement, which is the work of careless and violent nature. This place owes its foundation to the ferocity of mankind towards its own kind. For Dubrovnik was first settled by fugitives from the Greek city of Epidaurus, which is ten miles further south down the coast, and from the Roman city of Salonæ, when these were destroyed by the barbarians, and was later augmented by Slavs who had come to these parts as members of the barbarian forces. It was then monstrously harried by the still greater ferocity of fire and earthquake. Some of the fires might be ascribed to human agency, for the prosperity of the group—which was due to its fusion of Greek and Roman culture with Slav virility—meant that they were well worth attacking and therefore they had to make their rocky peninsula into a fortress with abundant stores of munitions. They were, therefore, peculiarly subject to fires arising out of gunpowder explosions. The Rector's palace was twice burned down for this reason during twenty-seven years. But such damage was trifling compared to the devastation wrought by earthquakes.

The bland little church beside the domed fountain at the City Gate was built in the sixteenth century as a thanksgiving by those who had been spared from an earthquake which, in a first convulsion, shook down houses that were then valued at five thousand pounds, and then continued as a series of shocks for over eighteen months; and there was apparently an earthquake of some degree in this district every twenty years. But the worst was the catastrophe of 1667. The sea was tilted back from the harbour four times, each time leaving it bone dry, and each time rushing back in a flood-wave which pounded many vessels to pieces against the docks and cliffs. The greater part of the public buildings and many private houses were in ruins, and the Rector of the Republic and five thousand citizens were buried underneath them. Then fire broke out; and later still bands of wolfish peasants from the mountain areas devastated by Venetian misrule and Turkish warfare came down and plundered what was left.

We know, by a curious chance, exactly what we lost in the way of architecture on that occasion. In the baroque church opposite the Rector's palace there is a two-foot-high silver statuette of St. Blaise, who is the patron saint of the city, and he holds in his hand a silver model of

Dubrovnik as it was before the earthquake. It shows us the setting for a fairy-tale. In particular it shows the Cathedral, which was built by Richard Cœur de Lion as a thanksgiving for his escape from shipwreck on this coast, as a thirteenth-century building of great beauty and idiosyncrasy, and the main street as a unique expression of commercial pride, a line of houses that were true palaces in their upper parts and shops and offices below. We can deduce also that there was an immense loss of pictures, sculptures, textiles, jewels, and books, which had been drawn by the Republic from West and East during her centuries of successful trading. Indeed, we know of one irreparable loss, so great that we cannot imagine what its marvellous content may have been. There existed in Bosnia a society that was at once barbarous and civilized, an indirect heir to Byzantine civilization and able to fight Rome on doctrinal points as a logic-chopping equal, but savage and murderous. This society was destroyed by the Turk. At the end of the fifteenth century, Catherine, the widow of the last King of Bosnia, murdered by his illegitimate son, who was later himself flayed alive by Mahomet I, fled to Dubrovnik and lived there till she went to Rome to die. Before she left she gave some choral books, richly illustrated and bound, to the monks of the Franciscan monastery, who had a famous library. If these books had survived they would have been a glimpse of a world about which we can now only guess: but the whole library perished.

What is the use of ascribing any catastrophe to nature? Nearly always man's inherent malignity comes in and uses the opportunities it offers to create a graver catastrophe. At this moment the Turks came down on the Republic to plunder its helplessness, though their relationship had till then been friendly. Kara Mustapha, the Turkish Grand Vizier, a demented alcoholic, pretended that the armed resistance the citizens had been forced to put up against the wretched looters from the mountains was in some obscure way an offence against Turkish nationals, and on this pretext and on confused allegations of breach of tariff agreements he demanded the payment of a million ducats, or nearly half a million pounds. He also demanded that the goods of every citizen who had been killed in the earthquake should be handed to the Sublime Porte, the Republic being (he suddenly claimed) a Turkish possession. For fifteen years the Republic had to fight for its rights and keep the aggressors at bay, which it was able to do by using its commercial potency and its diplomatic genius against the Turks when they were already rocking on their feet under the blows of Austria and Hungary. Those were its sole weapons. France, as professed defender of Christianity and order in Europe, should have aided the Republic. But Louis XIV would not lift his little finger to help her, partly because she had been an ally of Spain, partly because the dreary piece of death-in-life, Madame de Maintenon, supreme type of the she-alligator whom men often like and admire, had so inflamed him with pro-Jesuit passion that a mere rumour that the Republican envoy was a Jansenist was enough to make him cancel his mission.

The story of what happened to the four ambassadors who left to plead with the Turkish Government is one of the classic justifications of the human race: almost a promise that there is something to balance its malignity. Caboga and Bucchia were sent to Constantinople to state the independence of the Republic. They were, by a technique familiar to us today, faced with documents admitting that the Republic was a Turkish possession and told with threats and curses that they must sign them. They refused. Dazed and wearied from hours of bullying they still refused, and were thrown into a plague-stricken prison. There they lay for years, sometimes smuggling home dispatches written in their excrement on packing paper. Their colleagues, Bona and Gozzi, went to Sarajevo to make the same statement of independence to the Pasha of Bosnia, and were likewise thrown into captivity. They were dragged behind the Turkish Army on a war it was conducting with Russia on the Danube, and there thrown in irons into the dungeons of a fortress in a malarial district, and told they must remain prisoners until they had signed the documents which Caboga and Bucchia had refused to sign in Constantinople. There Bona died. A Ragusan priest who had settled in the district stood by to give him the last sacrament, but was prevented by the jailers. There is no knowing how many such martyrs might have been demanded of Dubrovnik and furnished by her, had not the Turks then been defeated outside Vienna by John Sobieski, King of Poland. Kara Mustapha was executed, and there was lifted from the Republic a fear as black as any we have felt today.

It is a glorious story, yet a sad one. What humanity could do if it could but have a fair course to run, if fire and pestilence did not gird our steps and earthquakes engulf them, if man did not match his creativeness with evil that casts down and destroys! It can at least be said that Dubrovnik ran well in this obstacle race. But there is not such exaltation in the spectacle when it is considered how she had to train for that victory, both so far as it was commercial and diplomatic in origin. Everywhere in the Dalmatian cities the class struggle was intense. The constitution of the cities provided for the impartial administration of justice,

legal and economic, to persons arranged in castes and made to remain there, irrespective of their merits, with the utmost rigid injustice. This was at first due to historical necessity. The first-comers in a
settlement, who had the pick of the economic findings and whatever culture was going, might really be acting in the public interest
as well as defending their own private ends, when they insisted on re-
serving to themselves all possible social power and not sharing it with
later-comers, who might be barbarians or refugees demoralized by years
of savage warfare. But it led to abuses which can be measured by the
continual rebellions and the horrible massacres which happened in every
city on the coast. In Hvar, for instance, the island where the air is so
sweet, the plebeians took oath on a crucifix held by a priest that they
would slaughter all the nobles. The Christ on the crucifix bled at the
nose, the priest fell dead. Nevertheless the plebeians carried out their
plans, and massacred many of the nobles in the Hall of Justice in the
presence of the Rector, but were overcome by a punitive expedition of
the Venetian fleet and themselves put to death or mutilated.

This caste system never led to such rebellions in Dubrovnik, partly
because the economic well-being of the community choked all discontent with cream, partly because they had little chance of succeeding;
but it existed in a more stringent form than anywhere else. The population was divided into three classes: the nobles, the commoners, and the
workers. The last were utterly without say in the government. They did
not vote and they could hold no office. The commoners also had no
votes, but might hold certain unimportant offices, though only if appointed by the nobles. The actual power of government was entirely
in the hands of the nobles. The body in which sovereignty finally rested
was the Grand Council, which consisted of all males over eighteen belonging to families confirmed as noble in the register known as the
Golden Book. This Council deputed its executive powers to a Senate
of forty-five members who met four times a week and at times of
emergency; and they again deputed their powers to a Council of Seven
(this had numbered eleven until the earthquake) who exercised judicial
power and performed all diplomatic functions, a Council of Three, who
acted as a tribune of constitutional law, and a Council of Six, who administered the Exchequer. There were other executive bodies, but this
is a rough idea of the anatomy of the Republic. It must be remembered
that these classes were separated in all departments of their lives as rigidly
as the Hindu castes. No member of any class was permitted to marry
into either of the other two classes; if he did so he lost his position in

his own class and his children had to take the rank of the inferior parent. Social relations between the classes were unthinkable.

It is interesting that this system should have survived when all real differences in the quality of classes had been levelled by general prosperity, when there might be commoners and even workers who were as rich and as cultured as any noble. It is interesting, too, that it should have survived even when the classes were cleft from within by disputes. When Marmont went to Dubrovnik in 1808 he found that the nobles were divided into two parties, one called the Salamancans and the other the Sorbonnais. These names referred to some controversy arising out of the wars between Charles V of Spain and Francis I of France, a mere matter of two hundred and fifty years before. It had happened that in the earthquake of 1667 a very large proportion of the noble class was destroyed, and it was necessary to restore it to strength by including a number of commoners. These the Salamancans, sympathizers with Spanish absolutism, would not treat as equals; but the Sorbonnais, Francophil and inclined to a comparative liberalism, accepted them fully. It is also a possible factor in the situation that the Sorbonnais had been specially depleted by the earthquake casualties and wanted to keep up their numbers. Be that as it may, the two parties were exactly equal in status and sat together on the Councils, but they had no social relations and did not even greet each other on the streets; and a misalliance between members of the two parties was as serious in its consequences as a misalliance between classes.

But this was far from being the only sop offered by the Republic to that disagreeable appetite, the desire of a human being to feel contempt for another not in fact very different from himself. The commoners in their turn were divided into the confraternities of St. Anthony and St. Lazarus, who were as rancorous in their relationship as the Salamancans and the Sorbonnais. The survival of this three-class system in spite of these dissensions suggests that it was actually a fusion of long-standing customs, native to the different races which composed the Republic: say a variation of the classical system of aristocracy grafted on some ancient Illyrian organization of which we now know nothing, which pleased the Slav late-comers, though themselves democratic in tendency, because of the solid framework it gave to internal bickerings. "Whether they agree or do not agree," an exasperated Roman emperor wrote of the first Slav tribes to appear within the Empire's ken, "very soon they fall into disturbances among themselves, because they feel a mutual loathing and cannot bear to accommodate one another."

The system, of course, was far from being merely silly. One may wonder how it survived; one cannot question the benefits it conferred by surviving. The Republic was surrounded by greedy empires whom she had to keep at arm's length by negotiation lest she perish: first Hungary, then Venice, then Turkey. Foreign affairs were her domestic affairs; and it was necessary that they should be conducted in complete secrecy with enormous discretion. It must never be learned by one empire what had been promised by or to another empire, and none of the greedy pack could be allowed to know the precise amount of the Republic's resources. There was therefore every reason to found a class of governors who were so highly privileged that they would protect the *status quo* of the community at all costs, who could hand on training in the art of diplomacy from father to son, and who were so few in number that it would be easy to detect a case of blabbing. They were very few indeed. In the fifteenth century, when the whole population was certainly to be counted by tens of thousands, there were only thirty-three noble families. These could easily be supervised in all their goings and comings by those who lived in the same confined area.

But it is curious that this ultra-conservative aristocratic government should develop a tendency which is often held to be a characteristic vice of democracy. Dubrovnik dreaded above all things the emergence of dominant personalities. The provisions by which this dread is expressed in the constitution are the chief differences which distinguish it from its obvious Venetian model. The Senate was elected for life, and there you had your small group of hereditary diplomats. But these elections had to be confirmed annually, and infinite precautions were taken lest any Senator should seize excessive power and attempt dictatorship. The Rector wore a superb toga of red silk with a stole of black velvet over the left shoulder, and was preceded in his comings and goings by musicians and twenty palace guards; but he held his office for just one month, and could be re-elected only after intervals of two years; and this brevity of tenure was the result of ever-anxious revision, for the term had originally been three months, had been reduced to two, and was finally brought down to the single month. He was also held prisoner within the palace while he held office, and could leave it only for state appearances, such as his obligatory solemn visit to the Cathedral.

The lesser offices were as subject to restriction. The judiciary and diplomatic Council of Seven was elected afresh every year, and could not be re-elected for another year. The Council of Three, who settled all questions of constitutional law, was also elected for but one year. The

Council of Six, who administered the state finances, was elected for three years. There were also certain regulations which prevented the dominance of people of any particular age. The Council of Seven might be of any adult age, but the youngest had to act as Foreign Secretary; but the Council of Three had all to be over fifty. These devices were entirely justified by their success. Only once, and that very early in the history of Dubrovnik, did a noble try to become a dictator; and then he received no support, save from the wholly unrepresented workers, and was forced to suicide. Later, in the seventeenth century, some nobles were seduced by the Duke of Savoy into a conspiracy to seize power, but they were arrested at a masked ball on the last day of Carnival, and executed by general consent of the community.

That terror of the emergent personality is not the only trait of this aristocratic society which recalls its contrary. There is a great deal in the history of Dubrovnik which had its counterpart among our Puritan capitalists. The nobles believed in education even more seriously than was the custom of their kind in other Dalmatian towns, though even there the standard was high: the Venetian Governor of Split is found complaining of young men who came back from their studies at Oxford filled with subversive notions. But they did not, as might have been expected, try to keep learning as a class prerogative. As well as sending their own sons to universities in Italy and France and Spain and England, they built public schools which were open to the children of all three classes. They also created a hospital system which included the first foundling hospital in the whole civilized world, and they were as advanced in their treatment of housing problems. After one of the earlier earthquakes they put in hand a town-planning scheme which considered the interests of the whole community, and their arrangements for a water supply were not only ahead of the time as an engineering project but made an attempt to serve every home.

They also anticipated philanthropists of a much later date and a wholly different social setting in their attitude to the slave-trade. In 1417 they passed what was the first anti-slavery legislation except for our own English laws discouraging the export of human cargo from Bristol. This was no case of damning a sin for which they had no mind, since a great deal of money could be made in the Mediterranean slave-trade, a considerable amount of which had come to certain Republican merchants living further north on the coast; and it must be remembered that, owing to the survival of the feudal system in the Balkans long after it had passed away from the rest of Europe, the state of serfdom was taken for granted by many of the peoples under the Republic's rule or in relationship with her. But the Grand Council passed a law providing that anybody selling a slave should be liable to a heavy fine and six months' imprisonment, "since it must be held to be base, wicked, and abominable, and contrary to all humanity, and to redound to the great disgrace of our city, that the human form, made after the image and similitude of our Creator, should be turned to mercenary profit, and sold as if it were brute beast." Fifty years later they tightened up this law and made the punishment harsher, adding the proviso that if a slave-trader could not recover his victims from captivity within a certain period after he had been directed to do so by the authorities, he was to be hanged. All through the next three centuries, until the Mediterranean slave-trade became wholly extinct, it was a favourite form of philanthropy among the wealthy Republicans to buy slaves their freedom.

There were other Whig preferences in Dubrovnik: the right of asylum, for instance, was strictly maintained. When the Turks beat the Serbs at Kossovo in 1389 one of the defeated princes, the despot George Brankovitch, took refuge in Dubrovnik and was hospitably received, though the Republic was an ally of Turkey. When the Sultan Murad II protested and demanded that he should be delivered up, the Senate answered, "We, men of Ragusa, live only by our faith, and according to that faith we would have sheltered you also, had you fled hither." But there is a quality familiar to us Westerners not only in the political but in the social life of the Republic. The citizens kept extremely comfortable establishments, with the best of food and drink and furniture, but their luxury was strictly curbed in certain directions. There was never any theatre in Dubrovnik till fifty years after the destruction of the Republic, when one was built by the Austrians. In the fifteenth century, which was a gay enough season for the rest of Europe, Palladius writes: "To make manifest how great is the severity and diligence of the Ragusans in the bringing up of their children, one thing I will not pass over, that they suffer no artistic exercises to exist in the city but those of literature. And if jousters or acrobats approach they are forthwith cast out lest the youth (which they would keep open for letters or for merchandising) be corrupted by such low exhibitions."

There must have been many an English family of wealthy bankers and manufacturers in Victorian days who ate vast meals and slept in the best Irish linen and were surrounded by the finest mahogany and the most distinguished works of Mr. Leader and Mr. Sidney Cooper (and, perhaps, thanks to John Ruskin, some really good Italian pictures), but who never set foot in a theatre or music-hall or circus. But an even more significant parallel between the Republic and England is to be found in the hobbies of the wealthier citizens. English science owes a great deal to the discoveries of business men, particularly among the Quakers, who took to some form of research as an amusement to fill in their spare time. So was it also in Dubrovnik. The citizens had a certain taste for letters, though chiefly for those exercises which are to literature as topiary is to gardening, such as the composition of classical or Italian verses in an extremely formal style; but their real passion was for mathematics and the physical sciences. They produced many amateurs of these, and some professionals, of whom the most notable was Roger Joseph Boscovitch, a wild Slav version of the French encyclopædists, a mystic, a mathematician and physicist, a poet and diplomat. In his writings and those of his compatriots who followed the same passion, there are pæans to science as the illuminator of the works of God, which have countless analogues in the writings of Englishmen of the same class in the eighteenth and early nineteenth centuries.

But the resemblance does not stop there. There is a certain case to be made against the bourgeois class of Englishmen that developed into the nonconformist liberals who followed Mr. Gladstone through his triumphs, and reared their sons to follow Lord Oxford and Mr. Lloyd George to the twilight hour of their faith. It might be charged against them that their philanthropy consisted of giving sops to the populace which would make it forget that their masters had seized all the means of production and distribution, and therefore held them in a state of complete economic subjection. It might be charged against them also that they were virtuous only when it suited their pockets, and that while they would welcome Kossuth or Mazzini or any other defender of oppressed people outside the British Empire, they were indifferent to what happened inside it. It might be charged against them that they cared little how much truth there was in the bitter description of our exports to the coloured races, "Bibles, rum, and rifles," so long as there was truth in the other saying, "Trade follows the flag." There is enough testimony to the virtue of this class to make such charges not worth discussing with any heat of spirit; but there was enough truth in them to make it impossible to regard the accused as an ideal group, and the society which produced them as paradisaical. It is even so with Dubrovnik.

The Republic was extremely pious. She spoke of her Christianity at all times, and in her Golden Book there is a prayer for the magistrates of the Republic which runs: "O Lord, Father Almighty, who hast chosen this Republic to serve Thee, choose, we beseech Thee, our governors, according to Thy Will and our necessity: that so, fearing Thee and keeping Thy Holy Commandments, they may cherish and direct us in true charity. Amen." Never was there a city so full of churches and chapels, never was there a people who submitted more loyally to the discipline of the Church. But there was a certain incongruity with this in their foreign policy. Had Dubrovnik the right to pose as a proud and fastidious Catholic power considering her relations with the Ottoman Empire, the devouring enemy of Christendom? The other Dalmatian towns were less complaisant than Venice in their attitude to the Turks, the Republic far more. She never fought the Turk. She paid him tribute, and tribute, and again tribute.

Every year two envoys left the city for Constantinople with their load of golden ducats, which amounted, after several increases, to fifteen thousand. They wore a special dress, known as the uniform of the divan, and had their beards well grown. They placed their affairs in order, embraced their families, attended mass at the Cathedral, and were bidden godspeed by the Rector under the arches of his palace. Then, with their cashier, their barber, numerous secretaries and interpreters, a troop of armed guards, and a priest with a portable altar, they set forth on the fifteen days' journey to the Bosporus. It was not a very dangerous journey, for the caravans of the Republic made it an established trade route. But the envoys had to stay there for twelve months, till the next two envoys arrived and took their place, and the negotiation of subtle business with tyrants of an alien and undecipherable race, while physically at their mercy, was a dangerous task, which was usually performed competently and heroically. This was not, however, the only business they transacted with the Turks. The envoys to Constantinople had also to do a great deal of bribery, for there was a sliding scale of tips which covered every official at the Porte from the lowest to the highest. This burden increased yearly as the Turkish Empire increased in size to the point of unwieldiness, and the local officials became more and more important. As time went on it was almost as necessary to bribe the Sandjakbeg of Herzegovina and the Pasha of Bosnia and their staffs as it was to make the proper payments to the Sublime Porte.

All this would be very well, if Dubrovnik had avowed that she was an independent commercial power in a disadvantageous military and naval position, and that she valued her commerce and independence so highly that she would pay the Turks a great ransom for them. But it is not so pleasing in a power that boasts of being fervent and fastidious in its Christianity. Of course it can be claimed that Dubrovnik was enabled by her relations with the Porte to render enormous services to the Christians within the territories conquered by the Turks; that wherever her mercantile colonies were established—and that included towns all over Bosnia and Serbia and Bulgaria and Wallachia and even Turkey itself—the Christians enjoyed a certain degree of legal protection and religious freedom. But on the other hand the Republic won for herself the right to pay only two or sometimes one and a half per cent on her imports and exports into and out of the Ottoman Empire, while all the rest of the world had to pay five per cent. It is no use. Nothing can make this situation smell quite like the rose. If Dickens had known the facts he might have felt about Dubrovnik as he felt about Mr. Chadband; and if Chesterton had attended to them he might have loathed it as much as he loathed cocoa.

Especially is this readiness to rub along with the Turks displeasing in a power which professed to be so fervent and fastidious in its Christianity that it could not let the Orthodox Church set foot within its gates. Theoretically, the Republic upheld religious tolerance. But in practice she treated it as a fair flower that was more admirable if it blossomed on foreign soil. Though Dubrovnik had many visitors, and even some natives, who were members of the Orthodox Church, they were not allowed to have any place of worship within the Republic. It curiously happened that in the eighteenth century this led to serious difficulties with Catherine the Great, when her fleet came to the Mediterranean and Adriatic to tidy up the remains of Turkish sea-power. Her lover Orloff was the Admiral in charge, and he presented the Republic with an agreement defining her neutrality, which included demands for the opening of an Orthodox church for public use in Dubrovnik, and the establishment of a Russian consulate in the city, to protect not only Russians but all members of the Orthodox Church. The second request was granted, the first refused. Jesuit influence, and the Pope himself, were again illustrating the unfailing disposition of the Roman Catholic Church to fight the Orthodox Church with a vehemence which could not have been exceeded if the enemy had represented paganism instead of schism, whatever suffering this campaign might bring to the unhappy peoples of the Balkan Peninsula.

The agreement Russia offered the Republic was in every other regard satisfactory; but for three years an envoy from Dubrovnik argued the point in St. Petersburg, and in the end won it, by using the influence of Austria and Poland, and the personal affection that the Prussian Ambassador to Russia happened to feel for the beauty of the city. It is pathetic how these Northerners love the South. In the end, after two more years, Orloff had to sign a treaty with Dubrovnik, by which she exchanged the right to trade in Russian waters for her sanction of the appointment of a Russian consul, who was to protect only Russian subjects, and who might build in his house a private chapel at which his own nationals might worship according to the Orthodox rite. History is looked at through the wrong end of the opera-glasses when it is recorded that the Republican envoy signed the treaty, went straight to Rome, and was given the warmest thanks for the services he and the Republic had rendered the Holy Catholic religion by "forbidding the construction of a Greek chapel." Such pettiness is almost grand. Owing to a change in Russia's foreign policy the consul was never appointed, and the Republic permitted instead the building of a tiny chapel in a deserted spot over a mile from the city walls. When, in 1804, the Republic was again asked to grant its Orthodox citizens the free practice of their religion it absolutely refused.

This intolerance led ultimately to the extinction of the Republic. At the Congress of Vienna the Tsar Alexander could have saved it, and the cause of this small defenceless state might well have appealed to his mystic liberalism; but he remembered that the Republic had obstinately affronted his grandmother, and that in order to persecute his own religion, and he withheld his protection. But it would be a mistake to suppose that in the defence of the Papacy the Republic acted out of fidelity to its religious principles and contempt for its worldly interests. It found —and here we find it achieving a feat of economy that has brought on its English prototypes many a reproach—that in serving the one it served the other. When an Austrian commissioner was taking over Dubrovnik after it had been abandoned by the French, he remarked to one of the nobles that he was amazed by the number of religious establishments in the city. The answer was given, "There is no cause for amazement there. Every one of them was as much good to us as a round-house." And indeed this was true. The Roman Catholic fervour of this state that lay on the very border of the Orthodox territory guaranteed her the protection of two great powers, Spain and the Papacy. Again there is a smell not of the rose.

This equivocal character of the Republic is worth considering, because it affects an argument frequently used in the course of that soft modern propaganda in favour of Roman Catholicism which gives testimony, not to the merits or demerits of that faith, but to the woolliness of modern education. It is sometimes put forward that it is right to join the Roman Catholic Church because it produces pleasanter and more mellow characters than Protestantism. This, of course, is a claim that the Church itself would regard with contempt. The state of mind demanded from a Roman Catholic is belief that certain historic events occurred in fact as they are stated to have occurred by the teachers of the Church, and that the interpretation of life contained in their teachings is literally and invariably true. If membership in the Church inevitably produced personalities intolerable to all other human beings, that would have no bearing on the validity of the faith. But those who do not understand this make their bad argument worse by an allegation that Roman Catholicism discourages two undesirable types, the Puritan and his complicated brother, the hypocritical reformist capitalist, and that Protestantism encourages them. Yet the Puritan appears throughout the ages under any form of religion or none, under paganism and Christianity, orthodox and heretical alike, under Catholicism and Protestantism, under deism and rationalism, and in each case the authorities have sometimes encouraged and sometimes discouraged him. There is indeed some excuse for the pretence that Protestantism has had a special affection for the reformist capitalist, because geographical rather than psychological conditions have made him a conspicuous figure in the Northern countries which resisted the Counter-Reformation. But here in Dubrovnik, here in the Republic of Ragusa, is a complete chapter of history, with a beginning and an end, which shows that this type can spring up in a soil completely free from any contamination of Protestantism, and can enjoy century after century the unqualified approbation of Rome.

EXPEDITION

EXPEDITION

I. Savtat

THE road runs along the coast between rocky banks dripping with the golden hair of broom. The hillside above and below us was astonishing in its fertility, although even here the rain was diluting the spring to a quarter of its proper strength. There was everywhere the sweet-smelling scrub, and thickets of oleander, and the grey-blue swords of aloes; and on the lower slopes were olive terraces and lines of cypresses, spurting up with a vitality strange to see in what is black and not green. Oaks there were—the name Dubrovnik means a grove of oaks; and where there were some square yards of level ground there were thick-trunked patriarchal planes, with branches enough to cover an army of concubines. The sea looked poverty-stricken, because, being here without islands, it had no share in this feast served up by the rising sap. There was presented a vision of facility, of effortless growth as the way to salvation. This coast, in ancient times, was a centre of the cult of Pan.

There were, however, other interesting residents of a supernatural character. Somewhere up in the mountains on this road is the cave in which Cadmus and his wife suffered their metamorphosis. They were so distressed by the misfortunes of their children, who were persecuted by Hera, that they begged the gods to turn them into snakes. Ovid made a lovely verse of it. When Cadmus had suffered the change

> . . . ille suæ lambebat coniugis ora
> inque sinus caros, veluti cognosceret, ibat
> et dabat amplexus adsuetaque colla petebat.
> quisquis adest (aderant comites), terrentur; at illa
> lubrica permulcet cristati colla draconis,
> et subito duo sunt iunctoque volumine serpunt,
> donec in adpositi nemoris subiere latebras,
> nunc quoque nec fugiunt hominem nec vulnere lædunt
> quidque prius fuerint, placidi meminere dracones.[1]

---

[1] "He licked his wife's face, and crept into her dear familiar breasts, enfolded

It is an apt symbol of the numbness that comes on the broken-hearted. They become wise; they find comfort in old companionship; but they lose the old human anatomy, the sensations no longer follow the paths of the nerves, the muscles no longer offer their multifold reaction to the behests of the brain, there is no longer a stout fortress of bones, there is nothing but a long, sliding, writhing sorrow. But what happened to Cadmus was perhaps partly contrived by the presiding deity of the coast, for he was the arch-enemy of Pan, since he invented letters. He made humankind eat of the tree of knowledge; he made joy and sorrow dangerous because he furnished the means of commemorating them, that is to say of analysing them, of being appalled by them.

That was not an end of the strange events on the coast. We learn from St. Jerome's life of St. Hilarion that when (in the fourth century) the holy man went to Epidaurus, which was a town founded by the Greeks not far from here, he found the whole district terrorized by a monster living in a cave near by, who could draw peasants and shepherds to his lair by his breath. It was certainly Cadmus; literature has always found readers. St. Hilarion went to the mouth of the cave and made the sign of the cross and bade the dragon come forth. It obeyed and followed the saint as meekly as might be back to Epidaurus: all literature worth naming is an expression of the desire to be saved. There the saint said to the townspeople, "Build a pyre"; and when they had done that, he said to the dragon, "Lie down on that pyre." It obeyed. The townspeople set the pyre alight, and it lay quietly till it was burned to ashes. Without doubt it was Cadmus, it was literature. It knew that it was not a dragon, it was a phœnix and would rise restored and young from its ashes; it knew that pagan literature was dying and Christian literature was being born.

Since then Epidaurus has changed its name twice. It was destroyed by the barbarians in the seventh century and its population fled ten miles further north and founded Dubrovnik, or Ragusa. But after a time some stragglers returned to the ruins of the sacked city and built another of a simpler sort, which came to be known as Ragusa Vecchia. Now it is called Savtat, which is said to be a Slavonic version of the word "*civitas*." We stopped there and found that the story about St. Hilarion and the

---

her and sought the throat he knew so well. All who were there—for they had friends with them—shuddered with horror. But she stroked the sleek neck of the crested reptile, and all at once there were two snakes there with intertwining coils, which after a little while glided away into the woods near by. Now, as when they were human, they neither fear men nor wound them and are gentle creatures, who still remember what they were."

dragon was perfectly true. It cannot be doubted. The town lies on a double-humped dromedary of a peninsula, and the road can be seen where the dragon trotted along behind the saint, looking as mild as milk but sustained by its inner knowledge that not only was it to be reborn from the flames, but that those who kindled them were to know something about death on their own account. It was aware that when we visited the scene fifteen hundred years later we should be able to see in our mind's eye the tall villas which it passed on the way to its martyrdom, and the elegant and serious people who held their torches to the pyre; and it knew why. It knew that one day the sailors and crofters would come to live among the ruins of the town and would delve among the burnt and shattered villas and take what they would of sculptures and bas-reliefs to build up their cottage walls, where they can be seen today, flowers in the buttonhole of poverty. It knew that the peasants' spades would one day attack a part of the peninsula which, in the Greek town, had been the jewellers' quarter; and that afterwards intaglios on the hungry breasts and rough fingers of people who had never known what it was to satisfy necessity, would evoke a dead world of elegant and serious ladies and gentlemen, otherwise sunk without trace. "Lie down," St. Hilarion was obliged to say to the dragon, "lie down, and stop laughing."

Yet even that was not the last event to happen here as it does nowhere else. Two seafaring families of this place became rich and famous shipowners, and just after the war a woman who had been born into the one and had married into the other conceived the desire that Mestrovitch should build a mausoleum for herself, her father, her mother, and her brother. She held long discussions with the sculptor, and then she and her father and her brother all died suddenly, for no very probable medical reason; and the mother had only time to make the final arrangements for the execution of the plan before she joined them. There is something splendid and Slav about this. They had resolved to provoke an analysis of death by their own deaths, and hastened to carry out their resolution.

Mestrovitch made the mausoleum in the form of a Chapel of Our Lady of the Angels, standing among the cypresses in the cemetery on one of the two summits of the peninsula. It is characteristic of him in the uncertainty with which it gropes after forms: there are some terrible errors, such as four boy musician angels who recall the horrid Japaneseries of Aubrey Beardsley. There is no getting over the troublesome facts that the Turkish occupation sterilized South Slav art for five hundred years, and that when it struggled back to creativeness it found itself separated by Philistine Austria from all the artistic achievements that the rest of Europe had been making in the meantime. But there are moments in the Chapel which exquisitely illustrate the theory, the only theory that renders the death of the individual not a source of intolerable grief: the theory that the goodness of God stretches under human destiny like the net below trapeze artists at the circus. The preservation offered is not of a sort that humanity would dare to offer; a father would be lynched if he should do so badly for his son. Yet to die, and to know a meaning in death, is a better destiny than to be saved from dying. This discussion Mestrovitch carries on not by literary suggestion, but as a sculptor should, by use of form.

But this coast belongs to Pan. In this mausoleum Cadmus goes too far, he delves into matters which the natural man would forget and ignore, and he is punished. The sexton in charge of this cemetery, whose work it is to show visitors the tomb, is a cheerful soul who has taken up mortuary interests as if they were football or racing. He has himself tried his hand at sculpture, and his carvings are all excruciating parodies of Mestrovitch, criticisms which none of his enemies have ever surpassed in venom; and, as every artist knows, there are tortures which a dragon dreads far more than the pyre.

II. Perast

FROM Savtat the road goes inland and passes one of those Dalmatian valleys which cannot be true, which are an obvious Munchausen. In winter they are lakes, not swamps but deep lakes, which can be swum and fished and rowed over in quite sizable boats; I have seen one as long as Derwentwater. In spring an invisible presence pulls out a plug, and the water runs away through the limestone and out to sea by miles of subterranean passages, and instead of Derwentwater there is dry and extremely cultivable land. Thereafter we came back to the sea and the town of Hertseg Novi, where wistaria and fruit blossoms and yellow roses frothed over the severely drawn diagram of military works, to which the Bosnians and the Turks and the Venetians and the Spaniards have all contributed in their time. In the distance we saw, and did not visit because the hour was wrong, the sixteenth-century monastery of St. Savina, where King Alexander of Yugoslavia delivered to himself an intimation of his approaching death. He had visited it many times, but when he went there just before he embarked for France, he did not pull the rope that rings the bell to announce the coming of a guest. He walked past it and rang the passing-bell.

It is to be noted that his very presence there is an indication of some of the difficulties inherent in the State of Yugoslavia. This was the first Orthodox monastery we had yet seen in the whole of our journey through the country. The piety which made him visit it could not have endeared him to his Catholic-Croat subjects in the North and on the coast; and they would not have shared in the passionate interest he felt in the treasures of this church, which comprise some holy objects in the possession of the Nemanyas, the great dynasty that made the Serbian Empire, because those emperors had no historical association with them. Yet if the Karageorges had not been sustained by the Orthodox Church and their pride in their medieval past they could never have driven out the Turks or defended themselves in the Great War or freed their fellow-Slavs from the Austrian yoke. There are, as Metchnikoff said, disharmonies in nature, and probably the greatest of them is our tendency to expect harmony in nature.

We ran along a coast that was pretty in a riverside way, though it was edged with the intended cruelty of naval warfare, with dockyards and out at sea the iron sharks of torpedo-boats and submarines. But then it suddenly became lovely, we were in the Bocca di Cattaro, the Boka Katorska, the winding natural harbour, of which one has read all one's life; and like a Norwegian fjord, it made an effect that was to the ordinary landscape as ballet-dancing is to walking. The channel became wilder in shape as it became milder in surface, it narrowed to a river and widened to a bay, then flung itself away like a shawl and lay cast down between rocks in an unpredictable line. Above us the mountain-side was cut with ledges where spring stood at different stages, sometimes showing the clearest green of early woodlands, laced with wild fruit-blossom, sometimes only as the finest haze over winter darkness of tree and soil; and high above all, pricking the roof of the sky at its full height, was the snow-covered peak of Mount Lovchen. But to Norway there was added here the special Dalmatian glory: a great deal of the coast is edged with a line of Venetian Gothic palaces and churches.

The channel drew to its narrowest. Here a King of Hungary once closed it with a chain. We passed a waterfall, which, according to the custom of this limestone country, burst straight from the living rock, and came on Rishan, one of the oldest inhabited towns in the world. It was the capital of old Illyria, the seat of Queen Teüta. It is a little place that has had the breath beaten out of its body, for it has been invaded again and again since the time of the Goths onward, and has suffered also earthquake. It is a grotesque fact that when the Crown Prince Rudolf was taught Croat, the court chose as his tutor not a learned professor from Vienna or Zagreb, or any of the cultivated gentlemen to be found in the Dalmatian cities, but a country squire from this town.[1] Battered though it is, it keeps the exquisite imprint of the coastal taste, and it has something of the hardy quality of the town opposite Korchula where the sea captains lived; nets hang bronze over the golden and lilac stone.

Perast a few miles further along the fjord is finer and larger, with a surrealist touch added to its Venetian Gothic charm. For beside the harbour an unfinished church, hardly more than an open arch, stands in front of a large and completely finished church, in very curious relations to its campanile, like one distracted before a superior, like Ophelia before the Queen; and many of the palaces have been cleft asunder by earthquakes, and are inhabited by Judas trees and fig trees and poplars

---

[1] I was about to discover the reason for this from a Viennese historian when the Anschluss came, and there was silence.

and wistaria vines, which are wildly contortionist, hanging over a richly carved balustrade and forcing an entrance back to the house through a traceried window a story higher. But Perast offers a touch of familiarity to the ear, and to the eye. Its name comes once into the life of Peter the Great, who, in the course of one of his five-year plans, sent sixteen young nobles here to go to sea with the local sea captains to learn the art of navigation. The boys must have blinked at the South, at the sea, at the discipline, all new to them. And set in the bay are two islands, lying two or three hundred yards out, both covered with low buildings, one bare of all but stone, the other guarded by some cypresses. At the second every visitor must feel a startled, baffled stirring of recognition which afterwards they will probably repudiate.

But the recognition is right. This is the island on which Arnold Böcklin based his horrid vision of what happens to Bubbles and His Majesty King Baby when the goblins get them because they don't watch out: "*Die Toteninsel*," the Isle of Death. But the original is a curious contrast to the picture. The island is as if one met the reverse of a common experience, it is like seeing a photograph which represents a woman as bloated and painted, and finding that she is in fact a sunburned young athlete. It is a chaste, almost mathematical arrangement of austerely shaped stones and trees. A boatman rowed us out, and we found it the most proper and restrained little Benedictine abbey of the twelfth century, ruined, but still coherent. We walked about it for a little, and found some stately tombstones that belonged, the boatman said, to the families that lived in the palaces on the mainland, which we could see lying on the shore and on the hillside among the spring woods. The names on the tombs were all Slav, Venetian though the place seemed to the eye.

But our boatman plainly wished us to make a move, he kept on looking over his shoulder at the other island, and explaining that the baroque church there was very beautiful, and that many miracles had been performed in it. "He does not like us being here," I said; "perhaps there are snakes." But when we rowed to the other island we found he had wished to take us to it simply because he lived there, and his dog had been wearying for his company. He had been quite right in thinking this important, for it was a unique animal. Its coat, which was of drab tow, struck one as uncoiffed. Apparently dogs must pay some attention to their toilet, since it could be seen at a glance that this one paid none, being preoccupied with holy things. It had fervent sherrycoloured eyes and was the very dog for a miraculous shrine, for it had such a rich capacity for emotional life that it could hardly have retained any critical sense of evidence.

If this dog had a fault, it lay in giving to God's creatures too much of the feelings that it should have reserved for the Creator. It greeted the boatman, who could not have been away from it for more than half an hour, and offered us its friendship, as it might have broken an alabaster box of ointment over our feet and washed them with its hair. It had a baroque excessiveness, perfectly matched to the place where it lived. This island is artificial, banked up round a small rock, and it is covered with a marble pavement, on which there stands a Renaissance church, holy yet swelling its lines like the bosom of a well-nourished female saint. There is a lovely and insane piece of furniture, or masonry, left out on this pavement: a large marble table, upheld by crouching giants. Inside, the church is lined with some Italianate pictures, themselves passable, and set against a background of some two thousand votive tablets, worked in silver, an encyclopædia of the silversmith's art and the moods of the pious. There is among them one large work which is a masterpiece: it is a bas-relief showing the Turks coming down the mountains to attack Perast and being driven back. It is Renaissance work that has been preserved from its own sins by the virility of the people who practised it.

As we left, the dog promised to pray for our own salvation and expressed its intention of lighting a candle before the altar of Our Lady for the safety of its master during his journey to the shore and back. I suggested that we should ease its emotional strain by taking it in the boat with us, but this caused it great distress, and even seemed to shock the boatman. I suppose it had taken a vow not to leave the island. As we rowed away it ran round in circles, barking wildly, its head down, while behind it a totally superfluous archway, the curve of its span as sweet as the drip of syrup from a spoon, framed the grey glass of the sea by the shores of ancient Rishan. I blushed a little for the dog's abandonment, and was glad that no cat was by to sneer. She must have been a thorn in the side of her spiritual adviser.

III. Kotor

THERE is a city named Dobrota, which is a string of Venetian palaces and churches along the coast, four miles long. It is a city, it is gloriously a city, for it was made so by the Republic on account of its exploits in naval warfare against the Turks. In one of its churches is the turban taken from Hadshi Ibrahim, who fell at Piræus by the swords of two soldiers from this parish. And the place is not dead, though the earthquake struck here also, and the stained purple of the Judas tree appears suddenly between cleft walls. The Yugoslavian Navy and the liners draw many of their crews from Dobrota. The sea gives these places an unending life.

In Kotor, too, there might be death. It was once a great city. It was part of the great medieval Serbian Empire, and after that was destroyed by the Turks it belonged to Hungary and then to Venice, and became superbly rich. The route from Dubrovnik to Constantinople ran through it, and it carried on a caravan trade on its own account, which it combined with sea trade to Italy. There are in the town thirty chapels built, none meanly, by private families. But all this was stopped by Napoleon's attack on foreign trade. That, and the actual fighting he brought down on this unoffending coast, destroyed a gentle and eclectic culture. Later, the rule of Austria paralysed any movement towards recovery. A great many of the mountain tribes about here were irreconcilable, particularly on the hills by Rishan, and Austria policed the coast with a persistent nagging inefficiency that kept it poor and undeveloped and sullen.

It lies at the fjord-head, pressed almost perpendicularly against the barren foothills under the mountains which are scaled by the famous road to Tsetinye; and it is cooped up by military fortifications. Always it is a little cold. The sun shines on it only five hours a day in winter, and summer is not long enough to correct the accumulated chill. A labyrinth of alleys and handkerchief-wide squares leads from beauty to beauty. There is a tenth-century cathedral, rough but with a fine front, two towers joined by a portal that forms an arch. Inside there is a doorway from a ninth-century church that stood on the same site, which is superbly carved; among a design of interlacing strands, like our Celtic borders but of superior rhythm, two devils snatch at two escaping souls; all persons concerned are violent but serene. There is a treasury,

untidy as the jewel-case of a rich woman who has become careless of
such things through age and trouble, still stuffed, in spite of Napoleon's
army and its requisitions: I have never seen such a show of votive arms
and legs made in silver, and there were some touching crosses that had
been borne hither and thither in the long wars between the Christians
and the Turks. And there is a bishop's palace beside it, with good capon
lined, and grown with climbing flowers.

Further on among the cold alleys there is a twelfth-century Orthodox church. Here in Kotor there are many Orthodox. It has a tiny
separate church within its aisle, a box within a box, a magic within a
magic. It reminded me of what I had forgotten, the difference between
the dark, hugged mystery of the Eastern Church and the bold explanation proffered by the lit altars of the Western Church. Round an icy
corner was a Romanesque church built in the fourteenth century yet
adorned with the eagles of pagan Rome. Here there is the crucifix of a
suffering Christ, with a crown of real thorns and hair made of shavings,
which is ascribed to Michelangelo by a learned monk of the seventeenth
century, who must have been a great liar; and here one mounts some
steps before a side altar and looks down through glass on the Blessed
Osanna, a Montenegrin saint who died nearly four hundred years ago,
but keeps about her rags and tatters of skin and bones a look of excited
and plaintive sweetness. It is odd how Catholicism and Orthodoxy
modify the Slav character. In the Orthodox parts of Yugoslavia they
do not believe that it is the part of women to lead consecrated lives
though they should be pious, and there are very few convents.

"Nothing ever happens in Kotor," one would think. We thought it
proven by our guide's insistence that on one day of the year, in February, something does happen in Kotor. Then the Guild of Sailors
parades the streets in medieval costume, bearing the weapons their ancestors used to fight the Turks, and there is a ceremony at the cathedral, unique, and I believe not strictly permissible, when the relics from
the treasury are laid on the altar and are censed alternately by two
leading citizens, one Roman Catholic and one Orthodox. We are far
from the seats of authority here, and Slavs are individualist. "Is it still
a great show?" we asked doubtfully. "Surely," said our guide. "We have
lost our merchants, but we still have our sailors, which is more important."

It was an agreeable answer to hear from a man who was wearing an
overcoat so threadbare that it showed its weft. He proved he meant it
by taking us through the Town Gate to the quay, and saying proudly,

"Here are our sailors." They were walking in the pale evening sunshine, with the mountains behind them curving over the fjord like a blown wave: they were indolent as highbred horses when they are not ridden, and their faces were quietly drunken with stored energy, which they would know how to release should they one day be at Piræus, and a pirate pass them wearing a turban. "If I had not been born in war-time, so that as a child I had many sicknesses," said the guide, "I too should have been a sailor."

IV. Home by Gruda

Our chauffeur was the son of a Swabian, which is to say a German belonging to one of those families which were settled by Maria Theresa on the lands round the Danube between Budapest and Belgrade, because they had gone out of cultivation during the Turkish occupation and had to be recolonized. His father had come to Dubrovnik before he was born, and he can never have known any other people but Slavs, yet quite obviously Slavs struck him as odd and given to carrying on about life to an excessive degree. He himself, particularly when he spoke in English, attempted to correct the balance by under-statement. Hence, when we approached the village of Gruda, on our way from Dubrovnik to Kotor, he turned his head and said, "Nice people." He meant, it proved, that the men and women of this district were undistinguishable in appearance from gods and goddesses. This was one of those strange pockets one finds scattered here and there at vast intervals in the universe, where beauty is the common lot.

"But why," the chauffeur was asking himself, "make a fuss about that?" He put the question to himself with a kind of stolid passion, when we passed through the village again on our way home to Dubrovnik, and a group of three young girls, lovely as primroses in a wood, came towards us, laughing and stretching out their hands and crying out, "Pennies, pennies," as if they were not only begging but were ridiculing the ideas of beggary and benevolence alike. Since we were on the return journey we knew we had time to waste, and hammered on the glass and made the chauffeur stop. He slowed up under protest. "They will beg," he said. "Why not?" said my husband. They were, indeed, most prettily prepared to do so, for each of them carried a little bouquet of flowers for an excuse.

"Pennies, pennies!" they cried, laughing, while we stared at them and adored them. This was no case of a racial tendency imposing itself on the mass, each germ-cell had made an individual effort at beauty. One was black, one was chestnut, one was ash-blonde; they were alike only in their golden skins, their fine eyebrows, their full yet neat mouths, the straightness of their bodies within their heavy black woollen gowns. "Have you any pennies, my dear? I have none," said my husband, full of charitable concern. "Not one," I answered, and I turned to the chauffeur. "Give me three tenpenny pieces," I said. "Three tenpenny pieces!" he exclaimed very slowly. "But you must not give them three tenpenny pieces. Three tenpenny pieces! It is very wrong. They should not beg at all. Begging is disgraceful. And even if it were excusable, three tenpenny pieces is far too much."

There was much to be said for his point of view. Indeed, he was entirely right and we were wrong. But they were so beautiful, and in spite of their beauty they would be poor all their lives long, and that is an injustice I never can bear. It is the flat violation of a promise. Women are told from the day they are born that they must be beautiful, and if they are ugly everything is withheld from them, and the reason scarcely disguised. It follows therefore that women who are beautiful should want for nothing. "Please, I would like to give it to them," I besought the chauffeur, "just three tenpenny pieces; it's not much for us English with the exchange as it is."

He did not answer me at once. His nature, which was so profoundly respectful of all social institutions, made him hate to refuse anything to an employer. At last he said, "I have only one tenpenny piece on me." As I took it we both knew that we both knew that he lied. Glumly he started the engine again, while the lovely girls stood and laughed and waved good-bye to us, a light rain falling on them, the wet road shining at their feet, the creamy foam of the tamarisk on the bank behind them lighter in the dusk than it is in the day, but the yellow broom darker. "I wonder how old those girls were," said my husband, a few miles further on. "Let's ask the chauffeur. Since he's a native he ought to know." The chauffeur answered, "They were perhaps fifteen or sixteen. And if they are encouraged to be impudent when they are so young, what will they be like when they are old?"

Dubrovnik II

THE day after our expedition we went to see the treasury of the Cathedral. This is now fairly easy, though it can be seen only once or twice a week at a fixed hour; it is typical of the stagnancy which covered Dalmatia under Austrian rule that before the war it was hardly to be visited, since the clergy took it for granted in that darkened world that a traveller was more likely to be a thief than a sightseer. A visit still takes time, for Dalmatians, like Croatians, sometimes find that difficulty about being at a particular place at a particular hour for a particular purpose which they believe to be characteristic of the Serb. With a crowd of fellow-tourists we sat about for half an hour or more after the prescribed moment, in the great baroque Cathedral, a creamy, handsome, worldly building. Then a priest, not old but already presenting a very prominent stomach, came in with the keys and took us through the safe-doors into the treasury, which is divided down the middle by a low spiked barrier. We waited in a line along this, while the priest went behind it and opened a large number of the cupboards which lined the room from floor to ceiling. He took from them object after object and brought them over to us, carrying them slowly along the barrier so that each of us could see them in detail.

Some of these objects were very beautiful, notably a famous reliquary containing the head of St. Blaise, which is the shape of a skull-cap six inches high and six inches across, and is studded with twenty-four enamel plaques of eleventh-century Byzantine work, austere and intense portraits of the saints. There were some other good Byzantine and Serbo-Byzantine pieces, which the priest seemed to reckon as less interesting than the numerous examples of commonplace Renaissance work in the treasury. Though the Catholic priests in Croatia and Dalmatia are pleasant and well-mannered they have none of that natural taste and aptitude for connoisseurship which are often found in quite simple priests in France and Italy. This one, indeed, felt little tenderness towards the arts. He showed us presently a modern crucifix, highly naturalist but very restrained and touching, which had been made by a young man of the town in his early twenties; and when the stout Swiss woman beside me asked if the sculptor had fulfilled his promise, he replied, "Ah, no, he died at twenty-four of drink. It's always so, with these artists." "Yes, indeed!" agreed the Swiss, and they shrugged their shoulders and nodded darkly, preening their flabbiness in superiority over a race who must necessarily follow a discipline stricter than they could ever have imagined.

But these people believed themselves to be lovers of the arts; presently the priest brought from the cupboards an object which he dandled and beamed upon while he showed it to the spectators, who responded by making the noise that is evoked by the set-piece of a firework display. I stretched my neck but could see nothing more than a silver object, confused in form and broken in surface. When it came to the Swiss woman I could see that it was a basin and ewer which are mentioned in many guide-books as the pearl of this collection. They are said to have been left by a certain archbishop to his nephew in 1470, but a blind and idiot cow could tell at once that they are not so. Such disgraces came later.

Nothing could be more offensive to the eye, to the touch, or to common sense. The basin is strewn inside with extremely realistic fern-leaves and shells, among which are equally realistic eels, lizards, and snails, all enamelled in their natural colours. It has the infinite elaborateness of eczema, and to add the last touch of unpleasantness these animals are loosely fixed to the basin so that they may wobble and give an illusion of movement. Though Dubrovnik is beautiful, and this object was indescribably ugly, my dislike of the second explained to me why I felt doubtful in my appreciation of the first. The town regarded this horror as a masterpiece. That is to say they admired fake art, naturalist art, which copies nature without interpreting it; which believes that to copy is all we can and need do to nature; which is not conscious that we live in an uncomprehended universe, and that it is urgently necessary for sensitive men to look at each phenomenon in turn and find out what it is and what are its relations to the rest of existence. They were unaware of our need for information, they believed that all is known and that on this final knowledge complete and binding rules can be laid down for the guidance of human thought and behaviour. This belief is the snare prepared for the utter damnation of man, for if he accepts it he dies like a brute, in ignorance, and therefore without a step made towards salvation; but it is built into the walls of Dubrovnik, it is the keystone of every arch, the well in every cloister. They surrounded themselves with real art, the art that moves patiently towards discovery and union with reality, because to buy the best was their policy, and they often actually bought the best. But they themselves pretended that they had arrived before they had started, that appearances are reality. That is why Dubrovnik, lovely as it is, gives the effect of hunger and thirst.

But the priest assumed that I would wish to look long on the basin, and bent towards me over the barricade to put it as close to me as possible; and I learned how far worse than æsthetic pain the vulgarer physical sort can be. My right hand was transfixed with agony. I had rested it on the top of one of the spikes in the barricade, and now it was being impaled on the spike by the steady pressure of the priest's immense stomach. I uttered an exclamation, which he took for a sign of intense appreciation evoked by his beautiful basin, and with a benevolent smile he leant still closer, so that I could see the detestable detail more plainly. His stomach came down more heavily on my hand, and my agony mounted to torment. I tried to attract his attention to what was happening by spreading out my fingers and twitching them, but this seemed to make no impression whatsoever on the firm rubbery paunch that was pressing upon them.

This filled me with wonder. It was odd to arrive at middle age and find that one had been wrong about much that one had believed about human anatomy. I tried to speak, but the only words that came into my mind came in an incorrect form which I immediately recognized and rejected, "*Ton ventre, dein Bauch, il tuo ventre, tvoy drob*, I must not say that," I told myself, "I must say *votre ventre, Ihr Bauch, il suo ventre, vash drob*." But at that it still seemed an odd thing to say to a priest before a crowd of people. I found myself, in fact, quite unable to say it, even though I taunted myself with displaying, too late in life, something like the delicacy which made Virginia refuse to swim with Paul from the shipwreck, because she was ashamed of her nudity. I uttered instead a low moan. The priest, certain now that I was a person of extreme sensibility, swayed backwards and then forwards. My husband, even more certain on that point, dug me savagely in the ribs. I uttered a piercing scream.

The priest recoiled, and seemed about to drop the basin, but my pleasure was mitigated by the fear that my husband was going to strangle me. I held out my hand, which was bleeding freely from a wound in the palm. "Ah, pardon!" said the priest, coming forward bowing and smiling. He was taking it lightly, I thought, considering the importance which is ascribed to like injuries when suffered by the saints. "But, my dear, what was it?" asked my husband. "The priest's stomach pressed my hand down on the spike," I said feebly. "It can't have done!" exclaimed my husband. "He would have felt it!" "No," I said, "about that we were both wrong." "What was it?" asked the Swiss woman beside me. "It was the priest's stomach," I said, imprudently perhaps, but I was beginning to feel very faint.

She looked at me closely, then turned to her husband. He, like everybody else in the room except the priest, who had returned to his cupboards, had his eyes fixed on me. I heard her say, "She says it was the priest's stomach." He looked at me under knitted eyebrows, and when he was nudged by his neighbour I heard him answer the inquiry by repeating, "She says it was the priest's stomach." I heard that neighbour echo incredulously what he had been told, and then I saw him turn aside and hand it on to his own neighbour. Though the priest came back with the ewer which was the companion to the basin and fully as horrible, containing a bobbing bunch of silver and enamelled grasses, he was never able to collect the attention of his audience again, for they were repeating among themselves, in all their several languages, "She says it was the priest's stomach." It seemed unfair that this should make them look not at the priest but at me. "Let us go," I said.

Out in the open air I leaned against a pillar and, shaking my hand about to get rid of the pain, I asked my husband if he did not think that there was something characteristic of Dubrovnik, and dishonourable to it, in the importance it ascribed to the basin and the ewer; and we discussed what was perhaps the false finality of the town. But as we spoke we heard from somewhere close by the sound of bagpipes, and though we did not stop talking we began to move in search of the player. "But the Republic worked," my husband said, "you cannot deny that the Republic worked." "Yes," I agreed, "it worked." The music drew us across the market-place, which lies just behind the Cathedral, a fine irregular space surrounded by palaces with a robust shop-keeping touch to them, with a flight of steps rising towards the seaward wall of the town, where baroque domes touch the skyline. There were some fiercely handsome peasants in the dark Dalmatian costume sitting with their farm produce at their feet, and some had heard the bagpipes too and were making off to find them. We followed these, and found a crowd standing outside a building with a vaulted roof, that looked as if in the past it had formed part of some ambitious architectural scheme, perhaps a passageway between two state offices. Now it seemed to be used as a stable, for there was horse's dung on the floor; but that would not explain why there was an upturned barrel on the floor, with a penny bottle of ink and a very large scarlet quill-pen lying on a sheet of newspaper spread over the top. Just inside the open doors stood a very old man, dressed in the gold-braided coat and full black trousers of a Bosnian, playing bagpipes that were made of nicely carved pearwood and faded blue cloth. He had put the homespun satchel all peasants carry down on the floor; the place did not belong to him. He played very gravely, his brow contorted as if he were inventing the curious Eastern line of his melody, and his audience listened as gravely, following each turn of that line.

"Look at them," I said; "they are Slavs, they believe that the next Messiah may be born at any minute, not of any woman, for that is too obvious a generation, but of any impersonal parent, any incident, any thought. I like them for that faith, and that is why I do not like Dubrovnik, for it is an entirely Slav city, yet it has lost that faith and pretends that there shall be no more Messiahs." "But wait a minute," said my husband; "look at these people. They are all very poor. They are probably the descendants of the workers, the lowest class of the Republic. That means that they have never exercised power. Do you not think that they may owe to that very fact this faith which you admire, this mystical expectation of a continuous revelation that shall bring man nearer to reality, stage by stage, till there is a consummation which will make all previous stages of knowledge seem folly and ignorance? The other people in Dubrovnik had to exercise power, they had to take the responsibility. Perhaps none can do that unless he is sustained by the belief that he knows all that is to be known, and therefore cannot make any grave mistake. Perhaps this mystical faith is among the sacrifices they make, like their leisure and lightheartedness, in order to do the rest of us the service of governing us."

"Then it should be admitted that governors are inferior to those whom they govern," I said, "for it is the truth that we are not yet acquainted with reality and should spend our lives in search of it." "But perhaps you cannot get people to take the responsibility of exercising power unless you persuade the community to flatter them," said my husband, "nor does it matter whether the governed are said to be lower or higher than their governors if they have such faces as we see in the crowd, if wisdom can be counted to dwell with the oppressed." "But they are hungry," I said, "and in the past they were often tortured and ill-used." "It is the price they had to pay for the moral superiority of the governed," said my husband, "just as lack of mystical faith is the price the governors have to pay for their morally unassailable position as providers of order for the community. I think, my dear, that you hate Dubrovnik because it poses so many questions that neither you nor anybody else can answer."

Herzegovina

HERZEGOVINA

Trebinye

ALL tourists at Dubrovnik go on Wednesdays or Saturdays to the market at Trebinye. It is over the border in Herzegovina, and it was under a Turkish governor until the Bosnians and Herzegovinian rebels took it and had their prize snatched from them by the Austrians in 1878. It is the nearest town to the Dalmatian coast which exhibits what life was like for the Slavs who were conquered by the Turks. The route follows the Savtat road for a time, along the slopes that carry their olive terraces and cypress groves and tiny fields down to the sea with the order of an English garden. Then it strikes left and mounts to a gorgeous bleakness, golden with broom and gorse, then to sheer bleakness, sometimes furrowed by valleys which keep in their very trough a walled field, preserving what could not be called even a dell, but rather a dimple, of cultivable earth. On such bare rock the summer sun must be a hypnotic horror. We were to learn as we mounted that a rainstorm was there a searching, threshing assault.

When the sky cleared we found ourselves slipping down the side of a broad and fertile valley, that lay voluptuously under the guard of a closed circle of mountains, the plump grey-green body of a substantial river running its whole length between poplars and birches. We saw the town suddenly in a parting between showers, handsome and couchant, and like all Turkish towns green with trees and refined by the minarets of many mosques. These are among the most pleasing architectural gestures ever made by urbanity. They do not publicly declare the relationship of man to God like a Christian tower or spire. They raise a white finger and say only, "This is a community of human beings and, look you, we are not beasts of the field." I looked up at the mountain and wondered which gully had seen the military exploits of my admired Jeanne Merkus.

That, now, was a girl: one of the most engaging figures in the margin of the nineteenth century, sad proof of what happens to Jeanne d'Arc if she is unlucky enough not to be burned. She was born in 1839, in Batavia, her father being Viceroy of the Dutch East Indies. Her mother came of a clerical Walloon family, and was the divorced wife of a professor in Leiden University. Jeanne was sixth in the family of four boys and four girls. When she was five her father died, and she was brought home to Holland, where she lived with her mother at Amster- dam and The Hague until she was nine. Then her mother died and she went to live with an uncle, a clergyman, who made her into a passion- ate mystic, entranced in expectation of the second coming of Christ.

It happened that when she was twenty-one she inherited a fortune far larger than falls to the lot of most mystics. Her peculiar faith told her exactly what to do with it. She went to Palestine, bought the best plot of ground she could find near Jerusalem, and built a villa for the use of Christ. She lived there for fifteen years, in perpetual expectation of her divine guest, and conceiving as a result of her daily life a bitter hatred against the Turks.

When she heard of the Bosnian revolt she packed up and went to the Balkans, and joined the rebels. She came in contact with Lyubibratitch, the Herzegovinian chief, and at once joined the forces in the field, at- taching herself to a party of comitadji led by a French officer. We have little information as to where she fought, for very little has been writ- ten, and nothing in detail, about this important and shameful episode of European history. We have an account of her, one winter's night, struggling single-handed to fire a mine to blow up a Turkish fortress among the mountains when all the rest of her troop had taken to their heels, and failing because the dynamite had frozen. It is almost our only glimpse of her as a campaigner.

Jeanne's more important work lay in the outlay of her fortune, which she spent to the last penny in buying Krupp munitions for the rebels. But as soon as the revolt was a proven success the Austrians came in and took over the country, and in the course of the invasion she was cap- tured. She was set free and allowed to live in Dubrovnik, but she eluded the authorities and escaped over the mountains to Belgrade, where she enlisted in the Serbian Army. There the whole population held a torch- light serenade under her window, and she appeared on the balcony with a round Montenegrin cap on her fair hair.

But there was to be no more fighting. The action of the great powers had perpetuated an abuse that was not to be corrected till thirty-five years later, and then at irreparable cost to civilization, in the Balkan wars and the first World War. There was nothing for Jeanne to do, and she had no money to contribute to the nationalist Balkan funds. The Turks had seized the house in Jerusalem which she had prepared for Christ, and, not unnaturally, would pay her no compensation. We find her moving to the French Riviera, where she lived in poverty. Sometimes she went back to Holland to see her family, who regarded her visits with shame and repugnance, because she talked of her outlandish adventures, wore strange comitadji-*cum*-deaconess clothes, smoked big black cigars, and was still a believing Christian of a too ecstatic sort. It is said that once or twice she spoke of her lost spiritual causes before young kinsfolk, who followed them for the rest of their lives. The relatives who remained insensible to her charm carried their insensibility to the extreme degree of letting her live on Church charity at Utrecht for the last years of her life, though they themselves were wealthy. When she died in 1897 they did not pay for her funeral, and afterwards they effaced all records of her existence within their power.

It is important to note that nothing evil was known of Jeanne Merkus. Her purity was never doubted. But she never achieved martyrdom, and the people for whom she offered up her life and possessions were poor and without influence. She therefore, by a series of actions which would have brought her the most supreme honour had she acted in an important Western state as a member of the Roman Catholic Church in the right century, earned a rather ridiculous notoriety that puts her in the class of a pioneer bicyclist or Mrs. Bloomer.

We passed certain coarse cliffs with lawns between which were once Austrian barracks. "Now I remember something I was told about this place," I said. "What was that?" asked my husband. "Nothing, nothing," I said. "I will tell you later." "Look, you can see that the Austrians were here," said my husband; "there are chestnut trees everywhere." "Yes, there's been a lot of coffee with *Schlagobers* drunk under these trees," I said as we got out of the car at the market-place. We were walking away when our Serbian chauffeur called to us, "You had better take this man as a guide." This surprised us, for we had come only to see the peasants in their costumes, and any interesting mosques we could find, and the guide was a miserable little creature who looked quite unable to judge what was of interest and what was not. "Is it necessary?" asked my husband. "No," admitted the chauffeur unhappily, but added, "This is, however, a very honest man and he speaks German, and it will cost you only tenpence." He mentioned the sum with a certain cold emphasis, evidently recalling the scene with the three lovely girls of Gruda.

But he was, I think, reacting to the complicated racial situation of

Yugoslavia. He was a Swab, and had lived out his life among the Croatians and Dalmatians; and all such Slavs who had never known the misery of Turkish rule harbour an extremely unhappy feeling about the fellow-Slavs of Bosnia and Herzegovina and Macedonia, who have so often suffered a real degradation under their Turkish masters. It is as if the North and East of England and the South Coast were as they are now, and the rest of our country was inhabited by people who had been ground down for centuries by a foreign oppressor to the level of the poor white trash of the southern states or South Africa. Were this so, a man from Brighton might feel acutely embarrassed if he had to take a Frenchman to Bath and admit that the ragged illiterates he saw there were also Englishmen. Different people, of course, show this embarrassment in different ways. If they are the hating kind they quite simply hate their unpresentable relatives. But this chauffeur was a gentle and scrupulous being, and he settled the matter by regarding them as fit objects to be raised up by charity. Doubtless he would give somebody here his mite before he left; and he felt this to be a good opportunity to direct to a useful channel the disposition to wastefulness which he had deplored at Gruda.

The guide turned out to be as we had thought him. It was a poor day for the market. A storm had been ranging over the mountains all night, and as the year was still early and the crops light, most of the peasants had not thought it worth while to get up at dawn and walk the seven or eight miles to Trebinye. There were a few handsome women standing with some vegetables before them, soberly handsome in the same vein as their plain round caps and their dark gathered dresses, gripped by plain belts. We saw a tourist level a camera at two of these. They turned away without haste, without interrupting their grave gossip, and showed the lens their backs. These were very definitely country women. They wore the typical peasant shoes of plaited thongs, and by their movements it could be seen that they were used to walking many miles and they bore themselves as if each wore a heavy invisible crown, which meant, I think, an unending burden of responsibility and fatigue. Yet there were women among them who were to these as they were to town ladies, country women from a remoter country. The eyes of these others were mild yet wild, like the eyes of yoked cattle, their skin rougher with worse weather than the others had seen and harsher struggles with it; and their bodies were ignorant not only of elegance but of neatness, in thick serge coats which were embroidered in designs of great beauty but were coarse in execution, if coarse is used not in the sense of vulgarity but to suggest the archaic, not to say the prehistoric. There was a difference among the men also. Some seemed sturdy and steadfast as the rock, others seemed the rock itself, insensitive, except to the weathering power of the frost and sun.

There were also about the market-place plenty of Moslems, the men wearing the red fez, the women in the black veil and the overall made of a straight wide piece of cotton pulled in at the waist by a drawstring. "Turks," said the guide, and he was talking nonsense. Nearly all the Moslems in Yugoslavia except in the extreme south, in Macedonia, are Slavs whose ancestors were converted by the Turks, sometimes in order to keep their properties, sometimes because they were Bogomil heretics and wanted defence against Roman Catholic persecution. This is pre-eminently the case in Bosnia and Herzegovina; the true Turks left at the time of the Austrian occupation. "Look!" said my husband, and I found that he was enraptured at the sight of the fezes and the veils, for though he had spent some time in Istanbul and Ankara, that had been since the days of the Ataturk and his reforms. "Do you think the veil adds charm to the female?" I asked. "Yes, in a way," he answered; "they all look like little Aberdeen terriers dressed up to do tricks, with those black muzzles sticking out." One stopped, and offered to sell him some white silk handkerchiefs of offensive aspect, with tatting at the corners. His taste in linen is classical; she was not fortunate. Nor were any of the six others who sought to sell him such handkerchiefs at various points in Trebinye. "I don't like their handkerchiefs and I don't like them," he decided. "No doubt they're perfectly respectable, but they waggle themselves behind all this concealment with a Naughty Nineties sort of sexuality that reminds me of Ally Sloper and the girls, and the old Romano, and the Pink 'Un and the Pelican."

This was not the last we were to see of that peculiar quality. After our guide had so far exhausted the possibilities of Trebinye that he was driven to taking us down a street to see a boot-shop and saying reverently, "Batya," we decided we would go back to Dubrovnik. But we changed our minds because a little Moslem boy handed us a leaflet which announced that tourists could visit an old Turkish house in the town, formerly the home of a famous pasha, which was complete with its original furniture and its original library. We found it in the suburbs, standing among gardens where spring was touching off the lilac bushes and the plum trees: a house perhaps a hundred or a hundred and fifty years old. It was a very pleasing example of the Turkish genius for building light and airy country houses that come second only to the work of our own Georgians, and in some ways are superior, since they hold no dark corners, no mean holes for the servants, no rooms too large to heat.

This stood firm and bright and decent, with its projecting upper stories, the windows latticed where the harem had been, and its two lower stories that had their defended Arabian-nights air of goods made fast against robbers. Across a countryish courtyard, almost a farmyard, was the servants' house, where the kitchens and stables were. Down an outer staircase ran a pretty, smiling girl of about sixteen, unveiled but wearing trousers, which here (though not in other parts of Yugoslavia) are worn only by Moslem women. Behind her came an elderly man wearing a fez and a brocade frock-coat. On seeing us the girl broke into welcoming smiles, too profuse for any social circle that recognized any restrictions whatsoever, and left us with a musical comedy gesture. Her trousers were bright pink. "Turkish girl," said the man in the frock-coat, in German. "Then why is she unveiled?" asked my husband. "She is too young," said the man in the frock-coat, his voice plump to bursting with implications.

We wavered, our faces turning back to Trebinye. "Come in, come in," cried the man in the frock-coat, placing himself between us and Trebinye. "I will show you all, old Turkish house, where the great pasha kept his harem, all very fine." He drove us up the stairs, and shepherded us through the main door into a little room, which in its day had been agreeable enough. Pointing at the latticed windows he said richly, "The harem was here, beautiful Turkish women wearing the beautiful Turkish clothes." He opened a cupboard and took out a collection of clothes such as may be found in any old-clothes shop in those provinces of Yugoslavia that were formerly occupied by the Turks. "Very fine, all done by hand," he said of the gold-braided jackets and embroidered bodices. "And look, trousers!" He held up before us a garment of white lawn, folded at the ankle into flashy gold cuffs, which can never have been worn by any lady engaged in regular private harem work. "Transparent," he said. It was evident that he was affected by a glad pruritis of the mind. Coyly he sprang to another cupboard and brought out a mattress. "The bed was never left in the room," he said; "they took it out when it was needed." There was unluckily a third cupboard, with a tiled floor and a ewer. "This was the bathroom, here is where the Turkish lady kept herself clean, all Turkish ladies were very clean and sweet." He assumed a voluptuous expression, cocked a hip forward and put a hand on it, lifted the ewer upside-down over his head, and held the pose.

Undeterred by our coldness, he ran on to the next room, which was the typical living-room of a Turkish house, bare of all furniture save a bench running along the walls and an ottoman table or two, and ornamented by rugs nailed flat to the wall. I exclaimed in pleasure, for the view from its window was exquisite. The grey-green river we had seen from the heights above the city ran here through meadows deep in long grasses and pale flowers, and turned a mill-wheel; and the first leaves of the silver birches on its brink were as cool to the eye as its waters. Along this river there must have once wandered, if there is any truth in Oriental miniatures, a young prince wearing an ospreyed fez and embroidered garments, very good-looking now though later he would be too fat, carrying a falcon on his wrist and smugly composing a poem about the misery of his love.

"I should be obliged," said the man in the frock-coat, "if the well-born lady would kindly pay some attention to me. Surely she could look at the view afterwards." "Shall I throw him downstairs?" asked my husband. "No," I said, "I find him enchantingly himself." It was interesting to see what kind of person would have organized my life had I been unfortunate enough, or indeed attractive enough, to become the inmate of a brothel. So we obeyed him when he sharply demanded that we should sit on the floor, and listened while he described what the service of a formal Turkish dinner was like, betraying his kind with every word, for he took it for granted that we should find all its habits grotesque, and that our point of view was the proper one. "And now," he said, rising and giving a mechanical leer at my ankles as I scrambled off the floor, "I shall show you the harem. There are Turkish girls, beautiful Turkish girls."

At a window in the passage he paused and pointed out an observation post in the roof of the servants' house. "A eunuch used to sit there to see who came into the house," he said. "A eunuch," he repeated, with a sense of luxuriance highly inappropriate to the word. He then flung open a door so that we looked into a room and saw three girls who turned towards us, affected horror, and shielded their faces with one hand while with the other they groped frantically but inefficiently for some coloured handkerchiefs that were lying on a table beside them. Meanwhile the custodian had also affected horror and banged the door. "By God, it is the Pink 'Un and the Pelican," said my husband. Then the custodian knocked on the door with an air of exaggerated care, and after waiting for a summons he slowly led us in. "Typical beautiful Turkish girls," he said. They were not. Instead of wearing the black veil that hides the whole face, which almost all Yugoslavian Moslems wear, they wore such handkerchiefs as Christian peasant women use to cover their hair, but knotted untidily at the back of the head so that their brows and eyes were bare. "Now they are cultivating our beautiful Turkish crafts," he explained. They were not. Turkish embroidery and weaving are indeed delicious; but two of these wenches held in their hands handkerchiefs of the offensive sort that my husband had rejected in the market-place, and the third was sitting at a loom on which a carpet which ought never to have been begun had been a quarter finished.

After we had contemplated them for some time, while they wriggled on their seats and tittered to express a reaction to my husband which both he and I, for our different reasons, thought quite unsuitable, the custodian said, "Now, we will leave the ladies by themselves," and, nodding lecherously at me, led my husband out of the room. I found this disconcerting but supposed he had taken my husband away to show him some beautiful Turkish "feelthy peectures," in which case they would be back soon enough. As soon as we were alone the girls took off their veils and showed that they were not ill-looking, though they were extremely spotty and had an inordinate number of gold teeth. They suggested that I should buy some of the offensive handkerchiefs, but I refused. I meant to ask my husband to give them some money when he came back.

To pass the time I went over to the girl at the loom and stood beside her, looking down on her hands, as if I wanted to see how a carpet was made. But she did nothing, and suddenly I realized she was angry and embarrassed. She did not know how to weave a carpet any more than I do; and the girls with the handkerchiefs did not know how to sew, they were merely holding them with threaded needles stuck in them. They all began to laugh very loudly and exchange bitter remarks, and I reflected how sad it is that slight knowledge of a foreign tongue lets one in not at the front door but at the back. I have heard poems recited and sermons preached in the Serbian language which were said to be masterpieces by those who were in a position to judge, and I have been unable to understand one word. But I was able to grasp clearly most of what these young women were saying about me, my husband, my father, and my mother.

The scene was horrible, because they looked not only truculent, but unhappy. They were ashamed because I had detected that they could not sew or weave, for the only women in the Balkans who cannot handle a needle or a loom are the poorest of the urban population, who are poorer than any peasant, and cannot get hold of cloth or thread because they have no sheep. The scene was pitiful in itself, and it was pitiful in its implications, if one thought of the fair-mannered and decent Moslem men and women in Trebinye and all over Yugoslavia, sad because they knew themselves dead and buried in their lifetime, coffined in the shell of a perished empire, whose ways these poor wretches were aping and defiling. I could not bear to wait there any longer, so I left them and walked through the house, calling for my husband. The search became disagreeable, for I opened the door of one or two rooms, and found them full of trunks and bundles lying on the bare floor, stuffed with objects but open and unfastened, as if someone here had meditated flight and then given up the plan on finding that the catastrophe which he had hoped to escape was universal.

I called louder, and he answered me from a room by the main door. "What did he take you away for?" I asked. "He didn't take me away for anything but to give you the thrilling experience of seeing those wenches unveiled," said my husband. The custodian came forward and said, "I have been showing your husband these beautiful Turkish books; they have been in this house for many centuries." He thrust into my hand a battered copy of the Koran, which fell open at a page bearing a little round label printed with some words in the Cyrillic script. "Oh, Lord! Oh, Lord," I said. "This is the stamp of a Sarajevo second-hand book-shop." "Really, this is all too bloody silly," said my husband; "it is like charades played by idiot ghosts round their tombs in a cemetery." We went out into the courtyard, followed by the custodian, who seemed at last to realize that we were not pleased by his entertainment. "Do they speak Serbian or not?" he asked our guide. "No, I don't think so," he was answered. He looked puzzled and decided to assume that life as he knew it was continuing in its usual course. So he gave us the Turkish greeting by raising his hand to his forehead, exposing that national custom to our patronage or derision, he did not care which it was so long as we tipped him, and he said, "Now you have met a Turkish gentleman and seen how all Turkish gentlemen used to live." My husband gave him money, and we walked away very quickly. The guide said, "Were you pleased with the visit? It is interesting, is it not?" My husband asked, "Who is that man?" "He used to be the servant of the owner of the house," said the guide. "Who is the owner?" my husband asked. "He is a Moslem baron," said the guide. "Once his family was very rich, now he is very poor. He furnished this house and put his servant in charge of it, and I think the money he gets from it is nearly all that he has. He lives far out in the country, where it is very cheap."

When we were driving out of the town I said, "I hate the corpses of empires, they stink as nothing else. They stink so badly that I cannot believe that even in life they were healthy." "I do not think you can convince mankind," said my husband, "that there is not a certain magnificence about a great empire in being." "Of course there is," I admitted, "but the hideousness outweighs the beauty. You are not, I hope, going to tell me that they impose law on lawless people. Empires live by the violation of law." Below us now lay the huge Austrian-built barracks, with the paddocks between them, and I remembered again what I had hated to speak of as we drove into Trebinye, when we were out to have an amusing morning. Here the Herzegovinians had found that one empire is very like another, that Austria was no better than Turkey. Between these barracks the Austrian Empire killed eighty people for causes that would have been recognized on no statute book framed by man since the beginning of time.

When the news came in 1914 that the Archduke Franz Ferdinand and his wife had been assassinated by Serb patriots at Sarajevo, the Austrian authorities throughout Bosnia and Herzegovina arrested all the peasants whom they knew to be anti-Austrian in sentiment and imprisoned some and hanged the rest. There was no attempt at finding out whether they had been connected with the assassins, as, in fact, none of them were. Down there on the grass between the barracks the Austrians took as contribution from Trebinye seventy Serbs, including three women, such women as we saw in the market-place. Someone I met in Sarajevo on my first visit to Yugoslavia had had a relative killed there, and had kept photographs of the slaughter which the Yugoslavian Government had found among the Austrian police records. They showed the essential injustice of hanging: the hanged look grotesque, they are not allowed the dignity that belongs to the crucified, although they are enduring as harsh a destiny. The women looked particularly grotesque, with their full skirts; they looked like icons, as Constantine had said Slav women should look when dancing. Most of them wore an expression of astonishment. I remember one priest who was being led through a double line of gibbets to his own; he looked not horrified but simply surprised. That indeed was natural enough, for surprise must have been the predominant emotion of most of the victims. They cannot have expected the crime, for though it was known to a large number of people these were to be found only in a few towns, far away from Trebinye; and when they heard of it they can never have dreamed that they would be connected with it.

"The scene was a typical illustration of the hypocrisy of empires, which pretend to be strong and yet are so weak that they constantly have to defend themselves by destroying individuals of the most pitiable weakness," I said. "But an empire," my husband reminded me, "can perform certain actions which a single nation never can. The Turks might have stayed for ever in Europe if it had not been for the same combination of forces known as the Austrian Empire." "But there was no need for them to combine once the Turks were beaten," I objected; "in the nineteenth century the Turks were hopelessly beaten, and the Porte was falling to pieces under the world's eye, yet the Austrians were flogging their peoples to keep them in subjection exactly as if there were a terrifying enemy at their gates." "Yes, but by that time there were the Russians," said my husband. "Yes, but Tsarist Russia was a rotten state that nobody need have feared," I said. "That, oddly enough, is something that no nation ever knows about another," said my husband; "it appears to be quite impossible for any nation to discover with any accuracy the state of preparedness for war in another nation. In the last war both Great Britain and Serbia were grossly deceived by their ideas of what support they were going to receive from Russia; and Germany was just as grossly deceived by her ally Austria, who turned out to be as weak as water." "But how absurd the behaviour of nations is!" I exclaimed. "If I ran about compelling people to suffer endless inconveniences by joining with me in a defensive alliance against someone who might conceivably injure me, and never took proper steps to find out if my companions were strong enough to aid me or my enemies strong enough to injure me, I would be considered to be making a fool of myself." "But the rules that apply to individuals do not apply to nations," said my husband; "the situation is quite different." And indeed I suppose that I was being, in my female way, an idiot, an excessively private person, like the nurse in the clinic who could not understand my agitation about the assassination of King Alexander of Yugoslavia. But it is just to admit that my husband was indulging his male bent in regard to international affairs, and was being a lunatic.

When we were well on our way back to our hotel at Gruzh, past Dubrovnik and among the lovely terraced gardens of its suburb Larpad, my husband said, "When we were in that idiot house at Trebinye, which was like *Hamlet* without the Prince of Denmark, a brothel with the sexual intercourse left out, I could not help thinking of that poor chap we came on in that farm over there." We had a night or two before walked up to the top of Petka, a pine-covered hill at the edge of the sea, and after seeing the best of the sunset had strolled over the olive groves towards Dubrovnik and dinner. We had missed our path and when the dark fell we were wandering in an orchard beside a farm, obviously very old, and so strongly built that it had a fortress air. The place bore many touches of decay, and the steps between the terraces crumbled under our feet; we took one path and it led us to a lone sheep in a pen, the other brought us to a shut wooden door in a cavern-mouth. We felt our way back to the still mass of the farm, and we heard from an open window the rise and fall of two clear voices, speaking in a rhythm that suggested a sense of style, that recognized the need for restraint, and within that limit could practise the limitless freedom of wit. Both of us assumed that there were living in this house people who would certainly be cosmopolitan and polyglot, perhaps ruined nobles of Dubrovnik, or a family from Zagreb who had found a perfect holiday villa.

We knocked confidently at the door, and prepared to ask the way in German. But the door was opened by a man wearing peasant costume and a fez, and behind, the light of an oil-lamp hung on a wall shone down on a room paved with flagstones, in which a few sacks and barrels lay about in a disorder that suggested not so much carelessness as depression. At the back of the room sat a woman who gracefully turned away her head and put up her hand to hide her face, with a gesture that we were later to see parodied and profaned by the girls in the Turkish house at Trebinye. The man was a tall darkness to us, and he remained quite still when my husband spoke to him in German and Italian. Then I asked him in my bad Serbian how we might get to Dubrovnik, and he told me slowly and courteously that we must go round the corner of the house and follow a landward wall. Then I said "*Sbogom,*" which means "With God" and is the Serbian good-bye. He echoed it with the least possible touch of irony, and I perceived I had spoken the word with the wrong accent, with a long lift on the first syllable instead of a short fall.

We moved away in the darkness, turned the angle of the house, and found a cobbled path beside the wall. As we stood there a door in the house behind us suddenly opened, and there stood the tall man again. "Good!" he said, and shut the door. It had been done ostensibly to see that we were on the right path, but really it had been done to startle us, as a child might have done it. It was as if this man who was in his body completely male, completely adult, a true Slav, but had the characteristic fire and chevaleresque manners of the Moslem, had not enough material to work on in this half-ruined farm, and had receded into childishness of a sort one can dimly remember. As one used to sit in the loft and look down on the people passing in the village street, and think, "They can't see me, I'm sitting here and looking at them and they don't know it; if I threw an apple at their feet they wouldn't guess where it came from," so he, this tall man sitting in this fortress, had told himself, "They won't know there is a door there, they will be startled when I open it," and the empty evening had passed a little quicker for the game.

I said, looking down the slopes towards the sea. "It was odd a Moslem should be living there. But it is a place that has only recently been re-settled. Until the Great War this district was largely left as it was after it had been devastated in the Napoleonic wars. Ah, what a disgusting story that is! See, all day long we have seen evidences of the crimes and follies of empires, and here is evidence of how murderous and imbecile a man can become when he is possessed by the imperial idea." "Yes," said my husband, "the end of Dubrovnik is one of the worst of stories."

When France and Russia started fighting after the peace of Pressburg in 1805 Dubrovnik found itself in a pincer between the two armies. The Republic had developed a genius for neutrality throughout the ages, but this was a situation which no negotiation could resolve. The Russians were in Montenegro, and the French were well south of Split. At this point Count Caboga proposed that the inhabitants of Dubrovnik should ask the Sultan to grant them Turkish nationality and to allow them to settle on a Greek island where they would carry on their traditions. The plan was abandoned, because Napoleon's promises of hand-some treatment induced them to open their gates. This meant their commercial ruin, for the time, at least, since after that ships from Du-brovnik were laid under an embargo in the ports of all countries which were at war with France. It also meant that the Russian and Montenegrin armies invaded their territory and sacked and burned all the summer palaces in the exquisite suburbs of Larpad and Gruzh, hammering down the wrought-iron gates and marble terraces, beating to earth the rose gardens and oleander groves and orchards, firing the houses themselves and the treasures their owners had accumulated in the last thousand years from the best of East and West. The Russians and Montenegrins acted with special fervour because they believed, owing to a time-lag in popular communication and ignorance of geography, that they were thus defending Christianity against the atheism of the French Revolution.

When Napoleon was victorious the inhabitants of Dubrovnik expected that since they had been his allies they would be compensated for the disasters the alliance had brought on them. But he sent Marshal Marmont to read a decree to the Senate in the Rector's palace, and its first article declared: "The Republic of Ragusa has ceased to exist." This action shows that Napoleon was not, as is sometimes pretended, morally superior to the dictators of today. It was an act of Judas. He had won the support of Dubrovnik by promising to recognize its independence. He had proclaimed when he founded the Illyrian provinces that the cause of Slav liberation was dear to him; he now annulled the only independent Slav community in Balkan territory. He defended his wars and aggressions on the ground that he desired to make Europe stable; but when he found a masterpiece of stability under his hand he threw it away and stamped it into the mud.

There is no redeeming feature in this betrayal. Napoleon gave the Republic nothing in exchange for its independence. He abolished its constitution, which turned against him the nobles, from whom he should have drawn his administrators, as the Venetians had always done in the other Adriatic cities. Hence, unadvised, he committed blunder after blunder in Dalmatia. In a hasty effort at reform he repealed the law that a peasant could never own his land but held it as a hereditary tenant, and therefore could never sell it. In this poverty-stricken land this was a catastrophe, for thereafter a peasant's land could be seized for debt. He also applied to the territory the Concordat he had bullied Pius VII into signing, which bribed the Church into becoming an agent of French imperialism, and caused a passionately devout population to feel that its faith was being tampered with for political purposes. This last decree was not made more popular because its execution was in the hands of a civil governor, one Dandolo, a Venetian who was not a member of the patrician family of that name, but the descendant of a Jew who had had a Dandolo as a sponsor at his baptism and had, as was the custom of the time, adopted his name. These errors, combined with the brutal indifference which discouraged Marmont's efforts to develop the country, make it impossible to believe that Napoleon was a genius in 1808. Yet without doubt he was a genius till the turn of the century. It would seem that empire degrades those it uplifts as much as those it holds down in subjection.

Road

Because there was a wire from Constantine announcing that he would arrive at Sarajevo the next day, we had to leave Dubrovnik, although it was raining so extravagantly that we saw only little vignettes of the road. An Irish friend went with us part of the way, for we were able to drop him at a farmhouse fifteen miles or so along the coast, where he was lodging. Sometimes he made us jump from the car and peer at a marvel through the downward streams. So we saw the source of the Ombla, which is a real jaw-dropping wonder, a river-mouth without any river. It is one of the outlets of the grey-green waters we had seen running through Trebinye, which suddenly disappear into the earth near that town and reach here after twenty miles of uncharted adventure under the limestone. There is a cliff and a green tree, and between them a gush of water. It stops below a bridge and becomes instantly, without a minute's preparation, a river as wide as the Thames at Kingston, which flows gloriously out to sea between a marge of palaces and churches standing among trees and flowers, in a scene sumptuously, incredibly, operatically romantic.

Our sightseeing made us dripping wet, and we were glad to take shelter for a minute or two in our friend's lodgings and warm ourselves at the fire and meet his very agreeable landlady. While we were there two of her friends dropped in, a man from a village high up on the hills, a woman from a nearer village a good deal lower down the slopes. They had called to pay their respects after the funeral of the landlady's aunt, which had happened a few days before. Our Irish friend told us that the interment had seemed very strange to his eyes, because wood is so scarce and dear there that the old lady had had no coffin at all, and had been bundled up in the best table-cloth. But because stone is so cheap the family vault which received her was like a ducal mausoleum. The man from the upland village went away first, and as the landlady took him out to the door our Irish friend said to the woman from the foothills, "He seems very nice." "Do you think so?" said the woman. Her nose seemed literally to turn up. "Well, don't you?" asked our friend. "We-e-e-ell," said the woman, "round about here we don't care much for people from that village." "Why not?" asked our friend. "We-e-e-ell, for one thing, you sometimes go up there and you smell cabbage soup, and you say, 'That smells good,' and they say, 'Oh, we're just having cabbage soup.' " A pause fell, and our friend inquired, "Then don't they offer you any?" "Oh, yes." "And isn't it good?" "It's very good. But, you see, we grow cabbages down here and they can't up there, and they never buy any from us, and we're always missing ours. So, really, we don't know what to think."

Mostar

I WAS so wearied by the rushing rain that I slept, and woke again in a different country. Our road ran on a ledge between the bare mountains and one of these strange valleys that are wide lakes in winter and dry land by summer. This, in spite of the rain, was draining itself, and trees and hedges floated in a mirror patterned with their own reflections and the rich earth that was starting to thrust itself up through the thinning waters. We came past a great tobacco factory to Metkovitch, a river port like any other, with sea-going ships lying up by the quay, looking too big for their quarters. There we stopped in the hotel for some coffee, and for the first time recognized the fly-blown, dusty, waking dream atmosphere that lingers in Balkan districts where the Turk has been. In this hotel I found the most westward Turkish lavatory I have ever encountered: a hole in the floor with a depression for a foot on each side of it, and a tap that sends water flowing along a groove laid with some relevance to the business in hand. It is efficient enough in a cleanly kept household, but it is disconcerting in its proof that there is more than one way of doing absolutely anything.

Later we travelled in a rough Scottish country, where people walked under crashing rain, unbowed by it. They wore raincoats of black fleeces or thickly woven grasses, a kind of thatch; and some had great hoods of stiffened white linen, that made a narrow alcove for the head and a broad alcove for the shoulders and hung nearly to the waist. These last looked like inquisitors robed for solemn mischief, but none of them were dour. The women and girls were full of laughter, and ran from the mud our wheels threw at them as if it were a game. Moslem graveyards began to preach their lesson of indifference to the dead. The stone stumps, carved with a turban if the commemorated corpse were male and left plain if it were female, stood crooked among the long grasses and the wild irises, which the rain was beating flat. Under a broken Roman arch crouched an old shepherd, shielding his turban, which, being yellow, showed that he had made the pilgrimage to Mecca.

The rain lifted, we were following a broad upland valley and looked over pastures and a broad river at the elegance of a small Moslem town, with its lovely minarets. It was exquisitely planned, its towers refined by the influence of the minarets, its red-roofed houses lying among the plumy foliage of their walled gardens; it was in no way remarkable, there are thousands of Moslem towns like it. We left it unvisited, and went on past an aerodrome with its hangars, past the barracks and the tobacco factory that stand in the outskirts of any considerable Herzegovinian town, and were in Mostar, "*Stari most*," old bridge. Presently we were looking at that bridge, which is falsely said to have been built by the Emperor Trajan, but is of medieval Turkish workmanship. It is one of the most beautiful bridges in the world. A slender arch lies between two round towers, its parapet bent in a shallow angle in the centre.

To look at it is good; to stand on it is as good. Over the grey-green river swoop hundreds of swallows, and on the banks mosques and white houses stand among glades of trees and bushes. The swallows and the glades know nothing of the mosques and houses. The river might be running through unvisited hills instead of a town of twenty thousand inhabitants. There was not an old tin, not a rag of paper to be seen. This was certainly not due to any scavenging service. In the Balkans people are more apt to sit down and look at disorder and discuss its essence than clear it away. It was more likely to be due to the Moslem's love of nature, especially of running water, which would prevent him from desecrating the scene with litter in the first place. I marvelled, as I had done on my previous visit to Yugoslavia, at the contradictory attitudes of the Moslem to such matters.

They build beautiful towns and villages. I know of no country, not even Italy or Spain, where each house in a group will be placed with such invariable taste and such pleasing results for those who look at it and out of it alike. The architectural formula of a Turkish house, with its reticent defensive lower story and its projecting upper story, full of windows, is simple and sensible; and I know nothing neater than its interior. Western housewifery is sluttish compared to that aseptic order. Yet Mostar, till the Austrians came, had no hotels except bug-ridden shacks, and it was hard to get the Moslems to abandon their habit of casually slaughtering animals in the streets. Even now the average Moslem shop is the antithesis of the Moslem house. It is a shabby little hole, often with a glassless front, which must be cold in winter and stifling in summer, and its goods are arranged in fantastic disorder. In a stationer's shop the picture-postcards will have been left in the sun till they are faded, and the exercise-books will be foxed. In a textile shop the bolts of stuff will be stacked in untidy tottering heaps. The only exceptions are the bakeries, where the flat loaves and buns are arranged in charming geometric patterns, and the greengroceries, where there is manifest pleasure in the colour and shape of the vegetables. There are, indeed, evident in all Moslem life co-equal strains of extreme fastidiousness and extreme slovenliness, and it is impossible to predict where or why the one or the other is going to take control. A mosque is the most spick-and-span place of worship in the world; but any attempt to postulate a connexion in the Moslem mind between holiness and cleanliness will break down at the first sight of a mosque which for some reason, perhaps a shifting of the population, is no longer used. It will have been allowed to fall into a squalor that recalls the worst Western slums.

The huge café of our hotel covered the whole ground floor, and had a billiard-table in the centre. For dinner we ate the trout of the place, which is famous and, we thought, horrible, like fish crossed with slug. But we ate also a superb cheese soufflé. The meal was served with incredible delay, and between the courses we read the newspapers and looked about us. Moslems came in from the streets, exotic in fezes. They hung them up and went to their seats and played draughts and drank black coffee, no longer Moslems, merely men. Young officers moved rhythmically through the beams of white light that poured down upon the acid green of the billiard-tables, and the billiard balls gave out their sound of stoical shock. There was immanent the Balkan feeling of a shiftless yet just doom. It seemed possible that someone might come into the room, perhaps a man who would hang up his fez, and explain, in terms just comprehensible enough to make it certain they were not nonsensical, that all the people at the tables must stay there until the two officers who were playing billiards at that moment had played a million games, and that by the result their eternal fates would be decided; and that this would be accepted, and people would sit there quietly waiting and reading the newspapers.

Here in Mostar the really adventurous part of our journey began. Something that had been present in every breath we drew in Dalmatia and Croatia was absent when we woke the next morning, and dressed and breakfasted with our eyes on the market square beneath our windows. It might be identified as conformity in custom as well as creed. The people we were watching adhered with intensity to certain faiths. They were Moslem, they were Catholic, they were Orthodox. About marriage, about birth, about death, they practised immutable rites, determined by these faiths and the older faiths that lie behind them. But in all other ways they were highly individualistic. Their goings and comings, their eating and drinking, were timed by no communal programme, their choice of destiny might be made on grounds so private as to mean nothing to any other human being. Such an attitude showed itself in the crowds below us in a free motion that is the very antithesis in spirit to what we see when we watch people walking to their work over London Bridge in the morning. It showed too in their faces, which always spoke of thought that was never fully shared, of scepticism and satire and lyricism that felt no deed to have been yet finally judged.

It showed itself also in their dress. Neither here nor anywhere else do single individuals dare while sane to dress entirely according to their whim; and the Moslems keep to their veils and fezes with a special punctilio, because these mark them out as participants in the former grandeur of the Ottoman Empire. But here the smallest village or, in a town, a suburb or even a street, can have its own fantasy of costume. The men go in less for variations than the women, for in the classic costume of these parts the male has found as becoming a dress as has ever been devised for him. The stiff braided jacket has a look of cere- mony, of mastership about it, and the trousers give the outer line of the leg from the hip to the ankle and make it seem longer by bagging be- tween the thighs. But the women presented us with uncountable varia- tions. We liked two women, grey-haired and harsh-featured, who looked like Margate landladies discussing the ingenious austerities of the day's menus, until a boy wheeled away a barrow and we could see their long full serge bloomers. Other women wore tight bodices and jackets and baggy trousers, each garment made of a different sort of printed ma- terial, such as we use for country curtains; but though these wore the Moslem trousers they were Christians, for their faces were unveiled, and they covered their heads loosely with what we know as Paisley shawls. The Moslems slid about black-muzzled, wearing their cotton wrappers, which were usually striped in coldish colours, greys and slate-blues and substanceless reds, except for those who wore that cos- tume one sees in Mostar and not again when one leaves it, unless one's journey takes one very far: to Turkestan, I have heard it said.

The costume is as stirring to the imagination and as idiotically un- practical as any I have ever seen. The great point in favour of Moslem dress in its Yugoslavian form is a convenience in hot weather, which in these parts is a serious consideration, for even in Mostar the summer is an affliction. The cotton overall keeps the hair and the clothes clean, and the veil protects the face from dust and insects and sunburn. This is not true of the heavy horse-hair veil worn in the real East, where the accumulation of dust is turned by the breath of the mouth and nostrils to actual mud, but the light black veil of voile or cotton does no harm and a great deal of good. There is, however, no such justification for the traditional Mostar costume. It consists of a man's coat, made in black or blue cloth, immensely too large for the woman who is going to wear it. It is cut with a stiff military collar, very high, perhaps as much as eight or ten inches, which is embroidered inside, not outside, with gold thread. It is never worn as a coat. The woman slips it over her, drawing the shoulders above her head, so that the stiff collar falls forward and projects in front of her like a visor, and she can hide her face if she clutches the edges together, so that she need not wear a veil. The sleeves are allowed to hang loose or are stitched together at the back, but nothing can be done with the skirts, which drag on the ground.

We asked the people in the hotel and several tradesmen in Mostar, and a number of Moslems in other places, whether there was any local legend which accounted for this extraordinary garment, for it seemed it must commemorate some occasion when a woman had disguised herself in her husband's coat in order to perform an act of valour. But if there was ever such a legend it has been forgotten. The costume may have some value as a badge of class, for it could be worn with comfort and cleanliness only by a woman of the leisured classes, who need not go out save when she chooses. It would be most inconvenient in wet weather or on rough ground, and a woman could not carry or lead a child while she was wearing it. But perhaps it survives chiefly by its poetic value, by its symbolic references to the sex it clothes.

It has the power of a dream or a work of art that has several interpretations, that explains several aspects of reality at one and the same time. First and most obviously the little woman in the tall man's coat presents the contrast between man and woman at its most simple and playful, as the contrast between heaviness and lightness, between coarseness and fragility, between that which breaks and that which might be broken but is instead preserved and cherished, for the sake of tenderness and joy. It makes man and woman seem as father and daughter. The little girl is wearing her father's coat and laughs at him from the depths of it, she pretends that it is a magic garment and that she is invisible and can hide from him. Its dimensions favour this fantasy. The Herzegovinian is tall, but not such a giant as this coat was made to fit. I am barely five-foot-four and my husband is close on six-foot-two, but when I tried on his overcoat in this fashion the hem was well above my ankles; yet the Mostar garment trails about its wearer's feet.

But it presents the female also in a more sinister light: as the male sees her when he fears her. The dark visor gives her the beak of a bird of prey, and the flash of gold thread within the collar suggests private and ensnaring delights. A torch is put to those fires of the imagination which need for fuel dreams of pain, annihilation, and pleasure. The austere yet lubricious beauty of the coat gives a special and terrifying emphasis to the meaning inherent in all these Eastern styles of costume which hide women's faces. That meaning does not relate directly to sexual matters; it springs from a state of mind more impersonal, even metaphysical, though primitive enough to be sickening. The veil perpetuates and renews a moment when man, being in league with death, like all creatures that must die, hated his kind for living and transmitting life, and hated woman more than himself, because she is the instrument of birth, and put his hand to the floor to find filth and plastered it on her face, to affront the breath of life in her nostrils. There is about all veiled women a sense of melancholy quite incommensurate with the inconveniences they themselves may be suffering. Even when, like the women of Mostar, they seem to be hastening towards secret and luxurious and humorous love-making, they hint of a general surrender to mortality, a futile attempt of the living to renounce life.

Bosnia

BOSNIA

Road

A MOSLEM woman walking black-faced in white robes among the terraces of a blossoming orchard, her arms full of irises, was the last we saw of the Herzegovinian plains; and our road took us into mountains, at first so gruffly barren, so coarsely rocky that they were almost squalid. Then we followed a lovely rushing river, and the heights were mitigated by spring woods, reddish here with the foliage of young oaks, that ran up to snow peaks. This river received tributaries, after the astonishing custom of this limestone country, as unpolluted gifts straight from the rock face. One strong flood burst into the river at right angles, flush with the surface, an astonishing disturbance. Over the boulders ranged the exuberant hellebore with its pale-green flowers.

But soon the country softened, and the mountains were tamed and bridled by their woodlands and posed as background to sweet small compositions of waterfalls, fruit trees, and green lawns. The expression "sylvan dell" seemed again to mean something. We looked across a valley to Yablanitsa, the Town of Poplars, which was the pleasure resort of Mostar when the Austrians were here, where their officers went in the heat of the summer for a little gambling and horse-racing. Before its minarets was a plateau covered with fields of young corn in their first pale, strong green, vibrant as a high C from a celestial soprano, and orchards white with cherry and plum. We drove up an avenue of bronze and gold budding ash trees and lovely children dashed out of a school and saluted us as a sign and wonder. We saw other lovely children later, outside a gipsy encampment of tents made with extreme simplicity of pieces of black canvas hung over a bar and tethered to the ground on each side. Our Swabian chauffeur drove at a pace incredible for him, lest we should give them pennies.

A neat village called Little Horse ran like a looped whip round a bridged valley, and we wondered to see in the heart of the country so

295

many urban-looking little cafés where men sat and drank coffee. The road mounted and spring ran backwards like a reversed film; we were among trees that had not yet put out a bud, and from a high pass we looked back at a tremendous circle of snow peaks about whose feet we had run unwitting. We fell again through Swissish country, between banks blond with primroses, into richer country full of stranger people. Gipsies, supple and golden creatures whom the window-curtains of Golders Green had clothed in the colours of the sunrise and the sunset, gave us greetings and laughter; Moslem women walking unveiled towards the road turned their backs until we passed, or if there was a wall near by sought it and flattened their faces against it. We came to a wide valley, flanked with hills that, according to the curious conformation, run not east and west nor north and south but in all directions, so that the view changed every instant and the earth seemed as fluid and restless as the ocean.

"We are quite near Sarajevo," I said; "it is at the end of this valley." Though I was right, we did not arrive there for some time. The main road was under repair and we had to make a detour along a road so bad that the mud spouted higher than the car, and after a mile or so our faces and topcoats were covered with it. This is really an undeveloped country, one cannot come and go yet as one chooses.

Sarajevo I

"Look," I said, "the river at Sarajevo runs red. That I think a bit too much. The pathetic fallacy really ought not to play with such painful matters." "Yes, it is as blatant as a propagandist poster," said my husband. We were standing on the bridge over which the Archduke Franz Ferdinand and his wife would have driven on the morning of June the twenty-eighth, 1914, if they had not been shot by a Bosnian named Gabriel Princip, just as their car was turning off the embankment.

We shuddered and crossed to the other bank, where there was a little park with a café in it. We sat and drank coffee, looking at the *Pyrus Japonica* and the white lilacs that grew all round us, and the people, who were almost as decorative as flowers. At the next table sat a Moslem woman wearing a silk overall striped in lilac and purple and dull blue. Her long narrow hand shot out of its folds to spoon a drop from a glass of water into her coffee-cup; here there is Turkish coffee, which carries its grounds in suspension, and the cold drop precipitates them. Her hand shot out again to hold her veil just high enough to let her other hand carry the cup to her lips. When she was not drinking she sat quite still, the light breeze pressing her black veil against her features. Her stillness was more than the habit of a Western woman, yet the uncovering of her mouth and chin had shown her completely un-Oriental, as luminously fair as any Scandinavian. Further away two Moslem men sat on a bench and talked politics, beating with their fingers on the headlines of a newspaper. Both were tall, raw-boned, bronze-haired, with eyes crackling with sheer blueness: Danish sea captains, perhaps, had they not been wearing the fez.

We noted then, and were to note it again and again as we went about the city, that such sights gave it a special appearance. The costumes which we regard as the distinguishing badge of an Oriental race, proof positive that the European frontier has been crossed, are worn by people far less Oriental in aspect than, say, the Latins; and this makes Sarajevo look like a fancy-dress ball. There is also an air of immense luxury about the town, of unwavering dedication to pleasure, which makes it credible that it would hold a festivity on so extensive and costly a scale. This air is, strictly speaking, a deception, since Sarajevo is stuffed with poverty of a most denuded kind. The standard of living among the working classes is lower than even in our great Western cities. But there is also a solid foundation of moderate wealth. The Moslems here scorned trade but they were landowners, and their descendants hold the remnants of their fortunes and are now functionaries and professional men. The trade they rejected fell into the hands of the Christians, who therefore grew in the towns to be a wealthy and privileged class, completely out of touch with the oppressed Christian peasants outside the city walls. There is also a Jewish colony here, descended from a group who came here from Spain after the expulsory decrees of Ferdinand and Isabella, and grafted itself on an older group which had been in the Balkans from time immemorial; it has acquired wealth and culture. So the town lies full-fed in the trough by the red river, and rises up the bowl of the blunt-ended valley in happy, open suburbs where handsome houses stand among their fruit trees. There one may live very pleasantly, looking down on the minarets of the hundred mosques of Sarajevo, and the tall poplars that march the course of the red-running river. The dead here also make for handsomeness, for acres and acres above these suburbs are given up to the deliberate carelessness of the Moslem cemeteries, where the marble posts stick slantwise among uncorrected grass and flowers and ferns, which grow as cheerfully as in any other meadow.

But the air of luxury in Sarajevo has less to do with material goods than with the people. They greet delight here with unreluctant and sturdy appreciation, they are even prudent about it, they will let no drop of pleasure run to waste. It is good to wear red and gold and blue and green: the women wear them, and in the Moslem bazaar that covers several acres of the town with its open-fronted shops there are handkerchiefs and shawls and printed stuffs which say "Yes" to the idea of brightness as only the very rich, who can go to dressmakers who are conscious specialists in the eccentric, dare to say it in the Western world. Men wash in the marble fountain of the great mosque facing the bazaar and at the appointed hour prostrate themselves in prayer, with the most comfortable enjoyment of coolness and repose and the performance of a routine in good repute. In the Moslem cookshops they sell the great cartwheel tarts made of fat leaf-thin pastry stuffed with spinach which presuppose that no man will be ashamed of his greed and his liking for grease. The looks the men cast on the veiled women, the gait by which the women admit that they know they are being looked upon, speak of a romanticism that can take its time to dream and resolve because it is the flower of the satisfied flesh. This tradition of tranquil sensuality is of Moslem origin, and is perhaps still strongest among

Moslems, but also on Jewish and Christian faces can there be recognized this steady light, which makes it seem as if the Puritans who banish pleasure and libertines who savage her do worse than we had imagined. We had thought of them as destroying harmless beauty: but here we learned to suspect that they throw away an instruction necessary for the mastery of life.

Though Sarajevo has so strong a character it is not old as cities go. It was originally a mining town. Up on the heights there is to be seen a Turkish fortress, reconditioned by the Austrians, and behind it are the old workings of a mine that was once exploited by merchants from Dubrovnik. This is not to say that it had ever any of the casual and reckless character of a modern mining town. In past ages, before it was realized that though minerals seem solid enough their habits make them not more reliable as supports than the rainbow, a mining town would be as sober and confident as any other town built on a hopeful industry. But it was neither big nor powerful when it fell into the hands of the Turks in 1464. The capital of Bosnia was Yaitse, usually but unhelpfully spelt Jajce, about ninety miles or so north in the mountains. But after the conquest Sarajevo became extremely important as a focal point where various human characteristics were demonstrated, one of which was purely a local peculiarity, yet was powerful and appalling on the grandest scale.

It happened that the Manichæan heresy, which had touched Dalmatia and left its mark so deeply on Trogir, had struck even deeper roots in Bosnia, where a sect called the Bogomils had attracted a vast proportion of the people, including both the feudal lords and the peasants. We do not know much about this sect except from their enemies, who were often blatant liars. It is thought from the name "Bogomil," which means "God have mercy" in old Slavonic, and from the behaviour of the surviving remnants of the sect, that they practised the habit of ecstatic prayer, which comes easy to all Slavs; and they adapted the dualism of this heresy to Slav taste. They rejected its Puritanism and incorporated in it a number of pre-Christian beliefs and customs, including such superstitions as the belief in the haunting of certain places by elemental spirits and the practice of gathering herbs at certain times and using them with incantations. They also gave it a Slav character by introducing a political factor. Modern historians suggest that Bogomilism was not so much a heresy as a schism, that it represented the attempt of a strong national party to form a local church which should be independent of either the Roman Catholic or the Orthodox Church.

Whatever Bogomilism was, it satisfied the religious necessities of the mass of Bosnians for nearly two hundred and fifty years, notwithstanding the savage attacks of both the Roman Catholic and the Orthodox Churches. The Roman Catholic Church was the more dangerous of the two. This was not because the Orthodox Church had the advantage in tolerance: the Council of Constantinople laid it down that Bogomils must be burned alive. It was because the political situation in the East became more and more unfavourable to the Orthodox Church, until finally the coming of the Turks ranged them among the objects rather than the inflictors of persecution. The Latin Church had no such mellowing misfortunes; and though for a time it lost its harshness towards heretics, and was, for example, most merciful towards Jews and Arians under the Carlovingians, it was finally urged by popular bigotry and adventurous monarchs to take up the sword against the enemies of the faith.

At the end of the twelfth century we find a King of Dalmatia who wanted to seize Bosnia complaining to the Pope that the province was full of heretics, and appealing to him to get the King of Hungary to expel them. This began a system of interference which was for long wholly unavailing. In 1221 there were none but Bogomil priests in Bosnia, under whom the country was extremely devout. But the zeal of the Church had been fired, and in 1247 the Pope endeavoured to inspire the Archbishop of Bosnia by describing to him how his predecessors had tried to redeem their see by devastating the greater part of it and by killing or carrying away in captivity many thousands of Bosnians. The people, however, remained obstinately Bogomil, and as soon as the attention of the Papacy was diverted elsewhere, as it was during the Waldensian persecutions and the Great Schism, they stood firm in their faith again. Finally it was adopted as the official state religion.

But the Papacy had staked a great deal on Bosnia. It had preached crusade after crusade against the land, with full indulgences, as in the case of crusades to Palestine. It had sent out brigades of missionaries, who had behaved with glorious heroism and had in many cases suffered martyrdom. It had used every form of political pressure on neighbouring monarchs to induce them to invade Bosnia and put it to fire and the sword. It had, by backing Catholic usurpers to the Bosnian throne, caused perpetual disorder within the kingdom and destroyed all possibility of dynastic unity. Now it made one last supreme effort. It supported the Emperor Sigismund of Hungary, who held Croatia and Dalmatia, and who wished to add Bosnia to his kingdom. This was not a step at all likely to promote the cause of order. Sigismund was a flighty adventurer whose indifference to Slav interests was later shown by his sale of Dalmatia to Venice. But the Pope issued a Bull calling Christendom to a crusade against the Turks, the apostate Arians, and the heretic Bosnians, and the Emperor embarked on a campaign which was sheer vexation to the tortured Slav lands, and scored the success of capturing the Bosnian king. The Bosnians were unimpressed and replaced him by another, also a staunch Bogomil. Later Sigismund sent back the first king, whose claim to the throne was naturally resented by the second. The wretched country was again precipitated into civil war.

This was in 1415. In 1389 the battle of Kossovo had been lost by the Christian Serbs. For twenty-six years the Turks had been digging themselves in over the border of Bosnia. They had already some foothold in the southern part of the kingdom. A child could have seen what was bound to happen. The Turks offered the Bogomils military protection, secure possession of their lands, and full liberty to practise their religion provided they counted themselves as Moslems and not as Christians, and did not attack the forces of the Ottoman Empire. The Bogomils, having been named in a Papal Bull with the Turks as common enemies of Christendom and having suffered invasion in consequence, naturally accepted the offer. Had it not been for the intolerance of the Papacy we would not have had Turkey in Europe for five hundred years. Fifty years later, the folly had been consummated. Bosnia was wholly Turkish, and the Turks had passed on towards Hungary and Central Europe. It is worth while noting that a band of Bogomils who had been driven out of Bosnia by a temporary Catholic king, while their companions had been sent in chains to Rome to be "benignantly converted," valiantly defended the Herzegovinian mountains against the Turks for another twenty years.

But the story does not stop there. It was only then that a certain peculiar and awful characteristic of human nature showed itself, as it has since shown itself on one other occasion in history. There is a kind of human being, terrifying above all others, who resist by yielding. Let it be supposed that it is a woman. A man is pleased by her, he makes advances to her, he finds that no woman was ever more compliant. He marvels at the way she allows him to take possession of her and perhaps despises her for it. Then suddenly he finds that his whole life has been conditioned to her, that he has become bodily dependent on her, that he has acquired the habit of living in a house with her, that food is not food unless he eats it with her.

It is at this point that he suddenly realizes that he has not conquered her mind, and that he is not sure if she loves him, or even likes him, or even considers him of great moment. Then it occurs to him as a possibility that she failed to resist him in the first place because simply nothing he could do seemed of the slightest importance. He may even suspect that she let him come into her life because she hated him, and wanted him to expose himself before her so that she could despise him for his weakness. This, since man is a hating rather than a loving animal, may not impossibly be the truth of the situation. There will be an agonizing period when he attempts to find out the truth. But that he will not be able to do, for it is the essence of this woman's character not to uncover her face. He will therefore have to withdraw from the frozen waste in which he finds himself, where there is neither heat nor light nor food nor shelter, but only the fear of an unknown enemy, and he will have to endure the pain of living alone till he can love someone else; or he will have to translate himself into another person, who will be accepted by her, a process that means falsification of the soul. Whichever step he takes, the woman will grow stronger and more serene, though not so strong and serene as she will if he tries the third course of attempting to coerce her.

Twice the Slavs have played the part of this woman in the history of Europe. Once, on the simpler occasion, when the Russians let Napoleon into the core of their country, where he found himself among snow and ashes, his destiny dead. The second time it happened here in Sarajevo. The heretic Bosnian nobles surrendered their country to the Turks in exchange for freedom to keep their religion and their lands, but they were aware that these people were their enemies. There could be no two races more antipathetic than the Slavs, with their infinite capacity for inquiry and speculation, and the Turks, who had no word in their language to express the idea of being interested in anything, and who were therefore content in abandonment to the tropism of a militarist system. This antipathy grew stronger as the Turks began to apply to Bosnia the same severe methods of raising revenue with which they drained all their conquered territories, and the same system of recruiting. For some time after the conquest they began to draw from Bosnia, as from Serbia and Bulgaria and Macedonia, the pick of all the Slav boys, to act as Janizaries, as the Prætorian Guard of the Ottoman Empire. It was the fate of these boys to be brought up ignorant of the names of their families or their birth-places, to be denied later the right to marry or own property, to be nothing but instruments of warfare for the Sultan's use, as inhuman as lances or bombs.

To these exactions the Bosnians submitted. They could do nothing else. But the two Bosnian nobles who had been the first to submit to the Turks came to this mining town and founded a city which was called Bosna Sarai, from the fortress, the *Sarai*, on the heights above it. Here they lived in a pride undiminished by conquest, though adapted to it. It must be remembered that these people would not see themselves as renegades in any shocking sense. The followers of a heresy itself strongly Oriental in tone would not feel that they were abandoning Christianity in practising their worship under Moslem protection, since Mohammed acknowledged the sanctity of Christ, and Moslems had no objection to worshipping in Christian churches. To this day in Sarajevo Moslems make a special point of attending the Church of St. Anthony of Padua every Tuesday evening. The Bosnian Moslems felt that they had won their independence by a concession no greater than they would have made had they submitted to the Roman Catholic Church. So they sat down in their new town, firm in self-respect, and profited by the expanding wealth of their conquerors.

It was then, no doubt, that the town acquired its air of pleasure, for among the Turks at that time voluptuousness knew its splendid holiday. An insight into what its wealth came to be is given us by a catastrophe. When Kara Mustapha, the Vizier who tormented Dubrovnik, was beaten outside Vienna his camp dazzled Europe with a vision of luxury such as it had never seen, such as perhaps it has never known since. His stores were immense; he travelled with twenty thousand head apiece of buffaloes, oxen, camels, and mules, a flock of ten thousand sheep, and a country's crop of corn and sugar and coffee and honey and fat. His camp was the girth of Warsaw, wrote John Sobieski to his wife, and not imaginable by humble Poles. The Vizier's tent—this I know, for I once saw it in Vienna—was a masterpiece of delicate embroidery in many colours. There were also bathrooms flowing with scented waters, gardens with fountains, superb beds, glittering lamps and chandeliers and priceless carpets, and a menagerie containing all manner of birds and beasts and fishes. Before Kara Mustapha fled he decapitated two of his possessions which he thought so beautiful he could not bear the Christian dogs to enjoy them. One was a specially beautiful wife, the other was an ostrich. The scent of that world, luxurious and inclusive, still hangs about the mosques and latticed windows and walled gardens of Sarajevo.

But however sensuous that population might be, it was never supine. Sarajevo, as the seat of the new Moslem nobility, was made the headquarters of the Bosnian Janizaries. These Janizaries, however, singularly failed to carry out the intention of their founders. Their education proved unable to make them forget they were Slavs. They insisted on speaking Serbian, they made no effort to conceal a racial patriotism, and what was more they insisted on taking wives and acquiring property. Far from inhumanly representing the Ottoman power in opposition to the Bosnian nobles, they were their friends and allies. The Porte found itself unable to alter this state of affairs, because the Janizaries of Constantinople, who were also Slavs, had a lively liking for them and could not be trusted to act against them. It had no other resources, for it had exterminated the leaders of the Bosnian Christians and in any case could hardly raise them up to fight for their oppressors.

Hence there grew up, well within the frontiers of the Ottoman Empire, a Free City, in which the Slavs lived as they liked, according to a constitution they based on Slav law and custom, and defied all interference. It even passed a law by which the Pasha of Bosnia was forbidden to stay more than a night at a time within the city walls. For that one night he was treated as an honoured guest, but the next morning he found himself escorted to the city gates. It was out of the question that the Ottoman Empire should ever make Sarajevo its seat of government. That had to be the smaller town of Travnik, fifty miles away, and even there the Pasha was not his own master. If the Janizaries of Sarajevo complained of him to the Sublime Porte, he was removed. Fantastically, the only right that the Porte insisted on maintaining to prove its power was the appointment of two officials to see that justice was done in disputes between Christians and Moslems; and even then the Commune of Sarajevo could dismiss them once they were appointed. Often the sultans and viziers must have wondered, "But when did we conquer these people? Alas, how can we have thought we had conquered these people? What would we do not to have conquered these people?"

Things went very well with this mutinous city for centuries. Its independence enabled it to withstand the shock of the blows inflicted on the Turks at Vienna and Belgrade, which meant that they must abandon their intention of dominating Europe. There came a bad day at the end of the seventeenth century, when Prince Eugène of Savoy rode down from Hungary with his cavalry and looked down on the city from a foothill at the end of the valley. Then the Slavs proved their unity in space and time, and the Bosnians rehearsed the trick that the Russians were later to play on Napoleon. The town, Prince Eugène was told, had been abandoned. It lay there, empty, to be taken. Prince Eugène grew thoughtful and advanced no further, though he had been eager to see this outpost of the East, whose atmosphere must have been pleasing to his own type of voluptuousness. He turned round and went back to the Danube at the head of a vast column of Christian refugees whom he took to Austrian territory. Perhaps that retreat made the difference between the fates of Prince Eugène and Napoleon.

After that a century passed and left Sarajevo much as it was, plump in insubordination. Then came the great reforming sultans, Selim III and Mahmud II, who saw that they must rebuild their house if it were not to tumble about their ears. They resolved to reorganize the Janizaries and, when that proved impossible, to disband them. These were by now a completely lawless body exercising supreme authority over all lawfully constituted administrative units. Also the sultans resolved to reform the land and taxation system which made hungry slaves of the peasants. Nothing would have been less pleasing to Sarajevo. The Janizaries and the Bosnian nobility had worked together to maintain unaltered the feudal system which had perished in nearly all other parts of Europe, and the proposal to remove the disabilities of the Christian peasants re-awakened a historic feud. The Bosnian Moslem city-dwelling nobles hated these Christian peasants, because they were the descendants of the Catholic and Orthodox barons and their followers who had opened the door to the invader by their intolerance of Bogomilism.

Therefore the Janizaries and the Moslem nobles fought the sultans. The Janizaries refused to be disbanded and when their brothers had been exterminated in Constantinople the prohibited uniform was still to be seen in Sarajevo: the blue pelisse, the embroidered under-coat, the huge towering turban, decorated when the wearer was of the higher ranks with bird-of-paradise plumes, the high leather boots, red and yellow and black according to rank. In time they had to retreat from the town to the fortress on the heights above it, and that too fell later to the troops of the central authority; Bosnian nobles were beheaded, and the Pasha entered into full possession of the city where for four centuries he had been received on sufferance. But after a few months, in July 1828, the Sarajevans took their revenge and, aided by the citizens of a neighbouring town called Visok, broke in and for three days massacred their conquerors. Their victory was so terrible that they were left undisturbed till 1850, and then they were defeated by a Turkish Empire which itself was near to defeat, and was to be drummed out of Bosnia by peasants not thirty years later. At last the two lovers had destroyed each other. But they were famous lovers. This beautiful city speaks always of their preoccupation with one another, of what the Slav, not to be won by any gift, took from the Turk, and still was never won, of the unappeasable hunger with which the Turk longed throughout the centuries to make the Slav subject to him, although the Slav is never subject, not even to himself.

Sarajevo II

WE knew we should try to get some sleep before the evening, because Constantine was coming from Belgrade and would want to sit up late and talk. But we hung about too late in the bazaar, watching a queue of men who had lined up to have their fezes ironed. It is an amusing process. In a steamy shop two Moslems were working, each clapping a fez down on a fez-shaped cone heated inside like an old-fashioned flat-iron and then clapping down another cone on it and screwing that down very tight, then releasing the fez with a motherly expression. "What extremely tidy people the Moslems must be," said my husband; but added, "This cannot be normal, however. If it were there would be more shops of this sort. There must be some festival tomorrow. We will ask the people at the hotel." But we were so tired that we forgot, and slept so late that Constantine had to send us up a message saying he had arrived and was eager to go out to dinner.

When we came downstairs Constantine was standing in the hall, talking to two men, tall and dark and dignified, with the sallow, long-lashed dignity of Sephardim. "I tell you I have friends everywhere," he said. "These are two of my friends, they like me very much. They are Jews from Spain, and they speak beautiful soft Spanish of the time of Ferdinand and Isabella, not the Spanish of today, which is hard and guttural as German. This is Dr. Lachan, who is a banker, and Dr. Marigan, who is a judge. I think they are both very good men, they move in a sort of ritual way along prescribed paths, and there is nothing ever wrong. Now they will take us to a café where we will eat a little, but it is not for the eating they are taking us there, it is because they have heard there is a girl there who sings the Bosnian songs very well, and it is not for nothing that there are so many mosques in Sarajevo; this is truly the East, and people attach great importance to such things as girls who sing the Bosnian songs, even though they are very serious people."

The men greeted us with beautiful and formal manners, and we went down the street to the café. It could be seen they liked Constantine half because he is a great poet, half because he is like a funny little dog. But at the door they began to think of us and wonder if they should take us to such a place. "For us and our wives it is nice," they said, "but we are used to it. Perhaps for an English lady it will seem rather strange. There

are sometimes dancers . . . well, there is one now." A stout woman clad
in sequined pink muslin trousers and brassière was standing on a platform
revolving her stomach in time to the music of a piano and violin, and as
we entered she changed her subject matter and began to revolve her
large firm breasts in opposite directions. This gave an effect of hard,
mechanical magic; it was as if two cannon-balls were rolling away from
each other but were for ever kept contingent by some invisible power
of attraction. "Your wife does not mind?" asked the judge and the
banker. "I think not," said my husband. As we went down the aisle one
of the cannon-balls ceased to revolve, though the other went on rolling
quicker than ever, while the woman cried out my name in tones of familiarity and welcome. The judge and the banker showed no signs of
having witnessed this greeting. As we sat down I felt embarrassed by
their silence and said, in explanation, "How extraordinary I should come
across this woman again." "I beg your pardon?" said the judge. "How
extraordinary it is," I repeated, "that I should come across this woman
again. I met her last year in Macedonia." "Oh, it is you that she knows!"
exclaimed the judge and the banker, and I perceived that they had
thought she was a friend of my husband's.

I was really very glad to see her again. When Constantine and I had
been in Skoplje the previous Easter he had taken me to a night club in the
Moslem quarter. That form of entertainment which we think of as peculiarly modern Western and profligate was actually far more at home in
the ancient and poverty-stricken Near East. In any sizable village in
Macedonia I think one would find at least one café where a girl sang and
there was music. In Skoplje, which has under seventy thousand inhabitants, there are many such, including a night club almost on a Trocadéro
scale. In the little Moslem cabaret we visited there was nobody more
opulent than a small shopkeeper, but the performers numbered a male
gipsy who sang and played the gusla, a very beautiful Serbian singer, a
still more beautiful gipsy girl who sang and danced, and this *danseuse de
ventre*, who was called Astra. When Astra came round and rattled the
plate at our table I found she was a Salonika Jewess, member of another
colony of refugees from Ferdinand and Isabella who still speak Spanish,
and I asked her to come and see me the next day at my hotel and give me
a lesson in the *danse de ventre*.

She was with me earlier than I had expected, at ten o'clock, wearing a
curious coat-frock, of a pattern and inexpert make which at once suggested she had hardly any occasion to be fully dressed, and that she
would have liked to be a housewife in a row of houses all exactly alike.

The lesson in the *danse de ventre* was not a success. I picked up the movement wonderfully, she said; I had it perfectly, but I could not produce the right effect. "*Voyez-vous, Madame,*" she said, in the slow French she had picked up in a single term at a mission school, "*vous n'avez pas de quoi.*" It is the only time in my life that I have been reproached with undue slenderness; but I suppose Astra herself weighed a hundred and sixty pounds, though she carried no loose flesh like a fat Western woman, but was solid and elastic. After the lesson had failed we sat and talked. She came of a family of musicians. She had a sister who had married an Englishman employed in Salonika, and now lived in Ealing and had two pretty little girls, like dolls they were so pretty, Milly and Lily. It was terrible they were so far away. She herself was a widow, her husband had been a Greek lorry driver who was killed in a road accident after three years of marriage. She had one son, a boy of ten. It was her ambition that he should go to a French school, in her experience there was nothing like French education "*pour faire libre l'esprit.*" In the meantime he was at a Yugoslavian school and doing well, because he was naturally a good and diligent little boy, but she wanted something better for him.

It was very disagreeable, her occupation. She did not state explicitly what it included, but we took it for granted. It was not so bad in Greece or Bulgaria or in the North of Yugoslavia, in all of which places she had often worked, but of late she had got jobs only in South Serbia, in night clubs where the clients were for the most part Turks. She clapped her hand to her brow and shook her head and said, "*Vous ne savez pas, Madame, à quel point les Turcs sont idiots.*" Her complaint, when I investigated it, was just what it sounds. She was distressed because her Turkish visitors had no conversation. Her coat-frock fell back across her knee and showed snow-white cambric underclothing and flesh scrubbed clean as the cleanest cook's kitchen table, and not more sensuous. She was all decency and good sense, and she was pronouncing sound judgment.

The judgment was appalling. The Turks in South Serbia are not like the Slav Moslems of Sarajevo, they are truly Turks. They are Turks who were settled there after the battle of Kossovo, who have remained what the Ataturk would not permit Turks to be any longer. They are what a people must become if it suspends all intellectual life and concentrates on the idea of conquest. It knows victory, but there is a limit to possible victories; what has been gained cannot be maintained, for that requires the use of the intellect, which has been removed. So there is decay, the

long humiliation of decay. At one time the forces of Selim and Suleiman
covered half a continent with the precise and ferocious ballet of perfect
warfare, the sensuality of the sultans and the viziers searched for fresh
refinements and made of their discoveries the starting points for further
search, fountains played in courtyards and walled gardens where there
had been till then austere barbarism. At the end an ageing cabaret dancer,
the homely and decent vanishing point of voluptuousness, sits on a bed
and says with dreadful justice: "*Vous ne savez pas, Madame, à quel point
les Turcs sont idiots.*"

When Astra came to our table later she told me that she hoped to be
in Sarajevo for some weeks longer, and that she was happier here than she
had been in Skoplje. "*Ici,*" she pronounced, "*les gens sont beaucoup plus
cultivés.*" As soon as she had gone I found at my shoulder the Swabian
chauffeur from Dubrovnik, whom we had paid off that afternoon. "Why
is that woman talking to you?" he said. He always immensely disconcerted me by his interventions. I was always afraid that if I said to him,
"What business is this of yours?" he would answer, in the loathsome
manner of a miracle play, "I am Reason" or "I am Conscience," and that
it would be true. So I stammered, "I know her." "You cannot know
such a person," he said. "Do you mean you have been in some café where
she has performed?" "Yes, yes," I said, "it was in Skoplje, and she is a very
nice woman, she has a son of whom she is fond." "How do you know she
has a son?" asked the chauffeur. "She told me so," I said. "You do not
have to believe everything that such a person tells you," said the chauffeur. "But I am sure it is true," I exclaimed hotly, "and I am very sorry
for her." The chauffeur gave me a glance too heavily veiled by respect
to be respectful, and then looked at my husband, but sighed, as if to
remind himself that he would find no help there. Suddenly he picked up
my bag and said, "I came to say that I had remembered I had forgotten
to take that grease-spot out with petrol as I had promised you, so I will
take it outside and do it now." He then bowed, and left me. I thought,
"He is really too conscientious, this is very inconvenient for now I have
no powder." But of course he would not have thought it necessary for
me to have any powder.

But my attention was immediately diverted. A very handsome young
man had come up to our table in a state of extreme anger; he was even
angrier than any of the angry young men in Dalmatia. He evidently
knew Constantine and the judge and the banker, but he did not give
them any formal greeting. Though his hair was bronze and his eyes
crackled with blueness, and he might have been brother to the two

Moslems we had seen talking politics in the park that afternoon, he cried out, "What about the accursed Turks?" The judge and the banker made no reply, but Constantine said, "Well, it was not I who made them." The young man insisted, "But you serve our precious Government, don't you?" "Yes," said Constantine, "for the sake of my country, and perhaps a little for the sake of my soul, I have given up the deep peace of being in opposition." "Then perhaps you can explain why your Belgrade gangster politicians have devised this method of insulting us Bosnians," said the young man. "We are used," he said, stretching his arms wide and shouting, "to their iniquities. We have seen them insulting our brothers the Croats, we have seen them spitting in the faces of all those who love liberty. But usually there is some sense in what they do, they either put money in their pockets or they consolidate their tyranny. But this crazy burlesque can bring them no profit. It can be done for no purpose but to wound the pride of us Bosnians. Will you be polite enough to explain a little why your horde of thugs and thieves have formed this curious intention of paying this unprovoked insult to a people whose part it should be to insult rather than be insulted?"

The judge leaned over to me and whispered, "It is all right, Madame, they are just talking a little about politics." "But what has the Government done to insult Bosnia?" I asked. "It has arranged," said the banker, "that the Turkish Prime Minister and Minister of War, who are in Belgrade discussing our military alliance with them, are to come here tomorrow to be received by the Moslem population." "Ah," said my husband, "that accounts for all the fezes being ironed. Well, do many people take the visit like this young man?" "No," said the banker, "he is a very extreme young man." "I would not say so," said the judge sadly.

At that moment the young man smashed his fist down on the table and cried into Constantine's face, "Judas Iscariot! Judas Iscariot!" "No," said poor Constantine to his retreating back, "I am not Judas Iscariot. I have indeed never been quite sure which of the disciples I do resemble, but it is a very sweet little one, the most *mignon* of them all." He applied himself to the business of eating a line of little pieces of strongly seasoned meat that had been broiled on a skewer; and when he set it down wistfulness was wet in his round black eyes. "All the same I do not like it, what that young man said. It was not agreeable. Dear God, I wish the young would be more agreeable to my generation, for we suffered very much in the war, and if it were not for us they would still be slaves under the Austrians."

Cautiously the banker said, "Do you think it is really wise, this visit?"

Constantine answered wearily, "I think it is wise, for our Prime Minister, Mr. Stoyadinovitch, does not do foolish things." "But why is it objected to at all?" said my husband. "That even I understand a little," said Constantine, "for the Turks were our oppressors and we drove them out, so that we Christians should be free. And now the heads of the Turkish state are coming by the consent of our Christian state to see the Moslems who upheld the oppressors. I see that it must seem a little odd." "But how is it possible," said my husband, "that there should be so much feeling against the Turks when nobody who is not very old can possibly have had any personal experience of their oppressions?"

The three men looked at my husband as if he were talking great nonsense. "Well," said my husband, "were not the Turks booted out of here in 1878?" "Ah, no, no!" exclaimed the three men. "You do not understand," said Constantine; "the Turkish Empire went from here in 1878, but the Slav Moslems remained, and when Austria took control it was still their holiday. For they were the favourites of the Austrians, far above the Christians, far above the Serbs or the Croats." "But why was that?" asked my husband. "It was because of the principle, *Divide et impera*," said the banker. It was odd to hear the phrase from the lips of one of its victims. "Look, there were fifty or sixty thousand people in the town," said the banker. "There were us, the Jews, who are of two kinds, the Sephardim, from Spain and Portugal, and the others, the Ashkenazi, who are from Central Europe and the East, and that is a division. Then there were the Christian Slavs, who are Croats and Serbs, and that is a division. But lest we should forget our differences, they raised up the Moslems, who were a third of the population, to be their allies against the Christians and the Jews."

Their faces darkening with the particular sullenness of rebels, they spoke of their youth, shadowed by the double tyranny of Austria and the Moslems. To men of their position, for both came from wealthy and influential families, that tyranny had been considerably mitigated. It had fallen with a far heavier hand on the peasants and the inhabitants of the poorer towns, and there it meant a great deal of imprisonment and flogging, and occasional executions. But to these people there had been a constant nagging provocation and a sense of insult. The Moslems were given the finest schools and colleges, the best posts in the administration were reserved for them, they were invited to all official functions and treated as honoured guests, the railway trains were held up at their hours of prayer. The Turkish land system, which grossly favoured the Moslems at the extense of the Christians, was carefully preserved intact by

his Catholic Majesty the Emperor Franz Josef. And it was a special
source of bitterness that the Austrians had forced their way into Bosnia
after the Slavs had driven out the Turks, on the pretext that they must
establish a garrison force to protect the Christians there in case the Turks
came back. That they should then humiliate the Christians at the hand
of those Moslems who had stayed behind seemed to these men an inflam-
ing piece of hypocrisy which could never be forgotten or forgiven.

They evidently felt this deeply and sincerely, although they themselves were Jewish. The situation was obviously one of great complexity.
That was apparent when they likened the Turks to dogs and swine, and
spoke the words with more than Western loathing, as the Turks would
have done. "When I went to Berlin to study for my degree," said the
banker, "I used to feel ashamed because the Germans took me as an equal,
and here in my house I was treated as an inferior to men with fezes
on their heads, to Orientals." In that statement too many strands were
twisted. Later my husband asked, "But are the Moslems a sufficiently important and active group for it to matter whether they are encouraged
or not?" The lawyer and the banker answered together, "Oh, certainly,"
and Constantine explained, "Yes, they are very, very clever politicians,
much cleverer than we are, for Islam taught them something, let us say
it taught them not to run about letting off guns just because one of them
had a birthday. Our Government has always to conciliate the Moslems.
In the present Cabinet Mr. Spaho is the Minister of Transport, and he is
a Moslem from this town." "A most excellent man," agreed the judge
and banker, beaming. All that they had spoken of for so long in such a
steady flow of hatred was forgotten in a glow of local patriotism.

At last it was time to go. "No, your Mr. Stoyadinovitch has not done
well," said the banker finally. "It is not that we do not like the Moslems.
Since the war all things have changed, and we are on excellent terms.
But it is not nice when they are picked out by the Government and
allowed to receive a ceremonial visit from the representative of the
power that crushed us and ground us down into the mud." We rose, and
Astra in her sequins and pink muslin bounced from the platform like a
great sorbo-ball to say good-bye. I wanted to give her a present, but
remembered that the chauffeur had taken my bag away to clean it, so I
told her to come and see me at the hotel next day. As we went out the
Swabian chauffeur suddenly reappeared, rising from a table which was
concealed by the bushes and creepers which were set about to give the
cabaret the appearance of an open-air beer-garden. He handed back my
bag with a triumphant smile, and I perceived that he had hidden himself

for this very reason, that I should not be able to find him and get my money if I felt a charitable impulse towards my unsuitable friend.

"And please note," he said, his eyes passing uneasily from my husband to me and then back again, deeply distressed by our lack of sense, "it would be a good thing to stay indoors tomorrow morning, for the Turkish Prime Minister and War Minister are coming to visit the Moslems and there might be a disturbance. At any rate, it is not for you, there will be great crowds." He spoke with authority out of the mass of his ideal world, which was almost as solid as if it were real because it had been conceived by his solid mind: a world in which people with money were also reasonable people, who did not give alms to the unworthy and stayed indoors when it was not so safe outdoors. And his blindish-looking eyes begged us to remember that we were English and therefore to refrain from acting like these Slavs.

Sarajevo III

I WOKE only once from my sleep, and heard the muezzins crying out to the darkness from the hundred minarets of the city that there is but one God and Mohammed His prophet. It is a cry that holds an ultimate sadness, like the hooting of owls and the barking of foxes in night-time. The muezzins are making that plain statement of their cosmogony, and the owls and the foxes are obeying the simplest need for expression; yet their cries, which they intended to mean so little, prove more conclusively than any argument that life is an occasion which justifies the hugest expenditure of pity. I had nearly fallen asleep again when my husband said out of his dreams, "Strange, strange." "What is strange?" I said. "That Jewish banker," he replied, "he said so proudly that when he was a student in Berlin he felt ashamed because he was treated there as an equal when here he was treated as inferior to the Moslems. I wonder what he feels about Germany now."

In the morning we were not late, but Constantine was down before us, breakfasting in the café. One of the reasons why people of the Nordic type dislike Constantine is that he is able to do things out of sheer vitality for which they require moral stimulus. His good red blood can fetch him out of bed without a moment of sombre resolution, his vigorous pulse keeps him going without resort to perseverance. The writings of the early Christian Fathers show that few things irritated them like a pagan who was in full possession of the virtues. But though he was vigorous this morning he was not gay. "Look at all the flags," he said, "it is a great day for Sarajevo. See how I show you all." But he spoke glumly.

I suspected that he was secretly of his friends' mind about the day's doings; and indeed it was not exhilarating to look out of the café windows and see a stream of passing people, and none of the men without fezes, all of the women veiled. I do not mind there being such men and women, but one sees them with a different eye when they are in a majority and could put at a disadvantage all those not of their kind. "I can understand that such a ceremony as this can revive all sorts of apprehensions," I said tactlessly. "We had better go," said Constantine, ignoring my remark. "The party from Belgrade are not coming to the railway station, they stop the railway train at a special halt in the middle of the boulevards, near the museum, and it is quite a way from here."

For part of the way we took a cab, and then we had to get out and walk. Because Constantine had his Government pass and we were to be present at the reception at the station, we were allowed to go down the middle of the streets, which were entirely lined with veiled women and men wearing fezes. Only a few Christians were to be seen here and there. "There seem to be a great many Moslems," I said, after the first two or three hundred yards. The crowd was close-packed and unified by a common aspect. The faces of the men were flattened, almost plastered by an expression of dogged adherence to some standard; they were all turned upwards to one hope. The women were as expressive in their waiting, though their faces were hidden. A light rain was falling on their silk and cotton overalls, but they did not move, and only some of them put up umbrellas, though most of them were carrying them. It was as if they thought of themselves already as participants in a sacred rite. Some of the spectators were arranged in processional order and held small, amateurish, neatly inscribed banners, some of them in Turkish script; and a great many of them carried Yugoslavian flags, very tidily, not waving them but letting them droop. There were many children, all standing straight and good under the rain. I looked at my watch, and I saw that we had been walking between these crowds for ten minutes. There are thirty thousand Moslems in Sarajevo, and I think most of them were there. And they were rapt, hallucinated, intoxicated with an old loyalty, and doubtless ready to know the intoxication of an old hatred.

We came to the halt at the right moment, as the train slid in and stopped. There was a little cheering, and the flags were waved, but it is not much fun cheering somebody inside the tin box of a railway carriage. The crowd waited to make sure. The Moslem Mayor of Sarajevo and his party went forward and greeted the tall and jolly Mr. Spaho, the Minister of Transport, and the Yugoslavian Minister of War, General Marits, a giant who wore his strength packed round him in solid masses like a bull. He looked as Göring would like to look. There were faint, polite cheers for them; but the great cheers the crowd had had in its hearts for days were never given. For Mr. Spaho and the General were followed, so far as the expectations of the crowd were concerned, by nobody. The two little men in bowlers and trim suits, very dapper and well-shaven, might have been Frenchmen darkened in the colonial service. It took some time for the crowd to realize that they were in fact Ismet Ineunue, the Turkish Prime Minister, and Kazim Ozalip, his War Minister.

Even after the recognition had been established the cheers were not given. No great degree of disguise concealed the disfavour with which these two men in bowler hats looked on the thousands they saw before them, all wearing the fez and veil which their leader the Ataturk made it a crime to wear in Turkey. Their faces were blank yet not unexpressive. So might Englishmen look if, in some corner of the Empire, they had to meet as brothers the inhabitants of a colony that had been miraculously preserved from the action of time and had therefore kept to their road.

The Moslem Mayor read them an address of welcome, of which, naturally, they did not understand one word. This was bound in any case to be a difficult love-affair to conduct, for they knew no Serbian and the Sarajevans knew no Turkish. They had to wait until General Marits had translated it into French; while they were waiting I saw one of them fix his eye on a distant building, wince, and look in the opposite direction. Some past-loving soul had delved in the attics and found the green flag with the crescent, the flag of the old Ottoman Empire, which these men and their leader regarded as the badge of a plague that had been like to destroy their people. The General's translation over, they responded in French better than his, only a little sweeter and more birdlike than the French of France, and stood still, their eyes set on the nearest roof, high enough to save them the sight of this monstrous retrograde profusion of fezes and veils, of red pates and black muzzles, while the General put back into Serbian their all too reasonable remarks. They had told the Moslems of Sarajevo, it seemed, that they felt the utmost enthusiasm for the Yugoslavian idea, and had pointed out that if the South Slavs did not form a unified state the will of the great powers could sweep over the Balkan Peninsula as it chose. They had said not one word of the ancient tie that linked the Bosnian Moslems to the Turks, nor had they made any reference to Islam.

There were civil obeisances, and the two men got into an automobile and drove towards the town. The people did not cheer them. Only those within sight of the railway platform were aware that they were the Turkish Ministers, and even among those were many who could not believe their eyes, who thought that there must have been some breakdown of the arrangements. A little procession of people holding banners that had been ranged behind the crowd at this point wrangled among itself as to whether it should start, delayed too long, and finally tried to force its way into the roadway too late. By that time the crowd had left the pavements and was walking under the drizzle back to the city, slowly and silently, as those who have been sent empty away.

We had seen the end of a story that had taken five hundred years to tell. We had seen the final collapse of the old Ottoman Empire. Under our eyes it had heeled over and fallen to the ground like a lay figure slipping off a chair. But that tragedy was already accomplished. The Ottoman Empire had ceased to suffer long ago. There was a more poignant grief before us. Suppose that such an unconquerable woman as may be compared to the Slav in Bosnia was at last conquered by time, and sent for help to her old lover, and that there answered the call a man bearing her lover's name who was, however, not her lover but his son, and looked on her with cold eyes, seeing her only as the occasion of a shameful passage in his family history; none of us would be able to withhold our pity.

Sarajevo IV

"I AM so glad that this is a bad spring," I said, "for otherwise I should never have seen snow on the roof of a mosque, and there is something delicious about that incongruity." "But it is killing all the plum blossom you like so much to see," said Constantine, "and that is a terrible thing, for in Bosnia and Serbia we live a little by our timber and our mines, but mostly by our pigs and our plums. But for you I am glad of the bad weather, for if it had been better you would have wanted to be out on the hills all the time, and as it is you have got to know my friends. Will you not agree that life in this town is specially agreeable?" "Yes," said my husband, "it is all that I hoped for in Istanbul, but never found, partly because I was a stranger, and partly because they are reformists and are trying for excellent motives to uproot their own charm." "I have liked it all," I said, "except that afternoon when the Turkish Ministers were here and I went to see the mosque in the bazaar. Then I felt as if I had insisted on being present while a total stranger had a tooth out. But that was my fault."

I had thoughtlessly chosen to see the mosque that afternoon, and had found the whole courtyard full of Moslems who were waiting there because a rumour had spread that the Turkish Ministers were going to visit it. On their faces lay that plastered, flattened look of loyalty to a cause which I had noticed in the crowd at the railway station that morning. But it was mingled now with that stoical obstinacy a child shows when it insists on repeating a disappointing experience, so that it can have no doubt that it really happened. It seemed indecent for a Christian to intrude on them at such a moment, and for a woman too, since the whole Moslem theory of the relationship of the sexes falls to pieces once any man has failed in a worldly matter. I had even hesitated to admire the mellow tiles and fretted arches of the façade or to go into the interior, so like a light and spacious gymnasium for the soul, to see the carpets presented by the pious of three centuries: what have been the recreations of the warrior must seem a shame to him when his weapons have been taken away.

But this was the one time when staying in Sarajevo was not purely agreeable. The visit was, indeed, like being gently embraced by a city, for all classes had borrowed from the Moslem his technique for making

life as delightful as might be. Our Jewish friends were strict in their
faith but their lives were as relaxed, as obstinately oriented towards the
agreeable, as Mohammed would have had his children in time of peace.
We went up to visit the banker in his large modern offices, which indeed
almost amounted to a sky-scraper, and his welcome was sweet without
reserve, and this was not due to mere facility, for he was a very wise man,
sometimes almost tongue-tied with the burden of his wisdom, as the old
Jewish sages must have been. It was only that till the contrary evidence
was produced he preferred to think us as good as any friends he had. He
was no fool, he would not reject that evidence if it came; but it had not
come.

There were brought in, as we sat, cups of a sweet herbal infusion, as
distinct from all other beverages as tea or coffee. We exclaimed in delight, and he told us, "It is a Turkish drink that we all give to our visitors
in our offices in Sarajevo. It is supposed to be an aphrodisiac." He was
amused, but without a snigger, at the custom he followed. "Think of it,"
he said. "I told that to a German engineer who was here last month, and
he went out and bought two kilos of it. An extraordinary people." He
went on to speak of his city, which he saw with the eye of a true lover,
as astonished by its beauty as any stranger. That we should see it well
he had arranged for two young women relatives of his to take us round
the sights, and he produced them forthwith. They were entrancing.
For theme they had the free, positive, creative attractiveness of the
Slav; their style had been perfected in the harem. They had husbands
and loved them, the banker was no more than kin and a friend, and my
husband himself would admit that they felt for him only as the courtier
speaks it in *As You Like It,* "Hereafter, in a better world than this, I
shall desire more love and knowledge of you." But though they kept
well within the framework of fastidious manners, they reminded the
banker and my husband that it must have been very pleasant to keep a
covey of darlings in silks and brocades behind latticed windows, who
would laugh and scuttle away, though only to an inner chamber where
they could be found again after a second's search, and sing and touch the
strings of the gusla and mock the male and be overawed by him, and
mock again, in an unending, uncriticized process of delight.

I record a wonder. The work of the bank was well done. That, with
my cold inner eye that trusts nothing, least of all my own likings, I
checked later. The banker was a man of exceptional ability and integrity
and he worked hard according to the severest Western standards. But he
appeared to keep his appointments with life as well as, and even during,

THE PERISTYLE OF DIOCLETIAN'S PALACE

Marshal Marmont's Belvedere at Trogir

his business engagements. Several times we went out with the two young women, and we always went back to the office and found the hot herbal tea, and coffee served with little squares of Turkish delight on toothpicks, and much laughter, and a sense of luxurious toys. Once we went in and found half a dozen pictures of Sarajevo, bought by the banker out of his infatuation with the city, stacked on the big sofa and against the walls, and it was as if the caravans had come in from the North with a freight of Frankish art. The two women ran about from one to another of these novelties, they took sides, they became partisans of this picture and intrigued against that. There was an inherent fickleness in their admiration. They would tire of the familiar, but no doubt it is more important for the artist to have the new encouraged.

"What do you think of them?" the banker asked me. I wished he had not. They were the work of a Jewish refugee from Berlin, and though his perception was delicate and his brush subtle, each canvas showed him the child of that spirit which had destroyed him. There was the passion for the thick black line, the Puritan belief that if one pays out strength when making an artistic effort one will create a strong work of art. He had put a cast-iron outline to the tree on his canvas, and because it took vigour to make such an outline, and because cast-iron is an unyielding substance, he believed that the result was virile painting, even though his perception of the tree's form had been infantile in its feebleness. It is the same heresy that expresses itself in the decree that had driven him into exile. Because it is a vigorous act to throw the Jews out of Germany and because it causes pain and disorder, it is taken as a measure of virile statecraft, although its relevance to the troubles of the country could be imagined only by an imbecile.

Something of this I said, and the banker motioned my husband and myself to step with him to the window, leaving the two women to bicker like birds over the pictures. With the grave smile, which could not possibly become laughter, of a sage confessing his own folly, he said, "I have remembered again and again a foolish thing I said when we first met. I told you that when I went to Berlin as a student I rejoiced as a Jew at being treated as an equal, while I was treated as an inferior here. That must have amused you. It was a piece of naïveté like a man boasting of his friendship with one who has spared no pains to show him that he considers him a fool, a bore, an oaf." He looked out for a moment on the mosques, on the domes of the old caravanserai among the tiled roofs of the bazaar, on the poplars standing over the city like the golden ghosts of giant Janizaries. "But it is puzzling, you know, not to be able to look to Germany as one's second home, when it has been that to one all one's life long. But one can come home to one's hearth, and I am fortunate that Sarajevo is mine."

He went back and stood before the pictures, the young women each taking an arm, one fluting that he must hang the picture of the little Orthodox church over his desk, the other screaming that he must throw it away, he must burn it, he must give it to one-eyed Marko the scavenger. I thought he was promising himself too little. In this office there lingered something of the best of Turkish life; and in his integrity, in his dismissal of the little, in the seriousness which he brought to the interpretation of his experience, there was preserved the best of what a German philosophical training could do for a man of affairs. It seemed to me exquisitely appropriate that the vulgar should call the Jews old-clothes men. Since it is the peculiar madness of us other races to make ourselves magnificent clothes and then run wild and throw them away and daub ourselves with mud, it is well that there should be some old-clothes men about.

These Jews of Sarajevo are indeed an amazing community. I could bring forward as evidence the Bulbul and her mate, the two human beings who more than any others that I have ever met have the right arrangement and comforting significance of a work of art. They were not only husband and wife, they were kin; and this common blood had its own richness and its own discipline, for they came of a family that was considered among orthodox Jews as orthodox Jews are considered by liberal Jews, as the practitioners of an impossibly exacting rule. "His father," said Constantine of the Bulbul's mate, who was named Selim, "was the most hieratic Jew that can ever be. All to him from the rising to the setting of the sun was a ritual, and he was very dominant, he made it so for all the world. I have seen it happen that when Selim was swimming in the sea at Dubrovnik, and he saw his father standing on the beach, and immediately he began to swim in a very hieratic manner, putting his hands out so and so, very slowly, and lifting his head out of the water and looking very gravely down his nose."

This was credible, for Selim's dignity was magnificent but not pompous, as if it were an inherited garment and its previous wearers had taken the stiffness out of it. He was a very tall man with broad shoulders, broad even for a man of his height. His build suggested the stylized immensity of a god sculpted by a primitive people, and his face also had the quality of sculpture; though his wit and imagination made it mobile, it was at once the tables of the law and the force that shattered them.

He had an impressive habit, as we discovered the first night we went out to dinner with him and his wife, of stopping suddenly as he walked along the street when he had thought of something important and staying quite still as he said it. The spot where he halted became Mount Sinai, and in his leisurely and massive authority could be seen the Moses whom Michelangelo had divined but could not, being a Gentile and therefore of divided and contending will, fully create in the strength of his law-fulness.

But the fascination of himself and his wife lay initially in their voices. There is a special music lingering about the tongues of many of these Spanish Jews, but no one else gave it such special performance. Selim had constrained his gift a little out of deference to the Western tenet that a man should not be more beautiful than can be helped and that a certain decent drabness should be the character of all he does, but from his wife's lips that music came in such animal purity that we called her the Bulbul, which is the Persian word for nightingale. Voices like these were the product of an existence built by putting pleasure to pleasure, as houses are built by putting brick to brick. A human being could not speak so unless he or she loved many other sounds—the wind's progress among trees or the subtler passage it makes through grasses; note by note given out by a musical instrument, each note for its own colour; the gurgle of wine pouring from a bottle or water trickling through a marble conduit in a garden—all sorts of sounds that many Westerners do not even hear, so corrupted are they by the tyranny of the intellect, which makes them inattentive to any message to the ear which is without an argument. Listening to her, one might believe humanity to be in its first unspoiled morning hour. Yet she was accomplished, she used her music with skill, and she was wise, her music was played for a good end. She built for grave and innocent purposes on a technique of in-genuity which had been developed in the harem.

The Bulbul was not as Western women. In her beauty she resembled the Persian ladies of the miniatures, whose lustre I had till then thought an artistic convention but could now recognize in her great shining eyes, her wet red lips, her black hair with its white reflections, her dazzling skin. This brightness was like a hard transparent veil varnished on her, wholly protective. Even if someone had touched her, it would not have been she who was touched. Within this protection, she was liquid with generosity. She was continually anxious to give pleasure to her friends, even were they so new and untried as ourselves. If we were in a café and a man passed with a tray of Turkish sweetmeats, her face became tragical till she was sure that she could call him back and give us the chance of tasting them. If we were driving down a street and she saw the first lilies of the valley in a flower shop, she would call on the driver to stop that she might buy us some, with an imperativeness found more usually in selfishness than in altruism. When she had brought us to the café where a famous gipsy musician was singing, she relaxed like a mother who has succeeded in obtaining for her children something she knows they should have. The seasons irked her by the limitations they placed on her generosity: since it was not mid-winter she could not take us up to the villages above Sarajevo for skiing, and since it was not mid-summer she could not open her country house for us. Had one been cruel enough to point out to her that one would have been happier with a million pounds, and that she was not in a position to supply it, she would for a moment or two really have suffered, and even when she realized that she had been teased her good sense would not have been able to prevent her from feeling a slight distress.

Yet there was nothing lax about this woman. Though she lived for pleasure and the dissemination of it, she shone with a chastity as absolute as that radiated by any woman who detested pleasure. She had accepted a mystery. She had realized that to make a field where generosity can fulfil its nature absolutely, without reserve, one must exclude all but one other person, committed to loyalty. That field was marriage. Therefore when she spoke to any man other than her husband she was all to him, mother, sister, friend, nurse, and benefactress, but not a possible mate. She was thus as virginal as any dedicated nun, and that for the sake not of renunciation but of consummation. But her nature was so various that she comprised many opposites. Sometimes she seemed the most idiosyncratic of natures; standing on a balcony high over a street, we looked down on the pavement and saw her walking far below, with a dozen before her and behind her, darkly dressed like herself, and we were able to say at once, "Look, there is the little Bulbul." But there were other times when everything she did was so classical, so tried and tested in its validity, that she seemed to have no individuality at all, and to be merely a chalice filled with a rich draught of tradition.

There was, indeed, a great range of human beings to be seen in Sarajevo, all of sorts unknown to us. In Dubrovnik we had visited an antique shop kept by a young man called Hassanovitch, of admirable taste, and my husband had bought me the most beautiful garment I have ever possessed, a ceremonial robe of Persian brocade about a hundred and fifty years old, with little gold trees growing on a background faintly purple as a wine-stain. We bought it in a leisurely way, over several evenings, supported by cups of coffee and slices of Banya Luka cheese, which is rather like Port Salut, brought in by his little brothers, of which there seemed an inordinate number, all with the acolyte's air of huge quantities of original sin in suspension. He had given us a letter of introduction to his father, the leading antique dealer of Sarajevo, who invited us to his house, a villa up among the high tilted suburbs.

There we sat and enjoyed the crystalline neatness and cleanliness of the prosperous Moslem home, with its divans that run along the wall and take the place of much cumbrous furniture, and its wall decorations of rugs and textiles, which here were gorgeous. We told the father about his son and how much we had admired his shop, and we mentioned too a feature of our visits that had much amused us. Always we had found sitting by the counter a beautiful girl, not the same for more than a few evenings, an English or American or German tourist, who would look at us with the thirsty and wistful eye of a gazelle who intends to come down to the pool and drink as soon as the hippopotami have ceased to muddy the water. The elder Mr. Hassanovitch stroked his beard and said in gratified accents, "And the kitten also catches mice," and took me to the women's quarters so that I could tell his wife, the mother of his fourteen children. She was an extremely beautiful woman in her middle forties, peace shining from her eyes and kneaded into the texture of her smooth flesh; and she was for me as pathetic as the women of Korchula, who believed that they had earned their happiness because they had passed certain tests of womanhood, and did not realize how fortunate they were in having those tests applied. Like those others, she was unaware that these tests would be irrelevant unless the community felt a need for the functions performed by women, and that infatuation with war or modern industry can make it entirely forgetful of that need.

But our last impression of Mr. Hassanovitch was not to be merely of benign domesticity. From the moment of our meeting I had been troubled by a sense of familiarity about his features, and suddenly my husband realized that we had seen his face many times before. When the Archduke Franz Ferdinand and his wife came to the Town Hall of Sarajevo on the morning of June the twenty-eighth, 1914, Mr. Hassanovitch was among the guests summoned to meet them for he was already an active Moslem politician, and he is standing to the right of the doorway in a photograph which has often been reproduced, showing the doomed pair going out to their death. That day must have been a blow to him. The contention of our Jewish friends that the Austrians had pampered the Moslems at the expense of the Christians, and had made them zealous supporters, is borne out by the constitution of the assembly shown by that photograph; and other photographs taken that morning show that when Princip was arrested the men in the crowd who are throwing themselves on him are all wearing the fez.

But I think he would have preferred it to the day he had just endured. The friends accompanying us, who knew him well, spoke to him of the visit of the Turkish Ministers, and he answered them with words that were blankly formal, a splendid bandage of his pain and their possible embarrassment at having provoked it. It was surprising that the visit had evidently been as keen a disappointment to such an expert and informed person as it was to the people in the street. Yet I suppose an Irish-American politician would suffer deep pain if time should bring to power in Eire a president who wanted to break with the past and sent an emissary to the States to beg that the old Catholic nationalism should be forgotten; and that he would even shut his eyes to the possibility that it might happen. The analogy was close enough, for here, just as in an Irish ward in an American town, one was aware that the actions and reactions of history had produced a formidable amount of politics. One could feel them operating below the surface like a still in a basement.

But history takes different people differently, even the same history. The Sarajevo market is held on Wednesdays, at the centre of the town near the bazaar, in a straggling open space surrounded by little shops, most of them Moslem pastrycooks', specializing in great cartwheel tarts stuffed with spinach or minced meat. The country folk come in by driblets, beginning as soon as it is fully light, and going on till nine or ten or eleven, for some must walk several hours from their homes: more and more pigeons take refuge on the roofs of the two little kiosks in the market-place. There are sections in the market allotted to various kinds of goods: here there is grain, there wool, more people than one would expect are selling scales, and there are stalls that gratify a medieval appetite for dried fish and meat, which are sold in stinking and sinewy lengths. At one end of the market are stuffs and embroideries which are chiefly horrible machine-made copies of the local needle-work. The Moslem women are always thickest here, but elsewhere you see as many Christians as Moslems, and perhaps more; and these Christians are nearly all of a heroic kind.

The finest are the men, who wear crimson wool scarfs tied round their heads and round their throats. This means that they have come from villages high in the mountains, where the wind blows down from

the snows; and sometimes the scarf serves a double purpose, for in many
such villages a kind of goitre is endemic. These men count themselves
as descendants of the Haiduks, the Christians who after the Ottoman
conquest took refuge in the highlands, and came down to the valleys
every year on St. George's Day, because by then the trees were green
enough to give them cover, and they could harry the Turks by brigand-
age. They reckon that man can achieve the highest by following the
path laid down in the Old Testament. I cannot imagine why Victorian
travellers in these regions used to express contempt for the rayas, or
Christian peasants, whom they encountered. Any one of these Bosnians
could have made a single mouthful of a Victorian traveller, green umbrella and all. They are extremely tall and sinewy, and walk with a
rhythmic stride which is not without knowledge of its own grace and
power. Their darkness flashes and their cheekbones are high and their
moustaches are long over fierce lips. They wear dark homespun jackets,
often heavily braided, coloured belts, often crimson like their headgear,
the Bosnian breeches that bag between the thighs and outline the hip
and flank, and shoes made of leather thongs with upcurving points at the
toes. They seem to clang with belligerence as if they wore armour. In
every way, I hear, they are formidable. Their women have to wait on
them while they eat, must take sound beatings every now and again,
work till they drop, even while child-bearing, and walk while their
master rides.

Yet, I wonder. Dear God, is nothing ever what it seems? The women
of whom this tale is told, and according to all reliable testimony truly
told, do not look in the least oppressed. They are handsome and sinewy
like their men; but not such handsome women as the men are handsome
men. A sheep-breeder of great experience once told me that in no species
and variety that he knew were the male and female of equal value in
their maleness and femaleness. Where the males were truly male, the females were not so remarkably female, and where the females were truly
females the males were not virile. Constantly his theory is confirmed
here. The women look heroes rather than heroines, they are raw-boned
and their beauty is blocked out too roughly. But I will eat my hat if
these women were not free in the spirit. They passed the chief tests I
knew. First, they looked happy when they had lost their youth. Here,
as in all Balkan markets, there were far more elderly women than girls;
and there is one corner of it which is reserved for a line of women all
past middle life, who stand on the kerb hawking Bosnian breeches that
they have made from their own homespun, and exchange the gossip of

their various villages. Among them I did not see any woman whose face was marked by hunger or regret. All looked as if they had known a great deal of pain and hardship, but their experience had led none of them to doubt whether it is worth while to live.

It was quite evident as we watched them that these women had been able to gratify their essential desires. I do not mean simply that they looked as if they had been well mated. Many Latin women who have been married at sixteen and have had numbers of children look swollen and tallowy with frustration. Like all other material experiences, sex has no value other than what the spirit assesses; and the spirit is obstinately influenced in its calculation by its preference for freedom. In some sense these women had never been enslaved. They had that mark of freedom, they had wit. This was not mere guffawing and jeering. These were not bumpkins, they could be seen now and then engaging in the prettiest passages of formality. We watched one of the few young women at the market seek out two of her elders: she raised her smooth face to their old lips and they kissed her on the cheek, she bent down and kissed their hands. It could not have been more graciously done at Versailles; and their wit was of the same pointed, noble kind.

We followed at the skirts of one who was evidently the Voltaire of this world. She was almost a giantess; her greyish red hair straggled about her ears in that untidiness which is dearer than any order, since it shows an infatuated interest in the universe which cannot spare one second for the mere mechanics of existence, and it was tied up in a clean white clout under a shawl passed under her chin and knotted on the top of her head. She wore a green velvet jacket over a dark homespun dress and coarse white linen sleeves, all clean but wild, and strode like a man up and down the market, halting every now and then, when some sight struck her as irresistibly comic. We could see the impact of the jest on her face, breaking its stolidity, as a cast stone shatters the surface of water. The wide mouth gaped in laughter, showing a single tooth. Then a ferment worked in her eyes. She would turn and go to the lower end of the market, and she would put her version of what had amused her to every knot of women she met as she passed to the upper end. I cursed myself because I could not understand one word of what she said. But this much I could hear: each time she made her joke it sounded more pointed, more compact, and drew more laughter. When she came to the upper end of the market and her audience was exhausted, a blankness fell on her and she ranged the stalls restlessly till she found another occasion for her wit.

This was not just a white blackbird. She was distinguished not because she was witty but by the degree of her wit. Later on we found a doorway in a street near by where the women who had sold all their goods lounged and waited for a motor bus. We lounged beside them, looking into the distance as if the expectation of a friend made us deaf; and our ears recorded the authentic pattern, still recognizable although the words could not be understood, of witty talk. These people could pass what the French consider the test of a civilized society: they could practise the art of general conversation. Voice dovetailed into voice without impertinent interruption; there was light and shade, sober judgment was corrected by mocking criticism, and another sober judgment established, and every now and then the cards were swept off the table by a gust of laughter, and the game started afresh.

None of these women could read. When a boy passed by carrying an advertisement of Batya's shoes they had to ask a man they knew to read it for them. They did not suffer any great deprivation thereby. Any writer worth his salt knows that only a small proportion of literature does more than partly compensate people for the damage they have suffered by learning to read. These women were their own artists, and had done well with their material. The folk-songs of the country speak, I believe, of a general perception that is subtle and poetic, and one had only to watch any group carefully for it to declare itself. I kept my eyes for some time on two elderly women who had been intercepted on their way to this club in the doorway by a tall old man, who in his day must have been magnificent even in this land of magnificent men. Waving a staff as if it were a sceptre, he was telling them a dramatic story, and because he was absorbed in his own story the women were not troubling to disguise their expressions. There was something a shade too self-gratulatory in his handsomeness; no doubt he had been the *coq du village* in his day. In their smiles that knowledge glinted, but not too harshly. They had known him all their lives: they knew that thirty years ago he had not been so brave as he said he would be in the affair with the gendarmes at the ford, but they knew that later he had been much braver than he need have been when he faced the Turks in the ruined fortress, they remembered him when the good seasons had made him rich and when the snows and winds had made him poor. They had heard the gossip at the village well pronounce him right on this and wrong over that. They judged him with mercy and justice, which is the sign of a free spirit, and when his story was finished broke into the right laughter, and flattered him by smiling at him as if they were all three young again.

I suspect that women such as these are not truly slaves, but have found a fraudulent method of persuading men to give them support and leave them their spiritual freedom. It is certain that men suffer from a certain timidity, a liability to discouragement which makes them reluctant to go on doing anything once it has been proved that women can do it as well. This was most painfully illustrated during the slump in both Europe and America, where wives found to their amazement that if they found jobs when their husbands lost theirs and took on the burden of keeping the family, they were in no luck at all. For their husbands became either their frenzied enemies or relapsed into an infantile state of dependence and never worked again. If women pretend that they are inferior to men and cannot do their work, and abase themselves by picturesque symbolic rites, such as giving men their food first and waiting on them while they eat, men will go on working and developing their powers to the utmost, and will not bother to interfere with what women are saying and thinking with their admittedly inferior powers.

It is an enormous risk to take. It makes marriage a gamble, since these symbols of abasement always include an abnegation of economic and civil rights, and while a genial husband takes no advantage of them—and that is to say the vast majority of husbands—a malign man will exploit them with the rapacity of the grave. It would also be a futile bargain to make in the modern industrialized world, for it can hold good only where there are no other factors except the equality of women threatening the self-confidence of men. In our own Western civilization man is devitalized by the insecurity of employment and its artificial nature, so he cannot be restored to primitive power by the withdrawal of female rivalry and the woman would not get any reward for her sacrifice. There is in effect no second party to the contract. In the West, moreover, the gambling risks of marriage admit of a greater ruin. A man who is tied to one village and cannot leave his wife without leaving his land is not so dangerous a husband as a man who can step on a train and find employment in another town. But the greatest objection to this artificial abjection is that it is a conscious fraud on the part of women, and life will never be easy until human beings can be honest with one another. Still, in this world of compromises, honour is due to one so far successful that it produces these grimly happy heroes, these women who stride and laugh, obeying the instructions of their own nature and not masculine prescription.

Sarajevo V

ONE morning we walked down to the river, a brightening day shining down from the skies and up from puddles. A Moslem boy sold us an armful of wet lilac, a pigeon flew up from a bath in a puddle, its wings dispersing watery diamonds. "Now it is the spring," said Constantine, "I think we shall have good weather tomorrow for our trip to Ilidzhe, and better weather the day after for our trip to Yaitse. Yes, I think it will be well. All will be very well." When he is pleased with his country he walks processionally, like an expectant mother, with his stomach well forward. "But see what we told you the other night," he said as we came to the embankment and saw the Town Hall. "Under the Austrians all was for the Moslems. Look at this building, it is as Moslem as a mosque, yet always since the Turks were driven out of Bosnia the Christians have been two-thirds of the population. So did the Catholic Habsburgs deny their faith."

Actually it is the Moslems who have most reason to complain of this Town Hall, for their architecture in Sarajevo is exquisite in its restraint and amiability, and even in modern times has been true to that tradition. But this was designed by an Austrian architect, and it is stuffed with beer and sausages down to its toes. It is harshly particoloured and has a lumpish two-storied loggia with crudely fretted arches, and it has little round windows all over it which suggest that it is rich beyond the dreams of avarice in lavatories, and its highly ornamented cornices are Oriental in a pejorative sense. The minaret of the mosque beside it has the air of a cat that watches a dog making a fool of itself.

Within, however, it is very agreeable, and remarkably full of light; and in an office high up we found a tourist bureau, conducted with passion by a man in the beginnings of middle life, a great lover of his city. He dealt us out photographs of it for some time, pausing to gloat over them, but stopped when Constantine said, "Show these English the room where they held the reception which was the last thing the Archduke Franz Ferdinand and the Archduchess Sophie saw of their fellow-men." The head of the tourist bureau bowed as if he had received a compliment and led us out into the central lobby, where a young man in a fez, a woman in black bloomers, and an old man and woman undistinguishable from any needy and respectable pair in South Kensington shuffled up

331

the great staircase, while a young man quite like an Englishman save that he was carrying a gusla ran down it. We went into the Council Chamber, not unsuccessful in its effort at Moslem pomp. "All is Moslem here," said the head of the tourist bureau, "and even now that we are Yugoslavian the mayor is always a Moslem, and that is right. Perhaps it helps us by conciliating the Moslems, but even if it did not we ought to do it. For no matter how many Christians we may be here, and no matter what we make of the city—and we are doing wonderful things with it —the genius that formed it in the first place was Moslem, and again Moslem, and again Moslem."

But the three reception rooms were as libellous as the exterior. They were pedantically yet monstrously decorated in imitation of certain famous buildings of Constantinople, raising domes like gilded honeycomb tripe, pressing down between the vaults polychrome stumps like vast inverted Roman candles. That this was the copy of something gorgeous could be seen; it could also be seen that the copyist had been by blood incapable of comprehending that gorgeousness. Punch-drunk from this architectural assault I lowered my eyes, and the world seemed to reel. And here, it appeared, the world had once actually reeled.

"It was just over here that I stood with my father," said the head of the tourist bureau. "My father had been downstairs in the hall among those who received the Archduke and Archduchess, and had seen the Archduke come in, red and choking with rage. Just a little way along the embankment a young man, Chabrinovitch, had thrown a bomb at him and had wounded his aide-de-camp. So when the poor Mayor began to read his address of welcome he shouted out in a thin alto, 'That's all a lot of rot. I come here to pay you a visit, and you throw bombs at me. It's an outrage.' Then the Archduchess spoke to him softly, and he calmed down and said, 'Oh, well, you can go on.' But at the end of the speech there was another scene, because the Archduke had not got his speech, and for a moment the secretary who had it could not be found. Then when it was brought to him he was like a madman, because the manuscript was all spattered with the aide-de-camp's blood.

"But he read the speech, and then came up here with the Archduchess, into this room. My father followed, in such a state of astonishment that he walked over and took my hand and stood beside me, squeezing it very tightly. We all could not take our eyes off the Archduke, but not as you look at the main person in a court spectacle. We could not think of him as a royalty at all, he was so incredibly strange. He was striding quite grotesquely, he was lifting his legs as high as if he were doing the goose-step. I suppose he was trying to show that he was not afraid.

"I tell you, it was not at all like a reception. He was talking with the Military Governor, General Potiorek, jeering at him and taunting him with his failure to preserve order. And we were all silent, not because we were impressed by him, for he was not at all our Bosnian idea of a hero. But we all felt awkward because we knew that when he went out he would certainly be killed. No, it was not a matter of being told. But we knew how the people felt about him and the Austrians, and we knew that if one man had thrown a bomb and failed, another man would throw another bomb and another after that if he should fail. I tell you it gave a very strange feeling to the assembly. Then I remember he went out on the balcony—so—and looked out over Sarajevo. Yes, he stood just where you are standing, and he too put his arm on the balustrade."

Before the balcony the town rises on the other side of the river, in a gentle slope. Stout urban buildings stand among tall poplars, and above them white villas stand among orchards, and higher still the white cylindrical tombs of the Moslems stick askew in the rough grass like darts impaled on the board. Then fir-woods and bare bluffs meet the skyline. Under Franz Ferdinand's eye the scene must have looked its most enchanting blend of town and country, for though it was June there had been heavy restoring rains. But it is not right to assume that the sight gave him pleasure. He was essentially a Habsburg, that is to say, his blood made him turn always from the natural to the artificial, even when this was more terrifying than anything primitive could be; and this landscape showed him on its heights nature unsubdued and on its slopes nature accepted and extolled. Perhaps Franz Ferdinand felt a patriotic glow at the sight of the immense brewery in the foreground, which was built by the Austrians to supply the needs of their garrison and functionaries. These breweries, which are to be found here and there in Bosnia, throw a light on the aggressive nature of Austrian foreign policy and its sordid consequences. They were founded while this was still Turkish, by speculators whose friends in the Government were aware of Austria's plans for occupation and annexation. They also have their significance in their affront to local resources. It is quite unnecessary to drink beer here, as there is an abundance of cheap and good wine. But what was Austrian was good and what was Slav was bad.

It is unjust to say that Franz Ferdinand had no contact with nature. The room behind him was full of people who were watching him with the impersonal awe evoked by anybody who is about to die; but it may be imagined also as crammed, how closely can be judged only by those who have decided how many angels can dance on the point of a needle, by the ghosts of the innumerable birds and beasts who had fallen to his gun. He was a superb shot, and that is certainly a fine thing for a man to be, proof thât he is a good animal, quick in eye and hand and hardy under weather. But of his gift Franz Ferdinand made a murderous use. He liked to kill and kill and kill, unlike men who shoot to get food or who have kept in touch with the primitive life in which the original purpose of shooting is remembered. Prodigious figures are given of the game that fell to the double-barrelled Mannlicher rifles which were specially made for him. At a boar hunt given by Kaiser Wilhelm sixty boars were let out, and Franz Ferdinand had the first stand: fifty-nine fell dead, the sixtieth limped by on three legs. At a Czech castle in one day's sport he bagged two thousand one hundred and fifty pieces of small game. Not long before his death he expressed satisfaction because he had killed his three thousandth stag.

This capacity for butchery he used to express the hatred which he felt for nearly all the world, which, indeed, it is safe to say, he bore against the whole world, except his wife and his two children. He had that sense of being betrayed by life itself which comes to people who wrestle through long years with a chronic and dangerous malady; it is strange that both King Alexander of Yugoslavia and he had fought for half their days against tuberculosis. But Franz Ferdinand had been embittered by his environment, as Alexander was not. The indiscipline and brutality of the officials who controlled the Habsburg court had been specially directed towards him. It happened that for some years it looked as if Franz Ferdinand would not recover from his illness, and during the whole of this time the Department of the Lord High Steward, believing that he would soon be dead, cut down his expenses to the quick in order to get the praises of the Emperor Franz Josef for economy. The poor wretch, penniless in spite of the great art collections Franz Ferdinand had inherited, was grudged the most modest allowance, and even his doctor was underpaid and insulted. This maltreatment had ended when it became obvious that he was going to live, but by that time his mind was set in a mould of hatred and resentment, and though he could not shoot his enemies he found some relief in shooting, it did not matter what.

Franz Ferdinand knew no shame in his exercise of this too simple mechanism. He was ungracious as only a man can be who has never conceived the idea of graciousness. There was, for example, his dispute with Count Henkel Donnersmark, the German nobleman who was a wild young diplomat in Paris before the Franco-Prussian War, returned there to negotiate the terms of the indemnity, astonished the world by marrying the cocotte La Païva, and changed into a sober and far-seeing industrialist on the grand scale. This elderly and distinguished person had bought an estate in Silesia, and had made it pay for itself by selling the full-grown timber and replacing it by a careful scheme of reafforestation. This estate he leased to the Archduke at a rent calculated on the assumption that so much game existed on the property and would do so much damage to the saplings. As the Archduke enormously increased the stock of game, and practically no new trees could grow to maturity, the Count very reasonably raised the rent. This the Archduke, who had the wholly whimsical attitude to money often found in royal personages, conceived to be a senseless piece of greed. He gave notice to terminate his lease and decided to punish the landlord by ruining the estate as a sporting property. The remainder of his tenancy he spent in organizing battues which drove all the beasts of the field up to his guns to be slaughtered in such numbers that slaughter lost its meaning, that the boundary between living and dying became obscured, that dazed men forgot that they were killing. But he and his staff found that the forces of life outnumbered them, so he let part of the shoot to a Viennese manufacturer, a man with whom he could not have brought himself to have relations for any other reason, on condition that he pursue the same crusade of extermination. That, however, was still not enough, and the employees of the hunt were set to kill off what was left of the game by any means, abandoning all sporting restraints. Because the forest still twitched with life, because here and there the fern was trodden down and branches stirred by survivors of the massacre, the Archduke suffered several attacks of rage which disgusted all witnesses, being violent as vomiting or colic.

It may be conceived therefore that, even as the game which St. Julian Hospitaller had killed as a cruel hunter appeared before him on the night when he was going to accomplish his destiny and become the murderer of his father and mother, so the half million beasts which had fallen to Franz Ferdinand's gun according to his own calculations were present that day in the reception hall at Sarajevo. One can conceive the space of this room stuffed all the way up to the crimson and gold vaults and stalactites with the furred and feathered ghosts, set close, because there were so many of them: stags with the air between their antlers stuffed with woodcock, quail, pheasant, partridge, capercailzie, and the like; boars standing bristling flank to flank, the breadth under their broad bellies packed with layer upon layer of hares and rabbits. Their animal eyes, clear and dark as water, would brightly watch the approach of their slayer to an end that exactly resembled their own. For Franz Ferdinand's greatness as a hunter had depended not only on his pre-eminence as a shot, but on his power of organizing battues. He was specially proud of an improvement he had made in the hunting of hare: his beaters, placed in a pear-shaped formation, drove all the hares towards him so that he was able without effort to exceed the bag of all other guns. Not a beast that fell to him in these battues could have escaped by its own strength or cunning, even if it had been a genius among its kind. The earth and sky were narrowed for it by the beaters to just one spot, the spot where it must die; and so it was with this man. If by some miracle he had been able to turn round and address the people in the room behind him not with his usual aggressiveness and angularity but in terms which would have made him acceptable to them as a suffering fellow-creature, still they could not have saved him. If by some miracle his slow-working and clumsy mind could have become swift and subtle, it could not have shown him a safe road out of Sarajevo. Long ago he himself, and the blood which was in his veins, had placed at their posts the beaters who should drive him down through a narrowing world to the spot where Princip's bullet would find him.

Through Franz Ferdinand's mother, the hollow-eyed Annunziata, he was the grandson of King Bomba of the Sicilies, one of the worst of the Bourbons, an idiot despot who conducted a massacre of his subjects after 1848, and, on being expelled from Naples, retired into a fortress and lived the life of a medieval tyrant right on until the end of the fifties. This ancestry had given Franz Ferdinand tuberculosis, obstinacy, bigotry, a habit of suspicion, hatred of democracy, and an itch for aggression, which, combined with the Habsburg narrowness and indiscipline, made him a human being who could not have hoped to survive had he not been royal. When he went to Egypt to spend the winter for the sake of his lungs it appeared to him necessary, and nobody who knew him would have expected anything else, to insult the Austrian Ambassador. By the time he had passed through his twenties he had made an army of personal enemies, which he constantly increased by his intemperate and unin-structed political hatreds. He hated Hungary, the name of Kossuth made him spit with rage. When receiving a deputation of Slovaks, though they were not a people whom he would naturally have taken into his confidence, he said of the Hungarians, "It was an act of bad taste on the part of these gentlemen ever to have come to Europe," which must remain an ace in the history of royal indiscretion.

He had a dream of replacing the Dual Monarchy by a Triune Monarchy, in which the German and Czech crown lands should form the first part, Hungary the second, and the South Slav group—Croatia, Dalmatia, Bosnia, and Herzegovina—the third. This would have pleased the Croats, and the Croats alone. Most German Austrians would have been infuriated at having to combine with the Czechs and to see the South Slavs treated as their equals; Hungary would have been enraged at losing her power over the South Slavs; and the non-Catholic South Slavs would have justly feared being made the object of Catholic propaganda and would have resented being cut off from their natural ambition of union with the Serbs of Serbia. By this scheme, therefore, he made a host of enemies; and though he came in time to abandon it he could not quickly turn these enemies into friends by making public his change of mind. As he was the heir to the throne, he could announce his policy only by the slow method of communicating it to private individuals.

He abandoned his plan of the Triune Monarchy, moreover, for reasons too delicate to be freely discussed. In 1889, when he was thirty-three, he had paid some duty calls on the Czech home of his cousins, the Archduke Frederick and the Archduchess Isabella, to see if he found one of their many daughters acceptable as his bride. Instead he fell in love with the Archduchess's lady-in-waiting, Sophie Chotek, a woman of thirty-two, noble but destitute. He insisted on marrying her in spite of the agonized objection of the Emperor Franz Josef, who pointed out to him that, according to the Habsburg House Law, the secret law of the Monarchy, a woman of such low birth could not come to the throne as consort of the Emperor.

It was not a question of permission that could be bestowed or withheld, but of a rigid legal fact. If Franz Ferdinand was to marry Sophie Chotek at all he must do it morganatically, and must renounce all rights of succession for the yet unborn children of their marriage; he could no more marry her any other way than a man with a living and undivorced wife can marry a second woman, though the infringement here was of an unpublished dynastic regulation instead of the published law. But some mitigation of this severe judgment came from an unexpected quarter. The younger Kossuth declared that, according to Hungarian law, when the Archduke ascended the throne his wife, no matter what her origin, became Queen of Hungary, and his children must enjoy the

full rights of succession. This weakened the vehemence of Franz Ferdinand's loathing for Hungary, though not for individual Hungarians. He
still meant to revise the constitutional machinery of the Dual Monarchy,
but he no longer wished to punish the Hungarians quite so harshly as to
take away from them the Croats and Slovaks. But this was not a consideration he could publicly name. Nor, for diplomatic reasons, could
he confess later that he was becoming more and more fearful of the growing strength of Serbia, and was apprehensive lest a union of South Slav
provinces should tempt her ambition and provide her with a unified ally.
So, by his promulgation of an unpopular policy, and his inability to
announce his abandonment of it, the first beaters were put down to the
battue.

His marriage set others at their post. Franz Ferdinand had far too dull
a mind to appreciate the need for consistency. That was once visibly
demonstrated in relation to his passion for collecting antiques, which he
bought eagerly and without discrimination. When he paid a visit to a
country church the simple priest boasted to him of a good bargain he had
driven with a Jew dealer, who had given him a brand-new altar in exchange for his shabby old one. Immediately Franz Ferdinand sat down
and wrote to the Bishop of the diocese asking him to give his clergy an order not to part with Church property. But he was quite amazed when
later this order prevented him from carrying out the sacrilegious purchase of a tombstone which he wished to put in his private chapel. He
showed a like inconsistency in regard to his marriage. His whole life was
based on the privileges that were given to the members of the Habsburg
family because the Habsburgs had been preserved in a certain state of
genealogical purity which Austria had agreed to consider valuable. He
could not understand that, as this purity was the justification of those
privileges, they could not be extended to people in whom the Habsburg
blood had been polluted. He took it as a personal insult, a bitter, causeless
hurt, that his wife and his children should not be given royal honours.

Nor did his inconsistencies end there. Himself a typical product of
Habsburg indiscipline, he nevertheless made no allowances when his
relatives and the officials of the court reacted to his marriage with a like
indiscipline. He had here, indeed, a legitimate object for hatred, in a
character as strange as his own. Franz Josef's Chamberlain, Prince Montenuovo, was one of the strangest figures in Europe of our time; a character that Shakespeare decided at the last moment not to use in *King
Lear* or *Othello*, and laid by so carelessly that it fell out of art into life.
He was a man of exquisite taste and æsthetic courage, who protected

the artists of Vienna against the apathy of the court and the imprudence of the bourgeoisie. The Vienna Philharmonic under Mahler was his special pride and care. But he was the son of one of the bastard sons mothered by the wretched Marie Louise, when, unsustained by the opinion of historians yet unborn that she was and should have been perfectly happy in her forced marriage with Napoleon, she took refuge in the arms of Baron Niepberg. To be the bastard son of a race which was so great that it could make bastardy as noble as legitimacy, but which was great only because its legitimacy was untainted with bastardy, confused this imaginative man with a passionate and poetic and malignant madness. He watched over the rules of Habsburg ceremonial as over a case of poisons which he believed to compose the elixir of life if they were combined in the correct proportions. "And now for the strychnine," he must have said, when it became his duty to devise the adjustments made necessary by the presence at the court of a morganatic wife to the heir of the throne. Countess Sophie was excluded altogether from most intimate functions of the Austrian court; she could not accompany her husband to the family receptions or parties given for foreign royalties, or even to the most exclusive kinds of court balls; at the semi-public kind of court balls which she was allowed to attend, her husband had to head the procession with an Archduchess on his arm, while she was forced to walk at the very end, behind the youngest princess. The Emperor did what he could to mitigate the situation by creating her the Duchess of Hohenberg: but the obsessed Montenuovo hovered over her, striving to exacerbate every possible humiliation, never happier than when he could hold her back from entering a court carriage or cutting down to the minimum the salutes and attendants called for by any state occasion.

It is possible that had Franz Ferdinand been a different kind of man he might have evoked a sympathy that would have consoled him and his wife for these hardships: but all his ways were repellent. When his brother, Ferdinand Charles, a gentle soul with literary tastes, doomed to an early death from consumption, fell in love with a woman not of royal rank, Franz Ferdinand was the first to oppose the misalliance and made violent scenes with the invalid. When it was pointed out that he had married for love he answered angrily that there could be no comparison between the two cases, because Sophie Chotek was an aristocrat and his brother's wife was the daughter of a university professor. Such lack of humour, which amounts to a lack of humours in the Elizabethan sense, isolated him from all friends; so instead he created partisans. He had been given, for his Viennese home, the superb palace and park known as the Belvedere, which had been built by Prince Eugène of Savoy. He now made it the centre of what the historian Tschuppik has called a shadow government. He set up a military Chancellery of his own; and presently the Emperor Franz Josef, who always treated his nephew with an even remarkable degree of tenderness and forbearance, though not with tact, resigned to this his control over the army. But the Chancellery dealt with much more than military matters. Franz Ferdinand attracted every able man in Austria who had been ignored or rejected by the court of Franz Josef, and thanks to the stupidity and bad manners of that court these were not contemptible in quality or inconsiderable in numbers. Helped by Franz Ferdinand to form a running point-by-point opposition to the mild policy of Franz Josef, these men carried into effect his faith in half measures; and they drafted a programme for him which was indiscreetly spoken of as a scheme of reform designed for preventing the dissolution of the Austro-Hungarian Empire, to be applied as soon as Franz Josef was dead and Franz Ferdinand had ascended the throne.

This way of life set still more beaters around him. It automatically roused the animosity of all at the court of Franz Josef, and many of his own partisans became his overt or covert enemies. He became day by day less lovable. His knowledge that he could not leave the royal path of his future to his children made him fanatically mean and grasping, and his manner became more and more overbearing and brutal. He roused in small men small resentments, and, in the minds of the really able men, large distrust. They realized that though he was shrewd enough to see that the Austro-Hungarian Empire was falling to pieces when most of his kind were wholly blind to its decay, he was fundamentally stupid and cruel and saw his problem as merely that of selecting the proper objects for tyranny. Some of them feared a resort to medieval oppression; some feared the damage done to specific interests, particularly in Hungary, which was bound to follow his resettlement of the Empire. Such fears must have gained in intensity when it became evident that Kaiser Wilhelm of Germany was taking more and more interest in Franz Ferdinand, and was visiting him at his country homes and holding long conversations with him on important matters. The last visit of this kind had occurred a fortnight before the Archduke had come to Sarajevo. There is a rumour that on that occasion the Kaiser laid before Franz Ferdinand a plan for remaking the map of Europe. The Austro-Hungarian and German Empires were to be friends, and Franz Ferdinand's eldest son was to become King of a new Poland stretching from the Baltic to the Black Sea, while the second son became King of Bohemia, Hungary, Croatia, and Serbia, and Franz Ferdinand's official heir, his nephew Charles, should be left as King of German Austria. It is certain that Kaiser Wilhelm must, at that moment, have had many important things on his mind, and that it is hardly likely that he would have paid such a visit unless he had something grave to say. It is definitely known that on this occasion Franz Ferdinand expressed bitter hostility to the Hungarian aristocracy. It is also known that these remarks were repeated at the time by the Kaiser to a third person.

The manners of Franz Ferdinand did worse for him than make him enemies. They made him the gangster friends that may become enemies at any moment, with the deadly weapon of a friend's close knowledge. Franz Ferdinand's plainest sign of intelligence was his capacity for recognizing a certain type of unscrupulous ability. He had discovered Aehrenthal, the clever trickster who as Austrian Minister had managed to convert the provisional occupation of Bosnia and Herzegovina into annexation behind the backs of the other great powers in 1907. Since Aehrenthal on his deathbed had recommended Berchtold to succeed him, that incompetent war-monger might also be counted as one of the works of Franz Ferdinand. But an even greater favourite of his was Conrad von Hötzendorf, whom he made the Chief of General Staff. This creature, who was without sense or bowels, fancied himself not only as a great soldier but as a statesman, and would have directed the foreign policy of his country had he been allowed. He was obsessed by the need of preserving the Austro-Hungarian Empire by an offensive against Serbia. "Lest all our predestined foes, having perfected their armaments should deliver a blow against Austria-Hungary," he wrote in a memorandum he presented to Franz Josef in 1907 which was followed by many like it, "we must take the first opportunity of settling accounts with our most vulnerable enemy." In the intervening seven years this obsession flamed up into a mania. In 1911 Franz Josef, with the definite statements that "my policy is pacific" and that he would permit no question of an offensive war, obtained Aehrenthal's consent and dismissed Conrad from his post, making him an Inspector-general of the Army. But Franz Ferdinand still stood by him, and so did all the partisans of the Belvedere, who numbered enough industrialists, bankers, journalists, and politicians to make plain the decadence of pre-war Vienna. Berchtold was so much impressed by Conrad that in 1912 he was once more appointed Chief of General Staff. He was preaching the same gospel. "The way out of our difficulties," he wrote to Berchtold, "is to lay Serbia low without fear of consequences."

But at this time Franz Ferdinand's convictions took a new turn. He was becoming more and more subject to the influence of the German Kaiser, and Germany had no desire at that time for war, particularly with a Balkan pretext. He admired the Germans and thought they probably knew their business. This infuriated Conrad, who thought that Franz Ferdinand ought to persuade Germany to support Austria, so that he could feel confident even if their offensive war against Serbia spread into a general conflagration, which shows that he knew what he was doing. But in 1913 Berchtold had to tell Conrad, "The Archduke Franz Ferdinand is absolutely against war." At this Conrad became more and more desperate. His influence over Berchtold had been sufficient to make him refuse to see the Prime Minister of Serbia when he offered to come to Vienna to negotiate a treaty with Austria, covering all possible points of dispute. He persuaded Berchtold, moreover, to withhold all knowledge of this pacific offer from either Franz Josef or Franz Ferdinand. This is the great criminal act which gives us the right to curse Berchtold and Conrad as the true instigators of the World War. But Conrad was no less crude when in 1913 he used a trifling incident on the Dalmatian coast to attempt to get the Emperor Franz Josef to mobilize against Serbia and Montenegro. This coercion Franz Josef, with a firmness remarkable in a man of eighty-seven, quietly resisted, even though Berchtold supported Conrad, and this time Franz Ferdinand was in agreement with the old man.

Shortly after this another incident lowered Conrad's stock still further. Colonel Redl, the Chief of General Staff to the Prague Corps, who had been head of the Austrian espionage service, was found to be a spy in the pay of Russia. He was a homosexual, and had fallen into the hands of blackmailers. He was handed a loaded revolver by a brother officer and left alone to commit suicide. This caused Franz Ferdinand to fly into one of his terrible attacks of rage against Conrad, who had been responsible both for Redl's appointment to the espionage department and for the manner of his death. He was incensed that a homosexual should have been given such a position partly for moral reasons, and partly because of the special liability of such men to blackmail; and it offended his religious convictions that any man should have been forced to commit suicide. This last was hardly a fair charge to bring against Conrad, since the loaded revolver was an established Army convention in the case of shameful offences. But thenceforward the two men were enemies.

There was no doubt about this after the autumn of 1913. At the Army manœuvres in Bohemia Franz Ferdinand grossly insulted and humiliated his former friend, but refused to accept his resignation. He, however, made it clear that the only reason for the refusal was fear of a bad effect on the public mind. In June 1914 Conrad was eating his heart out in disappointment, bearing a private and public grudge against the man who had disgraced him and who would not engage in the war against Serbia which he himself believed necessary for his country's salvation.

It must be realized that he was a very relentless man. He himself has told of a conversation he had with Berchtold about the unhappy German prince, William of Wied, who was sent to be King of Albania. "Let us hope there will be no hitch," said Berchtold. "But what shall we do if there is?" "Nothing at all," said Conrad. "But what if the prince is assassinated?" asked Berchtold. "Even then we can do nothing," said Conrad. "Somebody else must take the throne in his place. Anybody will suit us as long as he is not under foreign influence." The conversation is the more grievous when it is understood that they had just refused William of Wied's very reasonable request that he might live on a yacht rather than lodge among his reluctant subjects.

Such enemies surrounded Franz Ferdinand; but it cannot be laid at their door that he had come to Sarajevo on June the twenty-eighth, 1914. This was a day of some personal significance to him. On that date in 1900 he had gone to the Hofburg in the presence of the Emperor and the whole court, and all holders of office, and had, in choking tones, taken the oath to renounce the royal rights of his unborn children. But it was also a day of immense significance for the South Slav people. It is the feast-day of St. Vitus, who is one of those saints who are lucky to find a place in the Christian calendar, since they started life as pagan deities; he was originally Vidd, a Finnish-Ugric deity. It is also the anniversary of the battle of Kossovo, where, five centuries before, the Serbs had lost their empire to the Turk. It had been a day of holy mourning for the Serbian people within the Serbian kingdom and the Austrian Empire, when they had confronted their disgrace and vowed to redeem it, until the year 1912, when Serbia's victory over the Turks at Kumanovo wiped it out. But, since 1913 had still been a time of war, the St. Vitus's Day of 1914 was the first anniversary which might have been celebrated by the Serbs in joy and pride. Franz Ferdinand must have been well aware that he was known as an enemy of Serbia. He must have known that if he went to Bosnia and conducted manœuvres on the Serbian frontier just before St. Vitus's Day and on the actual anniversary paid a state visit to

Sarajevo, he would be understood to be mocking the South Slav world, to be telling them that though the Serbs might have freed themselves from the Turks there were still many Slavs under the Austrian's yoke.

To pay that visit was an act so suicidal that one fumbles the pages of the history books to find if there is not some explanation of his going, if he was not subject to some compulsion. But if ever a man went anywhere of his own free will, Franz Ferdinand went so to Sarajevo. He himself ordered the manœuvres and decided to attend them. The Emperor Franz Josef, in the presence of witnesses, told him that he need not go unless he wished. Yet it appears inconceivable that he should not have known that the whole of Bosnia was seething with revolt, and that almost every schoolboy and student in the province was a member of some revolutionary society. Even if the extraordinary isolation that afflicts royal personages had previously prevented him from sharing this common knowledge, steps were taken to remove his ignorance. But here his temperament intervened on behalf of his own death. The Serbian Government—which by this single act acquitted itself of all moral blame for the assassination—sent its Minister in Vienna to warn Bilinski, the Joint Finance Minister, who was responsible for the civil administration of Bosnia and Herzegovina, that the proposed visit of Franz Ferdinand would enrage many Slavs on both sides of the frontier and might cause consequences which neither Government could control. But Bilinski was an Austrian Pole; Ferdinand loathed all his race, and had bitterly expressed his resentment that any of them were allowed to hold high office. Bilinski was also a close confidant of old Franz Josef and an advocate of a conciliatory policy in the Slav provinces. Thus it happened that, when he conscientiously went to transmit this message, his warnings were received not only with incredulity but in a way that made it both psychologically and materially impossible to repeat them.

Franz Ferdinand never informed in advance either the Austrian or the Hungarian Government of the arrangements he had made with the Army to visit Bosnia, and he seems to have worked earnestly and ingeniously, as people will to get up a bazaar, to insult the civil authorities. When he printed the programme of his journey he sent it to all the Ministries except the Joint Ministry of Finance; and he ordered that no invitations for the ball which he was to give after the manœuvres outside Sarajevo at Ilidzhe were to be sent to any of the Finance Ministry officials. It is as if a Prince of Wales had travelled through India brutally insulting the Indian Civil Service and the India Office. There was a thoroughly Habsburg reason for this. Since the military authorities were in charge of all the arrangements, it had been easy for Franz Ferdinand to arrange that for the first time on Habsburg territory royal honours would be paid to his wife. This could not have happened without much more discussion if the civil authorities had been involved. The result was final and bloody. Bilinski could not protest against Franz Ferdinand's visit to Sarajevo when he was not sure it was going to take place, considering the indelicate rage with which all his approaches were met. This inability to discuss the visit meant that he could not even supervise the arrangements for policing the streets. With incredible ingenuity, Franz Ferdinand had created a situation in which those whose business it was to protect him could not take one step towards his protection.

When Franz Ferdinand returned from the balcony into the reception room his face became radiant and serene, because he saw before him the final agent of his ruin, the key beater in this battue. His wife had been in an upper room of the Town Hall, meeting a number of ladies belonging to the chief Moslem families of the town, in order that she might condescendingly admire their costumes and manners, as is the habit of barbarians who have conquered an ancient culture; and she had now made the proposal that on the return journey she and her husband should alter their programme by going to the hospital to make inquiries about the officer wounded by Chabrinovitch. Nothing can ever be known about the attitude of this woman to that day's events. She was a woman who could not communicate with her fellow-creatures. We know only of her outer appearance and behaviour. We know that she had an anaphrodisiac and pinched yet heavy face, that in a day when women were bred to look like table-birds she took this convention of amplitude and expressed it with the rigidity of the drill sergeant. We know that she impressed those who knew her as absorbed in snobbish ambitions and petty resentments, and that she had as her chief ingratiating attribute a talent for mimicry, which is often the sport of an unloving and derisive soul.

But we also know that she and Franz Ferdinand felt for each other what cannot be denied to have been a great love. Each found in the other a perpetual assurance that the meaning of life is kind; each gave the other that assurance in terms suited to their changing circumstances and with inexhaustible resourcefulness and good-will; it is believed by those who knew them best that neither of them ever fell from the heights of their relationship and reproached the other for the hardships that their marriage had brought upon them. That is to say that the boar we know as Franz Ferdinand and the small-minded fury we know as Countess Sophie Chotek are not the ultimate truth about these people. These were the pragmatic conceptions of them that those who met them had to use if they were to escape unhurt, but the whole truth about their natures must certainly have been to some degree beautiful.

Even in this field where Sophie Chotek's beauty lay she was dangerous. Like her husband she could see no point in consistency, which is the very mortar of society. Because of her noble birth, she bitterly resented her position as a morganatic wife. It was infamous, she felt, that a Chotek should be treated in this way. It never occurred to her that Choteks had a value only because they had been accorded it by a system which, for reasons that were perfectly valid at the time, accorded the Habsburgs a greater value; and that if those reasons had ceased to be valid and the Habsburgs should no longer be treated as supreme, then the Choteks also had lost their claim to eminence.

Unfortunately she coupled with this inconsistency a severely legalistic mind. It can be done. The English bench has given us examples. She had discovered, and is said to have urged her discovery on Franz Ferdinand, that the oath he had taken to renounce the rights of succession for his children was contrary to crown law. No one can swear an oath which affects the unborn; this is, of course, perfectly just. It did not occur to her that, if the maintenance of the Habsburgs required the taking of unjust oaths, perhaps the Habsburg dynasty would fall to pieces if it were forced to live on the plane of highest justice, and that her children might find themselves again without a throne.

Countess Sophie Chotek must therefore have had her hands full of the complicated hells of the humourless legalist; it must have seemed to her that her environment was always perversely resisting the imposition of a perfect pattern, to her grave personal damage. She had, however, a more poignant personal grief. She believed Franz Ferdinand to be on the point of going mad. It is on record that she hinted to her family lawyer and explicitly informed an intimate friend that in her opinion her husband might at any moment be stricken with some form of mental disorder. This may have been merely part of that corpus of criticism which might be called "Any Wife to Any Husband." But there were current many stories which go to show that Franz Ferdinand's violence had for some time been manifest in ways not compatible with sanity. The Czech officials in charge of the imperial train that had brought Franz Ferdinand from Berlin after a visit to the German Emperor reported to the chief of the Czech Separatist Party that when Franz Ferdinand had alighted at his destination they found the upholstery in his compartment cut to pieces by sword thrusts; and in a visit to England he struck those who met him as undisciplined in a way differing in quality and degree from the normal abnormality which comes from high rank.

This woman had therefore a host of enemies without her home, and within it an enemy more terrifying than all the rest. That she was in great distress is proven by a certain difficulty we know to have arisen in her religious life. It was one of the wise provisions of the early Church that the orthodox were not allowed the benefits of communion or confession except at rare intervals. There is obviously a sound and sensible reason for this rule. It cannot be believed that the soul is sufficiently potent to be for ever consummating its union with God, and the forgiveness of sins must lose its reality if it is sought too rapidly for judgment to pronounce soberly on guilt. Moreover limiting the approach to the sacraments prevents them from becoming magical practices, mere snatchings at amulets. By one of the innovations which divide the Roman Catholic Church from the early Church, Pope Leo X removed all these restrictions, and now a devotee can communicate and confess as often as he likes. But the Countess Sophie Chotek availed herself of this permission so extremely often that she was constantly at odds with the Bishop who guided her spiritual life. At their hotel out at Ilidzhe a room had been arranged as a chapel, and that morning she and her husband had attended mass. Not one day could go without invoking the protection of the cross against the disaster which she finally provoked by her proposal that they should visit the wounded aide-de-camp in hospital.

There was a conversation about this proposal which can never be understood. It would be comprehensible only if the speakers had been drunk or living through a long fevered night; but they were sober and, though they were facing horror, they were facing it at ten o'clock on a June morning. Franz Ferdinand actually asked Potiorek if he thought any bombs would be thrown at them during their drive away from the Town Hall. This question is incredibly imbecile. If Potiorek had not known enough to regard the first attack as probable, there was no reason to ascribe any value whatsoever to his opinion on the probability of a second attack. There was one obvious suggestion which it would have been natural for either Franz Ferdinand or Potiorek to make. The streets were quite inadequately guarded, otherwise Chabrinovitch could not have made his attack. Therefore it was advisable that Franz Ferdinand and his wife should remain at the Town Hall until adequate numbers of the seventy thousand troops who were within no great distance of the town were sent for to line the streets. This is a plan which one would have thought would have been instantly brought to the men's minds by the mere fact that they were responsible for the safety of a woman.

But they never suggested anything like it, and Potiorek gave to Franz Ferdinand's astonishing question the astonishing answer that he was sure no second attack would be made. The startling element in this answer is its imprudence, for he must have known that any investigation would bring to light that he had failed to take for Franz Ferdinand any of the precautions that had been taken for Franz Josef on his visit to Sarajevo seven years before, when all strangers had been evacuated from the town, all anti-Austrians confined to their houses, and the streets lined with a double cordon of troops and peppered with detectives. It would be credible only if one knew that Potiorek had received assurances that if anything happened to Franz Ferdinand there would be no investigation afterwards that he need fear. Indeed, it would be easy to suspect that Potiorek deliberately sent Franz Ferdinand to his death, were it not that it must have looked beforehand as if that death must be shared by Potiorek, as they were both riding in the same carriage. It is of course true that Potiorek shared Conrad's belief that a war against Serbia was a sacred necessity, and had written to him on one occasion expressing the desperate opinion that, rather than not have war, he would run the risk of provoking a world war and being defeated in it; and throughout the Bosnian manœuvres he had been in the company of Conrad, who was still thoroughly disgruntled by his dismissal by Franz Ferdinand. It must have been quite plain to them both that the assassination of Franz Ferdinand by a Bosnian Serb would be a superb excuse for declaring war on Serbia. Still, it is hard to believe that Potiorek would have risked his own life to take Franz Ferdinand's, for he could easily have arranged for the Archduke's assassination when he was walking in the open country. It is also extremely doubtful if any conspirators would have consented to Potiorek risking his life, for his influence and military skill would have been too useful to them to throw away.

Yet there is an incident arising out of this conversation which can only be explained by the existence of entirely relentless treachery somewhere among Franz Ferdinand's entourage. It was agreed that the royal party should, on leaving the Town Hall, follow the route that had been originally announced for only a few hundred yards: they would drive along the quay to the second bridge, and would then follow a new route by keeping straight along the quay to the hospital, instead of turning to the right and going up a side street which led to the principal shopping centre of the town. This had the prime advantage of disappointing any other conspirators who might be waiting in the crowds, after any but the first few hundred yards of the route, and, as Potiorek had also promised that the automobiles should travel at a faster speed, it might have been thought that the Archduke and his wife had a reasonable chance of getting out of Sarajevo alive. So they might, if anybody had given orders to the chauffeur on either of these points. But either Potiorek never gave these orders to any subordinate, or the subordinate to whom he entrusted them never handed them on.

Neither hypothesis is easy to accept. Even allowing for Austrian *Schlamperei*, soldiers and persons in attendance on royalty do not make such mistakes. But though this negligence cannot have been accidental, the part it played in contriving the death of Franz Ferdinand cannot have been foreseen. The Archduke, his wife, and Potiorek left the Town Hall, taking no farewell whatsoever of the municipal officers who lined the staircase, and went on to the quay and got into their automobile. Franz Ferdinand and Sophie are said to have looked stunned and stiff with apprehension. Count Harrach, an Austrian general, jumped on the left running-board and crouched there with drawn sword, ready to defend the royal pair with his life. The procession was headed by an automobile containing the Deputy Mayor and a member of the Bosnian Diet; but by another incredible lapse neither of these officials nor their chauffeurs were informed of the change in route. When this first automobile came to the bridge it turned to the right and went up the side street. The chauffeur of the royal car saw this and was therefore utterly bewildered when Potiorek struck him on the shoulder and shouted, "What are you doing? We're going the wrong way! We must drive straight along the quay."

Not having been told how supremely important it was to keep going, the puzzled chauffeur stopped dead athwart the corner of the side street and the quay. He came to halt exactly in front of a young Bosnian Serb named Gavrilo Princip, who was one of the members of the same conspiracy as Chabrinovitch. He had failed to draw his revolver on the Archduke during the journey to the Town Hall, and he had come back to make another attempt. As the automobile remained stock-still Princip was able to take steady aim and shoot Franz Ferdinand in the heart. He was not a very good shot, he could never have brought down his quarry if there had not been this failure to give the chauffeur proper instructions. Harrach could do nothing; he was on the left side of the car, Princip on the right. When he saw the stout, stuffed body of the Archduke fall forward he shifted his revolver to take aim at Potiorek. He would have killed him at once had not Sophie thrown herself across the car in one last expression of her great love, and drawn Franz Ferdinand to herself with a movement that brought her across the path of the second bullet. She was already dead when Franz Ferdinand murmured to her, "Sophie, Sophie, live for our children"; and he died a quarter of an hour later. So was your life and my life mortally wounded, but so was not the life of the Bosnians, who were indeed restored to life by this act of death.

Leaning from the balcony, I said, "I shall never be able to understand how it happened." It is not that there are too few facts available, but that there are too many. To begin with, only one murder was committed, yet there were two murders in the story: one was the murder done by Princip, the other was the murder dreamed of by some person or persons in Franz Ferdinand's entourage, and they were not the same. And the character of the event is not stamped with murder but with suicide. Nobody worked to ensure the murder on either side so hard as the people who were murdered. And they, though murdered, are not as pitiable as victims should be. They manifested a mixture of obstinate invocation of disaster and anguished complaint against it which is often associated with unsuccessful crime, with the petty thief in the dock. Yet they were of their time. They could not be blamed for morbidity in a society which adored death, which found joy in contemplating the death of beasts, the death of souls in a rigid social system, the death of peoples under an oppressive empire.

"Many things happened that day," said the head of the tourist bureau, "but most clearly I remember the funny thin voice of the Archduke and his marionette strut." I looked down on the street below and saw one who was not as the Archduke, a tall gaunt man from the mountains with his crimson scarf about his head, walking with a long stride that was the sober dance of strength itself. I said to Constantine, "Did that sort of man have anything to do with the assassination?" "Directly, nothing at all," answered Constantine, "though indirectly he had everything to do with it. But in fact all of the actual conspirators were peculiarly of Sarajevo, a local product. You will understand better when I have shown you where it all happened. But now we must go back to the tourist bureau, for we cannot leave this gentleman until we have drunk black coffee with him."

As we walked out of the Town Hall the sunshine was at last warm and the plum blossom in the distant gardens shone as if it were not still wet with melted snow. "Though the hills rise so sharply," I said, "the contours are so soft, to be in thi; city is like walking inside an opening flower." "Everything here is perfect," said Constantine; "and think of it, only since I was a grown man has this been my town. Until then its beauty was a heartache and a shame to me, because I was a Serb and Sarajevo was a Slav town in captivity." "Come now, come now," I said, "by that same reckoning should not the beauty of New York and Boston be a heartache and shame to me?" "Not at all, not at all," he said, "for you and the Americans are not the same people. The air of America is utterly different from the air of England, and has made Americans even of pure English blood utterly different from you, even as the air of Russia, which is not the same as Balkan air, has made our Russian brothers not at all as we are. But the air of Bosnia is the same as Serbian air, and these people are almost the same as us, except that they talk less. Besides, your relatives in America are not being governed by another race, wholly antipathetic to you both. If the Germans had taken the United States and you went over there and saw New England villages being governed on Prussian lines, then you would sigh that you and the Americans of your race should be together again." "I see that," I said. I was looking at the great toast-coloured barracks which the Austrians set on a ledge dominating the town. They seemed to say, "All is now known, we can therefore act without any further discussion": a statement idiotic in itself, and more so when addressed to the essentially speculative Slav.

"All, I tell you," said Constantine, "that is Austrian in Sarajevo is false to us. Look at this embankment we are walking upon. It is very nice and straight, but it is nothing like the embankment we Yugoslavs, Christian or Moslem, would make for a river. We are very fond of nature as she is, and we do not want to hold up a ruler and tell her that she must look like that and not stick forward her bosom or back her bottom. And look, here is the corner where Princip killed the Archduke, and you see how appropriate it was. For the young Bosnian came along the little street from the real Sarajevo where all the streets are narrow and many are winding and every house belongs to a person, to this esplanade which the Austrians built, which is one long line and has big houses that look alike, and seeing an Arch-Austrian he made him go away. See, there is a tablet on that corner commemorating the deed."

I had read much abuse of this tablet as a barbarous record of satisfaction in an accomplished crime. Mr. Winston Churchill remarks in his book on *The Unknown War* (*The Eastern Front*) that "Princip died in prison, and a monument erected in recent years by his fellow-countrymen records his infamy and their own." It is actually a very modest black tablet, not more than would be necessary to record the exact spot of the assassination for historical purposes, and it is placed so high above the street-level that the casual passer-by would not remark it. The inscription runs, "Here, in this historical place, Gavrilo Princip was the initiator of liberty, on the day of St. Vitus, the 28th of June, 1914." These words seem to me remarkable in their restraint, considering the bitter hatred that the rule of Austria had aroused in Bosnia. The expression "initiator of liberty" is justified by its literal truth: the Bosnians and Herzegovinians were in fact enslaved until the end of the war which was provoked by the assassination of the Archduke Franz Ferdinand. To be shocked at a candid statement of this hardly becomes a subject of any of the Western states who connived at the annexation of these territories by Austria.

One must let the person who wears the shoe know where it pinches. It happened that as Constantine and I were looking up at the tablet there passed by one of the most notable men in Yugoslavia, a scholar and a gentleman, known to his peers in all the great cities of Europe. He greeted us and nodded up at the tablet, "A bad business that." "Yes, yes," said Constantine warily, for they were political enemies, and he dreaded what might come. "We must have no more of such things, Constantine," said the other. "No, no," said Constantine. "No more assassinations, Constantine," the other went on. "No, no," said Constantine. "And no more Croats shot down because they are Croats, Constantine," rapped out the other. "But we never do that," wailed Constantine; "it is only that accidents must happen in the disorder that these people provoke!" "Well, there must be no more accidents," said his friend. But as he turned to go he looked again at the tablet, and his eyes grew sad. "But God forgive us all!" he said. "As for that accident, it had to happen."

I said to Constantine, "Would he have known Princip, do you think?" But Constantine answered, "I think not. He was ten years older, and he would only have known a man of Princip's age if their families had been friends, but poor Princip had no family of the sort that had such rich friends. He was just a poor boy come down from the mountains to get his education here in Sarajevo, and he knew nobody but his school-fellows." That, indeed, is a fact which is of great significance historically: the youth and obscurity of the Sarajevo conspirators. Princip himself was the grandson of an immigrant whose exact origin is unknown, though he was certainly a Slav. This stranger appeared in a village on the borders of Bosnia and Dalmatia at a time when the Moslems of true Turkish stock had been driven out by the Bosnian insurrectionary forces, and occupied one of the houses that had been vacated by the Turks. There must have been something a little odd about this man, for he wore a curious kind of silver jacket with bells on it, which struck the villagers as strange and gorgeous and which cannot be identified by the experts as forming part of any local costume known in the Balkans. Because of this eccentric garment the villagers gave him the nickname of "Princip," which means Prince; and because of that name there sprung up after the assassination a preposterous legend that Princip's father was the illegitimate son of the murdered Prince Rudolf. He was certainly just a peasant, who married a woman of that Homeric people, the Montenegrins, and begot a family in the depths of poverty. When Austria came in and seized Bosnia after it had been cleared of Turks by the Bosnian rebels, it was careful to leave the land tenure system exactly as it had been under the Turks, and the Bosnian peasants continued on starvation level. Of Princip's children one son became a postman, and married a Herzegovinian who seems to have been a woman most remarkable for strength of character. In her barren mountain home she bore nine children, of whom six died, it is believed from maladies arising out of undernourishment. The other three sons she filled with an ambition to do something in life, and sent them down into the towns to get an education and at the same time to earn money to pay for it. The first became a doctor, the second a tradesman who was chosen at an early age mayor of his town. The third was Gavrilo Princip, who started on his journey under two handicaps. He was physically fragile, and he entered a world distracted with thoughts of revolution and preparations for war.

The two most oppressive autocracies in Europe were working full time to supply themselves and all other European countries with the material of revolution. Russia was producing innumerable authors who dealt in revolutionary thought. The Austrian Empire was producing innumerable men who were capable of any revolutionary act, whether in the interests of military tyranny or popular liberty. The Russian influence came into Bosnia through several channels, some of them most unexpected. For political purposes the Russian imperial family maintained a boarding school for girls at the top of the road from Kotor, in Tsetinye, the capital of Montenegro, where many of the aristocratic families of Dalmatia and Bosnia and Herzegovina and even Croatia sent their daughters to be educated. As all familiar with the perversity of youth would expect, the little dears later put to use the Russian they acquired at that institution to read Stepniak and Kropotkin and Tolstoy. This was but a narrow channel, which served only to gain tolerance among the wealthier classes for the movement which swept through practically the whole of the male youth of the Southern Slavs and set them discussing nihilism, anarchism and state socialism, and experimenting with the technique of terrorism which the advocates of those ideas had developed in Russia.

In this last and least attractive part of their activities the Bosnians show at a disadvantage compared to their Russian brothers during the period immediately before the war: they appear more criminal because they were more moral. Among the Russian revolutionaries there had been growing perplexity and disillusionment ever since 1906, when it was discovered that the people's leader, Father Gapon, owing to the emollient effects of a visit to Monte Carlo, had sold himself to the police as a spy. In 1909 they received a further shock. It was proved that Aseff, the head of the largest and most powerful terrorist organization in Russia, had from the very beginning of his career been a police agent, and though he had successfully arranged the assassination of Plehve, the Minister of the Interior, and the Grand Duke Serge, he had committed the first crime partly because he was a Jew and disliked Plehve's anti-Semitism, and partly because he wanted to strengthen his position in revolutionary circles in order to get a higher salary from the police, and he had committed the second to oblige persons in court circles who had wanted to get rid of the Grand Duke. This made all the sincere revolutionaries realize that their ranks were riddled with treachery, and that if they risked their lives it was probably to save the bacon of a police spy or further a palace intrigue. For this reason terrorism was practically extinct in Russia for some years before the war.

But the Southern Slavs were not traitors. It is true that there existed numbers, indeed vast numbers, of Croats and Serbs and Czechs who attempted to raise funds by selling to the Austro-Hungarian Empire forged evidence that their respective political parties were conspiring with the Serbian Government. But their proceedings were always conducted with the utmost publicity, and their forgeries were so clumsy as to be recognized as such by the most prejudiced court; they presented telegrams, which were supposed to have been delivered, on reception forms instead of transmission forms, and they put forward photographs of patriotic societies' minutes which bore evidence that the original documents must have been over three-foot-three by thirteen inches: a nice size for reproduction but not for a society's minutes. Neither the officials of the Empire nor the Slav nationalists ever took any serious measures against these disturbers of the peace, and they seem to have had such a privileged position of misdoing as is given in some villages to a pilferer, so long as he is sufficiently blatant and modest in his exploits so that he can be frustrated by reasonable care, and the community loses not too much when he scores a success.

But the real traitor and *agent provocateur*, who joined in revolutionary activities for the purpose of betraying his comrades to authority, was rare indeed among the South Slavs, and therefore terrorist organizations could function in confidence. They honeycombed the universities and the schools to an extent which seems surprising, till one remembers that, owing to the poverty of the inhabitants and the defective system of education imposed by the Austrian Empire, the age of the pupils at each stage was two or three years above that which would have been customary in a Western community.

The terrorism of these young men was given a new inspiration in 1912 and 1913 by the Balkan wars in which Serbia beat Turkey and Bulgaria. They saw themselves cutting loose from the decaying corpse of an empire and uniting with a young and triumphant democratic state; and by the multiplication of society upon society and patriotic journal upon patriotic journal they cultivated the idea of freeing themselves by acts of violence directed against their rulers. This, however, did not alter that horrible dispensation by which it is provided that those who most thirstily desire to go on the stage shall be those who have the least talent for acting. The Croats and Serbs are magnificent soldiers; they shoot well and they have hearts like lions. But they are deplorable terrorists. Much more individualist than the Russians, the idea of a secret society was more of a toy to them than a binding force. They were apt to go on long journeys to meet fellow-conspirators for the purpose of discussing an outrage, and on the way home to become interested in some other aspect of the revolutionary movement, such as Tolstoyan pacifism, and leave their bombs in the train. When they maintained their purpose, they frequently lost not their courage but their heads at the crucial moment, perhaps because the most convenient place for such *attentats*, to use the Continental word for a crime directed against the representative of a government, was among crowds in a town, and the young Slav was not used to crowds. He felt, as W. H. Davies put it of himself in urban conditions, "like a horse near fire." Such considerations do not operate now. The Great War hardened the nerves of a generation in the dealing out of death, and it trained the following generation with its experience plus the aid of all the money and help certain foreign nations could give them. The Croats and Macedonians trained in Italy and Hungary who killed King Alexander of Jugoslavia represented the highest point of *expertise* in terrorism that man has yet attained.

But in the days before the war the South Slavs were touching and ardent amateurs. Typical of them was young Zheraitch, a handsome Serb boy from a Herzegovinian village, who decided to kill the Emperor Franz Josef when he visited Bosnia and Herzegovina in 1910. With that end in mind he followed the old man from Sarajevo to Mostar, and from Mostar to Ilidzhe, revolver in hand, but never fired a shot. Then he decided to kill the Governor of Bosnia, General Vareshanin, who was specially abhorrent to the Slavs because he was a renegade Croat. He waited on a bridge for the General as he drove to open the Diet of Sarajevo. The boy fired five bullets at him, which all went wide. He kept the sixth to fire at his own forehead. It is said that General Vareshanin got out of his car and walked over to his body and savagely kicked it, a gesture which was bitterly remembered among all young South Slavs. This poor boy was typical of many of his fellows in his failure. In June 1912 another Bosnian tried to kill the Ban of Croatia in the streets of Zagreb, and killed two other people, but not him. In August 1913 a young Croat tried to kill the new Ban of Croatia, but only wounded him. In March 1914 another young Croat was caught in the Opera House at Zagreb just as he was about to shoot the Ban and the Archduke Leopold Salvator. And so on, and so on. The Balkan wars altered this state of affairs to some extent. A great many young Bosnians and Herzegovinians either swam across the river Drina into Serbia, or slipped past the frontier guards on the Montenegrin borders by night, in order to join irregular volunteer bands which served as outposts for the Serbian Army as it invaded Macedonia. All these young men acquired skill and hardihood in the use of weapons. But those who stayed at home were incurably inefficient as assassins.

Princip was not among the young Bosnians who had gone to the Balkan wars. He had soon become weary of the school life of Sarajevo, which was reduced to chaos by the general political discontent of the pupils and their particular discontents with the tendentious curriculum of the Austro-Hungarian education authorities. He took to shutting himself up in his poor room and read enormously of philosophy and politics, undermining his health and nerves by the severity of these undirected studies. Always, of course, he was short of money and ate but little. Finally he felt he had better emigrate to Serbia and start studies at a secondary school at Belgrade, and he took that step in May 1912, when he was barely seventeen. One of his brothers gave him some money, and he had saved much of what he had earned by teaching some little boys; but it must have been a starveling journey. In Belgrade he was extremely happy in his studies, and might have become a contented scholar had not the Balkan War broken out. He immediately volunteered, and was sent down to a training centre in the South of Serbia, and would have made a first-rate soldier if gallantry had been all that was needed. But his deprived body broke down, and he was discharged from the Army.

Princip's humiliation was increased to a painful degree, it is said, because another soldier with whom he was on bad terms grinned when he saw him walking off with his discharge and said, "*Skart*," throw-out, bad stuff. Though he went back to Belgrade and studied hard and with great success, he was extremely distressed at his failure to render service to the Slav cause and prove his worth as a hero. It happened that in Serbia he had become a close friend of a young printer from Sarajevo called Chabrinovitch, a boy of his own age, who had been banished from Bosnia for five years for the offence of preaching anarchism. Much has been written about this youth which is not too enthusiastic, though it might be described as querulous rather than unfavourable. His companions found something disquieting and annoying about his high spirits and his garrulity, but it must be remembered that those who are very remarkable people, particularly when they are young, often repel more ordinary people by both their laughter and their grief, which seem excessive by the common measure. It is possible that what was odd about Chabrinovitch was simply incipient greatness. But he was also labouring under the handicap of an extremely hostile relationship to his father. In any case he certainly was acceptable as a friend by Princip, and this speaks well for his brains.

They had a number of Sarajevan friends in common, whom they had met at school or in the cafés. Among these was a young schoolmaster called Danilo Ilitch, a neurotic and irascible and extremely unpopular ascetic. He is said to have served in the Serbian Army during the Balkan War, but only as an orderly. From the beginning of 1914 he was engaged in an attempt to form a terrorist organization for the purpose of committing a desperate deed, though nobody, least of all himself, seemed to know exactly what. Among his disciples was a young man called Pushara, who one day cut out of the newspaper a paragraph announcing the intended visit of Franz Ferdinand to Bosnia, and posted it from Sarajevo to Chabrinovitch in Belgrade. It is said by some that he meant merely to intimate that there would be trouble, not that trouble should be made. It is also to be noted that one of his family was said to be an Austrian police spy. If he or somebody connected with him had been acting as an *agent provocateur* they could not have hoped for better success. Chabrinovitch showed the paragraph to Princip, and they decided to return to Sarajevo and kill Franz Ferdinand.

But they needed help. Most of all they needed weapons. First they thought of applying to the Narodna Obrana, the Society of National Defence, for bombs, but their own good sense told them that was impossible. The Narodna Obrana was a respectable society acting openly under Government protection, and even these children, confused by misgovernment to complete callousness, saw that it would have been asking too much to expect it to commit itself to helping in the assassination of a foreign royalty. Moreover they both had had experience of the personalities directing the Narodna Obrana and they knew they were old-fashioned, pious, conservative Serbs of the medieval Serbian pattern, who were more than a little shocked by these Bosnian children who sat up till all hours in cafés and dabbled in free thought. When Chabrinovitch had gone to the society to ask a favour, an old Serbian captain had been gravely shocked by finding the lad in possession of Maupassant's *Bel Ami* and had confiscated it.

It is unfortunate that at this point they met a Bosnian refugee called Tsiganovitch who had heard rumours of their intention and who offered to put them in the way of getting some bombs. He was a member of the secret society known as the "Black Hand," or was associated with it. This society had already played a sinister part in the history of Serbia. It was the lineal descendant of the group of officers who had killed King Alexander and Queen Draga and thus exchanged the Obrenovitch dynasty for the Karageorgevitch. The Karageorges, who had played no part in this conspiracy, and had had to accept its results passively, had never resigned themselves to the existence of the group, and were continually at odds with them. The "Black Hand" was therefore definitely anti-Karageorgevitch and aimed at war with Austria and the establishment of a federated republic of Balkan Slavs. Their leader was a man of undoubted talent but far too picturesque character called Dragutin Dimitriyevitch, known as "Apis," who had been for some time the head of the Intelligence Bureau of the Serbian General Staff. He had heard of Ilitch and his group through a Bosnian revolutionary living in Lausanne, Gachinovitch, a boy of twenty-two who had an extraordinary power over all his generation among the South Slavs, particularly among the Bosnians; his posthumous works were edited by Trotsky. It was by his direction that Chabrinovitch and Princip had been approached by Tsiganovitch, and were later taken in hand, together with another Bosnian boy of nineteen called Grabezh who had just joined them, by an officer called Tankositch, who had been concerned in the murder of King Alexander and Queen Draga.

Tankositch took the boys into some woods and saw how they shot—which was badly, though Princip was better than the others. Finally he fitted them out with bombs, pistols, and some prussic acid to take when their attempts had been made so that they might be sure not to break down and blab in the presence of the police. Then he sent them off to Sarajevo by what was known as the underground route, a route by which persons who might have found difficulty in crossing the frontier, whether for reasons of politics or of contraband, were helped by friendly pro-Slavs. The boys were smuggled through Bosnia by two guards who were under orders from the "Black Hand," and with the help of a number of Balkan peasants and tradesmen, who one and all were exceedingly discomfited but dared not refuse assistance to members of a revolutionary body, they got their munitions into Sarajevo.

This journey was completed only by a miracle, such was the inefficiency of the conspirators. Chabrinovitch talked too much. Several times the people on whose good-will they were dependent took fright and were in two minds to denounce the matter to the police, and take the risk of revolutionary vengeance rather than be hanged for complicity, as indeed some of them were. Ilitch was even less competent. He had arranged to fetch the bombs at a certain railway junction, but he fell into a panic and did not keep the appointment. For hours the sugar-box containing the weapons lay in the public waiting-room covered with a coat. The station cat had a comfortable sleep on it. Unfortunately Ilitch recovered his nerve and brought the bombs to his home, where he kept them under the sofa in his bedroom. He had swelled the ranks of those who were to use their arms by some most unsuitable additions. He had enrolled a Moslem called Mehmed Basitch, a peculiar character who had already shown a divided mind towards terrorism. In January 1913 he had gone to Toulouse with a Moslem friend and had visited the wonderful Gachinovitch, the friend of Trotsky. He had received from the leader weapons and poison for the purpose of attempting the life of General Potiorek, the Military Governor of Bosnia, but on the way he and his friend had thought better of it and dropped them out of the carriage window. Ilitch had also enrolled two schoolboys called Chubrilovitch and Popovitch, and gave them revolvers. Neither had ever fired a shot in his life. The few days before the visit of the Archduke Ilitch spent in alternately exhorting this ill-assorted group to show their patriotism by association and imploring them to forget it and disperse. He was himself at one point so overcome by terror that he got into the train and travelled all the way to the town of Brod, a hundred miles away. But he came back, though to the very end he seems at times to have urged Princip, who was living with him, to abandon the *attentat*, and to have expressed grave distrust of Chabrinovitch on the ground that his temperament was not suited to terrorism. It might have been supposed that Franz Ferdinand would never be more safe in his life than he would be on St. Vitus's Day at Sarajevo.

That very nearly came to be true. On the great day Ilitch made up his mind that the assassination should take place after all, and he gave orders for the disposition of the conspirators in the street. They were so naïve that it does not seem to have struck them as odd that he himself proposed to take no part in the *attentat*. They were told to take up their stations at various points on the embankment: first Mehmed Basitch, then Chabrinovitch, then Chubrilovitch, then Popovitch, and after that Princip, at the head of the bridge that now bears his name, with Grabezh facing him across the road. What happened might easily have been foretold. Mehmed Basitch never threw his bomb. Instead he watched the car go by and then ran to the railway station and jumped into a train that was leaving for Montenegro; there he sought the protection of one of the tribes which constituted that nation, with whom his family had friendly connexions, and the tribesmen kept him hidden in their mountain homes. Later he made his way to France, and that was not to be the end of his adventures. He was to be known to Balkan history as a figure hardly less enigmatic than the Man in the Iron Mask. The schoolboy Chubrilovitch had been told that if Mehmed Basitch threw his bomb he was to finish off the work with his revolver, but if Mehmed Basitch failed he was to throw his own bomb. He did nothing. Neither did the other schoolboy, Popovitch. It was impossible for him to use either his bomb or his revolver, for in his excitement he had taken his stand beside a policeman. Chabrinovitch threw his bomb, but high and wide. He then swallowed his dose of prussic acid and jumped off the parapet of the embankment. There, as the prussic acid had no effect on him, he suffered arrest by the police. Princip heard the noise of Chabrinovitch's bomb and thought the work was done, so stood still. When the car went by and he saw that the royal party was still alive, he was dazed with astonishment and walked away to a café, where he sat down and had a cup of coffee and pulled himself together. Grabezh was also deceived by the explosion and let his opportunity go by. Franz Ferdinand would have gone from Sarajevo untouched had it not been for the actions of his staff, who by blunder after blunder contrived that his car should slow down and that he should be presented as a stationary target in front of Princip, the one conspirator of real and mature deliberation, who had finished his cup of coffee and was walking back through the streets, aghast at the failure of himself and his friends, which would expose the country to terrible punishment without having inflicted any loss on authority. At last the bullets had been coaxed out of the reluctant revolver to the bodies of the eager victims.

Sarajevo VI

"Do you see," said Constantine, "the last folly of these idiots?" There is a raw edge to the ends of the bridge, an unhemmed look to the masonry on both sides of the road. "They put up a statue of the Archduke Franz Ferdinand and his wife, not in Vienna, where there was a good deal of expiation to be done to those two, but here, where the most pitiful amongst us could not pity them. As soon as we took the town over after the liberation they were carted away." They may still be standing in some backyard, intact or cut into queer sculptural joints, cast down among ironically long grass. There was never more convincing proof that we do not make our own destinies, that they are not merely the pattern traced by our characteristics on time as we rush through it, than the way that the destinies of Franz Ferdinand and Sophie Chotek continued to operate after their death. In their lives they had passed from situation to situation which invited ceremonial grandeur and had been insanely deprived of it in a gross ceremonial setting, and it was so when they were in their coffins. They were sent to Vienna, to what might have been hoped was the pure cold cancellation of the tomb. They were, however, immediately caught up and whirled about in a stately and complicated vortex of contumely and hatred that astonished the whole world, even their world, accustomed as it was to hideousness.

The Emperor Franz Josef cannot be blamed for the insolence which was wreaked on the coffins on their arrival in Vienna. A man of eighty-seven whose wife had been assassinated, whose son was either murdered or was a murderer and suicide, cannot be imagined to be other than shattered when he hears of the assassination of his heir and nephew, who was also his enemy, and his wife, who was a shame to his family. The occasion drew from Franz Josef a superb blasphemy: when he heard the news the thought of the morganatic marriage came first to his mind, and he said that God had corrected a wrong which he had been powerless to alter. But the guilt of the funeral arrangements at Vienna must rest on Prince Montenuovo, the Emperor's Chamberlain, who had tormented Franz Ferdinand and Sophie Chotek during their lives by the use of etiquette, and found that by the same weapon he could pursue them after their death.

Nothing but actual insanity can explain Prince Montenuovo's perversion of the funeral arrangements. He was not only a cultured man, he had shown himself at times humane and courageous. In March 1913 he had acted for Franz Josef in his resistance to Conrad's attempt to drag Austria into an unprovoked war with Serbia and Montenegro, and he had performed his duties with great tact and sense and principle. It would have been supposed that such a man, on finding himself charged with the duty of consigning to the grave the bodies of a husband and wife with whom he had been on contentious terms for many years, would feel compelled to a special decorum. Instead he could find no impropriety too wild for any part of the ceremony.

He arranged that the train which brought the bodies home should be delayed so that it arrived at night. It came in horribly spattered by the blood of a railwayman who had been killed at a level crossing. Montenuovo had two initial reverses. He prescribed that the new heir, the Archduke Charles, should not meet the train, but the young man insisted on doing so. He tried also to prevent Sophie Chotek's coffin from lying beside her husband's in the Royal Chapel during the funeral mass, but to that Franz Josef would not consent. But he had several successes. Sophie's coffin was placed on a lower level to signify her lower rank. The full insignia of the Archduke lay on his coffin, on hers were placed the white gloves and black fan of the former lady-in-waiting. No wreath was sent by any member of the imperial family except Stephanie, the widow of the Crown Prince Rudolf, who had long been on atrocious terms with her relatives. The only flowers were a cross of white roses sent by the dead couple's two children, and some wreaths sent by foreign sovereigns. The Emperor Franz Josef attended the service, but immediately afterwards the chapel was closed, in order that the public should have no opportunity to pay their respects to the dead.

Montenuovo attempted to separate the two in their graves. He proposed that Franz Ferdinand should be laid in the Habsburg tomb in the Capucine church, while his wife's body was sent to the chapel in their castle at Arstetten on the Danube. But to guard against this Franz Ferdinand had left directions that he too was to be buried at Arstetten. Montenuovo bowed to this decision, but announced that his responsibility would end when he had left the coffins at the West Terminus station. The municipal undertaker had to make all arrangements for putting them on the train for Pochlau, which was the station for Arstetten, and getting them across the Danube to the castle. But Montenuovo provided that their task was made difficult by holding back the procession from the chapel till late at night. As a protest a hundred members of the highest Hungarian and Austrian nobility appeared in the costumes that would have been the proper wear at an imperial funeral, thrust themselves into the procession, and walked on foot to the station.

The coffins and the mourners travelled on a train that delivered them at Pochlau at one o'clock in the morning. They found that the station had not been prepared for the occasion, there were no crape hangings or red carpets. This was extremely shocking to a people obsessed with etiquette and pomp. But they soon had more solid reasons for resentment. The moment when the coffins were laid on the platform was the signal for a blinding and deafening and drenching thunderstorm. The disadvantages of a nocturnal funeral became apparent. Nobody in charge of the proceedings knew the village, so the mourners could not find their way to shelter and had to pack into the little station, impeding the actual business of the funeral. It had been proposed to take the coffins to a neighbouring church for a further part of the religious services, but the hearses could not be loaded in the heavy rain, and indeed the mourners would not have known where to follow them in the darkness. So the bewildered priests consecrated the coffins in the crowded little waiting-room among the time-tables and advertisements of seaside resorts. At last the rain stopped, and a start was made for the castle. But there was still much thunder and lightning, and the sixteen horses that drew the hearses were constantly getting out of control. It was dawn when the cavalcade was brought safely to a quay on the Danube, and in the quietness the horses were coaxed on to the ferry-boat by attendants who had water running down round their feet in streams from their sodden clothing. The mourners, left on the bank to wait their turn, watched the boat with thankfulness. But when it was in the middle of the stream there was a last flash of lightning, a last drum-roll of thunder. The left pole-horse in front of the Archduke's hearse reared, and the back wheels slipped over the edge of the ferry-boat. Till it reached the other side it was a shambles of terrified horses, of men who could hardly muster the strength to cling to the harness, and cried out in fatigue and horror as they struggled, of coffins slipping to the water's edge.

It is strange that it was this scene which made it quite certain that the Sarajevo *attentat* should be followed by a European war. The funeral was witnessed by a great many soldiers and officials and men of influence, and their reaction was excited and not logical. If Franz Ferdinand had been quietly laid to rest according to the custom of his people, many Austrians would have felt sober pity for him for a day, and then remembered his many faults. They would surely have reflected that he had brought his doom on himself by the tactlessness and aggressiveness of his visit to the Serbian frontier at the time of a Serbian festival; and they might also have reflected that those qualities were characteristic not only of him but of his family. The proper sequel to the *Walpurgisnacht* obsequies of Franz Ferdinand would have been the dismissal of Prince Montenuovo, the drastic revision of the Austrian constitution and reduction of the influence wielded by the Habsburgs and their court, and an attempt at the moral rehabilitation of Vienna. But to take any of these steps Austria would have had to look in the mirror. She preferred instead to whip herself into a fury of loyalty to Franz Ferdinand's memory. It was only remembered that he was the enemy of Franz Josef, who had now shown himself sacrilegious to a corpse who, being a Habsburg, must have been as sacred as an emperor who was sacred because he was a Habsburg. It was felt that if Franz Ferdinand had been at odds with this old man and his court he had probably been right. Enthusiasm flamed up for the men who had been chosen by Franz Ferdinand, for Conrad von Hötzendorf and Berchtold, and for the policy of imperialist aggression that they had jointly engendered. Again the corpse was outraged; he could not speak from the grave to say that he had cancelled those preferences, to protest when these men he had repudiated put forward the policy he had abandoned and pressed it on the plea of avenging his death. The whole of Vienna demanded that the pacifism of Franz Josef should be flouted as an old man's folly and that Austria should declare war upon Serbia.

The excuse for this declaration of war was the allegation that the conspirators had been suborned to kill Franz Ferdinand by the Serbian Government. During the last twenty years, in the mood of lazy and cynical self-criticism which has afflicted the powers that were apparently victorious in 1918, it has been often pretended that there were grounds for that allegation. It has been definitely stated in many articles and books that the Serbian Government was aware of the murderous intentions of Princip, Chabrinovitch, and Grabezh, and itself supplied them with bombs and revolvers and sent them back to Bosnia. Sometimes it is suggested that the Russian Government joined with the Serbian Government to commit this crime.

Not one scrap of evidence exists in support of these allegations.

One of the most celebrated contemporary writers on European affairs sets down in black and white the complicity of the Serbian and Russian Governments. I have asked him for his authority. He has none. A famous modern English historian, not pro-Serb, tells me that ever since the war he has been looking for some proof of the guilt of Serbia, and has never found it, or any indication that it is to be found.

It is clear, and nothing could be clearer, that certain Serbian individuals supplied the conspirators with encouragement and arms. But this does not mean that the Serbian Government was responsible. If certain Irishmen, quite unconnected with Mr. De Valera, should supply Irish-Americans with bombs for the purpose of killing President Roosevelt, and he died, the United States would not therefore declare war on Eire. A connexion between the Irishmen and their Government would have to be established before a *casus belli* would be recognized. But no link whatsoever has been discovered between the Serbian Government and Tsiganovitch and Tankositch, the obscure individuals who had given Princip and Chabrinovitch and Grabezh their bombs. They were, indeed, members of the "Black Hand," the secret society which was savagely hostile both to the Karageorge dynasty and the political party then in power. That this hostility was not a fiction is shown by the precautions taken against discovery by the Serbian sentries who helped the conspirators over the frontier.

There are only two reasons which would give ground for suspicion of the Serbian Government. The first is the marks on the bombs, which showed definitely that they had been issued by the Serbian State Arsenal at Kraguyevatch. That looks damning, but means nothing. Bombs were distributed in large numbers both to the comitadji and regular troops during the Balkan War, and many soldiers put them by as likely to come in handy in the rough-and-tumble of civil life. A search through the outhouses of many a Serbian farm would disclose a store of them. Tankositch would have had no difficulty in acquiring as many as he liked, without any need for application to the authorities. The other suspicious circumstance is the refusal of several Serbian officials to disclaim responsibility for the crime, and the assumption by others of a certain fore-knowledge of the crime which was first cousin to actual responsibility for it. This can be discounted in view of the peculiar atmosphere of Balkan politics. A century ago no political leader could come forward among the Slavs unless he had distinguished himself in guerrilla warfare against the Turks, warfare which often involved what would be hard to tell from assassination. For this reason politicians of peasant origin, bred in the full Balkan tradition, such as the Serbian Prime Minister, Mr. Pashitch, could not feel the same embarrassment at being suspected of complicity in the murder of a national enemy that would have been felt by his English contemporaries, say Mr. Balfour or Mr. Asquith. After all, an Irish politician would not find a very pressing need to exculpate himself from a charge of having been concerned in the murder of Sir Henry Wilson, so far as the good-will of his constituents was concerned. But no hint of any actual meeting or correspondence by which Mr. Pashitch established any contact, however remote, with the conspirators has ever been given; and as any such contact would have involved a reconciliation with those who before and after were his enemies, there must have been go-betweens, but these, in spite of the loquacity of the race, have never declared themselves. There was a Mr. Liuba Yovano-vitch, Minister of Education under Mr. Pashitch, who could not stop writing articles in which he boasted that he and his friends in Belgrade had known for weeks ahead that the conspiracy was hatching in Sara-jevo. But unkind researchers have discovered that seven years before he put in exactly the same claim concerning the murder of King Alexander and Queen Draga, and that members of that conspiracy had indignantly brought forward proof that they had nothing to do with him. Mr. Yovanovitch, in fact, was the Balkan equivalent of the sort of English-man who wears an Old Etonian tie without cause.

On the other hand there were overwhelming reasons why the Serbian Government should not have supported this or any other conspiracy. It cannot have wanted war at that particular moment. The Karageorges must have been especially anxious to avoid it. King Peter had just been obliged by chronic ill-health to appoint his son Alexander as his regent and it had not escaped the attention of the Republican Party that the King had had to pass over his eldest son, George, because he was hope-lessly insane. Mr. Pashitch and his Government can hardly have been more anxious for a war, as their machine was temporarily disorganized by preparations for a general election. Both alike, the royal family and the Ministers, held disquieting knowledge about the Serbian military situation. Their country had emerged from the two Balkan wars vic-torious but exhausted, without money, transport, or munitions, and with a peasant army that was thoroughly sick of fighting. They can have known no facts to offset those, for none existed. Theoretically they could only rely on the support of France and Russia, and possibly Great Brit-ain, but obviously geography would forbid any of these powers giving her practical aid in the case of an Austrian invasion.

In fact, the Karageorges and the Government knew perfectly well that, if there should be war, they must look forward to an immediate defeat of the most painful sort, for which they could receive compen-sation only should their allies, whoever they might be, at some uncertain time win a definite victory. But if there should be peace, then the Karageorges and the Government could consolidate the victories they had won in the Balkan wars, develop their conquered territory, and organize their neglected resources. Admittedly Serbia aimed at the ultimate absorption of Bosnia and Herzegovina, Montenegro and the South Slav provinces of the Austro-Hungarian Empire. But this was not the suitable moment. If she attained her aims by this method she would have to pay too heavy a price, as, in fact, she did. No country would choose to realize any ideal at the cost of the destruction of one-third of her population. That she did not so choose is shown by much negative evidence. At the time the murder was committed she had just let her reservists return home after their annual training, her Commander-in-chief was taking a cure at an Austrian spa, and none of the Austrian Slavs who had fought in the Balkan War and returned home were warned to come across the frontier. But the positive evidence is even stronger. When Austria sent her ultimatum to Serbia, which curtly demanded not only the punishment of the Serbians who were connected with the Sarajevo *attentat*, but the installation of Austrian and Hungarian officers in Serbia for the purpose of suppressing Pan-Slavism, Mr. Pashitch bowed to all the demands save for a few gross details, and begged that the exceptions he had made should not be treated as refusals but should be referred for arbitration to The Hague Tribunal. There was not one trace of bellicosity in the attitude of Serbia at this point. If she had promoted the Sarajevo *attentat* in order to make war possible, she was very near to throwing her advantage away.

The innocence of the Serbian Government must be admitted by all but the most prejudiced. But guilt lies very heavy on the "Black Hand." There is, however, yet another twist in the story here. It seems fairly certain that that guilt was not sustained of full intent. We may doubt that when "Apis" sent these young men to Bosnia he believed for one moment that they would succeed in their plan of killing Franz Ferdinand. He was just as well aware as the authorities of the military and economic difficulties of his country, and probably wanted war as little as they did. But even if he had been of another mind he would hardly have chosen such agents. The conspirators, when they first attracted his attention, numbered only two weakly boys of nineteen, Princip and Chabrinovitch. He had learned that their only revolutionary connexions in Sarajevo were through Ilitch; and as this information came from Gachinovitch, the exile who knew everything about the unrest in Bosnia, he must have learned at the same time how inexperienced in terrorism Ilitch was. "Apis" must also have known from his officers that Princip was only a fair shot, and that Chabrinovitch and the third boy who joined them later, Grabezh, could not hit a wall. He must have realized that in such inexpert hands the revolvers would be nearly useless, and the bombs would be no better, for they were not the sort used by the Russian terrorists, which exploded at contact, but the kind used in trench warfare, which had to be hit against a hard object before they were thrown, and then took some seconds to go off. They were extremely difficult to throw in a crowd; any soldier could have guessed that Chabrinovitch would never be able to aim one straight.

Yet "Apis" could have got any munitions that he wanted by taking a little trouble, and, what is more, he could have got any number of patriotic Bosnians who had been through the Balkan wars and could shoot and throw bombs with professional skill. I myself know a Herzegovinian, a remarkable shot and a seasoned soldier, who placed himself at the disposition of the "Black Hand" to assassinate any oppressor of the Slav people. "*Dans ces jours-là*," he says, "*nous étions tous fous.*" His offer was never accepted. It is to be wondered whether "Apis" was quite the character his contemporaries believed. Much is made of his thirst for blood, and he was certainly involved, though not in any major capacity, in the murder of King Alexander and Queen Draga. But the rest of his reputation is based on his self-confessed participation in plots to murder King Nicholas of Montenegro, King Constantine of Greece, the last German Kaiser, and King Ferdinand of Bulgaria. The first three of these monarchs, however, died in their beds, and the last one is still with us. It is possible that "Apis" was obsessed by a fantasy of bloodshed and treachery, which he shrunk from translating into fact, partly out of a poetic preference for fantasy over fact, partly out of a very sensible regard for his own skin.

There is, indeed, one circumstance which tells us that the "Black Hand" took Princip and his friends very lightly indeed. Over and over again we read in the records of these times about boys who took out revolvers or bombs with the intention of killing this or that instrument of Austrian tyranny, but lost heart and returned home without incident. There must have been many more such abortive attempts than are recorded. The "Black Hand" was the natural body to which such boys would turn with a request for arms; it would be interesting to know how often they had handed out munitions which had never been used. Repetition had, it seems, bred carelessness in classification. For when Princip and Chabrinovitch took the prussic acid which Tsiganovitch and Tankositch had given them, it had no effect on either. It is said vaguely that it had "gone bad," but prussic acid is not subject to any such misfortune. In the only form which is easy to obtain, it does not even evaporate quickly. What Tsiganovitch and Tankositch had given the boys was plain water, or something equally innocuous. They would not have made this substitution if they had believed in the effectiveness of the conspiracy. They must have known that if the boys succeeded and were tortured and talked they would have reason for the gravest fears: which, indeed, were realized. "Apis" was executed by the Serbian Government three years later, after a mysterious trial which is one of the most baffling incidents in Balkan history; nothing is clear about it save that the real offence for which he was punished was his connexion with the Sarajevo *attentat*. Tankositch and Tsiganovitch also paid a heavy price in their obscurer way.

Only one person involved in this business did what he meant to do: Princip believed he ought to kill Franz Ferdinand, and he shot him dead. But everybody else acted contrary to his own will. The dead pair, who had dreamed of empire stretching from the Baltic to the Black Sea, surrendered the small primary power to breathe. If the generals about them had had any hope of procuring victory and the rule of the sword they were to fail to the extraordinary degree of annihilating not only their own army but their own nation. The conspirators wanted to throw their bombs, and could not. Ilitch, whose flesh quailed at the conspirator's lot, was compelled to it by the values of his society, distracted as it was by oppression. In Vienna Montenuovo raised a defence of criminal insolence round the sacred Habsburg stock, and uprooted it from Austrian soil, to lie on the rubbish-heap of exile. There was an exquisite appropriateness in this common fate which fell on all those connected with the events of that St. Vitus's Day; for those who are victims of what is known as St. Vitus's disease suffer an uncontrollable disposition to involuntary motions.

Sarajevo VII

"YOU must come up to the Orthodox cemetery and see the graves of these poor boys," said Constantine. "It is very touching, for a reason that will appear when you see it." Two days later we made this expedition, with the judge and the banker to guide us. But Constantine could not keep back his dramatic climax until we got there. He felt he had to tell us when we had driven only half-way up the hillside. "What is so terrible," he said, "is that they are there in that grave, the poor little ones, Princip, Chabrinovitch, Grabezh, and three other little ones who were taken with them. They could not be hanged, the law forbade it. Nobody could be hanged in the Austrian Empire under twenty-one. Yet I tell you they are all there, and they certainly did not have time to die of old age, for they were all dead before the end of the war."

This, indeed, is the worst part of the story. It explains why it has been difficult to establish humane penal methods in countries which formed part of the Austrian Empire, and why minor officials in those succession states often take it for granted that violence is a part of the technique of administration. The sequel to the *attentat* shows how little Bosnians had to congratulate themselves for exchanging Austrian domination for Turkish.

When the Serbian prussic acid failed, both Princip and Chabrinovitch made other attempts at suicide which were frustrated. Princip put his revolver to his temple, and had it snatched away by a busybody. Chabrinovitch jumped into the river and was fished out by the police. He made at that point a remark which has drawn on him much heavy-footed derision from German writers owing to a misunderstanding over a Serb word. A policeman who arrested him said in his evidence at the trial, "I hit him with my fist, and I said, 'Why don't you come on? You are a Serb, aren't you?'" He said that Chabrinovitch answered him in a phrase that has been too literally translated, "Yes, I am a Serbian hero." This has been taken by foreign commentators as proof of Chabrinovitch's exalted folly and the inflamed character of Serbian nationalism. But the word "*Yunak*" has a primary meaning of hero and a secondary meaning of militant nationalist. The words the policeman intended to put into Chabrinovitch's mouth were simply "Yes, I am a Serbian nationalist," so that he could say that he had then asked, "Where did you get your gun?" and that he had been answered, "From our society." Cha-brinovitch gave a convincing denial that the conversation, even in this form, ever took place. Thus is the face of history thickly veiled.

The two youths, beaten to unconsciousness, were taken to prison; which on the morrow of St. Vitus's Day was as good a place to be as any in Sarajevo. For there broke out an anti-Slav riot which in its first impulse destroyed the best hotel in Sarajevo and the office of a Serb newspaper, and the next day merged into an organized pogrom of the Serb inhabitants of Sarajevo. There was, of course, some spontaneous feeling against them. Many Moslems grieved over the loss of their pro-tector, and a number of devoutly Catholic Croats regretted their co-religionist for his piety; it is known that some of these, notably a few Croat clerical students, joined in the rioting. But General Potiorek had had to contrive the rest. The bulk of the demonstrators consisted of very poor Catholics, Jews, and Moslems, many of whom had come to town to work in the new factories and had fallen into a pitiful slough of misery. Those unhappy wretches were told by police agents that if they wanted to burn and loot authority would hold its hand, and, more than that, that they had better burn and loot good and hard, lest a misfortune should fall on the town.

This warning was more heavily impressed on the people by the thousands of troops that had been brought into the town now that Franz Ferdinand and Sophie Chotek were dead and beyond need of protection. There were enough of them to line three-deep the long route by which the coffins passed from the Cathedral to the railway station. Many of them were Croat and Austrian, and afterwards they walked about with fixed bayonets, singing anti-Serb songs. They did not interfere with the rioters. Rather were they apt to deal harshly with those who were not taking a sufficiently active part in the riot. It was doubtless easy to take the hint and enjoy the licence. Human nature is not very nice.

But the full blame for the riot cannot be laid on these helpless victims of coercion. The leading Serb in Sarajevo owned a house, a hotel, a café, warehouses, and stables, in different parts of the town. All were visited, and all were methodically sacked from cellar to roof. Street fighters do not work with such system. Then those who appeared with pickaxes and slowly and conscientiously razed to the foundations houses belong-ing to the Serbs were not stopped by the authorities. In this way material damage was inflicted on the town to the amount of two hundred thousand pounds. So little was the rioting spontaneous that many Croats and Jews and Moslems risked their lives by giving shelter to Serbs; but so many lives were lost that the figures were suppressed.

Not a single rioter was jailed nor a single official, military or civil, degraded for failure to keep order. It is not surprising that like riots broke out during the next few days in every provincial town and sizable village where the Croats and Moslems outnumbered the Serbs. This is said to have been a device of General Potiorek to placate the authorities and dissuade them from punishing him for his failure to protect Franz Ferdinand. But it is doubtful if he had any reason to fear punishment, for he was promoted immediately afterwards. Meantime hundreds of schoolboys and students were thrown into prison, and were joined by all eminent Serbs, whether teachers or priests or members of religious or even temperance societies. As soon as war broke out there were appalling massacres; in such a small place as Pali, the winter sports village above Sarajevo, sixty men and women were killed. Wholesale arrests filled the fortresses of Hungary with prisoners, of whom more than half were to die in their dungeons.

The Austrian excuse for this war was self-defence; but it is hard to extend it to cover the riots at Sarajevo. It is carrying self-defence too far to use a pickaxe and demolish the house of the man whom one regards, surely by that time only in theory, as an aggressor. Moreover, already the arrested youths had been interrogated and it must have been suspected by the authorities that the conspiracy might consist of a few isolated people of no importance. Before the provincial riots that suspicion must have become a certainty. For the prisoners had talked quite a lot. They, and those friends of theirs who had been arrested later, had been put to torture. Princip was tied to an oak beam so that he stood tiptoe on the ground. Grabezh was made to kneel on a rolling barrel, so that he continually fell off in a stifling cloud of dust, and was put in a strait-jacket that was pulled in again and again; and shepherd dogs, of the sort that are often terribly strong and savage in Bosnia and Serbia, were let loose in his cell when he was faint with pain and lack of sleep. Chabrinovitch apparently escaped such tortures, because the garrulity of which his friends complained came in useful; from the very beginning he told the police a great deal, and they did not find out till the end of the trial that it was not true. He concocted a very clever story that the Freemasons had ordered the murder of Franz Ferdinand because he was so militant a Catholic, which diverted suspicion from Belgrade. But Ilitch was also arrested, and the threat of torture was enough to make him tell everything. Let him who is without fear cast the first stone; but it meant that all the peasants and tradesmen who had reluctantly helped in the journey from the frontier, all the schoolboys who had chattered with him about revolt at the pastrycook's, joined the conspirators in jail. Some of them, however, would have been arrested in any case, for the Austrian Army had by now crossed the Serbian frontier and seized the customs records, which made them able to trace the route. The conspirators passed a time of waiting before the trial which would have been unutterably terrible to Western prisoners, but which these strange, passionate, yet philosophical children seem to have in a fashion enjoyed, though at one time hope deferred must have made their hearts sicken. In their cells they heard the guns of the Serbian Army as it crossed the Drina, and they expected to be rescued. But the sound of the firing guns grew fainter and died away, and later Serbian prisoners of war were brought into the prison.

On the twelfth of October the trial began. It is typical of the insanity of our world that, ten weeks before this, Austria had declared war on Serbia because of her responsibility for the *attentat*, although these were the first proceedings which made it possible to judge whether that responsibility existed. The trial was for long veiled from common knowledge. Only certain highly official German and Austrian newspapers were allowed to send correspondents. Chabrinovitch, in the course of one of his very intelligent interventions in the trial, talked of the secret sittings of the court, and when the president asked him what he meant, he pointed out that no representatives of the opposition press were present. To this the president made the reply, which is curiously like what we have heard from the Nazis very often since, "What, according to your ideas, is a court open only when the representatives of the opposition are allowed to come in?" There were naturally no English or French correspondents at that time; and there were apparently no American journalists. None could follow Serbo-Croat, so they took their material from their German colleagues. The most dramatic event of our time was thus completely hidden from us at the time when it most affected us; and it has only been gradually and partially revealed. The official reports were sent to Vienna and there they disappeared. Not till the early twenties was a carbon copy found in Sarajevo. This can be read in a French translation; care should be taken in consulting a German version, for one at least abounds in interpolations and perversions devised in the interest of upholding Chabrinovitch's fabrications about Freemasonry.

The only account of it in English is contained in Mr. Stephen Graham's admirable novel *St. Vitus' Day*.

It is perhaps for this reason that there are many false ideas abroad to-day concerning the conspiracy. It is imagined to have been far more formidable than it was. People say, "You know Franz Ferdinand had no chance, there were seven men in the street to shoot him if Princip failed." This is what the Moslems in the Town Hall thought, but it is not true. Princip was not the first but the last in the line of assassins, and all the rest had proved themselves unfitted for their job. It is also held that the conspirators were dangerous fanatics of maniacal or at least degenerate type. But actually their behaviour in court was not only completely sane but cheerful and dignified, and their evidence and speeches showed both individual ability and a very high level of culture. Even those who hate violence and narrow passions must admit that the records of the trial open a world which is not displeasing.

It is, of course, disordered. As a schoolboy goes into the dock he is asked according to form whether he has any previous convictions. Yes, he has served a fortnight in prison for having struck a teacher in a political disturbance in a class-room. One peasant, charged with helping the conspirators to dispose of the bombs, wept perpetually. It was the fate of his simple law-abiding sort to be ground between the upper and the nether millstones of an oppressive government and revolutionary societies so desperate that they dared to be almost as oppressive. When they asked him why he had not denounced the party to the police when he saw the bombs, he said, "But with us one cannot do a thing like that without the permission of the head of the family." He was sentenced to be hanged, and though his sentence was reduced to twenty years' imprisonment, he died in prison. Other prisoners showed the essential unity of the Slav race by talking like Dostoevsky characters, by falling out of a procession that marched briskly to a temporal measure and settling down to discuss spiritual matters, no more quickly than the slow pulse of eternity. When the president of the court said to one of the schoolboys, "But you say you're religious . . . that you're a member of the Orthodox Church. Don't you realize that your religion forbids the killing of a man? Is your faith serious or is it on the surface?" the boy thoughtfully answered, "Yes, it is on the surface." Another expounded the mysticism of Pan-Slavism, claiming that his nationalism was part of his religion, and his religion was part of his nationalism. How poorly Austria was qualified to bring order into these gifted people's lives—and there was no reason for her presence if she could not—is shown by the shocking muddle of the court procedure. Dates were hardly ever mentioned and topics were brought up as they came into the heads of the lawyers rather than according to any logical programme.

Nobody made any recriminations against Ilitch, though it was apparent he had behaved far from well. Some of the prisoners fought for their lives, but with a certain dignity, and on the whole without sacrifice of their convictions. It is very clear, however, that Princip was in a class apart. Throughout the trial he was always selfless and tranquil, alert to defend and define his ideas but indifferent to personal attacks. He never made a remark throughout the trial that was not sensible and broad-minded. It is interesting to note that he declared he had committed his crime as a peasant who resented the poverty the Austrians had brought on his kind.

Chabrinovitch, however, was a very good second, in spite of the unfavourable impression he often made. That impression one can quite understand after one has read the records. At one point he held up the proceedings to make a clever and obscure joke that did not quite come off, of the sort that infuriates stupid people; but it is also clear that he was extremely able. He kept his Freemasonry myth going with remarkable skill; and Princip carried on a debate which the left-wing youth of England and France came to only much later. Chabrinovitch had in the past been a pacifist. Indeed, though a passionate Pan-Serb, he had dissuaded many of his fellow-students from enlisting in Serbia's ranks during the Balkan wars. He was still so much of a pacifist that he was not sure whether his act in attempting the life of Franz Ferdinand had been morally defensible. It was, if it were ever right to use force; but of that he was never fully persuaded. In his speech to the court before it pronounced judgment this point of view was very apparent. He did not ask for mercy, and he quite rightly laid the blame for his crime on the poisoned atmosphere of the oppressed provinces, where every honest man was turned into a rebel, and assassination became a display of virtue. But Princip had always been of the opinion that this was not the time for Bosnians to delve into first principles. He had never been a pacifist, and as a boy had argued coldly and destructively with the Tolstoyan group in Sarajevo. He simply said: "Anyone who says that the inspiration for this *attentat* came from outside our group is playing with the truth. We originated the idea, and we carried it out. We loved the people. I have nothing to say in my defence."

The trial went as might have been expected. Consideration of the speeches of the counsel for the defence show that it was very nearly as difficult in Austria for a prisoner charged by the Government to find a lawyer to put his case as it is in Nazi Germany. The Croat lawyer who was defending one prisoner showed the utmost reluctance to plead his cause at all. He began his speech by saying, "Illustrious tribunal, after all we have heard, it is peculiarly painful for me, as a Croat, to conduct the defence of a Serb." But there was one counsel, Dr. Rudolf Zistler, who bore himself as a hero. With an intrepidity that was doubly admirable considering it was war-time, he pointed out that the continual succession of trials for high treason in the Slav provinces could only be explained by misgovernment; and he raised a vital point, so vital that it is curious he was allowed to finish his speech, by claiming that it was absurd to charge the prisoners with conspiracy to detach Bosnia and Herzegovina from the Austrian Empire, because the legal basis of the annexation of these provinces was unsatisfactory, and in any case the annexation had never been properly ratified. Apparently the first proposition can be disputed, but the second is sound enough. Neither the Austrian nor the Hungarian Parliament ever voted on the necessary Act of Annexation. It was only a technicality, just another piece of *Schlamperei;* but it adds yet one more fantastic touch to the event that Princip had had a legal right to be where he was in Sarajevo, and that Franz Ferdinand had had none.

Nothing, of course, was of any avail. Ilitch, together with a schoolmaster, a retired bioscope exhibitor, the peasant who wept, and one more stoical, who had all played a part in harbouring and transporting the munitions, was sentenced to the gallows, and the first three of them were hanged in Sarajevo four months later. The last two were reprieved and sentenced to imprisonment for twenty years and for life, respectively. Princip, Chabrinovitch, and Grabezh would have been hanged had they not been under twenty-one. As it was they received sentences of twenty years' imprisonment, one day of fast each month, and twenty-four hours in a dungeon on every anniversary of the twenty-eighth of June. The rest of the conspirators were sentenced to terms of imprisonment ranging from life down to three years. These were not excessive sentences. In England Princip would have very rightly been sent to the gallows. Nevertheless, the sequel is not such as can be contemplated without horror and pity. Thirteen conspirators were sent to Austrian prisons. Before the end of the war, which came three and a half years later, nine of them had died in their cells.

How this slow murder was contrived in the case of Princip is known to us, through Slav guards and doctors. He was taken to an eighteenth-century fortress at Theresienstadt between Prague and Dresden. The Austrians would not leave him in Sarajevo because they already saw that the war was not going as they had hoped, and they feared that Bosnia might fall into Serbian hands. He was put in an underground cell filled with the stench of the surrounding marshes, which received the fortress sewage. He was in irons. There was no heating. He had nothing to read. On St. Vitus's Day he had sustained a broken rib and a crushed arm which were never given proper medical attention. At Theresienstadt the arm became tuberculous and suppurated, and he contracted a fungoid infection on the body. Three times he tried to commit suicide, but in his cell there lacked the means either of life or of death. In 1917 his forearm became so septic that it had to be amputated. By this time Chabrinovitch and Grabezh were both dead, it is said of tuberculosis. Grabezh at any rate had been a perfectly healthy boy till his arrest. Princip never rallied after his operation. He had been put in a window-less cell, and though he could no longer be handcuffed, since the removal of his arm, his legs were hobbled with heavy chains. In the spring of 1918 he died. He was buried at night, and immense precautions were taken to conceal the spot. But the Austrian Empire had yet to make the last demonstration of *Schlamperei* in connexion with the Sarajevo *attentat*. One of the soldiers who dug the grave was a Slav, and he took careful note of its position; he came forward after the peace and gave his information to the Serbs. They were able to identify the body by its mutilations.

Princip appears to have suffered greatly under his imprisonment, though with courage. In his death, as in everything we hear reported of his life, there was a certain noble integrity of experience. He offered himself wholly to each event in order that he might learn in full what revelation it had to make about the nature of the universe. How little of a demented fanatic he was, what qualities of restraint and delibera-tion he brought to his part in the *attentat*, is revealed by the testimony of the Czech doctor who befriended him in prison. From the court records one would suppose him to be without personal ties, to be per-haps an orphan, at any rate to be wholly absorbed in politics. Yet to the Czech doctor he spoke perpetually of his dear mother, of his broth-ers and their children, and of a girl whom he had loved and whom he had hoped to marry, though he had never kissed her.

Chabrinovitch took his punishment differently, and almost certainly a little more happily. It chanced that in prison he had momentary contact with Franz Werfel, the greatest of post-war Austrian writers, who was working there as hospital orderly. In an essay Werfel has recorded his surprise at finding that the Slav assassin, whom he had imagined as wolfish and demented, should turn out to be this delicate and gentle boy, smiling faintly in his distress. It can be recognized from his account that Chabrinovitch used in prison that quality which annoyed his less-gifted friends, which was the antithesis, or perhaps the supplement, of Princip's single-mindedness. He took all experience that came his way and played with it, discussed it, overstated it, understated it, moaned over it, joked about it, tried out all its intellectual and emotional potentialities. What these youths did was abominable, precisely as abominable as the tyranny they destroyed. Yet it need not be denied that they might have grown to be good men, and perhaps great men, if the Austrian Empire had not crashed down on them in its collapse. But the monstrous frailty of empire involves such losses.

At the cemetery we forgot for a moment why we were there, so beautifully does it lie in the tilted bowl of the town. It is always so in Sarajevo. Because of the intricate contours of its hills it is for ever presenting a new picture, and the mind runs away from life to its setting. And when we had passed the cemetery gates, we forgot again for another reason. Not far away among the tombs there was a new grave, a raw wound in the grass. A wooden cross was at its head, and burning candles were stuck in the broken clay. At the foot of it stood a young officer, his face the colour of tallow. He rocked backwards in his grief, though very slightly, and his mouth worked with prayer. His uniform was extremely neat. Yet once, while we stared at him in shocked distress, he tore open his skirted coat as if he were about to strip; but instantly his hand did up the buttons as if he were a nurse coolly tending his own delirium.

This was a Slav, this is what it is to be a Slav. He was offering himself wholly to his sorrow, he was learning the meaning of death and was not refusing any part of the knowledge; for he knew that experience is the cross man must take up and carry. Not for anything would he have chosen to feel one shade less pain; and if it had been joy he was feeling, he would have permitted himself to feel all possible delight. He knew only that in suffering or rejoicing he must not lose that control of the body which enabled him to be a good soldier and to defend himself and his people, so that they would endure experience along their own path and acquire their own revelation of the universe.

There is no other way of living which promises that man shall ever understand his destiny better than he does, and live less familiarly with evil. Yet to numberless people all over Europe, to numberless people in Great Britain, this man would be loathsome as a leper. It is not pleasant to feel pain, it is the act of a madman to bare the breast to agony. It is not pleasant to admit that we know almost nothing, so little that, for lack of knowledge, our actions are wild and foolish. It is not pleasant to be bound to the task of learning all our days, to be under the obligation to go on learning even though it involves making acquaintance with pain, although we know that we must die still in ignorance. To do these things it is necessary to have faith in what is entirely hidden and unknown, to cast away all the acquisitions and certainties which would ensure a comfortable existence lest they should impede us on a journey which may never be accomplished, which never even offers comfort. Therefore the multitudes in Europe who are not hungry for truth would say: "Let us kill these Slavs with their dedication to insanity, let us enslave them lest they make all wealth worthless and introduce us at the end to God, who may not be pleasant to meet."

The judge and the banker said, "Look, they are here." Close to the palings of the cemetery, under three stone slabs, lie the conspirators of Sarajevo, those who were hanged and five of those who died in prison; and to them has been joined Zheraitch, the boy who tried to kill the Bosnian Governor General Vareshanin and was kicked as he lay on the ground. The slab in the middle is raised. Underneath it lies the body of Princip. To the left and the right lie the others, the boys on one side and the men on the other, for in this country it is recognized that the difference between old and young is almost as great as that between men and women. The grave is not impressive. It is as if a casual hand had swept them into a stone drawer. There was a battered wreath laid askew on the slabs, and candles flickered in rusty lanterns. This untidiness means nothing. It is the Moslem habit to be truthful about death, to admit that what it leaves of our kind might just as well be abandoned to the process of the earth. Only to those associated with a permanent system, who were holy men or governors or great soldiers, do Moslems raise tombs that are in any sense monuments, and they are more careful to revere these than to keep them in order. After all, a stone with a green stain of weed on it commemorates death more appropriately than polished marble. This attitude is so reasonable that it has spread from the Moslems to the Christians in all territories where they are found side by side. It does not imply insensibility. The officer swaying in

front of the cross on the new grave might never be wholly free of his
grief till he died, but this did not mean that he would derive any satisfaction at all in making the grave look like part of a garden. And as we
stood by the shabby monument an old woman passing along the road
outside the cemetery paused, pressed her face against the railings, looked
down on the stone slab, and retreated into prayer. Later a young man
who was passing by with a cart loaded with vegetables stopped and
joined her, his eyes also set in wonder on the grave, his hand also making
the sign of the cross on brow and breast, his lips also moving.

On their faces there was none of the bright acclaiming look which
shines in the eyes of those who talk of, say, Andreas Hofer. They
seemed to be contemplating a mystery, and so they were; for the Sarajevo *attentat* is mysterious as history is mysterious, as life is mysterious.
Of all the men swept into this great drawer only one, Princip, had
conceived what they were doing as a complete deed. To Chabrinovitch
it had been a hypothesis to be used as a basis for experiment; his vision
of it came from the brain only, and not from the blood. To some of the
others it had been an event interesting to imagine, which would certainly not be allowed to happen by the inertia we all feel in the universe,
the resistance life puts up against the human will, particularly if that
is making any special effort. To the rest, to the unhappy peasants and
tradesmen who found themselves quite involuntarily helping the boys
in their journey from the Serbian frontier, it must have seemed as if
the troubles of their land had fused into a mindless catastrophe, like
plague or famine. But the deed as Princip conceived it never took place.
It was entangled from its first minute with another deed, a murder which
seems to have been fully conceived by none at all, but which had a
terrible existence as a fantasy, because it was dreamed of by men whose
whole claim to respect rested on their realistic quality, and who abandoned all restraint when they strayed into the sphere of fantasy. Of
these two deeds there was made one so potent that it killed its millions
and left all living things in our civilization to some degree disabled. I
write of a mystery. For that is the way the deed appears to me, and to
all Westerners. But to those who look at it on the soil where it was
committed, and to the lands east of that, it seems a holy act of liberation;
and among such people are those whom the West would have to admit
are wise and civilized.

This event, this Sarajevo *attentat*, was in these inconsistencies an apt
symbol of life: which is loose and purposeless, which weaves a close
pattern and doggedly pursues its ends, which is unpredictable and il-

logical, which follows a straight line from cause to effect, which is bad, which is good. It shows that human will can do anything, it shows that accident does everything. It shows that man throws away his peace for a vain cause if he insists on acquiring knowledge, for the more one knows about the *attentat* the more incomprehensible it becomes. It shows also that moral judgment sets itself an impossible task. The soul should choose life. But when the Bosnians chose life, and murdered Franz Ferdinand, they chose death for the French and Germans and English, and if the French and Germans and English had been able to choose life they would have chosen death for the Bosnians. The sum will not add up. It is madness to rack our brains over this sum. But there is nothing else we can do except try to add up this sum. We are nothing but arithmetical functions which exist for that purpose. . . . We went out by the new grave where the young officer was trying to add up the sum in the Slav way. A sudden burst of sunshine made the candle-flames sadder than darkness. He swayed so far forward that he had to stay himself by clutching at the cross. His discipline raised him and set him swinging back to his heels again.

Ilidzhe

WE were going to see the village outside Sarajevo where the Austrians built a racecourse and where Franz Ferdinand stayed the night before he died. The road was so extravagantly bad that we bounced like balls, and Constantine had a star of mud on his forehead as he told us, "Sarajevo has a soul like a village, though it is a town. Now, why has a village the sort of soul that it has? Because it is irrigated, because there flow through it rivers of water and rivers of air. If there is water running through a city it is no longer water, it is not clear, it might evoke demonstrations of fastidiousness from a camel; if there is air blowing through the city it cannot be called wind, it loses its force among the houses. So it is with movements in the mind, they become polluted and effete. Religion instead of being an ecstasy and a cosmology becomes ethical, philosophical, penitential. But in Sarajevo," he continued, as the car lifted itself out of a rut with a movement not to be expected from a machine, credible only in a tiger leaping out of a pit, "there is a vivifying conception which irrigates the city and makes it fresh like a village. Here Slavs, and a very fine kind of Slav, endowed with great powers of perception and speculation, were confronted with the Turkish Empire at its most magnificent, which is to say Islam at its most magnificent, which is to say Persia at its most magnificent. Its luxury we took, its militarism and its pride, and above all its conception of love. The luxury has gone. The militarism has gone. You saw at the railway station the other morning what had happened to the pride. But the conception of love is still in the city, and it is a wonderful conception, it refreshes and revivifies, it is clean water and strong wind."

"What is peculiar about this conception of love?" asked my husband, who had just been thrown on his knees to the floor of the car. "It is," said Constantine, failing to remove his stomach from the small of my back, "the conception of love which made us as small boys read the *Arabian Nights* with such attention, so that Grandmamma always said, 'How he reads and reads, we must make a priest of him.' Is it not extraordinary, by the way, that all over Europe, even in the pudic nurseries of your own country, that this should be regarded as a children's book? It is as if our civilization felt fear that it had carried too far its experiment of bringing up children in innocence, but would not admit it, and called in another race to administer all that knowledge which had been suppressed, in an exotic and disguised form, so that it could be passed off as an Eastern talisman engraved with characters which naturally cannot be read, though they are to be admired æsthetically." "About this conception of love," said my husband, struggling up to a seated position and wiping the mud off his glasses, "you mean the old crones arriving with messages and the beautiful women in darkened rooms, and the hiding in jars?" "Yes, that is it," said Constantine, "the old crones, very discreet, the pursuit of the occasion that demanded faith, the flash of eye below a veil lifted for only a second, the wave of a scarf from a lattice, which was at once a promise of beauty and a challenge to cunning and courage, for there might be a witty ambush hiding in jars and there might be death from a eunuch's sword. It is too beautiful.

"Too beautiful!" he repeated, beaming as one cradled in content though at the moment he was actually suspended in the air. "It is a conception of love which demands that it should be sudden and secret and dangerous. You from the West have no such conception of love. It seems to you that love must be as slow as the growth of a plant: a man and woman must come throughout many months to a full understanding of each other's natures and take serious vows to fulfil each other's needs. You think also that a man insults a woman if he wishes to make love to her without delay, and that a woman is worthless if she gives herself to a man before they have killed a great part of the calendar. In this there is much truth. I remember that when I was a young man in Paris, it sometimes happened that though I had two mistresses there were times when I went out into the street and took the first woman I met, and it was because I am in part a barbarian and so I could not wait. That was nothing. But love can be sudden and quite different from that. It can be so ecstatic that it can come into full being at a single encounter, that it needs only that encounter to satisfy the lovers.

"If you offered them a lifetime together you could not offer them more than the night that follows when the old crone has opened the door. No, the car is not going to turn over. And when you come back next year the road will be better. We are a young country, and we will do all, but we have not yet had the time. Such love could properly be engendered by a single glance from the eyes. Indeed it could not claim to be this kind of love, this ultimate affinity, if the most infinitesimal contact was not enough to declare it. That is why it must be sudden.

"It must be secret because jealousy is a part of both this sudden love and the other, slow-moving kind. A man who performs the miracle of keeping a woman happy for forty years cannot bear it that on one night during those forty years another man should be necessary for her happiness; and a man who meets a woman once and makes that meeting as fabulous in her memory as a night spent in the moon cannot bear it that he should not be the father of the eleven children whose noses she wipes. Hence these men must not know of each other. We roar like bulls about our honour, but so it is.

"Also this love must be dangerous, or it would not be itself. That is not to say that one does not value a thing unless one has paid a great price for it—that is vulgar. But if a woman did not know that to lift her veil before a stranger was perhaps to die, she might perhaps lift it when she had received no intimation of this great and sudden love: when she was merely barbarian. And indeed neither she nor her lover could fully consummate this kind of love without a sense of peril. They would not shut the eyes of reason and precipitate themselves into the abyss of passion, unless they knew this might be their last chance to experience it or, indeed, anything else.

"It is a more marvellous conception of love, I think, than anything other nations know. The French make love for the sake of life; and so, like living, it often falls to something less than itself, to a little trivial round. The Germans make love for the sake of death; as they like to put off civilian clothes and put on uniform, because there is more chance of being killed, so they like to step out of the safe casual relations of society and let loose the destructive forces of sex. So it was with *Werther* and *Elective Affinities,* and so it was in the years after the war, when they were so promiscuous that sex meant nothing at all. And this is not to speak ill of the French and Germans, for the love of life and the love of death are both necessary things. But this conception unites love of life and death in a single experience. Such lovers are conscious at once of the extremity of danger and that which makes danger most terrible and at the same time most worth challenging."

"But that is the essence of all adventure," said my husband, "and indeed it is the essence of——" "Yes, yes, what you say is very true," said Constantine, as he always does when he intends that the person who is talking to him shall talk no more. "It is this conception of love which gives life to the city of Sarajevo. How far this tradition exists today I cannot tell. But I think that even now old women are sometimes sent with messages that must be read by only one person, and I think that the plum trees would not blossom so freely round those little restaurants on the hillside above the town if some god or goddess had not been placated by sacrifice." "You think," said my husband, "the rose never grows one-half so red." "But I am sure," continued Constantine, "that the conception gives the town a special elegance. The men and women in it have another dimension given to their lives, because they have kept in their hearts the capacity for this second kind of love. They are not mutilated by its suppression, and they have hope. All of them may yet have this revelation, and some of them have actually had it. I think that is why so many of the women here have lips and eyes that shine like children's, and why the men are not bitter or grudging or hurried. A sensuality that is also a mysticism," he cried, "what can a race invent better for itself? But here is Ilidzhe, here is our marvellous Ilidzhe!" He leaped in one second from well-buttered reverie to shaking indignation. "Ilidzhe, our Potemkin village! They built it to show the foreign visitors how well they had imposed civilization on our barbarism, just as Potemkin built villages on the steppes to impress the foreign ambassadors with Russian prosperity, hollow villages that were built the day before and were pulled down the day after. Come, look at their civilization, at our barbarity!"

The spa waited for us behind the scrubby, half-forested edge of a park, and indeed it was not pleasing. In earlier days it had certainly been better kept; it now looked like any of the other Yugoslavian spas, which are patronized by the peasants and small shopkeepers, and showed a certain homely untidiness, though nothing worse. But the place was unengaging in its architectural essence. A string of shapeless hotels was joined by a covered corridor to a central restaurant and pump-room, a pudding of a place. Every building was smothered in heavy porches and balustrades and balconies of craftless but elaborate woodwork. The hotels were all closed at the moment, they did not open till the heat brought people out of the city; and we strolled about looking for the proprietor of the Hotel Bosnia, the largest of the hotels, at which Franz Ferdinand and Sophie Chotek had spent their last night. "I think that they have kept the chapel that was made for their coming," said Constantine, "and I know they keep their room as it was, for I have seen it. It was the suite reserved always for the royal family and for the governor, and it was altogether Moslem, but a terrible Moslem. It was like a place I have seen in your London, when I was there for five days during the war, called the Kardomah Café: all little inlaid tables and a clutter of many things, whereas, as you have seen, the chief furniture of a Moslem house is the light. Also I would like you to meet my friend who is the director of the spa, he has a very beautiful wife and her sister, who would like to talk to you about Tennyson's *Idylls of the King*. They read nothing else, they would be Enid and Guinevere." He waved his arms as if he were wearing long flowing sleeves, and pulled out his neck to its most swanlike. "But here is a man with keys."

They fitted, however, only the door of a little shop in the Hotel Bosnia's arcade; but the man was glad to have a talk. "He says," said Constantine, "that they do their best to keep the place neat, but that there is not enough money to do much. Many people come here in summer, but they are not rich, like the nobles who used to come here from Austria and Germany and England to see how beautifully Bosnia was being governed by the Austrian Empire. But he would not have it different, though he has been here since a child and loves the place, for he is a very patriotic Yugoslav. But really it is disgusting, this Ilidzhe. They did nothing for the country, but they built these hotels and the race-course which I am going to show you presently, and all the grand people came and looked at it and said, 'Ah, it is so in Bosnia, all weeded gravel paths and new houses and good beer, it is too good for these cattle of Slavs.' " He mimicked the tone of a fine lady, turning his face from side to side and twirling an imaginary open parasol.

The man with the keys had been watching. He suddenly threw down his keys on to the pavement and began to shout straight past us to the horizon: like the young man at Trsat, like the young man on the boat whose soup was cold, like the hotel manager from Hvar. "Yes, yes," he cried, "and they had our men and women brought in to dance the kolo to them, we were for them the natives, the savages, and we had to dance for them as if we were bears at a fair." He bent and picked up the keys, then remembered something and threw them down again. "And what they did to us as soldiers! They made us become soldiers, and when a man goes into battle he may be called before his God, and they made us Christians wear the fez! Yes, the fez of the accursed Turks was the headgear of all our four Bosnian regiments!"

He picked up his keys for the second time and led us along the corridor to the railway station, which indeed was very grand, in the manner of Baden-Baden or Marienbad. "I find this grotesquely unpleasing," I said. "I did not bring you here to please you," said Constantine, "when I take you to see things that were left by the Turks and the Austrians it is not to please you, it is so that you shall understand. And now, will you please look where I tell you? This station is very untidy, is it not?

The paint has gone and there are no flowers growing in wire cages. Will you please look at the chestnut tree that stands in the middle of this piece of gravel outside the station? Do you see that there are growing round it many weeds? Now, I apply a test. If you are saved, if you know what the soul is and what a people is, you will be able to see that that tree is better now, standing among weeds, than it was when it was spick and span; for these weeds are the best we can do, they are all the order we can yet attain in Bosnia, and the spickness and spanness came from another people, and were therefore nothingness, they could not exist here, because they were not part of the national process." "There I cannot agree," I said. "I do not believe that it was wrong of the English to drain India and abolish suttee, I do not believe that the Pères Blancs did wrong in medicining the sicknesses of Africa." "Do I not know such things must be done?" said Constantine. "We Yugoslavs are stamping out malaria in Macedonia and we are raising up peasants that have been trodden into the mud by the Turks. But it should be done by one's people, never by strangers." "Rats," said my husband; "if a people have wholly gone under, without a fringe that has kept its independence and its own folk-ways, strangers must butt in and help it get on its feet again. The trouble is that the kind of stranger who likes helping unfortunate people usually does not get leave to set about it unless other members of his group see a military or commercial advantage to be got out of it. But if you mean that the Bosnians had enough force and enough remnants of the old Slav culture to look after themselves once they got the Turks off their necks, and that the Austrians had nothing to give them and had no business here, then I'm with you." "Ah, you have said something true and so untidy," complained Constantine, "and what I said was not quite true, but so beautifully neat."

But it was where the racecourse drew its white diagram on the gardeny plains that the irrelevance of the Austrian intervention appeared most apparent. The scene was now enchanting. All over the course sheep and cattle were grazing on the turf, ringing faint little bells as they were pressed on by comfortable, slow-moving greed, or met the active air, not quite a wind, which flowed quietly down the great tawny valley that led back to Sarajevo. Where there was not grass the earth showed red; and the poplars stood like jets of chill green-gold light. Scattered on the plains were the rough white farms and cottages of Christians; and on every slope which promised a fine view there stood a Moslem villa, smoothly and solidly white among the white clouds of its orchard. One such villa stood on a little hill close by the racecourse, as compact a delight as if an enormous deal of spring had been boiled down till it would fill just a little pot, according to the method of making rose-leaf jam.

And the white rails, of course, recalled another delight. I saw a string of horses going like a line of good poetry, under a cloudless morning on Lambourne Downs. I remembered what the author of the Book of Job had said about the horse: "The glory of his nostrils is terrible. He paweth in the valley, and rejoiceth in his strength. . . . He saith among the trumpets, Ha, ha; and he smelleth the battle afar off, the thunder of the captains, and the shouting. . . ." A pleasure, undoubtedly, but how irrelevant to the starving Bosnian peasant, and how irrelevant, how insolent to Sarajevo. The scenery before me was distressing in its evocation of Austrian society as it was in the time of Franz Josef, as Metternich had foreseen it must become if the Empire was not allowed some measure of freedom. Banality rose from the tomb and stood chattering about the lawns: women with heavy chins and lively untender eyes and blonde frizzes of hair under straw boaters, wearing light blouses and long skirts and broad waistbands, men with the strongly marked expressions of ventriloquists' dummies, with sloping shoulders and ramrod backs. They chattered loudly, with the exaggerated positiveness of those who live in a negative world. They were Catholics who could nourish among them a *"Los von Rom"* movement, they were cosmopolitans who lived by provincial standards, they were bound by etiquette and recognized no discipline, they were the descendants of connoisseurs yet neither produced nor appreciated great art, they sacrificed all civil interests to a military caste that proved as soon as war broke out to be wholly civilian in everything but its splendid and suicidal valour.

These people had come to govern, to change, to civilize such men and women as we had seen in Sarajevo: the Jews with their tradition of fine manners and learning; the Moslems with their houses full of light and their blossoming gardens and dedication to peaceful nature; the old women we had seen in the market-place, whose souls had attained to wit; the men whose long strides were endurance itself, who would know, like our friend with the keys, that an honest man must not dance before tyrants nor go to his God in the fez. These women in blouses and skirts had come as examples of the fashion to those who had worn Persian brocades since West was on visiting terms with East; the ramrod men had come to command such as the officer who had stood swaying by the new grave. The builders of these horrible hotels, of the little covered corridor that looked as if one end of it might have led to the old Druce's Bazaar in Baker Street, had come to Sarajevo, the town of a hundred mosques, to teach and not to learn.

Treboviche

LATER that afternoon we drove out of Sarajevo by the road that leads to Treboviche, the mountain which rises too near the town and too steeply to be seen from it. The craned neck can see only its foothills. Half-way up we stopped the automobile and stood on a grassy ledge to see the orchards and villas lying beneath us, all little pots of spring jam, like the villa by the racecourse. On a ledge above us were standing some gipsies, eight or nine girls in jackets and trousers of printed curtain stuffs, and two men who were jumping and gesticulating in front of them, the upturned toes of their leather sandals looking like cockspurs. Something about the gestures of Constantine's plump little arms as he showed us the city brought them tumbling about us. A good many people of the lettered sort recognized Constantine from his caricatures in the papers; but the unlettered see him for what he is with astonishing quickness. He has only to swing an eloquent hand at a street-corner and there are men and women about us looking at him with an expression which sums up the twofold attitude of ordinary folk to the poet: a mixture of amused indulgence, as of a grown-up watching a child at play, and ecstatic expectation, as of a child waiting for a grown-up to tell it a fairy-story. These gipsies ran down the grassy slope and stood about us giggling in a circle of crimson and plum and blue and green and lemon and cinnabar, the wind blowing out their full trousers and making them hug their shawls under the chin. They bring a lovely element into a community which allows them to exist without sinking into squalor. It is as if one could go out and make love to a flower, or have foxes and hares to play music at one's parties.

The higher rocks above the road were pale green with hellebores, and there were primroses and cowslips and cyclamen, and at last the faded mauve flames of crocus. Then we came to the snow, lying thinly on scars and under pinewoods. Where it deepened we left the car and walked past a house which might have been a Swiss chalet, had it not been for the music that someone within was plucking from the strings of a gusla, to a peak shoulder crusted in ice and deep with snow where there was a shadowed seam. About us were the smouldering Bosnian uplands, their heathy heights red with last year's autumn, though in some valleys the first touch of spring had given a spinney or an alp a hard mineral viridity. These heights and valleys run neither north nor south nor west nor east, but in all ways for a mile at a time, so that the landscape turns like a merry-go-round. Beyond these broken and burning highlands lay a wall of amber cloud, and above this rose two unknown ranges, one reflecting on its snows the brightness of an afternoon that was for us already dimmed, the other crimson with an evening that had not yet reached us. Sarajevo we could not see: the valley that runs down from it was a vast couch for a white river, until it twisted and broke and broadened and couched several rivers, which in winding spread their whiteness in mist. Over all the nearer highlands was cast a web of paths joining the villages across the tawny distance; and from some of them, though they were a mile or two away, came sounds of playing children and barking dogs.

Cold, we went back to the chalet and drank warming coffee under the pictures of the boy King and his mother and his murdered father. They are found in every public place in Yugoslavia, even Croatia. I think they are present in anti-Serb territory because they are sold by some charitable society which nobody wishes to refuse, but in other parts, where there lingers the medieval conception of the king as a priest of the people, they have nearly the status of holy pictures. At the back of the room sat a handsome young man playing the gusla and singing, apparently the proprietor, and two very pretty young women, all with that characteristically Slav look which comes from the pulling of the flesh down from the flat cheekbones by the tense pursing of the mouth. On the face of the murdered King there was the same expression, hardened to woodenness by the fear of death coming from assassination without or tuberculosis within.

Constantine drank his coffee, pushed away his cup, and said, "When you look at things, try to remember them wholly because you have soon to go home to England. I think of a story I heard from a monk of how King Alexander came to see the frescoes in his monastery which contained portraits of our Serbian kings of our old Empire, in the thirteenth century, which are real portraits, mind you. Before one he stood for three-quarters of an hour, looking terribly, as one would look on one's father if he came back from the dead, sucking him with the eyes. The monk asked him if he had a special cult for this king, and he said, 'No. For all kings of Serbia must I have a cult. All kings I must understand, in order that the new dynasty be grafted on the old. And this king I must make a special effort to understand, since nothing that is written of him makes him quite clear to me.' You see, he was a mystic,

and because the channel of his mysticism was Yugoslavia, nobody outside Yugoslavia can understand him."

He put his elbows on the table and rumpled his little black curls.
"Nobody outside Yugoslavia understands us," he complained. "We have
a very bad press, particularly with the high-minded people, who hate
us because we are mystics and not just intelligent, as they are. *Ach!*
that Madame Geneviève Tabouis, how she writes of us in her Paris
newspaper! She suspects us of being anti-democratic in our natures,
when we Serbs are nothing but democratic, but cannot be because the
Italians and the Germans are watching us to say, 'Ah, here is Bolshevism, we must come in and save you from it.' And really she is not being
high-minded when she makes this mistake, she makes it because she
hates the Prime Minister, Mr. Stoyadinovitch; and it is not that she hates
him because he is a bad man, she hates him just because they are opposites. She is little and thin and fine, he is a great big man with a strong
chest and much flesh that all comes with him when he moves; she finds
all relationships difficult, and all men and women follow him as if he
were a great horse; she is noble when she loves her country, and when
he loves his country it is as natural as when he sweats; and *en somme*
he likes wine and can drink it, all sorts of wine, red wine, white wine,
champagne, little wines of our country and great wines of France, and
she must drink only a little drop of mineral water from a special spa,
and of that she has a special source. So they hate each other, and since
she is idealistic and is therefore ashamed that she should hate people for
the kind of marrow they have in their spines, she pretends to herself she
hates Yugoslavia. And yet she is great in her way. But not so great, my
pardon to your wife, my dear sir, who I know is a lady writer also,
as Mr. Stoyadinovitch."

I never heard anybody else in Yugoslavia speak well of Stoyadinovitch
except Constantine; but Constantine was sincere. He laid his cheek on
the table, and drew his folded hands back and forward across his forehead. "There is something," I said, "which has been worrying me ever
since I stood by the tomb of the *attentateurs*, and what you said at Ilidzhe
this morning has intensified my perplexity. Listen. The predominantly
German character of the Habsburg monarchy, and the concessions it
had to make to the Hungarians, meant that the Austro-Hungarian Empire oppressed its Slavs and feared the kingdom of Serbia as a dangerous
potential ally to these discontented subjects. At the same time there were
economic conditions in the Austro-Hungarian Empire which meant that
there must be sooner or later a revolt, in which these discontented Slavs

would be specially likely to bear the brunt of the fighting. Therefore precisely this war that happened in 1914 was bound to happen sooner or later." "But certainly," said Constantine, "it had nearly happened in 1912, when Franz Ferdinand's friends all but succeeded in starting a preventive war over Albania." "Then it mattered not at all what happened in Sarajevo on June twenty-eighth, 1914," I said. Constantine was silent for a minute. The man behind us stopped playing his gusla, as if he understood what had been said. Constantine said, "In a sense you are right. The little ones need not have died. And of the two big ones the poor angry one could have gone on shooting his beasts, and the poor striving one could have continued to strive after the little things the other poor ones did not want her to have. We should have had the World War just the same." "What a waste!" I said. "Well, Sarajevo is the one town I know that could bear with equanimity the discovery that her great moment was a delusion, a folly, a simple extravagance," said Constantine. "She would walk by her river, she would sit under the fruit tree in her courtyard, and she would not weep." But after a pause he added, "But she is not an imbecile. If she would not weep it is because of her knowledge that we are wrong. By the *attentat* she took the war and made it a private possession of the South Slavs. Behind the veil of our incomprehensible language and behind the veil of lies the Austrians and Hungarians have told about us and our wrongs, the cause of the war —more than that, the reason for the war—is eternally a mystery to the vast majority of the people who took part in it and were martyrized by it. Perhaps that is something for us South Slavs, to know a secret that is hidden from everybody else. I do not know. How I wish," he said, standing up, "that we could stay here tonight. There are such honest little rooms upstairs, with coarse clean sheets, and it is so quiet. That is to say there are many noises, but they all have a meaning, it is this bird that cries or that, whereas the noises in a city mean nothing. But if we are going to Yaitse tomorrow we must go down to the town."

It was not yet dark. As we came down we could still see the cyclamen and the primroses and the cowslips on the banks of the road, looking sweetly melancholy as flowers do when seen by other than full light. When we were half-way down the dusk was deep blue, and we stopped the car when we came to the knoll where we had stood beside the gipsies, in order to look down on the scattered lights of Sarajevo. But our chauffeur called out to us from the car, pointing at the city. "He is asking you to listen to the bells," said Constantine. "They are sounding all over the city, and it is a great thing for him because when the Turks were here there might be no church bells. This man's father, or his grandfather, told him of the time, sixty years ago, when they were not allowed, and he feels proud that they are there now."

Travnik

On our way out of Sarajevo the next morning we stopped to buy oranges, and I filled my lap with white violets and cowslips and marigolds; and so we started on a morning's drive through valleys which might have been landscaped by Capability Brown, so prettily were the terraces set and planted, so neat was the line the climbing woodlands drew against the hilltop moor. This is in part due to geological accident, but it is also true that hereabouts man has the neatest of hands. He is extremely poor, but he can work miracles with his restricted materials. We came presently to a little spa called Kiselyak, a very old spa, which was popular, particularly among the Jews, in the Turkish times. I suppose that in the last twenty-five years the mass of people who had stayed there were on the same financial level as those in America who have an income of forty dollars a week or under. The place was as pretty as a musical-comedy set. In the main street there was a long low Park Hotel, plastered white as snow, with a brightly striped mattress taking the air at every window, which it seemed could not have been put there in answer to mere necessity, so gay was the pattern.

To admire it, we left the car, and crossed a little stream to a pinewood where there stood an artlessly built bath-house and drinking-fountains. On the bridge there was an elderly Moslem contemplating the running water. Always, in this part of the world, where there is running water, there is an elderly Moslem contemplating it. He joined our party without intrusiveness, and pointed out to us a café near by, a wooden summer-house built over the stream in a thicket of willows which he rightly thought particularly pleasing, and then he took us over to the drinking-booths and found a Christian gardener who unlocked them and gave us cups of water. It had a fortifying taste of metal. We strolled along a path through the pinewood and came on a black marble monument from which a gold inscription had been savagely excised. The Moslem and the gardener, who had been following us at a few paces' distance, came forward to tell us that it had been put up to commemorate a victory of the Austrian Army over the Bosnian insurgents. "Would you rather have things as they are now?" said Constantine. They agreed that they would, and we all sat down on a bench, while I finished my cup of water.

"I want to stay here, I do not want to go on," I said. "It is the Moslem who is making you feel like that," said Constantine, "that is the great art of the Moslem; and mind you, that is very interesting, for, look at him, he is a Slav like the gardener, who has it not. It is the Turks and his religion that have taught him to sit and do nothing so very nicely. He would be content to sit here all day, just as we are doing now; and indeed it would be most pleasant, for we would listen to the stream and watch the clouds above the tree-tops, and we would smoke and some-times we would exchange polite remarks." We stayed there, just as he said, for nearly half an hour. The feeling was as in one of the delightful households to be found in Bath, where there are beautiful manners and beautiful furniture and a complete sense of detachment from modern agitation. But there was not the anxiety about income tax which usually mars such interiors. The Moslem was as poor as can be, even here: he was in neatly mended rags, his leather sandals were tied up with string.

On our way again, such poverty was all about us. The mosques were no longer built of stone and bricks, but were roughly plastered like farm buildings, with tiled roofs and rickety wooden minarets. But they had still a trace of elegance in their design; and there were fine embroideries on the boleros the women wore over their white linen blouses and dark full trousers, and on the shirts of the black-browed men. With some of these people we could not get on friendly terms. If they were in charge of horses they looked at us with hatred, because the horses invariably began to bolt at the sight of the automobile, however much we slowed down. We sent two hay-carts flying into the ditch. So rarely had these people seen automobiles that they looked at us with dignified rebuke, as at vulgarians who insisted on using an eccentric mode of conveyance which put other travellers to inconvenience. But the people who had no horses to manage looked at us with peculiar respect, since automo-biles passed so rarely that it seemed to them certain that my husband and Constantine must be important officials from Belgrade. With a styl-ized look of sternness the men saluted and stood to attention while we passed. "Look at their faces," said Constantine; "they think that all the time they must die for Yugoslavia, and they cannot understand why we do not ask them to do that, but that now we ask another thing, that they should live and be happy."

The road climbed to a wide valley, where spring winds were hurry-ing across wet emerald pastures, and through woods sharply green where winter had left them, and bronze where it still dawdled. Little pink pigs and red foals ran helter-skelter before our coming, and men and women in gorgeous clothes, more richly coloured than in the lower valleys, chased after them, but paused to laugh and greet us. In the distance loomed mountains, holding on their ledges huge blocks of monastic buildings. These are among the few relics of the Austrian occupation other than barracks; it was here that the Empire made the headquarters of their attempt to Catholicize the Bosnians who belonged to the Orthodox Church. The Dominicans and the Franciscans, who had been here for seven hundred years, were reinforced, not altogether to their own pleasure, by the Jesuits.

At the base of these mountains we touched it, the town which for good reason was called by the Turks Travnik, or Grassy-town. Narrow houses with tall and shapely slanting tiled roofs sit gracefully, like cats on their haunches, among the green gardens of a garden-like valley. Here, in this well-composed littleness, which lies snug in the field of the eye, can be enjoyed to perfection the Moslem counterpoint of the soft horizontal whiteness of fruit blossom and the hard vertical whiteness of minarets. This town was the capital of Bosnia for two centuries under the Turks, the seat of the Pasha from the time that Sarajevo would not have him, and it has a definite urban distinction, yet it is countrified as junket. "This is where the Moslem at Kiselyak would like to have a house," said my husband, "if he ever let himself want anything he did not have."

We had been invited to luncheon with the father and mother of the lovely Jewess in Sarajevo whom we called the Bulbul, and we found their home in an apartment house looking over the blossoming trench of the valley from the main road, under a hill crowned with a fortress built by the old Bosnian kings. We found it, and breathed in our nostrils the odour of another civilization. Our appearance there caused cries of regret. The father stood in the shadow of the doorway, a handsome man in his late fifties, whose likeness I had seen often enough in the Persian miniatures, gazelle-eyed and full-bodied. In the delicious voice of the Sephardim, honey-sweet but not cloying, he told us that he was ashamed to let us in, for we would find nothing worthy of us. He had thought we meant to call at his factory, which was a couple of miles outside the town, so he had ordered a real meal, a meal appropriate to us, to be cooked there, and he had left an explanation that he could not be with us, as his wife had broken her ankle and till she was well he would eat all his meals with her. He bowed with shame that he should have blundered so. But a voice, lovely as his own but a woman's, cried from the darkened room beyond and bade him bring the strangers in. It was at once maternal, warm with the desire to do what could be done to com-

fort our foreignness, and childlike, breathless with a desire to handle the
new toy.

She lay on a sofa, fluttering up against the downward pull of her injury, as hurt birds do; and she was astonishing in the force of her beauty.
She was at least in her late forties, and she was not one of those prodigies
unmarked by time, but she was as beautiful, to judge by her effect on
the beholder, as the Bulbul. That could not really be so, of course. As a
general rule Horace must be right, for reasons connected with the fatty
deposits under the skin and the working of the ductless glands, when he
writes, "*O matre pulchra filia pulchrior.*" Yet in this case he would have
been wrong. He should have ignored his metre and written of "*mater
pulchrior pulcherrimæ filiæ,*" for there was the more beautiful mother
of the most beautiful daughter. The Bulbul was the most perfect example conceivable of the shining Jewish type, but so long as one looked
on this woman she seemed lovelier than all other women. Her age was
unimportant because it did not mean to her what it means to most Western women: she had never been frustrated, she had always been rewarded
for her beautiful body and her beautiful conduct by beautiful gratitude.

My husband and I sat down beside her, smiling as at an unexpected
present; and she apologized to us for the poor meal she would have to
improvise, and cried over our heads directions to her cook in a voice
that floated rather than carried, and then settled to ask us questions which
were by Western standards personal, which were extremely sensible if
she wished to be able to like us quickly before we left her house. In a
painted cage a canary suddenly raised fine-drawn but frantic cheers for
the universe, and they checked it with gentle laughter that could not
have hurt its feelings. The canary, it seemed, her husband had brought
home to divert her while she must lie on the sofa. The room was littered
with gifts he had fetched her for that purpose: a carved flute, a piece
of brocade, an eighteenth-century book of Italian travel with coloured
illustrations, an amber box—a trifle, I should say, for each day she had
been kept in the house. Their household rocked gently on a tide of giving and receiving.

They watched us sadly while we ate, uttering coos of regret for the
meal that was really worthy of us, waiting uneaten in the factory. But
we were not discontented. We were given home-made spaghetti, those
eggs called "Spanish eggs" which are boiled for three days in oil and
come out greaseless and silky to the palate, lamb chops from small ethereal
lambs who probably had wings, sheep's cheese, pure white and delicately
sharp, peaches and quinces foundered in syrup that kept all their summer

flavour, and raki, the colourless brandy loved by Slavs. As we ate we
told them of our meetings with their daughter in Sarajevo, and they
stretched like cats in pride and pleasure, owning that all we said of her
was true, and reciting some of her accomplishments that they thought
we might not have had the chance to observe. Nothing could have been
less like the uneasy smile, the deprecating mumble, which is evoked in
an Englishman by praise of his family.

But this was a long way from England. Constantine went on to tell
the gossip he had picked up in Sarajevo, and the more ambassadorial
gossip he had brought from Belgrade, and while they rewarded his perfect story-telling by perfect listening, I looked about the room. It was
certainly provincial; anything that had reached the room from Vienna,
Berlin, Paris, or London had taken so long to get there and had been
so much modified by the thought of the alien taste for which it was
destined that it would be antiquated and bizarre. But built into this room,
and inherent in every word and gesture of its owners, was a tradition
more limited in its scope than the traditions of Vienna, Berlin, Paris, or
London, but within its limits just as ancient and sure and competent.
Whatever event these people met they could outface; the witness to that
was their deep serenity. They would meet it with a formula compounded
of Islam and Judaism. Their whole beings breathed the love of pleasure
which is the inspiration of Sarajevo, which was perhaps the great contribution the Turks had to make to culture. But it was stabilized, its
object was made other than running water, by the Jewish care for the
continuity of the race. It was a fusion that would infuriate the Western
moralist, who not only believes but prefers that one should not be able
to eat one's cake and have it. I went later to comb my hair and wash
my hands in these people's bathroom. A printed frieze of naked nymphs
dancing in a forest ran from wall to wall, and several pictures bared
the breasts and thighs of obsoletely creamy beauties. Naïvely it was
revealed that these people thought of the bath as the uncovering of
nakedness, and of nakedness as an instrument of infinite delight. It was
the seraglio spirit in its purity; and it was made chaste as snow by the
consideration that these people would have offered this flesh of which
they so perfectly understood the potentialities to burn like tallow in
flame if thereby they might save their dearer flesh, their child.

So one can have it, as the vulgar say, both ways. Indeed one can have
a great deal more than one has supposed one could, if only one lives, as
these people did, in a constant and loyal state of preference for the agreeable over the disagreeable. It might be thought that nothing could be

easier, but that is not the case. We in the West find it almost impossible, and are caught unawares when we meet it in practice. That was brought home to me by this woman's tender gesture of farewell. First she took all the lilac from a vase beside her sofa and gave them to me, but then felt this was not a sufficient civility. She made me lay down the flowers, and took a scent-bottle from her table and sprinkled my hands with the scent, gently rubbing it into my skin. It was the most gracious farewell imaginable, and the Western world in which I was born would not have approved.

There sounded in my mind's ear the probable comment of a Western woman: "My dear, it was too ghastly, she seized me by the hands and simply drenched them with some most frightful scent. I couldn't get rid of it for days." Their fastidiousness would, of course, have been bogus, for the scent was exquisite, a rich yet light derivative from Bulgarian attar of roses. These people were infallible in their judgment on such matters, having been tutored for centuries by their part in the luxury trade between Bosnia and Tsarigrad, as they named Constantinople; and she had assumed that persons of our kind would have a like education and would recognize that this scent was of the first order. She had also assumed that I would like to receive a gift which showed that somebody who had not known me two hours before now liked me. She assumed, in fact, that I too preferred the agreeable to the disagreeable. Remembering the grey ice that forms on an Englishman's face as he is introduced to a stranger, I reflected that she was too audacious in her assumption.

Before we left the town her husband took us for a stroll. A lane wound among the mosques and villas through gardens that held much plum blossom and lilac and irises and, here and there, among the shrubs, the innocent playfulness of witch-balls. Travnik had changed its aspect now, as a town does after one has eaten salt in one of its houses. It is no longer something painted on one's retina, it is third-dimensional, it is a being and a friend or an enemy. We climbed up to the old castle, which is a fortress now, and were met by very grave young soldiers. Slav soldiers look devout and dedicated even when they are drunk; these sober boys, guarding their white town and pale-green valley, were as nuns. There had been an intention of calling on the commandant, but the young soldiers said he was asleep. They looked at us for some time before they told us this, and spoke sadly and with an air of pronouncing judgment; and I think that perhaps they thought that their commandant was a sacred being, and that it would be a profanation to disturb him for the sake of three men not in uniform and a woman no longer young. They bade us good-bye with a worried air, as if they wished they were sure they had done right. All to them was still of great moment.

We followed a little path down a grassy hill, miraculously untainted as glades are on the edge of Moslem towns, to a big pool lying among trees. It was fed by three springs, each bursting from the mauve shelter of a clump of cyclamen. It was dammed by a steep stone wall, broken at one end by a channel through which the waters burst in a grooved sliver that looked to be as solid as crystal. We admired it for a long time as if it were a matter of great importance; and then we went down to the main road and found a café which had settled itself in snug melancholy at the corner of a Moslem graveyard, near by the pompous canopied tombs of a couple of pashas.

There we sat and drank black coffee and ate Turkish delight on toothpicks, while a gentle wind stirred the flowering trees that met above the table, and set the grasses waving round a prostrate pillar which had fallen by one of the pashas' tombs. There strolled up and sat down some of those mysterious impoverished and dignified Moslems who seem to have no visible means of support, but some quite effective invisible means. They watched us without embarrassment; we were unembarrassed; and the men talked of country pastimes. Here, the Bulbul's father said, was real game for shooting in winter.

There is deep snow here in winter-time, it seems; and the beasts come down from the heights and loiter hungrily on the outskirts of the town. A friend of his had sauntered a few yards out of his garden, his gun loaded with pellets. He paused to look at a black bush that had miraculously escaped the snow. It stood up and was a bear, a lurch away. His friend raised his gun and shot. The pellets found the bear's brain through the eye, he staggered, charged blindly, and fell dead. He himself had been driving down to his factory one November afternoon when he saw a pack of wolves rushing down the mountain on a herd of goats. He stopped his car and watched. They came straight down like the water we had seen rushing down by the dam. They leaped on the goats and ate what they wanted. He had heard the goats' bones cracking, as loud, he said, as gunshots. When the wolves had eaten their fill they rushed up the mountain again, dragging what was left of the goats. It took only five minutes, he thought, from the time he first saw them till they passed out of sight.

He pointed up to the mountains. "It is only in winter you see them," he said, "but all the same they are up there, waiting for us and the goats."

We looked in wonder at the heights that professed the stark innocence of stone, that was honeycombed with the stumbling weighty hostility of bears, the incorporated rapacity of wolves. And as we lowered our eyes we saw that we were ourselves being regarded with as much wonder by other eyes, which also were speculating what the sterile order of our appearance might conceal. A gaunt peasant woman with hair light and straight and stiff as hay and a mouth wide as a door had stopped in the roadway at the sight of us. She was so grand, so acidulated, so utterly at a disadvantage before almost anyone in the civilized world, and so utterly unaware of being at a disadvantage at all, that I made Constantine ask her to let herself be photographed. She whinnied with delight, and arranged herself before the camera with her chin forward, her arms crossed, her weight on her heels, acting a man's pride; I think nothing in her life had ever suggested to her that there is a woman's kind of pride.

She was poor. Dear God, she was poor. She was poor as the people in Rab. Her sleeveless white serge coat, her linen blouse, the coarse kerchief she had twisted round her head, were stained with age. The wool of the embroidery on her coat was broken so that here and there the pattern was a mere fuzz. Garments of this sort have a long life. To be in this state they must have been worn by more than one generation. She had probably never had new clothes in all her days. This was not the most important aspect of her. There were others which were triumphant. It could be seen that she was a wit, a stoic, a heroine. But for all that it was painful to look at her, because she was deformed by the slavery of her ancestors as she might have been by rheumatism. The deep pits round her eyes and behind her nostrils, the bluish grooves running down her neck, spoke of an accumulated deprivation, an amassed poverty, handed down like her ruined clothes from those who were called rayas, the ransomed ones, the Christian serfs who had to buy the right to live. To some in Bosnia the East gave, from some it took away.

Yaitse (Jajce) I

BEYOND Travnik the road rose through slashing rain to a high pass, beset before and behind with violet clouds, rent and repaired in the same instant by the scissors of lightning. The open faces of the primroses were pulpy under the storm, the green bells of the hellebore were flattened against the rocks. In the valley beyond we ran into a high blue cave of stillness and sunshine, and came on a tumbledown village, shabby and muddy and paintless and charming, called Vakuf. *"Vakuf"* is a Turkish word meaning religious property; I have never heard anything that made me more positively anxious not to study Turkish than the news that the plural of this word is *"Evkaf."* It is called by that name because the land hereabouts was given by pious Moslems to provide for the maintenance of mosques and charitable institutions, and some hundreds of the labourers that tilled it lived in this village. Under the Austro-Hungarian Empire these properties were specially nursed, and the labourers given preferential treatment. They were, indeed, the only agricultural workers whose position was in any way better under the Austrians than it had been under the Turks. Nowadays the property is well looked after by the Moslem Political Party, but the village has fallen into that state of gentle disorder rather than actual squalor, which is characteristic of Ottoman remains in Bosnia.

The violent rains had set the main street awash with mud, and we saw nobody but an old man with the white twist in his turban that denotes the Moslem priest, tiptoeing across the morass, with the air of a disgusted cat, to a rickety wooden mosque. He looked agreeable; but the town was irritating to the female eye, with its projecting upper stories where the rotting latticed harem windows are ready to fall out of their rotten casements. It is impudent of men to keep women as luxuries unless they have the power to guarantee them the framework of luxury. If men ask women to give up for their sake the life of the market-place they must promise that they will bring to the harem all that is best in the market-place; that, as all intelligent Moslems have admitted, is the only understanding on which the harem can be anything but a field of male sexual gluttony and cantankerousness. But if they fail to keep that ambitious promise, which there was indeed no obligation to make, they should surrender the system and let women go back to freedom and get what they can. A harem window with a hole boarded up and a lattice tied by a rag to its casement is a sign of the shabby failure that has broken faith with others, like a stranded touring company.

After Vakuf we passed through a valley that was like a Chinese landscape, with woods leaning to one another across deep vertical abysses; and suddenly we found ourselves at the waterfall which is the chief glory of Yaitse. That town stands on a hill, divided by a deep trench from a wide mountain covered by forests and villages, and a river rushes down from the town and leaps a hundred feet into a river that runs along the trench. The chauffeur and Constantine ran about the brink uttering cries. All South Slavs regard water as a sacred substance, and a waterfall is half-way to the incarnation of a god. My husband and I went a stroll, hobbling over the slippery stones, to see the smooth lap and the foaming skirts of the waters from a distance, and when we looked back we saw that Constantine had taken a seat on a rock; and by the waving of his little short arms and the rolling of his curly black bullet head we knew that near him a bird was fluttering over the falls, exulting in the coolness, in the blows the spray struck on its almost weightless body, in the challenge that was made to its wing-courage. From the turn of his plump wrists and the circles described by his short neck, we knew it beyond a doubt. His hands and his head told us too when the wind swung out the fall from the cliff and it floated like a blown scarf, and what delicious fear was felt by the bird. Constantine is a true poet. He knows all about things he knows nothing about.

We heard laughter. On the mountainside beyond the river three peasant girls were taking a walk, in bright dresses which showed a trace of Turkish elegance, which recalled that the word used for "well-to-do" in this district means literally "velvet-clad," and Constantine's bird-ballet had caught their eye. They had huddled into a giggling group and watched him for some minutes, then burst into teasing cries, and waved their arms and rolled their heads in parody. Then when Constantine stood up and roared at them in mock rage, they squealed in mock fear, and fled along the path, across a flowery field, into a glade, and again across a field. In alarm the birds that had been fluttering through the spray flew out into the void of the abyss and divided to the right and left. The three girls took hands and laughed over their shoulders, louder than ever, with their heads thrown back, and entered a deep wood, and were not seen again. Constantine slumped forward, his head on his knees, and seemed to sleep.

When it grew cold we roused him, and walked slowly towards the town under flowering trees. The word *"Yaitse"* (or *"Jajce"*) means either little egg or, in poetry, groin, or testicle. I am unable to say what sort of poetry. The town is extravagantly beautiful. It stands on an oval hill that is like an egg stuck on the plateau above the river, and its houses and gardens mount over the rounded slope to a gigantic fortress; and it has the shining and easy look of a land where there is enough water. There is a royal look to it, which is natural enough, for it was the seat of the Bosnian kings, and an obstinacy about the wholemeal masonry of the city walls and the fortifications which is also natural enough, for it resisted the Turks for a painful century and in 1878 met the Austrians with dogged, suicidal opposition. Now it has a look of well-being, which is partly a bequest from the colony of wealthy Turkish merchants who settled here, and partly a sign that, what with pigs and plums and a bit of carpet-weaving and leather-working, things here are not going so badly nowadays.

The Austrians tried to direct their tourist traffic here, and that is why Yaitse owns an immense old-fashioned hotel with a Tirolean air. When I saw the high bed with gleaming sheets, so suggestive of ice-axes and early rising, I would willingly have lain down and gone to sleep, but already Constantine, who is never tired, had found a guide. This was a pale and emaciated lad, probably phthisical, for tuberculosis is the scourge of this land. All day long one sees peasants sitting on the ground, even shortly after rain, yet they rarely have rheumatism; but tuberculosis is as murderous as it is in the Western Isles. It seems to be the stuffy nights in the overcrowded houses that do it. The lad was the worse off for being a Christian; he had not that air of being sustained in his poverty by secret spiritual funds that is so noticeable in the poverty-stricken Moslem. Coughing, he led us through the white streets, in front of a fan of children that stared but never begged, to a gardenish patch, where steps led down into the ground.

We found ourselves walking through black corridors and halls, cold with the wet breath of the living rock. Black vaults soared above us, in hard mystery. From a black throne a sacrifice had been decreed, on a black altar it had been offered, in a black sepulchre it had been laid by; and throne and altar and sepulchre were marked with black crescent moons and stars. "These are the catacombs of the Bogomils," said the guide. That I believe is not certain; they are probably the funeral crypt of some noble Bosnian family, stripped of its skeletons by the Turks. But they revealed the imaginative bent which would find hermetic belief attractive. This subterranean palace came as near as matter could to realizing the fantasy, dear to childhood and never quite forgotten, of a temple excavated from the ebony night, where priests swathed and silent, though putatively *basso profundo*, inducted the neophyte by torchlight, through vast pillared galleries dominated by monolithic gods, to the inmost and blackest sanctuary, where, by bodiless whisper or by magic rite brightly enacted against the darkness, The Secret was revealed.

I felt agreeably stimulated. "This ought to be a setting for a wonderful play," I thought; but it would not develop past the image of the pale and powerful Master of Mysteries, sitting on his black throne and thundering his awful judgment. I could think of no event that would seem adequate as cause for pallor extreme enough to equal the blackness of the living rock, and I was forced to ask myself why, if this Master of Mysteries was so powerful, he had to do his work downstairs. I remembered that when Mozart wrote *The Magic Flute* in exploitation of our love for the crypto-cavern and the solemn symbol, he and his librettist had finally to turn their backs on the unresolved plot and go home whistling with their hands in their pockets. I remembered, too, that this strand of fancy had at first been identified with Christianity, but swung loose when Christianity became respectable and a church was as much a state building as a mint or a law-court. Then it identified itself with heresy; and, when religious tolerance had spread over Europe and heresy became dissent, it adopted political unrest and revolution as its field. Thus it happened that the secret societies of Europe, particularly those which had been formed in the universities, were responsible for '48. Now I was faced with a material expression of this fantasy, and realized my own inability to use it as a stepping-stone to any new imaginative position; I could see how it was that '48 led merely to '49, and to '50, and to all the other flat and doleful years; and how it was that left-wing movements, which are so often tinged with romanticism, fade away after the initial drama of their seizure of power.

"Come," said Constantine, "there are so many things to be seen in Yaitse, you cannot wait. There are two friends of mine who run a chemical factory here, you shall meet them tomorrow, and they have uncovered an altar of Mithras near here on the hillside, which I think you should see." As we came out of the crypt we saw that the afternoon had nearly become evening. There was a grape-bloom on the light, and the little children who were waiting for us cast their giants of shadows on the cobbles. We went on through the lanes till we found an orchard, opened a gate in the palings, and followed a path to the shed.

Inside it was quite dark, and the guide gave us candles. We raised them, and the light met the god of light.

It was the standard sculptured altar of Mithras. A winged young man, wearing a Phrygian helmet, his cloak blown out by the wind, sits on the back of a foundering bull, his left knee on its croup, his right leg stretched down by its flank so that his booted foot presses down on its hoof. With his left hand he grips its nostrils and pulls its head back, and with his right he is plunging a knife into its neck just above the shoulder. Mithras is not an Apollo, but a stocky divine butcher, and his divinity lies solely in his competence, which outdoes that of ordinary butchers. This is the supreme moment in his career. He so causes the earth. From the blood and marrow that ran forth from the bull's wound was engendered the vine and the wheat, the seed emitted by him in his agony was illuminated by the moon and yeasted into the several sorts of animal, while his soul was headed off by Mithras's dog, who had hunted down his body, and was brought into the after-world to be guardian god of the herds, and give his kind the safety he himself had lost.

The bas-relief is enormously impressive. It explains why this religion exerted such influence that it is often said to have just barely failed to supplant Christianity. That is an over-statement. It had no following among the common people, its shrines are never found save where there were stationed the soldiers and functionaries of the Roman Empire, and it generally excluded women from its worship. But it was the cherished cult of the official classes, that is to say the only stable and happy people in the dying state; and it must have had some of the dynamic force of Christianity, because it had so much of its content. The Christians hated it not only because it offered a formidable rivalry but because this sacrificial killing of the bull was like a parody of the crucifixion; and that was not the only uncomfortable resemblance between the two faiths. Tertullian says that "the devil, whose work it is to pervert the truth, invents idolatrous mysteries to imitate the realities of the divine sacraments. . . . If my memory does not fail me he marks his own soldiers with the sign of Mithras on their foreheads, commemorates an offering of bread, introduces a mock resurrection, and with the sword opens the way to the crown." He was also annoyed because virginity was practised by certain followers of Mithras. There is no pleasing some people.

But Mithraism has its own and individual attraction. Power, which is perhaps the most immediately attractive concept we know, is its subject matter. Mithras is the Lord of Hosts, the God of Victory, he who sends down on kings and princes the radiance that means success. This slaughter of the bull is a fantasy of the power that never runs to waste, that can convert defeat itself to an extreme refreshment. Mithras conquers the bull, which is to say, the power of mind and body conquers the power of the body alone. But it is not tolerable that any power of whatever sort should be wasted, particularly in the primitive and satisfying image of the bull, so there is invented a magic that makes him the source of all vegetable and animal life at a moment which it then becomes trivial to consider as his death. He even destroys death as he dies, for as the guardian god of the herds he guarantees the continued existence of his powerful species. Power rushes through this legend like the waterfall of Yaitse, falling from a high place but rising victoriously unhurt, to irrigate and give life.

It was so dark that even by candlelight one could see little: but the best way to see sculpture is not with the eyes but with the finger-tips. I mounted on the plinth and ran my hands over the god and the bull. Strength welled out of the carving. The grip of the god's legs on the bull recalled all the pleasure to be derived from balance, riding and rock-climbing and skiing; the hilt of the dagger all but tingled, the bull's throat was tense with the emerging life. My hands passed on from the central tableau. Right and left were the torch-bearers, one holding his torch uplifted, as symbol of dawn and spring and birth, the other letting it droop, as symbol of dusk and winter and death. How did this faith alter the morning? How did it improve the evening? What explanation of birth could it furnish, what mitigation of death? My finger-tips could not find the answer.

The central tableau showed that power was glorious and the cause of all; but all must be caused by power, for power is the name given to what causes all. That is to say, the central tableau proves that $x = x = x$. There are no other terms involved which can be added or subtracted or multiplied. The imagination came to a dead stop, as it had done in the crypt which we had just left. I remembered that there had been tacked on to the Asiatic elements in Mithraism a system something like Freemasonry, which put the faithful through initiatory ceremonies and made them in succession Ravens, Occults, Soldiers, Lions, Persians, Runners of the Sun, and Fathers. Each rank had its sacred mask, legacy from the tradition of more primitive cults. But when one had put on one's Lion's Head and walked about in procession, what did one do? One went home. So Mithraism waned, defended by martyrs who died as nobly as any Christians, and Christianity triumphed, by virtue of its complexity, which gives the imagination unlimited material.

We went through the fruit trees, their blossom rosy now with evening, and climbed to the heights of the town, between high houses with
steep tiled roofs, new churches, and old mosques. Women, often veiled,
leaned over balconies, out of suddenly opened casements; little dogs,
harlequined with the indications of a dozen breeds, ran out of neat little
gardens and bade us draw and deliver. We came at last to the fortress
that lifts a broad breast of wall and two hunched shoulders of strong
towers on the summit of the hill. This was built by the Bosnian kings,
who were warmed by a reflection of Byzantine culture, and it was occupied for centuries by the Turks; but, with the irrelevance scenery
sometimes displays, its interior is a perfect expression of French romanticism. As we walked round the broad turfed battlements we looked
on rough mountains that a fading scarlet and gold sunset clothed with
a purple heather made of light; and from the town below came the virile
and stoical cries of Slav children. But within the enceinte all was black
and white and grey, grace and melancholy.

It contained a deeply sunken park, such as might have surrounded a
château in France. In it there were several stone buildings fallen into
stately disrepair in the manner of the ruins in a Hubert Robert picture;
there was a long cypress avenue, appropriate for the parting of lovers,
divided either by the knowledge that one or both must die of a decline,
or by the appearance of the ghost of a nun; and there were lawns on
which ballet-girls in tarlatan should have been dancing to the music of
Chopin. It evoked all sorts of emotion based on absence. As the colour
faded from the sky, and it became a pale vault of crystal set with stars
blurred with brightness as by tears, and the woods lay dark as mourning
on the grey mountains, it was as if the park beneath had carried its point
and imposed its style on its surroundings. The moon was high and shed
on these lawns and cypresses and ruins that white bloom, that finer frost,
that comes before the moonlight. We felt an aching tenderness, which
was a kind of contentment; Constantine began to speak of the days when
he was a student under Bergson, as he always did when he was deeply
moved.

But the mind pricked on, as in the black crypt and before the Mithraic altar, to use this scene as a point of departure for the imagination.
And again I found no journey could be made. A ruin is ruined, nothing
of major importance can be housed in it. If the two lovers were consumed by a fatal illness, that was the end of them. If the ghost of a nun
appeared she would perhaps reveal a secret, such as the position of the
grave of her child, which would be rendered completely unimportant

by the fact that she was a ghost, since the existence of an after-life would
make everything in this life of trifling importance; or she would disappear, which would leave matters precisely as they had been. The dancers
would sometime have to stop dancing, to retreat on their slowly shud-
dering points into the shadow of the cypresses, until the undulating fare-
wells of their arms were no longer moonlit. None of the component
parts of this lovely vision admitted of development. Better men than I
am had felt it. The romantics are always hard put to it to begin their
stories, to find a reason for the solitude and woe of their characters; that
is why so often they introduce the motive of incest, a crime only really
popular among the feeble-minded, and open to the objection that after
a few generations the race would die of boredom, each family being restricted to a single hereditary hearth. And the romantics can never finish
their stories; they go bankrupt and put the plot in the hands of death, the
receiver, who winds it up with a compulsory funeral.

We went back to a hotel, pausing to blink through the night at a
kind of shop window in a church, a glass coffin let into the wall, where
there lies the last Bosnian king, a usurper and persecutor, yet honoured
because he was a Slav ruler and not a Turk. For half an hour I lay on
the steep and shining bed in my room, and then came down to eat the
largest dinner I have eaten since I was a little girl. There was chicken
soup, and a huge bowl of little crimson crayfish, and very good trout,
and a pile of palatschinken, pancakes stuffed with jam like those at Split
which the waiter had tried to make me lay up against the hungers of the
night, and some excellent Dalmatian wine. I said to Constantine something of what I had felt at the sights of Yaitse, and he answered: "Yes,
it is strange that there are sensations quite delightful which are nevertheless not stimuli; that there are spectacles which make us shiver with
pleasure of a quite refined and intricate sort and yet do not open any
avenue along which our minds, which are like old soldiers, and like to
march because that is their business, can travel. And listen, I will tell
you, it is very sad, for we need more avenues. Since some of the avenues
that our minds can march down very happily are bad places for us to go.

"Let me tell you a story of Yaitse. This was a great place to the Turks.
For them it was the key to Central Europe, and so for many years they
would have it. For seven years it was defended by a Bosnian general,
Peter Keglevitch, and at last he came to the end. He knew that if there
was another attack he could not meet it. Just then he heard that the
Turkish troops had left their camp and were massing in one of the ra-
vines to make a surprise sally on the fortress with ladders. So he sent

a spy over to talk with the Turks and tell them that he had seen they had gone from their camp, and had been very glad, and had told all his soldiers, 'Now you may laugh and be glad, for the enemy has gone far away, and you may sing and drink and sleep, and tomorrow, which is St. George's Day, your women and girls may go out as usual, to the mountains in the morning according to our custom and wash their faces in the dew and dance and sing.' But the Turks were doubtful, and they lay in wait at dawn, and they saw all the women and girls of Yaitse come out of their houses in their most beautiful clothes, and go down the steep streets to the lawns and terraces beyond the river, yes, where those most impudent ones were this afternoon. There they washed their dear little faces in the dew, and then some struck the strings of the gusla, and others sang, and others joined their hands and danced the kolo. Poor little ones, their fingers must have been very cold, and I do not know if they sang very well, for each of them had a knife hidden in her bosom, to use if her plan miscarried.

"Then, when the Turks heard them singing and saw them dancing they thought that what the spy had said must be true, and the fortress would be like a ripe fruit in their hands. But since they were always like wolves for women, they left their ladders and they ran down to rape the poor little ones before they started looting and killing in the town. When they were in the woodlands and marshes down by the river the Christians rose from their ambush and destroyed them. And the little ones who had been so brave went back to the city they had saved, and for a few more years they were not slaves.

"Now, that is a story that will send the mind marching on, particularly if it belongs to a good and simple man or woman. Peter Keglevitch was a cunning man, and it is right to be cunning, that the Turks and such evil ones may be destroyed. The little ones were very brave, and to save their city and their faith they risked all; and it is right to be brave, because there is always evil. And it is all so beautiful; for the little ones were lovely as they sang and danced, and they were trusted by their Slav men, so that there must have been an honourable love between them, and the desire of the Turks makes us think of other things of which we would be ashamed and which are nevertheless very exciting and agreeable. And St. George's Day is a most beautiful feast, and our mountains are very beautiful, and Yaitse is the most beautiful town. And so a man can give himself great pleasure in telling himself that story, and he can imagine all sorts of like happenings, with himself as Peter Keglevitch, with all the loveliest little ones being brave for his sake, and all his enemies lying dead in the marshes, with water over the face; and on that he can build up a philosophy which is very simple but is a real thing; it makes a man's life mean more than it did before he held it. Now, will you tell me what in peace is so easy for a simple man to think about as this scene of war? So do not despise my people when they cannot settle down to freedom, when they are like those people on the road of whom I said to you, 'They think all the time they must die for Yugoslavia, and they cannot understand why we do not ask them to do that but another thing, that they should live and be happy.' You have seen that all sorts of avenues our artists and thinkers have started lead nowhere at all, are not avenues but clumps of trees where it is pleasant to rest a minute or two in the heat of the day, groves into which one can go, but out of which one must come. You will find that we Serbs are not so. We are simpler, and we have not had so many artists and thinkers, but we have something of our own to think about, which is war, but a little more than war, for it is noble, which war need not necessarily be. And from it our minds can go on many adventures. But you must go to bed now, you look tired."

Yaitse (Jajce) II

"YOU must wake up at once," said my husband. But it was not next morning. The room was flooded with moonlight, and my watch told me that I had been in bed only half an hour. "Get up and dress," my husband urged me, "there is a female dentist downstairs." In his hand I noticed he held a glass of plum brandy. "She has a voice like running water," he continued, "and she says she will sing us the Bosnian songs, which in this region are particularly beautiful." "What is all this about?" I asked coldly. "She is the sister of Chabrinovitch, the boy who made the first attempt on Franz Ferdinand's life, and then threw himself into the river. She is the wife of the medical officer here and practises herself. Somebody in Sarajevo wrote and told her we were coming. Come down quickly. I must go back to her, Constantine is telephoning to his bureau in Belgrade, and she is all alone."

He left me with such an air of extreme punctiliousness that I was not surprised when I came downstairs to find a very attractive woman. She was not young, she was not to any pyrotechnic degree beautiful, but she was an enchanting blend of robustness and sensitiveness. She possessed the usual foundation of Slav beauty, lovely head bones. Her skin was bright, her eyes answered for her before her lips had time, and she had one of those liquid and speeding voices that will never age; when she is eighty it will sound as if she was an unfatigued and hopeful girl. In pretty German she said that she had come to take us to her house, where we could drink coffee and meet her husband, and so we went out into the moonlit town.

She was a little shy of us, since Constantine was still telephoning and we had to go alone. Like a foal she ran ahead, on the excuse that she knew the way; but kindness drew her back as we were going up an alley. "You would like to see," she said, and pointed to a small window in a white wall. We had already remarked a sound of chanting, and we found that we were looking into a mosque, where about a hundred Moslems were attending their evening rite. Through the dim light we could see their arms stretch up in aspiration, and then whack down till their whole bodies were bowed and their foreheads touched the floor in an obeisance that was controlled and military, that had no tinge of private emotion about it. The sound of their worship twanged like a bow. They rose again, relaxed, and we thought the prayer must be over; but again they strained up tautly, and again they beat the floor. It looked as if it were healthy and invigorating to perform, like good physical jerks, which, indeed, the Moslem rite incorporates to a greater degree than any other liturgy of the great religions. Five times during the day a Moslem must say prayer, and during these prayers he must throw up his arms and then get down to the ground anything from seven to thirteen times. As the average man likes taking physical exercise but has to be forced into it by some external power, this routine probably accounts for part of the popularity of Islam. We watched till a fezed head turned towards us. It was strange to eavesdrop on a performance so firmly based on self-confidence of success and solidarity with the big battalion, and feel diffident, not because one was on the side of failure and the beaten battalion, but because the final issue of the battle had been not as was expected. We went on to an apartment house that stood several stories high in the shadow of the fortress, and were taken into a home that recorded a triumph, which perhaps belonged truly to yesterday, but had certainly not been completely annulled by today.

It was a room that could be found anywhere in Europe. It had light distempered walls and a polished floor laid with simple rugs; it was hung with pictures in the modern style, bright with strong colours; the furniture was of good wood, squarely cut by living hands; there was a bowl of fruit on the sideboard; there were many books on the shelves and tables, by such writers as Shaw and Wells, Aldous Huxley and Ernest Hemingway, Thomas Mann and Romain Rolland and Gorky. This sort of room means the same sort of thing wherever it is, in London or Paris, Madrid or Vienna, Oslo or Florence. It implies a need that has been much blown upon since the last war ended and reaction got its chance; but it certifies that its owners possess honourable attributes. They have a passion for cleanliness, a strong sense of duty, a tenderness for little children that counter-balances the threat made to young life by the growth of the town, a distaste for violence, a courageous readiness to criticize authority if it is abusing its function. Such a room implies, of course, certain faults in its owners. They are apt to be doctrinaire, to believe that life is far simpler than it is, and that it can be immediately reduced to order by the application of certain liberal principles, which assume that man is really amenable to reason, even in matters relating to sex and race. They are also inclined to be sceptical about the past and credulous towards the present; they will believe any fool who tells them to fill themselves with some contorted form of cereal and despise the ancient word that recommends wine and flesh. These are, however, slight faults, easily corrected by experience, compared to the dirt and irresponsibility, violence and carelessness towards children, cowardice and slavishness, on which these people wage war.

Only the malign bigot hates such rooms. Even those who believe that there is more in life than such people grant must admit that these rooms are worthy temples to subsidiary gods. There are those who sourly remark that Bolshevism was made in such rooms. It is not true. The Russian exiles who were responsible for that sat on unmade beds in flats as untidy as Versailles or any medieval castle. They were the powerful people who never tidy up, who only happened for the moment to be out of power. But those who live in these swept and garnished rooms wish only to serve. In the hereafter they shall be saved when all the rest of us are damned.

It could be seen that the doctor husband was of salvation, like his wife: his handsome face spoke of kindliness, discipline, and hope. They gave us coffee, and we told them of the beauty of our journey, and they told us how homesick they had been when they had to leave Bosnia to take their training at the University in Belgrade, and how happy they had been to come back and practise here. They spoke of their work with a sternness which seemed strange in people who are in their own country, which we hear only from colonists and missionaries in Africa or Asia. But they were in the position of colonists and missionaries, because Austria left Bosnians in the position of Africans or Asiatics. "They did nothing for us," said the doctor, "nothing, in all the thirty-six years they were here. You can test it. Look for the buildings they left behind them. You will find a great many barracks, some tourist hotels, and a few—pitifully few—schools. No hospitals. No reservoirs. No houses for the people." They told us that when they had left Bosnia after the war to study in Serbia they had been astonished at the superior lot of the Serbian peasant. His country had been sacked and invaded, but nevertheless he was better fed and better clad than his Bosnian brother. "Liberation meant to us," said the dentist, "release from being robbed." I thought grimly of the many books written by English travellers between 1805 and 1914 which stoutly maintained that the Bosnians and Herzegovinians were so much better off, first under Turkey and then under Austria, than the free Serbs. It would be pleasant if this could be proved quite unconnected with the circumstance that the Turks and the Austrians knew how to entertain a Western visitor, while the free Serbs lacked the money and experience.

At length Constantine came in, and they greeted him affectionately. After we had drunk the ceremonial round of coffee that was brought in for him, he spoke to the dentist in Serb and she turned to us with a face suddenly flushed, the eyes and mouth happy and desperate, as in a memory of a love-affair that had been unfortunate but glorious. "Constantine says I am to tell you about my brother," she said. "But the story is so long, and it is so difficult for foreigners to realize. This will help you to understand some of it." She took from the book-case an album of photographs of the *attentat* that had been sent to her after the war by the Chief of Police at Sarajevo, and spread it out before us, and then walked up and down, her hands over her face, quivering in that lovely nervousness which, save when her sense of duty was organizing her, governed her being. Most of the photographs we had seen before; they showed the streets of Sarajevo, with the two poor stuffed and swollen victims being pushed on to their deaths, and the frail and maladroit assassins laying hold of the lightning for one minute, and then falling into the power of the people in the streets, who on this day looked so much more robust and autonomous than either the victims or the assassins that they might have belonged to a different race. But there were in addition some ghastly pictures of the terror that followed the assassination, when, long before any inquiry into the crime, hundreds of Bosnian peasants who had barely heard of it were put to death. There were some particularly ghastly pictures of men who had never known anything but injustice, misgovernment by the Turks and Austrians, poverty, and this undeserved death, and were now saying in grim pride with their wry necks and stretched bodies, "Nevertheless I am I." There were also pictures of some peasant women who hung from the gallows-tree rigid as saints on icons among their many skirts. There were several photographs of the fields round the barracks at various towns where these mass-executions took place, each showing the summer day thronged as if there were a garden-party going on, with the difference that every single face was marked with the extremity of agony or brutality. The interest and strangeness of the pictures were so great that I swung loose from what I was and for a moment looked about me, lost as one is sometimes when one wakes in a train or in an unfamiliar hotel; it might have been that we were all dead and that I was looking at some records of the death-struggle of our race.

Coming close to me, the dentist cried, in that voice which was delicious even when what she said was acutely painful, "But we have no record of the worst part, of what happened to him in prison. That should be known, for if such things happen it is not right that they should not be known. But it is dreadful to me to wonder what he did suffer, for you cannot think how delicate and fragile he was, my little brother. He was so—fine. If it had not been for the oppression never would he have done anything violent. So it was easy for them to kill him in prison." I asked, "Is it true, what they say, that he was bound to die, because before he went into prison he had tuberculosis?" "No, no, no," she protested, "never did he have anything of the sort before they got hold of him, never!" Then, correcting her impulsiveness by a lovely effort of self-discipline, she explained, "I have asked myself again and again, in the light of my medical training, if he suffered from anything of the sort, and quite honestly I do not think so, I cannot remember any definite symptoms at all. He was not robust, and he had a tendency to catarrh and bronchitis, but really there was nothing more than that. But it is the habit of our people to say when they see a boy or girl who is thin and weakly, 'He looks consumptive,' and the Austrians took advantage of that to excuse themselves."

It has always interested me to know what happens after the great moments in history to the women associated by natural ties to the actors. I would like to know what St. Monica had to do after her son, St. Augustine, heard the child in the garden say, "*Tolle lege, tolle lege*," and was converted to Christianity; how she treated with the family of the little heiress whom St. Augustine was then obliged to jilt, how she dismissed the concubine with whom he had been passing the difficult time of his engagement, how she gave up the lease of the house in Milan. These are the things you are never told. I said to the dentist, "Tell me what happened to you and your mother after the *attentat*." She said, "You cannot think how terrible it was for my poor mother. She knew nothing of politics, she had been married when she was a young girl, she had had many children, my father was a very stern man who would hardly let her speak and never spoke to her save to order her and scold her, she was quite dazed. Then suddenly this happened! Her eldest child tried to kill the Archduke and his wife—apart from anything else, she felt it was too grand for us, it could not happen. Then, that same evening, they came and arrested my father, and it was as if the end of the world had come, she had not known what it was to be without a man, without her father or her husband. I was no use to her. I was a girl, and indeed I was only fifteen. She was like a terrified animal. But then the next morning a neighbour climbed into her back garden and said, 'Come, you must escape, a mob is coming to kill you,' and she and I had to take the five children that were younger than me and my brother, and get them down the back garden and out through another house into the street beyond where another friend sheltered us. As we got clear we heard the mob wrecking our home. Then she was very brave. But for long she simply could not understand what had happened. Nothing in her life had prepared her for it.

"Later on, before she died, she saw that my brother had been very brave and had done something that history demanded, but at first it was only a disgrace and a disaster. You see, for long she was stunned by the terrible things that happened to us. We were taken with many other Bosnians to an internment camp in Hungary, and she and I had to earn money by working all day as laundresses, but even so my little brother and sisters were always hungry, and so were we, and many people died all round us. It was like Hell, and we grieved for my poor brother Nedyelyko, for we did not know what had happened to him, and even now, beyond the fact that he is dead, we do not know. Then at the end of the war it was still terrible, for one day they simply came to us and turned us loose, drove us out of the camp with no money and nowhere to go, and no clear idea of what had happened, and we were so weak and foolish and confused with suffering. That was a nightmare. Then, when we had found my father, we settled down again and all lived together in the same house. But it was not for long, she was a dying woman, and she lived only a year or two. I will show you a photo that we had taken of her on her deathbed only a few days before she died."

The dentist rose to fetch it, and Constantine said to me, prepared to hate me if I was unsympathetic, "It is the habit of our people to take photographs of their beloveds not only at weddings and at christenings, but in death too, we do not reject them in their pain." It marked a real division between our kinds. I could not imagine any English person I knew having had this photograph taken, or preserving it if by chance it had been taken, or showing it to a stranger. The mother's face was propped up against pillows, emaciated and twisted by her disease, which I imagine must have been cancer, like the petal of a flower that is about to die; her eyes reviewed her life and these circumstances that were bringing it to an end, and were amazed by them. The children's faces, pressing in about her sharp shoulders and her shrunken bosom, mirrored on their health the image of their mother's disease and were amazed by her amazement. But no part of their grief was being rejected by them, it was running through them in a powerful tide, it was adding to their power. Constantine need not have been alarmed, I felt this difference between his people and mine as a proof of our inferiority. To be afraid of sorrow is to be afraid of joy also; since we do not take photographs of our deathbeds, it is hardly worth the trouble to take photographs of our weddings and christenings. "Think of it," said the dentist, "there is such a sad and funny thing I remember about that photograph! We sent for the photographer and gathered round the bed; and afterwards we found that my father was hurt because we had not told him that the photographer was coming and he could not be included in the picture. It did not occur to him that to us he was the instrument of her martyrdom, that we would have thought it as odd to have him in a picture of her agony as it would be for the wife of a shepherd who has been fatally mauled by a wolf to include the animal in a last photograph of him. It showed how innocent he was in his severity, how it was all part of a role he had chosen and stuck to because he had not the sensitiveness to realize the consequences."

"This is what he was like," said the doctor, who had been turning over the portfolio out of which his wife had taken her mother's picture. He handed us a photograph of a man in peasant costume, with a face as completely "made-up" by an aggressive expression as Mussolini's, standing in a defiant pose in front of some banners bearing Serbian inscriptions of a patriotic nature. "He was a very stern Bosnian patriotic man," said Constantine; "see, these are the banners of his secret nationalist society. *Es musste mit ihm immer trotzen sein, immer trotzen.*" The dentist picked it up, looked at it for a minute as intently as if she had never seen it before, shook her head and put it down. "In the house, never a gentle word," she said. She buried her face in her hands, but began to laugh. "I can think of things that seemed terrible to me at the time, but now they seem funny. There was the time when I was chosen to recite for my class at the school prize-giving." "Yes," said the doctor, "tell them that, it always makes me laugh!" "Yes, please do," we said.

"It was when we still lived at Trebinye," said the dentist, "and already my brother and I were very ambitious, we meant to be educated, so I worked very hard, and I was top of my class. Therefore I was chosen to say a recitation at the prize-giving which was a great affair, all the functionaries came to it and even some of the officers and their wives, to say nothing of all the townspeople. But, of course, I was miserable when I heard that I was chosen, because I knew that all the other little girls who were chosen to recite for their class would have pretty new dresses and light shoes and stockings for the occasion, and I knew I would have nothing. We had nothing, none of us, never. We had only to ask for something and Father immediately felt that made it a duty to refuse it, lest we become spoilt and self-indulgent. It was no good asking our mother to speak for us. That would make it doubly certain we should not get what we wanted, he would then want to prove that he was master in his own house.

"But I began to see he was proud I had been chosen. I found out that he was taking about with him the local newspaper in which the choice of pupils was announced and showing it to his friends. So very, very timidly I approached him. I was not honest. Usually I was honest with him, however much he beat me. But this time—ah, I wanted so much a little soft, fine dress! So I went and I told him how I wanted a new dress and new shoes, and I thought I should have them, because the Austrians and Hungarians would be there and they would sneer at me as a Serb, if I was in my old clothes. And that impressed him. 'Yes,' he said, 'I see it, you must have a new dress, and new shoes, and new stockings. It must be done.' I shall never forget how my heart leaped up when I heard him say this.

"But I had not reckoned it was still my father who said I could have these things, and therefore it followed that they could not possibly be the things which I wanted and which would give me pleasure. The poor dear man began to think of these shoes and these stockings and this dress as expressions of his *Weltanschauung*. He became very smiling and mysterious, he treated me as if he were about to confer some benefit on me which I was not old enough to understand as yet, but which would astonish me when I came to full knowledge of it. Then at last a day came, just before the prize-giving, when he took me out to see what he had been preparing for me. We went to a bootmaker who had already made for me a pair of boots, immensely large for me so that I should not grow out of them, made so strongly that if I had walked through a flood I should have come out with dry feet, cut out of leather so tough and thick that it might have been from an elephant or a rhinoceros. For weeks he had been inquiring which cobbler in Trebinye made the stoutest footwear, used the most invincible leather. I put them on, saying in my heart, 'This cannot be true.'

"Then he took me to a tailor who tried on me a dress that was as incredibly horrible as my boots. For weeks the poor man had been going about the drapers' shops, in search of material that was strongest, that would never wear out. He had found out something with which one could build a battleship, I cannot tell you what it was like. It hardly went into folds. This had been made into a dress for me by a tailor, who had been chosen because he was an old man who made no concessions to modern taste and cut clothes as the people in the hill villages wore them, more like the cloths you put on horses and cattle. By the instructions of my father he had made my dress far too big for me, so that I should not grow out of it for years, and it even had deep hems, that felt like planks, so that the skirt would be long enough for me when I was a grown woman. It had even great insets in the bodice, for the days when my bosom should develop, that stuck out like capes.

"I cannot tell you what I felt like as I had this horror tried on me. But it was only a day or two before the prize-giving; and if there had been weeks and months before it happened, I still could have done nothing. For never had I seen my father in such a good humour, and this terrified me. I felt that interference in this state would lead to something so horrible that it could not be faced. My brother was very kind to me about it and I wept in his arms, but my mother was no use to me, because she was so dazed by my father, she said nothing but 'Hush, hush, you must not anger him!' So on the day of the prize-giving I crept into my school weeping. All my teachers and my school-fellows were very kind to me; they understood at once, for my father was well known for his severity. But the time came for me to speak my recitation, and then I had to stump on the platform in these horrible new boots that would have been suitable for a peasant working in one of our flooded valleys. I was scarlet, and with reason, for I must have been the most ridiculous sight in the world, less like a little girl than a fortress. But I stood there, and it seemed to me that this was just another battle in the endless war that I would have to carry on with my father all my life if I wanted to do anything, so I began my recitation as well as I could.

"I believe the audience was very kind. But I really knew nothing of what was happening, for I was caught up into an extraordinary state. I felt as if my mind was gagged, as if there was a bar preventing my feelings flowing in the natural direction, which was of course, for a child in such a situation, hatred. What was holding me back was the sight of my father in the audience. He was sitting far back, of course, because naturally as a patriotic Serb he would not sit in front where the Austrian and Hungarian functionaries would sit, but he sat in the front of the seats where the townspeople were, because he was much respected. So I could see him distinctly, and I could see that his face was alight as I had never seen it before, with a sense that at last, just for once in his troubled life, everything was going well, his daughter had wanted something sensible, and he had granted her desire, and added more to it, so that from then on he might be sure of getting more of that gratitude and obedience he craved. I could not love him, but I could not hate him. Oh, the poor dear, the poor dear!"

She burst into distressed and loving laughter; and her fingers, as if without her own knowledge, turned over the photograph of her mother, laying it with its face down, as if to protect the dead woman from the ancient enemy whose personality was being evoked by these memories. "My father had so many funny ways," she went on. "You have perhaps noticed how greatly our people, however poor they are, love to be photographed. It was so with him also. Whenever things seemed to be going well he wanted to take us all to the photographer's and be photographed in the midst of his children. But then when he quarrelled with any of us he would go round the house cutting our photographs out of the groups. But he would never destroy them; perhaps he was too much of a peasant, with primitive ideas of magic, and to burn the images of his children or to throw them into a waste-paper basket would have seemed too much like killing them. He kept them in a box, and when he took us back into favour he would paste them back into the group, so that some of our photographs presented a most extraordinary appearance. I would see one day that my little sister had gone, and then she would be back, and then she would be pasted in again—oh dear, oh dear, the poor man!"

Again she laughed into her hands; and again her husband said, a smile on his sane and handsome face, "It was extraordinary how it had never occurred to him that family life might be conducted agreeably. Once in Belgrade, long after the war, he came in and found me sitting in the café we frequented, and he asked me where my wife was. I said, 'I had an appointment to meet her here at six and she has not come yet.' He said, 'But it is already half-past. Tonight you must box her ears for this.' Then I said, 'But I married your daughter precisely because I know that she would never keep me waiting except for a very good reason, and in any case I am quite happy sitting here reading my papers and drinking my coffee, and furthermore I do not like striking women, particularly when I love them. So why should I give your daughter a box on the ears?' That horrified him. If I had said something really nasty, something really cruel and base, I could not have upset him more. He felt I was striking at the foundations of society."

"Yet, do you know," said the dentist, "in his last years he accepted everything. He used to talk of my whole life, of my profession, and even of my marriage as if it were something for which he had worked and planned." "Yes, indeed," said the doctor, "some months before he died we went out and had a meal alone together as my wife was away, and he said to me, 'Well, you know you have reason to thank me. I have brought my daughter up so that she is a good sensible girl, not just interested in foolishness as so many women are, and now you have a wife with a professional standing you can be proud of, whom you can treat as an equal.' " "Now what do you think of that?" said the dentist happily. But her face changed. She held up her forefinger. "Is not that one of my little ones?" "Yes," said the doctor, "I believe I heard a cry a minute ago, but I was not sure." "You might have told me," said the dentist, in a tone that was a little sister to reproach. "Would you care to see our babies?" she asked me, and as we went along the passage she explained to me, "They are not really our babies. My sister, the very lovely one who has her head against my mother's shoulder in that photograph I showed you, married and had four children, and recently died. So, as her husband has to live in the town and has to work very, very hard, we have adopted them."

The children were lying in two beds in a large room, with their four bright heads pointing to the four quarters of the compass. The little one had her feet right up on the pillow and her head down on her sister's stomach. They stirred and fretted a little as the dentist turned on the light, but they had the more than animal, the almost vegetable serenity, of well-kept children, which Tennyson described when he wrote of "babes like tumbled fruit in grass." As the dentist put them right way up and tucked them in, she laughed; and she said, after she put out the light and we were tiptoeing along the passage, "It is such a joke, you know, to have a ready-made family like this. To have the four children, that is grave and wonderful, but to have all of a sudden four little toothbrushes, and four little pairs of bedroom slippers and four little dressing-gowns, it is all like a fairy-story." She came back into the living-room much more placid than when she had left it. "Now you will hear some Bosnian songs," she said, her voice soaring as if it were glad that her mind were giving it liberty to sing.

Yaitse (Jajce) III

WHEN I awoke and saw the sun a pale-green blaze in the tree-tops below our windows, my husband was already awake and pensive, lying with his knees up and his hands clasped behind his head. "That was interesting last night," he said. "She loved her brother, but still to her the important person was the brow-beating father. She had to talk of him because he seemed to her the prime cause of everything in the house, and even the Sarajevo *attentat* seemed to her simply a consequence of him." "I remember there is an odd passage in the trial which shows that her brother was of the same opinion. Here, pass it, it is lying on the chair." I saw, for we had taken with us Mousset's French translation of the court proceedings. "Yes," I said, "it is right at the end. The father makes a few dreary contentious appearances in the evidence of other people, bullying, raging, having his son shut up in the police station because he had offended a pro-Austrian servant in their house and had refused to apologize, and so on. Then at the end they read a deposition made by the father, notably certain passages significant as regarding the father's opinion of the son. He complained of his children's ingratitude, and he expressed the hope that they in their turn might be treated in the same way by their own children." I thought of the plump children I had seen the night before, deep in their contented sleep in the airy bedroom, and shuddered on behalf of the dead. "The president of the court asked Chabrinovitch, 'Do you see what an ungrateful son you are?' and Chabrinovitch made rather an astonishing answer. He said, 'I do not wish to accuse my father, but if I had been better brought up, I would not be seated on this bench.' It was an odd thing for a man to say whose case it was that, granted the annexation of Bosnia, it was inevitable that he and his friends should murder the Archduke. It is the fashion now to sneer at Freud, but nobody else could have predicted that in the mind of Chabrinovitch his revolt against his father and his revolt against the representative of the Habsburgs would seem one and the same, so that when a question was put to him in court that associated the two revolts, he answered not with the reason of an adult, but with the excuse of a defiant child. How exactly this bears out the psychoanalytic theory that they who attack the heads of states are not acting as a result of impersonal political theory so much as out of the desire to resolve emotional disturbances set up by childish resentment against their parents!'"

"But wait a minute, wait a minute," said my husband. "I have just thought of something very curious. It has just occurred to me, does not Seton-Watson say in his book *Sarajevo* that Chabrinovitch was the son of a Bosnian Serb who was a spy in the service of the Austro-Hungarian Government?" "Why, so he did!" I exclaimed. "And now I come to think of it, Stephen Graham says so, too, in *St. Vitus' Day*." "This is most extraordinary," said my husband, "for Seton-Watson is never wrong, he is in himself a standard for Greenwich time." "And Stephen Graham may slip now and then, but in all essential matters he is in his own vague way precise," I said. "Yet all the same this cannot be true," said my husband; "this girl was talking under the influence of a memory so intense that it was acting on her like a hypnotic drug, I do not think she could have lied even if she had wanted to do so. And she never mentioned it; on the contrary she mentioned several things that were inconsistent with it, and she showed us that photograph of her father standing among the banners of a Serb patriotic society, which if he were a police spy would be a piece of Judas treachery such as the sister of Chabrinovitch could not bear to keep in her home, much less show to strangers."

"No, indeed," I said, "I do not believe that if she had known him to be a police spy she would have mentioned him to us. But there's something else than that. Chabrinovitch was a youth without reticence, and in the court at Sarajevo he did not care what he said against the Government. If his father had been a Government agent I believe he would have denounced him to the world, just as a young Communist would have denounced his father as a counter-revolutionary. Yet never once in all the pages of Chabrinovitch's evidence, and in any of the countless comments he made on the evidence of other witnesses, did he say, 'My father was a traitor to the Slav cause!' He says that he complained that his father hoisted both the Serbian and Austrian flags on his house, but that was not an individual act on the part of his father, it was a matter of conforming to a police regulation, which we know most people in Sarajevo obeyed. But there is no other act of his father's that is denounced by Chabrinovitch." "Could they perhaps not have known?" proceeded my husband. "The dentist at least must have considered the question," I said, "for if Seton-Watson and Stephen Graham spread this story it must be because they have heard it on good authority and from several sources. It must have come before her notice some time." "It is a mystery," said my husband; "but let us get up, once we get downstairs we will find Constantine and probably he will be able to clear up the mystery."

We found Constantine downstairs having a breakfast which was as admirable as the dinner. "You have stumbled upon something very intriguing, and very disgusting, and very frightening," said Constantine, "and lovely too, because it is the instrument of the martyrdom of a saint. But may I ask you, do you not find the coffee and the bread excellent?" "Yes, yes," we said. "My people know how to live," he purred, and continued. "It unfortunately happened that after the war we were all running hither and thither, and we had many other things to do besides write down what we had been doing. So the writing of the history of what happened at Sarajevo fell into the hands of a few who were clever enough to look to the future. Now, because there were no papers, because the reports of the trial were then lost to us, there was nothing for serious historians to work upon, and the field was free to anybody who had been in Bosnia at the time of the *attentat* and had come in contact with the conspirators. One of these was a young man who had certainly known the *attentateurs*, and who had himself been involved in the revolutionary movements of the students. It cannot be denied he has studied the subject very fully, and all foreigners who are writing about the *attentat* come and consult him. But unfortunately it happened that soon after the war this young man met Chabrinovitch's sister and fell madly in love with her. Many men have felt so about her; it is her voice, that makes one feel as if she was a *vila*," (the Serbian fairy, a kind of wood nymph) "and would dance with one for ever in the glades. But she could not love him, already she would marry with the doctor whom you saw last night. Long, long this other young man tried to change her heart for him, but it could not be done. So he went away, and then it appeared to him that the whole family of Chabrinovitch was not so wonderful, and he wished to destroy them with his scorn. So in everything he writes and tells, Chabrinovitch seems not such a hero after all. Just a little shade of scorn here, just a little touch of impatience there, and he spoils Chabrinovitch."

"I recognize that you are telling the truth," I exclaimed. "I can see that the descriptions of a jerky, fretful, loquacious, hysterical Chabrinovitch might be a jaundiced view of a vivacious, temperamental, and fluent personality such as his sister." "Yes," said Constantine, "there has been nothing grossly untrue said about Chabrinovitch, but it has all been made a little nasty and puny, and to this same cause I put down the story that Chabrinovitch's father was a police spy. I do not believe it, for I know that his daughter has heard it, and I know that she is such a good and true woman that she would not deny it unless she had investigated it and found it baseless, and if she had not found it baseless she would never have spoken his name again."

"What a cruel lie!" I exclaimed. "Oh, it will not be exactly a lie," said Constantine. "I do not think that this man would deliberately tell a lie. But he loved this woman, and because she does not love him he wants to prove that she and everything about her is worthless, and in this state of mind he thinks that facts bear a significance which he would certainly not see in them had he gained what he wanted. Here, I imagine, he has simply misinterpreted some incident, or rather given it greater weight than it merits. Think of Chabrinovitch's father. He was a monstrous egotist, *ein Subjektivist* without limit or restraint; it appeared to him that every part of the universe which was not him had shown the basest treachery by separating itself. We have seen how his children, who as you see from this specimen I have shown you (as I will show you all, all in my country) were really extremely serious, seemed to him ungrateful and unnatural. It is not to be imagined that when he was in a patriotic society, his comrades would not sometimes, and perhaps often, seem to be conspiring against him and their common cause, simply because they disagreed with him on some minute point of policy. It might quite well then happen that as a threat to his comrades he declared that he might leave the whole of them in the lurch and go off, and inform against them at the local police office. This threat may have been taken in earnest by some simple people, who might be misled by subsequent happenings into believing that he had carried it out, though he never did so. Other people, not simple but malevolent, may have spread stories that he had done so; for it cannot be expected that such a man would not make many bitter enemies. Moreover, it may have happened, perhaps just on one occasion, that Chabrinovitch's father may have denounced to the police some man in the Bosnian revolutionary movement whom he thought a danger to it. This is a method that was very often used by the revolutionaries in Russia under the Tsardom, to rid themselves of comrades whom they considered undesirable, on account of indiscretion or some form of indiscipline. Here amongst our people it was very rarely used; but remember this man was an exception, he was a law unto himself, it is just possible that he may have done it. Still, that he practised any sort of conscious treachery against his fellow-Serbs, and that he was in receipt of payment from the Austro-Hungarian authorities, that I do not believe." "What a shame that such a story should be told!" I said.

"No, not a shame," said Constantine, "it is something that could not be helped. For if a woman does not do a man the little favour of handing him over her body and her soul, regardless of whether she likes him, it appears to him the unvarnished truth that she is a leper, that her father is a hunchback who sold his country, that her mother was a cripple who nevertheless was a whore. Besides, I think between this man and Chabrinovitch there was to start with a little bit of dislike. I think he either gave evidence or made a deposition, and that Chabrinovitch commented on it in a way that makes one feel there had been a lack of sympathy——"

But at this point our table was approached by one of those pale persons in subfusc Western clothes, closely resembling the minor characters in a Maeterlinck drama, who carry messages in the Balkan countries. He said something to Constantine which made him burst into happy exclamations, and gave him a note. "Drink up your coffee, you English people are always eating," cried Constantine. He had been oddly showing his delight at the note by tearing it up into small pieces. "My two very good friends who are chemical manufacturers here are eager to see me, and they ask us to go down to the Temple of Mithras, so that they may show it to you more properly, but of course it is me they want to see, for we were very great friends when we were young in Russia." He hurried us out to our car and to the chemical factory, which stood among the grass and orchards on the outskirts of the town, incongruously urban, built with a gratuitous solidity that was considered appropriate to industrial architecture in Central Europe during the nineteenth century. But the two managers were not there, and Constantine stood, in an ecstasy of disappointment, crying, "But they told me to come here," and searching in his pockets for the note he had received. "You tore the note up at the hotel," I said. "You English are fantastic," said Constantine. "Why should I have done that?" By good fortune there drove up at the moment a large car, out of which there bounded, almost vertically, two huge men who fell upon Constantine and kissed him and smacked his bottom and cried out lovingly with voices such as loving bears might have. They paid no attention to my husband and me for some time, so delighted were they with this reunion with one whom they had evidently looked on as a little brother, as a fighting cock, and as a magician. They turned to us and cried, "Such a comrade he was, in Russia! Ah, the good little poet!"

But after a time Constantine told them that we must be moving on soon, and they became flushed with the prospect of half an hour's abandonment to their secret passion, which was archæology in general, and the Mithraic temple in particular, and with great loping strides they led us along a lane and down a field to the orchard. They came from the most Western Slav territories; one was a Croat, and the other, the taller, came from Slavonia, which used to be in Hungary; but both looked extremely and primitively Slav, as we think Russians ought to be. The taller, indeed, belonged to that order of Russian which looks like a gigantic full-bodied Chinaman. When we got to the orchard it was found that the key to the gate had been left at the factory, but they lifted up their voices and roared like bears in pain, and there came running up the hillside a workman in a beautiful braided plum-coloured peasant costume. When he had learned what was the matter he went away and returned with an axe and proceeded to break down a portion of the wooden fence round the orchard, which was of quite respectable solidity. While he was cutting, there approached us an extremely handsome and venerable old Moslem priest, well suited by the twist of white in his turban that announced his office, who, after greeting the men in our party, joined us, for no comprehensible reason, since he showed a profound indifference to both us and to what we were doing. When the gap was made we all filed through it, except for the Moslem priest. To him the sight of a statue representing the human form was forbidden, so he sat down with his back to the temple on a tree-trunk under a cloud of plum blossom.

It was too plain, the Mithraic mystery, this morning. The night before I had seen with my eyes the outlines and felt with my finger-tips the planes that made a massy hieroglyphic meaning strength. Now I could see the emotional overtones of the design, and its details. The god's face was empty of all but resolution, and resolution is not enough to fill a face; and that the bull's sexual organs were excessive in size would hardly be denied, even by another bull, and the scorpion that attacked them was as gargantuan. Grossness was being grossly murdered, with gross incidentals. No wonder women were not admitted to this worship, for it was distinctively masculine. All women believe that some day something supremely agreeable will happen, and that afterwards the whole of life will be agreeable. All men believe that some day they will do something supremely disagreeable, and that afterwards life will move on so exalted a plane that all considerations of the agreeable and disagreeable will prove petty and superfluous. The female creed has the defect of passivity, but it is surely preferable. There is a certain logic behind it. If a supremely agreeable event occurs it is probable that the

KORCHULA

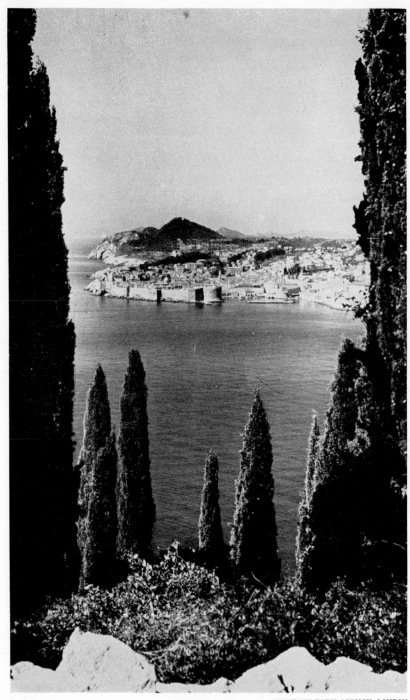

DUBROVNIK

human beings within its scope will be sweetened, and that therefore life will be by that much more harmonious. But there is no reason to suppose that a supremely disagreeable event will do anything, except strain and exhaust those who take part in it. It is not true that the vine and the wheat spring from the blood and marrow of a dying bull, the beasts from its sperm. The blood and marrow and sperm of the dead clot and corrupt, and are a stench.

The two giants exhibited this lunatic altar respectfully, because they too were male. But suddenly they caught sight of Constantine, who had climbed on an upturned basket, nosing in the side lines for additional symbols, and at the sight of his Pan-like plumpness they cried out, "Ah, the good Constantine, he is just the same as ever!" They spread out their arms and called to him, and he came down and let them smack and embrace him all over again. All three began to cry out, "Do you remember? Do you remember?" I was listening, and was quite unable to profit by it, to a passage of history that is, so far as I know, uncommemorated in Western history, yet is of considerable interest. After the Serbian Army had been driven out of its own country by the German and Austrian invaders and had reached the Adriatic by the famous retreat through Albania, a number of the survivors were sent to Russia. When the Revolution broke out some of these Serbians joined the Whites, and some the Reds. A number who had been in touch with Russian revolutionary propaganda at home played quite conspicuous roles in the Kerensky party. When the Bolsheviks seized power some were killed, and others followed Lenin; but they too were for the most part killed in the next few years. Only a few survive, and those whom one meets have escaped only by luck and preternatural daring.

The three survivors under my eyes were laughing so much that they had to lean against each other to keep on their feet. They felt they owed us an explanation, and the Croat wheezed out between his guffaws, "*Nous étions ensemble tous les trois dans la fortresse de St. Paul et de St. Pierre à Petrograd.*"[1] "*Oui, Madame,*" added the taller one, the Slavonian, "*moi et notre bon petit Constantin, nous étions enfermés dans la même cellule. Et après nous étions condamnés à mort, tous les deux.*"[2] At this point Constantine remembered a joke so rich that he staggered about and caught his breath while he tried to tell it to us. Pointing at the

[1] "We were all three together in the fortress of St. Peter and St. Paul at Petrograd."

[2] "Yes, Madame, I and our good little Constantine were shut up in the same cell, and afterwards we were condemned to death, both of us."

Slavonian, he gasped, *"Figurez-vous, il était deux fois condamné à mort. Deux fois! Deux fois!"* [1] At the thought of it they collapsed and sat down on the ground at the foot of the altar, crying with laughter. At last the Slavonian pulled himself together and said to us apologetically, wiping his eyes, *"Ah, que voulez-vous, Madame? On était jeune."* [2]

---

[1] "Just think of it, he was condemned to death twice. Twice! Twice!"
[2] "You know how it is, Madame! We were only young."

Yezero

THAT morning we followed the river of the waterfall some miles towards its source. It filled the trough of a broad and handsome valley, and interrupted itself every half-mile or so with shallow cascades, handsomely laid out in bays and scallops, and shaded by willow-gardens. In the lower reaches of the valley there are strung across these cascades lines of four or five mills, little wooden huts on piles, with a contraption working underneath which is a primitive form of the turbine. "It is here among my people," said Constantine in his fat, contented voice, "that the principle of the turbine was invented, hundreds of years ago." But the mills stand very high-shouldered nowadays, for some years ago Yaitse was shaken with twenty-three earth tremors, and a landslide altered the course of the river. To please Constantine we stopped the car and went into one of the mills, but lost heart, because there was a beautiful young man lying on the floor under a blanket, who woke up only to give a smile dazzling in its suggestion that we were all accomplices, and closed his eyes again. So we went on our way by the river, widened now into a lake, which held on its rain-grey mirror a bright yet blurred image of the pastoral slopes that rose to the dark upland forest, and which seemed, like so much of Bosnia, almost too carefully landscape-gardened. At the end it split with a flourish into two streams, which were linked together by a village set with flowering trees, its minaret as nicely placed as the flowers on those trees.

Some of its houses spoke, by lovely broken woodwork and tiled roofs fistulated with neglect, of a vital tradition of elegance strangled by poverty; and this was still alive in certain houses which in their decent proportions and their unpretentious ornament, kept trim by cleanliness and new plaster, recalled, strangely enough, some of the more modest and countrified dwellings in Jane Austen's Bath. There were lilacs everywhere, and some tulips. There was nobody about except some lovely children. From the latticed upper story of one of the houses that were rotting among their lilacs there sounded a woman's voice, a deep voice that was not the less wise because it was permeated with the knowledge of pleasure, singing a Bosnian song, full of weariness at some beautiful thing not thoroughly achieved. They became credible, all those Oriental stories of men who faced death for the sake of a woman whom they

433

knew only as a voice singing behind a harem window. Later, standing on a bridge, watching water clear as air comb straight the green weeds on the piers, we heard another such voice coming from a trim Christian house, divided from a wooden mosque by a line of poplars. This was more placid and less young, but was still urgent, urgent in its desire to bring out beauty from the throat, urgent to state a problem in music. Both these women made exquisite, exciting use of a certain feature peculiar to these Balkan songs. Between each musical sentence there is a long, long pause. It is as if the speaker put her point, and then the universe confronted her with its silence, with the reality she wants to alter by proving her point. Are you quite sure, it asks, that you are right? Are you quite sure it is not worth while being right about this thing? Then the melodic line gathers itself up and tries again to convert the inert mass of the silence by the intensity of its argument.

In an inn by the river we drank coffee. A gendarme came to see who the strangers might be, a huge old soldier with one eye missing and fierce grey moustaches. "Well, how goes it, old moustachioed one?" asked Constantine, laying his arm about the old man's shoulders. Something in the turn of his words gave credit to the old man as a soldier and a rebel and a descendant of the Haiduks, and he blushed and laughed with pleasure. The innkeeper's son, a pleasant boy in his teens, made himself agreeable by showing us the brown trout and the big crayfish wriggling in the floating box of their reserve. On the opposite bank was a prosperous Moslem house, bright as a Christmas present just off the tree, with a garden where the plants grew with a decorative precision we expect only from cut flowers in a florist's vase. It possessed a pavilion on the water's edge, and I was reminded, for the second time, of Jane Austen's Bath. Such little seemly shelters for those who love coolness and shade and the power to look out and not be looked at may be found on the banks of the Avon and on the park walls of great houses, where the traffic goes by. Indeed Bath and the surrounding country, with its towns that may be small but could not be taken for bumpkinish villages, and its enjoyment of private yet not greedy delights, such as walled gardens, is the most Moslem part of England that I know.

A veiled woman had flitted in, her puny shoulders rounded by the weight of something she carried under her overall. There was a murmuring with the innkeeper's wife in a corner, the veiled woman flitted off again, carrying herself straighter. There had been left for our inspection three boleros which a woman in the village, of a fine family now poverty-stricken, wished to sell. We laid them out on a bench and were abashed to see the value, for the price was a pound. All were of velvet, dark rose, soft scarlet, purple, and they were sewn so thickly with gold braid that the velvet appeared only as a steady factor behind the design which sprung and thrust and never lost its vital purpose in mere incrustation. Into the purple jacket some woman had put great cunning. Purple and gold are heavy matters, so she had placed here and there, by threes and sixes, tiny buttons of lavender and rose, always in a manner that lightened the burden on the eye, sometimes together, sometimes apart. "The woman who did this might still be alive in the village," I said. "I see they are old, but perhaps she sewed the jacket when she was very young." But I was wrong, for it was lined with an early nineteenth-century chintz. "How maddening that a person like that should have been swept away by time," I said; "but her work I shall save, I shall take that home and show it to people, and they will all like it, and I will leave it in my will to someone who will like it, and so it will be rescued from the past." "Of that you cannot be sure," said Constantine, "the past takes enormous mouthfuls. There may come a day when nobody will think that bolero beautiful, when it will seem simply tedious, or ludicrous, or even evil to those who lift it from the rag-bag.

"You are thinking that there are standards which do not change. But I will tell you a story of the town we have just left, of Yaitse, which will prove to you that objects which are beautiful and even sacred in the eyes of a whole people may lose their value in quite a few generations. When Bosnia fell to the Turks many of the Franciscan monks stayed where they were, but one house in Yaitse fled to the coast and set sail for Venice. They fled in order to save the dear treasure of their church, which was the body of St. Luke. It had been given to them by a daughter of George Brankovitch, the despot of Serbia, who had redeemed it for thirty thousand ducats from the Turks when they had seized it in Epirus. But when the poor Franciscans came to Venice, all was not well for them, and they were attacked as if they were pagans and had brought with them a false god. For there was already another body of St. Luke in Italy; some Benedictines at Padua had him already, and had had him for three hundred years, and he was the object of an impassioned cult of the people.

"The Yaitsean Franciscans had to defend their title at a trial before the Papal Legate at Venice which lasted three months. At the end the Papal Legate said, 'It is right what you say, your treasure is the true St. Luke.' But always the Franciscans were kept very poor and very unhappy, for the Paduans tried again and again to get the judgment reversed. At that I cannot wonder, for they had a strong point in their favour. Their body was headless, the Yaitsean Luke was whole, he had all; but about 580 the Emperor Tiberius had given St. Gregory the head of St. Luke, which was still in the Vatican, and which was still shown to the people as his true head even after the Papal Legate had pronounced that the whole body from Yaitse was the true St. Luke. No doubt he was in a position where he found it difficult to be logical, for another church in Rome had long been curing the sick by an arm of St. Luke, which was now certainly the third.

"There is nobody today to whom that story would not seem absurd, except very simple people, too simple people, idiots. Those who believe in the power of relics and who are solemn will beg you not to talk of such things, not to recall how the stupidities of our ancestors made foolish a beautiful thing. But most people, whether they are believing or not, will only laugh. But the people of five hundred years ago did not see anything ridiculous in a dead man with two heads and three arms, all working miracles; and they did not feel suspicious because many monks made much money out of such dead men. They saw something else, which made them add a head and a head and make it one head, and two arms and one arm, and make it two arms, and we do not know what that something was. For me, I hate it when I read history and I see that now there is nothing where once there was something. It shows me that man has been eating food which has done him no good, which has passed out of him undigested."

ROAD

A man fishing from a boat in the middle of the lake stood up and with wide sleeves waved what looked like a greeting; but he must have been a supernatural being in control of the elements, and very disagreeable in disposition, for at that moment a rage of rains broke on us. We saw nothing of our road till, at Vakuf, Christian women wearing woven aprons of bright winy colours, Moslem men with fezes, Moslem women with black muzzles, stood in mud during a moment's sunshine, marketing tiny piles of vegetables, lean and hungry livestock. Then it rained again, and we saw as little of the new road we took when we turned aside at Vakuf, save once when we left the car and stood by a thicket of blackthorn that climbed over great tombs resting on stone platforms. They are said to house the Bogomil dead, and they have the massive and severe quality which belongs to all manifestations of their heresy. But the blackthorn, polished silver in a sudden outpouring of sunshine, redeemed them. Then we came on a town that lay on the flat of a plain with the tedium of a military station which strategy has dumped where natural man would never halt. "This," said Constantine, "was an important garrison in Austrian days."

It was time for the midday meal, and we stopped at the hotel, which was quite big. We went into a dining-room where a surprisingly large number of people, including a good many military officers, were sitting at a small table and eating in a silence broken only by furtive whispers. I thought that they had perhaps come to the town to attend the funeral of some great personage, and after we sat down I asked Constantine if this could be the case, but he answered as softly, "No, I think there must be some generals here." And it was so. Presently four officers, of whom two were generals, rose from a table and went out; as soon as they had passed through the door conversation soared and filled the upper air, noisy as a flock of London pigeons. Our wine was given us long before our food, and proved to be very palatable, red and sweetish, not like any French wine but quite good. We were wondering where it came from, for its name gave no indication, when we received a visit by the landlady. I found her suddenly, leaning over the back of my chair, an elderly Jewess, with a chestnut wig, rapidly undulant in her cringing. We asked her about the wine, and she answered, "It is from Hungary." "What?" said Constantine. "But it cannot be from Hungary, it is too cheap; it cannot have had any duty paid on it, it must be from Yugoslavia." "No," she said, "it is from Hungary, it is from the Voivodina."

Somebody called her away, and she left, with a gait so conditioned by continual cringing that even between tables she bowed from right to left and pressed her clasped hands forward in objectless obeisances. Constantine said, "But why does she call the Voivodina Hungary? It has been ours since the war, it is the centre of Banat. She must have some reason to hold to the old Austrian days." We then thought for some time of nothing but our food, which was excellent, not in the Balkan but in the Central European way. There was vegetable soup without paprika, lamb stew of a Viennese type, and superb Apfelstrudel. But while we were eating it the Jewess came back and wavered about us, and my husband said to her, "What beautiful German cooking you are giving us, and what beautiful German you speak. May I ask where you learned your German?" "It is my native language," she said, and explained that she had been born in a certain town on the borders of Austria and Hungary. "But I have been here for fifty-two years. Fifty-two years, my dear," she repeated coquettishly, and slowly drew her hand down my arm with the rancid tenderness of the procuress. There could be felt the iron hand in the dirty velvet glove. It was sickening to reflect how often in those fifty-two years she must have brought to the exigencies of brothel life all they needed. One could see her wiping up the vomit of drunkenness, striking some soft white body into the required posture and conducting some forcible examination in search of venereal disease, jerking a frightened child by the arm and telling her not to whimper, carrying basins and perhaps performing direct services in the matter of hopeless and murderous abortions. "I am glad you drink my poor wine. I am glad you eat my little bit of an Apfelstrudel," she carnied, and bowed backwards to the door. "Yes," said Constantine, "you are perfectly right. I expect she came here when she was a little girl of sixteen or so, to be with the officers. I think she must have been very beautiful. And then as she got older she managed a house. So the Austrians spread culture among us barbaric Slavs. So she would hunger always for her dear Austrians, and say that the Voivodina is in Hungary."

As he spoke the old woman came back, followed by an elderly man, a middle-aged man, and two women in their late thirties or early forties, who sat down at a table near us. We had come late, and by this time the dining-room was nearly empty, so she and her family were having their meal. The elderly man was evidently her brother and the others her children, but they were malevolent parodies of her. In the stock that had produced her vigour some poison had been working which had spared only herself. Her features, which in her heyday must have had a Semiramic richness and decision, were in these others splayed into Oriental rubbish. Heaps of bone, they carried long stooping bodies on uncertain feet that turned out at obtuse angles. It was apparent when the meal was brought to them that the parody had been carried to a cruel height. They could not eat properly. Often the soup missed their mouths and ran down their chins into their plates. As the landlady sat at the head of the table, lifting the good soup she had made to her lips with a steady hand, looking on them with weary and tender eyes, and occasionally indicating some dropped food with a word or a proffered napkin, it appeared that to herself her life might seem like the triumphant bearing of a cross, a moral victory of which she might be proud. It was a point not to be denied too hastily. Nevertheless, she was cruelty; she was filth.

Sarajevo VIII

WE were at a party at the Bulbul's. She had a house on the quay by the river, not far from the corner where Franz Ferdinand was killed, a modern house which owed its handsomeness to the Turkish tradition, for it was full of light and clear of unnecessary furniture, and in the large reception room on the first floor there was a raised dais by the windows, running right across the floor, which is a common and charming feature of Moslem houses. What furniture there was was the best obtainable of its kind, but that kind is not good. There is no fine European furniture in the Balkans except a few baroque pieces in Croatia and Dalmatia. It is a contrast with the North of Europe, where the wealthy Danish and Swedish merchants and Russian landowners spread the knowledge of Chippendale and Sheraton right across the Baltic. The Turkish domination cut the Balkans off from that or any other European artistic tradition; and when the Balkan peoples came in contact with it, it was through the intervention of Central Europe, where there has never been any good furniture except the baroque and the Biedermeier, which were based entirely on fantasy rather than on sound principles of design and thus could found no school of cabinet-making. Taste degenerated more rapidly in Austria during the nineteenth century than in any other country, with the possible exception of Russia, so she imposed on the Balkans a corrupt fashion in these matters. A bookcase and a sideboard made by a man who knows nothing of what the masters of his craft have discovered in the past are apt to be merely large boxes; and if that man believes that quantity can be a substitute for quality, those boxes are apt to be very big and clumsy indeed.

But the little Bulbul had bought the best furniture that this dispensation produces, and her carpets and hangings were all beautiful in the Oriental style; and there was in every clean and sunlit square inch of the house a sense of housewifery that was conscientious yet leisurely, inspired not by irritable dislike of dirt but through sensuous preference for cleanliness. She herself was unhurried, in a crisp dress that made her edible beauty cool without chill, like the flesh of a melon. Her husband was gracious and sculptural, gentle, even soft, and yet immovable, imperishable, as a granite monolith might be that was carved in the likeness of a tender and amiable god. They had other guests, his sister and her son, who was studying science at Zagreb; in each of them giant liquid eyes and a purposeful scimitar slimness transmitted the Sarajevo tradition of prodigious good looks. It is the misfortune of the Jews that there are kinds of Jews who repel by their ugliness, and the repulsion these cause is not counterbalanced by the other kinds who are beautiful, because they are too beautiful, because their glorious beauty disconcerts the mean and puny element in the Gentile nature, at its worst among the English, which cannot stand up to anything abundant or generous, which thinks duck too rich and Chambertin too heavy, and goes to ugly places for its holidays and wears drab clothes. Many Gentiles, very many English, might have come out of this room hating the people inside for no other reason than their physical perfection.

The talk, also, might have been too good for a Western visitor. The artist among these people so far as talking was concerned was Constantine, who could exploit his own brilliance with the ancient cunning of the Oriental story-teller; but everybody in the room knew how to support the star; they not only understood what he was saying, they knew the play, they could give him his cues. Such conversation demanded attention, discrimination, appreciation, all forms of expenditure which we Westerners, being mean, are apt to grudge. But, indeed, the main objection an English person might have felt against this gathering was its accomplishment and its lack of shame at showing it. When we rose from the table we went into the sunlit room with the dais, and drank coffee which had had an egg beaten into it so that its black bitterness should be mitigated more subtly than by milk, and then, as the saying goes, we had a little music. A little music!

The Bulbul took up her gusla and, in a voiçe exquisitely and deliberately moderate, she sang many Bosnian songs. She did not sing them like the women in Yezero, for she was not Slav and she had not made that acceptance of tragedy that is the basis of Slav life. It was as if she were repeating in a garden what she had heard the wild Slavs wailing outside the walls. Mischievously she sang a love-song with her eyes fixed on my husband's face, because it is the custom of the country to sing such songs looking steadfastly into the beloved's face. Everybody laughed because it was understood that an Englishman would find this embarrassing, but he acquitted himself gallantly, and they clapped him on the back and told him they thought him a good fellow. This too recalled Jane Austen's Bath; such a pleasantry might have enlivened a drawing-room in the Crescent.

Presently the Bulbul put her gusla in her husband's hands and said,

"Now you," and with adoring eyes she turned to her guests and explained, "I sing and sing well, but he not only sings, he has a voice." It was true. He had a voice like drowsy thunder, forged by a god only half awake. He sang a Serbian song, longer than most, about the pasha of the town where Constantine was born, Shabats. He was a drunkard and a gambler: the song suggests a mind dazed, as one has seen people in the modern world, at casinos and over card-tables, by a certain amount of alcohol and the ecstatic contemplation of number, divided from any substance. He had played away his fortune; he sat penniless in the shell of his splendour. He suffered like a morphinomaniac deprived of his drug because he could not gamble, so with the leisurely heartlessness of the drunkard he ordered that his mother be taken down to the slave-market and sold as a servant. But his wife, who was young and beautiful and noble, came and, with the even greater leisureliness of the heart-broken, told him that she must be sent to the slave-market and sold instead of his mother; for there is disgrace and there is disgrace, and one must choose the lesser. The song presents ruin in a framework of decorum, it takes up the melancholy of drunkenness and the coldness of long-standing vice and examines them as if they were curiously coloured flowers.

But in a later song he paused, smiled, repeated the last phrase, and sang a phrase from a song by Schumann which was like a translation of the other into its different idiom. The science student ran to the piano, and everybody joined in snatches of Schumann's songs. They went on well with "The Two Grenadiers," with Constantine in the middle of the room, acting it as well as singing it, until he spread out his arms and thundered, *"Mein Kaiser, mein Kaiser gefangen,"* and the foolish little white dog which was the Bulbul's only apparent weakness woke up in its basket and leapt forward barking, anxious to lend any help that was needed. They laughed; they were not ashamed to laugh, laughter is agreeable, and they had come here to enjoy agreeable things together. Then they began to sing again, but this time in mockery, pursuing German romanticism from lyric to lyric, passing from "Myrtillen und Rosen" to "Poor Peter." Constantine, very stout and very red with lunch and happiness, and still accompanied by the kindly and questioning dog, enacted poor Peter. (*"Der arme Peter wankt vorbei, Gar langsam, leichenblass und scheu."*) [1] In spite of all their clowning they were singing their four parts exquisitely, and their parody was a serious criticism of the romantic spirit. But Constantine put up a prohibitory hand and said,

---

[1] "Poor Peter totters slowly by, pale as a corpse, and full of fear."

"Enough. Now let us restore ourselves by contact with the genius of the great Nordic One. Are we not all Aryans?" And they passed into a compost of scenes from the *Ring*, which went very well considering that Constantine was singing the character of Carmen. Why Carmen? They knew. It was because Nietzsche in a famous passage expressed a belief that what Wagner needed was an infusion of the spirit of Bizet. Therefore in this performance of the *Ring* Siegfried and Brünhilde were sustained through their troubles by the companionship of the gipsy, and "Yo-ho-eo" mingled with the "Habañera." Such musical virtuosity and such rich literary allusiveness is, in my experience, rarely the sequel of English lunch-parties.

There came into the room as we applauded, quiet-footed and with his perpetual air of gentle cheerfulness about all particular issues and melancholy about our general state, our friend the banker, whom we had not seen for some days. The Bulbul detached herself from the singers for a moment and came to have her hand kissed, and stood by us for a little till they haled her back, and she left us with the prettiest smile of real regret thrown over her shoulder, though she was glad to sing again. I think her idea of perfect happiness would have been to find herself simultaneously feeding every mouth in the universe with sugar plums. The banker watched his friends with a smile for a moment or two, and then asked us how we had enjoyed our trip through Bosnia. I said, "It was beautiful beyond anything. Travnik was lovely and Yaitse better still. But best of all I liked the sister of Chabrinovitch." "You are like the dwarf in the fairy-tale who declared, 'Dearer to me than any treasure is something human,' " he said. "I am sure you are right, you will not see better than her in any journey. She is truly noble." I spoke also of Yezero and the jackets, of Vakuf and the women with the wine-coloured aprons, and lastly of the terrible old woman at the inn where we had eaten. "You are quite right," he said, "she would be what you suppose. Indeed, I think I have heard of this woman. I will speak to you now of things that you will not read about in any of the books that were written by English travellers who visited Bosnia while the Austrians were here." "Which, if I may say so, were not very intelligent," I agreed. I had that morning been reading one which I thought imbecile. The author had circulated in fatuous ecstasy among the Austrian and Hungarian officials, congratulating them on having introduced the mulberry tree, which had been a most prominent feature of the Bosnian landscape under the Turk, and congratulating the Governor's wife, "called, not unjustly, the 'Queen of Bosnia,' " on teaching handicrafts to such women as had

made the purple bolero at Yezero. "You see, we were not an easy people to govern any time in the occupation before or after the annexation. The soldiers were all paid as if they were on active service, and the
functionaries also were given specially high salaries. This meant that a
great many camp-followers came down to our country to batten on
these men who had plenty of money and no natural ways of spending
it. It had something of the atmosphere of the Klondike rush. And there
were many, many prostitutes among these, and of these many were
Hungarians, not that they are a people lacking in virtue, but that the
land system left many of the peasants so poor that they had to send
their daughters out to service in the world or see them starve. So it happens that for us Hungarian is the language of gallantry, even as French
is in London."

He paused. The singers had stopped their opera, and were singing old
favourites. "Let us sing 'Wow—wow—wow—,'" said Constantine, and
nobody could for a moment fail to realize that he meant "Ay, ay, ay."
"The fault," continued the banker, "is not with these women, who are
often exceedingly kind and good, and achieve every kind of moral victory that they are permitted, but with the Austro-Hungarian Empire,
which, although pretentiously Roman Catholic, violated all Catholic
counsels of chastity by itself organizing a system of brothels in our
country, which could not be excused on the grounds of the necessities
of the troops. Certainly the brothels they opened in Sarajevo were far
in excess of the requirements of the garrison and the functionaries.
There were five very large expensive ones, which were known as The
Red Star, The Blue Star, The Green Star, and so on, and two for the
common soldiers, The Five Matches and The Last Groschen. It was a
wicked thing to do to our town, for before that we had not such things.
We Jews have our traditional morality, which was then undisturbed.
The Serbs and Croats are a chaste, patriarchal people; where a man
will kill any other man who has taken the virtue of his wife or daughter
there must be a harsh kind of purity. All cases where our codes broke
down were met by the gipsies, whose part it is alone among the nations
of the world to exorcise dishonour. But we had never known prostitu-
tion, and there is something extremely exciting to a young man in the
knowledge that he can acquire the enjoyment of a beautiful girl by payment of a small sum. To many of us, also, the furniture of the brothels
was a revelation of Western luxury. Those who did not belong to families who had been wealthy for a long time had never seen big mirrors
before, or gold chairs covered with red velvet, and they were profoundly

impressed. I am afraid that his Catholic Majesty the Emperor Franz
Josef did not sin only against purity when he organized these brothels;
he committed also the sin of conspiring for the souls of others. For I
am sure the intention was to corrupt all the young men of Sarajevo
so that our nationalist spirit should be killed and Bosnia should be easy
to govern. But this would not be only a political move; the thought of
the corruption would in itself be delicious, for the Austrian hates the
Slav, every German hates the Slav, with an appetite that simple death,
simple oppression cannot satisfy."

He added, "But I wonder if you can understand how mighty hatred
can be. I think you English do not, for you have long been so fortunate
that nobody else's hatred could touch you, and you had yourselves no
reason to hate anybody. Let me point out to you that in your journey
to Travnik and Yaitse there was one thing you did not see. You saw
nothing of the kingdom of Bosnia. You saw a few fortresses, and perhaps
a church or two, and probably the funeral vaults of the Vakchitch family. There is nothing else to see. Yet once the Doge of Venice wrote to
the Pope, 'Under our eyes the richest kingdom of the world is burning!'
and he meant Bosnia. Conquest can swallow all. The Turks consumed
Bosnia. The Austrians did what they could to consume that little which
remained, but they then had weak mouths. But sometimes I fear lest
some of their blood have grown strong jaws like the Turks."

Serbia

SERBIA

TRAIN

WE left Sarajevo in the early morning, picking our way over the peasants who were sleeping all over the floor of the station. Nothing we believe about peasants in the West is true. We are taught to think of them as stolid, almost physically rooted to the soil, and averse from the artificial. Nothing could be less true, for the peasant loves to travel, and travels more happily by train than on horseback. In old Spain I first remarked it. At the junctions trains used to stand packed as they are in the English Midlands, where there are myriad commercial occasions to set people travelling; but these had nobody in them except peasants who can have had the slenderest material motives to leave their homes. In the account of the Sarajevo trial the mobility of the prisoners and the witnesses is far greater than that of anybody in England below the more prosperous middle classes. Now that the country is self-governing and there are fewer restrictions, every train and motor omnibus is stuffed with people amiable with enjoyment, as if they were going to a Cup Tie, but with no Cup Tie whatsoever in view.

The journey out of Sarajevo is characteristic, leisurely and evasive and lovely. The train starts at the bottom of the bowl in which the city lies, and winds round it and comes out at a nick in the rim. There is a high station at the nick, and there one looks down for the last time on the hundred minarets, the white houses, and the green flames of the poplars. Thereafter the train travels through a Swiss country of alps and pinewoods, with here and there a minaretted village, until it goes into a long wooded gorge, which has one superb moment. Where two rivers meet they thunder down on each side of a great rock that has been sharpened by ages of their force to a razor-edged prow. Sometimes we looked at the scenery and sometimes we slept, and often we listened to Constantine, who throughout our entire journey, which lasted thirteen hours, talked either to us or some of the other passengers. The first time

I was in Yugoslavia Constantine took me down to Macedonia so that I could give a broadcast about it, and when we arrived at Skoplje I thought I would have to run away, because he had talked to me the whole time during the journey from Belgrade, which had lasted for twelve hours, and I had felt obliged to listen. Now I know that in conversation Constantine is like a professional tennis-player, who does not expect amateurs to stand up to his mastery for long, who expects to have to play to relays, so sometimes I did not listen to him, until I caught one of the formulas which I know introduce his best stories.

"When you are in Belgrade," said he to my husband, "you will meet my wife. My wife she is a German. She was very, very beautiful, and she is of a very old German family, and they did not wish her to marry me, so I rapted her from them in an aeroplane. And for long they would not be good with me, and I was not always very fortunate in the efforts I made to win them. You see, my mother-in-law she is the widow of a Lutheran pastor, and I know well that is a different religion from mine, but I think there are only two Christian religions in Europe, and one is the Orthodox Church and the other is the Roman Catholic Church. Now I know that my mother-in-law is not an Orthodox, for one of the things that disgusts her with me is that I am Orthodox, so it seems to me that to be Lutheran is to be some kind of Catholic. Perhaps a Catholic that lets his pastor be married. So one day my wife and I are staying with my mother-in-law among the mountains, and my mother-in-law and I are having breakfast on the balcony, before my wife has come down, and there is sunshine, and the coffee is so good, and there are many flowers, and I am so happy that I say to myself, 'Now is the time to make myself pleasant to the old lady,' so I say to her that I see in the papers that the Pope is ill, and that I am sorry, because I think very well of the Pope, and I give her instances of all the things that have made me think the Pope is a good and wise man. I point to the snow peaks in the distance, and I say that to climb such heights is a great achievement, and so often had done the Pope, for he is a great mountaineer; and from that I pass on to the Papal Edicts, and praise their wisdom and discretion. And my mother-in-law says nothing to me, but that does not surprise me, because often I talk all, and others not at all. But then my wife comes down and my mother-in-law stands up and cries to her, 'Look at the savage you have married, that sits there and on such a beautiful morning praises in my very face the Pope, who is the devil!'

"And from her side the efforts to be friends with me are often not very good, though in time she came to like me. It is so with the white beer. Do you know white beer? It is the last of all that is *fade* in the world, and it is adored by the *petite bourgeoisie* in Germany. They go to the beer-gardens in the woods and by the lakes and with their little eyes they look at the beauties of their Germany, and they drink white beer, which is the most silly thing you can drink, for it does not taste of anything and cannot make you drunk. It is just like the life of the *petit bourgeois* in liquid form, but it is gross in its nothingness, so that some of them who have shame do not like it, and order raspberry syrup to add to it. But there are those who are not ashamed of being *fade* and they would not spoil it with a flavour, and they order '*ein Weisses mit ohne . . .*' *Mit ohne, mit ohne,* could you have anything that is better for the soul of the *petite bourgeoisie* that is asked what it wants and says, 'I want it with without.' That is to be lost, to be damned beyond all recovery, and yet there they are very happy, they sit in their beer-gardens and ask for *mit ohne*. It is altogether delicious, it is one of those discords in the universe that remind us how beautifully God works when He works to be nasty. Once I said this in front of the mother-in-law, and do you know ever after she gives me to drink this horrible white beer. And my wife has tried to tell her she should not do so, and my mother-in-law says, 'You are foolish, I have heard him say he likes very much *mit ohne*,' and my wife she says, 'No, you have it wrong, it is the expression *mit ohne* he likes,' and my mother-in-law says, 'How can you say such nonsense, why should he be pleased when people say they will have white beer without raspberry syrup?' And to that there is nothing to be said, so I must drink white beer, though I am a Serb and therefore not a *petit bourgeois,* but a lord and a peasant."

We were passing through lumber country, by a river on which we saw the lumbermen steering great rafts of logs over the rapids. "Some day you must travel so," said Constantine, "in the calm places you will hear the men singing so wonderfully." We passed through Vishegrad, a lumber town with many stacks of new logs and old houses, with minarets and a wide brown bridge over which there rode on a pack-horse a Moslem who must have been very old, or from the far south, for alone of all Bosnian Moslems I have ever seen he wore the head-dress which preceded the fez among the Turks, the turban. Then I slept a little and woke up in a little town where there was not a minaret, where there was no more trace of Islam than there would be in a Sussex village. We were, in fact, in Serbia. We went and stood on the platform and breathed the air, which was now Serbian air. It is as different from Bosnian air as in Scotland the Lowland air differs from Highland air; it is drier and, as they say of pastry, shorter. Anybody who does not know that it is one pleasure to fill the lungs up at Yaitse or Loch Etive and another to fill them down at Belgrade or the Lammermuir Hills must be one of those creatures with defective sensoria, who cannot tell the difference between one kind of water and another. On the platform a ceremony was going on, for there was travelling on our train an officer, a light-haired boy in his twenties, who had once been in the garrison of this town, and had afterwards been moved south and was returning northward to take up some new and more exalted duty. The people of the town had heard beforehand that he would be passing through and had gathered with their children to congratulate him on his promotion. It could be grasped, chiefly from their cheering when the train arrived and left, that they had liked him very much; but when he was standing in front of them he and they alike were transfixed with shyness, evidently arising from the sense of sacredness of military glory, for from what they said it appeared that he had reached a rank extraordinary for so young a man. He was extremely touching as he stood before them solemn with honour, his compact body whittled down from broad shoulders to a slim waist and lean haunches by discipline and exercise. He had one of those Slav faces that puzzle the Westerner, for he had the stern eyes and brows and cheekbones with which we expect hard, thin lips, but his mouth was full and sensitive. I liked the look of him as he stood there in his neat, olive uniform; I liked the faces of the children lifted to him, tranced by the thought of his austere and defensive destiny. There are better things in life than fighting, but they are better only if their doers could have fought had they chosen.

"My town is Shabats," said Constantine, and I listened, for all his best tales begin with those words. "In Shabats we were all of us quite truly people. There were not many people who spoke alike and looked alike as there are in Paris and in London and in Berlin. We were all of us ourselves and different. I think it was that we were all equal and so we could not lift ourselves up by trying to look like a class that was of good repute. We could only be remarkable by following our own qualities to the furthest. So it is in all Serbian towns, so it was most of all in Shabats, because we are a proud town, we have always gone our own way. When old King Peter came to visit Shabats he spoke to a peasant and asked if he did well, and the peasant said he did very well, thanks to the trade in pigs and smuggling. We do not at all care, yet we care much. The peasant would tell the King he smuggled and broke his law, but he would die for the King. In the war we were a very brave town. The French decorated us as they decorated Verdun.

"I would like to take you to see Shabats. But it is not as it was. I mean I do not know it now. You might not be disappointed by a visit, but I should be, because I should not be able to introduce you to all the people that were there when I was young, and that now are dead. Some of them were so very nice, and so very strange. There was an old man that I was very fond of, yes, and I loved his wife too. He had made something of a fortune out of making Army clothing, and he made it honestly, for he was a good, patriotic man, and did not cheat the poor soldiers. So with his money he could follow his mania, which was for the new thing, for Science, for the machine, for the artificial, the modern. You may not remember it, for I think it came earlier with you than with us, but there was some time ago a rage for such things. It was partly due to your H. G. Wells and his imitators, and it was partly due to our ideas about America, which we then believed to be entirely covered with sky-scrapers and factories. I had it myself a little, which is how I became friendly with the old man, for I spoke of such things before him and after that he used to send for me sometimes to come to his home and eat, because he had been to Belgrade, or Novi Sad, and had brought back a tin of vegetables or fruit, so I used to sit down with him and his wife in the midst of the country which grows the best fruit and vegetables in the world and we used to smack our lips over some pulpy asparagus and turnipy peaches from California, and talk of the way the world was going to be saved when we all lived in underground cities and ate preserved food and had babies artificially germinated in tanks and lived for ever.

"I was only a boy then and I grew out of it, but the old man was firm in the faith, and his wife, who, I think, never believed in it at all but who loved him very dearly, followed him. I have said he was very rich, and so he was able to have the first sewing-machine in our town, and then the first gramophone, and then the first motor car, which, as we then had no roads for motoring, was of no use to him, but sent him into ecstasy. But there were many other objects on which he gratified his passion, far more than you would believe. His house was full of them. He had many very odd clocks; one I remember very well, the dial of which was quite hidden, which told the time only by throwing figures of light on the ceiling, which was all very well in the dark, but cannot have been much use to my friends, who always went to bed early and slept like dogs till the sunrise. He also fitted his house with a water-closet, which he was always changing for a newer pattern. Some of these water-closets were very strange, and I have never in my life seen anything like them since, and I cannot imagine what ideas were in the inventors' minds. In some kinds one had to go so and so, and why in a water-closet should one go so and so? Surely that is the one place in the world where a man knows quite simply what he has to do. The clothes of my friends were very strange also. He would not wear peasant costume, of course, but as soon as he had adopted Western costume, he rebelled against that also, and he had ties that fastened with snappers and trousers that were made in one with a waistcoat. But he was worse about his wife's dress. He made her wear knickerbockers under her skirts which our women used not to do, and which for some reason shocked them. Trousers they knew from the Turks, and skirts they knew, but trousers under the skirts, that they thought not decent. And when he heard of brassières those too he sent for, and made his wife wear them, and as she was an old peasant woman, very stout, they had to be enormously enlarged, and even then they remained clearly to be seen, never quite accommodated to her person. And he was so proud of having everything modern that he could not help telling people that she was like an American woman, and was wearing knickerbockers and brassières, and then the poor thing grew scarlet and suffered very terribly, for our women are modest. But she endured it all, for she loved him very much.

"I know how she loved him, for I became involved in her heart. You know that young men are very callous, and when I had got out of my boyhood it no longer seemed to be glorious to eat tinned vegetables, and I laughed at my old friend behind my hand. When I came from Paris after my first year at the Sorbonne, I went to see them and out of wickedness I began to tell them preposterous stories of new machines which did not really exist. Some of them might have existed, indeed some of them have come to exist since then. I remember I told them an American had discovered a system by which houses and trains were always kept at the same temperature, no matter what the weather is like outside. It is air-conditioning, it is now quite true, but then it was a lie. And I went on so, telling more and more absurd stories, until I said, 'And of course I was forgetting, there is the artificial woman that was invented by the celebrated surgeon Dr. Martel. That is quite wonderful.' And my old friend said to me, 'An artificial woman? What is that? A woman that is artificial! For God's sake! Tell us all about it!' So

I went on and on, telling many things that were not at all true, and that were not honest, and my friend listened with his eyes growing great, and then I looked at his wife and her eyes were great too, and they were full of pain. Then my old friend said to me, 'But you must get me one, you must get me an artificial woman!' He could afford all, you see, and I realized she had known that he was going to say that, and that she was terribly sad, because she knew that she was his real wife and that she would not be able to keep him from an artificial mistress. So I said it was not ready yet, that Dr. Martel was working on it to improve it, and that it could not be bought, and then I sweated hard to tell him something that would make him forget it, and drank more plum brandy, and I pretended to be drunk. But before I left he came round to my house and he told me to bring him back an artificial woman, that he did not care at all how much it cost, and that he would sell all he had to be possessed of such a marvel.

"So it was every time I came back from Paris on my holidays. I would go to their house and he would talk of other things for a time, but only as a little boy who has been well brought up, and knows that he must talk to the uncle for a little while before he asks, 'And did you not forget my toy train?' But sooner or later he would say, 'Now about the artificial woman. Is she ready yet?' And I would shake my head and say, 'No, she is not yet ready.' Then I would see his wife's face grow so happy and young and soft. She had him a little longer. Then I would explain that Dr. Martel was a very conscientious man, and a very great surgeon, and that such men like to work very slowly and perfectly. And then I would put my hand up so that she would not hear, and I would tell him some story that would not be very decent, of how the artificial woman had broken down under experiment, but the old man would listen with his eyes right out of his head, and she would go away to the kitchen and she would fetch me the best of her best, some special preserve or a piece of sucking-pig that she had meant to keep for the priest, because I said that the artificial woman was not yet ready. And I saw that she was getting very fond of me, like a mother for her son, and I grieved, for I did not like to have brought this sorrow to her by a silly joke. I felt very ashamed when she came to see me at a time when the cold wind had made me bad with my lungs, and it was as if I should go like my sister, who had died when she was sixteen, and I said to her, 'Aunt, you are too good to me. I have done nothing for you,' and she answered with tears in her eyes, 'But you have been as good to me as a son. Do you think I am so simple that I do not know the artificial woman must long ago be finished, with such a clever man as you say working on it? You tell my husband that it is not so only because you know that I could not bear to have such a creature in my house.' There was nothing at all that I could say. I could not confess to her that I had been a monkey without making it plain to her that her husband had been an ass. As many people in the town laughed at him, and she was more aware of it than he was and hated them on his account, I could not admit that I had been of their party, she would have felt betrayed. So I could do nothing but kiss her hand and tell her that always, always I would protect her heart from the artificial woman.

"The last year of my studies was the last year before the war, and then I did not come back for my holidays at all, I was studying too hard philosophy under Bergson and the piano under Wanda Landowska, and then for years I was a soldier and all people were swept away, and it did not seem to matter to ask how or where they were. So it was not till years after that I heard what had happened to my two old friends. It is a terrible story to me, not only because I had a sort of love for them, but because it is typical of us Slavs. We are a light people, full of *légèreté* till it becomes heavy as lead, and then we jump into the river for no reason, and if our *légèreté* had not grown heavy as lead one would say for the sake of sport, but that has altered the case. Do you remember, no, we none of us can remember it, but we all have read of it, that at the end of the century people believed that something had happened to humanity and that we were all decadent and that we were all going to commit suicide? *Fin de siècle*, the very phrase means that. Everything takes a long time to reach this country and this talk arrived here very late, in 1913, and in the meantime it had been translated into German and it had become heavy, and morbid, and to be feared. It came to this poor silly old man and he learned that the most modern thing to do was to kill yourself, and so he did it. He became very melancholy for a time, working at it as other old men work at learning chess, and then went into his stable and hanged himself, to be modern, to have an artificial death instead of a natural. I think he was probably sure that there was immortality, for though he believed he was a freethinker I do not believe it ever crossed his mind that he would not live after death. And soon after his wife also hanged herself, but I do not think there was anything modern about her reasons, they could not have been more ancient. In Shabats many strange things happened, very many strange things indeed, but I think that of all of them not nothing was not never more sad."

I slept, and woke up into a world of mirrors. They stretched away on each side of the railway, the hedges breathing on them with their narrow images. We were passing through the floods that every year afflict the basin of the Danube and its tributaries, and to me, who love water and in my heart cannot believe that many waters can be anything but pleasure heaped upon pleasure, there came a period of time, perhaps twenty minutes or half an hour, of pure delight. During this period I remained half asleep, sometimes seeing these floods before me quite clearly yet with an entranced eye that was not reminded by them of anything I had learned of death and devastation since my infancy, sometimes falling back into sleep and retaining the scene before my mind's eye with the added fantasy and unnameable significance of landscapes admired in dreams. The scene was in fact if not actually unearthly, at least unfamiliar, in aspect, because of the peculiar quality of the twilight. Light was leaving the land, but not clarity. For some reason, perhaps because there was a moon shining where we could not see it, the flooded fields continued to reflect their hedges and any height and village on their edge as clearly as when it had been full day; and though the dusk was heavier each time I opened my eyes I could still see a band of tender blue flowers which grew beside the railway. By mere reiteration of their beauty these flowers achieved a meaning beyond it and more profound, which, at any rate when I was asleep, seemed to be immensely important though quite undefined and undefinable, like the sense of revelation effected by certain refrains in English poetry, such as "the bailey beareth the bell away."

But presently the floods were blotted out from me, as thoroughly as if a vast hand had stretched from the sky and scattered earth on the waters till first they were mud and then land. Then Constantine came back into the compartment after an absence I had not noted, his face purplish, his black eyes hot and wet, his hands and his voice and his bobbing black curls lodging a complaint against fate. He sat down on the feet of my husband, who till then had been asleep, and he said, "On this train I have found the girl who was the first real love of my life. She was of my town, she was of Shabats, and we went to school together, and when we grew to the age of such things, which among us Serbs is not late, we were all for one another. And now she is not young any more, she is not beautiful, she has more little lines under her eyes even than you have, but it can be seen that she was very beautiful indeed, and that she is still very fine, very fine in the way that our women sometimes are, in the way that my mother is fine, very good for her husband, very good for her children, and something strong beyond. You know my mother was a very great pianist. It seems to me it would have been very well for me if I had made this girl my wife before the war and had come back to her, for I had terrible times when I came back from the war and it would have been good if I had had a grand woman like this to stand by me. But she would not have me; though we had been sweethearts for two years I knew that when I left Shabats to go to the Sorbonne she was glad to see that I am going, and all the way to Paris I was glad that it looked very well and as it should be, and I the man was leaving her the woman and going to a far place and having new adventures, because I knew that was how it was not and that she was tired of me. Never did I write to her because I was afraid she would not answer.

"But now when I saw her here on the train I knew that it was a pity it was so, and I said to her, 'Why did you treat me so? When I was young I was very handsome and my father was very rich and already you knew I was a poet and would be a great man, for always I was a *Wunderkind*, but you did not want me, though I think that once you loved me. What had you?' At first she would not tell me, but I asked her for a long time, and then she said, 'Well, if you trouble me so for so long a time, I will tell you. There is too much of you! You talk more than anybody else, when you play the piano it is more than when any other person plays the piano, when you love it is more than anybody else can make, it is all too much, too much, too much!' Now, that I cannot understand. I talk interesting things, for I have seen many interesting things, not one man in a hundred has seen so many interesting things, your husband has not seen so many interesting things. And I play the piano very well, also when I love with great delicacy of heart, and in passion I am a great experience for any woman. And you must ask my dear wife if I am not a kind man to my family, if I do not do all for my little sons. Now, all these things are good things, how can I do them too much? And I am sure that at first she loved me, and when she saw me here in this train she was so glad to see me that her eyes shone in ecstasy. Why then did she become weary and let me go to Paris with all things finished between us? Why does she now become cross and tell me there is too much of me? Why have I so many enemies, when I would only do what is good with people, and when I would ask nothing but to be gentle and happy? I will go back and ask her, for she cannot have meant just what she said, for it was not sensible, and she is a very fine sensible woman."

When he had gone my husband sighed, and said, "Good old Constantine. Now in all my life I have never got on a train and met a woman I used to love. Indeed, the nearest I have ever come to it was once going down to Norfolk when I met my old matron at Uppingham. That was indeed quite agreeable. But really, I prefer it that way. It seems to me that the proper place for the beloved is the terminus, not the train." "I am, however, travelling with you on this occasion," I reminded him. "Yes, my dear, so you are," he said, closing his eyes.

I myself slept after a time; and when I awoke he was still asleep and it was night, and a conductor was telling me that we were near Belgrade. We packed our books and collected our baggage and went to look for Constantine. He had fallen asleep in the corner of another compartment, and was now sitting half awake, running his hand through his tight black curls and smiling up at the lamp in the roof. There was no sign of the first woman he had ever loved, and he said, "As I woke up I thought of a beautiful thing that happened to me when I was a student in Paris. Bergson had spoken in one of his lectures of Pico della Mirandola who was a great philosopher in the Renaissance but now he is very hidden. I do not suppose you will ever have heard of him because you are a banker, and your wife naturally not. He did not say we must read him, he just spoke of him in one little phrase, as if he had turned a diamond ring on his finger. But the next morning I went to the library of the Sorbonne and I found this book and I was sitting reading it, and Bergson came to work in the library, as he did very often, and he passed by me, and he bent down to see what book I had. And when he saw what it was he smiled and laid his hand so on my head. So, I will show you." Passing his plump hand over his tight black curls, he achieved a gesture of real beauty. "That happened to me, nothing can take it away from me. I am a poor man, I have many enemies, but I was in Paris at that time, which was an impossible glory, and so Bergson did to me." He sat with his heels resting on the floor and his toes turned up, and his black eyes winking and twinkling. He was indestructibly, eternally happy.

The railway station at Belgrade is like any big railway station anywhere. It was odd to step back from a world where everything had its strong local flavour into scenes which were familiar precisely because they were so flavourless, so international in the pejorative sense of the word. In the colourless light descending its vaults there waited Constantine's wife, Gerda, a stout middle-aged woman, typically German in appearance, with fair hair abundant but formless, and grey eyes so light and clear that they looked almost blind, vacant niches made to house enthusiasms. She wore a grey coat and skirt and a small hat of German fashion, and among the dark hurrying people she stood as if drawing contentment from her own character, from her advantageous difference. When we got out of the train Constantine ran to her and hugged her, and she smiled over his shoulder at us in resigned amusement. Then she greeted me, and my husband was introduced to her, and it might have been a tea-party in Hamburg or Berlin, with the same proud stress on a note which nobody not German can define. It is not magnificence; the slightest touch of the grand manner would be regarded as absurd. It is not simplicity; massive elaboration is required in furniture, in dress, in food. It is not the moderation of the French bourgeoise, for that is based on craftsmanship, on a sense that to handle material satisfactorily one must keep one's wits about one and work coolly and steadily; these people at such tea-parties have no sense of dedication to the practical and financial problems of a household, they have an air of regarding it as an ideal that by handsome expenditure they should buy the right to be waited upon. Yet there is nothing wild, nothing extreme, about them or Gerda, only aims that are respected by the mass, such as continuity and sobriety. There is a positive element, even impressive in its positiveness, that welds these negatives into a dynamic whole; but I have no idea what it is.

We stood still together while Constantine and my husband looked for a lost suitcase, in an amiable yet uneasy silence. She took my book from my hand, looked at the title, and handed it back to me with a little shake of the head and a smile, full of compassionate contempt. It was a book called *The Healing Ritual*, by Patience Kemp, a study of the folk-medicine of the Balkan Slavs, which traced the prescriptions and practices it described back to early Christianity, to pre-Christian mythology, and to the culture of Byzantium and Greece and the Orient. Puzzled by Gerda's expression, for it seemed to me a most admirable book, I asked, "Have you read it?" "No," she said, smiling and shaking her head again, "but I do not believe it. I am not a *Mystik*." "But it is not that sort of book at all," I said, "it is by a graduate of the School of Slavonic Studies, who is also a trained anthropologist, and she has travelled all over the country collecting legends and customs and analysing them." Gerda continued to smile, bathed in satisfaction at the thought of her superiority to Miss Kemp in her poetic fantasy, to me in my credulity. "But it is a work of great learning," I insisted. Miss Kemp could obviously look after herself and I could not care what

Gerda thought of my intelligence, but there seemed to me something against nature in judging a book without having read it and in sticking to that judgment in spite of positive assurances from someone who had read it. "It is published by a firm called Faber," I continued; "they do not publish books such as you imagine this to be." She turned away so that she stood at right angles to me, her smile soared up above us: I could see her spirit, buoyed up by a sense of the folly of myself, of Miss Kemp, of Messrs. Faber, mounting and expanding till it filled the high vaults of the railway station. Unconstrained by any sense of reality, there was no reason why it should not.

Belgrade I

WHEN we were having breakfast in our bedroom a chambermaid came in about some business, one of those pale women with dark hair who even in daylight look as if one were seeing them by moonlight, and we recognized each other and talked affectionately. It was Angela, a Slovene, who had been very kind to me when I was ill in this hotel with dengue fever last year. She was the gentlest and sweetest of women and for that reason had developed a most peculiar form of hysteria. Perhaps because of her experience as a tiny child in the war she was a true xenophobe, she could not imagine anything more disgusting than a member of another race than her own. But she did not like to feel anything but love for her fellow-creatures, so she transformed her loathing for them into a belief that they exude powerful and most unpleasant odours. This belief made her life as a chambermaid an extraordinary olfactory adventure, for to this hotel there came people of all nationalities. She staggered from room to room on her round of duties, almost in need of a gas-mask when she came to making the beds. Her political convictions led her to think very poorly of the Bulgarians, the Italians, and the Greeks, and therefore it appeared to her that these people smelt like manure-heaps, like the area round a gasometer, like a tanner's yard. Particularly was this so with the Greeks. When she spoke of her daily work in the suite then occupied by a wealthy young Greek merchant her face assumed a look of poignant physical apprehension, as if she were a miner talking of the firedamp which might provoke a disaster. The Hungarians seemed to her to have a strong smell, which, however, was not unpleasant, only extremely different from the smell a human being ought to exhale. But the Germans and Austrians were definitely very gross in her nostrils, and the French smelt wicked and puzzling, as I imagine a chemist's shop might to a country woman who knew the uses of hardly any of the articles it exhibited.

About the natives of countries more remote she knew less, so she smelt less, and about such people as the Swedes and Finns her nose invented what were to full odours as suspicions are to certainties. To test her, I told her that I was not truly English, but half Scottish and half Anglo-Irish. This distracted her, because she had never heard of the Scottish or Irish, and while she was won to Scotland by my explanation of the resemblance between the Scottish and the Bosnians, it rightly seemed to her that to be Anglo-Irish was to be like an Austrian or Hungarian landowner among the Slovenes or Croats, or to be a Turkish landowner among the conquered Slavs. She would cry out as she made my bed, "I have it, I know what you smell like," and it would always be something valuable but ambiguous, not universally appreciated, such as some unusual herb, some rarely used kind of wood. But there would be some strain of pleasantness in the comparison, due to her belief that the Scottish resembled the Bosnians. And no matter how I and other borderline cases smelt, her toil was not repellent, since the foul miasma given out by the foreign guests of the hotel was exorcized and exquisitely replaced by the fragrance, stronger than that of rosery or herb garden because it was imaginary, which hung about the rooms occupied by Croats, Serbs, and Slovenes.

"I feel happier about your illness now that I have been here and seen that the hotel is very good, and that the people are so very friendly," said my husband, "but it looked terrible when I read in the papers before I had got your letter that you were ill in a hotel in Belgrade. I thought of Belgrade then as the Viennese talk of it, as the end of the earth, a barbarian village." "I am sorry I tried to keep it from you," I said, "but after all I too had a shock when I read of my illness in the paper. For it said that I was in the care of two doctors: but there were three gentlemen coming in every day and baring my bosom and laying their heads against my heart, and I had hoped they were all members of the medical profession. On the whole I have never been more happily ill than I was here. When my temperature was very high and I really felt wretched, Angela and two other chambermaids and a waiter came and stood at the end of my bed and cried nearly the whole afternoon. Also my nurse cried a lot. I liked it enormously." "But you always say you hate scenes," said my husband. "So I do, when I am well, there are so many other things to do," I answered; "but when I am ill it is the only incident that can cheer and reach me under the blankets. And really it is sensible to show emotion at serious illness. Death is a tragedy. It may be transmuted to something else the next minute, but till then it is a divorce from the sun and the spring. I also maintain that it would have been a tragedy for myself and for a few other people if I died in my early forties, so it was quite logical for susceptible people to burst into tears at such a prospect and neglect the bells that their more robust clients were pressing. I am quite sure that it must be more exhilarating to die in a cottage full of people bewailing the prospect of losing one and the pathos of one's destruction than to lie in a nursing-home with everybody pretending that the most sensational moment of one's life is not happening."

"I see that," said my husband, "but you must remember that if people behaved like that they would not be able to bear the strain of patiently nursing the victims of long illnesses." "That is what is called taking the long view," I said, "and I do not believe it is so superior to the short view as is supposed. I remember once going a walk in Greece with two Englishwomen, one of them the enchanting Dilys Powell, to see a marble lion that lies somewhere near the foot of Mount Hymettus, when from a long way off we had seen some peasants about their business of repainting and cleaning a little church that had been erected to commemorate the feat of a Christian saint, who had turned to marble this lion (which was in fact archaic and many centuries older than any Christian). Suddenly one of their number who was walking away from the church towards a farm stopped in horror, just where the grass grew long at the edge of the road, looked down, and cried out to his companions, who also looked down and then also cried out. Some went down on their knees on the ground, others ran back to the church and returned carrying things. When we got there we found that the first peasant had stopped because he had come on an old man who had fallen in a faint by the roadside, from hunger and thirst and weariness. He was, as one of the peasants explained to us, one of 'those without corn,' a peasant who for some reason has no land and must tramp the country seeking to be employed by others. The English ladies might find it difficult to believe, he said, speaking with embarrassment, that such people existed, since we were from a rich country, but in a poor country like Greece there were some of them. This I found extremely embarrassing. But I forgot that, in my pleasure in the delightful kindness they were showing the old man, the way they were folding coats and cloaks to make a bed for him, and holding up to his mouth bottles of wine and pieces of bread, and crying out what a shame it was that he should have to be wandering on such a day and without food.

"Then one of my companions said, 'Yes, they are like this, very kind to people in trouble at first, but they are like children, they soon get tired. So-and-so of the British colony in Athens was taken ill with fever when he was walking in the mountains, and some peasants took him in and looked after him with extraordinary care for a few days, and then they simply turned him out.' I felt a jar at that, for it seemed to me that here was a difference between primitive and civilized practice, which was, on the whole, to the advantage of the primitive. For there are more short illnesses than long, at least in circumstances where one is obliged to be dependent on strangers; and sympathy seems to me more necessary for acute pains than for chronic suffering, which gives one time to muster one's defences. That, indeed, is something about which I feel bitterly. Twice it happened to me, before I married you, that people who were close friends of mine wrote inquiring how I was and what my plans were, and I had to write back to them telling that an extraordinary calamity had befallen me, something almost as extraordinary as that a wicked stepmother had sent me out into the woods in winter with instructions not to come back till I had gathered a basket of wild strawberries, and infinitely agonizing as well. On neither occasion did I receive any answer: and when I met my friends afterwards each told me that she had been so appalled by my news that she had not been able to find adequate words of sympathy, but that I was not to think she was anything but my friend and would be till death. And indeed both women are still my friends. It, however, only gives me a modified pleasure, it presents me with the knowledge that two people know me very well and enjoy my society but are not inspired by that to do anything to save me when I am almost dying of loneliness and misery, and that this unexhilarating relationship is likely to persist during my lifetime. It seems to me it would have been much better for me if I had had someone who would have cried out and said it was a shame that I should be so unhappy, as the peasants did when they found the old man by the roadside."

My husband said, "I wonder. I wonder very much indeed. This has all something to do with economics." "What on earth?" I said derisively. "I am moved, and your friends were moved, by fear of exceeding emotion," he explained, "and I believe it is because Western people always regard their emotion exactly as they do their material wealth. Now in a highly artificial capitalist society such as we live in, one's money comes to one piece by piece, and if one spends it one might not be able to replace it, because the circumstances in which one made it may not be repeated, and in any case it takes a long time to store up capital, so that considering the shortness of life a piece of extravagance may never be corrected. But a peasant's material wealth comes from the soil; he therefore knows that if he is wasteful one year the summer and autumn will bring him replenishment, and even the hazard of drought and frost and flood does not amount to anything so threatening as the immense discrepancy between capital and income, the enormous amount that has to be saved for a competency. So even a rich and lavish man may be more uneasy in his mind about expenditure than a very poor and economical peasant. And I fancy that therefore all of us in the Western world know an instinct to skimp our emotional expenditure which the peasant has not. It is true therefore that my feeling that Angela and the waiters and the nurses were doing something wrong in crying round your bed has no logical basis at all, and is a stupid transference and confusion." "Yet there are practical conveniences," I said, "because in towns we could not cry out and wail and weep as one could in a village. Think how strangers to Paris feel it the most frightening of towns instead of the least, simply because Parisians quarrel and grieve exactly as they would if they were the inhabitants of some hamlet of thirty houses, and the cries echo back from the tall houses and the pavements, exaggerated to the intensity of Hell."

The telephone rang and my husband answered it. Putting it down, he said, "Constantine's wife is coming up to see us." I sat down at the dressing-table and began to powder my face, but my eye was caught by the view from the window. Belgrade straggles over a ridge between the Danube and its tributary the Sava, and the Hotel of the Serbian King is high on that ridge, so between the blocks of the flats and houses on the opposite side of the street I looked at the flat plate of the floods. The waiter who had come to take away our breakfast tray followed the line of my eye and said, "Yes, it is unfortunate, you will be able to have no fresh caviare, for while the river is high they cannot get it." My husband exclaimed, "What, do you get caviare here?" "You had better ask," the waiter replied, "where else can you get it? It is well known that Serbian caviare is the best in the world."

When he had gone we rejoiced at this patriotic remark and I at last remembered to show my husband a verse I found quoted in a book by a Serbian author called Mitchitch:

> Le ciel serbe est couleur d'azur
> Au dedans est assis un vrai dieu serbe
> Entouré des anges serbes aux voix pures
> Qui chantent la gloire de leur race superbe.

We were laughing over this when Gerda came in, and we repeated it to her. She smiled and said, "So you have got over your liking for the Serbs?" "Not at all," I said. "But it is stupid to be like that," she said, "you cannot like people who are stupid." "Yes, we can," said my husband, with an air of quietly asserting our rights.

It did not seem possible to carry on this conversation on fruitful lines, so we spoke of other things; and presently, according to a charming German custom, she rose from her seat and shook hands with me in thanks for a handbag I had sent her from London some time before. Then we showed her some things we had bought in Bosnia, a Persian tile picture of a prince on his white horse, delicately holding out a fruit to a bird that delicately received it with his beak, in the most delicate of landscapes, and my coat of cloth of gold; and it was all very agreeable. We were lifted for a moment into that state of specifically German contentment that I had remarked in Gerda at the station, in which my husband was perfectly at ease, from sheer habit, since he had lived so much in Germany, but in which I am acutely uncomfortable, as I do not understand its basis and I feared I might put my foot through it at any moment. Its basis, on this occasion I think, was a sense that we were a group of the elect, connoisseurs of objects which many people would not at all appreciate, and able at the minute to command leisure for our enjoyment. She looked happy and much younger, and I remembered Constantine's boasting of her beauty. Suddenly I remembered friendship and how beautiful it is, in a way that is difficult in London or any capital where one suffers from an excess of relationships, and I realized that it was probably a great comfort for this German woman, so far from home, to talk with my husband, whose German is like a German's and of her own kind, for he learned it in Hamburg and she was of Bremen.

These thoughts made me say, next time there was a pause, "It was very pleasant in Sarajevo to see how many friends Constantine had, and how much they loved him." But Gerda made no answer. My husband thought she had not heard, and began to enumerate the families and individuals we had met in Bosnia, and the affectionate things they had said of Constantine to us. She remained perfectly impassive, so impassive that it seemed as if she was perhaps hiding some painful emotion; and my husband, afraid lest she had some idea that these friends of Constantine's were not friendly to her, said, "And those who had met you spoke very regretfully because they had not seen more of you." He told her truthfully that the Bulbul's father and mother, who had entertained Gerda at Travnik when Constantine and she came to Bosnia on their honeymoon, had asked after her with a special warmth. Gerda shrugged her shoulders and said, "I cannot remember them." "What a pity!" I exclaimed, "they are such a wonderful pair," but before I could say very much about them she interrupted me, by asking coldly and wearily as if I had been talking for a long time about something I should have known would bore her, "It is twelve years ago since I saw these people, how can I possibly be interested in them?" Impatiently she made arrangements that we should visit her for tea that afternoon, and soon after rose and left.

"I do not understand that," said my husband later, as we walked out of the hotel towards the park that lies beside it, the Kalemegdan, which is the special glory of Belgrade and indeed one of the most beautiful parks in the world. "Usually a wife or husband is delighted, if only for superficial and worldly reasons, when the other partner has many friends. Unless of course there is hatred between them. Do you think Gerda perhaps really hates Constantine?" "I do not know," I said. "Constantine thinks that she adores him. She certainly gives you the impression she would adore her husband if she could, and Constantine certainly adores her." "I have it!" exclaimed my husband. "Most of the people I mentioned were Jews. What an odd, what an allusive thing it is to be a German nowadays." "It is like asthma," I said. "Suddenly they begin to strangle spiritually, and you have to remember it is because they are allergic to Jews. But there is more than that to it. She was happy with us, together we formed a group of people who were like the groups who are approved in her own country. Suddenly by talking of Constantine's friends we deserted the camp and went over to the enemy, we took sides with the Jews and the Slavs who are constantly afflicting her with their strangeness, who make up the bitterness of her exile." "Yes, but it is a pity she does not fit her emotions better into the framework of society," said my husband, "for surely she would bring no other accusation against the Jews and the Slavs than that they do not fit into the framework of society. But it does not matter, she is probably a very nice woman and has many good points."

But now we were in the park, and its charm was separating us from everything outside it, as good parks should do. We went through an area which is common to all parks, no matter where they may be, where nurses watch their children play among lilac bushes and little ponds and the busts of the departed nearly great, whose living prototypes sit beside the nurses on the benches, writing, or reading in books taken out of shiny leather portfolios. Then there is a finely laid-out flower garden, with a tremendous and very beautiful statue to the French who died in Yugoslavia during the Great War, by Mestrovitch, showing a figure bathing in a sea of courage. Many people might like it taken away and replaced by a gentler marble. But the pleasantness of this park is such an innovation that it has hardly earned the right to put all grimness from its gates. For this is the old fortress of Belgrade, which till the end of the Great War knew peace only as a dream.

Ever since there were men in this region this promontory must have meant life to those that held it, death to those that lost it. Its prow juts out between the two great rivers and looks eastward over the great Pannonian Plain (superb words, the flattest I know) that spreads across Hungary towards Central Europe. Behind it is the security of broken country and forest. Here, certainly not to begin at the beginning, the Illyrians made a stand against the Romans and were driven out. Here the Romans made a stand against the Huns and the Avars, and were driven out. Here the Slavs joined the Huns and were oppressed by them, and for a brief space enjoyed peace under the Byzantines, but were submerged by the Hungarians, until war between Byzantium and Hungary brought a victorious Greek army to the foot of this rock. Then the Serbs came, and knew imperial glory under the Nemanya dynasty; here the petty Serbian kings who had failed to uphold that glory made their last stand before the Turks. But the Hungarians, with typical Christian frivolity, claimed it for nearly a hundred years, harrying the Serbs so that they could not beat back the Turkish army. Hence Belgrade fell to Suleiman the Great in 1521. The Hungarians paid their scot five years later, when the Turks beat them at Mohacs and kept them in servitude for a hundred and fifty years. Then the tide turned, the maniac Vizier Kara Mustapha was defeated outside Vienna and brought to this very place to be strangled. Then in 1688 the Austrians swept them out and took the fortress, but lost it two years later, and it was not retaken till Prince Eugène of Savoy came down on it in 1717.

So far the history of Belgrade, like many other passages in the life of Europe, makes one wonder what the human race has lost by its habit of bleeding itself like a mad medieval surgeon. But it may be that not much has been wasted which we miss. Those that are preserved to unfold the buds of their being often produce very repulsive blossoms. In 1739 by a hideously treacherous agreement the Austrians handed Belgrade and its Serb inhabitants to Turkey. This was, however, not such a calamity for the Serbs as appears, for they had been so oppressively governed by the Austrians that many had already fled into Turkish territory, though the treatment they received there could be described not as good, but better.

In 1792, however, the Austrians conferred some benefits on the Serbs by a treaty which they had designed simply for their own security.

They arranged that no Janizaries should be admitted to the garrison of Belgrade or any other Serbian town. This was to save the Austrians from a frontier that could immediately become aggressive in time of war, it virtually imposed a no-man's-land. But to the Serbs it meant liberation from the unchecked tyranny of the dominant military caste. In the next few years the Belgrade Pashalik became happy and prosperous under Hadji Mustapha Pasha, one of the few Turks who ever showed signs of a talent for colonial administration. He was so much beloved by his Christians that he was known as "the Mother of Serbs," an odd title for an intensely military people to bestow on the bearded representative of another. But there was a shift in palace politics far away in Constantinople, and the treaty was annulled. The Janizaries came back. They stole by fraud into this fortress, murdered the wise Hadji Mustapha, and set up a looting, murdering, raping tyranny over the countryside.

It was against them that Karageorge, Black George, the founder of the dynasty, a pig-farmer of genius, led his revolt in 1804. He besieged this fortress and it was handed over to him in 1806. He freed his whole country down to Parachin and Krushevats, in 1810. But when Serbia became the ally of Russia against Turkey in 1813, she was betrayed by Russian incompetence, and the Turks came back to Belgrade. They took a terrible revenge for Karageorge's revolt. They massacred all the men who were not quick enough to take refuge in the Shumadiya, as it is called, the Wooded Place, the country lying south of Belgrade which formed most of the old kingdom of Serbia; and they sold many of the women and children into slavery. But later another Serbian leader arose, one Milosh Obrenovitch, and he induced Russia to support him in a revolt against the Ottoman Empire. It was successful. It was too successful. Russia had not wanted Serbia to be free, but to be absorbed into the Tsardom. But the Serbs had shown such mettle that Belgrade could not be mistaken for anything but the capital of a free Serbia. She was therefore cheated out of the victory she had earned. To prevent her from being too free she was forced to let a garrison of Turkish troops remain in Belgrade fortress.

This led to incidents. It could not have been otherwise. And the great powers were always there to turn them, sometimes out of greed and baseness, sometimes out of sheer idiocy, into wounds and humiliations. Their guilt can be judged from the conduct of the English in June 1862. One evening in that month two Turkish soldiers sitting at a fountain fell into a dispute with a Serbian youth and killed him. In the subsequent disorder a Serbian policeman was killed and another wounded. This started a race riot which lasted all night. The Serbian Cabinet and the foreign consuls and the Turkish Pasha joined together to take measures to stop it, and peace was believed to be restored when the garrison of the fortress suddenly opened fire on Belgrade. For four hours the unhappy town was bombarded. Not until the foreign consuls took the courageous step of pitching their tents on the glacis between the town and the fortress were the guns silenced. After this the British Foreign Office took a step memorable in its imbecility. Lord John Russell, without making any inquiries whatsoever, decided that the incident had occurred because the Serbians had violated their treaty obligations to Turkey, and he put forward the strange decision that Austria should invade Serbia. Fortunately Austria perceived that she could not choose a more dangerous moment, and sent no troops. It is a relief to remember that four years later English influence induced the Porte to withdraw from Serbia altogether. Foreign students of our politics must be puzzled to find that this change in attitude was due to the substitution of a Conservative for a Liberal Government.

But this withdrawal did not yet bring peace to the fortress. In front of it lay Hungary and Austria, greedy for it. Behind it lay Russia, greedy for it. Both wanted to snatch the Balkans from the hands of the dying Ottoman Empire. When the young Serbian state tried to placate Austria, Russia raged. In its rage it financed the Bulgars to turn against the Serbs, filling them with hopes of Balkan ascendancy which have ever since complicated and embittered the international situation. Later the great powers met at the Congress of Berlin and gave Bosnia and Herzegovina to the Austrian Empire, and thereby left Serbia helpless and humiliated. In 1905 Serbia resisted Austrian commercial aggression by a tariff war which was known as "the pig war," and formed a customs Anschluss with the Bulgars. So Austria's hatred for Serbia grew day by day, till in 1914 Princip's bullet acted as a catalytic to Central European passions, and the Austrian monitors bombarded the fortress from the Danube. In 1915 it was occupied by Austrian troops, not to be freed until 1918. Now its ramparts and glacis shelter in their mellow bluish-rose brickwork a sequence of little flower-gardens, which stuff the old ravelins and redoubts with pansies and tulips and forget-me-nots. It is the prettiest and most courageous piece of optimism I know: but for all that I think the Yugoslavs wise to have Mestrovitch's statue by, to remind them of the imbecile ferocity of their kind.

There is another statue by Mestrovitch in Kalemegdan. It is the war memorial of Yugoslavia itself, the glorious naked figure. It can be seen only imperfectly, it stands on the very top of a column, at the prow of the promontory, high up above the waters, which it faces; on the park it turns its back, and that is all the observer can see. This is not according to the intention of the sculptor, nor is it a sacrifice made to symbolism, though it is very apt that the Yugoslavian military spirit should look out in vigilance and warning towards Hungary and Austria. It happens that the statue is recognizably male, so the municipality of Belgrade refused to set it up in the streets of the town, on the ground that it would offend female modesty. But the Serb is not only a peasant in prudery, he is an artist, he has some knowledge of handicrafts, so he saw that it was natural for a man cutting out the shape of a man to cut out the true shape of a man; the councillors felt therefore no Puritan hatred of the statue, and their peasant thrift told them that it would be wicked waste to throw away a statue well carved in expensive material by an acknowledged master. So up it went, buttocks to the fore.

And beautiful it looked, outlined against the landscape, which lay under the floods as a human being in a bath; the face of the land, its trees and houses, were above the water, but the body was wholly submerged. These floods were even threatening the low platform that lies below the slope which drops, purple with lilacs, from the prow of Kalemegdan. But the low grey barracks down there were still occupied; on the nacreous surface of an exercise-ground there walked in twos and threes a number of soldiers wearing round Cossack caps and long full-skirted coats opening over scarlet breeches. The scene had the air of the beginning of a ballet, because each body was so tautly sprung in its trained perfection. There were two dovecotes in the compound, one a pleasant faded jade-green, the other earth-brown. Sometimes some soldiers would halt underneath one of these cotes and cry out or clap their hands so that the doves whirred out and travelled a low arc to a corrugated iron roof. But for the most part these young men strolled about talking with a peculiar intensity that was untinged by homosexuality but spoke of male friendships more acute and adventurous than anything we know in the West. To look at them was to understand the military conspiracies that have been the special difficulty of Serbia during the last fifty years.

By now the surface of the floods was hacked into choppy waves, which became a coarse trembling silver where the sunlight pierced the grey-violet clouds. We shuddered and took refuge in the fortress. It is immense. It is shaped by the Oriental tradition which obliged a ruler to symbolize his greatness by the size of his habitation. Some of it the Yugoslav Government has not yet had time or money to take in hand. A labyrinth of corridors and cells is as the Turks left it seventy years ago; but in other parts there are arsenals, barracks, offices, tennis-courts, and a museum which holds, as a grisly and suspicious exhibit, the automobile in which King Alexander was assassinated at Marseille. It is not to be comprehended why the French authorities let it leave the country. It is an old-fashioned vehicle—seven years old in 1934 and clumsily refitted with new coachwork after a smash—which had actually been used for the transport of better-class criminals. The French chauffeur is known to have protested against being made to drive a king in such a piece of old iron. It is right that the automobile should be in Belgrade, for it beautifully symbolizes the way the Western powers have dealt with the Balkans. There also, in the landward ramparts, is a charming zoo of the Whipsnade sort. Grey skies bring out the colour of flowers and animals: a lion and lioness drinking at a stream shone like topazes. But it was no use, the day was growing colder, we went back to our hotel.

Belgrade II

WE ate too large a lunch, as is apt to be one's habit in Belgrade, if one is man enough to stand up to peasant food made luxurious by urban lavishness of supply and a Turkish tradition of subtle and positive flavour. The soups and stews and risottos here are as good as any I know. And the people at the tables round about one come from the same kitchen: rich feeding, not too digestible, but not at all insipid. Some of them, indeed, are definitely indigestible, beings of ambiguous life, never engaged in any enterprise that is crystalline in quality. It is said that Belgrade is the centre of the European spy system, and it may be that some of these people are spies. One about whom such a doubt might be harboured came up to me while we were eating our chicken liver risotto, an Italian whom I had last seen at a night club in Vienna. I remembered our meeting because of his answer to my inquiry as to what he was doing in Austria. "I come from Spain, but I have never good fortune," he said. "I hoped to bring here a bull-fight, but the bull, he will not come." This did not, of course, refer to a startling example of animal sagacity, but to the change noticeable in the attitude of the customs officials as the animal passed from territories where bull-fighting is done to where it is not. The unhappy beast had started on its journey as a symbol of life, glorious in the prospect of meeting a sacrificial death, and ended it as something like a fallen girl, to be rescued by bloodless humanitarians. Today when I asked the Italian a like question about his presence he made a more optimistic answer. "I am about to take up very, very great concessions," he said. "A pyrites mine in Bosnia." "But," I thought, "the pyrites, he will not come."

This man was an adventurer for the reason that most Westerners turn adventurers: he was too weak and silly to fit into the grooves of ordinary life, to be accepted in the company of the really important business men, the industrialists and financiers who would take up the concessions in Bosnia if they were worth anything, and who are also to be seen lunching at this hotel. But the native Yugoslavs who are offering them their country's resources over the table seem also to be adventurers, though for another reason. They would deviate from the strict pathway drawn by business necessity not because they were too negative but too positive for daily life. They are robust men who speak and laugh and eat and drink a great deal, so that by early middle life they have the lined faces of actors and are full-bodied. The vitality of these Yugoslavs to be seen at midday in this or any other big Belgrade hotel is in astounding contrast to any English gathering of the sort. Englishmen, if they happen to be physically dynamic, usually disclaim it by their manners. These Yugoslavs have never had an ache or pain in their lives. Yet all the historical factors involved should by rights have produced an opposite effect; for all the Yugoslavs over forty must have taken part in a military campaign of the most appalling nature, and all adults who were below that age had undergone as boys privations and dangers such as never threatened French or English or German children.

I could understand why English diplomats, too often the most delicate of a delicate class, hated being *en poste* among the Balkan peoples; but I could guess also at another reason why they should hate it. These Yugoslavs were not only very well, they were certain in any circumstances to act vigorously; and it would be impossible to foresee what form that action would take. In the Yugoslavian villages one felt certain of the peasants' vigour and the predictability of their conduct. They might be intensely individual in their emotions and their expression of them, but they would follow a tested tradition. Here one had no such certainty. These men in the hotel dining-room were not united by the acceptance of any common formula. This gave them the alien and enigmatic character of wild animals: the lion and lioness, drinking at the stream in the Kalemegdan were not more sealed from one in their feeling and thinking than these jolly, healthy men. I asked myself in vain, "What will they do?" And I asked myself also the more important question, "What would they feel that they could not do?" I remembered what English people who had lived in the Balkans had told me of dishonesty and punctilio, of grossness and delicacy, avarice and handsomeness, co-existent in the same person, of statesmen who had practised extremes in patriotism and in peculation not at different times in their career but on the same day, of brutality that took torture and bloodshed in its stride and suddenly turned to the tenderest charity. Surely this meant that not only I, but the Yugoslavs, were unable to answer the question. They were not yet familiar with the circumstances of urban life. It could hardly be otherwise, since thirty-five years ago there was not a town in Serbia the size of Rockford, Illinois. The Yugoslavs could not be blamed, therefore, if they had not worked out a tradition of conduct to fit those circumstances.

Urban life takes a deal of learning. We saw further evidence of that when we went out to see the procession of children that always on this day, April the twenty-fourth, marches through the street along the ridge of Belgrade, to receive the blessing of the Patriarch at the Cathedral, which is near the park. We took up our places near the central square among a mob of infatuated parents, and languidly kind big brothers and sisters who were too old to walk in the procession, and bubbling and dancing little brothers and sisters who were too young, and had for the most part been given balloons for compensation. There was a great deal of apprehension about, for every child had had new clothes bought for this occasion, and this worst of springs ranged drably overhead, sometimes spilling great heavy pennies of rain; and the procession was forty minutes late.

All that was forgotten, however, every time one of the children in the crowd lost grip of its balloon, and we all saw it rise slowly, as if debating the advantages of freedom, over the wide trench of the cleared street. Then we all laughed, and laughed louder when, as usually happened, since the wind was short of breath, the balloon wobbled and fell on the heads of the crowd on the other side of the road, and was fetched back by its baby owner. There was one such recovery which caused great amusement. A red balloon was blown higher than any of the others, as high as the first-floor windows, and then travelled across the street very slowly, with jerks and hesitations, while its owner, a little boy in a sky-blue serge coat, staggered exactly beneath it, his anxious body expressing all the consternation a man might feel when the stock market is breaking. "It's going. It's gone. No, it isn't. See, it's going to be all right. No, there isn't a chance." The puce-faced old soldier who held the line in front of us shook and heaved, producing laughter from some place one would never keep it unless one was in the habit of packing things away as safely as possible. Three schoolgirls who had been stiff in adolescent affectation laughed as comfortably as if they were women already.

But in spite of all this good-humour the occasion was not as pretty as we had hoped, because the little children were so remarkably fragile and pasty-faced. "It is perhaps because they have been waiting so long in the cold," suggested my husband. But that was not the reason, for the children who were walking briskly in the procession were just as pallid and dull of eye and hair. "I cannot understand it!" I said. "Why should the Serbs, who are so superbly healthy when they grow up, be such weakly children?" A Frenchwoman standing beside us in the crowd said primly, with that air of having put in her thumb and taken out a plum which we in England have not used with ease since the days of Maria Edgeworth, "It is because they keep their children indoors all winter. You would not believe how little they understand the importance of giving the little ones plenty of air and exercise." After a moment's complacent pause, she added, "And vegetables too. That is another thing of which they are ignorant. The children are given enormous quantities of meat, and some salad, yes, but green vegetables they hardly eat at all."

That was to say, in fact, that the Serbs had not mastered the technique of bringing up children in town, which indeed is hard enough to learn so far as winter is concerned. For in the country a peasant's child must go out into the cold, whatever the day be like, to help with the crops or the livestock. It gets air and exercise without ever having the need for them propounded. But a great deal of information has to be stated and realized before a man and woman living in town see that it is their duty to commit the obvious unkindness of sending a child out into the cold for no reason at all. The matter of food is perhaps not so urgent as the Frenchwoman alleged; for it is said that the paprika, with which the Serb flavours his soups and his stews, compensates for the lack of green vegetables. But the excess of meat is also a real injury to the child, which it is very hard for its parents to avoid inflicting. For in the country a peasant can eat a great deal of meat and profit by it, and it is not easy for him when he comes to town to realize that this source of his strength has suddenly become a danger to him.

They are learning a new technique, and the conditions of their education are not ideal. "What a calamity it is that the Serbs consider it of such importance to have a great capital," I said to my husband; "think of all the new ministries, and look at these poor teachers." "Unfortunately the Serbs are perfectly right," said my husband. "The old pre-war Belgrade was in no way discreditable to any Serbs except those who five hundred and fifty years ago were beaten on the field of Kossovo, and let the Turks stream north. But it was always being brought up against her in every German or Austrian or French or English book on the Balkans, and it was perpetually alluded to by diplomats. But I agree with you, these teachers are a most unhappy sight." For just as remarkable as the pallor and fragility of the children was the neediness of the schoolmasters and schoolmistresses who were in charge of them.

They bore themselves with dignity, and their faces were for the most part thoughtful and dedicated. This was to be expected, for the profession of teacher offers not the steady job which the peasant longs for above all else when he leaves the soil, but has a special heroic prestige. Before the Balkan wars all the young bloods of both sexes with a turn for letters took teaching diplomas and went down to Old Serbia and Macedonia, which were still Turkish provinces. The great powers had forced Turkey to permit the establishment of schools with foreign staffs for the benefit of the Christians among their subjects; but the result was hardly what could have been expected from such a benevolent intervention. No area since the world began can have been at once so highly educated and so wildly uncivilized. Macedonia was important to all Europe, because a power that got a foothold there had a chance of falling heir, by actual occupation or by economic influence, to the territories of the dying Ottoman Empire. So the land was covered with schools staffed by nationalist propagandists, who, when they hailed from the neighbouring Balkan powers, took their duties with more than normal pedagogic ferocity. Macedonia had a large population of Christian Slavs, who were mainly of Serb or Bulgarian or Greek character, though they often exchanged characters if they shifted or their districts fell under different domination. Serbia and Bulgaria and Greece therefore all founded schools which aimed at making the Macedonian infants into Serbs or Bulgars or Greeks who could be counted on to demand the transfer of the province to whatever state had secured their adherence. Quite a number of the schoolmasters and schoolmistresses in these competitive establishments were shot, or were not shot only because they shot first. This situation was not wholly ended by the war. Until a few years ago the I.M.R.O. or Internal Macedonian Revolutionary Organization, which wished to take Macedonia from Yugoslavia and make it Bulgarian, often attacked Yugoslav schools and murdered the staff, and yet many Serbian teachers volunteered to put in some years of duty in the South before they settled down at home. So the teacher in Yugoslavia is often a hero and fanatic as well as a servant of the mind; but as they walked along the Belgrade streets it could easily be seen that none of them had quite enough to eat or warm enough clothing or handsome lodgings or all the books they needed.

It must be admitted that this city, with its starved professional classes, its lavish governmental display, and its pullulation of an exploiting class, sometimes presents an unattractive appearance. I did not like Belgrade that evening when I sat in the hotel lounge and watched the bar fill up with high-coloured, thick-necked, stocky little men whose black mous-

taches were lustreless as apes' hair. There had been some sort of conference upstairs in a private room, with two foreign visitors, one pale and
featureless and round, like an enormous Dutch cheese, the other a Jew
as Hitler sees Jews. I think the dreams raised at that conference would
never be realized in all their rosiness. No party was going to be left, as
the others hoped, with the horns and the hooves as his share of the
carcass. But everybody would do pretty well, except the general public
here and in the rest of Europe, which was going to provide the carcass. And the rest of Europe can look after itself. It has had its opportunities, and if it has never used them to tidy up its financial system, so
much the worse for it. The heavier offence is against Yugoslavia, a new
country that has to make its body and soul.

The extent of the damage that is done to the state by these financial
and industrial adventurers is not easy to compute. I do not believe that
it is nearly so much in terms of money as the Yugoslavs outside Belgrade allege. The great fortunes in Yugoslavia come from shipping and
timber, and are as legitimate as such riches are in England or America.
For the rest, there are only sporadic and unimpressive evidences of
wealth, however gained. There may be some large villas in Belgrade
whose owners could not explain how they came to be able to build
them; but then there are very few large villas in Belgrade. Nor are
there many large cars, or expensive restaurants, or jewellers, or furriers.
It looks to me as if all the city's speculators absorb a much smaller proportion of their country's goods than England and the United States
cede as a matter of course to the City and to Wall Street. But to a community of peasants it may well seem that such rewards for the middle-
man are altogether exorbitant; and indeed the political consequences of
such a privateering strain in society are altogether disastrous for a new
country.

If the politicians of a state are dominated by ideas, then few parties
form. There are certain natural classifications which establish themselves: those who are for repression and those who are for freedom,
those who are for the townspeople and those who are for the peasants,
those who are for the army and those who are for finance and industry,
and so on. Sometimes these groups stand sharply defined and sometimes
they coalesce into fewer and larger groups. But there is only a limited
number of such classifications, and of the combinations that can be
formed from them. But if there are a thousand financiers and industrialists in a country, they can, especially when they are Slavs, turn political
life into a multiplicity of small slippery bodies like a school of white-

bait. In the ten years after the granting of the Yugoslavian constitution in 1921 twenty-five different governments held office. There is nothing more necessary for the country than a steady agrarian policy; there have been as many as five Ministers of Agriculture in thirteen months.

It was to end this gangsterish tumult that King Alexander took the disastrous step of proclaiming a dictatorship in 1929. This introduced what seemed to be a change for the better, but most Yugoslavs would say that it produced no change at all, for it ultimately put into the saddle Stoyadinovitch, who was hated throughout the length and breadth of the country. That hatred was extraordinarily widespread. I have literally never heard any Yugoslav, except Constantine and a very simple-minded judge from a Dalmatian town, express admiration for him. He was hated chiefly because he was said to be a tyrant and enemy of freedom. He was said to have suppressed freedom of speech and freedom of the press by throwing his opponents into jail, where they were often starved and beaten. It is extremely difficult to weigh the justice of these accusations. It must be conceded at once that if a man is imprisoned in Yugoslavia he is likely to be maltreated. A bad penal tradition has been inherited both from Turkey and from Austria. I have known a most enlightened Serb official who had had the greatest difficulty in persuading his subordinates that it was not good form to use torture for the purpose of extracting confessions. It added to the complexity of the situation that when they were not torturing their prisoners they would treat them with a fatherly kindness unknown in our Western prisons.

Whether Stoyadinovitch imprisoned many people or not was hard for a stranger to tell. My impression was that the regime was far more indulgent than German Nazism or Italian Fascism. I have heard malcontents loudly abuse the government freely when sitting in a café or by an open window giving on a lane, and I have often received through the ordinary post letters in which my Yugoslav friends abused the Prime Minister and signed their names. I have been told several stories of atrocities which on investigation turned out to be either completely untrue or exaggerated. For example, I was told in Croatia of a Croat who had been exiled to a Macedonian town and was forced to report to the gendarmerie every two hours; but a pro-Croat anti-Government Macedonian living in that town could not trace him, and had never heard of anybody undergoing that peculiar punishment. I was also told of a man who had been given a long term of imprisonment for having abused Stoyadinovitch to his companion as they sat at dinner in a restaurant; but actually the magistrate had done no more than advise him not to talk so loud next time.

But sometimes the hand of Stoyadinovitch fell very heavily indeed. It sometimes fell vexatiously on the intellectuals. I have known of a provincial lawyer of the highest character who was sent to prison for two months for treasonable conversation on the evidence of an ignoble personage who had before the war been an Austrian spy in Belgrade. The real damage done to the intellectuals lay not in the number of such cases or the severity of the sentences but in the insecurity arising from the knowledge that they could happen at all. But I believe that the hand fell with a murderous heaviness on the working classes. An English friend of mine once came on a tragic party of young men being sent down from a Bosnian manufacturing town to Sarajevo by a night train. All were in irons. The gendarmes told him that they were Communists. I expect they were nothing of the sort. Real Marxian Communism is rare in Yugoslavia, for it is not attractive to a nation of peasant proprietors and the Comintern wastes little time and energy in this field, but the word is extended to cover the mildest of left activities. These young men had probably done nothing worse than try to form a trade union. It was against such as these, I believe, that the Stoyadinovitch regime brought up its full forces.

Consideration of this bias brought one to the reason that the more serious-minded among the Yugoslavs gave for their hatred of Stoyadinovitch. They knew that their abominable prison system could not be reformed in a moment, they knew that they were often difficult and ungracious under government. But they could not forgive him for representing the thick-necked, plundering little men in the bar. Those men were his allies, and they were united against the rest of Yugoslavia. They were against the peasants, against the starving schoolmasters, against the workmen who had been brought to town and poverty like lambs to the slaughter.

It is plausible, yet I do not think it is true. Certainly Stoyadinovitch represented the financial and industrial interests of Belgrade, but he may not have meant to be his country's enemy. I have known Englishmen and Frenchmen who have done business with him, and they all received honest, even handsome treatment at his hands, which seemed to be part of a certain Augustan attitude, hardly consonant with carelessness for his country's interest. The truth was, I suspect, that he was astonishingly naïve, and that his naïveté was cut to an old-fashioned pattern. The clue to that was supplied every evening to anybody who would listen to it by the radio. The Yugoslavian news bulletins had in 1937 certain peculiarities. There was very little given out about the boy King and his mother, Queen Mariya: there was far more to be heard about the Regent, Prince Paul, and his family. This was a great mistake. I believe that it was the result of a very proper desire to give young King Peter some sort of unpublicized boyhood, but it was misinterpreted by the rural and provincial population who considered it was a sign that Prince Paul was ambitious and might wish to usurp the throne. But there was never nearly so much about any member of the royal family as there was about Mr. Stoyadinovitch. I have never turned on the radio in Yugoslavia without hearing a full account of everything the Prime Minister had done on the previous day, delivered in accents that would have been appropriate had he been a Commander-in-chief that had just driven an invading army over the frontier.

That might be taken as just another manifestation of the sham Cæsarism which is a commonplace of our age; and, indeed, towards the end of Stoyadinovitch's regime he had the unhappy notion of packing his meetings with youths who chanted, in a concert that was most uncharacteristic of the Slav, "*Vodyu! Vodyu! Vodyu!*" as it might be, "*Führer! Führer! Führer!*" But there was a difference. Here we had a relic of the pre-Cæsarean age that has passed from the rest of Europe. "Mr. Stoyadinovitch," Constantine once said to me, "admires capitalism." "Admires capitalism?" I echoed. "Why, how can he do that? Capitalism is an attempt at solving the problem of how man shall get a steady living off an earth that does not care a jot for him, and it may be said, until some Communist state has worked out its theory with better results than Russia, that we know of none more successful. But surely it is nothing like as good as what we want for ourselves, surely it can only be regarded with disappointment, not admiration." "So you think," said Constantine, "but so does not Mr. Stoyadinovitch. He knows that we are a poor country, since the Turks have taken all for five centuries, and he thinks it would be beautiful if much foreign money came here and bred more money, and if we had many factories such as they have in America, splendid white palaces full of machinery so intricate that when it moves it is like symphonies being played in steel, pouring out new and clean things for our people, pouring out golden streams of wages that all could be bought." "But sometimes money does not breed," I said, "sometimes it dies in childbirth, and the community is left with a whole lot of corpses on hand. And as for such factories, they may look like palaces but the people who work inside could never be taken for princes and princesses, and the stream of wages, which is golden in the same sense that the Danube is blue, often washes them back in the evenings to filthy slums." "You are a woman, you want all to be pretty," said Constantine, "you do not see the beauty of ruthlessness, and as for money, Mr. Stoyadinovitch is a very clever man. He would see that there are no depressions as there have been in America."

There is something here, touching in its inexperience, which is very different from Fascism or Nazism. Mussolini and Hitler came to power because they offered the victims of capitalism a promise of relief by a magical rite of regimentation. But this is an innocent who does not know that such victims can ever be numerous enough to exercise a determining force in society. He thinks of them as failures, as weak and impotent, and so they may be in their personal lives; but if they form a seething and desperate mass they may develop a dynamic power surpassing that engendered by success. Under this delusion he conducts himself with an extraordinary imprudence. He does not understand that it is wise to allow as many of the failures as possible to convert themselves by organization to something more like success, and so he fails—and in this he resembles many members of the propertied classes both in England and in America—to understand that trade unionism is not a disintegrating but a stabilizing force.

How should such men as these in the bar know otherwise? When the Industrial Revolution had dawned on the Western powers, the Serbs were Turkish slaves; to this day eighty-seven per cent of Yugoslavs are agricultural workers; Leskovats is called the Manchester of Yugoslavia and is no such thing, but a pleasant good-weathered little town of under twenty thousand inhabitants who have no difficulty in keeping their faces clean; never has Belgrade known a time when, from the uplifting windows of sky-scraper hotels it does not possess, ruined bankers dropped like the gentle dew from heaven upon the place beneath. It may be asked why these adventurers might not have learned of the inconveniences of capitalism from books and newspapers. Certain mistakes the printed word never kept anyone from committing. *Manon Lescaut* never deterred a man from loving a whore, no ageing woman sent away a young lover because she had read *Bel Ami*. There exists a mountain of economic publications which prove that in our modern world of shrinking markets and increasing production it would be impossible to found John Company; the Germans plan to draw such wealth from colonial expansion.

I felt a rush of dislike towards the men in the bar who were instruments of this error. I detected in them a strong physical resemblance to certain types found in Western cities during the last century, to pictures representing the financial adventurers who dominated Paris under the Second Empire, to the photographs of City men which can be seen in the illustrated papers of the nineties, named as founders of enterprises not now extant. Idiotically, they were not only copying a system that was far from ideal, they were themselves imitating those who had proved incapable of grasping such success as the system offers. I could imagine the hotel making the same error. It would repudiate its good fat risottos, its stews would be guiltless of the spreading red oil of paprika, it would employ chambermaids who would not howl by the beds of ailing clients and whose muzzles would not twitch in animal certainty before a Greek, in doubt before a Finn. It would not then resemble a good French hotel, it would become international, a tethered wagon-lit, like the large Spanish hotels.

Belgrade, I thought, had made the same error. It had till recently been a Balkan village. That has its character, of resistance, of determined survival, of martyred penury. This was a very sacred Balkan village; the promontory on which it stood had been sanctified by the blood of men who had died making the simple demand that, since their kind had been created, it might have leave to live. Modern Belgrade has striped that promontory with streets that had already been built elsewhere much better. I felt a sudden abatement of my infatuation for Yugoslavia. I had been enchanted on my first visit with the lovely nature and artifice of Bosnia, and I had recognized in Macedonia a uniquely beautiful life of the people. When the Macedonians loved or sang or worshipped God or watched their sheep, they brought to the business in hand poetic minds that would not believe in appearances and probed them for reality, that possessed as a birthright that quality which Keats believed to be above all others in forming a "Man of Achievement, especially in Literature, and which Shakespeare possessed so enormously." "Negative Capability," he called it, and it made a man "capable of being in uncertainties, doubts, without any irritable reaching after fact and reason." But Macedonia had been under the Ottoman Empire until 1913; it had till then been stabilized by Turkish misgovernment in precisely those medieval conditions which had existed when it was isolated by its defeat at Kossovo in 1389. Macedonia should perhaps be looked on as a museum not typical of the life outside it. It had had only twenty-five years of contact with the modern world. Serbia had known no such seclusion. It was liberated in 1815. For a century it had been exposed to the peculiar poisons of the nineteenth century. I had perhaps come a long way to see a sunset which was fading under my eyes before a night of dirty weather.

But some of this threatened degeneration was still a long way from consummation. This hotel may have longed to slip off its robust character and emulate the Savoy and the Crillon and the Plaza; but its attempt was not well under way as yet. A newcomer had arrived in the bar; the stocky little men were now greeting with cries of love and trust another of the kind who would have betrayed them for about the sum that would have made them betray him, lifting their glasses to him and slapping him on the back with the exaggeration of children playing the game "In the Manner of the Word." That I might have seen in London or Paris or New York. But in none of those great cities have I seen hotel doors slowly swing open to admit, unhurried and at ease, a peasant holding a black lamb in his arms. He took up his place beside the news-stand where they sold *Pravda* and *Politika*, the *Continental Daily Mail*, *Paris Soir*, the *New York Herald Tribune*. He was a well-built young man with straight fair hair, high cheekbones, and a look of clear sight. His suit was in the Western fashion, but he wore also a sheepskin jacket, a round black cap, and leather sandals with upturned toes; and to his ready-made shirt his mother had added some embroidery. He looked about him as if in search of someone. Twice he went to the door of the bar and peered at the faces of the stocky little men, so it was plain that he was waiting for one of their kind; and indeed the middle class in Yugoslavia is so near to its peasant origin that any of them might have had such a cousin or nephew. But the one he sought was not there, so he went back to his place by the news-stand. He stood still as a Byzantine king in a fresco, while the black lamb twisted and writhed in the firm cradle of his arms, its eyes sometimes catching the light as it turned and shining like small luminous plates.

Topola

As arranged, we called the next morning at Constantine's house ready to go with Gerda to see the half-finished Monument to the Unknown Soldier on the hill of Avala, twelve miles from Belgrade, and the Karageorgevitch Mausoleum on the hill of Oplenats. The expedition began badly. Gerda opened the door in trim, fresh clothes and was formally welcoming us in the hall when Constantine's old mother slipped in. Her mouth had suddenly watered for some kind of food, so she had tied a kerchief round her head and gone along to the market in her wrapper and slippers, and she had hoped to get back into the house without anybody being the wiser. But here we all were, being *hochwohlgeboren* in the passage. So Gerda looked at the floor with the air of blushing for shame, though her skin did not in fact show any alteration at all, and the poor old mother hung her Beethovenish head. This was all quite wrong, for she was really a magnificent pianist, and Balzac's dressing-gown is the one garment all artists have in common. One cannot create without a little sluttishness packed away somewhere. Neatness and order are delicious in themselves, but permissible only to the surgeon or the nurse. Schiller knew that when he kept rotting apples in his writing-desk, and opened the drawer when he needed inspiration, so that he could look on their brownness, inhale the breath of over-ripeness.

But Gerda had not been able to coerce Constantine. Shamelessly he called us into his study, and we found him fat and round and curly in his candy-striped pyjamas and dressing-gown, with little bouquets of black hair showing between his jacket buttons. "Ah, she is your girl too," said my husband, pointing to the photograph over Constantine's desk, which represented the Ludovisi triptych of Venus rising from the foam. "And why not?" said Constantine. "She is perfect, for what she is and what she is not. There is nothing in her pose of patriotism or propaganda or philosophy or religion, simply she says, 'I am rising to delight.' " His little fat hands paddled in the air, lifting him through the same tide as Venus, to the same sweet enamoured air. He, who is one of the ugliest of human beings, knows intuitively all that it is to be the goddess of beauty. "That sculpture is the very opposite of the frescoes that you have seen in South Serbia, that your husband will see in the mosaic copies that King Alexander made for the mausoleum at Oplenats.

For there is no delight, it is all patriotism and propaganda and philosophy and religion, but all the same there is rising, there is floating, there is an ecstasy, but it is a terrible one." His mouth was full of bread and coffee, but his hands paddled, and he rose up a beam of white light to a light that was whiter.

"You are an intelligent man, though you are a banker," he said to my husband, "so you will make no error at Oplenats, you will take these mosaics as an indication of what you will see in Macedonia, in South Serbia, not for themselves. All the Macedonian frescoes are painted, and these have been copied in mosaic. A painted fresco is a painted fresco and a mosaic fresco is a mosaic fresco, and a fresco that is meant to be painted and is worked in mosaic is a mongrel, and mongrels should be gay little dogs, not very large works of art. I suffered the tortures of the damned when I was in Germany and must arrange all for our King with the German manufacturer of mosaics, but I must own it was not only because of my artistic conscience, it was also because the manufacturer was the slowest man in the world. A tall, fat man he was with a great beard, and he spoke so . . . and so . . . and so . . . and once I could not help myself; I cried out, '*Mein Herr*, will you not speak a little faster, for I have many things to do,' and he answered, very angrily, but still very slowly, 'No, I cannot speak fast, for in the mosaic business we do all things very slowly, we make for eternity.' But you will see what he made. I am not sure that it was for eternity, I think it was only for ever, which is not at all the same."

On the porch he said, "It is fine weather, and it will be fine weather tomorrow, I am so glad that tomorrow we go to the Frushka Gora. That I have not told you about: there are some old monasteries of our people on some hills by the Danube, that are called the Frushka Gora, that is the Frankish Hills; they are very pretty in themselves, and they explain Belgrade and all that you will see today." So we drove off along the boulevards, which were crowded with leisurely people, for it was Sunday, and even those who had come to the market were taking it easy. For the same reason there were boys lolling at the open windows of the University Students' Hostel, in the lovely cat-like laziness only possible to highly exercised youth. From one window a boy, darker and more fiery than the rest, was leaning forward and making a burlesque harangue to a laughing group, who raised their hands and cried in mock-hatred, "Long live Stoyadinovitch!" Of such are the students whom the newspapers often describe as Communists, and a number of them would claim that title. Yet to Westerners nothing could be less accurate. These people are peasants who have in a sense enjoyed an unusual amount of class freedom. They were serfs only to the Turks, who were alien conquerors, and have not for centuries been subordinate to large landowners of their own blood, so they find it natural to criticize such of themselves as set up to be governors. Since they are South Slavs, they have never had a Peter the Great or Catherine the Great to teach them obedience to a centralized power. If they were to rebel against the Government they would act in small independent groups, as Princip and Chabrinovitch did, they would never joyously become subordinate atoms in a vast Marxist system. When they say they are Communists they mean that they are for the country against the town, for the village against Belgrade, for the peasant against the industrialist; and for that reason they one and all loathed Stoyadinovitch.

We were out of Belgrade, we were driving to the dark cone of distant Avala across a rolling countryside that was the spit and image of Lowland Scotland, though richer to the eye by reason of the redness of the earth. It bears signs of comfortable peasant proprietorship, and there came into my mind the verdict my Provençal cook had passed on a certain village on the Côte des Maures: *"C'est un bon pays; personne n'est riche là-bas mais tout le monde a des biens."* Fairer words cannot be spoken of a country, in my opinion; and I felt in great good humour. So, too, I was delighted to find, did Gerda. Her face was serene and she was making conventional German small-talk with my husband, and she was plainly passing through a specifically German experience which has always struck me as charming. Its simplest form is often displayed in old-fashioned German children's books. Little girls arrive in a coach at a Cologne hotel, with their hearts singing like birds within them: "Our papa," rises their carol, "is a Herr Geheimrath from Hanover, our mamma is everything a Frau Geheimrath should be, we are two well-behaved little girls, wearing beautiful new travelling ulsters, and we are going to see the Rhineland, which everybody knows is one of the most beautiful sights in the world, and all, all is heavenly." Neither the French nor the English ever get quite the same naïve, unpresumptuous joy in what one is and what one does, when both are unremarkable. We may rejoice in what we do, but we are too Augustinian not to detest what we are, or not to pretend such detestation. It pleased me enormously that Gerda was saying to herself as she drove along, "I come of an old family of Lutheran pastors, I am the wife of a Yugoslavian official, I am accompanying an Englishman, a cultured person and graduate of Oxford Uni-

versity and a banker, and his wife, who is a writer, and we are going to
see two interesting *Denkmals*, and it is a fine day."

The road swung round and round the cone of Avala, running between
woodlands, green with their first leaves and bronze with buds and
carpeted with blue periwinkles. We got out and climbed to the summit
over the unfinished gauntness of the engineering construction which is
to support the vast Mestrovitch memorial. At the very top we halted,
embarrassed by an unusual view of the fighting male. On the descending slope beyond stood two rows of soldiers, one facing the other, every
man of them holding in his hand something that flashed. An officer
cried out a word of command, which roared from his throat like a spell
designed for the instant precipitation of an ocean of blood. The soldiers
raised to their lips the things that flashed, which were tin mugs, and we
heard a strange sound which might have been made by birds singing
underground. Then the officer cried out for atrocity again, and a jet
of liquid, silver in the sunlight, spurted from each soldier's lips. They
were doing gargling drill against influenza. They saw us, but showed
no signs of self-consciousness. If the Serbian heroes of old had been
ordered by their Tsars to gargle in front of female tourists they would
have obeyed. Military service appears to be the only thing that makes
a Slav calm. The difference between the students we had seen at the
windows of the University Hostel and these soldiers was that which
might be remarked in France between the girl pupils of a *lycée*, gad-
ding and gossiping their way home through the streets of a provincial
town, and the still and stylized products of an extremely expensive
convent school.

We went down the hill again and paused beside a model of the
Mestrovitch memorial which was mounted on a truck. The roof of the
tomb is to be supported by immense calm caryatides, Serbian peasant
women, the mothers of these calm boys. We looked at the existing
memorial, which is rough and small, cut by some simple mason, and out
of curiosity I put my head into a little hut beside it. I wished I had not.
It housed the wreaths that had been laid on the memorial by various
official bodies. Through its gloom immortelles and ribbons lettered
with gold and striped with crude national colours emitted the nostril-
stopping smell of dust. By reason of the words spelled out by gold letters
and the combinations of the national colours, the spectacle was horrifying. These wreaths were displeasing in any case because they were
official, and had been ordered by preoccupied functionaries and sup-

plied as articles of commerce for a minor state occasion that would provoke no wave of real feeling in the people, but their provenance reminded one that the quality of Balkan history, and indeed of all history, is disgusting.

One wreath had been given by Nazi Germany, which had now absorbed the body of Austria, and which had been absorbed by the spirit of Austria; Vienna is speaking again, through Hitler as through Lueger and Schoenerer and Conrad von Hötzendorf, a message of self-infatuation and a quiver of hatreds for all but the chosen Teutonic people, the most poisonous being dedicated to the Slav. Another had been given by Italy, who had incessantly harried Dalmatia by her greed, who gave the assassins of King Alexander arms and the knowledge how to use them. It was a kind of filthy buffoonery almost unmatched in private life which had made these powers lay their wreaths on a grave sacred to a people whom they meant to send to its grave as soon as possible. It was an indictment of man that this people was forced to stand by when their enemies came to defile their holy place, simply because no political arrangement has been discovered which annuls the dangers arising out of Yugoslavia's proximity to Central Europe and Italy.

I became filled with feminist rage. I would have liked to deface the model of Mestrovitch's monument, which represented peasant women without contrition. Since men are liberated from the toil of childbirth and child-rearing, they might reasonably be expected to provide an environment which would give children the possibility to survive and test the potentialities of humanity. The degree of failure to realize that expectation revealed in this disgusting little room could not be matched by women unless ninety per cent of all births were miscarriages. Gerda, however, liked the wreaths. "Our father is a Herr Geheimrath. . . ." I put out my hand and touched the Italian offering, and murmured my distaste, but Gerda only wrinkled her nose and laughed slyly, like a little girl who sees something that her nurse has told her is dirty.

We drove away from Avala by a pleasant road that runs among water-meadows where willows mark the constant stream, and orchards with plump foliage smothering the last of the blossom, and vineyards naked and unpromising as graveyards, with their poles stripped bare for spring. Like the Pas de Calais, this Serbian countryside presents inconsistently neat cultivations and sluttish villages. The villages here are very large, for except in the neighbourhood of the big towns there are no scattered farmsteads. Wherever the peasant's land may be he lives in the village and drives his livestock home at night and out again in the morning. This custom proved its convenience during the Turkish occupation, for it enabled the Christians to put up a combined defence against night raids by irregular troops or bandits, but it had its origin further back than that. The basis of the Slav social system was the *Zadruga*, the family whose members shared equally in the labours and profits of a jointly owned estate, which was governed by an elected Elder, who was usually the oldest man in the group but might sometimes be a younger man who had shown exceptional ability, or might even be a woman. The Elder and his wife lived in a central house and the others inhabited either rooms joined to it or adjacent houses. The *Zadruga* naturally split up when the number of descendants began to press too heavily on the resources of the estate, but it usually included at least three generations and often numbered a hundred persons or more. The dreary identification between country life and solitude has therefore never depressed Serbia as it has other lands; and even quite insignificant villages run long main streets down a hill and over a stream and up the hill on the other side, where the cultivators of the trim orchards and vineyards loll outside tumbledown cafés, looking anything but trim themselves.

They were, indeed, not out to look trim. Ferocity was this district's line. They would have preferred to curdle the blood, just a little, by their manifest kinship with the Haiduks, with the great chief Karageorge himself. For we were already on the stage where that first liberator of Serbia had unveiled his violence and power. At a turn of the road we stopped to see the place where Karageorge was one day riding with his herdsmen behind his swine, just after the Janizaries had come back to power and murdered the pro-Serb Mustapha Pasha and were massacring every important Serb that they could find. Through the dust he saw the flashing weapons of a party of Turkish soldiers and without an instant's hesitation he and his herdsmen turned their horses' heads into the oak forests that bordered the road, leaving the swine to take care of themselves. Later we came to the village where Karageorge had met with two Serbian chiefs and five hundred of the rank and file, and had been chosen their Commander-in-chief in the first insurrection of 1804. This moody and valiant giant, who was no mere springing tiger but possessed real military genius, did not wish to accept that office, for curious reasons which have been reported for us by an actual witness. He said, "I want to go with you, but not before you," and when they pressed him for a reason he told them, "For one thing, you've not learned soldiering, and because of that, after some days, you will surrender to the Turks, then you know what will happen! And for another, if I accepted I certainly would do much not to your liking. If one of you were taken in the smallest treachery—the least faltering—I would kill him, hang him, punish him in the most fearful manner."

This was not a mere threat of disciplinary firmness; it was a confessional allusion to the violences which he had already committed under the stress of patriotism. Years before, when he was a youth, he had taken part in an uprising and had had to flee with his stepfather and their cattle towards the Austrian frontier. But when they came to the river Sava his stepfather's nerve failed him, and he announced he would turn back and seek pardon from the Turks. Karageorge did not believe that he would receive anything from the Turks but torture, so in desperation he took out his pistol and shot the old man dead. Then he went on to the next village and asked the headman to give the corpse burial, and left him all his cattle in payment. That Karageorge should at the moment of being chosen leader by his people have referred to their characteristic faults and his own, not in comfortable tones of conventional modesty but with an unimpassioned accuracy, is characteristically Slav. But East can meet West. The house where the three chiefs met has been pulled down and replaced by a towered school, closely resembling a small suburban public library.

We passed by a spa almost as unlike Bath or Vichy or Baden-Baden as the spa we had seen in Bosnia: no fine ladies and gentlemen were here in search of undefined recuperation, peasants were striding down a chestnut avenue towards the spring, solemnly conscious of what they expected its waters to do to their bowels, solemnly conscious of what their forefathers had known, that in water there are gods. There was a solid yet naïve *Kurhaus*, built by somebody who had gone to the West to see how these things were done, and had gaped at his model as well as studying. Since it was Sunday there were little boys offering trays of scones and rolls, for the Serbs love breadstuffs almost as much as the Scots; and others were selling miniature leather sandals of the type worn throughout Yugoslavia, with the upturned toe, which is useless though appropriate as a symbol of the x which is added to the usual human characteristics in the Slav. The evaluation of that x became an increasingly interesting problem as we drove along the lanes into Karageorge's village, Topola (which is one of the two Serb words for poplar), for there his kind stood in the mud, all with these cockspur points to their sandals, all with that Slav mystery heavy on their dark forelocks, across their scowling brows, hanging round a playground that had been Karageorge's stableyard. The main street took us to a village green, running uphill alongside a church with dome and walls battered and pitted with rifle-fire, and a galleried farmhouse that had been Karageorge's home and now bore the emblems of a Sokol headquarters. On a seat beneath some trees sat two parent wolves, an old man and woman, their ferocity silvered down to gentle and amiable dignity, emitting fire from the nostrils only now and then, finely dressed in the sheepskin and em-broidered homespun of peasant costume. The unknown quantity was not what one might have thought, for mere lawlessness and savagery do not age in majesty, with accumulated goods about them.

An old man came and took us into the church, which was full of the dark magic of the Orthodox rite, and told us that here Karageorge had come to take communion, and here his bones had rested ever since they had been laid there several years after his death, till they had been moved to the great new mausoleum on the hill of Oplenats half a mile away. "Where had they been in the meantime?" I asked. "In the ground," said the old man, "in a valley not far from here. He had come back from exile after Obrenovitch had become the leader of the Serbs, and Obreno-vitch sent a man to kill him, that he might placate the Sultan by sending him his head. But later Obrenovitch's wife grew alarmed, be-cause one of the children in her family grew ill, and she had the bones of Karageorge dug up and sent back to us here." Behind us in the dark-ness Gerda tittered. We turned in surprise and found her looking sur-prisingly fair. "They are such savages," she explained. The old man gazed at her perplexed, as if she might perhaps be ill or unhappy, and went on slowly with doubtful, kindly glances at her, to show us the screen that divides the whole altar from the church, the iconostasis. It was carved with artless sculptures of holy stories seen through peasant eyes, after the fashion of the fourteenth century, although the wood was new. "They were carved for us by three brothers," he said, "de-scendants of the three brothers who did the famous iconostasis and pulpit at the Church of the Holy Saviour in Skoplje, two hundred years ago. They have carried on the craft from father to son. Eight years they lived here, making this screen. Now they have been for many years at Nish, working on a screen that will be greater than this, but not more beautiful. For the Karageorgevitches they did their best." He opened the royal door in the iconostasis, that opens on the altar, and his face folded with grief. "Here once God gave us a great mercy. When our King Alexander went to Bulgaria we said mass here day and night dur-ing all the three days he was in Sofia, and although there are many

Bulgarians who hate us and have evil hearts, nothing happened to him, he came back to us in safety. But, God forgive us, when he went to France we did not say mass for him at all, for we thought he was among friends." Again history emitted its stench, which was here particularly noisome. Nothing a wolf can do is quite so unpleasant as what can be done to a wolf in zoos and circuses, by those who are assumed not to be wolfish, to be the civilized curators of wolfdom.

Before we got back into the car we stood for a minute on the green, looking at the fierce little church, at the fierce little farmhouse out of which some fierce boys were issuing, fresh from gymnastic exercises dynamized by patriotic fury, at the fierce and handsome ancients on the seat. "Now I see the truth of the old saying that there are more ways of killing a cat than by choking it with cream," said my husband. "Observe that in Bosnia the Slavs did choke the Turk with cream, they glutted him with their wholesale conversions and kept him outside of Sarajevo. But here cream just did not come into the question. The Serbs fought the Turks, and then they fought them, and then they fought them. What we see in these people is the normal expression to be looked for in a fighting army that has just come out of the trenches after a long hand-to-hand fight, and thinks it may yet be ambushed." But later, as we walked to the mausoleum where it lifts its white cupolas in a wooded park, as we passed under the dry grainy gold of its mosaic vaults, he said, "This, however, is something else. Has it anything to do with these people, this extraordinary place? Or is it just a fantasy of these Karageorgevitches?"

The church, which is dedicated to St. George, is quite new, and externally it is very beautiful. Fidelity to the Byzantine tradition is responsible for quite a number of very ugly small churches, for its reliance on pure form shows up any defects in the way of bad machine cutting and ugly stone; but it automatically imposes a certain majesty and restraint on a church which is given good material and skilled workmanship. Oplenats was built by old King Peter in 1912, but it was reduced to ruins during the Great War. In 1922 King Alexander rebuilt it, and added two features which had, apparently, not been in his father's mind when he originally planned it. King Alexander brought up the bones of Karageorge from the village church at Topola, and buried them under a plain block of marble in the right apse: that is to say, beside the royal throne which stands in any Orthodox church of dignity, which is here an impressive matter of green marble surmounted by a white-and-gold eagle. The only other Karageorgevitch whom King

Alexander thought worthy to be buried in the church itself, and not in the crypt, was King Peter, who lies under another plain block of marble in the left apse. This indicates a critical attitude which ruling monarchs do not usually adopt towards their dynasty: for there was another Karageorgevitch ruler, Alexander the son of Karageorge, but he was not a success.

The other contribution of King Alexander was the mosaics; King Peter planned no other decoration than the shot-riddled regimental banners, borne in the Balkan wars and the Great War, which hang from the marble pillars. These mosaics are indeed at first extremely disconcerting in their artistic impropriety. It is not mere pedantry to object to mosaic as a medium for copying painted frescoes, for the eye is perpetually distracted by its failure to find the conditions which the original design was framed to satisfy. These frescoes are Byzantine in origin: their proper title in the histories of art is Serbo-Byzantine. The flame-like forms that should have been fixed in appropriate tenuity by colours flame-like in their smoothness and transparency were falsified in their absence because they were represented in a material opaque and heterogeneous as sand. The man who ordered these mosaics to be made must have been lacking in any fine æsthetic perception. But they compose an extremely ably prepared encyclopædia of medieval Serbian art. Looking up at them one can say, "That Dormition of the Virgin comes from Grachanitsa, that sequence of the life of St. George comes from Dechani, that Flight into Egypt from Petch," and without receiving the intense pleasure which is given by the actual sight of these works of art, one is afforded useful information as to what sort of pleasure that is going to be.

"But why did this man want to hold up an encyclopædia of medieval Serbian art over his family vault?" asked my husband. "It seems to me as if an English king should build a mausoleum full of allusions to Richard Cœur de Lion." "Well, that is all the remote past they have," I said, "and they came straight out of that glory into the misery of Turkish conquest." "But is there any real continuity between the medieval Serbian Empire and these Serbs?" asked my husband. "Of course there is," I said; "you will see that once you get away from Belgrade." "But these frescoes are so beautiful," said my husband, "this is a true legacy from Byzantium. It is too patently sensitive for the great period of Byzantine art, but there is the right hieratic quality, the true desire to arrange all things in an order that shall disclose a relationship between the lowest and the highest, even God Himself." Then a thought struck him. "But where are these Serbo-Byzantine frescoes?" he asked. "In monasteries," I said, "some in Serbia; some of the most beautiful are in Studenitsa and Mileshevo and Zhitcha, but many are in Old Serbia and in South Serbia." "All on strictly Serb territory," said my husband, "so this building with its enormously costly mosaics can mean nothing whatsoever to any Croatians or Dalmatians or Slovenes. Yet it is the mausoleum of their King, and superbly appropriate to him. I see that though Yugoslavia is a necessity it is not a predestined harmony."

We went towards the crypt where King Alexander himself is buried, but the beauty of one of the frescoes caught my husband back. "But you never told me of this extraordinary thing," said my husband. "Here is a man whom I know only as a Balkan king with an unfortunate tendency to dictatorship. He appears to have conceived a gloriously poetic idea, such as only the greatest men of the world have ever had. He recovered the ancient lands of his people in the Balkan wars and tried —what was it Constantine once said?—'to graft his dynasty' on the stock of their ancient emperors so that what was dead lived again. It is quite a different idea from mere conquest. Those frescoes say to his people, 'This is what you were, so this is what you are.' But, tell me, was it anything more than a pedagogic fancy? Can those toughs we have seen outside really respond to such an idea?" "I am not sure," I said, "but I think he got it from them." "Nonsense," said my husband. "I refuse to believe that those young ruffians fret for lack of the Byzantine frescoes their ancestors enjoyed in the fourteenth century." "Well, I assure you they knew they had lost something," I said, "they all know by heart a lot of poetry." "They do not look as if they did," said my husband. "Oh, not Arthur Hugh Clough," I said, with a bitterness that referred to an attempt made by my husband to read me a poem by that writer which he had declared was tolerable, "but they know thousands of lines of folk-poetry about the defeat of the Serbs at Kossovo, and it gives an impression of a great civilization. I know that they tested the patients in the Serbian military hospitals during the war to see how many knew it, and it was something like ninety per cent." "Maybe," said my husband.

In the crypt lamps hanging above the tombs illumined long arcades. Mosaics on the walls and vaults shook with a feeble pulse in this uncertain light. There are numbers of Karageorgevitch dead lying here, and though it is only a hundred and twenty years since Karageorge died, not a few have lain here for many times the length of their lives.

This family, though so potent, was physically fragile. There are children, lads, young wives in their twenties, their names all trembling with that suggestion of weakness, headache, fever, which is given by tremulous lamplight. A stronger brightness was shed by the candles which blazed in an iron stand beside the grave of King Alexander, which lies at the altar end of the crypt, under slabs of onyx. Half a dozen men and women were lighting fresh candles and putting them in the stand, were crossing themselves and murmuring and kneeling and bringing their roughness down to kiss the shining onyx; such passion, I have heard, is shown by Lenin's tomb. The King lies beside his mother, as his will directed: she died of tuberculosis when he was fifteen months old. In this crypt, the foundation of this immense mass of marble erected to a parricide by his descendants, the core of this countryside on which defensive resentments grew like thick forests, all was plaintive and wistful, tender and nostalgic.

Franzstal

ABOVE us the day was blue and golden, as it had rarely been during this lachrymose spring. Around us it may have been so also, but we did not know. We were shut up in the courtyard of an inn. There was nothing remarkable about this courtyard. It was quite large; the rooms round it had a certain cosy quality, not at all Slav, as if they were built for a congestion which would not be at all contentious, but warm and animal and agreeable; on a line across the courtyard hung scarlet blankets and white sheets and towels embroidered in red cross-stitch; in flower-beds running by the walls primroses and tulips grew with an amusing stiffness. All that was worth seeing there could be seen in ten seconds.

Nor was this inn set in an interesting place. Outside there was a village consisting of one very broad and muddy street, lined with one-storied houses and shops. Sometimes a light cart passed, drawn by a mare with her foal running alongside, harnessed outside the poles; so do they accustom horses to the traffic from the beginning. Sometimes a herd of dirty and ill-tailored pigs roamed by, apparently free from all governance. There was really no reason to pay a visit to such a village, particularly on a Monday afternoon, when none of the population was visible to display such interesting characteristics as they possessed.

Nor was it for the food that we had come to this inn. On the table in front of the four of us, Gerda, Constantine, my husband, and myself, there were stacked platefuls of long undulant sausages that can never have been good specimens of their kind, that were particularly unpleasant at the moment, for they were neither quite warm nor quite cold. The liver sausage was peculiarly horrible, and left a layer of grease on the lips and palate.

My husband and I were not even there because we had made a mistake, and had been deceived by our ignorance of the country into believing that this village was interesting. We had not wished to come at all. It had been announced to us that we should. The evening before, on our return from Topola, we had been sitting at dinner in our hotel, uneasily discussing Gerda. During the day's expedition she had shown that she was disappointed with us. When we showed admiration or curiosity about Serbian things she behaved as if we were letting her down and betraying some standards which we should have held in common: as an exceptionally stupid Englishman might behave in India to tourists who showed an interest in native art or philosophy. "But she is worse than that," said my husband. "She said something to me this afternoon when you were making a sketch of the church at Topola which seemed to me profoundly shocking. She told me that the Serbs hold that the Austrians had no right to bombard Belgrade, as it was an unfortified town, and I could not understand whether this was just an attitude of the people or a serious opinion of informed men. So I asked, 'Does your husband think so?' She gave a queer, sly smile and said, 'Yes, he would say so, but then he is a good official.' That seemed to me the most utterly undisciplined and disloyal thing that the foreign-born wife of an official could possibly say." It was then that a waiter came to announce a telephone call from Constantine. When my husband came back he said, "Constantine tells me we will not be going to the Frushka Gora tomorrow, but the day after. Tomorrow he wants us to go and have lunch at a place called Franzstal." "Franzstal? Why Franzstal?" I said. "It is a suburb inhabited by the Swabs, the Germans who were settled here by Maria Theresa to colonize the lands that had been neglected by the Turks. But we will not see them if we go there by day, they will all be out at work in Belgrade or in the fields. Is there anything specially interesting there?" "That is what I asked Constantine," said my husband, "but he only said, as one who is doing his best, that the Swab girls wore from ten to twenty petticoats."

Next day we learned that the second part of our conversation was explained by the first, as we crossed the Danube and found our way to Zemun, which used to be the first town over the Hungarian frontier, and is now remarkable only for its enormous population of storks. Gerda wore an expression of sleepy satisfaction which increased as we drew nearer to Franzstal. Now, as she sat at this table in the courtyard, eating her tepid sausages, her face was soft with complete contentment. Constantine watched her and broke into a tender laugh. "Is it not extraordinary, the patriotism of Germans?" he asked us. "My wife is quite happy, because this little village is quite German and she feels she is surrounded by what is German." It was difficult to make a helpful response. I am fond of England myself, but I trust that if I lived in Rome I would not insist that some French or German visitors who happened to be in my power should cancel a trip to Tivoli or Frascati in order to spend the day in an English tea-room. "Would you believe it," continued Constantine fondly, "she would not consent to be my wife until I had admitted to her that Charlemagne was a German. They are like rocks, these Germans." A silence fell. My husband and I were both reflecting that in the Nazis' opinion Charlemagne was not a German but an oppressor of Germans. Since we dared not make a frivolous comment and could not make a serious one, our eyes grew vacant. Above us the misused day was glorious. We heard doors banging in the inn, somewhere a parrot began to scream. A girl in bunchy skirts came into the courtyard, put down a ewer, and pulled up an iron plate in the paving and drew herself some water from a well. "Look," said poor Constantine timidly, "she is wearing very many petticoats, it might be as many as ten or twenty."

Frushka Gora

WE STOOD in the disordered rooms of some sort of society called "The Serbian Queen Bee," and I had difficulty in fixing my attention on Constantine and the officials of the society as they explained to us precisely what it was. We had started at seven from Belgrade and had travelled for two hours to Novi Sad, a journey which might have been pleasant, for the train ran beside the hallucinatory landscape of the misted Danube floods, but which was not, because it became apparent that Gerda had decided to detest us. Every word and movement of hers, and even in some mysterious way her complete inaction, implied that she was noble, patient, industrious, modest, and self-effacing, whereas we were materialist, unstable, idle, extravagant, and aggressive. She was at that moment standing in the corner of the room behind the men who were talking to me, silently exuding this libellous charade.

The town, I understood they were telling me, had been founded by the Patriarch Arsenius III at the end of the seventeenth century. When the Serbians revolted against the Turks in 1689 and failed, the Emperor Leopold of Austria offered them asylum on his territories, with full rights of religious worship and a certain degree of self-government. There were already a number of Serb settlers there who had been introduced by the Turks when Hungary was theirs. The Patriarch accepted the offer and led across the Danube thirty thousand Serbian families, from all parts of the land, as far south as Macedonia and Old Serbia. Some of them had settled here in Neuestadt, as it had been called. A good many of them had fled back to Turkish territory, for the Emperor broke his promises, and the Austrians and Hungarians bled them white with financial and military levies and forbade them the use of the Orthodox rite. Only for a little time, under Maria Theresa's liberal son, the Emperor Joseph, did the refugee Serbs enjoy honest treatment. But they never forgot their language and their culture, and in 1823 they founded this literary society, "The Serbian Queen Bee." It was unfortunate that we had come to visit its headquarters just when it had been handed over to the house painter, they said anxiously.

We could get some idea of what the society had preserved, we replied; and pulled out some of the pictures that were stacked against the wall. We came again and again on typical portraits of the sort that pullulated on the whole of nineteenth-century Europe except France, where there were too many good eighteenth-century portrait-painters for artlessness to take the country by storm. Men who were nothing but moustaches and sloping shoulders, women who were nothing but smoothly parted coiffures and stiffly caged bodices, had their Slav characteristics contracted down to a liverish look. "They did not migrate here," murmured my husband, "until three hundred years after the destruction of the Serbo-Byzantine civilization. I expect the continuity was quite thoroughly broken, and that King Alexander was simply a doctrinaire acting on nationalist——" His voice broke. "Theory," he added, uncertainly. He had turned to the light a Byzantine Madonna, vast-eyed, rigid in the climax of an exalted rhythm. The Serbs had, indeed, not lost all their baggage on their way here.

"I will show you all," said Constantine, "all I will show you. Therefore we must hurry, for I will show you the Patriarchate at Karlovtsi, which has been the headquarters of the Serbian Church since the great migration of Arsenius, before we go to the monasteries of the Frushka Gora." So we soon left this town, which was very agreeable and recalled my own Edinburgh in its trim consciousness of its own distinction. Our road took us into pretty country, green and rolling, at the river's edge. Once we paused at a church that had the remarried look of a building that has changed its faith. It had been a mosque during the hundred and fifty years the Turks held Hungary; it has since the early eighteenth century been a Roman Catholic Church. The club-like atmosphere of a mosque still hung round it: it had a wide terrace overlooking the waters, where there should have been sitting impassive and contented men in fezes, drawing on some immense secret fund of leisure. We stood there for a moment, soothed by the miles of water, pale as light itself, on which stranded willows impressed dark emblems, garlands and true-lover's knots and cat's-cradles. We went back to our contest with mud, with the dark Central European ooze that is never completely mastered save by a drought so extreme as to be a still greater affliction, that rose now in thick waves before our wheels, that kept the upper hand even in the main street of Karlovtsi, though that was a handsome little town.

The Patriarchate was a nineteenth-century stone palace, built in the Byzantine style with Austrian solidity, rich in arch and balcony. We went up a flight of steps to the florid entrance and rang the bell, and looked round us at the gardens, which were very ornate in the formal

DUBROVNIK: the fountain of Onofrio de la Cava and Church of St. Saviour

Costume of Mostar

style, with many flower-beds laid out in intricate shapes and surrounded with low box hedges, and numbers of lilac bushes bearing peculiarly heavy purple flowers. The door did not open. We rang the bell again, we knocked with our fists, we went back to the car and sounded the hooter. Nothing happened, so we went into the gardens, Constantine clapping his hands and crying "Holla! Holla!" to the unresponsive palace. The gardens were mystifying, inside the beautifully tended box hedges the flower-beds were choked with weeds, a single garden chair, made of white painted wire in the Victorian fashion, was set quite alone on a wide gravel space, with an air of deluded sociability, as if it had gone mad and thought that there were about it many other garden chairs. Children came in from the street and followed us about. We could find no gardener, and the only door we could find opened into a large room with stone shelves used for storing an immense quantity of jam. We had given up all hope of entering, and had paused to inhale the scent of the prodigious purple lilacs, when an old man carrying an orange came out of a door we had not seen and told us that the Patriarch was in Belgrade, but there were some priests working at the printing-press near by, and he would fetch us one of them.

There came to us a tall monk, nobly beautiful, wearing a cloak of complicated design and majestic effect: all the garments worn in the Eastern Church are inherited from Byzantium and recall its glory. He had perfect manners, and was warm in his greeting to Constantine and Gerda, but his eyes lay on us with a certain coldness and reproach. I was surprised at this, for I had always found Orthodox ecclesiastics disposed to treat English people as if they were members of the same Church; but I supposed that here, at headquarters, they might be stricter in their interpretation of schism and heresy. But he was courteous, and told us that he would take us over the Patriarchate, and would like also to show us the printing-press, in which he took a special interest as he was head of Propaganda.

It lay behind the gardens, in a no-man's-land of alleys and outhouses, countryish and clean, with here and there more of those prodigious lilacs, and little streams running down to the Danube. From a courtyard filled with green light by a gnarled old fruit tree we went into a dusty office, where an old priest and a young one sat at rickety desks furnished with ink-wells and pens and blotting-paper that all belonged to the very dawn of stationery. Pamphlets of artless appearance, incompetently tied up in bales, were lying about not in disarray but in only amateurish array. We went down a step or two to the composing-room, where a man stood before the sloping trays and set up print in the fantastic Old Slavonic type used in Orthodox missals and in no secular writings whatsoever. We went up a step or two into a room where young girls bound the pamphlets, not very skilfully but most devoutly. Then in another room, either two steps up or two steps down but certainly not on the same level, we found a lovely twisted old man, deformed by the upward spiral of his spirit, as El Greco loved to paint his holy kind. He fed the printing machine with sheets as if he had to school himself to remember that the poor mindless thing could do its sacred work only at a certain pace. We might have been visiting the office of some small, fantastic cult carried on by a few pure and obstinate and unworldly people in some English town. Indeed, I know a shop in a Sussex village, owned by a sect which believes that the way to please God is by ritual water-drinking, which was the precise analogue of this modest and fanatic establishment. Yet this was the analogue of a printing-press owned by the Church of England and housed by the Archbishop of Canterbury in the grounds of Lambeth Palace.

We had still to wait for some minutes before the front door of the Patriarchate, though the priest had gone through the kitchen to send up a servant to open it. Then it slowly swung open, and a withered little major-domo looked out at us. It seemed to me that he pursed his lips when he saw my husband and myself. "Good morning," said Constantine, stepping inside, "and how is life going with you?" "Pol-ako, polako," answered the little man, that is, "Only so-so." "Why, he speaks like a Russian," said Constantine, and talked to him for a little. "Yes," he said, "he was a Russian officer, and he is very pious and he would like to be a monk, but he has a wife, so they have made him major-domo here." He was at least somewhere which might have re-minded him of his home. I have never been to Russia, but I have visited states which formed part of Tsarist Russia, Finland and Estonia and Latvia, and I am familiar with villas that have belonged to rich Rus-sians in France and Italy and Germany, and I can recognize a certain complex of decoration and architecture as Romanoff and nothing else.

It has elements that can be matched in other countries. Something like it can be seen in the older mansions built by the nineteenth-century barons on Riverside Drive and in the Middle West and the West; there is the same profusion of busy and perforate woodwork in the interior. There is a suggestion also of the photograph-frames and boxes made of shells which are to be bought at English seaside towns; and they recall also the presents that people give each other in German provincial shops, such as umbrellas with pink marble tops cut into stags' heads. There is a suggestion, in fact, of every kind of bad taste known to Western civilization, down to the most naïve and the most plebeian; and there is a curious absence of any trace of the classical and moderating influence which France has exercised on the rest of Europe, though it has suffered the gilt infection spread by the Roi Soleil. Yet there is also from time to time the revelation of a taste so superb that it puts the West to shame. There is here a passion which is the root of our love for beauty, and therefore of our effort for art; the passion for beautiful substances, for coloured gems, for shining stone, for silver and gold and crystal. There is not only this basis for art, there is art, there is a creative imagination that conceives vast and simple visions, as a nomad would see them, who, lifting his eyes from the plains, looks on the huge procession of the clouds. There is also a feeling for craft; this nomad was accustomed to pick up soft metal and twist it into the semblance of horses and wild beasts, shapes he could criticize, since he rode the one and hunted the other, so much that he knew their bodies as his own.

We are perhaps looking not at a manifestation of bad taste at all, but at the bewilderment of a powerful person with perfect taste who has been suddenly transported from a world in which there are only a few materials, and those in a pure state, to be shaped by that taste or ignored, into another world, crammed with small manufactured objects, the product of other people's tastes, which are so different from his that he cannot form any just estimate of their value. The powerful Russian people were kept from Western art by the Tartar occupation. They have never made full contact with it. This is no more than a giant's stupendous innocence; yet it is also a giant's stupendous vulgarity. He has resolved his doubts in too many cases by consideration of the money value of objects, or of the standards of people who may be of rank but who are historically ridiculous. But he is a giant, and it is something to be above the dwarfish ordinary stature.

There was, indeed, one room in the Patriarchate that was magnificent, a conference chamber with a superb throne and crimson curtains which might have been taken from one of the finest Viennese palaces, but was derived from a larger and more dramatic inspiration. The rest was faintly bizarre and sometimes that not faintly. We sat down in a small drawing-room, while Constantine talked to the priest and the

major-domo; and I remarked that the furniture was not what would
have been found in an English archbishop's palace. It was a suite made
from black wood, including chairs and tables and bookcases, all decorated with gilt carvings, three or four inches long, representing women
nude to the waist, with their breasts strongly defined. They were placed
prominently on the pilasters of the bookcases, on the central legs of
the round tables, on the arms of the chairs. They were a proof, of
course, of the attitude of the Orthodox Church regarding sexual matters, which it takes without excitement, and I am sure nobody had ever
cast on them a pornographic eye. But for all that they were naïvely
chosen as ornaments for an ecclesiastical home.

"But why," I said to Constantine, "are both the priest and the major-
domo looking at me and my husband as if they hated us?" "Oh, it is
nothing personal," said Constantine, "but they both hate the English."
"Ha, ha, ha!" said Gerda, laughing like somebody acting in an all-star
revival of Sheridan. "That I suppose you find very odd, that anybody
should hate the English." "But what do they know about the English?"
asked my husband. "The old officer hates very much the English," explained Constantine, "because he says that it was Sir George Buchanan
who started the Russian Revolution." We had to think for a minute
before we remembered that Sir George Buchanan had been our Ambassador at St. Petersburg in 1917. "But does he not think that perhaps
Kerensky and Lenin had a little to do with it?" asked my husband.
When it was put to him the major-domo shook his head and emitted
an impatient flood of liquid consonants. "He says," translated Constantine, "that that is nonsense. How could unimportant people like Kerensky and Lenin do anything like starting a revolution? It must have
been someone of real influence like Sir George Buchanan."

"Now, ask the priest why he hates the English," I said. "It is because
he believes that Lloyd George could have saved the Romanoff dynasty," said Constantine, "but I do not understand what he means."
"I know what he means," I said; "he has heard the story that the
Bolsheviks would have allowed the Tsar and Tsarina and their family
to come to England, and Lloyd George would not let them. But you
can tell him that there was not a word of truth in that story, that
Lloyd George's worst enemies have never been able to confirm it. The
Bolsheviks never offered to turn the poor souls over to us and there is
no shred of evidence that they would ever have done so if they had
been asked." But the priest only shook his head, his beautiful brown
eyes showing him as inaccessible to argument as if he were a stag. "It

is no use talking to these good people," said Constantine, "for this house is all for White Russia. The Patriarch is mad against the Bolsheviks, and he thinks that all European problems would be solved and that we would enter a Golden Age if only the Romanoffs were restored, and he cannot see why England has not done it." I thought apprehensively of the stacks of pamphlets in the printing-press, with their rough biscuit-coloured paper and their pale sticky type, and I wondered what astonishing information they gave out when they were designed, as they sometimes are, to instruct the Orthodox laity in political matters.

But before we left for the Frushka Gora, the priest in the grand cloak would have us see the Patriarchate church, which is next door to the palace; and once we were there all the ineffectiveness and art-lessness that we had seen, the clutching at broken toys and the kinder-garten assurance that life was simple when it was in fact most compli-cated, fell into its place and appeared legitimate. In the white-and-gold theatre of a baroque church the students of the theological seminary attached to the Patriarchate were assisting at a Lenten mass. The priests passed in and out of the royal door in the great iconostasis, which framed in gilt the richness of the holy pictures. As they came and went there could be seen for an instant the shining glory of the altar, so sacred that it must be hidden lest the people look at it so long that they forget its nature, as those who stare at the sun see in time not the source of light but a black circle. The students' voices affirmed the glory of the hidden altar, and declared what it is that makes the ador-able, what loveliness is and harmony. The unfolding of the rite brought us all down on our knees in true prostration, with the forehead bent to the floor. "It is only necessary to do this during Holy Week," gasped Constantine apologetically in my ear. "I am so very sorry." He thought that English dignity would be affronted by the necessity to adopt this attitude. But there could have been nothing more agreeable than to be given the opportunity to join in this ceremony, which, if nothing in the Christian legend were true, would still be uplifting and fortify-ing, since it proclaims that certain elements in experience are supremely beautiful, and that we should grudge them nothing of our love and service. It inoculated man against his constant and disgusting madness, his preference for the disagreeable over the agreeable. Here was the unique accomplishment of the Eastern Church. It was the child of Byzantium, a civilization which had preferred the visual arts to litera-ture, and had been divided from the intellectualized West by a widen-ing gulf for fifteen hundred years. It was therefore not tempted to use

the doctrines of the primitive Church as the foundation of a philosophical and ethical system unbridled in its claim to read the thoughts of
God; and it devoted all its forces to the achievement of the mass, the
communal form of art which might enable man from time to time
to apprehend why it is believed that there may be a God. In view of the
perfection of this achievement, the ecclesiastics of the Eastern Church
should be forgiven if they show the incompetence in practical matters
and the lack of general information which we take for granted in
painters and musicians. They are keeping their own order, we cannot
blame them if they do not keep ours.

The Frushka Gora, that is to say the Frankish Hills, which are called
by that name for a historical reason incapable of interesting anybody,
lie to the south of the Danube; and we had to drive across the range
to find the monasteries founded by the seventeenth-century migrants,
for they lie scattered on the southern slopes, looking back towards
Siberia. Once we were over the crest we found ourselves in the most
entrancing rounded hills, clothed with woods now golden rather than
green with the springtime, which ran down to vast green and purple
plains, patterned with shadows shed by a tremendous cloudscape,
slowly sailing now on its way to Asia. We stopped to eat at a hotel
high above a valley that fell in a golden spiral to the plains; and it
should have been agreeable, for this is a centre for walking-tours, and
we had around us many young people, probably teachers freed from
their duty because it was near Easter, and there is nothing so pretty
as the enjoyment people get out of simple outings in countries that
have been liberated by the Great War. It is so in all the Habsburg succession states, and it is so in the Baltic provinces that once were Russia, Finland and Estonia and Latvia. But we did not enjoy our outing
so much as we might have, because Gerda had been on the wrong side
of the peace treaties.

Constantine was saying, "And much, much did we Serbs owe to
those Serbs who were in Hungary, who were able to bring here the
bodies of their kings and their treasure and keep alive their culture,"
when Gerda crossly interrupted him. "But why were the Serbs allowed
to stay here?" "It is not a question of being allowed to stay here," said
Constantine, "they were invited here by the Austrian Empire." "Nonsense," said Gerda; "one does not invite people to come and live in
one's country." "But sometimes one does," said Constantine; "the Austrian Emperor wanted the Serb soldiers to protect his lands against the
Turks, so in exchange he promised them homes." "But if the Austrians

gave the Serbs homes then it was most ungrateful for the Yugoslavs to turn the Hungarians out of this part of the country," said Gerda, "it should still be a part of Hungary." "But we owe nothing to Hungary, for they broke all their promises to the Serbs," said Constantine, "and since the Austro-Hungarian Empire has ceased to exist and we reconstituted it according to the principle of self-determination and there were more Slavs here than any other people, this certainly had to become Yugoslavia."

To change the subject Constantine went on, "But there are Slavs everywhere, God help the world. You have the Wends in Germany, many of them, and some distinguished ones, for the great Lessing was a Wend. They are Slavs." "But surely none of them remember that," said my husband. "Indeed they do," said Constantine; "there was a Wendish separatist movement before the war and for some time after the war, with its headquarters in Saxony. I know that well, for in 1913 I went with a friend to stay in Dresden, and when we described ourselves as Serbs the hotel porter would not have it at all. He said, 'I know what you mean, and I have sympathy with all who stand with their race, but you will get me into trouble with the police if you say you are Serbs,' and he would hardly believe it when he looked at our passports and saw that there was a country called Serbia." "But if all the Wends are Slavs," said Gerda, "why do we not send them out of Germany into the Slav countries, and give the land that they are taking up to true Germans?" "Then the Slavs," I said, "might begin to think about sending back into Germany all the German colonists that live in places like Franzstal." "Why, so they might," said Gerda, looking miserable, since an obstacle had arisen in the way of her ideal programme for making Europe clean and pure and Germanic by coercion and expulsion. She said in Serbian to her husband, "How this woman lacks tact." "I know, my dear," he answered gently, "but do not mind it, enjoy the scenery."

She could not. Her eyes filled with angry tears, the lower part of her face became podgy with sullenness. We none of us knew what to say or do, but just at that moment someone turned on the radio and the restaurant was flooded with a symphony by Mozart, and we all forgot Gerda. Constantine began to hum the theme, and his plump little hands followed the flight of Mozart's spirit as at Yaitse they had followed the motion of the bird at the waterfall. We all drew on the comfort which is given out by the major works of Mozart, which is as real and material as the warmth given by a glass of brandy, and I wondered, seeing its efficacy, what its nature might be. It is in part, no doubt, the work of the technical trick by which Mozart eliminates the idea of haste from life. His airs could not lag as they make their journey through the listener's attention; they are not the right shape for loitering. But it is as true that they never rush, they are never headlong or helter-skelter, they splash no mud, they raise no dust. It is, indeed, inadequate to call the means of creating such an effect a mere technical device. For it changes the content of the work in which it is used, it presents a vision of a world where man is no longer the harassed victim of time but accepts its discipline and establishes a harmony with it. This is not a little thing, for our struggle with time is one of the most distressing of our fundamental conflicts, it holds us back from the achievement and comprehension that should be the justification of our life. How heavily this struggle weighs on us may be judged from certain of our preferences. Whatever our belief in the supernatural may be, we all feel that Christ was something that St. Paul was not; and it is impossible to imagine Christ hurrying, while it is impossible to imagine St. Paul doing anything else.

But that was not all there was in the music; it was not merely the indication of a heavenly mode. The movement closed. It was manifest that an argument too subtle and profound to be put into words—for music can deal with more than literature—had been stated and had been resolved in some true conclusion. If those of us who listened should encounter the circumstances which provoke this argument we would know the answer, we would not have to agonize to find it for ourselves if we had been sensitive enough to recognize it. But as the eardrums were taken over by the ordinary sounds of a restaurant, by chatter and clatter, it became apparent how little as well as how much the music had done for us. A particular problem had been solved for us, but in a way that made it completely unserviceable to those millions of people who do not like music, and that indeed was not as clear to all of us as it should have been if we were to get on with the business of living. To comprehend this solution we had all had to learn to listen to music for years, and when we wanted to recall it in time of need we had to exercise both our memories and our powers of interpretation. A tool should not make such demands on those that handle it. And of such solutions Mozart had found only a number, which was large when one considered how great the genius required for their finding, but small compared to the number of problems that vex mankind; and he was unique in his powers, none has excelled him. Art covers not even a corner of life, only a knot or two here and there, far apart and without relation to the pattern. How could we hope that it would ever bring order and beauty to the whole of that vast and intractable fabric, that sail flapping in the contrary winds of the universe? Yet the music had promised us, as it welled forth from the magic box in the wall over our heads, that all should yet be well with us, that sometime our life should be as lovely as itself. But perhaps no such promise had been given; perhaps it was only true that had a human voice spoken in such tones it would have been to express tender and protective love. If the musician used them in the course of his composition it might be only because he found they fitted in some entertaining arrangement of the scale.

At a point on the plains there was now heaped up a drift of dark cloud; and through this there ran a shaft of lightning. A storm was on us, and it was in alternate blackness and greenish crystal light that we began our journey to four of the monasteries of the Frushka Gora, a journey which was astonishing in the directness of its contact with the past. It was as if one should drive along the South Downs, turning off the main road and following by-roads in to the downlands at Sullington and Washington and Steyning, and should find buildings where persons involved in the tragedy of Richard II had but newly cast aside their garments in mourning, where the sound of their weeping was hardly stilled. It made for a strangeness which immediately caught the eye that all these monasteries, so far from Byzantium, are built in the Byzantine fashion, with the quarters for the monks or nuns and pilgrims built in a square round an open space with the church in the middle. Though some have been burned down and rebuilt in the style of the Austrian baroque, they keep to the original ground plan, and cannot be confused with anything of recent or Western inspiration.

The first monastery we visited had been rebuilt in Austrian fashion. It raised above its quadrangle roofs a cupola as ornate as a piece of white coral, dazzling now in the strange stormlight against an inky sky; and it lay among orchards, their tree-trunks ghostly with spray. It might have been in the Helenenthal, an hour from Vienna. But within we found that the Eastern idea was still in government, that a wall had been built before the altar to dam the flow of light, to store up a reservoir of darkness where mystery could engender its sacred power. It possessed some relics of a saint, a Herzegovinian soldier who had wandered hither and thither fighting against the Turk, first under a Serbian despot and then under a Hungarian king. The legend ran that the Turks took the town where he was buried and were terrified because rays of light proceeded from his grave, and went to their emir, who was overcome at finding who the dead man had been and gave his body to the monks of this monastery. For this emir was a renegade who had been taken prisoner by the Turks and had bought his life by renouncing his faith; and he was not only a Herzegovinian, he was actually kin to the dead man. The news of this wonder came to the Saint's widow, who was a refugee in Germany, and she sought out this monastery, in defiance of the Turks, and became a hermit near by, till she died and was buried here, near to her husband.

This might have happened yesterday, indeed it might have happened today, for the monastery is in the care of White Russian nuns, wearing a melancholy head-dress of a close black cap fitting over a black veil that falls about the shoulders, and still preoccupied by the distress of their exile. It was hard to keep their misfortunes distinct in our minds from those of the founders of the monastery, and indeed others had failed to do so. Constantine halted by a grave in the quadrangle to tell me that it housed an abbess who had been stricken down during the seventeenth-century migration; and two young novices who were standing by, girls who had been born after their parents' flight from their fatherland and had been drawn here by an inborn Tsarist nostalgia, exclaimed in surprise. They had thought her one of their own community who had died on her way from Russia.

The black sky was pressing lower, the cloisters gleamed at us through an untimely dusk. Constantine thought that if we were to be storm-bound it had better be in a monastery where there was more to see, and we hurried back to the car under the first heavy pennies of rain. Thunder and lightning broke on us as we ran into Krushedol, another monastery which has been burned and given an Austrian exterior while keeping its ancient core. But this was older than the others. When the leader of the Slav forces at the battle of Kossovo, the Tsar Lazar, was killed on the field, the rags of his power were inherited by his kin, and there was one unhappy heir, named Stephen, whose fate was lamentable even for that age. His father, forced to seal a treaty by giving the Sultan Murad his daughter as a bride, sent his son to bear her company; but in time the Sultan fell into war with his wife's father and put out the young man's eyes lest he should take up arms in the fight. In his private darkness he reeled across the Balkan Peninsula, sometimes a captive dragged from prison to prison, then, released, back to his father's camp on the Danube, then away with his father again to wander in exile. His father died; his two brothers, one blinded like himself by the Sultan, engaged in fratricidal war; his mother also died, it is thought of poison; his blind brother fled and became a monk on Mount Athos; his victorious brother died. Though this dead usurper had named an heir, a party of the nobles took Stephen, and, spinning him round as in the game of blind-man's-buff, made him declare himself Despot of Serbia. The Serbians, seeing themselves threatened with civil war in the face of their Hungarian and Turkish enemies, rushed on him and sent him out of their land, bound and under guard. Again he stumbled about the Balkan Peninsula, sometimes pushed back into Serbia by his heartless supporters and beaten out again by his reluctant subjects, always preserving his gentle, patient fortitude. At one time he seemed to find a lasting refuge in Albania, where the great hero Skanderbeg took a great liking to him and gave him his own daughter, the Duchess Angelina, for wife. But the Turks came to Albania also, and the blind man was homeless again, and was in Italy when death took him. Then his widow and his two sons, now penniless, started to wander afresh, and Hungarian charity maintained them here. One of the sons became a priest, and he founded this monastery, and in time all three of them were laid in the same tomb before the altar. In the dark church, that blazed with light because of the profligate but mellow gilding on the iconostasis, we were shown the Duchess Angelina's narrow and elegant hand, black and mummified, loaded with the inalienable rings of her rank.

But there was other royalty here. Under a round red stone on the floor was buried King Milan Obrenovitch, the king who was so little of a success that he was forced to abdicate in 1889, who wandered almost as much as Stephen, but on more comfortable routes, from Belgrade to Vienna and Paris, harried not by the Turks without but by the Turk within. Nor was his grave all we saw of him at Krushedol. There is a memorial to him in the church wall, erected by the Emperor Franz Josef. "Why not?" said Constantine. "Milan was all for Austria, he governed our country as an Austrian dependency." Later, in the treasury, which was not in the church but in the monastery, a flash of lightning dispersed the unnatural dusk and showed us the contorted trees of the wind-flogged woods outside, and inside a medley of Byzantine church vestments, medieval chalices and crosses, ancient manuscripts, and the cups and saucers, prettily painted with pale flowers in the Slav fashion, the silver teapots and coffee-pots, the wineglasses and decanters, of King Milan's last establishment. These had been sent here by the Emperor Franz Josef, to whom, by an act of testamentary whimsy, King Milan had left the entire contents of his home.

"It would be, quite simply, that he would hardly notice to whom he left them, so long as it was not to his wife, Natalia," said Constantine. "Is she buried here?" I asked. "No, not at all," said Constantine. The negative he used sounded delightful in this connexion. "She is not dead, she is living in Paris, very poor.[1] Only the other day the Government was obliged to prevent a German company from making a film about the Obrenovitches and she wrote a letter about it." "And she will never be buried here," said the Abbot, a grave person who had been a priest and had become a monk ten years ago, after the death of his beloved wife. "That is, unless she is granted the light before she dies, for she was converted to Roman Catholicism about thirty years ago. It was a strange thing to do, for our people had been kind to her, and had taken her part when her husband dealt wickedly with her."

In another room there was arranged all the furniture from King Milan's drawing-room; a salon of the eighties sat there in its stuffy and shiny richness, and from its walls there stared the portraits of the doomed family—King Milan, with the wide cat-grin of a tormented buffoon, the excessively, grossly beautiful Queen Natalia, their fat son Alexander, who was like his father in resembling a cat, though this time the cat had been doctored, and Queen Draga, who was so prosaic that even now, when we can recognize her expression as fear and know what she feared, her face remains completely uninteresting. "Our Mrs. Simpson," said Constantine, pointing to her picture. "Yes! yes! Our Mrs. Simpson," cried the Abbott, going into fits of laughter. There was also King Milan's bedroom, furnished in rosewood, and more portraits of these unhappy people, preserved in tragedy like flies in amber.

Before we went away I went into the treasury again to take a last look at the embroideries and caught sight of two photographs which showed Serb peasants and soldiers and priests walking through the snow, with expressions of extreme anguish, bringing the body of King Milan to his grave. "But how could they feel so passionately about Milan Obrenovitch?" I asked Constantine. "He had done ill by his country and ill in his personal life. I noticed that even the Abbot spoke of him as behaving wickedly." "It does not matter what Milan Obreno-

[1] Queen Natalia died in a convent in Paris in May 1941.

vitch was in himself," said Constantine. "He was our first-crowned king after the Turkish conquest. When we were free our power flamed like a torch in the hands of our Emperor Stephen Dushan, but afterwards it grew dim, and in the poor wretch who was the husband of the Duchess Angelina it guttered and went out. The dead torch was lit again by Karageorge, and it grew bright in the hand of his successor, Prince Michael Obrenovitch, and when Milan made himself King its light grew steady, though his was not the hand that was to bear it, and it was the same torch that our ancient dynasty of the Nemanyas had carried. So why should we care what else he had done? It was not Milan but their king whom these Serbs were following through the snow, it was the incarnation of Serbian power."

When the storm had lifted we drove out again on the plains, now lying under a purged and crystal air, in which all things were more than visible, in which each blade piercing the rich spring earth could be seen for miles in its green sharpness, in which the pools outside the villages carried not reflections but solid paintings of the blue sky and silver clouds. Then we turned back to the range of downs and entered it by a little valley, which presently ran into a cache of apple orchards, a lovely coomb as sweet as anything Devonshire or Normandy can show. Behind a white wall shielded by fruit trees and Judas trees we found a monastery enclosing an astonishing church, that had been built after the emigration had done its work on the migrated craftsmen's imagination; it was a fusion, lovely but miscegenic, of the Byzantine and the baroque styles, of fourteenth-century Eastern and seventeenth-century Western styles. While we gaped there came up to us a Russian monk, a young man who, like the nuns we had seen at the first monastery, must have been born after his parents had left Russia. He was beautiful, with the eyes seen only in Russians so far as I know, which look dangerous as naked lights carried on the stage, by reason of their extraordinary lambency. He told us with smiling remoteness that the Abbot was away; and we were disappointed, for the Abbot is a Pribitchevitch, one of a family that has been dominant in this Serb colony ever since the migration, and is the brother of a famous democratic politician who died in exile during the dictatorship of King Alexander. "That is a pity," said Constantine; "however, we can still show these English people what is interesting here." "But there is nothing interesting here," said the Russian monk, "we have only the body of a Serbian emperor." He spoke without insolence, his remark proceeded from a complete failure to form any sort of relationship with his surroundings, however hospitable they might have been, which is characteristic of a certain kind of White Russian *émigré*.

We said that we found that interesting enough; and he went with us into the exquisite mongrel church, and found it glowing and beautiful within. There were two handsome girls on step-ladders cleaning the windows, and they clattered down and followed us, smiling in welcome and at the same time murmuring in piety, as we went towards the sarcophagus of the Emperor. The Russian monk lifted its lid and showed us the body under a square of tarnished cloth of silver, but would not uncover it for us. He shrugged his shoulders and said that it was only done on the Emperor's day; he would have seemed on a par with a girl in a milliner's shop refusing to take a hat out of the window had it not been quite plain that, while he was flagrantly frivolous, religious ecstasy was not only within the range of his experience, it was never very far from him. But the two girls behind us sighed deeply in their disappointment.

"This is Urosh, the son of Stephen Dushan," said Constantine; "he was a poor weakling, and lost all his father's empire in a few years." "Yet he is venerated," I said. "But certainly," said Constantine. "But do the people who venerate him know what he did?" I asked. "Do these girls, for instance, know that he destroyed the Serbian Empire and paved the way to Kossovo?" "Well, I would not say they could pass an examination in the facts," said Constantine, "but certainly they know that he was weak and he failed. That, however, is not of the smallest importance. He was of our ancient dynasty, he was a Nemanya, and the Nemanyas were sacred. Not only were they the instruments of our national power, they have a religious significance to us. Some of them are described on their graves as '*saintement né*,' born in sanctity; and this Urosh, though he was quite simply killed by a usurper of his secular power, is called by our Church the martyr. This is not mere nationalist piety. It is due to the historical fact that the Nemanyas simultaneously enforced on us Serbs Christianity and unity. We were Christians before, of course, but we had not a living church of our own. Then this extraordinary family of little, little princelings from an obscure village below Montenegro on the Adriatic came and did in a few years as much as Rome has done for any state in centuries. The first Nemanya to rule Serbia, Stephen Nemanya, became a monk, when he abdicated in favour of his son Stephen, and is known as St. Simeon, and he is a true saint: the oil from his grave at Studenitsa does many miracles; and one of his sons became our St. Sava, and was a monk on Mount Athos, and left his monastery when his brother's throne seemed insecure and organized Serbia into such a close-knit fabric of church and state that, though the heirs of the throne were incompetent for sixty years afterwards, nothing could unravel it. But as well as a statesman Sava was a saint, and was a pilgrim and visited the monks of Thebaid. And his brother, too, King Stephen II, he also was a saint. When he lay dying he sent for St. Sava to make him a monk, but St. Sava came too late; but God vouchsafed that he should be raised from the dead to take his vows as a monk and so his corpse stood up and was consecrated. I tell you no people could be expected to forget the identification between saint and king, between religion and nationalism, which was made by our early history."

"Good-bye," said the Russian monk at the gateway, "the Abbot will be sorry not to have seen you, particularly as you are English. He has gone to the post-office now to complain because some English books have not arrived; I think they were sent to him by something called the Left Book Club." We left the hills and went back into the plains, which were again threatened by storm, and then returned to the hills by another valley, which was astounding in its likeness to a corner in the Wiltshire downs. Twisted thorn trees guard austere channels of turf; but the hillside that closed our road was broken by the fine-drawn ironmongery of a pithead, and we came into a mining village, as monotonous as such are in every country and continent, but here radiant with whitewash. Among its right angles we got lost, and stopped to ask our way to the Vrdnik monastery from a group of boys. One of them got on the footboards to guide us, and brought us down to a morass in the middle of the village, which we had to skirt carefully, for it was involved with a railway line. "Look up, look up," said the boy, pointing up to the hillside before us, "there stands Vrdnik, see how great its walls are, see how rich it is, with all its vineyards and orchards." As we walked up a gold-green avenue of poplars to the gateway he told us that he was going to be a monk, and so were all the boys with whom he had been walking when we found him. "Why is that?" asked Constantine. "Did your mothers promise you to God when you were born?" "No, no," he said. "It is our own idea. We love this monastery, we come to it whenever we can and we are always happy here, and we want to serve it all our lives."

Vrdnik is larger than the other monasteries, which is natural, since its unique possessions attract many pilgrims; and because of the wealth

drawn from these pilgrimages the large two-storied quadrangle is in
good repair, handsomely whitewashed, and laid out like a garden with
plum trees and Japanese quinces. The church is also different from the
others. It seems to reject the Byzantine prescription that magic must be
made in darkness. Direct light shines on the gilded iconostasis and on the
multicoloured thrones, and shines back amber from the polished marble
pavement. It can be so, for there is no need to manufacture magic here.
That already exists in the coffin lying before the iconostasis, which con-
tains the body of the Tsar Lazar who fell at Kossovo.

He lies in a robe of faded red and gold brocade. A dark cloth hides
his head and the gap between it and his shoulders. His mummified brown
hands, nearly black, are crossed above his loins, still wearing the bright
rings of his rank. His dwindled feet have been thrust into modern stockings, and over them have been pulled soft medieval boots of blue silk
interwoven with a gold thread. He is shrunken beyond belief; his hip-
bones and his shoulders raise the brocade in sharp points. He is piteous
as a knot of men standing at a street-corner in Jarrow or a Welsh mining
town. Like them he means failure, the disappointment of hopes, the
waste of powers. He means death also, but that is not so important. Who
would resent death if it came when all hopes had been realized and all
powers turned to use? There is an ideal point at which the fulfilment
of life must pass into the acceptance of death. But defeat is defeat, and
bitter; not only for the sake of pride, but because it blunts the sword of
the will, which is the sole instrument man has been given to protect
himself from the hostile universe and to impose on it his vision of redemption. When this man met defeat it was not only he whose will was
frustrated, it was a whole people, a whole faith, a wide movement of the
human spirit. This is told by the splendid rings on the Tsar Lazar's black
and leathery hands; and the refinement of the pomp which presents him
in his death, the beauty and gravity of the enfolding ritual, show the
worth of what was destroyed with him. I put out a finger and stroked
those hard dry hands, that had been nerveless for five hundred years. It
is written here that the lot of man is pitiful, since the odds are against
him, and he can command the success he deserves only if an infinite
number of circumstances work in his favour; and existence shows no
trace of such a bias.

In a dark and cramped treasury are some untidy ancient manuscripts,
on which a Tauchnitz edition of *The Hound of the Baskervilles* has curiously intruded, and certain possessions of the Tsar Lazar: the icon on
which he swore his nobles to loyalty before the battle, the beaker from

which he drank, the model of one of his cities. There is no reason to doubt that any of these are genuine. The Turks let Lazar's widow take his corpse and all his private treasures, and in the course of time she placed them in the monastery of Ravanitsa, which he himself had founded, in Serbia, far south of Belgrade on the way to Nish. It was often attacked and damaged by the Turks, and the migrants of 1683 took away its relics and built this new monastery, which for this reason is often also called Ravanitsa, to house them. I went down on my knees to peer at the precious objects through the glass case of the cupboard. The icon was damaged but enormously beautiful: in the background was a soaring close-pressed assembly of saints, conceived by an imagination disciplined and formalized by experience of ceremonial. There was also a panel of velvet, once crimson, now maroon, which was embroidered in silver-gilt thread with words, many words, a prayer, a poem.

It was sewn by the Princess Euphemia, the widow of a Serbian prince killed by the Turks, who had found refuge at the court of the Tsar Lazar. After Lazar had fallen at Kossovo she went with his widow Militza to the monastery of Lyubostinya, where they both became nuns. She was an embroideress of great genius. Two of the most famous pieces of early embroidery in Europe are her work: the curtain for the sanctuary doors in the church of Hilendar, the Serbian monastery on Mount Athos, and a cloth for laying on the altar during Lent, now in the monastery of Putna in Roumania. In the silence of the monastery she worked a pall to cover the severed head of the Tsar Lazar, and on it she wrote him a letter with her needle.

"You were brought up among all the good things of this earth, O Prince Lazar, O new-made martyr," she begins. "The power of the Lord made you strong and famous among all the kings of the world. You ruled over the land of your fathers and in all right ways did you give happiness to the Christian folk who were laid in your hands. In courage and piety did you go out to do battle against the snake Murad, the enemy of God's church, because your heart could not bear to see the hosts of Ismail ruling in Christian lands. You were determined that if you failed you would quit this crumbling fortress of earthly power and, red in your own blood, be one with the hosts of the Heavenly King.

"You had both your desires fulfilled. You slew the snake and you won from God the martyr's crown. So do not now forget your beloved children, who are left desolate by your death, while you are enjoying the everlasting delights of Heaven. Many troubles and sufferings have fallen on your beloved children, and their lives are passed in sorrow, for the sons of Ismail rule over them, and we sorely need your help. Therefore we beg you to pray the Ruler of Mankind for your beloved children and all who serve them in love and faith. For your children are girt about with many ills, and have forgotten, O martyr, your goodness to them. But though you have quitted this life, you know the troubles and sufferings of your children, and since you are a martyr, you can take certain freedoms with the Lord.

"So bow your knee before the Heavenly King who bestowed on you the martyr's crown; beg Him that your beloved children may live long and be happy and do His will; beg Him that the Orthodox Church may stand firm in the land of our fathers; beg Him, who is the Conqueror of All, that He give your beloved sons, Prince Stephen and Prince Vuk, the victory over all their enemies, seen and unseen. If the Lord gives us His help, we shall give you praise and thanks for it. Gather together the company of your fellows, the Holy Martyrs, and with them pray to the God that glorified you. Call St. George, rouse St. Demetrius, persuade the saintly Theodores, take with you St. Mercurius and St. Procopius; forget not the forty martyrs of Sebaste, in which town your beloved sons, Prince Stephen and Prince Vuk, are now vassals in the army of the Sultan. Pray that they may be given help from God, come, you, too, to our aid, wherever you may be.

"Look on my humble offerings and magnify them with your regard, for the praise I offer is not worthy of you, but is only the little that I can do. But as you, my dear Ruler and Holy Martyr, were ever generous of temporal and passing things, how much more freely so will you give us of those great and everlasting things which you have received from God. You abundantly gave me what my body needed when I came to you as a stranger in exile, and now I pray you both that you will save me and that you will calm the wild storm in my soul and in my body. Euphemia offers this from her heart, O blessed saint!"

Belgrade III

WHAT has made modern Belgrade, though no one could guess it by looking at the town, is a conscious attempt to restore the glories of the medieval Serbian Empire. The nostalgic frescoes of Oplenats truly reveal the dominating fantasy not only of the Karageorgevitches but of the Serbian people. The memory of the Nemanyas and their wealth and culture was kept alive among the peasants, partly by the Orthodox Church, which very properly never ceased to remind them that they had once formed a free and Christian state, and also by the national ballads. These poems are not quite so artless as they seem. They were composed by the Serbs, more or less collectively, quite a century after the battle of Kossovo, on the model of the *chansons de geste,* which reached the Balkan Peninsula through Dalmatia at a very early date. Thereafter the full force of the artistic genius of the nation, denied all other outlet, poured into this medium; and the late eighteenth century, which marked the decline of folk-song in the West, here brought it new strength, for the nationalist and liberal ideas popularized by the French Revolution found their perfect expression ready-made in the laments of this enslaved people. The Serbs who took part in the first rising against the Turks in 1804 were, therefore, nothing like primitives who were simply revolting against an immediate injustice. That revolt they were making; but also they were the heirs of a highly developed civilization, which they intended from the first to create anew.

It is possible that the monasteries of the Frushka Gora, the blackened body of the Tsar Lazar, exerted a direct influence on this rising. Karageorge, after the flight from Serbia during which he killed his stepfather, joined the Austrian Army; and though he deserted for a time and became a Haiduk in the mountains, because he believed that he was unfairly neglected in a distribution of medals, he ultimately rejoined his regiment and was accepted by his colonel, who was greatly impressed by his personality, and got him employment after the end of the Turco-Austrian War as a forest ranger in the Frushka Gora. He was there for some years before the mildness of the new Pasha of Belgrade, Hadji Mustapha, "the Mother of Serbia," tempted him to return to Serbia. He had therefore an ideological experience which is not conveyed in the usual description of him as a swine-herd; and indeed even his material

circumstances are not what the term suggests. He was a dealer in swine
on such a large scale that his income was probably equivalent to about
a thousand pounds a year at the time when he was chosen as the Commandant of Serbia. Though the common lot of the Christian inhabitants
of the Ottoman provinces was poverty-stricken, a certain number of
exceptions enjoyed quite a handsome degree of prosperity; and according to the usual paradox of revolutions it was these exceptions and not
the oppressed multitude who revolted.

It is not clear why the Serbs chose Karageorge for this office. He was
over forty. Though he had served in the Austrian Army he does not
seem to have won any particular distinction. He was of definitely unstable temperament: he was subject to fits of abstraction that lasted for
days, and to gusts of violence caused by flimsy suspicion. But he had
a superb physique. He was tall even for a race of tall men, with burning
eyes, wild coal-black hair, a face that was still handsome though deeply
scarred, and a strange vibrant voice. He was a born warrior, and war was
the breath of life in his nostrils. More than all else he liked to take part
in a cavalry charge, spring from his horse at the climactic moment, and
use his rifle in close combat; he shot with his left hand because his right
had been smashed to pieces in one of his early campaigns. He had the
prestige of high courage, and also that other strange, almost mystical
prestige which is accorded to a wealthy man who renounces the more
obvious enjoyments that his money might buy. It was the habit of these
prosperous Serb rebels to practise a certain imitation of the Turkish
pashas, to dress in silks and use gold harness and chased arms, and keep
a certain degree of state in their homes. Karageorge dressed and lived
and worked with his hand like a peasant.

These were intimations of a certain distinction, but not of the degree
or kind which Karageorge afterwards manifested. He showed himself
for nine years as one of the most remarkable men in European history.
He was brilliant not only as a fighting soldier but as a strategist; his use
of his forces to harass an enemy that outnumbered them sometimes by
three to one is among the most amazing triumphs of military genius,
and it is the more amazing since he had seen the inside of no staff college. He was also a skilful diplomatist, both in dealing with his own
people, whom he had to educate in the primal idea of unity, and in
playing off Austria and Russia against Turkey without compromising
Serbian independence. In the task of setting up some sort of governmental system to oust Turkish maladministration he acted like a far-

seeing statesman. There, indeed, he showed the first and most unexpected qualities of his genius.

It was evident that the strong individualities of the rebels threatened the country with another form of the anarchy they were seeking to correct. There was every possibility that it might be split up under regional military chiefs, who would wrangle among themselves and reduce the Balkan Christians to the same state of disunity that had left them helpless before the Turks four hundred years before. To control this situation Karageorge founded a Skupshtina or Parliament, of Chiefs, which met each New Year to settle all military matters, tactical, strategic, political, financial, and disciplinary. But this was obviously not a complete government, and shortly after a visit of certain Serbian chiefs to the Tsar led to the formation of another body. In the course of their journey they went to Kharkov, in Poland, and there they met a lawyer named Filipovitch, who was a native of Novi Sad, a descendant of the seventeenth-century Serb migrants. He suggested that he should accompany them home and found a legislative and judicial system in Serbia. They agreed, and took him back with them to Karageorge, who, loyal to the influences of the Frushka Gora, made him welcome and told him to get on with the job.

Filipovitch then sat down and drafted a constitution for the Serbian state. He invented a Soviet, or Council, of twelve persons elected and paid by different districts to manage the general affairs of the country. He inaugurated it, and became its Secretary. There is extant the correspondence in which he made financial provision for the Army by selling the houses and land owned by Turks in Serbian territory, fixed the taxes, organized a system of magistrates, and instructed the Soviet delegates in the exact nature of their rights while warning them against corruption. He also promulgated a legal code based on the Code Napoléon. It is difficult to think of any man in all history who undertook a more comprehensive labour single-handed; and it is interesting to find that Filipovitch was never a vociferous patriot. He appears to have accepted the post largely to escape the climate of Kharkov, which he found extremely disagreeable. But he had a truly legalist mind, in the highest sense, and he delighted in the task of imposing order on a disorderly society for order's sake; and it is quite apparent that that delight found a response in Karageorge's very different nature.

He supported Filipovitch enthusiastically in his educational schemes, which were ambitious. Till that time the only schools in Serbia were

held in the monasteries, and attendance at them involved great inconvenience, for the monks could not afford to house pupils who did not
help in the cultivation of their lands, and a scanty education took several years. The Soviet was instructed by Filipovitch to found an elementary school in every big town, and a secondary school of ambitious
curriculum in Belgrade. This greatly pleased Karageorge, for though
he himself could not read or write he was a great believer in education,
and he was always impressing on his followers, who were for the most
part as illiterate as himself, the advantages of having all business recorded
in writing.

Even after Filipovitch's premature death Karageorge continued to
work on his high plans. It became obvious as time went on that the
Senate did not counterbalance the Skupshtina as had been hoped. The
power of the rebel chiefs was, in fact, the only real power in the land,
and soon it controlled the Soviet indirectly just as it directly controlled
the Skupshtina. They seemed likely not only to split up the country
so that it would be helpless before external aggression, but also to become greedy and oppressive despots not to be distinguished from the
Turkish pashas. Karageorge met this threat by deposing two of the
most powerful chiefs, and by using his prestige as national Commandant
to dominate the Soviet and force on it regard for the interests of the
whole people. He took this attitude partly, no doubt, because the democratic tradition of the Slavs was working in him, but chiefly because he
knew as a soldier the importance of national unity to a country perpetually threatened by foreign dominance.

Karageorge kept at his task with unremitting grimness; and indeed he
must have seemed a grim figure, for the essence of his struggle was austerity. He was fighting against the Turks, the practitioners of pagan
luxury; and in the first part of his struggle he engaged those among the
Turks who were the most skilful in that practice, the rebellious Janizaries
who had given Sarajevo its intoxicating air of pleasure, and were rebel-
ling against the reformist Sultan Selim because he was endeavouring to
brace them to a new and Spartan dispensation. One of his followers has
left us an account of a night the Serbian Army spent during the campaign of 1805 on the heights above the town of Parachin, which was occupied by the Turks. When the trenches had been dug and Karageorge
had inspected them and seen that all was prepared for the morrow's
battle, he sat down on a cannon and asked his officers if there was any
plum brandy about. They fetched him a flask of plum brandy and some
corn-pone, and he drank and passed the flask to them, and shared the

corn-pone out. They looked down on Parachin, which was blazing with light in the darkness below. It seemed almost to be in flames, such was the brightness. Light was streaming out from the Pasha's palace, and they could hear the sound of pipes and flutes and drums. One of Karageorge's suite, a man who was called Stephen the Scribe and was kept simply as a secretary, being notoriously no good as a soldier, looked down on the town and said, "Do let me fire off this gun at the Turks!" Karageorge laughed at him, but he went on begging. "Do let me take one shot—just one—at the palace!" Karageorge jeered, "But you might kill the Pasha!" "Well, why not?" asked Stephen the Scribe. "Well," said Karageorge, "you mustn't do that. You might make his children orphans, and they'd have nobody to buy them shoes, and then they might catch cold running round barefoot and die of fever." But Stephen the Scribe teased him till he got his way, and very unskilfully pointed the gun and fired it. The ball cut through the air like lightning, and went straight for the Pasha's palace. In one instant the flutes and pipes and drums came to a stop, the lights went out, and there was darkness and silence. Very often Karageorge's rebellion must have seemed just such a murderous cannon-ball, that put an end to brightness and music, and established the night.

His end was not to be deduced from his beginning. After a time the war he had to conduct changed its form. The Serbs had begun their insurrection to rid themselves of the Dahis, the rebel Janizaries who had set themselves up as independent despots in defiance of the Sultan; but when they had beheaded the four chiefs they began to dream of freeing themselves from Turkey. Indeed, the treachery with which the Sultans treated them in spite of their services made them realize this as a necessity. This raised a problem which differed from year to year according to the situation of Europe. When Napoleon defeated Austria and the Turks were harried by Britain and Russia, then Serbia had reason for hope. But Napoleon's star waned, Russia was a preoccupied and often disloyal ally, and Turkey was reorganized by the great Sultan Mohammed II. Finally in 1813 a Serbian army of fifty thousand faced an army of treble that number. Defeat was certain, but the Serbians knew what it was to be outnumbered and could quite well have put up enough resistance to gain them a negotiated peace, had not Karageorge, quite simply and shamefully, run away. He fell back, when he should have been bringing up reinforcements to support a harassed body of troops who were making a magnificent stand before the main Turkish army. His officers suddenly found he had deserted them without a word of explanation. For a time he wandered about the country, and then fled over the Danube back to Novi Sad and the Frushka Gora.

Nobody knows the reason for Karageorge's conduct. He never published any justification of it. Till then his worst enemies had never charged him with cowardice or lack of care for his country. It is possible that fatigue had released that unstable element which had caused his early fits of melancholy and abstraction. His family life had been tragic. The murder of his stepfather had not been the only act of violence which he had been obliged to commit against his family. He had a ne'er-do-well brother who had crowned his career by committing rape. This was an offence which was regarded as being at least as serious as murder; it was so often committed by Moslems on Christians that for a Christian to rape a Christian was not only a sexual crime, it had a renegade flavour. So Karageorge ordered his brother to be hanged at the door of his house, and forbade his mother to mourn her son. This was the appointed procedure, and there was nothing remarkable about it, but the relationship of brother and brother among Slavs is peculiarly close, and even if his individual sensibility was calloused his racial self must have been appalled.

He had also led as extravagantly busy a life as, say, Napoleon, if one takes his illiteracy into account and considers what it would mean to be Commander-in-chief and Prime Minister under that handicap; and he was now fifty-one. He had added to his routine considerable demands on his detective capacities and a perpetual burden of apprehension. He had all the time to scan the rebel chiefs who were the medium through which he had to work, and judge whether they were loyal or disloyal, and if the latter, decide when he had best strike against them. Again and again he had to smother conspiracies, not only to save himself, but to protect the state. It would be no wonder if after nine years of this hag-ridden life he should forget his nature and sink into apathy. But it is perhaps also relevant that the dominant figure of the Kossovo legend which shaped him as all other Serbians was the Tsar Lazar, who was not victorious, who did not preserve his people, who lay a blackened and much-travelled mummy in the exile of the Frushka Gora. That dominance perhaps explains why the Serbs always respect Karageorge as the founder of their liberty, withdrawing no part of their homage because of his failure.

There is yet a pendant to this mysterious eclipse of a great man. Four years later Karageorge returned to Serbia. Since the country was then ruled by Milosh Obrenovitch, his deadly enemy, who hated him be-

cause he suspected him of the murder of his half-brother, he cannot but
have anticipated that he would meet his death. And the trip proves to
be even more suicidal than it appears at first sight if his ostensible reason
for returning is examined. Though the Greeks were, like the Serbs, in
revolt against the Turks, the Serbs had never trusted them. Since the
Turks had abolished the Serbian Patriarchate and put the Serbs under
Greek priests there were too many old scores about to make for a
successful alliance. Karageorge knew this and during his domination of
Serbia he had for this reason held his country free of all entanglements
with the Greek rebels. But in 1817, at a time when Milosh Obrenovitch
was engaged in the most delicate negotiations with the Sultan, Karageorge came back to Serbia as an agent of the Greek revolutionary society, the Ethniké Hetairia, to induce the Serbians to stage a rising at
the same time as a Greek revolt. He must have known that Milosh
Obrenovitch would have to silence him, not for his own interest but
for the sake of the country. He must have known how Milosh Obrenovitch was likely to silence him. He was killed by an unknown assassin
while he lay asleep in a cave.

But that suicidal streak was not peculiar to him. It showed, against
all expectation, in Milosh Obrenovitch also, though the two men were
utterly different in character. His palace still stands in Belgrade; it is a
Turkish house, with a projecting upper story, full of air and light with
many water conduits. In Belgrade there may be seen, on the first floor
of the Museum of Prince Paul, the robes worn by him and his wife.
Richer far than the gear of the Karageorges, which is shown alongside, they might have been worn by a Turkish pasha and the flower of
his harem. And indeed he gave his audiences like a pasha, seated cross-
legged on silk cushions, wearing the turban. Milosh had his eye set
on the quality that Karageorge had seemed likely to drive out of Serbia,
the luxury and pleasure which had made Sarajevo, which had lit the
lights at Parachin. He meant not to expel it but to transfer it from the
possession of the Moslems to the Christians.

He was capable of arranging the transference. He had only to follow
where Karageorge led, but he brought genius to his following. When
Karageorge fled across the Danube in 1813, and most of the chiefs who
had owned him as leader fled into exile like lost sheep, Milosh stood his
ground and calmly awaited the horror which he knew would burst on
the country once the Turks returned. There was a preliminary massacre,
with impalements and mutilations and roastings on spits; then there was
systematic banditry, the worst of it under a legalistic guise. All sorts of

Turks appeared, passing themselves off as landowners and merchants driven out by the rebel Serbs, who claimed land and wealth which had certainly never been theirs; and all those claims were allowed. The Serb population was beggared.

Milosh waited by, smiling and bland. He ingratiated himself with Suleiman, the new Pasha of Belgrade, who had been wounded by him on the battlefield and therefore respected him, and who trusted him because of his known enmity to Karageorge. Suleiman made him Governor of three large districts, and he repaid this honour by apparent subjection of the most absolute kind. He constantly exhorted the Serbians to lay down their arms and think no more of resistance to the Turks. When some rebels collected in one of his own districts, he went at once and persuaded them to surrender on a promise from Suleiman that they should be pardoned. That promise was broken. One hundred and fifty of them were beheaded, and nearly forty impaled; and Milosh himself was sent to Belgrade and kept in captivity. He bribed his way out. The resources on which all these rebels could draw were far larger than the modern reader would imagine. He returned to his home and found the people frantic with rage and terror, persuaded that there was again about to be a general massacre. Then he judged it well to act, and he put himself at their head. In six months he had driven out the Turks.

It must be owned that Milosh never faced such huge odds as Karageorge, and that he gained one of his most inexplicable victories because the Turkish Commander made a sudden flight, just as inexplicable as Karageorge's great defection. But Milosh showed military genius of the same impressive order as his rival, and later he showed himself a far greater diplomat and, by one supremely important act, at least as great a statesman. After his victory he made a technical avowal of subjection to the Sultan and then sat down to negotiate the independence of his country, with infinite guile and patience. He knew just how to play on Turkey's fear of Russia; and he never let himself forget that, in actual fact, it would not be easy for the Russian Army to come to Serbia's aid. He threatened to adhere to one or other of the great powers when Turkey was at ease in her foreign relations, but when she was perturbed he proffered the most soothing assurances of neutrality. He had an infallible nose for the right moment to bribe a pasha or roll a threatening eye on a vizier. It took him eighteen years to wring Serbian independence from the Porte, when not a soul in Europe had thought the Porte would give way to him till the Turkish Empire had dissolved. True, it was not complete independence that he gained. Turkey insisted on her right to garrison certain towns, notably Belgrade, and refused to promise not to poke her nose into Serbian affairs. But it was practical independence. Turkish officials and regular and irregular troops no longer roamed at large in the land.

Milosh's supreme act of statesmanship followed that victory. The Treaty of Adrianople which gave Serbia its effective freedom, burdened only by a few irksome but not serious restrictions, also handed over to Milosh extensive crown lands. He might have distributed them as baksheesh to his followers and founded a large class of landowners on whose power he could have relied. Instead he gave the lands to the people as small-holdings, and guaranteed Serbia as a peasant state, thereby giving her her happiness and her distinctive genius. This great service, as the culmination of a career so full of military and diplomatic gifts to his country, might have made him the most beloved ruler in Europe, had he not seen to it that his fame was far otherwise. He had for years been practising a highly offensive and unnecessary despotism. He was certainly responsible for the death of two of his political opponents; and even if a light hand with murder was not to be harshly judged on territory demoralized by Turkish occupation, there was no excuse for seizing a fellow-Serb's house and fields without a shadow of justification, or forcing peasants to labour for him at his will, or enclosing common forestland as pasture for his own swine.

As he became more and more powerful, he behaved with more and more fantastic improbity. It might have sobered him that the Sultan had appointed him first Prince of Serbia; but it only seemed to intoxicate him. He made his subjects pay their Turkish tribute in Austrian currency, but forwarded it in Turkish currency and pocketed the difference. He insisted on his right to punish his officers by beating. He enraged his subjects by establishing a monopoly on salt, a commodity which was scarce in Serbia and had to be imported from Wallachia, and by investing his ill-gotten profits in a Wallachian estate, to which he proposed to retire if he was deposed. This, surely, was putting the words into the people's mouth. He had a remarkable wife, Princess Lyubitsa, who had in her youth stood beside many a battlefield and urged on the warriors with heroic invective, who cooked her husband's meals and waited on him at table all her days, who was reputed to chastise any lady who caught her husband's eye with such terrible effect that some had been known to die. It is fairly plain that his absolutism made her think he had gone mad, and that she begged his friends to warn him that he was running his head into a noose.

But the noose was where he wanted his head to be. In 1838 a constitution was thrust upon him, in the course of a farce played out by the great powers. Russia and Turkey believed that if Serbia had a constitution they could in practice guarantee and interpret it; so the Tsar Nicholas and the Sultan Mohammed, the two great despots of Europe, forced constitutionalism on Serbia. Hence Palmerston and Louis Philippe, the two apostles of liberalism and Parliamentary control, found themselves forced to urge Milosh to become an absolute monarch. The fuss seems quite nonsensical; why it should be easier for an external power to influence a constitutional monarch than an absolute one is not clear, and the whole dispute was probably conjured up by some silly young man in one of the foreign offices. But Russia and Turkey won, and a constitution was presented to the delighted Serbian people.

Milosh refused to execute it. He tried, indeed, to suppress it altogether, but the opposition knew of it. A group of determined men gathered under a chief called Vutchitch, who had been one of Milosh's bravest and most devoted aides till his loyalty had been broken by the cruel and imbecile caprices of his master. One day they surrounded Milosh's house and sent away his guards of honour, and also those who were detailed to wait on the Princess Lyubitsa. She went to her husband to be by his side, and when he saw her he said, "Well, you see it was no use your siding with my enemies. They have taken away your guard of honour too." She burst into tears.

There was a long discussion concerning Milosh's fate. Some of the chiefs maintained that he should be put to death for the sake of national peace and unity. But he was the first prince Serbia had had since Kossovo, and the profound, even superstitious sense of dynasty which had been inherited by these Serbians made them regard him as by that token sacred. They decided he must abdicate in favour of his eldest son Milan, and go into exile. When they told Milosh he said, "If they no longer desire to have me, it is well, I will not intrude on them," and he signed the deed of abdication. Two days after, he crossed the Sava to Austrian territory. Many people, even Vutchitch, wept to see him. Nevertheless Vutchitch flung a stone into the river and cried out to Milosh, "When this stone floats you will come back to Serbia." "I shall die as Serbia's ruler," answered Milosh, and the boatmen rowed on, bearing him to his strange, imbecile, unsanctified renunciation.

Belgrade IV

THE action of Vutchitch and his followers in accepting Milosh's princedom as hereditary was more bizarre, more a matter of totem and taboo, than appears. For his heir was totally unsuited to be a ruler, at least at that moment. Always delicate, he was now so ill that he could not be told of his father's fall, and he died after some weeks without ever having learned that he was Prince of Serbia. His younger brother, Michael, was still a boy, and his accession involved the inconveniences bound to arise out of the appointment of counsellors who were practically regents. Quite suddenly Turkey insisted on appointing these counsellors, and named Vutchitch and a chief called Petronievitch, who was on good terms with the Turk and was strongly anti-Milosh. The Serbians disliked these counsellors because they were named by Turkey and held Turkish sympathies; Michael resented their existence because he wished to govern by himself, and had a personal grudge against them for their hostility to his father. A further complication existed because a conspiracy to remove Michael from the throne was being organized in an unexpected quarter. The other members of the Obrenovitch family marshalled themselves against him with a unity that sprang from an unusual and fascinating diversity of opinion. Two of Milosh's brothers had remained in Serbia; one of these was all in favour of deposing Michael because he himself had not been made a cabinet minister, another wanted to expel his nephew because he thought the boy would make a mess of it and one fine day all Obrenovitches would be massacred. And abroad the Princess Lyubitsa was deeply involved in the conspiracy, for the reason that, if there had to be shooting, she preferred her husband rather than her son to be the target.

The boy met this complicated situation with spirit. Actually he had inherited all his father's genius and brought a much better character to the using of it. He faced the pestilential Vutchitch, who had rebelled against Milosh with courage and patriotic passion, but now discounted that achievement by showing that rebellion was his only reaction to every circumstance; and he drove him into exile. But this very spirit raised the suspicions of the peasants, particularly as about that time it became necessary to depreciate Serbian currency and to raise the taxes, which Vutchitch had disingenuously lowered when he drove out Milosh in order to make the step popular. They feared that he was going to rob them of their money and their rights as impudently as his father, and when Vutchitch returned to Serbia in the guise of a defender of the constitution they took up arms and followed him. Michael knew Vutchitch was inspired by the Sultan and went out to fight him, confident that he would free his country from the last traces of Turkish suzerainty, and that his people must applaud him for it. He was amazed when the deluded peasants followed Vutchitch, and his own army, itself disaffected, ran away. With a certain significant dignity, he disbanded such of his troops as remained loyal and sent home all peasants who had come from the provinces to support him, and passed over to Austrian territory. It is one of the paradoxes of Balkan history that though the Serbians who rejected Michael were moved by ignorance and stupidity and negativism, later events proved they were performing an enormous service to their country.

Vutchitch then entered Belgrade in triumph and was acclaimed as "Leader of the Nation," but his profound instinct against simplicity prevented him from putting himself forward as Prince. It seemed good to him, for what reason it cannot be imagined, to force on the Skupshtina Alexander Karageorgevitch, the son of Karageorge, a man of thirty-six, upright and sensible and not contentious, but not impressive in personality. This set in motion the strange oscillation of Serbian sovereignty between the Obrenovitches and the Karageorgevitches which has been so misconceived in the West. It has been thought of as a sanguinary conflict between the two families. Even H. W. Temperley writes in his *History of Serbia*, "For a century the ghastly struggle was continued by the partisans of both houses, until the last living Obrenovitch was assassinated in our own day"; and elsewhere he deplores "this terrible blood feud." But in actual fact when Milosh Obrenovitch murdered Karageorge he committed the last crime that either family was to inflict on the other. Only one Karageorgevitch was ever to die by violence, and that was King Alexander of Yugoslavia; and he can hardly have been killed at Marseille by an Obrenovitch, for by then the breed was extinct. Two Obrenovitches died by violence, but there is no evidence that any Karageorgevitch was responsible. One Karageorgevitch was deposed and one Obrenovitch was forced to abdicate, but in neither case could the other family be blamed. Indeed the abdicating Obrenovitch handed over his throne to his son.

It may be doubted whether there was any effective enmity between the families till late in the second half of the nineteenth century. Cer-

tainly there was little at this time. Milosh Obrenovitch had persuaded
Karageorge's widow that he was guiltless of her husband's death; and
at his invitation she had brought her children back from Hungary to
Serbia, and had accepted a pension to keep them. During the reign of
young Prince Michael, Alexander Karageorgevitch had cheerfully and
loyally acted as the boy's Adjutant. He certainly did not rise to princedom by any attacks he had made on the Obrenovitches, and it needed
no effort on their part to account for his expulsion seventeen years
later in 1859. His reign began tediously with a great deal of hubbub
caused by Russia and Turkey. Dynastic Russia was shocked because
Serbia had cast aside a hereditary prince and thought that she ought to
have been consulted. Turkey had already recognized Alexander and told
Russia so. In the end Russia grumpily consented to recognize Alexander, though only after he had been chosen by a free election, on condition that the abominable Vutchitch and his colleague Petronievitch,
both pro-Turks, were sent into exile. Vutchitch had therefore gained
nothing by his continual intrigues and mischief-making. But when
these excitements settled down it was only to disclose a situation in
which Alexander's failure was inevitable.

The historians call him weak. It would be far more true to say that
in his reign Serbia discovered its weakness. It had come to life again not
as a great empire, but as a small nation; and it was to learn, what was to
become tragically clear in the twentieth century, that modern conditions make the independence of a small nation a bad joke. In 1848
Alexander and Serbia suffered a deep and inevitable humiliation. The
Magyars of Hungary rose against the Austrian Government; and as
their nationalist movement, under the leadership of the renegade Slav
Kossuth, showed the most bitter hostility to all Slavs, the Serbs of Novi
Sad and the Frushka Gora made haste to revolt against Hungary. It was
then that the Croats took the same resolve and marched into Hungary
under Yellatchitch. It was a shame and an agony to the Serbians that
their brothers, the descendants of the seventeenth-century migrants,
the guardians of the blackened body of the Tsar Lazar, should be in
danger, and that they should not go to help them. But Russia would
not have it so, lest Austria should defeat the Slavs and draw a conquered
Serbia into her orbit. So Alexander Karageorgevitch had to sit with
folded hands while the Danubian Serbs fought for life and lost. Twelve
thousand Serbian volunteers went to their aid, but Serbia as a state had
to behave like a coward.

Six years later it again seemed to his people that he had humiliated them. The Crimean War broke out and Serbia longed to take sides with Russia against Turkey. Serbia's incubus, Vutchitch, who had been exiled as pro-Turk and anti-Russian, had now got back to the country as anti-Turk and pro-Russian, and he persuaded the country to elect him as Prime Minister. Needless to say, he did nothing whatsoever to further its cause. He was a pure negativist. A Turkish army advanced towards Serbia on the south and an Austrian army confronted her across the river at Belgrade. Again Alexander had to remain inactive and frustrate national feeling.

The peasants could not understand that he was bowing to the inevitable. They only saw that he did not resist their ancient enemy, Turkey, and that he had shown complete subservience to Austria, whom they now hated almost as much as Turkey, and quite rightly. For though the Serbs of Novi Sad had helped Austria to defeat the Magyar revolt, Franz Josef had betrayed them as he betrayed the Croats who had shown him a like loyalty. He had after a few years handed them back to the Hungarians, who were now taking their revenge by a merciless process of Magyarization, which denied the Serbs their language, their religion, and their culture. The infuriated Serbians lost patience, and, needless to say, Vutchitch skipped forward to organize their discontent, and there was a conspiracy of Senators to murder Alexander. It failed, but it was made unnecessary by a meeting of the Skupshtina, which without a dissentient called on him to resign and demanded the recall of Milosh Obrenovitch.

Alexander Karageorgevitch obeyed without a shadow of resistance, and Milosh returned with his son Michael. The old man was now seventy-eight years of age, and the records show that he thoroughly enjoyed the day of his return. The Austrians refused to let him cross the river in their steamers, so he came over in a rowing-boat, just as on that day when he told Vutchitch that he would die the ruler of Serbia. On landing he made a deft speech which made it quite clear that he intended to disregard the Turkish pretension that the princedom of Serbia was not to be hereditary. "My only care," he said to the cheering crowds, "will be to make you happy, you and your children, whom I love as well as my only son, the heir to your throne, Prince Michael." That established the issue so firmly that the Turks could hardly care to dispute it. The old man then took up the routine where he had laid it down twenty years before, with all his characteristic zest. It is impossible not to feel pleasure in recording that one of his first actions was to throw Vutchitch into prison. There, very shortly, he died. The Turks wished to examine his body, but Milosh explained that it was better that they should not.

His reign lasted only twenty months, during which he gave himself great amusement and pleased his people by using his old insolent skill in diplomacy to inflict some important defeats on the Turks. It is as well that he ruled so short a time, for he had nothing to offer but that skill. If he had lived longer he must have been faced by that hard fact, the helplessness of the small nation, which had vanquished Alexander Karageorgevitch, and he must have been vanquished too, for he had no resources to meet it. But it was very different with his son Michael, who on his accession to the throne showed how well the tricksters and simpletons responsible for his exile in 1842 had worked for their country. For he had spent the intervening years in improving his education and visiting the Western capitals of Europe, in pursuit of the definite end of fitting himself for monarchy. The specific problem before him was the transformation of a medieval state into a state which would be modern enough to defend itself against modern empires. He attacked it with a genius that never failed until his death.

First, Michael gave Serbia internal order. He impressed on it the conception of law as a code planned to respect the rights of all which must be obeyed by all. No longer was the ruler to bring his enemies before judges who touched their hats and gave the desired sentence. He and all his subjects had to face a blindfold justice. He reorganized the political constitution, laying it down that the members of the Soviet were no longer to be responsible to the Sultan but to their own national authority, and that the Soviet was to be subordinate to the democratic Skupshtina. He also took a powerful step towards the establishment of order by setting up a regular army under French instructors. Till then the Serbian military forces had been a synthesis of private armies led by chiefs who submitted only fitfully to the discipline of a central command, and were always favourable material for a meddler like Vutchitch. This Michael did against the violent opposition of Austria, who wanted to annex Serbia, Turkey, who wanted to recover her, and Great Britain, who was Turcophile. Only Russia and France befriended her.

Second, he drove the Turks out of Serbia. For they were still in the fortresses of the principal towns. Two years after his accession there occurred the famous incident when the population of Belgrade were not unnaturally moved to demonstrations at the murder of two Serbians by two Turks, and the Pasha in command of Kalemegdan fortress thought fit to bombard the open town for five hours, until he was forcibly restrained by the foreign consuls. Michael was able to use this to prove just how intolerable it was for a vigorous and developing country to have to submit to these fantastical vestiges of an ill-regulated authority, and to represent the outrage in terms comprehensible to the Western powers. He followed this up by sending his beautiful and able wife, Julia Hunyadi, to London to influence British public opinion, which she was able to do through Cobden and Palmerston. Soon he had Great Britain, France, Russia, and even Austria lined up behind him in his demand that the Turks should withdraw their garrison; and he showed his father's diplomatic skill by making the demand in terms that enabled Turkey to grant it without lack of dignity.

Third, he found a new foreign policy. He knew he was his father's son and better, and that he could get everything he wanted from the great powers by wheedling and threatening. But that was not enough, for he knew it would hold good only so long as the empires were in a state of quiescence. When they should be moved by a real need for expansion his guile would be unavailing, they would sweep down on his little principality like robbers on a child. For that, however, his period of exile had suggested a remedy. After he had lost his throne in his boyhood he had first gone to live with his father among the Serbs of Hungary. He had visited the shrines of the Frushka Gora and had seen the relics of his people's ancient glory. Among the Serb scholars of Novi Sad and Budapest and Vienna he had learned how real these glories had been, how certainly the medieval Serbian Empire had been begotten by Byzantine civilization, and how near it had come to being heir and transmitter of that civilization, prevented only by the coming of the Turks. He learned enough to know that in the past the struggle for power in the Balkans had swung from east to west, and from west to east, and victory had rested now with the Serbs, now with the Bulgarians. The Bulgarians were a people of other than Slav origin, being akin to the Turks and Hungarians and Finns, but they were interpenetrated with Slav blood and spoke a Slav language. Now they had another bond with the Serbs, they had been conquered by the Turks; and they were still enslaved. Michael believed that it would be a glorious thing to unite the South Slav peoples. The independent state of Montenegro would certainly be his ally; and since he could not join hands with the Croatians and Dalmatians and Hungarian Serbs, because they were under the vigorous tyranny of the Austro-Hungarian Empire, it would perhaps be wiser to link up with the Bulgarians, who would be more accessible than the others because of the inefficiency of the Turkish administration, and for the same reason more eager for emancipating friends. Then again should there be a vast area, solidly Slav, magnificently free.

This dream, which was born of poetic and historical imagination, was immediately expanded by Michael's practical sense. Why should not past and present experience of Turkish oppression bind together small states, even though they were not Slav, into an effective union that should destroy the Turk? He planned a Balkan League that should join Serbia and Montenegro with Greece, which indeed was full of Slav blood, and Roumania, and should receive the Bulgarians, the Bosnians and Herzegovinians, the Macedonians and the Hungarian Serbs, as soon as these revolted against their oppressors. He actually came to an understanding with Greece and Roumania, and sent Serbian propagandists to work among all the enslaved Slav peoples, while he increased his military strength at home. A check was sharply applied to his plan when England and France, with incredible fatuity, joined Austria-Hungary in rebuking him. It is difficult to imagine why they did this, for a young and prosperous Balkan League able to defend itself must have been a most powerful factor for European peace. The Great War of 1914 could never have happened if Austria had had on her east a solid wall of people able to protect themselves, and had therefore had to accept her limitations. But so it was, and Michael had to neglect obvious opportunities for fulfilling his programme. He was about to fill in the time by revising his constitution and making it more democratic when, on the tenth of June 1868, he went for a walk in the Topchider, the delightful park outside Belgrade that looks across the river Sava at the town on its great ridge of rock. He was accompanied by his cousin and her daughter Katarina, a lame girl of brilliant intellect, with whom, it is said, he was in love, but whom he could not marry because the kinship was within the degree prohibited by the Orthodox Church. He had some time before been divorced, for reasons which are still mysterious, from his Hungarian wife, Julia Hunyadi, who subsequently married the Duke of Ahremberg and died in Vienna fifty-one years later, in 1919. Three men came up to the party and attacked all three with knives. Katarina was wounded, her mother and Prince Michael were killed. Again the Great War was brought nearer to us, another wall between us and that catastrophe was pulled down.

It has been alleged that this assassination was the work of Alexander Karageorgevitch, and indeed he was tried *in absentia* by a Serbian court and condemned. But no evidence was called which was worth a straw.

It is not easy to believe that this man, who was now sixty-one, and who had never been ambitious and was completely aware of his own unpopularity, decided to kill his successor, whom he knew to be adored by his people, and reclaim the throne at a time when a vast and exacting programme had been begun and would have to be triumphantly accomplished by any prince who wanted to save his neck. It is still more difficult to believe that Alexander Karageorgevitch arranged the assassination yet took no steps to seize the power of the murdered man, and, indeed, never left his estate in Hungary before or after the crime.

Alexander followed this up by an even stranger omission. Michael's marriage had been childless, and the Serbian Cabinet was forced into proclaiming as ruler young Milan, a boy of thirteen, the grandson of one of Milosh's brothers. The relationship was uninspiring in its remoteness, and indeed there were suspicions that it was actually nonexistent. But Alexander Karageorgevitch never appeared to take advantage of the countless opportunities offered him or any other malcontent during the boy's minority. The assassins may have called themselves partisans of the Karageorgevitches; and the Karageorgevitches certainly had partisans. Everybody at odds with Michael's administration, which was far too efficient to satisfy everybody, used to take trips to see Alexander Karageorgevitch and grumble over endless black coffees. But they were most likely to do this if they were old and remembered the good old days of corruption. The assassins of Michael Obrenovitch were young and vigorous; they were known to have relations with the Austrian police, and it was Austria who profited by Michael's death.

Belgrade V

EVERY Slav heart grieved at Michael's death; and apparently the powers that are not to be seen were also perturbed. At noon on the ninth of June 1868, a peasant called Mata, or Matthew, ran through the streets of a town called Ushitse crying out: "Brothers! Brothers! Rise up and save our Prince! They are cruelly murdering him! Look, they are slashing him with *yataghans!* Look, look, the blood! Help him, help him!" The police thought he had gone mad and arrested him; but his position looked more serious when next day there reached Ushitse the news that Michael had been stabbed to death in Topchider. Matthew was examined by the Mayor on the assumption that he must have been concerned in the conspiracy; but he was able to prove that nothing was less probable, and the whole countryside came forward to bear witness that he was a seer and often foretold events that had not yet happened or were happening far away. The Mayor then told Mata to say what he saw of the future, and had a secretary to take it down in writing; and he was so impressed that he sent the notes up to the Minister of the Interior. The Minister also was impressed. He ordered Matthew to be brought to Belgrade, and for some days the man sat in a room in the Foreign Office dictating to an official. The notes were filed in the archives, and only disclosed gradually to persons connected with the court or Cabinet. But the notes taken by the Mayor of Ushitse were not so well guarded. They became common knowledge and were finally published and sold all over the country.

Mata foresaw all of Balkan history for the next fifty years. He said: "Michael will be succeeded by a child, and for a time the country will be governed by three Regents. When he comes of age all will go ill. He is clever but unstable, and he will be a torment to Serbia, which will know nothing of peace or security so long as he is on the throne. He will lead several wars, will enlarge the country; and will be more than a Prince, he will be a King. But there will always be trouble. Finally he will abdicate and die in exile before he is old. He will leave but one son, born of a detested wife. This son will mean even more suffering to Serbia. His rule will plunge the country into disorder, and he too will make a disastrous marriage. Before the thirtieth year he will be dead, and his family will die with him. Another family will come to reign in

Serbia; but the new King will disappear after three years and then there will be agony unspeakable for our people. There will be revolts and bloodshed, and then a foreign power will invade our country. That foreign power will torture us. There will come such sad and hard times that those who are living will say when they pass a churchyard, 'O graves, open that we may lie down and rest. Oh, how happy are you who have died and are saved from our troubles and misfortunes!' But a better time will come. . . ."

He said other things, not yet fulfilled, which explain why nowadays one cannot buy the prophecies of Mata of Krema. It is no wonder that those who are threatened by them are apprehensive, for all that he said of Milan and his son came true. Milan was an unqualified disaster to his country. It is possible that he was not an Obrenovitch at all. His mother was a noble and beautiful and indecorous Roumanian, and there was some doubt as to whether his father also was not Roumanian, and the Obrenovitches in no way involved. When Milan was presented to the Skupshtina on coming of age, one of the deputies stayed in his seat and explained that he did not intend to rise till he had seen the young man's birth certificate. In any case, even had Milan been an Obrenovitch his upbringing would have prevented him from behaving like one. Their courage and vitality and craft were theirs only because they had lived the life of peasant soldiers. But Milan spent his childhood in not quite the best palace hotels of Paris and Vienna and Belgrade and Bucharest, alternately petted and neglected by parents who detested each other. Although it must have been realized how likely it was that he should succeed Michael, nobody seems to have regarded his education as a matter of any importance. He grew up with no virtue except an extreme æsthetic sensibility, which would have been revolted could he have caught sight of himself. In mind and body he was the perfect *rastaquouère*.

His marriage was indeed as disastrous as Mata had foretold. When he was nineteen, while his Ministers were negotiating with St. Petersburg to secure him the hand of a young Russian princess, he announced his engagement to Mademoiselle Natalia Keshko, the daughter of a Russian colonel belonging to the lesser ranks of the Moldavian nobility, who was a strange mixture of Slav and Roumanian and Levantine. As the couple left the Cathedral after their wedding a thunderstorm broke over Belgrade and the horses of the state carriage reared and bolted. The omen was not excessive. Natalia was a detestable child, and cruel to the child she had married. When he showed her the peculiar best of himself she answered with a sneer. Because he once heard her say she liked lilies of the valley he had a whole field planted with them, which is a gesture a *rastaquouère* might make if stirred to his depths. When he took her to see them at the perfect moment of their flowering she was puzzled and annoyed by this extravagance. A whole field of lilies of the valley! This coldness she manifested in all phases of their common life. Violently aphrodisiac in appearance, with the immense liquid leaf-shaped eyes and the voluptuous smoothness of the ideal odalisque, she bore within her the conventionality of the kind of Russian provincial society that is described in some of Tolstoy and much of Tchekov, and she deeply resented her husband's passion. They had but one child, Alexander, born when its father was twenty-one and its mother twenty. Thereafter Milan took a mistress, an ugly and intelligent Levantine Greek ten years older than himself, who was perhaps a Russian agent. Natalia, who was at once narrow and loose, knew no restraint in her public resentment of this situation, particularly when this mistress gave birth to a son. Belgrade was startled and shocked by the public brawls of their Prince and his wife. These were not peasant manners, but they were not fine manners either.

As a ruler Milan was not less a failure than as a husband. When the Bosnians and Herzegovinians revolted against Turkey he marched against the Turks from the north while Prince Nicholas of Montenegro marched on them from the south-west. Prince Nicholas made a brilliant success, and wrung an advantageous peace treaty out of them. Milan failed, and had to be saved from disaster by Russian intervention. That started a movement in Serbia for the dethronement of Milan in favour of Prince Nicholas, which soon lost its vigour owing to the flaws that were evident in the Montenegrin's character whenever he stopped fighting; and it started a much more lively and lasting movement in favour of recalling Peter Karageorgevitch, who had fought with the Bosnian rebels and shown himself remarkable as a soldier and as a man. It is hard to blame Milan either for his defeat or for the steps he took to remedy it. He was only twenty-one when he led out his troops against Turkey; and in a modern and orderly state genius has no chance to be precocious. If he had lived in the Old Serbia of Karageorge and Milosh he would have been fighting since he was fifteen or sixteen, and would have known that to keep his throne he had to placate or outwit a dozen wily old chiefs, and in either case earn their respect as well. That was the training Michael Obrenovitch had had; it was ironic that it had enabled him to sweep away such barbaric conditions, which as it proved were apparently necessary to equip a Serbian ruler, his heir not excepted, for the difficult task of modernizing his state.

A later campaign against the Turks was more satisfactory. But at treaty-making Milan was pitifully incompetent. He let the Treaty of San Stefano, which was signed between the Russians and Turks in 1878, take a form which inevitably was to destroy Michael Obrenovitch's dream of a union of the South Slavs for many years and perhaps for ever; for he did not prevent Russia's giving her vassal state, Bulgaria, extended boundaries to which not only the Serbs but the Greeks could legitimately object. The Balkan League was split in three before it was founded. Then came the infamous Congress of Berlin, which was called for no other reason than to frame a treaty which should deprive the democratic Slavs of their freedom and thrust them into subjection under the imperialism of Turkey and Austria-Hungary. Without the Balkan League to use as a counter Milan was utterly helpless, he was back in the position of poor Alexander Karageorgevitch.

It is not to be wondered at that in 1881 Milan signed a secret convention with Austria which handed over his country to be an Austrian dependency. He promised not to make any effort to redeem the Bosnians and Herzegovinians, in return for a vague promise of support for a war, which he was not likely ever to declare, against the Turks in Macedonia, and he agreed to submit his policy day by day to Austrian control. The Austrian military attaché in Belgrade used to call at the palace and give Milan his orders. It is suspected that Milan received, directly or indirectly, financial recompense for this treachery. This increased the dishonour of the transaction; but it would be superficial to take it as proof that Milan's motives were simply mercenary. There can be no doubt that he was chiefly moved by his sense that the great aggressive empires of Turkey, Russia, and Austria made it impossible for him to give his country that independence which it thought it his duty to guarantee.

A year after Milan sold his country down the river, down the Danube, he proclaimed himself King, and had himself anointed in the ancient church of Zhitcha, where all the Nemanyan dynasty had been crowned. It is a crimson church which stands among land like the fairest parts of the Lake District, solemnly dedicated to its royal ritual. A new door was pierced in the wall for each king to come to his coronation, and on his going out it was bricked up again. The people were not placated by Milan's elevation. He was notoriously given to drunkenness, he was spendthrift to the point of mania, his relations with his wife were already scandalous; and owing to his secret convention with Austria-Hungary his political conduct looked like the caprice of a lunatic. Most of his Ministers and all of the public had no idea of the agreement, and they were therefore completely mystified when, as constantly happened, their King suddenly abandoned a project which he had fully approved and which was indeed plainly in the interests of Serbia, or when he put forward a plan which appeared meaningless because its context was known only in the Ballplatz. It is typical of Austrian *Schlamperei* that those who gave Milan his orders took no trouble whatsoever to make them such as he could obey without coming to loggerheads with his people. In 1883 certain districts rose in rebellion which was savagely suppressed.

When little Alexander was nine years old his father and mother separated with the utmost indecency. Their venomous hatred and bad manners were such as Strindberg describes in his play *Divorce*. Natalia on one occasion abominably kidnapped the child and took him to Wiesbaden, and Milan equally abominably had him brought back by the German police. The only respite in these brawls was due to Milan's imbecile declaration of war against Bulgaria, which led to a disgraceful defeat in 1886. By 1888 Milan had exhausted all other means of persecuting his wife and conceived the idea that he must divorce her, though he had no grounds whatsoever, for she was entirely virtuous. He persuaded the Serbian Primate to regard as precedents certain cases of Russian Tsars who had been divorced by simple edicts of the Metropolitans. This deeply shocked his people, who now knew that their king was a thoroughly bad lot. His treasury was incessantly faced with cheques he had cashed in nearly every capital in Europe and with dunning letters from money-lenders; and his military defeat meant even more in a Balkan country than it would have in the West. It was apparent that even if Milan was contented with the situation his backers were not. In January 1890 he tried placating his subjects by giving them a liberal constitution, but three months afterwards, abruptly and without explanation, he abdicated in favour of his son, who was only twelve years old. It is probable that the new constitution and the abdication were Austrian attempts at coping with the steadily increasing interest that Serbia felt in the sober personality of Peter Karageorgevitch, who would certainly never be amenable to foreign influence if he ascended the throne.

The boy Alexander ruled until his majority, through three Regents, two of whom were military men known as "the tarnished generals" since certain unlucky incidents in the war against Bulgaria, while the third was a political boss who had always been Milan's henchman. They were hardly ideal substitutes for a father and a mother, as they very soon had to be. For Milan insisted when he left his son in their care that he should never be allowed to see his mother or hold any communication with her. This was probably not purely an act of domestic hatred. The quarrels between the two seem, particularly towards the end of their dreadful marriage, to have had some sort of political basis. Natalia was strongly Russophile, and it is probable that she found out the existence of the secret convention with Austria. Indeed some of her recorded utterances make it almost certain that she had. It may be that Milan feared she would impart this knowledge to the boy before he had the discretion to realize its full consequences.

Whatever the cause of this prohibition, Natalia turned it to the vulgarest account. She came to Belgrade and used to stand with her face pressed against the gates, looking up at the windows to see her adored son, whom she had done little or nothing to protect. She took a house near by and hung from a balcony when the young King went by on his daily drive. She also distributed secretly to the foreign newspaper correspondents information damaging to Serbia which she had learned in her position as Queen. Finally the Regents rushed through Parliament a bill providing that neither King Milan nor Queen Natalia should be allowed to reside even temporarily in Serbia. The inclusion of both parents enabled the Regents to avoid the accusation of partiality; and indeed they were probably feeling none too fond of Milan, who had been sent abroad with a handsome allowance but was running up enormous debts in Paris and Vienna. Once the Act was passed the Government asked Natalia to leave Belgrade, and when she refused they sent a police commissioner and his men to put her on a Danube steamer. She locked her door and the men had to climb over the roof to get into her house. They drove her away in a cab, and her beautiful grief inspired a mob of young men to make an attempt at rescue. After several of them had been killed and many wounded, she addressed the mob and begged them to disperse, declaring that to prevent any more of this dreadful bloodshed she would leave Belgrade at once.

When Alexander was seventeen, and a weak-kneed, stout, spectacled boy, he asked the Regents and the principal Ministers of the Cabinet to dine with him at the palace. They came to dinner in high spirits, for they were all Liberals, which is to say in this confusing country that they were not liberals at all, but Tammany politicians with a great deal

more machine than ideology, and they had just pulled off a smart ma-
noeuvre against the Radicals, who here are not radicals at all but anti-
Western, nationalist, democrat conservatives who base their programme
on the ancient Slav communist tendencies growing out of the Zadruga
system. But before they had finished dining the palace aide-de-camp
entered and spoke in a low voice to the boy, who nodded, rose to his
feet, and said, "Gentlemen, it is announced to all the garrisons in Serbia,
to all the authorities, and to the people, and I announce it here to you,
that I declare myself of full age, and that I now take the government
of the country into my own hands. I thank you, my Regents, for your
services, of which I now relieve you. I thank you also, gentlemen of
the Cabinet, for your services, of which you are relieved also. You will
not be allowed to leave this palace tonight. You can remain here as my
guests, but if not, then as my prisoners."

For a second the men were silent, then they jumped up and hurried
round the table towards the boy, crying out threats and protests. The
aide-de-camp drew his sword and stopped them, then went silently to
the folding doors on one side of the room and threw them open. Bayonets
glittered on the rifles of a company of soldiers. "I leave you in charge of
Lieutenant-colonel Tyirich, whose orders you will have implicitly to
obey, while I go to give the oath of fidelity to the Army," said the King,
and he left the hall. Next morning the Regents and the Ministers were
released, and went home through streets placarded with royal procla-
mations stating that King Alexander had watched the illegal actions of
the Liberal Government, and feared that if they had been suffered to
continue the country would drift into civil war, and therefore had
declared himself of age and taken the reins of power into his hands.
The people came out of their houses, read the proclamation, ran back
and hung out their flags, and then rushed to the courtyard before the
palace to cheer the Obrenovitch who after all had shown himself an
Obrenovitch.

There is but one explanation of this incident and the anticlimax that
followed it; there can be only one reason why Alexander made this
superb gesture and then never another, why he afterwards only acted
as if he wished to surpass his father in caprice and cruelty towards his
subjects. The clue is given by an utterance he made concerning this secret convention with Austria, and by certain of his actions which are
apparently conflicting. There seems to be no doubt that later he spoke
of his father's signature to the convention as "an act of treason." At the
time of his *coup d'état* he called the nationalist, democratic, anti-

Western radicals to power. But only a year later he illegally removed the radicals from power, and later he annulled the constitutional reforms of the past twenty years, suppressed the freedom of speech and freedom of the press, and governed with the Parliamentary help of an insignificant pro-Austrian party called the Progressives. Yet all this time Alexander was on the most affectionate terms with his mother, Natalia, who was pro-Radical and pro-Russian, and he frequently left the country to spend holidays with her, which were apparently not marred by any differences of opinion. Finally, to the country's amazement and rage, he recalled his father from his scandalous life abroad and made him Commander-in-chief. This was not altogether a disaster. Milan was far from being a fool. In between his orgies in Paris he had acquired a superb collection of pictures by the yet unrecognized masters of the nineteenth century; some of the finest Cézannes once belonged to him. And though he had not been a successful general on the field, his sense of style made him an excellent organizer of a peace-time army. But he took his fun in persecuting the Radicals and pro-Russians, many of whom he did to death. Serbia had never sunk lower since its foundation as a state.

These incidents fall into a comprehensible pattern if certain assumptions are made for which there is some independent evidence. It happened that in 1892 a copy of the secret convention had fallen into the hands of a Serbian nationalist and patriot, Prince Lazarovitch Hrbelianovitch, a descendant of the Tsar Lazar, and he had communicated it to the European press. Its existence was explicitly denied, both by the Serbian Regents and by the Austro-Hungarian Empire through the Parliaments of both Vienna and Budapest. If Alexander had discovered, perhaps by some secret communication from Natalia, that the convention indeed existed, it might well be that his young idealism revolted and he decided to appear before his country as their deliverer from the hidden tyrant. That would explain why he drove out his Regents and assumed power a year before the proper time, and why he favoured the anti-Austrian Radicals. But his first conversation with the Austrian Minister would show him the reality of the fear that had paralysed Alexander Karageorgevitch and disintegrated his own father. He was probably told that any public disclosure and repudiation of the convention would be treated as an unfriendly act by Austria and would be followed by an invasion, or by his murder and replacement by a Karageorgevitch. The boy, sobered, would try to compromise. He would keep silent about the convention, but he would continue his support of the Radicals. Austrian pressure slowly increased. Every year that Alexander reigned without disclosing the convention to his people put him in a worse position to assert his independence. He could not turn to his country and demand its support in his war against the foreign oppressor when it could be proved that he had for long been acting as the oppressor's agent. So he was forced backwards along a dark corridor, a pistol at his breast, to meet an unknown and horrid end, till suddenly he stopped. He struck the pistol away from the hand that held it, careless whether it might be picked up again or not. He had fallen in love with a woman who was Serbian and pro-Russian.

Belgrade VI

BY now the Serbians were deeply unhappy. They were a people who had lived by a tradition that had never failed them for five hundred years, that had never let them forget how much fairer than all the conquering might of Islam their Christian knightliness had been. They had lived by St. Sava and Stephen Dushan, by the King Marko and the Tsar Lazar. But Milan and Alexander Obrenovitch, who were perhaps not Obrenovitches at all, nor even Serbians, and who were entirely and essentially nineteenth-century, to such a degree that they both might have been minor characters in Proust, cannot possibly have been even faintly interested in these medieval personages. Milan was infatuated with the modern West, and he had surrounded himself with people who shared his infatuation and expressed it in ways less admirable than the purchase of Cézannes. His favourite Foreign Minister, Chedomil Miyatovitch, who supported him in the signature of the secret convention with Austria, once wrote a book on Serbia in which he speaks very ill of the Serbian Church. In shocked accents he tells how he took some "distinguished English gentlemen" to an ancient monastery and found there the Bishop of Nish, who bade him tell his friends "that it would be much better if, instead of sending us Bibles, they were to send us some guns and cannons." This was an answer which, of course, might have come from any bishop of the early Church. Leave to us the instruction of the people, it says, and help us to wage war against the heathen that sell the baptized into captivity. There were many such captives over the Serbian frontiers, in the hands of the Turks, not possibly to be redeemed until there was again a strong Christian power in the Balkans. Men like Miyatovitch wanted the Serbians to lay aside this grandiose subject matter which their destiny had given them for their genius to work upon; and instead they offered them, as an alternative, to be clean and briskly bureaucratic and capitalist like the West. It was as if the *Mayflower* and Red Indians and George Washington and the pioneer West were taken from the United States, and there was nothing left but the Bronx and Park Avenue.

The Serbian tradition was not killed. The Serbians did not forget the field of Kossovo. Simply they felt that every day Kossovo was desecrated by the indifference of the father and son who governed them in this curious unconstitutional partnership. They were also conscious, though they did not openly admit it, that they could not even flatter themselves that they were really governed by this pair. It is impossible that the interpretation of Alexander's capricious and terrified despotism should have escaped a people so subtle, so politically experienced, and so suspicious. But to admit it would have involved recognition that Serbia could never be independent, that though it had freed itself from Turkey now it must fall under the tutelage of Austria or Russia: and that was to insult the Tsar Lazar, to leave the defeat of Kossovo unredeemed for ever. The Serbians became moody, hallucinated, creative; and the real persecution they suffered at the hands of the anti-Russian and anti-Radical agents sent out by Milan tinged their fantasies with a certain colour, a certain brooding, cryptic violence.

When Alexander Obrenovitch was a little boy he and his tutor had often walked in the Royal Park outside Belgrade with an American newspaper correspondent named Stephen Bonsal and an English military attaché named Douglas Dawson, who was later to be the Controller of the Household of King George V. One day the two foreigners talked of the delights of swimming in the Danube, and they were shocked to find that the little boy could not swim. So they found him a pool among the trees, and in spite of the tutor's protests they gave him his first swimming lesson. They were distressed to see how badly the boy stripped. He was misshapen and top-heavy, with clumsy shoulders and long arms, meagre loins and thighs, and knock-knees. As soon as he could cross the pool, which was about thirty feet wide, he said proudly to his unhappy tutor, "Now you need not worry about telling the Regents that I am being given swimming lessons by these gentlemen, who are my friends. You can tell them that the King can swim."

Alexander never lost his delight in swimming. When he visited his mother at her home in Biarritz, as he did regularly after his dismissal of the Regents, he spent much of his time in the sea or lying on the sands in the sunshine. One of his companions was Queen Natalia's chief lady-in-waiting, a very pretty widow, ten years older than himself, named Draga Mashin. With her, as time went on, he fell deeply in love. She was the first woman in whom he had shown any interest. His reluctance to marry and his distaste for feminine society had led it to be generally believed that he was physiologically defective. But some time between the years 1894 and 1897 his passion for her became so overwhelming that he forced his way into her bedroom at night. She, however, took him by the shoulders, turned him out, and locked the door.

This is regarded by her enemies as proof of her subtle guile, but according to the King's own account she used a degree of muscular strength far greater than a designing woman would risk. Alexander came near to being in a position where he could say, "Perhaps you were right to dissemble your love, but why did you kick me downstairs?"

After this the story becomes obscure. Some time in the autumn of 1897 Queen Natalia discovered a letter from Alexander to Draga, and flew into a rage most curious in a middle-aged woman of great social experience. It is not clear why she was angry with Draga, who, however indiscreet she had been to evoke the letter, had answered it with the extreme discretion of staying where she was instead of going to Belgrade. But Natalia at once dismissed Draga, turned her out of the house, and sat down to write to all her friends that her lady-in-waiting had behaved to her like a traitress and a wanton. This at once threw Draga on her own resources, which amounted to about a hundred pounds a year, and closed to her the only circle where she might have found fresh employment. She was therefore obliged to return to her family in Belgrade. Queen Natalia, in fact, had made inevitable the relationship which she affected to loathe. For this reason some have suspected her of finding an ingenious device for planting a pro-Russian agent in her son's court and looking as if she were doing no such thing. But the suspicion is unfounded, for she evidently conceived a real resentment against her son, and never saw him again. There is no reason to see anything here but the tropisms of a stupid and vulgar woman.

It is hard to imagine a life more complicated than young Alexander's in the winter of 1897. His father, to whom he had become more attached since his quarrel with his mother, and who had only lately returned to the country as Commander-in-chief, had already begun to embarrass him as a Serbian patriot by pro-Austrian activities. Alexander went for a holiday to Merano, where Draga was staying, though she was still, according to his later and convincing accounts, not yet his mistress; and there he was visited by the Russian diplomat Isvolsky, then *en poste* in Bavaria, who fully realized the extent to which he was anti-Austrian and might become pro-Russian, and reported to his superiors that, although Draga had caused a breach between the young King and his pro-Russian mother, she was herself a pro-Russian influence. It seems probable that he arranged for certain transactions to be carried on through the mediation of Draga, in order to shield them from the observation of Alexander's father. This extreme intricacy of relationship was just what might have stirred the interest and sympathy of the Serbian people, but it had to be kept secret. So Alexander and Draga went back to Belgrade, to all appearances in the excessively simple characters of a tyrannous king and his venal mistress.

It is still not known when the reality came to correspond with the popular belief. Alexander declared it was three years after the night when she had turned him out of her bedroom at Biarritz, but that scene may have occurred any time between 1894 and 1897. It is possible that she did not surrender to him till long after her return to Belgrade, perhaps only a short time before their marriage in the summer of 1900. But the people had no reason to guess at the unexpected purity of their relationship. Draga lived in a pretty little house near the palace in a style which was plainly not within the reach of her own resources, and she was constantly visited by the King. They naturally concluded that she was his mistress; but the feeling aroused by their conclusion was not natural. Before long she was hated as few women since the beginning of time, as no cruel mother, as no murderess, has ever been loathed. I have heard of a Serbian scholar, born beyond the Danube, in Hungary, whose great work was crowned by the Belgrade Academy. Though he was a passionate patriot and free Serbia was sacred soil to him, he would not come to claim his honour. To him Belgrade was utterly polluted by the presence of Draga.

All over Europe spread this campaign of defamation; when the King married her not a country but looked down its nose. She was supposed to be a woman of low origin who had led a vicious life, and this impression was confirmed by the current photographs of her, which showed a bloated face, coarsening around the jaw. But there are other things than dissipation that thicken the features. Tears, for example. Certainly the first part of the story was not true, for she was by birth the equal of the Obrenovitches. Her grandfather, Nikola Lunyevitza, was a friend of Milosh Obrenovitch, a very prosperous cattle-breeder, who had ruined himself financing the rebellions against the Turks. Her more immediate antecedents had been painful, but quite respectable. Her father had died in a lunatic asylum, but till he went mad he had been an efficient and popular Prefect of Shabats. His collapse had left a large family poorly provided for, and Draga, who was one of the elder children, married at seventeen a mining engineer and civil servant. He was himself a worthless and depraved person, but he came of a quite successful family; his father was a noted doctor and one of his brothers had risen high in the Army.

There is an overwhelming consensus of opinion that there is no defence possible in the second part of the story. It is still held by the mass of people today in Serbia that she unquestionably had had many lovers before Alexander, and that she might fairly be called a woman of loose life. Though it is always rash to challenge such unanimous certainties, the student must wonder where and when Draga Mashin was able to live loosely. She was born in 1866. She married her husband some time before her eighteenth birthday in 1884. He immediately fell ill with a disorder due to alcoholism, and she nursed him, except during periods when she had to flee from his ill-treatment, till his death in 1885. When she became a widow she was left badly off, but not so badly off that she could not buy food and shelter; and her unfortunate position attracted the attention of Queen Natalia, who had her taught foreign languages and prepared for her duties as a lady-in-waiting. She was so constantly in attendance at the palace during this time that it was rumoured she was King Milan's mistress, although in fact King Milan hated her. In 1889 she began to travel about with Queen Natalia, and from 1890 lived under her roof at Biarritz. Her bad reputation can be taken as deserved only if it is accepted that from 1885 to 1889, between the ages of nineteen and twenty-three, she conducted herself so licentiously in Belgrade that it was still remembered in 1897. But Queen Natalia was chaster than snow, she was as chaste as sleet, and she was no more likely than Queen Victoria to have a woman of damaged reputation as her personal attendant. She was also noted for knowing everything that went on in Belgrade. If there existed in 1885 stories about Draga so rich and strange that they survived eight years of absence, it seems odd that Queen Natalia never heard them. It seems odder still that a young woman who had spent her youth in the arms of innumerable lovers should at the age of twenty-three be willing to take up her quarters for the rest of her life in what was virtually the nunnery of Queen Natalia's court, particularly when she was so beautiful that she could have set up as a cocotte in any capital of Europe.

There are discrepancies here which cannot be reconciled. We may be warned by the puerility of the case against her. Vladan Georgevitch, the Jewish scoundrel who was Progressivist Prime Minister and specialized in terrorism, theft of state papers, and blackmail, was driven to denouncing her for lending one of his family an immoral book by a Russian Nihilist: it was Mr. Gladstone's favourite, the *Journal* of Marie Bashkirtseff. It seems as if it might be wiser to pay heed to the curiously sober and lethargic expression noticeable even in the earliest photographs of Draga, and accept their indication that a woman who has known at the age of nineteen what it is to have an insane father and an alcoholic husband may develop a certain caution about the exploration of life. Her bad reputation had probably two sources: one limited though effective in a highly important sphere, the other unconfined as a comet, the poetry in the heart of the people, catching fire from a fiery destiny.

It has already been said that Draga Mashin had a brother-in-law in the Army: Colonel Alexander Mashin. He and most of his family hated her. It is hard to believe that this hatred can have been justified. A girl of seventeen cannot have offended greatly against a husband, much older than herself, who during their brief year of married life was suffering from the effects of alcoholic excess. It is likely that this emotion sprung from the reluctance of obstinate people to humble themselves before a stranger to whom one of their kind has done an injury. To Colonel Mashin this hatred was bound to seem justified when she became Alexander's mistress, for he was a partisan of the Karageorgevitches, though he had also received great kindness from King Milan. There is no doubt that Colonel Mashin, who was a good soldier and very popular in the Army, widely disseminated his sincere belief that she was abominable.

For the rest, the people hated Alexander Obrenovitch because he had taken from them their dream of avenging Kossovo, because he had destroyed the integrity of their free state, because he was laying low the representatives of their ancient ways, because he was vulgarizing their style, their austere Byzantine splendour, which made their men gaunt and minatory, their women still and patient, like the ancient kings and holy personages in the frescoes. Because the woman a man loves is in a sense his soul, or at any rate the answer to the call it makes, they thought of Draga as Alexander's soul, and therefore their enemy, and therefore utterly evil, as all of us in our simplicity conceive our enemies.

It is certain that she was aware of the people's hatred and was full of fear. It looks as if, with a not unnatural cynicism, she thought that her lover's passion would pass and that she would then be free. It is said that he gave her twenty thousand pounds; and it is probable that she hoped to spend the rest of her life quietly in some French wateringplace, where there was a casino at the end of an esplanade planted with palms, and pink villas with jalousies. This vision might well seem heavenly, for Balkan politics were thickening round her to a nightmare. In February 1899 the Austrian influence in the court, of which the chief representative was King Milan, insisted on a suspension of relations with Russia. In July of the same year King Milan was driving from

the Belgrade fortress to the palace when a young man stepped forward
and fired a revolver at him. The assassin was a revolutionary Russophile
Bosnian. Like all his kind save Princip, he missed. King Milan used the
event as a pretext for throwing many of his personal and political enemies
into jail, but he, and several of the Ministers who were in the best position to form an opinion, believed that it was his son Alexander who
had employed the assassin.

It is not easy to visualize family life as it was lived in the palace at
Belgrade during this period. However, calm was apparently restored, and
Alexander shuffled along quietly enough under instructions from Vienna
until March 1900, when Count Goluchowsky, the Austrian Foreign
Minister, was unfortunately inspired to send him a peremptory demand
that he should marry a German princess without delay. This was typical
of the extraordinary incompetence which the Austro-Hungarian Empire
always showed in its dealings with Serbia. It was notorious that Alexander was still passionately in love with his mistress, and as he was not yet
twenty-four years of age there was no reason whatsoever to hurry him
into marriage. But Alexander's Ministers obeyed the orders from Vienna
and extracted from him a promise that he would marry before the year
was out. They lacked the sound common sense of the Chief of the Belgrade Police, a simple peasant who believed that Draga owed her power
over Alexander to magic potions. When he heard of the promise he
blurted out, "Here, what's this? We all know that this creature has
bewitched the King so thoroughly that he firmly believes that he couldn't
even be a husband to another woman. If he has promised you to marry
within the year, he means to marry Draga Mashin."

He was right. On July the eighth Alexander announced to the world
his intention of marrying his mistress. He chose a moment when both
his father and his Prime Minister were on holiday in different parts of
the Continent. As he had taken the precaution of ordering them to be
supplied with different code books, they wasted a great deal of time
after hearing the news in sending each other incomprehensible messages.
But at home he had immediately to face a flood of opposition not to be
deflected by such easy means. We know how he met it in one case. He
addressed one of his Ministers in terms which were drawn from the
common language of lovers, which we may even recognize as having
been used in our own times by other lips.

"You know, Vukashin," he said, "that I have had neither childhood
nor youth like other men. . . . I have never had any ambition, not even
the ambition to reign as a King. I wear the crown, not because I love it,

but because it is my duty to do so. You must have noticed that yourself. . . . There now exists a woman whom I love more than anyone or anything in this world, the only woman with whom I can be perfectly happy, and only then can I consecrate my whole life to the interests of the people if she becomes my wife. In the whole world there is only one woman who can make me forget the bitterness of my past life, and make me feel happy. This woman has been hitherto my good angel, who gave me strength to bear patiently all that I had to bear. That woman is—Madame Draga, the daughter of Panta Lunyevitza. . . . I am inflexibly resolved to marry her. Don't insult me by attacks on her. . . . She is a pure and honourable woman, and only her enemies speak badly of her. . . . Only after she received proof that without her and her love I could not live, did she sacrifice herself to me. Yes, I am passionately in love with her, and without her I cannot live. There is now no power on earth which could prevent my marrying Draga, whatever the consequences may be. I would prefer to give up my crown and live with Draga, on an income of three hundred and sixty pounds a year, than have the throne and an apanage of forty-eight thousand pounds a year. I knew that my marriage with her would meet with extraordinary difficulties, therefore I have surrendered myself to her, body and soul, and therefore I have made it impossible for her to leave me. You ought to know that she persistently refused to become Queen. I alone know what difficulties I have had to gain her consent. And now, after I have at last broken down her resistance, you come and make difficulties! Have you no pity for me? Do you wish to force me to go away for ever? Because you ought to realize that if I cannot marry Draga as King, I will leave Serbia for ever, and marry her as a private individual."

His Ministers were unmoved by his eloquence. The whole country was filled by the news of the approaching marriage, by a black horror such as they would not have felt at a threat of invasion by the Turks. On the day the King proclaimed his betrothal to his people the Cabinet resigned, and sent two of their number to Draga Mashin with the message that she must leave the country without delay. It was in their minds that if she refused she must be kidnapped; and it must have been in her mind that her life was no longer safe. She consented at once to their demand, but she not unnaturally asked if she might not wait till her maid had packed up her clothes and papers, provided that meanwhile she went to a friend's house where the King would not be likely to seek her. Once she had her possessions, she said, she would gladly cross the river to Hungary. To this the two Ministers agreed.

But it was then that her tragic origins put out a hand to drag her down to her doom. She had two younger brothers who were Army officers. Both seem to have inherited the mental instability of their father. They were flighty, garrulous, arrogant, extremely indiscreet, and not at all abashed by their sister's curious position. There is no doubt that their behaviour had contributed largely to Draga's unpopularity. It was unfortunate that that very morning the worse of the two was with his sister, and that as she got into her carriage she whispered to him the name of the friend with whom she was going to take shelter while her maid packed for her. This was a natural enough precaution for one who knew herself to be in danger of kidnapping or death. It was not natural for her brother to give this name to the King when he called on his mistress two hours later. He drove at once to Draga's hiding-place and brought her home in his own carriage, and there and then put on her finger a diamond engagement ring, and left her under a strong armed guard.

For four days the capital was in a turmoil. It is indicative of the curious standards of this people that deputation after deputation visited the palace, urging the King not to marry the woman whom he adored, on the ground that she was old, his mistress, and of depraved habits, and that they were permitted to depart in impunity. This is not what one would have expected in a country where freedom of speech and the press had long been violated. But the Slavs are so inherently democratic that even under an autocracy there was an admitted right for the common man to discuss his ruler's affairs once they entered a phase of supreme importance. These deputations went away and formed various schemes for meeting the situation. Some wanted King Milan to be recalled and put in his son's place, others wanted Peter Karageorgevitch, others reverted to the original plan of exiling Draga, with the added precaution of putting Alexander under arrest till she was out of the country. There was no question but that the Army was to prevent the marriage by a rebellion. It only remained to settle how they were to do it.

Without any doubt a plan would have been devised which would have found general support, but on the fifth day an announcement was issued which hamstrung all opposition to the King's marriage. The Tsar Nicholas declared his approval of the engagement and sent an emissary to congratulate not only Alexander but Draga. More than that, the Tsar expressed his readiness to be "Kum" at their wedding; the Kum is the chief witness, who plays a more important part in a marriage celebrated according to the Orthodox rite than any equivalent

figure we know in the West, who is as it were the godparent of the
marital tie. The enemies of Alexander were almost all pro-Russian. They
could no longer oppose him now that he was obviously transferring his
allegiance from Austria to Russia; and the marriage showed in quite a
different light now that the Tsar was going to lend it his spiritual authority. A silence fell on Belgrade, not the less profound because it proceeded from bewilderment rather than from satisfaction. It had some
chance to settle, for King Milan never returned to Serbia. The Continental press published a letter which he was supposed to have sent his
son concerning his marriage, but which appears to have been written
for journalistic use; and he helped the Austrian authorities in a campaign of libel against Belgrade. His son directed his generals that if his
father attempted to re-enter Serbia he was to be shot like a mad dog.
But this scene, which would indeed have been not at all a surprising
climax to the family life of the Obrenovitches, was rendered impossible
by Milan's death in Vienna in 1901. Nothing could have been more
ironical than that his corpse and household possessions should have been
sent to Krushedol on the Frushka Gora, among the holy Serbian things
which had never interested him. But it can well be understood why the
Emperor Franz Josef sent them there. "Put them with the rest of the
Slav rubbish," he may have said. For Milan had failed in his duty of
keeping Serbia as an Austrian dependency, and henceforth he and all
Serbs were hateful and worthless in Habsburg eyes.

But the silence in Belgrade broke. The public loathing of Draga had
to find words to lift its corroding bitterness out of the heart. There is
no indication that Draga was not an admirable wife to Alexander. She
seems always to have treated him with an ungrudging maternal tenderness. There is no record of her having sided with the world against him
by showing consciousness of his lack of dignity or physical repulsive-
ness. But though certain Ministers recognized her virtues this did not
improve her popularity, for there were other counteracting forces.
There was a mysterious event which touched the primitive instincts of
the people. It was commonly believed that Draga was sterile as a result
of a surgical operation. This does not seem probable. If she had had
such an operation while she was in France it seems unlikely that anybody would hear about it except her immediate family, who would
hardly have broadcast it. This was the nineteenth century, in Belgrade
as anywhere else. But it is still more unlikely that it was performed before she went to France, for it is rarely required by very young women.
It is a little difficult to believe that if it had ever been performed Draga

would have ventured to announce shortly after her marriage that she was expecting a child, for the doctors and the nurses who had attended on her would have become potential dangers, threatening even her life. Furthermore, a famous French gynæcologist examined her and confirmed her opinion. Careless as fashionable doctors become, it is hard to imagine one failing to notice that an expectant mother lacked a womb; and it is not likely that he would have accepted a bribe, or that Alexander, who was in difficulties with his exchequer, could have raised one.

In the spring of 1901 there were rumours that Draga had been mistaken or had lied. The Tsar of Russia offered to lend the court two of his own physicians. Because he had been Kum at the wedding he would have had to be godparent to the first child, and it is possible that he had heard the gossip from Belgrade, thought he had been rash in backing the unpopular pair, and wanted to keep clear of any dubious proceedings. These two Russian doctors declared that Draga was not pregnant, but they explained clearly enough that this was not the result of a surgical operation but of a malady that might necessitate one. They also explicitly stated that the symptoms of this malady might easily have misled Draga into believing herself pregnant, and that the French gynæcologist's diagnosis might have been justified at the time when it was made.

The mischief was done. The people's mind was nursing an image that it always likes to hate and dandle in its hatred, the woman who is death, who is a whore and barren. They were moved to new folk-lore by this story, which troubled them by allusions to all sorts of dangers specially feared by the blood, to threats against kingship, to pollution of the race. Before long it was believed that Draga had been frustrated by the Tsar in an attempt to palm off as heir to the throne a child belonging to a sister of hers named Petrovitch. It is quite true that Madame Petrovitch was pregnant; and it may be true that in panic, finding her own hopes of pregnancy were false, Draga had thought of a "warming-pan baby." If that were so, only those who have never felt fear can blame her. Her situation was daily made more perilous by the conduct of her wretched brothers, who were certainly insane. The Serbian habit of expressing high spirits by discharging firearms into the air has alarmed many travellers, but these two young men indulged in it in a manner that alarmed even the Serbians. They also insisted that when they entered a café or restaurant the band should play the national anthem. If they did not start the rumour that one or other of them was to be adopted as heir to the throne, they at least behaved in a way that supported it and made it seem the beginning of anarchy.

From Draga's photographs it can be seen that she grew rapidly stout, old, wooden. A hostile newspaper published a serial written round the prophecies of Mata of Krema, and she brooded on the fate that had been foretold for her. She must have been aware, for she was not a fool, that her husband's reign was a tragic catastrophe. The change from dependence on Austria had done Serbia no whit of good. If Austria gave Alexander bad advice Russia gave him none at all, and that was worse, for though he had been on the throne ten years he had no knowledge of how to govern independently. The constitutional routine that steadied Russian absolutism was utterly unknown to him. For too long he had defended his crown and his very existence by alternate cringing and terrorism, and he could conceive no other procedure.

In 1901 he promulgated a new and democratic constitution, and almost immediately quarrelled with the Radicals whom the country elected to work it. Very soon he swept it out of existence and appointed a military dictatorship under General Tsintsar-Markovitch. The task of the Government was not to be performed. The finances of the country were in ruins, largely through the rogueries of Milan. The Army and Government officials were irregularly paid. Graft tainted every service. Nobody's liberty was safe. And both interior and foreign policy, owing to the long period of Austrian tutelage and Alexander's inability to profit by its termination, presented a completely bewildering spectacle to the people.

In April 1903 rioters were shot down in the streets of Belgrade. In May there was a General Election, with all returns grossly falsified by the Government. On the night of June the eleventh General Tsintsar-Markovitch went to King Alexander and told him that he could no longer face the task of ruling the country when the people were so solidly against him. This news distressed and angered the King, and he covered him with bitter abuse. But later he became calmer and admitted the reasonableness of the resignation, and asked only that his Prime Minister should carry on in office till a successor could be found. About ten o'clock the interview ended, and the King and Queen committed a last imprudence. Every evening a military band played in the gardens in front of the palace, while the crowds walked to and fro. The King and Queen went out on a balcony and sat there surrounded by Draga's sisters, including the one who was supposed to have assisted her in a plot to foist a false heir on the throne, and her two insanely ambitious brothers. Through the gathering darkness the people looked at the royal party with hatred that was strangling in its intensity, that had need to come to a climax. Meanwhile Tsintsar-Markovitch had gone to his home and sat up talking to his wife over a glass of wine. There were two reasons why they did not go to bed. Their eldest daughter, a girl of twenty-one, was married to a young officer named Milkovitch, who was that night on guard at the palace, and she was expected to give birth to her first child at any moment at her own home, which was in a neighbouring house. Also both Tsintsar-Markovitch and his wife felt sorrow over his resignation, and concern lest it should lead to royal disfavour.

In the cafés and garden-restaurants the usual summer crowds were sitting listening to the gipsy bands and watching the fireflies among the trees. There stands by Kalemegdan Park a hotel called the "Serbian Crown," which is distinguished by a certain romantic, haunted grace, as if the shutters had been flung back by ghosts keeping trysts made in a past and more passionate age. It has a long veranda which on warm nights is thrown open to the air, and there, on this night of June the eleventh, which was the anniversary of the murder of Prince Michael Obrenovitch thirty-five years before, sat a party of officers who attracted a great deal of attention. One of them was "Apis," Dragutin Dimitriyevitch, who ten years later was to give out guns and bombs to the lads from Sarajevo who wanted to kill Franz Ferdinand. They were drinking an enormous amount of plum brandy, and they called repeatedly for the tune which was played in honour of the Queen when she appeared in public, "Queen Draga's Kolo." Once at least they got up and danced the kolo, the Serbian national dance, forming a circle with their arms on each other's shoulders and their feet shuffling in an intricate rhythm. It was not extraordinary that they should dance the kolo. To this day soldiers will do that at any minute, outside their barracks or when they have to wait in a public place, say at a railway station. But it was extraordinary that these officers should dance Queen Draga's kolo, considering her unpopularity. It was explained for many of the onlookers by their drunkenness. A number of them were visibly drunk by eleven o'clock.

Shortly after that hour they left and walked towards the palace. They were joined by certain other parties of officers who had been spending their evening at various cafés and the Officers' Club. Some of them also were flushed and riotous, but some were quite sober and well able to play their appointed parts in the conspiracy. One of these was Draga's brother-in-law, Colonel Mashin. His motive in leading these soldiers against the palace may be taken as largely base. He had received large gifts of money from King Milan, who had often sent him on interesting missions; with exquisite inappropriateness he had been one of Serbia's representatives at The Hague International Peace Conference of 1899. All these benefits had stopped at the marriage of Alexander and Draga, when Milan left the country to die. This must have inflamed to fever-point his resentment against Draga for her failure to appreciate his brother's delirium tremens. Of Mashin nothing noble has ever been disclosed. But other leaders of the conspiracy were of a quite different sort. One lived to be a great man, of proven courage and wisdom, incorruptible in a time of temptation, never forgetful of his peasant origin, and always loyal to the peasants. His family speak of him as selfless, austere to himself, and tender with all others. Their followers also were of different qualities. Some were going to the palace in the expectation of murder and loot. Others went to demand the abdication of Alexander and to promise him and his wife a safe conduct over the frontiers on condition he did not name either of the Lunyevitza brothers as his successor. And of the eighty-six conspirators twenty-six had come up that day from scattered garrisons in answer to telegrams from Mashin telling them to get leave on any pretext and hurry to Belgrade, and were still not quite sure what was going to happen.

From the restaurant some went to the barracks of certain regiments to keep them from leaving for the defence of the palace when the alarm was given. Others went to the palace and gave the previously arranged signal, which was to bring them the King's equerry to open the outer door and lead them to the royal bedroom. But he had already repented of his consent to the conspiracy and had reacted to repentance in the manner of a Dostoevsky character. He had not betrayed his comrades to the King, he had simply sat in a chair in the entrance-hall and drunk himself into a state of unconsciousness, so that he would be unable to hear them when they came. Eventually they had to explode the locked door with a dynamite cartridge. This gave the alarm inside the palace and out. The King's aide-de-camp ran to the telephone but found the wires cut. Then the electric lights went out, either because the system had been damaged by the explosion or, some say, because the aide-de-camp turned off the central switch. Outside some gendarmes ran out of the neighbouring police station, saw a mob in the street, and began to fire. But what they thought was a mob was the Sixth Regiment, who had been brought out of barracks by one of the conspirators, and the soldiers answered fire. For a quarter of an hour there was a battle, but then the lie which had brought the Sixth Regiment to the palace spread to the police. They were told that King Alexander was turning Queen Draga out of the palace and that they had been sent for to keep peace in the town while she and her family were sent off to the frontier; and at once they ceased action. The same lie had disarmed the palace guard. All stood silent, bemused, cataleptic, because of their hatred of this woman.

The King's equerry was shocked out of his drunken sleep and staggered to the door. The conspirators cried out that he had betrayed them and "Apis" shot him dead. There is no record that this inveterate plotter of *attentats*, who dreamed all his life long of murdering crowned heads, ever killed anyone with his own hands except this dazed and unimportant man. Terrified, with the din of the street-fighting in their ears, they sent over to the house of a doctor near by and asked for candles. Since the doctor was told the story of Draga's expulsion, he gladly gave them. With these feeble lights the conspirators hurried into the palace, not knowing how long they had left for their work, and blundered about amongst the shifting shadows and the litter of furniture. The palace was a fine example of the school of interior decoration to which the dynasties of Europe seem irresistibly drawn, and they had to find their way among objects including many bead *portières*, a huge black bear that someone had shot during the Bulgarian War, marble fountains removed from old Turkish palaces, an immense number of occasional tables covered with bric-à-brac, tom-toms, and Turkish hookahs. They stumbled about, knocking things over, and tried to find their way to the royal bedroom. Sometimes enemies detached themselves from the shadows, loyal members of the palace guard, who were instantly killed. One was Milkovitch, husband of Tsintsar-Markovitch's eldest daughter, who was that night in childbirth.

Concerning these loyalists a divergence of opinion soon appeared. Some were merely for overpowering the King and Queen, others were for outright murder and did it. There must have been a certain amount of mutual distrust among the conspirators themselves by the time they struggled through the darkness to the royal bedroom and found that the King and Queen had gone. There was no question but that they had just left, for the bed was still warm, and a French novel had been thrown down on the bed-table, open and face-down. Now the conspirators had reason to feel real fear. If the King had got away and roused those soldiers who were still faithful, they would all lose their lives. They ordered the aide-de-camp, whom they had wounded in the shooting downstairs, to be brought upstairs and they questioned him. Though he was weak and in pain he lied glibly and sensibly to gain time. First he persuaded them to go down and search the cellars, which they did for an hour. When they were satisfied that there was nobody there they ran upstairs and ransacked the rooms again, some holding candles while the others drew their swords and poked them under sofas and pierced curtains with them, and beat them on the walls to detect secret doors. Their situation was becoming more and more desperate.

Meanwhile two officers had been sent with a company of soldiers to the house of Tsintsar-Markovitch. When they knocked at the door the General and his wife thought a messenger had come from their daughter's house. But owing to the conversation that they had been having about the results of his resignation, he was not surprised and he received them courteously and tranquilly. The senior officer told him that they had been sent to place him under arrest in his own house until it was time for him to go to the palace to hand over the seals of office. The General still showed no surprise and treated them as soldiers doing their duty, bidding them sit down while he gave them cigarettes. They smoked for a while. The senior officer showed signs of agitation which puzzled his junior, who did not know that they had been sent to kill the General. After a time the General rose and said, "I will go and order some coffee," and as soon as he turned his back on his guests the senior officer lifted his revolver and shot him three times. The assassin stood in great distress, crying out that he had been ordered to do this thing, while the junior officer knelt down and took the dying man in his arms. "Your Majesty, Your Majesty," Tsintsar-Markovitch said with his last breath, "I have been faithful to you. I did not deserve that you should do this thing to me." And in this error he died.

At the palace, King Alexander and Queen Draga were hiding in a little room that opened off their bedroom, scarcely more than a wardrobe, where her dresses were hung and her maid did her sewing and ironing. There had been a secret passage specially built by King Milan to meet just such an occasion as this, but Alexander had scornfully had it bricked up. The door to this wardrobe room was covered by the same wallpaper as the bedroom walls, and it completely deceived the conspirators, perhaps because they searched by candlelight. The King and Queen kept silent till they heard their enemies question their aide-de-camp and then go stumbling down to the cellars. Then the King went to the window and cried to the soldiers whom he saw dimly standing about in the gardens about the palace. But they were all some way off, and he was leaning from a dark window, and they had been told that the officers of the palace guard were protecting their King against a conspiracy started by Draga and her family. They stood silent and immovable. The hatred of Draga had become a wandering spell, an enchantment that played about the city, sealing the mouths and paralysing the bodies of all its inhabitants.

The royal pair seem to have given up the attempt to save themselves for a time and to have tried to clothe themselves decently. The King was wearing trousers and a red silk shirt, and Draga had found lying about a pair of white silk stays, a petticoat, and yellow stockings. She did not dare to open a cupboard to get out a dress, for fear of making a noise, and they were in darkness. Their torture lasted for about two hours. Then the Queen, who was standing at the window, saw an officer come into the gardens just below, and recognized him by his walk as the Commander of the Royal Guard. She leaned out and cried to him, "Come and save your King! He is in danger!" The Commander halted, looked up, and made sure that it was she. He raised his revolver and fired at her: or rather at the Austrian Empire, at our evil earth, at our polluted species, at sin. A wide shot, for she was in fact none of these things. It was no wonder he missed her.

This Commander went round to the entrance-hall and found the conspirators, with their drawn swords in their hands, wrangling with the dying aide-de-camp, who was on the point of persuading them to search another building near by. He told them that he had seen the Queen at a window near the royal bedroom. They ran back to it at once, but still could not find the wardrobe room. An axe was fetched from a woodshed in the palace courtyard, and one of the officers struck the walls till he came on the door. It was locked, and there is no evidence whether it was broken open or whether the King and Queen unbolted it under promise of safety. All that is known is that at the last they stood in their bedroom, the flabby spectacled young man and the stout and bloated middle-aged woman, fantastically dressed, and faced a group of officers whose shaking hands held guttering candles and drawn swords and revolvers.

Mashin was there, but so was a leader of the highest character. This man asked the King if he would abdicate, and was answered with the bitterest words a son ever spoke. "No; I am not King Milan, I am not to be overawed by a handful of officers." Then all the revolvers in the room fired at once, and Alexander fell into Draga's arms. He cried, "Mito! Mito! How could you do this thing to me?" Mito was the familiar name of Tsintsar-Markovitch. Alexander died in the belief that he had been assassinated by order of the man who had died an hour before, in the belief that he had been assassinated by order of Alexander. Then the revolvers fired again, and Draga dropped to the floor. A madness came on most of the men in the room. They stripped the bodies and hacked them with their swords, gashing the faces, opening their bellies. Some of them who did not run amuck shouted to them that they must all go away now that the deed was done, now that partisans of the King and Queen might come in and arrest them. This, however, did not do anything to restore decency to the scene. For with a dreadful sanity the men who had been stripping and slashing tumbled the naked corpses out of the window into the gardens below. This was sound common sense and guaranteed their own safety, for it showed that both King and Queen were dead and there was now no one to protect or be protected by, since there were no Obrenovitches left to succeed to the throne. But it added another indecency to the scene. Alexander's arms had always been much more developed than the rest of his body; and as there was a spark of life in him he clung to the balcony with one hand as he went over, and an officer had to sever his fingers with a sword before he would let go. When he had been cast down on the lawn his other hand closed on some blades of grass.

The morning broke; and although it was June some rain fell about four o'clock. That brought the Russian Minister out of his Legation, which looked across a chestnut avenue at the palace. He had been watching the tragedy all night through the slits in his shutters. Though he could certainly have taken steps to rescue the King and Queen, he had intervened neither then nor when he had been informed of the conspiracy, which had happened two or three days earlier. For a great number of people had known of it beforehand. Mr. Miyatovitch, who was then Serbian Minister in London, received a full description of it at a spiritualist séance held by Mr. W. T. Stead three months before. The medium, Mrs. Burchell, had visualized the scene with singular fidelity. Such at least was the opinion of everybody present who came from Finsbury Park, though a gentleman from Hounslow heard nothing. Other persons, however, received intimations later and from more materialistic sources. The Austrian Government knew of it, and certain movements of troops on its frontiers could be explained only by that foreknowledge. But it would not issue a warning to Alexander, its enemy. And the Russian Legation would not issue a warning to its highly unsatisfactory friend, who was so unpopular, so awkward, and, above all, so unlucky. But there is a point at which a gentleman must draw the line. Entering the garden, the Russian Minister went up to the officers who were standing about and pointed to the corpses. "For God's sake," he said, "carry them into the palace. Do not leave them here in the rain exposed to the gaze of the public." This sentence may well be preserved as a symbol of the kind and degree in which the great powers have acted as a civilizing influence in the Balkans.

Belgrade VII

THEREAFTER the city blossomed like the rose. Serbia was young again, it was refreshed, it tossed its head and threw off its sleep and faced the morning in its strength, because Draga was dead, because the bad woman had been killed. The actual ills that Alexander Obrenovitch had committed, or at any rate consented to, the imprisonments and floggings, the corruption and fraud, were quickly forgotten. For long the people have spoken as if he had been murdered because he was Draga's husband, and as if his murder were secondary to hers, and as if the murders were purgations of a plague, which was nothing but Draga.

This is a mystery. For Draga was insignificant. She is one of the most negative people who appear in history. At no point in her career does she seem to have said or done anything that could be remembered five minutes later. She represents prose in its defective sense, in its limitation to factual statement, in its lack of evocation and illumination. Her enemies found it difficult to make a case against her, because she provided them with no material from which any deduction could be made; and for the same reason her friends could build up no defence. When she went into a room she did nothing that was noble and nothing that was base, she stood up if standing was good, and she sat down if sitting was better. No man except Alexander seems to have loved her, and although a few women felt a protective kindness towards her they do not talk of her as in any way interesting.

Such a woman could not have committed a great crime, and indeed she never was accused of any. To plan the substitution of an heir to the throne would have been disgraceful, had she ever truly done so; but that can be left on one side, for Serbia's hatred of Draga was mature before she ever became Queen. It was ostensibly based on the immorality of her life as a young widow in Belgrade; and let us visualize exactly what that meant if it were real. A beautiful and dull young woman lived in a small room somewhere in Belgrade; on the walls there would be hung many family photographs and a poor bright rug or two, and on the wooden floor there would be one or two others of these poor rugs. There would come to her sometimes men who would perhaps be comely and young like herself, for she was not so poor as to need to take lovers against her inclination. There would follow some conversation, agonizing in its banality had one had to listen to it, but not criminal, not threatening to anyone's peace or life. It would not be unnatural if the couple soon abandoned the use of words, and turned to embraces, which would as like as not be purely animal in inspiration. Then, if the worst of what the Queen's enemies said was true, they went into another room, in which there was a bed, and lay down on it. Once they were there nature limited them to the performance of a certain number of movements which except to the neurotic are not abhorrent, which some people find agreeable and others disagreeable, which by common consent have to be judged ethically solely by their results, since they themselves carry hardly any but a momentary and sensational significance.

Now, this is admittedly not what one would hope to find in the past of a royal personage. A queen should know only the love that lasts, as a king should know only the courage that never fails. But it must be reiterated that Draga was hated before there was any probability that she should become Queen: and that makes the power of the scene over the popular imagination remarkable. It might have led to the birth of an illegitimate child, but it did not. It might have led to the transmission of venereal disease, but it did not. Still, the potentiality shadows it. But even so it is extraordinary that the Serbs should have been distraught and frenzied by a scene that was darkened by only the shadow of horror when they were so familiar with scenes that were black with its substance. They were used to murder, to the bullet that sped from the forest branches, to the rope that strangled the captive who the next day would be pronounced a suicide. They were used to the fraudulent trial, the lying witnesses, the bribed judge, the undeserved imprisonment, and the thieving fine. Yet it was Draga who sent their blood rushing to blind their eyes, who made them draw their swords in a completely supererogatory murder. For there was no reason whatsoever to kill Draga. Alexander it would perhaps have been impossible to leave alive, for his obstinacy and his sense of grandiose destiny would have made him cling to power if it meant wrecking his country's peace. But Draga could safely have been put on a train and sent off to spend the rest of her days between Passy and Nice. There was no reason at all why the conspirators should have spent that night of panic in the palace staggering about among the occasional tables and the bead *portières*, accumulating damnable guilt.

But it would be fatuous to deny the dynamic effect of the deed. There was at first the movement towards demoralization that would have been expected. The conspirators murdered not only the King and Queen and the Prime Minister, but also the Minister of War, and Draga's two brothers. These two young men were brought to the barracks of the regiment and confronted by the Commander of the Royal Guard, the same who had shot at Draga from her garden. "Their Majesties are now dead," he said to them with ferocious irony. "The moment has come for your Royal Highnesses to command. Do not hesitate. We are your faithful subjects. Pray give your orders. But if I may presume to advise you, you will not ask for more than a glass of water and a cigarette." They were then taken out into a courtyard and shot by a firing-party commanded by Lieutenant Tankositch, the friend of "Apis," who eleven years later was to aid him in giving arms to Princip and his friends for the Sarajevo *attentat*. After such a blood bath there was bound to be disorder and there was some looting of the palace and the houses of the murdered Ministers. But in a day the Army was brought to heel, and the business of government was competently carried on. A provisional Government was formed, and after a peculiar religious service, of a kind not prescribed in any missal, attended by the Ministers and conspirators, a deputation set off to Geneva to offer the throne to Peter Karageorgevitch.

It is incontestable that Peter Karageorgevitch had known nothing about the murders beforehand. His worst enemies never seriously alleged that he had been consulted, and several of the conspirators admitted that they never dared tell him. He was a man of fifty-seven, with an upright character and a complete incapacity for pliancy, and they were well aware that had he known of their intentions he would have stiffly denounced them to the proper authorities. For a royal pretender he had had a curious career. He was the grandson of the great Karageorge and the son of the Alexander Karageorgevitch who had ruled without zest from 1842 to 1858. Because of his father's democratic principles he had been brought up as much like a peasant child as possible, and had gone out from the palace to the national school every morning. At the time of his father's abdication he was sent to a boarding-school in Geneva, which was singularly successful in marking him for life. To the end of his days there was grafted on the essential Serb in him an industrious, conscientious, Puritan Swiss. He spent his holidays on his father's estate in Transylvanian Hungary and learned the elements of farming; but he elected to become a soldier, and at seventeen went to France and passed through the Military Academies of Saint-Cyr and Metz. He fought in the Franco-Prussian War, and was wounded and decorated, and laid the foundations of the rheumatism that was to cripple him in later life by swimming the Loire in midwinter to escape capture. We have an odd vignette of him bursting into a house in a French town one quiet evening during the campaign, explaining that he had heard from the streets the tones of a harmonium and begging that he might be allowed to play on it. He then spent a happy hour wheezing out Serbian national airs.

He remained inveterately serious and simple. It is doubtful whether he ever learned that a harmonium is not chic. But the rest of his family established itself in Paris and could have taught him that the right thing was a grand piano covered with a Japanese embroidery. His younger brother, Arsenius, became a dashing Russian officer, and later a well-known boulevardier; of his young cousins, Alexis and Bozhidar, much can be read in Marie Bashkirtseff's *Journal*. Indeed, one of the most interesting exhibits in Prince Paul's Museum at Belgrade, though it has some fine Corots and Degases and Van Goghs and Matisses, is a charming picture by Marie of the bearded young Bozhidar, leaning from a balcony threaded with orange nasturtiums, looking down on a Paris silvery with autumn. This boy grew to be a water-colourist of some merit and wrote several Loti-like books about travel in the East which consisted almost entirely of colour-adjectives; he was a close friend of Sarah Bernhardt, and was in much demand for masquerades because of his capacity for Arielesque gaiety. Alexis and he both spent money like water on highly amusing and refined objects. They were conspicuously not what would be expected of the grandchildren of a Serb pig-breeder and rebel chief. But all the genes characteristic of Karageorge seemed to have been transmitted in almost uncomfortable purity to Peter.

He spent some time in France after he left the Army, and studied the elements of law and social science. It was at this time that he translated John Stuart Mill's *Essay on Liberty* into Serbian. In 1875 he went to Bosnia and fought in the revolt against Turkey, and was unremittingly in command of a company of comitadji throughout the whole three years of the campaign. After the settlement he went to Serbia, not to advocate his claim to the throne but to see his native country again. He was soon expelled by the police. Five years later he went to Montenegro to help Prince Nicholas reorganize his army, and married one of his daughters. In 1889 his wife died of consumption, leaving him with three children, two boys and a girl. By this time he had taken an intense dislike to his father-in-law, whom he rightly considered dishonest and dishonourable, so he moved with his family to Geneva.

There he lived in great poverty. There was barely enough money to feed the family, and some people in Switzerland believe that Peter added to his income by some such work as the copying of legal documents. He also took his full share in his family responsibilities. He had taken furnished rooms, and an elderly cousin acted as nurse to the children, but there were three of them, and presently four; for his brother Arsenius had married in Russia a member of the plebeian but wealthy family of Demidoff, and they had separated, leaving a little boy (now Prince Paul) without a home. Peter brought them up with a tender, anxious, austere care. He gave them their first lessons, and he watched over their manners and morals with an unrelenting eye. A Serb and a Swiss, he thought that one must be a soldier, and that one must be good. The training that this faith brought on the four children is not altogether agreeable to contemplate. They were all over-worked. They had to attend the ordinary Swiss elementary school during the day, which was supposed to be a whole-time education, and in the evening they had to learn the Serbian language and history and literature from a Serbian governess and their father. They were also subjected to ferocious discipline. In 1896 their mother's sister Helen married the Crown Prince of Italy, and invited the children, of whom she was very fond, to the wedding at Rome. The little daughter was not allowed to go because her marks at school had been bad.

But he was kind and loving. To understand his severity towards his children it must be remembered that he intensely disapproved of his own family. He thought Arsenius might probably be saved in so far as he was a good soldier, but his Swiss side found much to disapprove of in his brother considered as a dashing Russian officer and the divorced husband of Aurora Demidoff. As for Bozhidar and Alexis, he thought they were degeneration itself. Alexis had married a very rich American lady, and to please her had tried to get Peter to stand back and let him assume the role of pretender, pointing out that he at least had the money to finance his claim. This had struck Peter as a most unholy proposal, and he coldly continued to instruct his children in the legend of Kossovo and deprive them of their meals if they were not in time for them, trusting that by such means he would prevent them from resembling their relatives. But it could not escape his notice that his elder son, George, showed undoubted signs of the unstable charm which he disliked in Alexis and Bozhidar, and, what was perhaps more serious, the moody violence that had darkened the genius of Karageorge.

It was perhaps for this reason that in 1898 Peter accepted an offer made by the Tsar to receive all three of his children in St. Petersburg, give them the freedom of the palaces, and educate them at the best Russian schools. It is certain that his liberal tendencies would have been better pleased if the children had been educated in Switzerland or France; but he could no longer face the responsibility of bringing them up on scanty food, in uncomfortable lodgings, and without advice, when there was this handsome alternative. But though this improved his family's lot it initiated a most uncomfortable routine for him. The little Paul could not at first be taken to Russia for reasons connected with his parents' troubles, and he remained in Geneva under the care of Prince Peter and his cousin till later. But Prince Peter had to take care that his children remained good Serbs and were not Russified, so he visited them in Russia in the holidays, travelling as cheaply as possible. These journeys were not wasted. His second son, Alexander, remained curiously impervious to Romanoff luxury, practised his father's frugality and chastity, and cultivated Serb circles in St. Petersburg. The Roman virtue of this man was real, and had its emanations.

The news of the Belgrade murders must have been unspeakably disgusting to Peter Karageorgevitch. He had never supported his claim to the Serbian throne by the most faintly dubious action. He had announced that he believed himself to be the rightful ruler of Serbia and that he was willing to take up the sceptre whenever the Serbian people demanded it; and there he had left it. Now he was faced with what is the nastiest thing in the world from an Army officer's point of view: an Army conspiracy. He was faced with what is the next nastiest thing from a soldier's point of view: the slaughter of unarmed civilians. Also one victim had been a woman, and there had been a great deal of drunkenness. It must have been the bitterest moment in his life when he went to his café to read the morning newspapers and found them black with this blot on his country, which—as it must have struck him after the first second's shock—was also a blot on his own name. When the Skupshtina elected him King he was faced with one of the most unpleasant dilemmas that has ever faced a decent man. He knew that if he accepted the throne the whole world would suspect him of complicity in the murders, he would be ostracized by all other reigning sovereigns, and he would be in the deadliest personal danger, since mutiny is no exception to the rule that the appetite grows by what it feeds on. But he knew that Serbia needed a good king and that there was nobody else likely to rule well except himself. He knew too that there were many people in Serbia who trusted him to save them from misgovernment. It is also possible that the Tsar had given his children their education on the understanding that he would go to Belgrade when the opportunity served and protect the country from the Austrian devourer of the Obrenovitches.

When the twenty-four delegates from the Skupshtina arrived in Geneva and offered Peter Karageorgevitch the Serbian crown, he stiffly accepted. Without temporizing, without waiting till European excitement had subsided, he took the train to Belgrade and got there thirteen days after the assassination. By that time all powers except Austria and Russia had withdrawn their diplomatic representatives as a mark of scorn. Peter greeted his people with a gravity which made it plain that it was for him to approve them rather than for them to approve him. His first legislative act was to remove the censorship on the foreign press. No newspapers from abroad were to be seized or blacked. "Serbia," said Peter, without explaining himself further, "shall henceforth know what other countries think of it."

His immediate problem was how to deal with the regicides. He never dealt with them in the complete and clear-cut way suggested by the over-zealous apologists of the Karageorgevitches. It is said in one history that he removed them all within three years. This is not true. Peter recognized that there were differences in guilt among the conspirators, and that some were high-minded men who had conceived the crime out of public spirit and had never intended it to be so bloody. Even under strong foreign pressure he refused to expel these men from office. One was the famous General Mishitch, who showed himself a great soldier in the Balkan wars and still greater in the World War. But others he recognized as base and sooner or later excluded from official favour: Mashin was one. And Peter would not persecute those who denounced the crime. When he was reviewing a regiment four months after his arrival a lieutenant left the ranks and shouted in his face that the blood of Alexander was still crying out for vengeance; the young man was removed from the Army but was not otherwise punished. Soon the baser regicides banded together to protect themselves, and in 1907 they assassinated the head of the anti-regicide group. Peter used that assassination, in conjunction with an Austrian attempt to eject him and give the Serbian throne to an Anglo-German, to sober public opinion. He told his people that if they insisted on behaving like wild beasts they must expect to be caged and put in charge of a keeper. But he himself was well aware that though he had thereby cleansed public opinion he had not succeeded in rounding up all the conspirators of dangerous character. Chief among these was Dragutin Dimitriyevitch, who was protected by the extraordinary personal fascination which made him a popular figure in the Army.

But the question of the regicides mattered far less than can be supposed. Incredible as it may seem, it was dwarfed by the astonishing achievements of which the people, refreshed by their sacrifice of Draga, found themselves easily and happily capable. Peter began a programme of reforms in the simplest, most Genevese spirit. When his major-domo came to him on the day of his arrival to inquire what sort of menus he preferred, he exclaimed, "Menus! Menus! I have no time for menus! Never speak of such things to me again." He can indeed have had very little time, for he started to reform Serbia on foot and by hand. He would walk without military escort to a hospital, and if he found all the doctors out, as was not unlikely to happen in those Arcadian days, he wrote in the visitors' book, "King Peter has been here." He would visit a school, and if he found the children playing and the teachers gloomily discussing their grievances, he wrote on the blackboard, "King Peter has been here." He went on, however, to deal with the grievance which most afflicted doctors and teachers, and indeed many civil servants and soldiers in Serbia, and explained a great deal of disordered conduct: he saw that they were paid regularly. Swiss honesty, which in the place of its origin sometimes seems too much of a good thing, affected the Serbians, after thirty-five years of Milan and Alexander, as picturesque and exotic. It was to them what their national costume is to us. They stood gaping, while by continuous probity Peter brought his own state to financial order and even won the respect of international financiers. Alexander had been unable to raise a loan in Vienna even by pledging the entire railway system of Servia, but Peter was cheerfully lent nine times the sum his predecessor had vainly importuned.

The Serbs rose to their dawn. They followed him along the new path that Serbia had not trodden for five hundred years, to the world where success, and golden, luxuriant success at that, was won not only by the sword but by the plough, the loom, the pen, the brush, the balance. For the first time since the Turkish conquest the lost civilization of Byzantium showed signs of revival, and at last it seemed as if the monotonous reciprocal process of tyranny and resistance were to be displaced by a truly polymorphous life. The Serbians spread their wings, they soared up to the sun. When Austria saw them it was enraged. It contrived a snare to get Serbia back under its tutelage. When King Peter reorganized his army, under the commandership of his brother, Arsenius Karageorgevitch, he proposed to buy some big guns from France; he also arranged a customs agreement of a most brotherly sort with Bulgaria. Vienna rapped him sharply over the knuckles. The agreement with Bulgaria must be cancelled, and the guns must be ordered from Austria. King Peter refused; so did his Prime Minister, Nicholas Pashitch, the Lloyd George of Serbia, a crafty idealist; so did the intoxicated Serbians. "The Obrenovitches are gone, the Karageorgevitches are here, we are no longer slaves," they said.

Austria then declared economic warfare on the Serbians. It looked as if it must conquer, and that easily. Serbia had only one industry, pig-breeding, and there was nothing simpler than raising the tariff against their livestock to prohibitive heights. That killed at one blow nine-tenths of their trade. However, the Serbians tightened their belts, and very soon found new markets in France, Egypt, and even England, while the price of meat mounted to preposterous heights in Austria. The "pig war" lingered on for five years, from 1905 to 1910. As its failure became manifest, Austria made it clear she had not accepted defeat. In 1908 the abominable Aehrenthal chose to annex Bosnia and Herzegovina; which, once annexed, were a threat to every state between Austria and the Black Sea. It meant that the Habsburgs, having failed to subdue Serbia by economic warfare, meant some day to settle the score by the use of arms. Again the Serbians spread their wings and soared up to the sun. "If there is Austria," they said, "there is also Russia. We have no need to cringe before any state; we are a strong people whose strength will buy us allies." And this indeed was true, now that they had a king who could not be bought and would not let his Ministers sell themselves.

This moment must have found King Peter at his happiest and his most sorrowful. The contrast between the disorganized and dishonoured Serbia which he had taken over from the Obrenovitches and the proud and virile state which was now making its own terms with the great power was, indeed, the sign of one of the most dramatic personal achievements in modern history. But it is quite possible that he was not altogether pleased by the company his triumph had brought on him. He had had to accept Russian upbringing for his children in his days of exile; now he had to accept Russian protection for his subjects. But the democratic Serb, the liberal Swiss, the translator of John Stuart Mill's *Essay on Liberty*, could not but disapprove of Russian absolutism; his frugality must have been repelled by the luxury of the Romanoffs; and he knew that the South Slavs had every reason to fear the Russian movement known as Pan-Slavism. That had become evident in the seventies, when the Turks had tried to kill Greek and Serb influence in Macedonia by

founding of the Bulgarian Exarchate, which was to make the government of the Macedonian churches independent of the Greek Patriarchate. This Exarchate was inevitably anti-Serb, as Serbs wanted self-
government for their own churches; and Russia lent her support to the
Exarchate, because it feared the Austro-Hungarian Empire and its dominance of Serbia and therefore wished to have no Serbs in Macedonia.
Hence it put up the money for Bulgarian churches, schools, and newspapers, which had no other object than to turn Serbs into Bulgarians. In
fact Russia had, in the name of Pan-Slavism, destroyed the unity between
the Serbs and the Bulgarians which was necessary if the South Slavs were
ever to maintain themselves against the Turks and the Austrians. Later
Russia sometimes retrieved her position, but she often backslid. This was
no stable ally of the sort that King Peter, King Rock, would have chosen.

He had another and more personal sorrow. His elder son, the Crown
Prince George, took a prominent part in politics and became the leader
and idol of the violent pro-war party. Of his charm and courage and
ability there was no doubt; and he was even sound in judgment. When
the rest of Europe still held blind faith in the efficiency of the Austrian
Army he predicted its collapse under the first prolonged strain. But the
fantastic strain in him which had grieved his father in the old days at
Geneva was flowering into a monstrosity not to be ignored. King Peter
could not deal with him in the summary manner that would have been
best; his popularity with the Army, and particularly among those officers
who had formed the more disreputable part of the regicidal conspirators,
would have made it dangerous to seclude him. But in 1909 he fell into
trouble. He killed his valet in an attack of rage. The most charitable account has it that he found the man reading his letters and kicked him
downstairs with no intention of inflicting on him any serious injury. The
King then inflexibly required that the Crown Prince should resign his
claim to the succession in favour of his brother Alexander, though he
felt obliged to let him retain his commission in the Army. It has been said
by envenomed critics of the dynasty that this was the result of Alexander's intrigues; but he was then a silent boy of twenty-one, who was still
a student at the Military Academy in St. Petersburg, and had paid only
a few brief visits to Serbia during the six years since his father's accession.
King Peter, who was now sixty-five, cannot have been altogether certain of the quality of the boy he now recalled from Russia to help him
against his internal and external enemies.

Now destiny took charge of his kingdom. The Austrian provocation
became more and more insolent. In January 1909 there had been a spec-

tacular trial in Zagreb where fifty-three Serb subjects of the Austrian Empire had been charged with conspiring against their country with the connivance of the Serbian Government, and thirty-one of them had been convicted on obviously forged or frivolous evidence. In March 1909 the Austrian Foreign Office handed the official historian of the Habsburg family, one Dr. Friedjung, forged documents which purported to prove the existence of a new conspiracy against the Empire not only directed but financed by certain members of the Serbian Government. King Peter and his Ministers issued a statement roundly calling the Austrians liars, and over fifty Serbian politicians backed up that statement by filing actions for libel against Dr. Friedjung in Vienna. The subsequent trial showed beyond a doubt that all his evidence was fabricated. Smiling, the Serbs went home, and prepared themselves for the war that must come. They believed that it would not come at once. Russia had been greatly annoyed by the annexation of Bosnia, and her annoyance was a fortress wall behind the Serbians, clearly visible to the Austrians.

There was work they could do in the meantime. Macedonia was still unredeemed, a Christian province in the hands of the Ottoman Empire: a hell of misgovernment, that had known no respite for five hundred years, save for a brief period of international control at the beginning of the twentieth century, which had been terminated by the Austro-Hungarian and German Empires for no other reason than the Teutonic hatred of the Slav. It was now in the deeper darkness that follows a false dawn. The Young Turk movement had suddenly swept away the Sultanate, and established a constitution promising liberty to all its subjects of whatever race. Very soon it appeared that the Young Turk was simply the son of the Old Turk, with a Prussian military training, and there was set on foot a ferocious scheme for denationalizing the Macedonian Christians. Serbia and Bulgaria not only abhorred this spectacle from the bottom of their Balkan souls, but were touched by it in their self-interest. If the Austrians were to have an empire stretching to the Black Sea they would first go down the valley of the Vardar through Serbia and get command of the Ægean at Salonika, and Serbia and Bulgaria would be impeded in their resistance to his invasion, because Macedonia, a strip of disordered country in the hands of their enemies, the Turks, would lie between them and their allies, the Greeks. There was no question but they must drive out the Turks; and with that resolution there came to the Serbs an extraordinary happiness. There is nothing like the peculiar gratification which fills us when we find ourselves able to satisfy the claims of reality by enacting a fantasy that has long warmed our imagination. The Serbians, to live in modern Serbia, must realize the poem that was written in the monasteries of the Frushka Gora, that was embodied in the dark body of the Tsar Lazar. They had not to choose whether they would make a day-dream into fact: they were under the necessity of choosing between life with that day-dream and death without it.

There has been no fighting in our time that has had the romantic quality of the Balkan wars that broke out in 1912. The Serbians rode southwards radiant as lovers. The whole West thought them barbarous swashbucklers, and fools at that, advancing on an enemy who had never been defeated, and had found some magic prescription for undeserved survival. That mattered nothing to these dedicated troops, wrapped in their rich and tragic dream. They were determined to offer themselves to the horrors of war in a barren land where the climate is bearable for only four months in the year, where there were dust-storms and malaria and men who had been turned by art to something more savage than savagery. Those horrors accepted them. The summer burned them, the winter buried them in snow; on the vile Turkish roads their commissariat often broke down for days and they had to live on roots and berries; the wounded and malarial lay contorted among the untender rocks; they suffered atrocities and committed them. But they were not perturbed. In their minds there lay the splendid image of Slav empire, potent in spite of time and defeat, like the Tsar Lazar in his coffin. It can be conceived as filling with a special glory, altogether Byzantine in its rigidity of forms and intense incandescence, the mind of the Crown Prince Alexander, for the Karageorgevitches permitted themselves no other poetry.

In three months the poem had completed itself. By December 1912 the Ottoman Empire, as Europe had known it for six hundred years, had been destroyed. The Serbians and Bulgarians and Greeks laughed in the astonished faces of the West. All should have gone magically well, had it not been that the quality that the West has shown in its dealings with the Balkans was too pervasive and enduring not to tarnish even the purest metal of achievement. It may be remembered that the Slavs had won this same victory once before, in 1876; and had been diddled out of their victory first by Russia's incompetence, which made them sign the unsatisfactory Treaty of San Stefano, and then by the criminal idiocy of all the great powers combined, and of England in particular, which replaced it by the infinitely more mischievous Treaty of Berlin, designed for the maintenance of Turkey in Europe. This had left all sorts of unsettled issues for the Serbians and Bulgarians to quarrel about; and the intrigues it engendered had placed upon the Bulgarian throne in 1887 a being of tortuous impulses and unlovely life called Prince Ferdinand of Saxe-Coburg-Gotha. During his reign he watered and tended corruption as if it were a flower. The disorder of Bulgarian politics, which is often cited as a reproach to the Balkans, was very largely an importation of this detestable princeling. He was always a tool of Austria, although his bias towards treachery makes all statements about his character difficult to frame; and after the Karageorgevitches had freed Serbia from the Austrian yoke he became one of Austria's most useful instruments in its increasingly frenetic anti-Russian and anti-Serbian policy. He had been forced to join with Serbia in the Balkan wars by the will of his people, and indeed his Austrian masters told him that there was no objection against it, provided he was ready to do a Judas-trick at the end. And this he did.

Ferdinand assured the Serbians and the Greeks that he had shifted his allegiance from Austria to Russia, signed pacts with them, and went to war at their side, though not as the most satisfactory ally imaginable. With money and munitions he was extremely stingy, but he was generous to a fault in the manufacture of "incidents" which faced too simply the problem of rousing public sympathy. A staff of his blackguards distributed bombs among trained bandits who exploded them in mosques, which not unnaturally inspired the infuriated Moslems to rush out and massacre Christians. This pleased neither the Christians who were massacred nor the Serbs and Greeks, who found themselves regarded with suspicion by neutral observers. Such, however, was the melodic line traced by Ferdinand's soul. Then, when the peace came he saw to it that discord between the Serbians and the Bulgarians should be its first result. The Treaty of San Stefano had awarded Bulgaria territory that gave her a position in the Balkans only to be justified if she had been the real liberator of the Peninsula, and the three peoples had gone into the war with a loose understanding that the Treaty might at last be carried into effect if Bulgaria provided that justification. But in that she failed. Ferdinand had mismanaged his gallant army so that they had in fact not even done their share of their fighting; and the decisive battle of the campaign, Kumanovo, had been won by the Serbians alone. It was natural that Serbia should demand some recognition of her special services in the peace treaties, which should take the form of a common frontier with her ally Greece and access to the sea at Salonika. This was an abso-

lute necessity to her existence, as Austria had recently created out of the wreckage of Turkish territory a puppet state of Albania, which was to be an Austrian stronghold that should control Serbia and Greece.

But Ferdinand impudently resisted these reasonable demands. The Judas-trick he had been asked to perform by Austria was the sowing of deep dissension between the Serbians and Bulgarians at the end of the war, if need be by the betrayal of his own subjects' good name. During the summer of 1913, while the peace treaties were being discussed, he spread among his troops all manner of lies about the Serbians. Then on June twenty-eighth, St. Vitus's Day, which was the anniversary of the defeat of the Christians on the field of Kossovo, which was to see the assassination of the Archduke Franz Ferdinand and Sophie Chotek, he issued certain orders which even his own kept Government was not allowed to know. Many Bulgarian officers dined with Serbian officers to celebrate the recovery of Kossovo; when they returned to their trenches they were told that the discovery of a conspiracy made it necessary for them to make a surprise attack on the Serbian regiments in the early morning. This is one of the vilest episodes in Balkan history; and it was not committed by a Slav. It was not a vestige of Balkan medievalism. It cannot be laid at the door of the Turk. It was the fruit of nineteenth-century Teutonism.

But the Serbians, knifed in the back, continued within their dream, to achieve their poem. The powerful magic of that dream, that incantatory poem, blunted the knife. They beat back the Bulgarians. The Greeks, the Turks, the Roumanians, closed in on Ferdinand, who was unperturbed. He believed his time was yet to come. He made a secret pact with the Emperor Franz Josef towards the end of 1913, that he should place all the resources of Bulgaria at the disposal of Austria and Germany, provided he was given a large portion of Serbian and Greek and Roumanian territory if he kept his throne, and a fat pension if his subjects expelled him. He then set to work to thrall Bulgaria to Germany by a loan, to which the assent of Parliament was given during a most peculiar scene. Ferdinand's Prime Minister faced the assembly with a revolver in his hand, but all the same the opposition deputies did considerable damage on the Ministerial Front Bench by using inkstands and books as missiles. The angels must have been greatly perplexed by the determination of European statesmen to civilize the Balkans by sowing them with German princelings; for in Belgrade, the only capital in the Peninsula ruled by a Slav, things were going better. It would be light-minded to deny that the second Balkan War cast for a time a red shadow of barbarism across Serbian life. That treacherous early-morning attack on the trenches, though the guilt lay on the Bulgarian crown and not on the people, engendered a hatred that met atrocity with atrocity; and the first Serbian official who went to settle the newly acquired territories behaved as if they were conquerors and not liberators. But the liberalism of King Peter was quietly attending to these natural inflammations of a national spirit which had suffered war; it is typical of the difficulties of his task and of the infinite incalculabilities of Balkan history that by far his most sagacious aide in dealing with the problem of the tyrannous and dishonest officials in Macedonia was one of the regicides. The tiger, blood on its claws, crossed itself; the golden beast became a golden youth; church and state, love and violence, life and death, were to be fused again as in Byzantium.

Hardly had the transformation been made when it was threatened; and the threat shocked and startled. It was known to all Europe, and to Serbia best of all, that the Central powers were preparing for an aggressive war, but it was not generally expected that they meant to act in 1914. What the intelligence services of the great powers had reported in these years has never yet been published, though this would be far more enlightening than any amount of diplomatic correspondence. But it is said that both France and Russia were for some reason convinced that Germany and Austria would not make war until 1916, and certainly that alone would explain the freedom with which Russia announced to various interested parties in the early months of 1914 that she herself was not ready to fight. So Serbia was in a trance of amazement when Franz Ferdinand and Sophie Chotek were killed at Sarajevo, and it became certain that the enemy was going to use the murder as a pretext for instant attack. There could have been no more hopeless moment. The Serbian peasant army had been fighting since 1912, and every soldier had either already gone home or was homesick. The arsenals were empty of arms, the treasury was empty of money to buy them. There was a difficult internal situation. King Peter was now completely crippled by the rheumatism he had contracted in swimming the Loire to escape capture during the Franco-Prussian War, and only ten days before he had appointed his younger son, Alexander, already recognized as Crown Prince in place of his elder brother George, as Regent; and since George had acquitted himself well in the Balkan wars his partisans were excited and angered. It looked as if the history of resurrected Serbia was to end in the same moment as it began.

Such was the authority of Russia that some Serbs were incredulous.

Nicholas Pashitch, the Prime Minister, did not believe that Austria's out-cry was serious, and was half-way to Athens on a visit to Venezelos when he had to be recalled to Belgrade, to deal with Count Berchtold's famous ultimatum. This had been framed in defiance of the report of a high official of the Austrian Foreign Office who had been sent to Sarajevo to investigate the crime and had come to the conclusion that it was "out of the question" to suppose a connexion between the Serbian Government and the assassins. The ultimatum made eleven demands. The Serbian Government was required:

(1) To admit a policy of incitement to the crime, and publish a con-fession of this and a promise of future good conduct which should be dictated from Vienna, and both published in the offi-cial journal at Belgrade and read to the Serbian Army by King Peter.

(2) To suppress all publications inciting to hatred of Austria-Hungary and directed against her territorial integrity.

(3) To dissolve the Society of National Defence (a perfectly re-spectable society which had no connexion whatsoever with the crimes), and to suppress all other societies engaged in propa-ganda against Austria-Hungary.

(4) To eliminate from the Serbian educational system anything which might foment such propaganda.

(5) To dismiss all officers and officials guilty of such propaganda, whose names might be communicated, then or later, by Vienna.

(6) To accept "the collaboration in Serbia" of Austro-Hungarian officials in suppressing this propaganda.

(7) To open a judicial inquiry concerning those implicated in the crime, and to allow Austro-Hungarian delegates to take part.

(8) To arrest without delay Major Tankositch and Milan Tsigano-vitch, the Serbians who had supplied the Sarajevo assassins with arms.

(9) To supervise the Serbian frontier so that no arms and explo-sives might pass, and to dismiss the customs officials who had helped the assassins.

(10) To give explanations regarding the "unjustifiable" language used by high Serbian officials after the crime.

(11) To notify Vienna without delay of the execution of all the above measures.

Serbia was given only forty-eight hours to accept or reject this ulti-matum.

It was not easy to accept. The fifth and sixth demands meant that Ser-bia must become a spiritual vassal of the Austrian Empire, in conditions that were bound before long to produce provocative incidents, with a sequel of bloodshed and annexation. Yet the Serbian Government accepted that ultimatum, with only three reservations. It pointed out that the constitution of the country made it impossible to comply with certain of the Austrian demands, such as interference with the freedom of the press, without legislative changes impossible to enact during the time-limit; but it was willing to submit these points to the arbitration of The Hague Tribunal. Pashitch took the humiliating document of his country's submission to the Austrian Legation a few moments before six o'clock on the evening of July the twenty-sixth; though the Legation was a quarter of an hour from the station the Austrian Minister and his staff were in the train on their way to the frontier by half-past six, a sign that the acceptance had been rejected. The three reservations were better than he had hoped; though it would not have mattered if there had been none at all, for the legal adviser of the Austrian Foreign Office had already handed in a memorandum as to how war could be declared on Serbia no matter what her reply to the ultimatum. "If Serbia announces her acceptance of our demands *en gros*, without any protest, we can still object that she did not within a prescribed time provide proofs that she carried out those provisions which had to be executed 'at once' or with all speed, and whose execution she had to notify to us 'without delay.'"

By such means Serbia was trapped, and the whole of Europe doomed. Count Berchtold and his friend Conrad von Hötzendorf, who were resolved upon hostilities, persuaded the Hungarian Minister, Count Tisza, to withdraw his opposition, and gained the consent of the old Emperor Franz Josef by a totally false statement that Serbian troops had fired on the Austrian garrison of a Danubian port; and the final declaration of war was dispatched on July twenty-eighth. The consequences were clearly foreseen by all these plotters against peace. If Austria attacked Serbia and stretched out its hand to the Black Sea, Russia was bound to intervene; for Russia did not want, for reasons that may seem far from frivolous in view of what has already been written in this volume, to have the Austrian Empire as a neighbour on another front, and it could not like to see Slavs subject to Teutons. Germany must join in on the pretext of aiding Austria, because it had its own appetite for Russian territory, having long hankered after the Baltic, and because it could now find a pretext for attacking France, who was Russia's ally and was showing dangerous signs of having recovered its strength after the defeat of 1870. Immediately millions of people were delivered over to the powers of darkness, and nowhere were those powers more cruel than in Serbia.

Belgrade was at once bombarded. An army of three hundred and fifty thousand men fought a rearguard action, without big guns to answer their enemy's artillery, with so few arms that some regiments had but one rifle to two men. They gave up Belgrade, their only town, their earnest that they were Byzantium reborn materially as well as spiritually, and pressed back, bitter and amazed. But Belgrade did not fall. It was left to be defended by a single division commanded by a colonel, who blew up the iron bridge across the Danube so that it blocked the river against Austrian traffic, and dressed the customs officials and such towns-folk as remained in extemporized uniforms so that Austrian spies reported a large garrison; and by a miracle it remained intact when the Serbian Army turned on its tracks, and, to the world's amazement, sprang at the Austrians' throats and drove them out of the country in less than a month. They even invaded Austrian territory and set foot in Bosnia and Herzegovina and the Serb parts of Hungary, and the Frushka Gora itself.

But the Austrian Empire had numbers. It had at this moment little else; it had so little virtue or wisdom or even common sense that again and again the student must marvel that this was the same state as eighteenth-century Austria. But what it had it used, and it sent back its armies in September. This time they enjoyed a certain disgraceful advantage. During the first invasion they had laid waste the country, pillaging the crops, burning the houses, murdering the civil population: over three hundred and six women are known to have been executed, as well as many people over eighty and children under five. So the Serbian Army had this time to retreat over a devastated countryside which could give it no food and offered it much discouragement, not diminished by the floods of civilian refugees, some Serbian, some from the Slav parts of the Austro-Hungarian Empire, all hungry and footsore and with tales to tell of the enemy's malign brutality. There might have been panic had it not been for the spirit of the Karageorgevitches and the higher command. King Peter hobbled up to some troops that were wavering under artillery fire to which their army had no answer, and said to them, after the manner of a Homeric general, "Heroes, you have taken two oaths: one to me, your king, and one to your country. From the first I release you, from the second no man can release you. But if you decide to return to your homes, and if we should be victorious, you shall not be made to suffer."

They did not go. To lead them General Mishitch, the grave and reluctant regicide whom King Peter had refused to dismiss, now appointed fourteen hundred young students as non-commissioned officers. Of these boys, who before the war had been studying at Belgrade, Vienna, Prague, Berlin, and Paris, one hundred and forty survived the war. Arms came suddenly to this army, sent from England. These men who were so spent that they no longer lived by their experience but by what is known to our common human stock, these boys who had no experience at all and therefore were also thrown back on that same primitive knowledge, alike they forgot the usual prudent opinion that dying is disagreeable, and valued death and life and honour as if they were heroes who had died a thousand years before or gods who were under no necessity to die. They flung themselves again on the Austrians. By the end of December they had retaken Belgrade. They took down the Hungarian flag that had floated above the palace and laid it on the steps of the Cathedral when King Peter went with his generals to the mass of thanksgiving for victory. They had to thank the Lord for a real suspension of natural law; for when the Austrians had withdrawn over the frontiers there remained behind rather more Austrian prisoners of war than there were Serbian soldiers.

It is not known what King Peter thought of the future. In his old age he had become more of a Serb, and the Genevan mark was not so strong as it had been. He was now wholly a warrior king, a Nemanya reborn. But it is said that the Crown Prince Alexander, the pale and pedantic graduate of St. Petersburg Military Academy, knew that the victory was no more than a breathing-space, and that there must follow another assault, which would mean defeat. This certainly must have become a growing horror when it was manifest that the country had received a wound deeper than any that could be inflicted by military action. Some of the Austrian troops had come from parts of Galicia where typhus was endemic, and they had brought the germs with them. Where food was scarce, water was polluted, and vast districts were littered with dead men and animals far beyond the power of scavenging, the fever spread. The hospital system, particularly in the recovered Turkish provinces, was utterly unable to cope with this inundation of disease, and indeed it killed a third of all Serbian doctors. There came out several foreign sanitary units, of which Dr. Elsie Inglis's Scottish Women's Hospital left an imperishably glorious name. Alexander, himself sickening of an internal malady, spent his days travelling up and down the country organizing a medical service.

In the summer of 1915 Austria approached Serbia with proposals for a separate peace. The Skupshtina rejected them one blazing day, at Nish, and expressed its resolution to continue the war till all Slavs were liberated from the Austrian yoke. This meant that Peter and Alexander and Pashitch had come to believe that the life of their nation was not worth preserving unless the tyrannical power that had threatened them throughout their entire existence were disarmed and disintegrated. They thought it better for the nation to go down into death for a time on the chance they might live again, if France and England and Russia destroyed the might of the Central powers.

In the heat and dust they waited. About them refugees wandered over a famined land; the soldiers who waited by their guns were worn out by three years of fighting in medieval conditions of sanitation and commissariat; and on the near frontiers massed enemies which their Allies, the British and the French, would not allow them to disperse. Incredible as it may seem, though Great Britain and France were fighting Germany, they still accepted the legend that Bulgaria was the most civilized and powerful of the Balkan states, though the only evidence ever adduced for such an estimate was that it is the most Germanized among them; and the Allies formed the curious notion that it would be the easiest thing in the world to persuade the Bulgarians to fight against the Germans in defence of the Serbians, who had beaten and humiliated them only two years before. They therefore forbade the Serbians to attack the Bulgarian armies which were massing on the border, and which could have been easily defeated, and when Serbia asked for a quarter of a million men to repel the impending invasion, they made the astonishing reply that they were arranging for the Bulgarians to supply these troops. This they attempted to do by offering Bulgaria territories which Roumania, Greece, and Serbia had acquired in the Balkan wars. This naturally turned Roumania and Greece against the Allies, and filled the hearts of the Serbians with perplexity and bitterness.

In September the invasion began. By October the Serbian Army, which now numbered a quarter of a million men, was faced with three hundred thousand Austro-German troops, under the great strategist Mackensen, and as many Bulgarians. It was now necessary for the country to die. The soldiers retreated slowly, fighting a rearguard action, leaving the civil population, that is to say their parents, wives, and children, in the night of an oppression that they knew to be frightful. Monks came out of the monasteries and followed the soldiers, carrying on bullock-carts, and on their shoulders where the roads were too bad, the coffined bodies of the medieval Serbian kings, the sacred Nemanyas, which must not be defiled. So was carried King Peter, whose rheumatic limbs were wholly paralysed by the cold of autumn; and so too, before the retreat was long on its way, was Prince Alexander. The internal pain that had vexed him all year grew so fierce that he could no longer ride his horse. Doctors took him into a cottage and he was operated on for appendicitis. Then he was packed in bandages wound close as a shroud, and put on a stretcher and carried in the procession of the troops. It is like some fantastic detail in a Byzantine fresco, improbable, nearly impossible, yet a valid symbol of a truth, that a country which was about to die should bear with it on its journey to death, its kings, living and dead, all prostrate, immobile.

The retreating army made its last stand on the field of Kossovo, where a short time before, in a different dream of the Creator, it had known victory: where the Tsar Lazarevitch had proved that defeat can last five hundred years. Above them circled enemy aeroplanes, evil's newest instrument. After a last rearguard action to shake off the Bulgarians, they turned to the wall of Montenegrin and Albanian mountains that rises between Kossovo and the Adriatic. Rather than face that icy path into exile, many of the soldiers and the civilian refugees turned and fled back towards Serbia and were butchered by the Moslem Albanians, who had been the favoured subjects of the Turks and bitterly resented the Serbian conquests in the Balkan wars. The rest of the Army obeyed the order that they must take this desperate step in the hope that some might survive and be reorganized on the Adriatic shore with the help of the British and French. When they came to the foot of the mountains the weeping gunners destroyed their guns with hand grenades and burning petrol. The motor-drivers drove their cars and lorries up to a corner where the road became a horse-trail on the edge of the precipice, jumped out, and sent them spinning into space. Then all set out on foot to cross the five-thousand-foot peaks that lay between them and the sea. Some took other routes, but on any of the roads their fate was the same. They trudged in mud and snow over the mountain passes, the December wind piercing their ragged uniforms. Many fell dead, some died of hunger. They were passing through one of the poorest parts of Europe, and the inhabitants had little to sell them, and in any case were instructed to withhold what they had by the King of Montenegro, who, though he was Serbia's ally and King Peter's father-in-law, had come to a treacherous understanding with Austria. The Serbians ate the raw flesh of the animals which fell dead by the track, they ate their boots. Some died of dysentery. Some were shot by Albanian snipers. Of the quarter of a mil-

lion Serbian soldiers, one hundred thousand met such deaths. Of thirty-
six thousand boys nearing military age who had joined the retreat to
escape the Austrians, over twenty thousand perished on this road. Of fifty
thousand Austrian and German prisoners, who had had to follow the
Serbians because their own military authorities had refused to exchange
them, the greater part never came down from the mountains.

When the survivors reached the coast they found that the Allies again
had failed them. The port they arrived at was blocked with shipping
sunk by Austrian submarines and it was impossible either to bring them
food or to ship them away. They had to trudge southwards, still hungry.
Too much of the responsibility for their safety rested on the Italians,
who had already signed the Treaty of London, and knew that if the
Serbian nation should by a miracle reconstitute itself it would certainly
dispute the allocations of Slav territory made by that imbecile document. At last the French and the British settled that the Serbians should
be sent to the Greek island of Corfu, since Greece was under obligations
to the Allies which not even their diplomacy could wholly annul. Still
hungry, they were put on boats to be taken out to the transports. It
happened, that when the first boatloads pushed off, not many hours had
passed since a food ship had been torpedoed in the channel outside the
harbour, and loaves of bread were still floating on the waves. Many of
the Serbians had never seen deeper water than a fordable stream, and
these jumped out of the boats to wade towards the bread, and sank immediately. Others, who knew the northern rivers or the lakes of Ochrid
or Presba, tried to hold back those who wanted to jump, and there
were struggles which overturned some of the boats. Thus many were
drowned.

On Corfu the Serbian Army fell down and slept. Some never awoke.
For quite a long time there was still not enough food, and there was a
shortage of fuel. Every night for weeks boats put out to sea weighed
down with those who had been too famished and diseased to recover.
The others stirred as soon as the spring warmed them, stretched, and
looked up into the sunshine, and were again golden and young and victorious, golden and ancient and crafty, as they had been in the Balkan
wars. Alexander, restored to health, travelled to Paris, Rome, and London, and urged on the Allies the value of an expeditionary force that
would use Salonika as a base and would strike up at the forces the Central powers were maintaining in Serbia. He carried his case, and his troops
were drilled, equipped again, inspired again. In summer they embarked
for Salonika. A year after they had been driven out of Serbia they were

back on Serbian soil, fighting the Bulgars. In November 1916 they put forth their strength and took Kaymakchalan, the Butter-churn, the mountain that dominates the southern plains of Macedonia and the road to the north, and had been thought impregnable. In effect the Near Eastern campaign was over. But the war was not sufficiently mature in its other theatres to make it safe to harvest the victory, so the Serbian Army sat in Macedonia and waited. In the summer of 1917 the Serbian Government and a committee of South Slavs issued a manifesto proclaiming a "Kingdom of Serbs, Croats, and Slovenes, a democratic and Parliamentary monarchy under the Karageorgevitch dynasty, giving equality of treatment to the three religions, Orthodox, Catholic, and Mussulman, and in the use of the Latin and Cyrillic alphabets." They announced, in fact, that the Austro-Hungarian Empire was destroyed and that out of its ruins they were making a kingdom of the South Slavs, such as had inherited the glory of Byzantium eight hundred years before. The poem was now written. In the autumn of 1918 the Serbian armies, as the spearhead of the Allied forces, drove into the enemy forces and scattered the Bulgars back to Bulgaria, the Austrians and Germans back to a land which was no land, which had lost all institutions, even all its characteristics, save that discontent which springs of conceiving poems too formless and violent ever to be written. The more poetic nation was in Belgrade thirteen days before the Armistice.

Belgrade VIII

WHAT sequel to this story would not be an anticlimax? There are heights which the corporate life has never surpassed and which it attains only at rare intervals. It is not so with the personal life, for the mind, in its infinite creativeness, can always transcend any external event. To King Peter, it may be, the war was only prelude to a greater experience. He had taken no part in the campaign of 1918, since by that time he could only hobble. He went to Greece, and did not leave it even when victory was achieved. The state entry into Belgrade took place without him. He lingered where he was till late in 1919, and then went north, but no further than Arandzhlovats, the simple and even shabby spa near the Karageorgevitches' old home at Topola. One day, without warning, he returned to Belgrade, which did not recognize him, for while he was in Greece he had grown a long white beard like a priest's. The Prince Regent and his people welcomed him, and begged him to take up residence in the palace, but that he would not do, for he said it would be wrong, since he was no longer King. It is proof of the strangeness of the Karageorgevitches, and their ambivalent attitude to their own royalty, that Alexander also would not move into the palace, though it was new and comfortable. He made his home in a simple one-storied house in the main street of the town, which he furnished hardly more comfortably than if it had been his staff headquarters in time of war.

Peter went to live in a villa overlooking Topchider, the park where Prince Michael of Serbia was murdered and little Alexander Obrenovitch learned to swim, and he became more and more of a recluse. He was not indifferent to his people; he cut off his beard because they complained that it disguised their beloved King from them. But all his forces were devoted to a relationship which it is hard to imagine. The Karageorgevitches were not now a united family. Alexander was busy forging the new state of Yugoslavia into a reality, and was working all day and half the night. Peter's brother, Arsenius, was not without the strain of frivolity that had made his cousins, Alexis and Bozhidar, such well-known boulevardiers, and he had returned to Paris, where he was to prove that there are many paths to a serene old age. The son of Arsenius and Aurora Demidoff, Prince Paul, was virtually secretary to the Prince Regent, and worked as hard as his chief. A cloud had fallen between

588

Peter's only daughter, Yelena, and her relatives. She, having married the
Grand Duke Constantine, had been caught up in the Russian Revolution.
Her husband had been killed and she had been put in prison, from which
she was released only through the intervention of a Serbian officer who
had joined the Bolsheviks. On her return to Belgrade it began to be whispered that the Karageorgevitches were greatly angered by some circumstance connected with her flight from Russia. Either they thought,
the story ran, that she had accepted her freedom on dishonourable terms
or that she had not honourably observed those terms. These were probably fantasies spun by outsiders to explain a quarrel that for insiders had
some more prosaic significance. But the fact remains that the Grand
Duchess soon left Yugoslavia for ever and settled in Switzerland. There
were none others in the family except Peter's elder son, George.

Peter had dispossessed George of his birthright and given his crown
to his younger brother; and daily George's mind was growing wilder
and more restless. It might have been judged dangerous that the father
and son should live together in the quiet villa at Topchider. But they
were very happy. Peter treated his son with a gentle devotion which
guided him away from tragedy. The old King was no longer what
Geneva and France had made him, he had lost the Western sense that a
man's life ought to describe a comprehensible pattern. He was not appalled when George laughed or wept louder than was reasonable, or sent
a bullet without cause out into the night. If his handsome son's spirit was
wandering where it could not be followed, it might be that he too was
seeking wisdom. They lived together in perfect love, and when the old
man lost his wits and fell mortally ill in the summer of 1921, George upheld him with his patient kindness. At the time of the death the Prince
Regent was in Paris, and the news threw him into a state of collapse so
complete that his doctor forbade him to travel back to Belgrade for the
funeral. So George was his father's chief mourner, and performed his
duties with great dignity. Thereafter he was seen no more among ordinary men. Enemies of Alexander say that this was due to fraternal hate,
but that is not the opinion of foreigners who came in accidental contact
with the elder brother.

Alexander was not permitted by his duties to cultivate the personal
life. He must struggle with the external world, so anticlimax was his lot;
and he resented it, for he was perhaps the last ruler in the world to be
inspired by a Homeric conception of life. The day should always be at
the dawn, all men should be heroes, the sword should decide rightly. He
found himself, on the contrary, smothered with small mean difficulties.

These were the harder to bear because he had foreseen them and would have avoided them if it had not been for the blindness of others. He was unable to proceed with the real business of state-making because, do what he would, he could not secure unity among the Croats and Slovenes and Serbs; but he himself had never wished to include the Croats and Slovenes in his kingdom. He had hoped, at the beginning of the war, not for a Yugoslavia, not for a union of all South Slavs, but for a Greater Serbia that should add to the kingdom of Serbia all the Austro-Hungarian territories in which the majority of the inhabitants were Serbs, that is Slavs who were members of the Orthodox Church. The school of thought to which he belonged rightly considered the difference between the Roman Catholic and the Orthodox Churches so great that it transcended racial or linguistic unity.

It cannot be doubted that this Greater Serbia would have been a far more convenient entity than Yugoslavia, but it could exist only on two conditions: it must be supported on the east by the Russian Empire, and divided on the west from German-speaking countries by Catholic Slav states. In 1917, however, the Tsardom fell in ruins, and of all the Slav subjects of the Austrian Empire the Czechs alone were sufficiently highly organized to convince the peacemakers that they could be entrusted with the governance of an independent state. So Serbia had need of the Catholic Slavs and they had need of her; and the Kingdom of the Serbs, Croats, and Slovenes, as Yugoslavia was then called, became inevitable. But that did not annul the temperamental incompatibilities of the Serbs and the Croats, which faced the King with a sea of troubles.

It is likely that Alexander was the less able to bear these dissensions with equanimity because of the personal tragedy that had befallen him during the war. We now know that while he was a student at the Military Academy in St. Petersburg he had fallen in love with one of the Tsar's daughters, though she was still a schoolgirl. He had mentioned it to his father, who had asked the Tsar if Alexander would be allowed to present himself as a suitor when the girl was of a proper age, and had received an encouraging answer. In January 1914 Mr. Pashitch, the Serbian Prime Minister, visited Russia to inquire whether, now that the Balkan wars were over, Alexander might begin his courtship, and the permission was given. It is probable that Alexander would have gone on this errand shortly after he had been declared Regent, had not the war broken out.

We cannot be certain that this courtship would have been successful, for we know that the Tsar's daughters were allowed to choose for themselves in such matters, and that the Tsarina wished none of them to marry outside Russia. But it is beyond doubt that this was for Alexander a real affair of the heart. He did not merely want to be the husband of one of the Tsar's daughters. He wanted to have this particular daughter as his wife. In March 1917 the news came that the Tsar had abdicated and that he and his family were in the hands of the revolutionaries. Some time in July 1918, while Alexander was in the sweltering heat of the Macedonian plains, all of them were put to death at Ekaterinburg. It seems reasonable to ascribe Alexander's hatred of Bolshevism at least as much to this event as to temperamental bias or political prejudices.

For a very long time no other woman seems to have convinced him that she existed. After his father's death he looked about for a wife, but plainly only for dynastic reasons; and though the Princess Marie of Roumania was very beautiful, he probably chose her rather for her English connexions and her Romanoff blood. But he became devoted to her, and derived very great happiness from his life with her and their three sons. She was indeed an excellent wife for him, as she had inherited from her mother, the famous Queen Marie, a great deal of the fluency and brilliance that he lacked. She liked driving a high-powered automobile over mountains down to the Adriatic, she was fond of flying. She had also an instinct for comfort which was welcome in the Balkans. Between the Karageorgevitches' barbarous and glorious old home at Topola and the tremendous Byzantine assertion of majesty and death at Oplenats there lies, set among orchards and vineyards, a cottage planned by the Queen, where she and Alexander and the children lived the kind of home life, uncultured but civilized and amiable, that Queen Victoria made common form for European royalty. It is as if the Karageorgevitches, usually immersed in the tide of their terrible and splendid experience, had for a moment come to the surface to breathe.

The King had his marriage to console him, and, perhaps, his ambition. For he was still ambitious. He had come a very long way in his thirty-odd years. He had spent his childhood as the son of a pretender almost comic in his destitution, in a poky flat in Geneva, as a youth he had been lifted to a step of the Romanoff throne, and as a young man he had overthrown an imperial dominance that had pressed on his people for five hundred years, and before he was yet a ripe man had driven back another empire, the most formidable of Continental powers, and thereby reincarnated the glory of the Emperor Stephen Dushan. It is said that he meant to travel still further. He would never consent to be crowned. Though he was so resolute that the Karageorgevitch stock should be grafted on the Nemanya dynasty, no fresh door was ever opened for him in the crimson wall of Zhitcha Cathedral and walled up when he left it an anointed king, according to ancient custom. There is reason to suspect that he was postponing the ceremony till he might be crowned not king but emperor, and that of an empire greater than Stephen Dushan ever knew.

Alexander took a great interest in the internal condition of Russia, and he was convinced that the Bolshevik regime would not last more than twenty or thirty years. During this time he hoped to make a Balkan Federation, a real union of South Slavs, which might go in and rescue the North Slavs when Bolshevism had collapsed. Then he would be crowned in Zhitcha as King of Serbia and Emperor of all the Russias.

This dream was not as insane as it sounds to Western readers. The South Slav loves the Russian, White or Red, but he does not think him as efficient as himself, and the task of overthrowing Bolshevism would not seem to him any greater than his conquest of the Turk. Nor was it purely aggressive. The King believed, and was right in his belief, that the Slavs needed to protect themselves against Italy, Hungary, and the German-speaking peoples; and the firmer they were in unity the better. But whatever his plans and their justification, they involved Herculean labours. His heart, however, approved of Herculean labours; what afflicted him beyond bearing was the business which fell to him in the meantime, of settling the small differences of small men.

The primary disease of Yugoslavia was the same that was wasting every European country which had taken part in the war: a shortage of young and middle-aged men. Three-fifths of Serbia's man-power had been lost, and nine-tenths of the university students who had been made non-commissioned officers. The Croats had suffered terribly fighting for the Austrian Empire. It was, as it always is in war, the flowers that had fallen. There were no young and able leaders coming up, the pre-war politicians were worn out with age and responsibility, second-rate adventurers were taking advantage of the dearth of better men to obtain office for the sake of profit, and the distracted rank and file wrangled over these unsatisfactory leaders. The King suffered at all times from the professional soldier's inability to distinguish between an argument and a mutiny; but now he had some real excuse for finding the political controversies of his subjects disquieting.

There was another element in the situation which was common to all combatant countries at this time; the old liberalism was faced with problems for which it had no solution. Although the King had been tempted

in his youth into a flirtation with his brother's Prætorian Guard type of Fascism, he had been educated as an old-fashioned liberal and probably would have remained one had circumstances allowed it. But they did not. It is extremely difficult to maintain the freedom of the press, when that is used by different parties to advocate the assassination of each other's leaders. It is extremely difficult not to throw people into prison without trial if disorder is so great that the law courts dare not convict the most guilty disturbers of the peace. And the King could not discuss his difficulties with his liberal subjects, because he was incapable of understanding intellectuals.

Artists he might have understood better. He had grown up in contemplation of a historic poem, and was passionately fond of music, and his cousin and closest friend, Prince Paul, was a lover of great painting. But with intellectuals he had nothing in common. He could not—and perhaps this was because he was something of an artist—understand why they could not suppress their faculty of criticism in order to follow a common purpose. Underneath the great mountain of Durmitor in Montenegro there lies a dark and glassy lake, mirroring many snow peaks, which are doubly pure in their reflection, with the purity of their own snow, with the purity of its black crystal waters. By this lake the King once camped for thirteen days. To one of the secretaries who brought state papers to his tent he said, his prim voice trembling, "If those intellectuals in Belgrade could come here and look at this lake as I have done they would not . . . they would not . . ." This is an idiotic remark from the point of view of those intellectuals who were defending the rights of man, who were protesting against innocent people being thrown into prison and the suppression of free speech. But it is not an idiotic remark from the point of view of a man who had realized the vision of the Frushka Gora.

The King was further handicapped by his inability, which was greater than one would have expected in a man of his age, to understand anything at all about the post-war left wing. He thought it sheer wickedness that many of his subjects should sympathize with Bolshevik Russia and that some should join the Communist Party. He asked why the very people who were most shocked if he used force against the Croats, no matter how mildly, should accept the Red massacres without a murmur, and he put the question without the capacity to listen to the answer, for he was thinking of a murdered girl. When he was told that this attitude was part of a revolt against poverty, he replied that there was no need for such a revolt, since people in his kingdom were much better off than they used to be, and if the country were allowed to settle down there was every hope that this might continue. In this he was perfectly accurate, yet quite irrelevant. A man who is hungry is suffering from an absolute discomfort, and cannot be comforted by the statement, or even believe it, that he was often hungrier when he was a boy, and that his father had been hungrier still.

Nor could the King understand why the intellectuals kept on talking about peace. In Belgrade there was once held an exhibition of German pictures which had been selected by a Serbian official in the Yugoslav Legation at Berlin. When the King visited it he made a conscientious inspection of the pictures, and then sent for this official. Instead of congratulating him he coldly censured him for including certain canvases by Käthe Kollwitz which were designed to expose the horrors of warfare. This and other manifestations of his distaste for pacifism were regarded by the left wing as proof of the bloodthirstiness of the man, but in that they were wholly mistaken. Few generals in modern history have experienced the horrors of warfare as fully as he had, and his was not the temperament which intoxicates itself with action. But he believed that it might be necessary again for Yugoslavia to fight for its life, and he therefore saw the discouragement of the fighting spirit as a step towards national suicide. He entirely forgot that it is the proper function of the intellectual to hold up certain moral values before the eyes of the people, even if it is not possible to realize them in action at the moment. But it must be conceded that his situation made that forgetfulness inevitable.

The King was, of course, entirely right in his assumption that Yugoslavia might have to fight for her life. Recent years, by bringing so many ill-favoured personalities to the fore, have made Mussolini seem by contrast genial and almost inoffensive, but we must not forget that he owes that character entirely to contrast. A face which might seem reassuringly normal in a criminal lunatic asylum might repel and terrify in a railway carriage. The part that Mussolini played in Yugoslavian affairs as soon as he had acceded to power was purely evil. He screamed insults at them for their possession of Dalmatia and constantly provoked riots and disorder; but that was the most innocent side of his relations with the country. There were two main centres of disaffection in Yugoslavia, Croatia and Macedonia, and in these Mussolini attempted to establish himself as a murderous enemy of civil peace. In Croatia he found it at first difficult to get a footing, for the rebels were for the most part men of high principle who had their wits about them and knew what happens when the lamb asks the fox for aid against the wolf. But the Macedonians were at

THE MITHRAIC ALTAR AT YAITSE DURING ITS EXCAVATION

MONASTERY IN THE FRUSHKA GORA

once more criminal and more innocent. Their case was pitiful, for it was the result of ancient virtues running to waste in an altered world. The Macedonians, a magnificent people, had prepared the way for the Balkan wars by a perpetual revolt, sometimes open, sometimes covert, against the Turk. This was organized by the Internal Macedonian Revolutionary Organization—known as I.M.R.O.—which was formed in 1893 by Bulgarian Macedonians, bloodthirsty men who were nevertheless great heroes and pitiable victims.

When the Turks were driven out as a result of the Balkan wars Macedonia was divided between Greece, Serbia, and Bulgaria; and Bulgaria greatly resented the terms of the division. Some Bulgars wanted a purely Bulgarian Macedonia; others wanted an independent Macedonia, a dream state which was to be entirely free, though it would have had to be financed and to a large extent repopulated from abroad; others again wanted a federated state, similar to a Swiss canton. All these parties consisted of those who had been revolutionaries all their born days and who could no more have taken to a conforming way of life than an elderly seamstress could become a ballet dancer. They were also subjected to great provocation by the harshness of the Yugoslavs in forcing the many Bulgarian inhabitants of their newly acquired territory to speak Serbian and alter their names to Serbian forms, and the incompetence of many of the Yugoslav officials, which was, indeed, no greater than that which had been shown by the Turks or would have been shown by the Bulgarians, but was none the less (and very naturally) resented. They therefore reconstituted I.M.R.O. as an anti-Yugoslav organization.

In no time they formed a guerrilla army which had its headquarters near the frontier and repeatedly crossed it on raids into Yugoslav Macedonia, burning and looting and killing just as in the old Turkish days. Of the damage done there can be no accurate estimate, for the peasantry was too terrorized to report its losses to the officials; but it is said that over a thousand violent deaths are known to have occurred between the years 1924 and 1934. This reign of horror might have gone unchronicled, for the government of neither Yugoslavia nor Bulgaria wished to publish the shameful inability to keep order, had it not been that passengers on the Athens Express gazed astonished, since they knew that Europe was theoretically at peace, on the unbroken line of barbed wire entanglements, block-houses, redoubts, and searchlight posts which followed the Yugoslav-Bulgarian frontier. Every bridge and tunnel and station was guarded by soldiers in full battle kit; and even so the passenger on the Athens Express sometimes ceased abruptly to gaze and wonder, for

I.M.R.O. liked to get bombs aboard the international trains, since explosions were reported in newspapers all over the world, and gave their cause publicity. But if the passenger was spared to continue his thoughts he might well have asked himself how I.M.R.O. could afford to maintain the standing army whose assaults made necessary this vigilant and elaborate defence, for the Macedonian peasantry was notoriously among the poorest in Europe.

There was, indeed, more reason for this question than even the prodigious view from the carriage window. I.M.R.O. published newspapers and pamphlets in Bulgaria and abroad. It maintained propaganda offices in all the Western capitals. It specialized in curious slow-motion assassinations that cost a great deal of money; a member would be sent to a distant place to murder an enemy of the cause and would be ordered not to do it at once, but to live beside him for some months before striking the blow. It also ran an expensive and efficient machine in Sofia which for many years dominated Bulgarian politics; indeed, I.M.R.O. became the Fascist Party of Bulgaria, murdering Stambulisky, the great leader of the Peasant Party, and routing the Communist Party, though that numbered a fourth of the electorate. In this last feat they were aided by the indecisiveness of the General Secretary of the Bulgarian Communist Party, one Dimitrov, later to be famous for his not at all indecisive part in the Reichstag trial. But that and all their other feats cost money. Some of this was given gladly by Macedonian supporters. Some of it was filched from Macedonians, whether supporters or not, by an efficient system of illegal taxation. The tax-collector who, whether he was a believer in a Bulgarian Macedonia or not, had kin in the country whose safety he valued produced two tax demands, one to be paid to the Bulgarian Government, and the other, amounting to ten per cent of the first, to be paid through him to I.M.R.O. But for a great part its funds were provided by Italy.

If Alexander sometimes acted brutally towards the insurgents he saw conspiring with foreign powers against the safety of his people, and towards the intellectuals who showed themselves so blind to the implications of these conspiracies, he cannot be altogether blamed. The situation was too confusing. It cannot have clarified it that no hostile act against a malcontent ever cost the King so dearly as the act of reconciliation he made with his arch-enemy, which seemed for long a great political triumph and was certainly his greatest moral triumph. This was the root of all the troubles that darkened the last six years of his life. From the first the leader of the Croat Peasant Party, Stephen Raditch, had been a thorn in the King's side. Not even Gandhi had a more magnetic effect on his followers, and though he guided them in all sorts of different directions he could claim consistency, for he never took them down a road that did not lead away from Serbia. Before the war he had been anti-Hungarian but fiercely pro-Austrian, with a deep veneration for the Habsburgs, and he had advocated the creation of a triune kingdom comprising Austria, Hungary, and a Greater Croatia which should include a conquered Serbia. After the war he preached an independent Croatia in the form of a republic where no taxes would be collected from peasants, prevented the Croat deputies from going to Belgrade and taking their seats in the Skupshtina, and attacked the Government in terms that, not at all inexplicably, led every now and then to his imprisonment.

In 1923 this situation should have been materially changed. He went to London and Mr. Wickham Steed, the former editor of *The Times*, one of the few Englishmen who understood Balkan conditions, urged him to give up his republicanism, and work to shear the Yugoslavian constitution of certain undemocratic features and convert it into a constitutional monarchy on the English pattern. Raditch afterwards said he was convinced. But he omitted to mention this change of heart when he returned to Yugoslavia, and he was imprisoned and his party was declared illegal, largely because he had come back by way of Russia. This punitive action of the King and his Government was unwise and ill-tempered, but was not as silly as it seems. Raditch's own account was that he had called on Lenin to advise him to abandon Bolshevism and set up a peasant republic. It seems certain that he was moved to this trip partly by his love of travel, which was inordinate. But detached observers among the Bolsheviks believed he came to Moscow in order to blackmail Belgrade with the fear of social revolution, and it appears that while there he joined the Peasant International. Once he found himself in prison, however, he sent for his nephew and dictated to him a confession of his belief in the monarchy and the constitution.

Immediately the King was told of this declaration he appointed Raditch Minister of Education and gave ministerial posts to three leading members of his illegal party. It is proof of the strange political nature of the Croats that, though this was the first indication Raditch's followers had received that he had completely changed his programme, they do not seem to have been disconcerted for more than a short time. Raditch went straight from prison to the King's palace, and there the two enemies sat down, talked for hours, and fell into an instant friendship. This was unbroken for five years. The royal household became very fond of him, and he constantly came to the palace simply as a familiar. He was a fine linguist, and the Queen liked speaking English with him. As his sight was failing she used to take his plate at meal-times and cut up his food for him. The King learned to like him better than he had liked any politician since the war.

In 1928 there fell the catastrophe. The country was in a disturbed state, and complained of many troubles. Some of these were inevitable: it had been necessary to unify the currencies of the country into a single unit, and a certain amount of inflation had followed. Some of these might easily have been avoided: the political parties were perpetually disintegrating into smaller and smaller factions, and this made it almost impossible for any government to maintain itself in power over any period sufficient for effective action. In ten years twenty-one political parties came forward to save Yugoslavia, and there were twenty-five changes of government. Raditch was still a Minister. It must be confessed that he had brought nothing new into political life, and that he had done little to distinguish himself from the Serbian Ministers he had for so long attacked. At this point, though he was theoretically left, he suddenly demanded a military dictatorship. "Our national army," he told the King, "which is our national shrine in its finest form, can perhaps alone provide a generally recognized leader, strong enough to drive away corruption unmercifully, as well as lawlessness, to destroy partisanship in administration, and to overcome the political terrorism which is turning our entire country into a huge penitentiary." This infuriated alike the political parasites and the sincere democrats of Yugoslavia, and to justify himself he carried on a campaign against corruption, defining the abuses which he thought made a dictatorship imperative, and named their perpetrators.

The baser newspapers called for his blood, desiring quite literally that someone should shed it. But it must be admitted that he himself conducted this campaign with less than perfect wisdom. He was violently provocative in a situation where the most pressing need was calm; and his violence was unrestrained. He was capable of standing up in Parliament and calling his fellow-Ministers swine. It was also unfortunate that the Germanic bias he derived from Austria made him speak contemptuously of all races outside the sphere of German influence. With difficulty, and only under the influence of the King and Queen, he had learned to accept the Serbians, but the remoter peoples of wilder Yugoslavia were hardly better than Negroes seen through the eyes of

Southerners. He used the term "Tsintsar" as an insult, as if it meant a kind of human mongrel, although the Tsintsari are a race of shepherds who have gone respectably about their business on the Macedonian uplands since the days of Byzantium. He was completely insensible to the poetry of the Yugoslavian idea, to the charity that inspired it in spite of its blunders and brutalities. It meant nothing to him, and to most Croats, that people had been rescued from the power of Islam and were restored to Christian civilization in the shelter of this state.

June is not a favourable month in Serbian history. On the twentieth of June 1928 a Montenegrin deputy named Punisha Rachitch, who was among those charged with corruption, entered the Skupshtina and fired five shots from a revolver. With these he killed outright a Croat deputy named Basarichek, a brilliant and beloved man, and Raditch's nephew Paul, he slightly wounded two other Croat deputies, and he mortally wounded Raditch himself. Six weeks afterwards this strange and inconclusive genius died. The King was constantly at his bedside, pale and trembling with grief. The wounded man gripped his hand when the pain was worst. During those weeks there went on a pathetic wrangle, which later events were to make bitterly ironical. "When you are well," the King said, "you must be Prime Minister." "No, no," answered Raditch, "it must be a general." He had already picked a general for the job, one Zhikovitch. But the others could see that all such talk was idle, and soon he was taken home to Zagreb to die. On his deathbed he uttered many wishes, which were also to be made bitterly ironical in later years, that none of his followers should seek to avenge his death, and that the Croats and the Serbs were to come to the fullest and most ungrudging reconciliation.

It is almost incredible that King Alexander should have been blamed for Raditch's death. He had much to lose by it and nothing whatsoever to gain. But there was brought up against him what is true enough, that a sinister association binds the name of Karageorgevitch to murder. Prince Michael of Serbia, King Alexander Obrenovitch and Queen Draga, the Archduke Franz Ferdinand and Sophie Chotek, all had been murdered and all had been enemies of the Karageorgevitches. It was also recalled that during the war, at Salonika, the famous "Apis," Dragutin Dimitriyevitch, had been found guilty of an attempt on Alexander's life, on what seemed strangely slight evidence, and had been shot. Slavs like telling each other bloodcurdling stories, and in the pleasure of these recitals it was forgotten that Raditch for five years had ceased to be the King's enemy.

All these suspicions of the King were held to be confirmed by the sentence passed on Punisha Rachitch. He was adjudged insane and sent to a lunatic asylum. This was regarded as a ruse adopted to evade the plain duty of exacting the death penalty. But many murders have been committed by rebels, including Croats, who have suffered nothing worse than imprisonment and it is just possible that Punisha Rachitch was insane. He was a man of outstanding ability who, in spite of having studied law in Paris, had remained essentially the chief of a primitive tribe, and he had done valuable work in establishing order on the new Yugoslav-Albanian frontier. This involved a certain amount of savage suppression, for the Albanians and pro-Austrian Montenegrins were raiding Serb villages, murdering travellers, and cutting down telephone wires. The educated comitadji often cracked. They saw more horrors and felt more fear than the subtilized mind can endure. In 1919, when Punisha Rachitch arrested an English captain who was touring the country on the business of an allied commission, his recorded proceedings suggest a certain degree of hallucinated arrogance.

But whether Rachitch was sane or mad hardly mattered; it mattered so much more that in either case it would have been extremely difficult for the King and the Government to inflict on him the death penalty. He was adored by the Montenegrin tribesmen who were his constituents. He was a man of superb physique, which always counts for much among virile communities, and of undoubted courage; and he had a high reputation as a shrewd and impartial judge of local disputes. In the eyes of these tribesmen he must have been perfectly justified in the murder he committed, for Raditch had attacked his honour. If Rachitch had been tried on charges of corruption by a legal tribunal they would have recognized another victory for the new state which was invading their lives and which, whether for better or worse, was proving irresistible. But the Government (of which, it must be remembered, Raditch was a member) never had prosecuted Rachitch. So there was, for the tribesmen, simply an old and familiar situation: two chiefs undermined each other's credit by abuse till the only way of finding the better man was by murder. The Government might be crotchety about such matters as graft, though that seemed unreasonable enough, since the tribesmen accepted the payment of tribute to strong individuals as a natural practice; but when it came to a large classic situation like murder among chiefs it was no use putting up new-fangled ideas. Because of this attitude the execution of Rachitch might have caused serious unrest among the Montenegrins: and here we are faced again with the early, pre-genial Mussolini. He was financing a large number of Montenegrin insurgents in order to further his designs on Albania, and would certainly have used the death of Rachitch to stir up well-armed revolt. It would so greatly have profited the King to tamper with justice and save Rachitch from his proper punishment on a false plea of madness that most people took it for granted that he took that course. There is no possible means, short of the appearance of Punisha Rachitch before an independent medical board, by which we can tell whether this is the case or not.

After that catastrophe nothing went right. The King was left alone on the political stage. The obvious step was to form a Coalition Ministry. It was impossible to appoint a Serb. Since a Roman Catholic had been killed by a member of the Orthodox Church, the whole faith must perform an act of penance. It proved impossible to appoint a Croat, for Raditch's successor, Machek, and all Croat deputies except a few freaks, withdrew to Zagreb and refused to take their seats again in the Skupshtina. It is hard to understand why they did this. It was contrary to Raditch's wishes; they cannot have thought that they owed it to their loyalty to him to flout the Serbs, for he had been murdered by a Montenegrin, and the Serbs were on notoriously bad terms with the Montenegrins; and had they collaborated with the Serbs at this time they could have extracted from them every concession they wanted short of actual home rule. These were the realities of the situation. But the Croat Peasant Party preferred to react to the baser newspapers, which continued to attack Raditch after his death, and to the Serbian political bosses who inspired them, though with the King against them these had little chance of survival.

There remained only the Slovenes, and their leader, Father Koroshets, was appointed Prime Minister. The Slovenes are a sensible and unexcitable people who had had better opportunities than their compatriots to live at peace. Much of the trouble between the Croats and the Serbs had arisen because their language was identical and Serb officials could be sent to administer Croat territory. But the Slovene tongue differs greatly from Serbo-Croat, and the Slovenes had been left to govern themselves in peace. It is only fair to the Serbs to recognize that the Slovenes are not of the same oppositionist temperament as the Croats and therefore can be trusted with self-government. But the Church had supplied the Slovenes with a leader not up to the standard of his followers. Anton Koroshets had been the confessor of the last Empress of Hungary, Zita, and he represented the sombre and reactionary type of Catholicism cultivated by the Habsburgs. His spirit was therefore blind to the fundamental problems presented by the ancient and the modern world and moved busily in an etiquette-ridden bourgeois nineteenth-century limbo which had no correspondence with reality. This made him a past master of political intrigue, and a calamitous and irritating statesman. It was his imbecile custom to respond to the challenge of troubled times by using manifestos which ascribed all his country's ills to revolutionary movements engendered by Communists, Jews, and Freemasons. But there are very few Communists in Yugoslavia; the Jews are a stable body of traders producing few intellectuals; there are practically no Freemasons in Croatia and Slovenia, and Serbia is the only place in the world where Freemasonry gathers together the forces of reaction. It happened that under Alexander Obrenovitch a pro-Austrian and anti-democratic politician was Grand Master of the Belgrade Lodge and used it as a centre of intrigue with the lodges of Vienna and Budapest, and at that time all masons of progressive sympathies resigned and have never rejoined. All Koroshets's interventions in Yugoslav politics were on this level, and it is not surprising that in this crisis he proved unable to lead the country.

His failure left the King with only one course to follow: to obey Raditch's advice and establish a military dictatorship. In January 1929, after six months' turmoil, he dissolved Parliament, and made General Zhikovitch his Prime Minister, to be responsible to the Crown and not to the deputies. This was a complete breach with the Karageorgevitch tradition, for it involved the infringement of the constitution and the dynasty had always been defenders of constitutionalism. The King, with his narrow and intense concentration on the idea of his royalty, must have known that he had put an axe to the root of his power the minute he decided to exercise it absolutely: and General Zhikovitch could do nothing to repair this injury. It is proof of the essential capriciousness of Raditch's character that he should have advised the King to entrust himself and his country to this obscure man. His respectable but undistinguished military career had brought him no prestige, and, while he had a passion for political intrigue, he was completely ignorant of political principles.

He was, however, a perfect instrument for the King. It is said that Raditch had proposed him as dictator only to expose his inefficiency and emptiness; and such tortuousness can be believed of Raditch. Completely at a loss, Zhikovitch had to obey the King. For a time there was a superficial improvement in Yugoslavian affairs, because the dictatorship put into effect various necessary reforms—many concerning public utilities—which had been held up in the Skupshtina by regional and personal rivalries. In the preceding ten years Parliament had passed only 110 laws. The King and Zhikovitch passed 118 laws and 535 minor decrees in twelve months, and most of these were in accordance with the people's wishes. They also promulgated new penal and civil codes. Then the Nemesis of dictatorship laid its paralysing hand on the King's shoulder. The dictator seizes power, and it is yielded to him, because Parliament has failed to solve certain fundamental problems which are vexing the people. But Parliament has failed in that task only because the human mind has not yet discovered the solution of those problems. Other minor problems can be deliberately left unsolved by individuals, classes, or regions which find that the *status quo* favours their interests. But nobody would be able to suppress the solution of a major problem, such as war or poverty, if only because the existence of an enormously complicated idea—such as the solution of a complicated problem must be—could not be kept a secret, since it must be the product of the spirit of the age acting on a number of intellectually active people. It is not possible that one man alone could have conceived such a solution, because the range of variation in our species is extremely small, particularly at the top of the scale. A dictator might have an idea that was not shared by the village idiot; but it is extremely unlikely that a dictator would have an idea which had not already occurred in some comparable form to an elected assembly of men, some of whom, since the intellect is of some use in competition, must be of intellectual eminence. The chief problems of Yugoslavia were its proverty and the antagonisms felt by sections of the population which had different cultures. When the King had cleared up the arrears of work that could be settled by a firm and legible signature, he looked these problems in the face and realized that he could solve them no better than the Skupshtina.

He made some gallant attempts. To tackle the economic problem, he tried to develop the country's industries, but luck was against him, for the world slump began in the autumn of 1929. In any case Yugoslavia is primarily an agricultural country, and cannot know prosperity until an answer is found to man's world-wide refusal to pay a fair price for the food he eats. He also took steps to heal the antagonisms among his subjects, which showed him a very strange man, pedantic, doctrinaire, morally earnest, intellectually naïve, and, at that moment, desperate and alone. The problem was enormously intricate. It sprang from the inclusion in the same state of two kinds of Slavs: Slavs who were the inheritors of the Byzantine tradition of culture and the primitive Christianity of the Orthodox Church, and had been informed with the tragic conception of life by the defeat of Kossovo and the ensuing five hundred years of slavery; and Slavs who had been incorporated in the Western bourgeois system by Austrian influence and were spiritually governed by the Roman Catholic Church, which owes its tone to a Renaissance unknown to the other Slavs, and were experienced in discomfort but not in tragedy. To reconcile these two elements, which were different as the panther and the lynx, the King enforced certain measures which bring tears to the eyes by their simplicity.

He changed the name of his state from the Kingdom of Serbs, Croats, and Slovenes to Yugoslavia, the country of the South Slavs; and, forbidding the use of the old regional names such as Serbia, Bosnia, and the rest, he cut it up into nine provinces, called after the rivers which ran through them, except for Dalmatia, which was called the Littoral. He forbade the existence of the old regional political parties. Thus he disclosed the innocent hope that if Croatia were called the Savska Banovina the inhabitants would forget that they were Croats, would cease to wish to vote for Machek, and would learn to respect the Macedonians, since they had become the inhabitants of the Vardarska Banovina; and thus he committed a terrible wrong towards his own people. It was a shameful thing that Serbia, with its glorious history of revolt against the Turks, should cease to be an entity, and that the Serbian regiments which had amazed the world by their heroism should have to send their colours to the museums and march under the new, and as yet meaningless, flag of Yugoslavia. There is no doubt that at this time the King went too far in his desire to conciliate the Croats. He relaxed his devotion to the Orthodox Church, so that he should not seem too alien from his Roman Catholic subjects. He also took a step that was offensive not only to the Serbs but to common sense when he tried to abolish the use of the Cyrillic script in the Serb districts and replace it by the Latin script used by the Croats and in Western Europe. This Cyrillic script has a great historical significance for the Serbs, for it is a modification of the Greek alphabet made by St. Cyril and St. Methodius for the use of their converts when they came to evangelize the Slavs in the ninth century. But it is also much better suited than the Latin script to render the consonants peculiar to the Slav languages, it is virtually the same that is used in neighbouring Bulgaria, and is almost the same as that used in Russia, and it can be mastered by any intelligent person in a couple of days.

While these measures widened the gulf between the King and his Serb subjects they did not bring him an inch nearer the Croats. Strangely enough, though it was Raditch himself who had urged the establishment of a military dictatorship, nobody was so hostile to it as his followers. It was then that Italy found an opportunity to get her foot into Croatia and play the same part there that she had played in Macedonia. She had an advantage in finding a willing ally in this enterprise in Hungary, who had lost Croatia and the rich Danubian territory of the Voivodina to Yugoslavia and longed for revenge, but otherwise the soil was more difficult. The Croats had practised a steady policy of resistance to Hungarian rule, but it was mainly passive; and their rulers had not, like the Turks, accustomed them to the idea of murder. Hence the terrorists hired by Italy and Hungary to organize a movement on I.M.R.O. lines had, at first, little success. Neither then nor later did they win over the main body of the Croat Peasant Party, or indeed of any Croat political party. It is said that after a year's work there were not more than thirty active adherents of the new organization; and though it established training camps in Italy and Hungary these could not be filled. At enormous expense agents were sent everywhere where Croats were seeking their fortunes, France, Belgium, South America, the United States, and recruited them with cock-and-bull stories of how the Serbs were massacring their brothers by the thousands. Even this was not too successful, and the Hungarian camp was driven to decoying Yugoslav peasants over the frontier and kidnapping them.

But the Croat terrorists had their successes. They were far from inefficient. They distributed treasonable newspapers and pamphlets all over the world, many most persuasively written. They started an able and unscrupulous propaganda office in Vienna, which wounded the King's feelings bitterly and succeeded in poisoning European opinion; and they practised here no less successfully than on the Bulgarian frontier the art of placing bombs on international trains. This caused the Yugoslavian Government endless trouble. It was usually foreigners who were injured, and that made trouble with their governments; and the foreigners who were not injured showed themselves curiously irritating in their reaction to the measures that were taken for their protection. An English or French liberal, asked to leave his carriage while a police officer searched under the seats and on the racks, was apt to write home attacking the tyranny of the King's regime, and to add comments on the glumness of the searcher, although men are apt to look glum when doing a job that may cost them their lives. There were also, as in Macedonia, constant deliveries of arms to the rebels on a vast scale. Bombs, grenades, rifles, machine-guns, were brought in by smugglers who frequently murdered Yugoslav frontier guards, and were deposited in arsenals from which they were drawn by terrorists, who used them for such purposes as the blowing up of an Orthodox church in Zagreb during a service and the firing of a barracks dormitory full of conscripts.

Nobody came forward to help the King. There was one man, Svetozar Pribitchevitch, the greatest liberal journalist and politician in post-war Yugoslavia, who might have been expected to furnish him with a policy. He was one of a great family, descendants of the emigrants who had been led to Hungary by the holy Arsenius in the seventeenth century, and he had played a fearless part in the movement for Slav independence within the Austro-Hungarian Empire. All he had to suggest was, however, that the King should abdicate and the kingdom be converted into a republic. This was, in fact, an impractical suggestion. The Orthodox Church gave the King a stable position as the God-appointed head of the state in the minds of his Serb subjects; and no possible president had emerged from the Yugoslavian politics of that time who could have supplied by his own qualities any substitute for even that amount of unifying force. But the King reacted to the blunder with an excessive rage. Pribitchevitch's newspaper was suppressed and he was placed under arrest in his own home. Later he became ill and the Yugoslavs were humiliated by a request from President Masaryk that he might be allowed to harbour the rebel in Czechoslovakia.

Everybody failed him. Zhikovitch resigned, hurting the King intolerably by a frank admission that together they had made a great mess of Yugoslavia. Father Koroshets demanded home rule for the Croats and the Slovenes, and again the King showed excessive rage, and ordered him to be interned in Dalmatia. There was some excuse for his resentment. Koroshets had always been treated handsomely by Yugoslavia, and his famous respect for institutions, which was the card with which he always trumped the democratic ace, might well have been extended to the Karageorgevitch dynasty. Then Machek, Raditch's successor, put in a claim for the Croat right of self-determination, and was arrested and sentenced to three years' imprisonment. At this both Croats and Serbs were outraged, but the King was implacable. It must be remembered in his defence that these programmes were completely unfeasible. The Catholic Slavs of the kingdom, who numbered five and a half million, had no sort of chance of maintaining their existence as an independent state. Inevitably some would have been absorbed by Italy and others by Hungary, and we have the spectacle of the four hundred thousand Slovenes at present in Italy and the memory of what the Croats and Serbs of the Voivodina suffered from Hungarian oppression before the war, to tell us exactly what such absorption would mean. These annexations would not only have meant misery for the annexed but would have brought enemy powers up to the hearthstone of the Serbian people, who would have been as badly off as they were in the middle of the nineteenth century. There remained the solution of federation. But it is asking a great deal of a sovereign to apply that to a region which has lent itself to insurrection financed and organized by a hostile foreign power.

So the King dealt with Croatia by the light of his own wisdom, which proved insufficient. He could not send an army to deal with the unrest. It would have ruined the national prestige to have admitted the existence of civil war, and indeed the actual state of affairs was a good deal short of that. Many people travelled through Croatia at this time without observing any disruption, and the bulk of the population never ran any physical risks whatsoever. So instead of soldiers the Government sent Serbian or pro-Serb gendarmerie, who without any doubt treated the Croats with hideous brutality. There were many reasons for this. For one, they were sincere believers in the Yugoslav idea, and thought that Slavs who wanted to desert their brother Slavs and forgather with non-Slavs were very wicked people, who would be the better for a beating. For another, the Croats met them with a hostility that terrified them, strangers as they were and far away from home, and they felt justified in using any methods that would disarm their enemies. It must be remembered that when they came to grips with the terrorists financed by Italy they were dealing with men who habitually practised mutilation and had been known to torture a man for three days before they killed him. Since a Serbian policeman in Croatia was faced with many different types of Croat dissidents and usually had no means of distinguishing between them, it is not surprising that very often mild and inoffensive liberals were subjected to treatment that would have been appropriate, and then only according to Mosaic law, when applied to professional assassins and torturers. This meant that a great many people, some of whom were entirely innocent, were beaten and ill-treated in Croatian police stations.

Yet another reason for the brutality of the police lay in the difficulty of maintaining discipline in a police force, which is always less easy to control than an army, since it works in smaller and more scattered groups. No order could be issued in Belgrade which would make it certain that Belgrade's orders were being obeyed in Croatia. There was also, as a disturbing factor, the appalling police tradition which lingered in a form that was bad enough in all territories which had once been Habsburg, and in a far worse form in all territories which had been

Turkish. The police were regarded as a body that had to get results satisfactory to the supreme power in the state, and that had better not be
questioned by lower powers on how it got those results lest it take its revenge. This encouraged a spirit of enterprise that was usually regrettable
in its manifestations; that was notably regrettable in Croatia when the
police themselves started murdering Croatian politicians whose removal
they thought likely to facilitate their tasks, and organized bands of gangsters called *chetnichi* who went about assaulting Croat patriots and
breaking up their meetings as they themselves could not do in uniform
for fear of being reported to the highest authorities.

It would be easy to exaggerate the extent of this situation. Atrocities
did not happen everywhere, or every day. It would not be easy to exaggerate the degree to which Raditch and Machek, by the mindlessness and
emotionalism of their leadership and their failure to turn the political
situation to their advantage, were responsible for the suffering of their
followers. But it was a detestable situation, and though the King did not
hear the whole truth about it, owing to the independence of the police,
he heard at least enough to make him realize that the policy of suppression was a mistake, and that he must make another attempt at a policy
of reconciliation, since even if that failed it would smell better than the
other. But he was strangely obstinate in his persistence. It has been suggested that there was an international explanation for his obstinacy, and
that he had mistaken the personal affection felt for him by Sir Nevile
Henderson, then British Minister in Belgrade, for approval of his political actions. According to this story he made the pathetic error of believing that his dictatorship won him favour in English eyes and was worth
maintaining if for that reason alone.

Every independent mind in Croatia was now anti-Serb, and had been
thrown into the arms of the foreign terrorists. In September 1931 the
King had had the unhappy idea of proclaiming a new constitution which
virtually annulled the principle of popular representation. A Senate was
established with eighty-seven members, no less than forty-one of whom
were to be nominated by the King. Ministers were responsible to the
King and not to Parliament, and were to be nominated by the King. The
ballot was no longer secret and voluntary, but open and obligatory.
With a free Parliament thus abolished, and freedom of speech and freedom of the press long ago become mere memories, the Croats had to
take what means they could to defend themselves by secret arming and
appeals to foreign opinion. This was precisely what Mussolini had designed, yet the King showed no signs of retraction.

He had lost the Croats, and he had not kept the Serbs. The new constitution struck the Serbians as an act horrible in itself, since democracy is as essential a part of their social structure as Christianity or agriculture, and doubly horrible because it had been perpetrated by a Karageorgevitch. A man who worked for many years with the King on a scheme for developing the education of the recovered territories, and who greatly loved him, told me that when he went to see him at the palace during this time he could hardly speak to him. "My voice kept on breaking, I could do nothing but stare at him, as if I were asking him, 'Is it really you who have done this thing?' And though he must have noticed my distress and was, I think, quite fond of me, he said nothing about it, but went on talking, pleasantly and calmly, like a teacher who has upset a child by doing something which it cannot understand and which she cannot yet explain to it." It is possible that there was an explanation. The King told certain people that he intended to give his country a constitution which would actually be more democratic than any previous one, as soon as circumstances convinced him that this step could be taken in safety, and he seems to have spoken as if he meant what he said. Though there are no grounds for supposing him to be a lover of democracy for its own sake, there are none for supposing him to have hated it. What seem political principles in a country which has established its right to existence may seem expedients in a country where the nationalist issue has not yet been settled. The King may have believed that democracy had its value as a national and dynastic tradition, and might well be restored when he had gathered the results of his foreign policy, and had built so strong a wall of peace on his threatened frontiers that he could afford a measure of internal conflict.

For the King was far more successful in settling his affairs abroad than at home. In the international sphere his naïveté did not betray him but inspired him. It sent him forward to offer his hand to ancient enemies, whose surprise disarmed them, so that they found the friendliness in them awakening and answering. He laid the foundations of a most necessary structure that might have subserved the peace not only of his people but of all Europe when he repudiated the hostility between Bulgaria and Yugoslavia that had been encouraged by Russia and envenomed by King Ferdinand. Here he was helped by the recent decline in the fortunes of I.M.R.O. This body had virtually lost its cause in Macedonia, because the Yugoslavian administration was rapidly improving, and the Yugoslav Macedonians, who are no fools, saw that they might live far from disagreeably if only they were not harried by perpetual guerrilla attacks and forced to pay extortionate illegal taxes. This is not to say that the Bulgarians in Yugoslav Macedonia gave up their desire that the territory in which they lived should be handed over to Bulgaria. Many have never been reconciled to Yugoslav rule. But most of them grew heartily sick of I.M.R.O., and joined their Serb neighbours in picking up rifles whenever a raiding party appeared and giving as good as they got.

I.M.R.O., thus repulsed, then turned its whole attention to its work in Bulgaria, where it had for long fulfilled the functions of a Fascist Party, and strengthened that party till it was a state within the state. Its financial resources were enormous, for it had foreign aid and levied illegal taxes on Bulgarian Macedonia as in Yugoslavian Macedonia; from the tobacco industry alone it raised over a million pounds in six years. But its chief resource was its ruthlessness, which, as time went on, made Bulgarian political life into a shambles. Sofia, which is a city full of delightful people, beautiful and extravagantly literate, lay in the power of a savage gang as if enslaved by sorcerers, and stared glassily at the assassinations that occurred nearly every day in the open streets. The whole of life was infected with fear and squalor. No shops could open without paying a tax to I.M.R.O., and all had to supply its followers with goods on the production of an official requisition. Every hotel-keeper had to reserve five rooms for I.M.R.O., two on the first floor for the leaders, three on higher levels for the rank and file. An ancient heroism took on itself the likeness of Al Capone. King Boris of Bulgaria, and indeed most Bulgarians, were deeply ashamed. Because I.M.R.O. had no hold on its followers other than its claim to liberate Yugoslavian Macedonia, King Boris decided to spike the movement's guns by declaring a new and unalterable policy of friendship with Yugoslavia. Henceforward the parasite state would have to fight its host to keep its life. The plundered peasants and shopkeepers, to say nothing of the tobacco industry, were deeply sensible of the conveniences offered by the friendship, even though they may have felt no sentimental attachment for Yugoslavia whatsoever. The leaders of I.M.R.O. were executed, imprisoned, or driven to flight, while their followers were beaten and disbanded; and Bulgaria turned towards a more normal way of life.

This reconciliation would not have been possible without King Alexander's eager acceptance of King Boris's advances. He did much to sweeten Bulgarian feeling by his visits to Sofia and Varna, which, indeed, were among the most fearless acts recorded of any sovereign. All the Balkan peoples like a man with courage. And when King Boris delayed to give proper diplomatic expression to the new friendship, owing to the influence of Italy on some Bulgarian politicians and the tropism of lifelong hatreds in others, King Alexander paid other visits that were designed to hurry him up. It was his aim to keep Italy at bay by uniting his neighbour states into a bloc resolved to keep the South-East of Europe inviolate. He went to Constantinople to see Mustapha Kemal, who smiled at him with eyes which revealed that the Balkans had once more played their trick on the Turk, and had been conquered only to rule; for those eyes were blue, and Ataturk, like some sultans, several viziers, and the flower of the Janizaries, was at least half Slav. He went to Greece, and set going negotiations that were ultimately consummated, in spite of the peculiarly unconcordant character of Greek politicians. Greece, Turkey, and Yugoslavia signed the Balkan Pact in 1933, and once Bulgaria found herself one against three she changed her mind and joined them in 1934.

But even these achievements cannot have convinced King Alexander that the world was as pleasant as he had believed it to be twenty years before, when he was a young man, at the end of the Balkan War: as pleasant as it must be if it is worth while lavishing on it the luxury of poetry, of such dreams as the vision of the Frushka Gora. It was not only that the path of his successes must inevitably lead him to a pact with Soviet Russia. That Mustapha Kemal had told him; and he could see that the support of Russia, no matter whether it was White or Red, was absolutely necessary to the Balkans if they were to make a stand against Western aggression. But there were more disagreeable aspects of his situation than that, which must have struck him at the very beginning of his diplomatic pilgrimage and made him conscious that certain glories had left the world, that nothing was now simple in shape and bright like a sword.

His very first meeting with the King of Bulgaria showed a certain dimming of the monarchic tradition, a certain muting of martial music as it had been heard through history. It happened that in 1930 King Boris had married Princess Giovanna of Italy, who was cousin to King Alexander, as their mothers had been sister princesses of Montenegro. The first meeting of the kings had to take place timidly, under the shelter of this cousinly relationship. It was represented that, on a return journey to Sofia from Paris and London, Queen Giovanna was overcome by her sense that blood was thicker than water, and felt that she must see King Alexander, whom in fact she cannot possibly have laid eyes upon since 1913 when he was twenty-five and she was six. In response King Alexander came down to the railway station and drank coffee with them in a waiting-room, specially decorated in the gloomy fashion habitual on such occasions, during the hour's halt the Orient Express always made at Belgrade. There had been some dealings between the two countries, but King Boris had not dared to make the more definite overtures which would have justified King Alexander in proposing a visit to the palace. But once they were all standing on the platform Queen Giovanna forced the diplomatic pace by kissing King Alexander as if she really meant it, putting her arms on his shoulders as if there were a strong good-will between them all which might do great things for them if they let it. King Alexander was stirred out of his usual formality into responsiveness, and in the waiting-room they talked and laughed together with the warmth of real loyalty. But there was defiance in their laughter. This meeting sprang from the revolt of one of the Italian royal family against Mussolini. Three heirs to the blood of kings were conspiring, not without trepidation, to give the people peace in spite of a blacksmith's son.

Such a spectacle could not have been imagined by the priests and emperors of Byzantium, nor by the Nemanyan kings, nor even by the Serbian peasants who raised Karageorge and Milosh Obrenovitch to be princes over them. Surely, they would have said, a king must be all-powerful; others might snatch his sceptre, but so long as he held it power was his. And surely, they and their subjects would have agreed, the people would never give birth to its own enemy. But now there was a new factor to confound all their certainties. There were two sorts of people. There was the people as it had been since the beginning of time, that worked in the villages, small towns, and capitals. But there was also a new people, begotten by the new towns which the industrial and financial developments of the nineteenth century had raised all over Europe: towns so vast and intricate that, in coping with the problems of their own organization, they lost all relationship to the country round them, so that even though they were called capitals they were not, for a head should have some connexion with its body; towns planned in the biological interest of only the rich, and careless of the souls and bodies of the poor. The new sort of people have been defrauded of their racial tradition, they enjoyed no inheritance of wisdom; brought up without gardens, to work on machines, all but a few lacked the education which is given by craftsmanship; and they needed this wisdom and this education as never before, because they were living in conditions of unprecedented frustration and insecurity. A man without tradition and craft is lost, and book learning is of little help to him, for he lacks the shrewdness to winnow what he reads.

Some among this new people, by a miracle that may be called grace, resist all these assaults on their stock, and are as the best of the old people. But there are those who succumb, never ripen, and are infantile, and so react to their frustration and necessity, as infants react to hunger, by screaming and beating out at what is nearest. One such, named Luccheni, had killed Elizabeth of Austria in 1898. But his kind had grown in power since then. This is not to say that they had become wiser, or had discovered a formula that would medicine their distress; it was only that there were more of them, and that, conscious of their numbers, they had learned to scream orders as well as complaints. So when King Alexander, having achieved the Balkan *entente*, visited France to discuss the new power's future relationship, he was struck down at Marseille not by a hungry vagrant, but by a ruler who was in a position to tyrannize over the royal blood of his country as he had tyrannized over its peasants and workmen. A form of government had arisen which was far more disgusting than any of the governments of the immediate past, though they had been nasty enough. The great powers had perpetuated Balkan misery by the Treaty of Berlin. They had been responsible for many ugly deaths in high places—Prince Michael of Serbia had been killed by Austrian conspiracy, Queen Draga and King Alexander Obrenovitch might have lived to old age had it not been for Austrian intrigue, Franz Ferdinand and Sophie Chotek were doomed by Austrian maladministration. They had been responsible for many ugly births in low places: Luccheni and Mussolini would never have come to be in a just economic system. But at least they knew when they had sinned that there was sin, at least they were aware that there was good and there was evil. But this the new rulers of the world did not know. "Violence," said Mussolini in the unmistakable accents of moral imbecility, "is profoundly moral, more moral than compromises and transactions." Time had rolled backward. It seemed likely that man was to lose his knowledge that it is wiser being good than bad, it is safer being meek than fierce, it is fitter being sane than mad. He was not only ignoring the Sermon on the Mount, he was forgetting what the Psalmist had known. And since these things are true it was certain that, once man had forgotten them, he would be obliged, with pains that must be immense, to rediscover them.

Belgrade knows all this, and looks forward to her future with apprehension. For, to tell the truth, it is a mournful city. Even in spring, when the young lovers walk among the flowers in Kalemegdan, and their elders sit in the restaurants talking politics with a new and rosy vehemence, because their nostrils are filled with the savour of roasting lamb and piglet, its underlying mood is an autumnal doubtfulness. The winter is going to be very long and hard. Is it going to be worth while living through it for the sake of what lies beyond? And those who wonder are not ignorant of what winter is, nor are they cowards. This mood is one of the deep traces left on the capital by Alexander Karageorgevitch's personality. It is still his city. If one of the medieval Serbians who painted the frescoes in the monasteries came to life and covered a wall with Belgrade, he would certainly show the murdered king floating on his bier above the city; and if the picture were to be a valid symbol it would show the King's tenacious and reserved face changed by doubtfulness, its reserve breaking to betray a doubt whether its tenacity had been of any avail.

Each Serbian ruler has proved something by his reign. More than once it was proved by this curious sovereignty, newer than the United States and as old as Byzantium, that a small state could defeat a vast empire; always it was proved that it is terrible, even in victory, to be a small state among great empires. It was given to Alexander to give new proof of these arguments, and to prove others also. By the expansion of his state beyond the limits of his people's culture, Serbia had been forced into guilt. It was, evidently, a moral necessity that small peoples should form small states, and the price exacted for the defence of morality looked to be more than men's bodies can afford to pay. This the King had known well as he drove stiffly through the streets of Belgrade. A dictator himself, he was the first ruler in Europe to learn how inimical dictatorship must be to all true order. He knows it still better as he floats over the city on his bier. For his murder went virtually unpunished. France hardly dared to try his assassins, and the League of Nations murmured timid words of censure, such as would offend no one.

Belgrade IX

WE grew eager to leave Belgrade, and start on the trip we were to take with Constantine through Macedonia and Old Serbia, though nothing unpleasant was happening to us here. There were indeed two disconcerting moments when we turned a corner too smartly and came on Constantine and Gerda in complete emotional disarray, Gerda weeping in disregard of the passers' frank Slav stares, Constantine red with misery. But we had taken it for granted that Constantine's life would cover the whole range of oddity, and would be painfully odd as well as pleasantly odd, so we were hardly even surprised. It was no personal experience that depressed us in the city, but the pervading air of anticlimax. Nothing real had happened here since King Alexander died. That was indeed more of a miracle than an anticlimax. His murderers had put him out of the way in order that the country should be left without a head and would be unable to defend itself when it was attacked, yet the attack was never made.

This inaction is still mysterious, though there are one or two obvious factors which must have recommended it. The first was the reaction of Yugoslavia to the King's death. It was not split asunder, but on the contrary drew closer in a unity it had not known since King Peter's abdication. Every part of the country, even Croatia, abandoned itself to grief. No state not fallen into animal sloth can lose its head, whether that be king or president, without some amount of visceral anguish, and the Slavs, being analytical, knew that though Alexander had committed many harsh and foolish acts he had been fundamentally the priest of his people. There are not only good men and bad men, there are bad good men and there are good bad men. A bad good man complies in each individual act with accepted ethical standards, but his whole life describes a pattern that cannot be pleasing to God. A good bad man may commit all manner of faults and crimes, but at bottom he lets nothing come before the duty of subjecting experience to the highest law; and the Yugoslavs knew that King Alexander belonged to this order. They were aware that though he had sent too many of them to prison, he had sought to give Yugoslavia an honourable destiny that would preserve its genius. So there was no revolt of the Croats, and the foreign royalties and statesmen who followed the King's bier through the streets of Belgrade were amazed by the strange, soft sound of a whole city weeping.

The other factor that preserved Yugoslavia from the long-planned assault was the secret attitude of the great powers, which was more audacious than their public showing. Immediately after the assassination the British Mediterranean Fleet took up its position in the Adriatic; and it is possible that the French found out more than they were meant to about the crime, and that they were able to demand a *quid pro quo* for erecting the scaffolding of obfuscation that surrounded the trial of the murderers at Aix-en-Provence. That their policy preserved peace at the moment does not exculpate it, for a war then would have been far less dangerous than later; and meanwhile every totalitarian ruffian in Europe rejoiced to see one of their kind strike down a foreign king in peace-time and go scot-free, and all honest men lost heart.

Here in Belgrade that shadow did not lift by an inch. For all the vehemence and intelligence of life it was at a deadlock. There were plenty of people daring to think, but no one acted, except perhaps the group of financial and industrial adventurers who are supposed to be represented by Stoyadinovitch, who "admire" capitalism, who are inspired by the myth that the capitalism which is dying all over Europe will revive for their benefit. Error often stimulates the organism more violently than the truth, as cancer produces a more spectacular reaction in its host than the healthy cell. Those who had truer foundations to their thought were simply waiting for their scepticism to be resolved. They used to draw their strength from France and England and Russia. But they were so deeply shocked by the failure of France and England to speak honestly before the League of Nations concerning King Alexander's murder that they no longer thought of those two countries, they only wondered. They could not derive any refreshment from us in the West till we should give them new proof of our value. They still thought much of Russia, but not as they did when the Balkans were perpetually fecundated by Russian mysticism or revolutionary theory, for Russia was by then so remote behind its Chinese wall of exclusiveness and secretiveness, it was like thinking of Paradise, or, as it may seem to others, of Hell.

Sometimes it seemed as if their inactivity was in part due to the mythic quality of the popular imagination. It is as if the people were saying to themselves, "A state must have a head, but we have none till our king is a man, so we cannot live like a state, we must hold our peace till young Peter can rule us." That is a wise enough decision;

but where the popular mind holds too firmly to its primitive enter-
tainments, its first fairy-tales, it strikes into folly. King Alexander left
three Regents to rule Yugoslavia till his son came to maturity: his cousin
Prince Paul, his doctor, and the Governor of Croatia (himself a Croat),
with a general in reserve. None of the non-royal Regents was outstanding in character or influence, so if they wished to oppose Prince Paul
it would have been impossible. The country felt, therefore, that Prince
Paul exerted the only effective power under the Regency; and this was
probably true. So far as strangers could see, he had acquitted himself
very creditably within the limits set by his distaste for his position. For
he had an exclusive interest in art which is very odd in a pure Slav, and it
is generally known that he would far rather have led the life of a con-
noisseur in Florence than be tied to a tedious administrative job in
almost pictureless Belgrade. Perhaps because of this desire to be doing
something else somewhere else, perhaps because of the prudence which
enabled him in the past to live calmly among the disturbed Karageorgevitches, he always responded to the forces working in Yugoslavia rather
than governed them. He was amiable to Stoyadinovitch, and bowed and
smiled to all the powers that Stoyadinovitch led up to him, even to
Italy and Germany.

This was not at all a foolish policy for a man who knows himself not
naturally a ruler, in an extravagantly perilous time of history. But the
myth-making mind of the people saw him as the Regent of the fairy-
stories, the Uncle of the Babes in the Wood, who longs to usurp his
charge's throne, who is in sympathy with usurpers at their crassest, with
Mussolini and Hitler. There was ascribed to him a savage spirit of reaction, fired from an anti-Bolshevism that regrets the Romanoffs and is
loyal to the Demidoffs. Yet it seems unlikely that a lover of Western
painting, whose law of life is obviously taste, should have felt such passionate nostalgia for the Philistine court of Nicholas III, and the circumstances of the separation between Arsenius Karageorgevitch and
Aurora Demidoff must have forbidden the unity that a son might
normally feel with his mother's family. From all appearances Prince
Paul's political ideas are derived not from Russia but from the upper-
and middle-class England he learned to know when he was at Oxford.
This is not to say that they were ideally applicable to the Balkan situation, but their inapplicability was of a different sort from Tsarist ob-
scurantism. There were no times when the liberalism of Belgrade failed
to be inspiring, for it is a robust tree with roots deep in the nature of
the Slav race; but there were times when it seemed as if this Liberalism

could never come into effective action again, because it had broken from the peasant tradition of sound sense and preferred those urban opinions which are only clever guesses.

"But you will see that all must go well here," I said to my husband, as I sat in front of my dressing-table in the hotel bedroom, putting on my hat to go out to tea with Gerda and Constantine, "as soon as we get to Macedonia. You will see that there is a Balkan genius so strong that its peoples can never perish, that they can take refuge from material death, and even intellectual or moral death, in its spiritual life." "That seems so strange to me," said my husband, "when I have all my life heard of Macedonia as a symbol of age-long misgovernment and ruin. I used to hear of it when I was a child, as a place where men butchered other men, whom they should have thought of as their brothers." "But that was not age-long," I said. "I remember that too. We heard our elders talking of the squalid disputes in Macedonia when we were somewhere about nine or ten, and I realize now that it was after the Mürzsteg agreement between Turkey and the great powers was signed in 1903. That was a terrible business. It provided for the policing of Macedonia by military forces sent out by the great powers, and it was drawn up by the Austro-Hungarian and Russian Foreign Ministers, Goluchowski and Lansdorff, at one of Franz Josef's hunting lodges. It happened that Goluchowski, who was a clever man, loved shooting above all things, and that Lansdorff, who was a stupid man, loved writing above all things. So Goluchowski went out with his gun every day and all day, and left Lansdorff to draft the agreement. Apparently he came back too tired to read it, and apparently all the other diplomats in Europe were equally fond of shooting, for they all passed an imbecile clause by which it was announced that as soon as Macedonia could be restored to order the Turkish administrative districts were to be delimited anew so that they might correspond with ethnographical districts. This automatically provoked civil war of the bloodiest character. For this clause terrified the Bulgars, Serbs, and Greeks in Macedonia, who knew that there are hardly any districts which are ethnographically pure in that part of the world, and saw themselves handed over to whatever race was in the majority, by however small a figure. Each group therefore attacked both the others, and killed off as many of them as possible, with the object of reducing them to unquestionable minorities. This went on for three years, till an Englishwoman called Lady Grogan visited Macedonia and informed the Foreign Office of the reason for the massacres, and the great powers drowsily collected themselves and withdrew the clause. But, of course, there had been endless pain and misery for five centuries before. It is astonishing that there should be anything waiting for us in Macedonia, but last time I was there I had the impression that there was more there than anywhere else."

We started early for our tea-party, because we wanted to visit the Prince Paul Museum and have a last look at the pictures and antiquities with which the Regent had filled one wing of the New Palace on the main street. Some he himself had collected, others were the remains of a collection which the Serbian state had gathered since 1842 but which was pillaged and damaged in the war. There were a lovely gold vessel found in Macedonia, relic of a pre-Mycenæan civilization not recorded in history, some beautiful gold work and enamels from Byzantium and medieval Serbia, some robes and furniture and arms of the earlier Karageorgevitches and Obrenovitches; some bad paintings by the Germans and Austrians, some very good paintings by the French and goodish paintings by the English, and some Slav paintings that had little individuality and were echoes of the German and Austrian and French work; and some Slav sculpture that had great individuality, but was contorted with its struggle to lay hold of a sound tradition. The serene certainty of the medieval work and the uncertainty of the modern work might have been distressing had we not recognized some friends who were manifesting the continuity of Serbian national life, which would doubtless make itself felt in time. During our stay in Belgrade we had sometimes visited a café for wine and hot spiced sausages towards midnight, and there had listened to the singing of two Roumanian sisters, fine girls, plump as table birds, who had a habit of putting their heads together and smiling widely, just as Phyllis and Zena Dare used to be photographed in my childhood. The night before, we had watched a young man, neatly dressed and confident yet manifestly no townsman, probably the son of the wealthiest peasant in some big village, fall under the charms of both these sisters, with a perfect impartiality which struck us as psychologically curious, but which was apparently accepted by the two girls without resentment. We had no doubt that his passion for them was of a practical nature; but here in the museum we found the three, in front of some medieval icons and reliquaries, and the young man was explaining to the two girls, with violent gestures and proud cries, that the first King of the Nemanyas was the father of St. Simeon, who had founded the monastery of Hilandar on Mount Athos. They appeared to be interested and impressed.

When we came to Constantine's house he opened the door to us, a happy little Buddha, as he always is when he is dispensing hospitality, and Gerda waited for us behind her tea-table, composed and gracious in a neat grey silk dress, with not a trace of tears. The two children played about the table, miraculous little creatures, since they reconciled and yet obstinately maintained apart the different elements in them. They can flash a glance which is at once German in its romantic activism, Jewish in its shrewd and swift calculation of probabilities, and Slav in its analytic penetration. They have an amusing coolness, of which I learned the very first time I ever met Constantine. I was taken to call on him at his office in connexion with the work I was doing on my first visit to Yugoslavia, so late in the morning that to finish our discussion we had to lunch together. So Constantine telephoned to his house and said, "Is that you, my little son? Tell your mother that I will not be home to lunch because I have run away with an Englishwoman." Sitting at the opposite side of the table, I heard the child's reply in the unknown language, cold as ice-water. "Do you think," he asked, "that the Englishwoman has any stamps?" That was the older boy, but the younger also had an air of being seriously aware of the necessity for imposing form on the extravagances of nature; and it could be seen, now the whole family was united, that they regarded Constantine and his mother as conduits of that extravagance. They were sage about this opinion. They were willing to admit that the prodigiousness of the pair was beneficent and entertaining, but they would not blind themselves to its need for control.

I grieved a little at their attitude, knowing them wrong, with an error that they had inherited from Gerda, with her Western tradition. Constantine may need control, owing to his circumstances, the most unfavourable of which is his surrender to the West; but Constantine's mother has shown herself able to endure so much that there can be no question of better adapting her to life. In her youth her beauty, which must have been superb, presented her with a gifted and loving husband, her son Constantine, and a daughter. Just before the war the scourge of the Balkans, tuberculosis, took the daughter. Then her husband and son went to the war; her husband died of typhus, and her son was sent to Russia and disappeared. Meantime her home was occupied by the Germans, she was without means, and though she found work as a nurse that ended with the war, she nearly starved till life became more normal and she succeeded in getting pupils for music lessons; and even then she was in misery, for not until three years after the peace did she hear that Constantine still lived. All this might conceivably have been borne by a peasant woman, disciplined from birth to silence under frustration. But this woman was a musician, an interpretative artist, whose discipline was all directed towards the public demonstration of what she felt. What might have been expected was that she would feel a transcendent kind of grief and die of it, a special death that would have been a fulfilment. But here she was, her face certainly tortured, but not so much because of her sufferings as because of the impossibility of finding out the exact truth about humanity, which is to say, the impossibility of finding a stable foundation for artistic endeavour.

"Then you can tell me something!" she exclaimed, when we told her that since I had last seen her we had been to Canada. "Is it possible that Scriabin is really the favourite musician of all Canadians?" We replied that nothing we had seen of Montreal and Toronto had prepared us for this conclusion. "For myself, I cannot really believe it," she explained, "but there came to Belgrade this winter a Canadian professor, and he assured me that in his country the favourite composer of all was not Beethoven or Mozart or Wagner but Scriabin, and that there existed a great society to popularize his works, called the Scriabin Society. But it is not possible, for Scriabin himself would have admitted that if he was anybody's *favourite* composer that person would not have been able to appreciate him. A people which ate lobster and champagne at every meal could never claim to be *fins gourmets* of lobster and champagne. Also, Scriabin is too *difficult*." Her fingers stood up, stiffly apart, each registering discomfiture before a technical problem. "Not enough people could play him, not enough people could listen to him, to become truly familiar with him. Besides, how absurd to think of a great country, largely covered with snow, many of whose inhabitants earn their living trapping wild animals, having Scriabin as its favourite composer."

"Yes, Mamma," said Constantine, "but are you not forgetting that Scriabin himself was the child of a great country covered with snow, where there was a good deal of trapping wild animals?" "Yes, yes," said the old lady, "but I do not believe that in the whole of Russia you would find one man who would claim that Scriabin was the favourite composer of Russians!" "But, perhaps, Mamma," said Constantine, "it is a different sort of animal that they trap in Canada." "A different sort of animal? But what would that matter?" exclaimed his mother in stupefaction, knitting her fine mind against this puzzle till she saw Constantine winking at us, and then she cried out, laughing, "Ah, wait till you are old, you will see what it is like when everybody mocks you, even your poor little idiot son!"

Very soon we had an idea that Gerda thought that this was not the proper way to entertain us. She thought the less of us for liking this wild talk about music, which could not really be of any value, because it made no references to the Ideal or the History of Music. It would have been better if we had made statements about specific musical occasions and had evoked them from her, and had thus established our common enjoyment of culture: if we had, for example, spoken of hearing a Beethoven symphony in Toronto or Montreal, and had asked her where she had heard it. She spoke presently of her surroundings as lacking precisely that kind of sophistication, when the conversation turned to food and the amount of cooking that was done in Yugoslavian households. Contemptuously she told us that when a Serbian family expected guests to tea, the housewife would put herself about to bake cakes and biscuits; but, as we would see, she said with a shrug of the shoulders, indicating the food on her table, which had been obviously bought from a shop, she was not so. Her cool tone drew a picture of how she would like to dispense hospitality. One would go down, well dressed, with a full purse, and all one's debts paid, to Kranzler if one lived in Berlin, to Dehmel if one lived in Vienna, to Gerbeaud if one lived in Budapest, and would greet the assistant, who would be very respectful because of one's credit, and would choose exquisite pastries and *petits fours*, which would not only be delightful when crushed against one's friends' palates, but would also be recognizably from Kranzler, or from Dehmel, or from Gerbeaud.

She was assuming that my husband and I would share her feeling, that we would be with her in upholding this cool, powerful, unhurried ideal against the Serbian barbarians who liked a woman to get hot over a stove, as if she could not afford to pay other women to work for her, which indeed was probably the case. It would have been difficult for us to explain how wrong we thought her. We like the Apfelkuchen of Kranzler, we have never gone to Vienna without buying the Nusstorte of Dehmel, we have shamefully been late for a friend's lunch in Budapest for the reason that we had turned into Gerbeaud's to eat meringues filled with cream and strawberries. But we knew that when one goes into a shop and buys a cake one gets nothing but a cake, which may be very good, but is only a cake; whereas if one goes into the kitchen and makes a cake because some people one respects and probably likes are coming to eat at one's table, one is striking a low note on a scale that is struck higher up by Beethoven and Mozart. We believed it better to create than to pay. In fact, England had had a bourgeoisie long before

Germany, and we had found out that the bourgeois loses more than he gains by giving up the use of his own hands; but there is no wider gulf in the universe than yawns between those on the hither and thither side of vital experience.

As Gerda spoke Constantine watched her with slightly excessive approval, nodding and smiling. He so obviously meant to reassure her and to recommend her to us that there came back to us the spectacle they had twice presented to us lately in the streets of Belgrade, dishevelled and disunited. It was astonishing to think that between such scenes these people should enjoy the glowing contentment with each other which now warmed this room; but of course there are millions of kinds of happy marriages. Only when we rose to go and Constantine told us that he would walk a little way back with us did we see that he was smiling not only at her but at us, and that his smile bore the same relation to a real smile as false teeth do to real teeth; it performed the function of indicating good-will, but the organism had failed in its normal spontaneous action. I could feel him still smiling through the darkness, as we strolled away from the cache of simple streets in which his pretty little house found itself, into the boulevard where grey concrete cakes of institutions and ministries shone with a blindish brightness behind the electric standards. When we came to the centre of the town, and looked across a circus where people were hurrying in and out of the yellow-lit cafés, at the slow and dark yet gay procession of the corso, he said, still with this undue facial cheerfulness, with the corners of his mouth turned up, "I must go back now." But he did not take the hand my husband offered him, but stared across the street at the Corso. Two gipsies, lean and dark as Sikhs, with red rags tied round their heads, padded past, wheeling a handcart in which there lay a bundle. It stirred, it sat up, it was an elderly and beautiful woman in richly coloured garments who looked at us with wild eyes that filled with solemn recognition, who swept out her arm in the gesture of a prophet, and cried out some words in Roumanian, which twanged with the spirit of revelation. For a second it seemed a supreme calamity that we could not understand her. But she softened, and fell back, and was a bundle again; she was simply drunk. Constantine said absently, as if his soul were entirely with the march of the Corso, "You know, my wife has made up her mind to come with us to Macedonia."

I stood transfixed with horror. Tears began to run down my cheeks. Macedonia was the most beautiful place that I had ever seen in my life, I had looked forward to showing it to my husband, and now we were to be accompanied by this disagreeable woman who liked neither of us. It was like having to take a censorious enemy on one's honeymoon. Not only was this proposal an outrage to a reasonable sentiment, it raised endless practical difficulties. The cars and cabs we could rely on in Macedonia would be small, too small for four, though comfortable enough for three. Gerda would have to be our guest, as Constantine was to be, and the relationship between host and guest is not easy for people who feel a strong mutual antipathy. And her contempt for everything Slav and non-German would be at its most peevish in Macedonia, which is the most Slav part of Yugoslavia, and which is not only non-German but non-Occidental, being strongly Byzantine and even Asiatic. "But she will not like it!" I exclaimed. "So I have told her many, many times!" wailed Constantine. My husband bent down over him, his spectacles shining with a light that looked menacing, that was in fact panic-stricken. "Your wife cannot come with us," he said. "But she will, she will!" cried Constantine. "All night she cries, because I will not take her, and I get no sleep. And she says she will suicide herself if I go without her! And I cannot let you go alone, for my Ministry wishes me to go with you! I tell you, she must come with us!" And he turned and left us, walking very fast. My husband and I stood staring at each other, feeling like the people in Kafka's books who are sentenced by an invisible and nameless authority for some unnamed sin to a fantastic and ineluctable punishment. It was not a thing that happens to one in adult life, being obliged to go on a journey with someone whom one dislikes and who has no sort of hold over one, sentimental or patriotic or economic.

So, at eight o'clock on the morning of Good Friday (according to the Orthodox calendar) the four of us started for Macedonia from Belgrade station. My husband and I had driven down from the hotel, past a corner of Kalemegdan Park that drops a steep bank towards the river, claret-coloured with tamarisk bloom. The early light lay as a happy presence on the wide grey floods round the city, and it shone on the Obrenovitch villa on the hill-top, which, like all Turkish villas, was exquisitely appropriate to everything freshest in nature, to spring and the morning. At the station we found that Gerda and Constantine had not arrived, and we sat down at the café on the platform and ate beautiful Palestinian oranges, their flesh gleaming like golden crystal. There appeared presently a young doctor of philosophy, a colleague of Constantine's, with whom I had had some official business, who came to say good-bye and bring me a bunch of red roses. He sat down with us and had some coffee, and we talked until it became evident that Constantine and Gerda were very late indeed, and we began to walk up and down, alarmed and exasperated.

They came at the last possible moment, and we had to jump into the train just as it went, the doctor of philosophy handing up the roses to the window after we had started. My husband and I busied ourselves packing away our baggage and putting out cushions and books, for we were to be nearly twelve hours in the train. But soon we became aware that Gerda was standing quite still, looking down at the roses with a resentful expression, and Constantine, with his arm round her, was attempting to console her. "Yes, it is very bad," he was saying, "certainly he should have brought you flowers also." My husband and I stared at him aghast, for it was obvious that the young doctor had come down to give me the roses as an impersonal and official act, and that he had refrained from bringing any to Gerda for the precise reason that she had some personal value for him. "But I am afraid," said Constantine, "that this young man really does not know how to behave so well as I had hoped, for look, these are not the flowers he should have given our friend." "*Nein, ganz gewiss nicht!*" agreed Gerda hotly, and they gazed down at the roses, shaking their heads.

"Tell me," said Constantine, turning to my husband, "what sort of flowers would it be considered right in your country for a man to give to a lady whom he does not know very well when he sees her off at a station?" My husband guffawed and said, "In our country he would go to a florist and ask for some nice flowers." Gerda looked disgusted, sat down, and stared out of the window. Constantine said in shocked and bewildered accents, "*O! Il y a des règles!*" "What are they?" asked my husband, laughing coarsely. From Constantine's explanations I learned that it was not by ill luck that I had been dogged through Central Europe by carnations, which I detest; I had brought them on myself by my marriage to a banker. Pains had been taken, which I had never perceived, to keep me from getting above myself, for it was ruled that the flowers which I received on my arrival in a town, and during my stay in it, should be modest. "It is only on departure," said Constantine, "that the bouquet should be really large. And there remains the question of colour, which is what disturbs us at this moment. There are certain colors, particularly in roses, which are purely personal, which are not suitable for gifts of ceremony. It is here that our young friend has offended. These roses are nearly crimson." My husband turned to me with an air of suspicion, but Constantine did not laugh. There was doubt in his eyes, as if he were wondering whether his wife were not right, and he had greatly exaggerated the degree of our refinement.

The lovely Serbian country, here like a fusion of Lowland Scotland and New England, with many willows rising golden green, and meadows white with daisies, and nymphean woods, ran past us for some hours. Then there was the call for lunch, and we went along to the restaurant car, to eat one of those pungent and homely meals that are served on the Balkan trains. As we sat down, a middle-aged man in a grey lounge suit stood up in his place and shouted at an elderly man in a braided purple peasant costume who went on with his meal. "It is nothing," said the waiter who was taking our order; "they are only two members of Parliament." "Yes," said Constantine, "the one in peasant costume is a well-known supporter of Mr. Stoyadinovitch, and the other is an opposition man." At this point the opposition man bent down to look at his opponent's plate, straightened himself, and cried, "I see you are eating an enormous amount of fish. No wonder you take no interest in measures for controlling the floods, I suppose you like floods because they bring us quantities of fish." He then sat down, but sprang up immediately to shout, "If you don't make better roads we in our banovina will become separatists. We've got a fine regiment, and one will be enough, for only the riff-raff of the Army would march for your lot." That was the end, and we all went on with our meal.

As we went back along the corridor a man ran out of his carriage and grasped Constantine by both hands. "Look at him well," said Constantine, "he is a typical old Serbian patriotic man." He was short and thickset, overweight but nimble, with a great deal of coarse black hair on his head and face. "See, he has not a grey hair on his head," Constantine went on, "and he is nearly an old man. I will get him to come and sit with us, for he likes me very much, and you can observe him." He remained with us for quite a time, bouncing up and down on his seat, as he passionately attacked the Stoyadinovitch Government, not for its reaction, but for its innovations. "The country has gone to the dogs," he cried, "now that there are so many non-Serbs in the Army! Think of it, there are Croat colonels. A Croat colonel, that is something ridiculous to think of, like a woman preacher! I tell you, the Croats are spoiled for ever by the Austrian influence, they are like fallen women, they cannot be raised." Every now and then he stopped to show my husband and myself some point in the landscape, which he thought strangers should not miss. "They look good people," he said of us; but sighed and added gloomily, "But after all they are from the West, they're Europeans, no doubt they are in sympathy with this horrible age when everything is questioned."

"Of course he is not at home in the present," Constantine explained to us, "he is one of our medieval heroes reborn." Though he was very rich and he had much to see to in his own district, all his youth he used to rush backwards and forwards between his home and Macedonia, where he was a comitadji and killed many Turks. He fought like a lion in the Balkan wars and the Great War, and after the peace he was made Ban of South Serbia (which is the administrative title of Macedonia) as a reward. "But," said Constantine, "his ideas were not modern enough for his position. He was splendidly brave, of course, and that was a great qualification, for there could not have been a more dangerous job, what with the I.M.R.O. and the wild Montenegrins and the Albanians. But in other ways he was too simple and too large, too Homeric. He wished to remake Macedonia as it had been five hundred years ago, and whenever he saw a ruined church or a castle that had belonged to the Serbs and had been destroyed by the Turks, he would take Turks and Moslem Albanians away from where they lived until he had enough labour to rebuild them, and then he made them work under armed guards. And when people said, 'But you must not do that,' he answered, 'But why not? They knocked them down, didn't they?'

"But King Alexander was very kind about it, and though he did not keep him there for long, since these things will now not do, he gave him other work that he could do better. And now this man is very happy building many churches, since he is very pious, and the Church and the state to him are one. He aims to make more foundations than our medieval King Milutin, who built thirty-seven monasteries." He bent across and asked the patriot what his record was, and the old man stroked his coal-black moustache with a flourish and announced, "Forty-six." "The one he loves most," said Constantine, "is a chapel near the field of Kossovo, where he has really let himself go. It cost two hundred pounds, and it is ornamented with frescoes, which gratify him in an old quarrel he has with the Church. You see, our medieval kings, the Nemanyas, were recognized as saints, except for the one who was a flagrant sinner and defied the Church, who was that same Milutin who built the thirty-seven monasteries. They were saints because they were heads of a theocratic society on the Byzantine model, and because they defended Christianity against the pagan Turks. So he cannot see why Karageorge and the Karageorgevitches, who also united the Church and state and who actually drove out the Turks, should not be recognized as saints too. But of course the Church of today will have nothing to do with such an idea, they think it is profane, and they tell him not to be so impious. However, down there his chapel is far away from everywhere, so he has had frescoes painted showing Karageorge himself, and Alexander Karageorgevitch and old King Peter, yes, and King Alexander, all with immense haloes like golden soup-plates. He had quite a well-known artist to paint them, and he knew it was wrong and did not want to do it, but this one roared at him like a bull, and snatched so at his belt as if he were finding his pistol, and the artist said, 'Oh, certainly they shall be saints, they shall all be saints!' Then when the Patriarch came down to consecrate the chapel this one covered all the frescoes that showed the new royal saints with banners, and all went well. But his mother, who is very *dévote*, she spends many hours lying on the floors of chapels praying these sins of his will be forgiven."

"Now tell your friends that we are coming to the heart of Serbia," the patriot bade Constantine. "This town we are coming into is Kraguye-vats," Constantine explained, "and it was the big town of the Shumadiya, that is to say the wooded district, where the most Serbian Serbs came from, the ones that were foremost in the revolt against the Turks. Now there are great munition works here." "Tell them to look over there at the memorial to King Alexander," said the patriot; "it is a good thing for foreigners to see, it makes him quite stout and broad as a king should be, though God knows the poor man was thin as a student. But now make them look out of the other window, for God's sake." "Why?" asked Constantine. "If they do that they won't see the memorial to the Serbian dead." "That's just what I am hoping," said the patriot. "But why?" asked Constantine again. "The figure of the Serbian mother is considered very fine." "It's just that figure I don't want them to see," insisted the other. "Serbian women have got good breasts, this creature they have put up looks like a toothpick." "Never would he think of a woman's breasts except from a patriotic point of view," explained Constantine. "His country is all to him. He is as pure as a good monk."

A little further on he got out at his own station. A peasant in a sheepskin jacket, a much younger man, was waiting for him and took his baggage, and watched him as he said good-bye to us, with a loving and loyal and condescending smile. "I am glad to be back!" cried the patriot. "This is a beautiful part of the country, you know! Some day you must all come and see me!" He smiled up at his local sky, and looked into the branches of one of the lindens that grew all along the platform, and was convulsed with pride. "These lindens! Fine, aren't they? I planted them all ten years ago!" "Ten? It is not possible!" exclaimed Constantine. "You must mean twenty!" "No, I mean ten," said the patriot, and turned to his servant. "It is not more than ten years since I planted these trees, is it, Sasha?" "It is twenty-two," said Sasha. "Sasha, you are a fool and the son of a fool!" cried the patriot. "It is twenty-two years since you planted these trees!" the peasant answered, his voice rising. "How can that be so," the patriot screamed, "when——" The train moved on and we re-established ourselves for another long session. "Would you not like to sit in this corner?" I asked Gerda. "I think you will see most from the window on this side." "That would be interesting, no doubt," said Gerda, "if one had the slightest intention of looking out of the window." The train ran on into the afternoon, into the evening, into the night, into Macedonia.

AUSTRIA

HUNGARY

R. Drava

• Zagreb

C R O A T I A

S L A V O N I A

R. Sava

B O S N I A

D A L M A T I A

• Sarajevo

R. Drina

HERZEGOVINA

A D R I A T I C

Boundary up to 1913

M O N T E N E

Dubrovnik
(Ragusa)

• Tsetinye

S E A

I T A L Y

AL

Miles

0   20   40   60   80   100